D1710417

CSU 85595 VOL 30

Special Physical Education
Physical Activity, Sports, and Recreation

Paul Jansma
The Ohio State University

Ron French
Texas Woman's University

PRENTICE HALL, Englewood Cliffs, New Jersey 07632

PJC PEN CAMPUS LRC

Library of Congress Cataloging-in-Publication Data

Jansma, Paul.
    Special physical education : physical activity, sports,
and recreation / by Paul Jansma, Ronald W. French.
      p.   cm.
    French's name appears first on the earlier edition.
    1. Physical education for handicapped persons.   I. French, Ronald
W. II. Title.
  GV445.F74 1994
  371.9'04486—dc20
  ISBN 0-13-827056-2   93-10842
                                        CIP

Acquisitions editor: Ted Bolen
Editorial/production supervision and
  interior design: Mary Anne Shahidi, Barbara Reilly
Cover design: Bruce Kenselaar
Production coordinator: Peter Havens
Editorial assistant: Nicole Gray

© 1994 by Prentice-Hall, Inc.
A Paramount Communications Company
Englewood Cliffs, New Jersey 07632

All rights reserved. No part of this book may be
reproduced, in any form or by any means,
without permission in writing from the publisher.

Printed in the United States of America
10 9 8 7 6 5 4 3 2 1

ISBN 0-13-827056-2

Prentice-Hall International (UK) Limited, *London*
Prentice-Hall of Australia Pty. Limited, *Sydney*
Prentice-Hall Canada Inc., *Toronto*
Prentice-Hall Hispanoamericana, S.A., *Mexico*
Prentice-Hall of India Private Limited, *New Delhi*
Prentice-Hall of Japan, Inc., *Tokyo*
Simon & Schuster Asia Pte. Ltd., *Singapore*
Editora Prentice-Hall do Brasil, Ltda. *Rio de Janeiro*

This book is dedicated to Paul's father,
Reverend Theodore J. Jansma,
who passed away January 28, 1994.

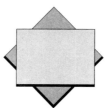

Contents

Preface

This book is written for regular physical educators who will be teaching pupils who are disabled. It is also an introductory text for those students who will be pursuing a career in special physical education. In addition, the information may be valuable for therapeutic recreators who provide physical activity programs to a variety of populations and occupational and physical therapists who use physical activities as a medium in their habilitation or rehabilitation programs. In this regard the emphasis of this text is on the development of functional community-based skills by special populations.

In other books in the area of special physical education there appears to be an overemphasis on providing the reader with special education, elementary games, and medical information with accompanying physical education and sports activities for special populations. In contrast, this book focuses on physical education and extracurricular activities for special populations by providing just

essential information needed for safe, successful, and satisfying programming. Further, the emphasis here is on bridging the gap between theory/research findings and direct instructional applications in special physical education.

This book has four parts. The first part introduces the reader to special physical education by presenting an overview of the differences between regular and special physical education and answers to such questions as: What is the need for special physical education? How is one trained in the specialization? What disabilities exist and what is their frequency? Past and current historical perspectives are then presented within the framework of society, disabilities, and special physical education.

The noncategorical approach in teaching physical education to special populations, with its stress on pupil needs, not pupil label or category, is the focus of the second part of this book. Physical educators should be able to individualize a program around the needs of all pupils, regardless of pupil category, label, or disability.

In the third part, focus then switches to categorical programming, in an effort to address the unique needs of pupils with specific identifiable disabilities. Such disabling conditions do affect an individual's ability to perform appropriately in physical education. For instance, because a child who is deaf typically requires adaptations different from those for a child who is visually impaired, it is important to understand such differences required for programming such pupils. Special needs of pupils who are disabled are recognized by all school districts in the United States and are defined by the U.S. Department of Education and each state.

The format of each chapter in the third part is similar. Background information is provided, followed by related characteristics and instructional strategies. The instructional strategies are presented as they relate to the psychomotor, cognitive, and affective domains of development. Next, specific indicated and nonindicated activity recommendations are provided. These activities are presented across each of the five areas specifically identified in the P.L. 101-476 definition of physical education. These areas are physical and motor fitness, fundamental motor skills and patterns, aquatics, dance, and individual and group games.

The last part of this book provides specific ways to manage and organize physical education and extracurricular activities, with an emphasis on individuals with special needs. The first topic addressed is behavior management. We believe that teachers' ability to manage pupils is the key to instruction and that the best teachers are the best behavior managers. An eclectic approach is taken in presenting information on this topic, but operant conditioning methods dominate the discussion. The second topic highlights the importance of the educational team to increase teaching efficiency and effectiveness. The rationale for using an educational team, types of teams, team members and their roles, and issues related to the functioning of such teams are addressed. The third topic is testing and evaluation. Physical educators must become aware of and be able to use developed instruments to assist in the appropriate placement of pupils, to make instructional decisions regarding appropriate activities for pupils, and to evaluate overall programs of special physical education. No longer should these integral aspects be ignored. Without testing and evaluation, physical education programming for pupils with special needs will continue to be haphazard at best.

Next considered is program administration. Numerous administrative areas are explored, ranging from program organization to grading to computer applications to financial support to legal liability and public relations. The belief is that good teaching emanates from a well-run program.

The last topic of emphasis is on extracurricular opportunities for special populations. Such opportunities do exist and are discussed across the areas of recreation, intramurals and extramurals, interscholastic sports, intercollegiate athletics, and amateur athletics.

Throughout the book a variety of individual interviews are presented. The purpose of the interviews is to give readers a more in-depth perspective on various topics and to introduce readers to some of those who work in the field. The series of interviews with representatives from different countries adds an international perspective.

We have written *Special Physical Education* in order to help you be a better teacher. That is, and will continue to be, our real motive.

Acknowledgments

Our editor, Ted Bolen, was a guiding force in the production of *Special Physical Education*. His support and patience are much appreciated. Thank you, Ted.

We would also like to acknowledge our gratitude to several chapter contributors: Dr. April Tripp, a consultant in special physical education in Maryland, for her extensive review of Chapter 7, on emotional disorders; Dr. Hester Henderson, from the University of Utah, for her extensive editing of Chapter 13, on behavior management; and Dr. James Decker, from East Carolina University, for his co-authorship of Chapter 17, on extracurricular activities. We also especially thank Dr. Lisa Silliman, a special physical educator in Texas, for her editorial reviews of a number of chapters, the taking of numerous photographs, and the typing of a number of the chapters. A special thanks is given to Dr. Hester Henderson for spearheading the instructor's manual. We know that, because of her work, many professors who adopt this text will be more efficient in their preparation of lectures and related tasks.

Numerous photographs, figures, and tables are included. The series of signs illustrated in Chapter 8 were made possible through the efforts of Dr. Steven Butterfield, from the University of Maine. In addition, we also want to highlight the fact that some of the photographs include contributions from our families. The collective contributions of the other individuals are too many to list. We simply say thanks.

Separate recognition also is afforded the interviewees in selected chapters. These include representatives from the United States and nine foreign countries. We believe that this unique feature of the book will be well worth the effort for the sake of this book's readership.

And finally, to our reviewers—Gail Clark, Louisiana Tech University; John Hall, University of Kentucky; Joseph R. Higgins, Columbia University; Leon E. Johnson, University of Missouri–Columbia; Barry Lavay, California State University–Long Beach; Wendell Liemohn, University of Tennessee; and Bob Rider, Florida State University—your advice was well received and heeded. Thank you.

Overview
of
Special Physical
Education

Before designing, implementing, and evaluating a physical education program that includes pupils who are disabled, a physical educator should have a basic understanding of what special physical education is, its historical evolvement, why it is so important, what types of pupils need special physical education, and the relation between special physical education and regular physical education. Such important information, the focus of the first part of this book, serves as the foundation for the programmatic and other information presented in the remainder of the text.

The first part of the book has two chapters. This first chapter provides definitions of regular and special physical education, as well as information on the need for special physical education, personnel development and employment, and the definition and scope of those primary disabilities highlighted in educational law. An historical and contemporary overview of societal attitudes toward individuals with disabilities and the evolvement of special physical education as a profession is presented in Chapter 2.

A large majority of pupils with disabilities now receive their physical education in a regular class setting, and one of the first regular classes into which pupils with mild to moderate disabilities are placed initially is physical education. One reason for this trend is that most children and youth can receive educational benefits from a comprehensive regular physical education program. Physical educators, therefore, can expect to have all types of pupils in their classes. For this they will need to be professionally prepared.

In addition, physical educators who specialize in teaching pupils with disabling conditions (special physical educators) are in demand to provide consultation services to regular physical educators who teach classes with pupils who are disabled. Special physical educators also are providing direct services to more pupils with severe and multiple disabling conditions. They need in-depth skills that cover the entire gamut of pupils with special needs. Clearly, intensive and comprehensive programs of preservice and in-service training are needed to prepare present and future teachers for this special type of physical education.

> After discussing regular physical education and its benefits, this chapter addresses four basic questions about physical education for pupils with special needs:
>
> What is this special type of physical education?
>
> What is the specific need for a special type of physical education?
>
> How should personnel be prepared in special physical education?
>
> What are the major disabling conditions represented among the school-aged population in the United States, and how prevalent are they?

REGULAR PHYSICAL EDUCATION

As in other curricular areas in education, physical education involves development of pupils in all areas—cognitive, affective, and psychomotor. The uniqueness of physical education is the major focus on the development of knowledge and skills in the psychomotor domain that can be carried over into extracurricular activities while in school, as well as in healthy postschool psychomotor practices. The psychomotor domain has four basic components: physical, motor, fitness, and play.

The *physical* component relates to the anatomical structure of individuals, which is related to static and dynamic posture and body mechanics. The *motor* component involves the quality of a person's movement and incorporates such basic factors as body image, spatial orientation, locomotor, nonlocomotor, and object control skill development. The *fitness* component refers to the quantity of movement that is demonstrated by an individual. The primary elements of a traditional physical fitness program involve strength, flexibility, cardiorespiratory endurance, agility, speed, muscular endurance, and power development. The *play* component represents an integration of the other developed components within a social context, traditionally involving games and sports.

The numerous benefits that individuals can derive from a physical education program have been recognized for decades. These benefits are as follows.

Psychomotor Benefits

There is little doubt that physical activity has a positive effect on the growth and development of infants, toddlers, children, youth, and adults. This is dramatically demonstrated by people who have been bedridden or who have had a body part immobilized for an extended period of time. Their affected body part begins to decrease in size and function, a process termed atrophy. In fact, it has been estimated that in the first week of bed rest, half the calcium is lost in a broken bone set in a cast (Bailey, 1976).

More generally, the psychomotor dimension of human development across its physical, motor, fitness, and play components is associated with frequent experiences, and often training, in numerous specific areas. Reflexive movement; rudimentary movement, including postural control; fundamental movement such as locomotor, nonlocomotor, and culturally determined movement involved in specific sports (e.g., pitching in baseball); physical fitness; aquatics; dance; and games are all applicable. Competence in these activities is vital to human life. Well-trained professionals can assist individuals who are disabled to learn skills in each of these areas. Just as nondisabled people are challenged, people who are disabled must learn to look good, move well, sustain their movement, and be able to play in activities within their potential capacities. This overall psychomotor competence enhances the possibility that those who are disabled will live a "normal" life.

Affective Benefits

A pupil's self-concept will affect all other dimensions of his or her development. For example, a child's acceptance into a peer group is dependent on his or her performance. Therefore, physical educators need to provide successful, positive experiences for each pupil while not using any techniques that preclude the development and maintenance of a healthy self-concept.

Physical education can help pupils learn desirable ways to deal with others and to develop moral values that society deems appropriate. It provides the opportunity for social interaction in a variety of environments and can help pupils, both disabled and nondisabled, learn to accept the individual differences among people.

Cognitive Benefits

Physical education can enhance intellectual development. Each time a child participates in a game or sport, thinking is required. Further, some authorities contend that fitness is related to intelligence factors, particularly mental alertness and concentration.

Until relatively recently, provision of physical education programs for children with disabling conditions had been a low pri-

FIGURE 1.1 Children who are disabled can no longer be left sitting on the sidelines.

ority. However with the passage of P.L. 94–142* (the Education for All Handicapped Children Act of 1975) came the recognition of the need for physical education for children with disabling conditions (and their legal right to education). In fact, physical education is the only curriculum area specifically mentioned in P.L. 94–142's definition of special education. Now, by federal and state laws, all children with disabilities must receive physical education and receive it in the least restrictive environment possible (see Figure 1.1). Physical education cannot be considered supplemental or totally neglected because of medical disability concerns, inadequate equipment and facilities, a lack of teacher competency in specialized programming, lack of funds, or any other reason.

DEFINING SPECIAL PHYSICAL EDUCATION

If a pupil cannot benefit from or safely participate in a regular physical education

---

*Public law, abbreviated P.L., refers to a federal law. The first number after the P.L. refers to the Congress that passed the law; the second number, to the sequence of the specific piece of legislation. Thus P.L. 94–142 was the 142nd piece of legislation introduced by the 94th Congress.

program, some form of special physical education must be provided. Special physical education is a specialty area within the field of physical education that was developed to provide programs for pupils with special needs. Three major types of programs exist within special physical education: adapted, corrective, and developmental (the terms do vary).

Adapted physical education refers to the modification of traditional physical activities to enable individuals with disabilities to have the opportunity to participate safely, successfully, and with satisfaction. For example, pupils who are visually impaired or who use wheelchairs may need modified equipment to play softball (see Figure 1.2) or additional equipment for bowling.

Corrective physical education—also called remedial physical education—refers mainly to the habilitation or rehabilitation of functional postural and body mechanics deficiencies. A child who has just had a cast removed and needs to rehabilitate an atrophied limb may be temporarily enrolled in this type of

class. Also, an adolescent with lordosis or kyphosis might be enrolled in a corrective physical education class for an extended period of time (see Figure 1.3). Today this type of special education program is not usually stressed.

Developmental physical education refers to a progressive physical fitness and/or gross motor training program to raise a pupil's ability to a level at or near that of peers. One developmental approach to exercise is illustrated in Figure 1.4.

Currently these types of special physical education programs are not always conducted in separate classes. Sometimes elements of all three are incorporated into one comprehensive program. For instance, at a special school for pupils who are orthopedically disabled, the instructor might provide individual programs for postural, physical fitness, and gross motor skill improvement, as well

FIGURE 1.3 Corrective physical education using stall bars to straighten body alignment.

FIGURE 1.2 Adapting a softball game by using a tee.

FIGURE 1.4 A developmental approach to exercise: varied types of sit-ups.

as adapt traditional sports and games. This might occur in one physical education class throughout a semester.

THE NEED FOR SPECIAL PHYSICAL EDUCATION

In the United States a growing positive attitude toward pupils with disabilities is reflected in the current trend toward placement in least restrictive environments (LREs) and individualization in all aspects of education, including physical education. This emphasis actually began a few decades ago, but became law with the passage in 1975 of P.L. 94–142. In essence, P.L. 94–142 is a civil rights law that says that each pupil identified as disabled has a right to an education that meets his or her own unique needs. But, of course, nothing is quite that simple. The LRE concept is complex, and placement in a *least* restrictive environment is not simply a ques-

tion of either integrating or segregating a pupil with a disabling condition. Yet, unfortunately, this is how the term is too often defined and used.

The LRE concept ideally involves a continuum of educational environments in which pupils could be placed based on their specific needs. An example of a physical education continuum of educational environments, modified from Deno's model (1970), is provided in Figure 1.5. The model in Figure 1.5 has two educational levels of service, with several options within each level. In Level I the three options are provided in totally segregated environments and there is very little opportunity for interaction between pupils who are disabled and nondisabled pupils. It is estimated that during the 1989–90 school year, 6.1 percent of pupils with disabilities in the United States were educated in these types of environments (U.S. Office of Special Education and Rehabilitative Services, 1992). Pupils in such environments were usually

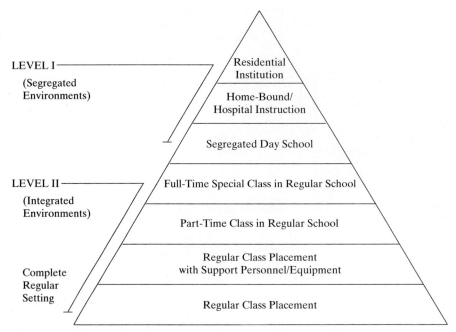

LEVEL I
(Segregated
Environments)

Residential
Institution

Home-Bound/
Hospital Instruction

Segregated Day School

LEVEL II
(Integrated
Environments)

Full-Time Special Class in Regular School

Part-Time Class in Regular School

Complete
Regular
Setting

Regular Class Placement
with Support Personnel/Equipment

Regular Class Placement

FIGURE 1.5 Continuum of physical education placements.

severely or profoundly disabled and were labeled as multiply disabled, deaf-blind, or orthopedically impaired.

In Level II there is some type of integration between pupils who are disabled and nondisabled. At the most restrictive stage within Level II, pupils who are disabled are educated in separate classes. They may interact with other pupils during lunch, recess, and special events, or ride the same school bus to and from home. In the next two options within Level II, pupils who are disabled are educated for all or part of the total day in regular class settings. At an even less restrictive stage, pupils who are disabled are placed full time in a regular class setting and are provided support personnel and/or special equipment in order to be educated appropriately in this environment. Support personnel could include a special physical educator, providing the regular physical educator with consultation services, or a school

psychologist, assisting the regular physical educator in designing and implementing a behavior management system. Special equipment could be an audio locator for a pupil who is visually impaired or a bowling ramp for a pupil in a wheelchair. (Chapter 4 is devoted to implementing and designing programs for pupils with disabilities taught in this type of educational setting, whether part or full time. A complete chapter is given over to this topic because of the large number of pupils who are placed in this type of environment.)

The last educational option within Level II involves complete integration into a regular physical education setting without any support personnel or special equipment. In such an environment the pupil is probably not disabled in physical education but is having an educational problem in another curriculum area. This is the stage of the LRE process that we consider to be truly mainstreamed.

The most recent concept related to LRE is based on the philosophy that all pupils who are disabled need to be fully included with nondisabled peers in their home school. Students who are mainstreamed attend general education classes throughout the school day in schools that may be far from their home school, where they are segregated from siblings and friends. With inclusion, pupils with disabilities attend their home schools with those of comparable age, and pupil ratios in the school reflects the proportion of individuals who are disabled in society (National Association of State Boards of Education, 1992).

In reality, placement of a pupil within such a physical education LRE continuum may involve a series of steps over time which could conceivably progress all the way from a residential institution (the most restrictive environment) to the regular classroom. In this regard, however, a child with a disabling condition should be moved to a less restrictive environment only when appropriate, with the goal of eventual placement in a regular setting without extra support. In truth, though, a certain percentage of pupils with disabilities will always require some special support and some pupils will need special programs throughout their schooling in more restrictive environments.

Overall, more and more pupils who have traditionally been placed in schools of their own will be attending regular public schools near their homes. Many of them, who may have trouble learning, are no different or barely different from nondisabled pupils in physical education skills. Others have distinct physical disabilities, and still others have sensory problems. Increasingly, all are receiving physical education in the public schools.

Regardless of the arguments against gradually integrating pupils with and without disabling conditions, the mandate for least restrictive placement seems here to stay. Physical educators must, therefore, face the reality that they will have pupils with disabilities in their classes. Toward that end, more special physical educators will have to be trained to help them. The views of Paul Surburg on the need for more special physical educators and related training are presented in the interview on page 8.

PERSONNEL DEVELOPMENT AND EMPLOYMENT

With the passage of P.L. 94–142 the role of the special physical educator has changed. Pupils in their classes are now more severely and profoundly disabled, and include children who traditionally had no program of physical education. On the other hand, pupils with mild and moderate disabilities, who used to be served by the special physical educator, have become the responsibility or shared responsibility of the regular classroom teacher or regular physical educator. The special physical educator continues in the role of consultant to these other teachers.

With the requirement that all children with disabilities must be provided with physical education, the number of positions open in special physical education has increased significantly. There were, and still are, many more positions available than can be adequately filled. For example, in the 1989 school year, just in the state of Texas more than 350 special physical education vacancies were identified by directors of special education. This was about the same number cited eight years earlier, an indication that the teacher shortage in this area is not improving.

Specific competencies that physical education generalists and special physical educators should possess were identified by the American Alliance for Health, Physical Education, Recreation and Dance (Adapted

Paul Surburg

Dr. Surburg is a professor of adapted physical education at Indiana University. He is known in the area of professional preparation at both the masters and doctoral levels.

1. *What are your views on the need for special physical education in the United States?*

The need for special physical education may be addressed from two perspectives. From a philosophical standpoint, a person can easily build a case for special physical education. Establishment of appropriate levels of physical and motor fitness, enhancement of fundamental motor patterns, and development of team and individual sport skills are essential components in a good physical education program which will benefit all pupils. Concerning pupils who are disabled, a more cogent argument may be made for physical education because their limitations may have physically or ecologically precluded the development of the aforementioned components of physical education.

From a practical standpoint, physical education is being placed on individualized educational programs (IEPs) which warrants some type of special physical education. While not all educators recognize the importance of special physical education, the need for this type of education does exist. This need is substantiated by the fact that a physical education teacher with this type specialization has no difficulty finding employment in all parts of this country.

2. *What are your thoughts related to the future training of special physical educators?*

As we move toward the twenty-first century, training of special physical educators will be conducted primarily at the graduate level. With increased demands for more stringent standards for teacher certification, increased educational requirements (which translate into more education courses) will be imposed upon physical education majors. A concurrent development already in evidence is the proliferation of knowledge in the discipline of physical education which again translates into more required courses in the undergraduate physical education curriculum. An overcrowding of the undergraduate curriculum will, therefore, necessitate graduate level preparation for the specialist in special physical education. This specialist will develop an area of expertise such as a preschool endorsement, all-grade license, or an adult certification for special populations.

With regard to the latter certificate, as P.L. 94–142 set the age range from 3 through 21 years for appropriate special education and P.L. 99–457 expanded special education services to the preschool years, extended coverage for adults is the next logical step in this expansion of services for persons with disabilities. This specialist will be increasingly well prepared to deal with the concept of wellness for special older populations. Specialized preparation in adult physical fitness, nutritional assessment, and a strong foundation in strategies and procedures to facilitate community integration objectives will be essential components in this person's area of preparation. The concept of the school as the only domain for the special physical educator will be as archaic in the twenty-first century as the straight leg sit-up is today.

3. *What about the training of regular physical educators, special physical educators, and others who are already in the field and are responsible for teaching special physical education?*

There still is a gap between what is expected of regular physical educators dealing with pupils who are disabled in mainstreamed settings and the preparation of these people. Data of surveys investigating the preparation of physical educators in special physical education present a bleak picture. At best teachers have only one special or adapted physical education course at the undergraduate level.

The initial impetus for in-service training from the passage of P.L. 94–142 has dissipated and for the last decade in-service training programs have not been given priority status. Only recently are some professionals attempting to provide more in-service programs in special physical education. There must be concerted efforts for this phase of training at local, state, and national levels to affect change in the level of preparation of regular physical educators.

Physical Activity Council, 1993; Hurley, 1981). In preparing this text, the authors used the Alliance's guidelines to provide the underlying structure in order to ensure that the reader will be knowledgeable in these areas. There is a clear differentiation between the generalist and specialist. The generalist needs to have basic knowledge about some pupils with disabilities. In contrast, the specialist must have in-depth knowledge about a wide variety of these pupils. In addition, the generalist should be able to apply basic knowledge in teaching pupils with mild and moderate disabilities in a regular physical education setting. The specialist applies in-depth knowledge to these pupils, too, but is also trained to teach pupils who are severely and multiply disabled. To develop these competencies, considerable preservice training

will be required of physical education generalists and special physical educators who are going into the field; and in-service education will be required of those who are already in the field.

Preservice Training

Many state boards of education require generalist physical educators to demonstrate specific competencies related to teaching pupils who are mildly or moderately disabled, before a teaching credential is awarded. For instance, these are some of the areas from which questions could appear on the Texas state certification examination: analyzing the structure, functions, and different disorders of the biological system; understanding common diseases and disorders and their effects on physical performance; and being able to identify principles and activities related to fitness and individual and group activities appropriate for various age groups and development levels.

Introductory courses in special physical education are being taught in most of the 3,200 colleges and universities in the United States that have teacher preparation programs (Jansma, 1988). To begin to develop Alliance-mandated competencies, such introductory courses should include the following elements (Jansma, 1988):

- *Noncategorical elements*: behavior managing; testing (gathering data); assessing; planning; instructing developmentally; evaluating; following up; understanding individualized education programs, laws and historical trends, and organization and administration of programs; and knowing extracurricular activities.
- *Categorical elements:* addressing the programming of at least the pupils most often found in physical education classes. These include pupils who are learning disabled, mentally retarded, severely emotionally disordered, and orthopedically disabled.

A number of colleges and universities are also offering physical education majors specialized courses of study, generally at the graduate level, that focus on designing and implementing programs for pupils with severe and multiple disabling conditions. There is also often a stress during preservice on learning how to provide consultation services to physical education generalists and other professionals who provide physical education services to pupils with special needs.

The need for trained professionals in this area is understandably great. In 1985, Bundschuh reported that 30 states had target-ed physical education for pupils with disabilities as a personnel priority area. Subsequent to this report in the state of Texas there was a need for more than 380 special physical educators (Jackson, French, and Pope, 1986). Further, based on a more recent survey by French (1991), the need for special physical educators has not decreased substantially. Because of the demand for competent special physical educators, the federal government provides grants to a few qualified colleges and universities to train personnel in this area.

In-Service Training

In-service training is needed to increase the competencies of those professionals who already provide physical education to pupils with special needs. Numerous studies have been conducted to identify the specific in-service needs of physical educators, special educators, and others teaching physical education to pupils with disabilities. Two high priorities are classroom management and competency in teaching physical fitness and fundamental motor skills. Two other important areas are safety precautions related to pupils with specific disabling conditions and administrative policies for placement of pupils with disabilities (Cowden 1980; Foederer, 1987).

In-service training is usually provided through workshops and consultation services. Workshops are usually on a specific topic of concern to a pretargeted group. They are on a short-term basis, usually from half a day to two days (Tymeson, 1988). Consultation is ordinarily on a one-on-one basis concerning a topic that is of immediate concern to a teacher or teachers. Consultation is often on an ongoing basis over an extended period of time. More and more school districts are employing special physical education specialists who provide both types of inservice training.

Credentialing

To ensure adequate preparation of individuals teaching physical education to pupils with disabilities, credentialing in the form of certification, endorsement, or validation in special physical education is now required in some states. For example, California, Illinois, Kansas, Ohio, Louisiana, New Mexico, and Michigan have a state credential in special physical education. In many other states that do not have a credential requirement, position papers are being written and proposals are being considered by state boards of education. The process of implementing a new teacher's certificate, endorsement, or validation is very slow because of various necessary procedural requirements. But with the number of professionals and parents interested in improving the physical education opportunities for their children, more and more states will be adopting some form of special physical education credential.

DISABLING CONDITIONS

Definitions

Exceptionality refers to a person who significantly deviates from others in physical, mental, emotional, and/or social development. This term includes both disabilities and giftedness. The major focus of this text is on pupils who have specific disabilities in educational settings and who cannot participate fully in a regular education program, including physical education.

It should be noted that "disabled" is used throughout this text because it is the term most widely used now by the federal government and within education. It should be considered synonymous with "impaired" and "handicapped." Others (A clarification, 1971), however, see clear and distinct differences among these three terms about which the reader should be aware:

1. An individual with an *impairment* has an identifiable organic or functional condition, such as a speech deficiency, learning disability, emotional problem, cerebral palsy, or amputation.
2. An individual with a *disability* has an impairment that restricts or limits ability to perform specific activities safely, successfully, or with satisfaction.
3. An individual with a *handicap* possesses an impairment or disability that adversely affects him or her emotionally and/or socially.

The federal government has defined various categories of disabilities that are widely used in educational settings. We use them throughout this book as well, and describe each condition more fully as we discuss each group.

- *Autism*: a developmental disability significantly affecting verbal and nonverbal communication and social interaction, generally evident before age 3, that adversely affects a child's educational performance. Other characteristics often associated with autism are engagement in repetitive activities and stereotyped movements, resistance to environmental change or change in daily routines, and unusual responses to sensory experiences. The term does not apply if a child's educational performance is adversely affected primarily because of a serious emotional disturbance.
- *Deaf-blindness*: concomitant hearing and visual impairment, the combination of which causes such severe communication and other development and educational

problems that the child cannot be accommodated in special education programs solely for children with deafness or children with blindness.

- *Deafness*: a hearing impairment that is so severe that the child is impaired in processing linguistic information through hearing, with or without amplification, and thus adversely affects a child's educational performance.

- *Hearing impaired*: an impairment in hearing, whether permanent or fluctuating, that adversely affects a child's educational performance.

- *Mental retardation*: significantly subaverage general intellectual functioning existing concurrently with deficits in adaptive behavior and manifested during the developmental period that adversely affects a child's educational performance.

- *Multiple disabilities*: concomitant impairments (mental retardation-blindness, mental retardation-orthopedic impairment, etc.), the combination of which causes such severe educational problems that the child cannot be accommodated in special education programs solely for one of the impairments. The term does not include deaf-blindness.

- *Orthopedic impairment*: a severe orthopedic impairment that adversely affects a child's educational performance. The term includes impairments caused by congenital anomaly (e.g., clubfoot, absence of some member), impairments caused by disease (e.g., poliomyelitis, bone tuberculosis), and impairments from other causes (e.g., cerebral palsy, amputations, fractures or burns that cause contractures).

- *Other health impairment*: having limited strength, vitality, or alertness, due to chronic or acute health problems (e.g., heart condition, tuberculosis, rheumatic fever, nephritis, asthma, sickle cell anemia, hemophilia, epilepsy, lead poisoning, leukemia, diabetes), that adversely affects a child's educational performance.

- *Serious emotional disturbance*: a condition exhibiting one or more of the following characteristics over a long period of time and to a marked degree that adversely affects educational performance: an inability to learn that cannot be explained by intellectual, sensory, or health factors; an inability to build or maintain satisfactory interpersonal relationships with peers and teachers; inappropriate types of behavior or feelings under normal circumstances; a general pervasive mood of unhappiness or depression; or a tendency to develop physical symptoms or fears associated with personal or school problems. The term includes schizophrenic. It does not apply to children who are socially maladjusted, unless it is determined that they have a serious emotional disturbance.

- *Specific learning disability*: a disorder in one or more of the basic psychological processes involved in understanding or in using language, spoken or written, that may manifest itself in an imperfect ability to listen, think, speak, read, write, spell, or to do mathematical calculations. The term includes such conditions as perceptual disabilities, brain injury, brain dysfunction, dyslexia, and developmental aphasia. It does not apply to children who have learning problems that are primarily the result of visual, hearing, or motor disabilities, of mental retardation, of emotional disturbance, or of environmental, cultural, or economic disadvantage.

- *Speech or language impairment*: a communication disorder such as stuttering, impaired articulation, a language impairment, or a voice impairment, that adversely affects a child's educational performance.

- *Traumatic brain injury*: an acquired injury to the brain caused by an external physical force, resulting in total or partial functional disability or psychosocial impairment, or both, that adversely affects a child's educational performance. The term applies to open or closed head injuries resulting in impairments in one or more areas such as cognition; language; memory; attention;

reasoning; abstract thinking; judgment; problem solving; sensory, perceptual, and motor abilities; psychosocial behavior; physical functions; information processing; and speech. The term does not apply to brain injuries that are congenital or degenerative or brain injuries induced by birth trauma.

- *Visual impairment, including blindness*: an impairment in vision that even with correction adversely affects a child's educational performance. The term includes both partial sight and blindness.

Note that these definitions reflect the functional abilities of each child, not just the disabling category or label itself. This is a fundamental philosophical change toward a more noncategorical approach in designing and implementing educational programs for children with disabling conditions. The reason for this very basic change is that categories in themselves are educationally irrelevant and overlap.

The use of the noncategorical approach is very important for a physical educator who has a class of pupils who are disabled in some way. The category or label of either one pupil or a group of pupils has little to do with the needs, abilities, and interests of each child within the class. Thus, in keeping with the noncategorical approach, pupils should be assigned to classes based on functional abilities that are relevant to the purpose of the class. For example, the teacher might be informed that the children in the class are motorically awkward and function two years behind their normal peers in motor skills. This is more helpful in planning class activities than just knowing that the pupils are mentally retarded or learning disabled.

In addition, some children do not conveniently fit into a single disability category. A pupil could have cerebral palsy and also be mentally retarded and have seizures. Thus,

TABLE 1.1   NUMBER OF PUPILS WITH DISABILITIES AGE 6–21 RECEIVING SPECIAL EDUCATION SERVICES DURING THE 1990–91 SCHOOL YEAR*

DISABLING CONDITION	TOTAL POPULATION	% OF DISABLED POPULATION
Learning disabled	2,144,377	49.10
Speech or language impairment	990,186	22.70
Mental retardation	552,658	12.70
Serious emotional disturbance	392,559	9.00
Other health impairments	56,312	1.30
Multiple disabilities	97,625	2.20
Hard of hearing and deaf	59,312	1.40
Orthopedic impairments	49,393	1.10
Visually disabled	23,686	.50
Deaf-blindness	1,522	.00
Total	4,367,630	100.00

*Autism and traumatic brain injury conditions have not yet been counted.

professional preparation by category would not optimally prepare a teacher to instruct pupils with a combination of disabilities in one class. Also to be considered is that, particularly in physical education, many of the same activities and teaching methods can be used with pupils who collectively represent a combination of disabling conditions because these pupils are typically more like their normal peers than they are different.

Scope of Disabling Conditions

It is difficult to determine the prevalence of children in the United States with any defined disabling condition. It is estimated that 12 percent of the total population of individuals from birth to age 22 are disabled. However, the percentage actually served in schools is less than 12 percent. In this regard, we offer two sets of data from the *Fourteenth*

TABLE 1.2   PERCENTAGE OF PUPILS AGE 6–21 SERVED IN DIFFERENT EDUCATIONAL ENVIRONMENTS BY DISABILITY: SCHOOL YEAR 1989–90

DISABILITY	*Educational Environments*					
	REGULAR CLASS	RESOURCE ROOM	SEPARATE CLASS	SEPARATE SCHOOL	RESIDENTIAL FACILITY	HOMEBOUND/ HOSPITAL
Specific learning disabilities	20.7%	56.1%	21.7%	1.3%	0.1%	0.1%
Speech or language impairments	76.8	17.7	3.8	1.5	0.1	0.1
Mental retardation	6.7	20.1	61.1	10.3	.14	0.4
Serious emotional disturbance	14.9	28.5	37.1	13.9	3.6	2.0
Hearing impairments	27.0	18.2	31.7	10.6	12.3	0.2
Multiple disabilities	5.9	14.3	43.7	29.5	3.9	2.7
Orthopedic impairments	29.6	18.9	34.7	9.9	1.0	5.9
Other health impairments	31.2	22.3	24.6	7.8	1.0	13.1
Visual impairments	39.3	23.7	21.1	4.5	10.8	0.6
Deaf-blindness	8.0	16.3	29.9	16.6	28.4	1.0
All disabilities	31.5	37.6	24.9	4.6	0.9	0.6

Includes data from 50 states, the District of Columbia, and outlying areas. Educational placements for children age 3–5 are not reported by disability.

Annual Report to Congress on the Implementation of The Individuals with Disabilities Education Act (U.S. Department of Education, 1992, pp. 6, 25). Table 1.1 shows the approximate number (4,367,630) and percentage of those age 6–21 served by disability category during the 1990–91 school year. The top four are learning disability, speech impairment, mental retardation, and serious emotional disturbance. Table 1.2 shows what we believe to be very interesting data for those who plan to teach in a regular school environment. The table indicates that during the 1989–90 school year 94 percent of U.S. pupils with disabilities (or suspected of having disabilities) from 6 through 21 years of age, were educated in regular school (Level II) environments. From general census data, these pupils generally had a mild or moderate disability. These numbers, types of disabilities, and settings in which educational programming occurs should serve notice to regular and special physical educators alike that a lot of work is ahead of us. The challenge is squarely on our shoulders.

A Past
and
Present
Perspective

Today thousands of children and youth who are disabled are being provided special physical education services geared toward their unique needs. Some of these pupils receive one-to-one physical education instruction every day as an integral part of their education. In other cases, pupils are appropriately grouped together or integrated with their nondisabled classmates. Some receive both one-to-one and group instruction.

Specialized services like this did not appear overnight. The history of this country's treatment of people with disabilities and the history of special physical education must be considered in order to understand the long-term trends that have contributed to the status quo. An integral, and perhaps the major, part of this history is of societal attitudes during different periods of history.

A HISTORY OF SOCIETAL ATTITUDES TOWARD DISABILITIES

Throughout history, the attitudes toward individuals who are disabled have varied, but typically they have been negative. Those with disabilities have been regarded as being a financial drain on society, even as objects of fear and bearers of evil spirits.

We can identify five periods in society's attitudes toward those with disabilities. The first was the primitive era of human history (prehistoric to 500 B.C.), during which people had a spiritual-medical-magical attitude about the causes of and cure for disabling conditions. It was assumed that disabilities were the work of gods or evil spirits. Infants with physical disabilities were usually killed at birth. Children who acquired a disabling condition that interfered with their ability to contribute to the community were usually put to death or banned from the group. Of course, abandonment usually resulted in death, as the children could not provide food and shelter for themselves.

During the second period (500 B.C. to A.D. 500) a more logical and natural explanation for the cause of disabling conditions was accepted, at least by some physicians and philosophers, such as Hippocrates and Galen. In Greece, infanticide was still widely practiced. The Spartans threw infants with disabilities into a river to drown or left them to perish on a mountainside (L'Abate & Curtis, 1975). Infanticide was also practiced by the early Romans. Fathers were permitted by law to kill an infant with deformities; and abandonment of children with disabilities was widespread.

Attitudes toward older persons with physical disabilities who were a deterrent to the goals of the community or who were nonproductive members were not any more humane than attitudes toward children. The Roman ruler Commodus used people who were crippled for target practice with his bow and arrows. The general Roman attitude toward those who were mentally retarded is depicted in the laws of Lycurgus, which permitted abandonment of the "idiot." Some wealthy Romans did take individuals who were mentally retarded into their homes, but only to use them as objects of amusement at social gatherings (L'Abate & Curtis, 1975).

The Greeks are recognized for the first significant movement toward a scientific view of emotional disorders (Redlich & Freedman, 1966). Greek physicians of this period increasingly emphasized physiological disorders as the cause of emotional disturbance. However, widely divergent treatments for those who were emotionally disturbed as well as people with seizures were prescribed. Some physicians recom-

mended specific physical environments, gentle and patient caretakers, and minimal use of restraints. Physical exercise and sports were also prescribed. Some physicians, though, used starvation, chains, flogging, head shaving, and bleeding.

During the next period of history (500 to 1500), the Middle Ages, cruelty and confusion remained the norm (Poynter & Keele, 1961). The movement to separate medicine from religion (which had begun with the Greek physicians and philosophers) had ended, and for all practical purposes disappeared. Theological rationalization and explanation returned to serve as the foundation for treatment.

This period was characterized by a mixture of attitudes toward people who were mentally retarded. One attitude was that of compassion, exemplified in the development of the first custodial care facilities. On the other hand, many people who were mentally retarded were also persecuted as witches. For individuals who were physically disabled, emotionally disabled, or seizure prone, prayer and religious ceremonies were seen as the best cure. Gradually the belief changed to the position that physical disabilities were natural, but that emotional disability and seizure proneness were caused by the supernatural (Redlich & Freedman, 1966).

The fourth period in history (1500 to the early 1900s) marks a turning point. The philosophy of Locke and Rousseau relating to the importance of "the dignity of all individuals" was accompanied by a positive shift in society's attitudes, coupled with a return to a more scientific explanation of disabling conditions. Custodial care was typically provided during this period.

An emotional disability, however, was still associated with religion by such leaders as Luther in Germany and Calvin in Switzerland. Those who were emotionally disabled were believed to be incompetents, "filled with Satan." Some physicians did begin to accept the notion that the cause could be a faulty functioning of the body fluids. The treatment, though, was basically the same as that suggested by Celius 2,000 years earlier. This included such remedies as drinking a cordial with such ingredients as the flesh and blood of vipers, canary wine, and honey (Henderson & Gillespie, 1956). Toward the end of this period, a movement was begun by reformers such as Pinel (see Figure 2.1) and Dix to provide medical attention rather than punitive treatment to those who were emotionally disabled.

Systematic training to increase the skills of children with mental retardation was initiated during this same period. In 1801, Itard (1962) published a description of his work with Victor, the Wild Boy of Aveyron. The text describes Itard's attempts to use sensory stimulation to increase the intellectual level of the child, who was functioning below the level of most domestic animals. Seguin extended Itard's ideas and developed a physiological approach to educating individuals with mental retardation. He took an eclectic view, combining principles of philosophy, medicine, and psychology in developing a theory of instruction (Talbot, 1964). In 1837, Seguin established the first successful school for individuals with mental retardation in France.

Montessori (1964), who believed that mental growth depends on the interaction of the individual with the environment, incorporated the sensory training of Itard and Seguin into her method of teaching children with mental retardation. She also developed sequential steps for numerous self-help and educational tasks and ranked each from simple to complex. Before a child could accept a new challenge, he or she had to complete and

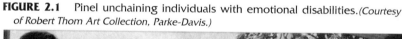

FIGURE 2.1 Pinel unchaining individuals with emotional disabilities. *(Courtesy of Robert Thom Art Collection, Parke-Davis.)*

master the task that preceded it. The basic principles of Montessori's method are still widely accepted in education (Hewett, 1974).

The first residential institution for people with disabilities in the United States was the American School for the Deaf in Hartford, Connecticut, which opened its doors in 1817. From this date to the Civil War other categorical residential institutions opened for individuals who were visually impaired, mentally retarded, or orthopedically involved. About 1899, public schools began to serve pupils with disabilities, as evidenced by the establishment of a public school for those with orthopedic disabilities in Chicago (Mackie, 1945).

The fifth period (early 1900s to the present) is a landmark era because of the increased care, treatment, and educational services provided all people with disabling conditions. During the first part of the 1900s, the numbers and types of services for individuals with disabilities increased, due in large part to the passage of federal laws that ensured the rights of those with disabilities and to the advocacy of parents and professionals associated with organizations committed to the civil rights of those with disabilities.

By the early 1960s, special classes throughout the United States enrolled approximately 400,000 pupils. Today approximately 5 million infants, toddlers, children, and youth are provided with special education. One main reason for the phenomenal increase in numbers of children served is medical and health service advances that have saved or prolonged the lives of individuals with disabilities. Another reason is the passage of more civil rights legislation since the 1970s, affecting more school-aged children than during any preceding decade in American history.

However, we should never become complacent. There have been pockets of neglect, even recently, particularly in those institutions where individuals who are seriously disabled reside year-round. A number of these residential institutions were investigated only to find conditions of severe deprivation or, at best, custodial care for those who were disabled. Blatt and Kaplan's (1966) classic photographic essay on institutions for those classified as mentally retarded revealed numerous deplorable conditions (see Figure 2.2). Blatt, Ozolins, and McNally followed up this investigation in 1980 and found only slightly improved conditions.

As a consequence of these investigations, and other related events, the 1981–92 period was declared "The Decade of the Handicapped" by UNESCO (The United Nations Educational, Scientific and Cultural Organization), and major reforms in special education followed, particularly in the United States. The emphasis on educating pupils with disabilities in least restrictive environments became the federal and state governments' first priority. This included the placement of these pupils into regular programs whenever possible, with accommodations as necessary. Along the same lines, an emphasis on deinstitutionalization resulted in many individuals being placed in the community in the most normalized setting possible for each of them. Concurrently, such organizations as TASH (The Association for Persons with Severe Handicaps) called for, and still work toward, the elimination of all residential institutions for those with disabling conditions in America.

In reaction to these events, special educators and other professionals now often highlight community-based training of skills most useful in pupils' everyday lives. This has come to be known as functional skill training, with the goal of successful transition of pupils from school to work and functioning to an increasing level in less restrictive work, residential, and play environments throughout the 24-hour day. Functional skill training

FIGURE 2.2 The snake pit. (Source: *B. Blatt and F. Kaplan, Christmas in Purgatory: A Photographic Essay on Mental Retardation, 3rd ed. Syracuse, NY: Human Policy Press, 1974. Used by permission.)*

now has become particularly popular as the most appropriate educational approach for pupils with serious disabilities.

HISTORY OF SPECIAL PHYSICAL EDUCATION

The history of special physical education can be divided into three eras based on medical and educational advances and changes in societal attitudes toward people with disabilities. Primitive and ancient times (prehistoric to 500 B.C.) is the first era. During this period there was little technique to develop or rehabilitate the motor and physical skills of peo-

ple with disabilities. The Greek and Roman period, the second era, occurred between 500 B.C. and A.D. 1500. It is characterized by a shift in the prevalent attitude toward the role of exercise. Exercise was used in treatment of numerous medical conditions. This attitude, though, was reversed at the end of the Roman period, with the beginning of Christianity. There was a renewed and continued interest in the therapeutic value of exercise during the third era (1500 to 1970). This era provided the foundation for today's special physical education programs. During this time the adapted, corrective, and developmental aspects of special physical education were more clearly defined.

Prehistory to 500 B.C.

Although special physical education in the schools has evolved as a formal discipline only in the past half century, its roots can be traced as far back as primitive history. In fact, we have documentation from approximately 7000 B.C., when stretching exercises were used to relieve pain in the limbs (Nissen, 1947). During this period, agility, strength, and endurance were demanded of every member of the tribal community. People who did not have or who lost these physical attributes were frequently put to death or abandoned to perish from hunger and exposure. Any medical treatment was a combination of magic and religion, involving conjuring magical charms, incantations, songs, and dances.

It was not until about 3000 B.C. that specific medical gymnastic programs were developed (Licht, 1965). The ancient Chinese believed that physical inactivity caused material to accumulate in the circulatory system. This material was thought to cause obstructions, which were the cause of all disease, and thus an exercise program was developed to remove the obstructions. The program was known as Cong Fu, which meant the art of exercising the body and the application of this exercise to the treatment of disease. The activities consisted of body positioning and breathing exercises.

By 2000 B.C., religion and magic were still reflected in medical practice. Early Babylonian writings were devoted to describing magic formulas for eliminating demons and avoiding the devil, which were considered the sources of disease (Singer, 1928). The Babylonian physicians were also priests, and these priest-physicians were responsible for the treatment of internal illness, which could be cared for only by a combination of magic and religious methods. Some lay "physicians" were responsible for treating external abnormalities, usually caused by injury. Any exercises that were prescribed were given by the lay physician. (This was also the case in the early Egyptian and Hebrew societies.)

500 B.C. to A.D. 1500

Religious medicine was still prominent in 500 B.C. The Greeks built temples to Asclepius, the god of healing, where body ailments were treated. Initially the methods were chiefly supernatural; later, diet, bathing, and exercise began to play major roles in treatment (Sigerist, 1961). Herodikus was the first Greek known to write on the relationship of exercise to medicine, and he prescribed special diets and exercise plans for the treatment of diseases (Robinson, 1944). Hippocrates, a famous pupil of Herodikus, recommended exercise to reduce the convalescent period of atrophied muscle. He stated that through appropriate exercises the body would become healthy and physically well developed and would age slowly (Licht, 1965). After Hippocrates' death, the use of exercise as a therapeutic technique began to decrease, despite the later support of great philosophers such as Socrates, Aristotle, and Plato.

The Romans, like the Greeks, combined supernatural and religious beliefs in their medical treatment. This is understandable, as most physicians in Rome during this period were Greek. It was not until 100 B.C., when Asclepiades (a Greek) included exercises such as walking and running in his treatment of specific medical conditions, that there was a widespread revival of the notion that exercises had therapeutic value (Osler, 1961). Celsus, another famous physician of the time and who supported the medical value of exercise, prescribed progressive exercises for individuals with hemiplegia and other paralyses.

In A.D. 150, Galen was the most respected physician in Rome; he was a follower of the principles of Hippocrates (see Figure 2.3). One of his most famous books, based on his experiences treating gladiators, dealt with therapeutic exercise. Galen also developed one of the first exercise classification systems, which consisted of three groups (Van Dalen, Mitchell, & Bennett, 1953, p. 93):

Those exercises that give muscle tone, such as diving, rope climbing, and resistive exercises; quick exercises, such as running, sparring, punching ball play, and noncompetitive wrestling; and violent exercise, which involves repetition of the exercises in #1 and/or uninterrupted drills involving #2 with weights.

During the Roman period of Christianity's history, interest in exercise and belief in its therapeutic value declined again. Early Christians returned to the idea that medicine and religion could not be separated. Their concern was for the soul and not for the body. St. Augustine, in the early 5th century, was a spokesman for the early Christians. He believed that man's dire state was due to the original sin of Adam and Eve and that humans from birth to death were not only inclined to evil but were totally depraved. The only way to righteousness, he believed, was through the gratuitous acts of God. The emphasis of life was on preparation for death. The medieval mind was filled with superstitions involving trolls, elves, giants, fairies, goblins, dragons, and vampires. This was the prevalent attitude for the next 800 years.

1500 to 1970

It was not until after 1500 that there was a renewed interest in the therapeutic value of

FIGURE 2.3 Galen treating a child medically.
(Courtesy of Robert Thom Art Collection, Parke-Davis.)

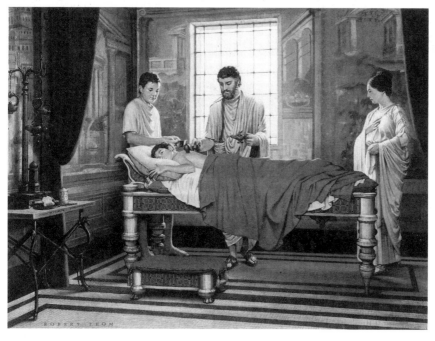

exercise. For instance, Mercurialis wrote a text entitled *De Arte Gymnastics.* In one section of the text, devoted to the therapeutic value of exercise, he established the following principles: (1) Each exercise should preserve the existing healthy state. (2) Exercise should not disturb the harmony among the principal humors (body fluids). (3) Exercise should be suited to each part of the body. (4) All healthy people should take exercise regularly. (5) Sick people should not be given exercises that might exacerbate existing conditions. (6) Special individualized exercises should be prescribed for convalescing patients. (7) Persons who lead sedentary lives urgently need exercise. With the exception of one,* all of Mercurialis' principles are still widely accepted.

Interest in the importance of exercise continued through the 1700s, sustained by the work of such individuals as Andre and Tissot (Licht, 1965). In the 1600s, Andre believed that of all the methods of curing many illnesses, none could equal physical exercise. He is given credit for coining the term *orthopedic.* In the 1700s, Tissot published *Medical and Surgical Gymnastics,* which addressed the role of exercise in curing disease. The beginning of special physical education is also associated with Tissot. He was the first individual known to prescribe modified sports and games for those with physical disabilities (in the 1780s).

The roots of twentieth-century corrective physical education go back to the work of Per Henrik Ling of Sweden (Wide, 1899). In the early 1800s, Ling developed medical exercises for the rehabilitation of abnormal body con-

ditions (Licht, 1965). Working at the Central Institute of Gymnastics of Stockholm, he extended the system of German gymnastics developed by Friedrich Jahn in the early 1800s, which was intended basically for able-bodied individuals. (A primary source on Swedish gymnastics is Weston, 1962.) Ling's exercises were first used in American institutions of higher education during the second half of the nineteenth century. In 1879, the first American corrective physical education department was established at Harvard University, under the directorship of Dudley Sargent. The major purpose of the program was to correct postural deficiencies and to improve general health.

Up to 1900, American physical educators were physicians, and physical education was essentially medically oriented with corrective exercises and posture training the central focus. Individuals who were primarily non-disabled by our present-day standards were those mostly served by this system. At the turn of the twentieth century, there was a further emphasis on corrective physical education in America using Jahn's and Ling's gymnastics systems and led by such noted individuals as McKenzie, Bancroft, Drew, Sargent, and Lippett.

World War I and the infantile paralysis epidemic of 1916 also contributed to the development of numerous other corrective departments of physical education in America. Until the early 1920s, these programs were still taught mainly by physicians interested in the goals of medical gymnastics. Their work was further advanced during the period from 1920 to 1950 by such individuals as Scott, Hitchcock, Lowman, Stafford, Rathbone, Kelly, and Clarke. Largely as a result of their work, the sole emphasis on education *of the physical* began to shift toward a philosophy that is more the norm today—education *through the physical.* This not only affected teacher training curricula but also

---

*The exception is the second principle. During the Middle Ages it was believed that there were four main body fluids (humors): blood; phlegm, a thick mucus from the respiratory passages; yellow bile; and black bile. Bodily health and temperament were thought to be regulated by these fluids.

the delivery of physical education services to pupils.

The two world wars significantly challenged the role of physical educators. Approximately 40 percent of the candidates for military service during World War I and four million potential inductees during World War II were considered unfit for military service. Similar results were reported for women volunteering to serve in the military. Most authorities considered poor school physical education programs to be responsible (Wheeler & Hooley, 1969). The need for physical reconditioning and training nationwide became obvious. During this same period, physical therapy became a respected and much used allied service connected with the medical profession. In the early years of World War II, the number of soldiers who received physical injuries increased so quickly that physical therapists could not meet all of their needs. As a result, the British medical profession turned to physical educators to assist in their rehabilitation. The use of physical educators in Great Britain was so successful that in 1937 the U.S. Army created a program to train corrective therapists. Trainees were army personnel with a background in physical education, coaching, or athletics. The program included courses in anatomy, kinesiology, medical terminology, physiology, and psychology. The major function of the graduates was to provide rehabilitation programs that would return soldiers to duty.

Howard Rusk, the director of Rehabilitation Medicine at New York University, is credited with developing the rehabilitation concept based on an interdisciplinary approach including "corrective therapy." By 1946, the U.S. Veterans Administration officially established a medical rehabilitation program with corrective therapy as an integral part.

After World War II, with the revealed state of unfitness and the successful use of corrective therapy in medical settings with physically disabled and other convalescing soldiers, the focus of corrective physical education activities shifted in educational settings. Aside from corrective physical education, other types of physical education soon appeared in schools to provide for all the psychomotor needs of pupils with disabling conditions. In 1947 a task force of experts in the area of physical education met to formulate a definition incorporating developmental activities, games, sports, and rhythms as an integral part of physical education for pupils with disabilities. This became the formally recognized definition of "adapted physical education." In 1952, the American Association for Health, Physical Education and Recreation endorsed a formal definition. "Adapted physical education" was defined as:

> a diversified program of developmental activities, games, sports, and rhythms suited to the interests, capacities, and limitations of students with disabilities who may not safely or successfully engage in unrestricted participation in the vigorous activities of the general education program (Committee on Adapted Physical Education, 1952, p. 15).

Adapted programs were intended for all types of special needs pupils, including the physically, mentally, emotionally, and socially disabled. In the same year, the same Association created a section devoted to special physical education within its organization.

The need for developmental physical education with an emphasis on physical fitness and motor ability was clearly made evident in the early 1950s when the Kraus–Weber Test (Kraus & Hirschland, 1954) was administered to thousands of American, European, and Oriental children. Based on the results of this test of minimum muscular strength and flexibility, American children were reported to be significantly inferior. These results caused national concern, and President Dwight Eisenhower formed the President's Council on Youth Fitness.* This council acted as a catalyst to affect the physical fitness of American youth and adults.

Not until the early 1960s did structured developmental physical education programs blossom and become incorporated with adapted and corrective physical education. During the 1950s and most of the 1960s the very notable names within these specializations included Arthur Daniels, Hollis Fait, Evelyn Davies, Warren Johnson, Lawrence Rarick, Julian Stein, Robert Holland, and Frank Hayden (Sherrill, 1988). Within the same time frame President John Kennedy and his family stimulated a national interest in movement programs for individuals who were mentally retarded, which included the creation of the Special Olympics in 1968. The Kennedy family, mostly through the Joseph P. Kennedy, Jr., Foundation, directly influenced special physical education also. In 1965 it helped start the Project on Recreation and Fitness for the Mentally Retarded, housed within the American Association for Health, Physical Education and Recreation. In 1966, this project, directed by Robert Holland, expanded from its sole categorical interest (mental retardation) and was renamed the Unit on Programs for the Handicapped. (Holland was succeeded by Julian Stein.) The Kennedy Foundation was also instrumental in lobbying efforts to include physical education as a prominent area of special education instruction in the Education for All Handicapped Children Act (P.L. 94–142).

Until the mid-1960s, only one special physical education course was required in

approximately half of the American colleges and universities with a physical education major. No sequenced specialization was available. In 1965, with the passage of the Elementary and Secondary Education Act (P.L. 89–10), funds became available to support training, research, and demonstration projects, which included the field of special physical education. Two years later, the Bureau of Education for the Handicapped (BEH) was created by P.L. 89–750 to perform similar functions exclusively for the benefit of those with disabilities. Some of the BEH-supported projects were in the area of special physical education. Perhaps most significantly, in 1967, P.L. 90–170 was passed. One section of this Mental Retardation Facilities and Community Mental Health Centers Construction Act established grants to institutions of higher education for the purpose of training special physical educators and conducting research within this area of study. This can rightly be called the beginning of true specialization within the field of special physical education as we know it today. Relatedly, as of the late 1960s to the present time, there has been a much more concerted effort to train special physical educators up to the doctoral degree and beyond (i.e., postdoctoral training).

These training efforts were complemented with the dissemination by the American Alliance for Health, Physical Education, Recreation and Dance of related training competencies for both the generalist and specialist in special physical education (Hurley, 1981; Horvat, 1991). In addition, doctoral competencies in special physical education also have been developed (Surburg, 1991) and are in current use at such major doctoral training universities as Oregon State University, Texas Woman's University, Indiana University, and the Ohio State University.

*The name has since been changed to the President's Council on Physical Fitness and Sports.

CONTEMPORARY SPECIAL PHYSICAL EDUCATION

Under one title or another, programs of special physical education have been steadily increasing in number and quality. During the 1970s and 1980s, there was substantial growth in this specialization for a variety of reasons, most of which can be traced to specific professional literature, leverage (lobbying), litigation (court), or the enactment of laws (legislation). These catalytic forces, which we can call the "four Ls," all have stemmed from increasingly positive social attitudes toward individuals with disabilities.

Literature

Historically, professional literature has been disseminated in order to make people more aware of events and to confront ignorant and stereotyped behavior. It has been an

FIGURE 2.4   Three key special physical education journals.

effective medium for helping people come to a new awareness and to reevaluate established attitudes. Today special physical educators have available a number of excellent published resources that deal directly with their specialization. Regular physical educators who have pupils with disabilities in their classes will find them useful.

1. The *Adapted Physical Quarterly* (see Figure 2.4) is published by Human Kinetics Publishers, Champaign, Illinois. A cross-disciplinary journal dealing with physical activity for those with disabilities, it has established itself as the foremost research journal within our specialization.

2. *Palaestra* (see Figure 2.4) is published quarterly by Challenge Publications, Ltd., Macomb, Illinois. This journal is devoted to the dissemination of information on special physical education, therapeutic recreation, and sports for those with disabilities.

3. *Clinical Kinesiology* (formerly *The American Corrective Therapy Journal*) is a quarterly publication of the American Kinesiotherapy Association (see Figure 2.4). It has traditionally devoted much of its space to the writings of special physical educators, including both discussion and research articles.

4. *The Advocate* is published quarterly by the National Consortium on Physical Education and Recreation for Individuals with Disabilities. This newsletter focuses on grant-related activities, legislation at the federal and state levels, credentialing, research, conferences, and lobbying in both special physical education and therapeutic recreation.

Three valuable resources from the American Alliance for Health, Physical Education, Recreation and Dance for the practitioner and researcher are *Update* (10 issues per year), the *Journal of Physical Education, Recreation and Dance* (9 issues per year), and the

Research Quarterly for Exercise and Sport. Collectively, these publications include information on current research and programs of physical education for individuals who are disabled. In addition, there are more than 40 textbooks in the area of special physical education with a copyright date of 1975 or later (see Sherrill, 1988, for a listing). Teachers of physical education for pupils with disabilities might wish to construct their professional libraries from all or some of these sources.

Leverage

Advocates of any cause are able to publicize their concerns as a group. This type of group is known as a special interest or lobby group, and its purpose is to influence a person or persons in order to accomplish goals. With respect to those with disabilities, citizen groups (parents), professional special interest groups (professional organizations), official government groups (government agencies), and consumer groups (individuals with disabilities) have been effective lobbyists.

Parents. Armed with an awareness of selected laws and grieved with the status of educational programming for their children with disabilities, parents throughout the United States have been a major catalyst for instructional improvement. We have personally witnessed the positive effects of such a group in causing immediate and long-range changes in major school districts (see Figure 2.5). By constantly communicating with school board members, directors of special education, school principals, teachers, and others, this group has been able to influence directly the employment of special physical educators, increase the further training of district physical educators in special physical education "best practices," and encourage the mainstreaming or inclusion of their children into regular physical education programs.

On the local, state, and national levels, parents are also contributing to professional organizations. Two of the largest of these are the Learning Disabilities Association and the Association for Retarded Citizens, which were formed to serve as advocates for the appropriate education of individuals with disabilities.

Professional Organizations. Numerous professional organizations have an impact on programs of special physical education. Most of these come from either physical education or special education. They work to enrich educational programs in the areas of direct programming, professional preparation, and research. They also function as lobbying groups. Some of these organizations are fully devoted to special physical education, and others involve many fields and, therefore, only partly serve the direct interests of special physical education.

FIGURE 2.5   A parent lobbying group.

The American Alliance for Health, Physical Education, Recreation and Dance is the largest single organization of its kind in the world and is composed of six associations. Splintered among three of these associations are four substructures that directly affect those with disabilities: Leisure for Special Populations, Correctional Recreation, Dance for Special Populations, and the Adapted Physical Activity Council. The latter is the most active across the three adapted physical activity areas (physical education, sport, recreation) and is most visible in the areas of conference planning, publications, and some special projects. It essentially replaced the original Unit on Programs for the Handicapped (1965–85).

Members and potential members of the alliance are encouraged to choose the Adapted Physical Activity Council as one of their two affiliation electives if they would like to receive ongoing information on programs of physical activity for individuals with disabilities. All physical educators, whatever their specialization, can receive up-to-date information related to their particular concerns if they belong to the Alliance and its regional and state branches. National headquarters is located at 1900 Association Drive, Reston, Virginia 22091.

Another organization, created in 1973, which significantly affects programs of special physical education is the National Consortium for Physical Education and Recreation for Individuals with Disabilities. During its first two years, it was known as the National Ad Hoc Committee on Physical Education and Recreation for the Handicapped. It originally brought together federal grant project directors in the areas of special physical education and therapeutic recreation from around the country. This consortium has functioned primarily as a lobbying group (see Figure 2.6) to maintain or increase funding levels for program support and to affect ongoing legislation, particularly at the federal level. For example, the consortium influenced the position of prominence of physical education in P.L. 94–142. Its contribution to the establishment of national credentialing for all special physical educators in the 1990s also is noted.

Another organization concerned with the mandates of P.L. 94–142 and which positively contributes to sport, special physical education, and therapeutic recreation is the Joseph P. Kennedy, Jr., Foundation. Located in Washington, D.C., the foundation has created multiple programs of value to the grass-roots physical educator. Some of the more well

FIGURE 2.6 A meeting of NCPERID.

known include the Special Olympics (see Chapter 17 and Figure 2.7), a revised program of physical activity entitled Let's Play to Grow (see Chapter 5), the Motor Activities Training Program (see Chapter 3), and the Unified Sports Program (see Chapter 17).

An international professional organization with a direct connection with America's special physical educators is the International Federation for Adapted Physical Activity. Since 1977, this organization has held biannual symposia bringing together recognized authorities from around the world to share new information concerning movement programs that crosses over the areas of special physical education, therapeutic recreation, and sport for individuals with disabilities. The latest symposium was held in August 1993 in Yokohama, Japan. Most of the major contributors to this organization's symposia and proceedings come from the United States, Canada, Australia, Scandinavia, and Germany.

A number of other professional organizations are valuable resources and advocates for parents, children, and professionals interested in special physical education. One is the Council for Exceptional Children, which originated in 1922, the largest special education organization in the world. Most professionals in the field join this council. It is locat-

FIGURE 2.7 Special Olympics. *(Photo from* Adapted Aquatics, *copyright 1977 by The American National Red Cross, reproduced with permission.)*

ed in Reston, Virginia, next door to the headquarters of the American Alliance for Health, Physical Education, Recreation and Dance. Another organization to be highlighted is the National Association of State Directors of Special Education. The goal, belief statements, and objectives generated from its 1991 Action Seminar on Physical Education and Sports for Students with Disabilities are important for all physical educators (special and regular) in the 1990s and beyond toward the end of ensuring that all school-aged pupils with disabilities participate in appropriate physical education programs, and all school-aged pupils have an equal opportunity to participate in school and community-based athletic programs as well (NASDSE, 1991). This association's headquarters is in Alexandria, Virginia.

Government Agencies. According to the U.S. Constitution, education is the responsibility of the states, not the federal government. State educational agencies (SEAs) are the major bodies that direct educational endeavors. Each state is divided into local educational agencies (LEAs), otherwise known as local school districts. The federal government, however, provides SEAs and LEAs various incentives to enrich educational programs. These incentives are based on the passage of legislation that allows tax dollars to be spent for specific programs. Considerable federal assistance in the form of grants and technical assistance is available through a number of national sources. Some provide allotments solely for educating individuals with disabilities, and many of these educational allotments are available for programs of special physical education.

Until 1979, the Department of Health, Education and Welfare (HEW) was the major government agency providing educational assistance. This assistance was specifically provided by agencies within the U.S. Office of Education. In 1979, HEW was separated into two cabinet-level departments, the Department of Education and the Department of Health and Human Services. The U.S. Office of Education was, in effect, elevated to cabinet level in the federal government, with a concomitant increase in overall influence.

As part of the Department of Education, the office that now has sole responsibility for the education of those with disabilities, is the Office of Special Education Programs (OSEP), known from 1967 to 1979 as the Bureau of Education for the Handicapped. The OSEP division that most directly influences grassroots-level programs of special physical education is the Division of Assistance to States. Aside from its monitoring responsibilities, this division annually disburses to complying states more than $1 billion related to the overall implementation of P.L. 94–142. Because programs of special physical education are accorded a prominent position in this law, substantial P.L. 94–142 monies theoretically "flow through" to enhance programs of physical education.

The OSEP Division of Personnel Preparation is also a direct advocate for physical education. This division is charged with disbursing grants to enhance the preservice and in-service training of teachers preparing to work with or already working with pupils who are disabled. Millions of dollars are granted every year nationally from this division for such purposes, some of which directly flows to special physical education teacher trainers. For more perspective, see the interview with special physical education's chief advocate within this division, Martha Bokee.

Martha B. Bokee

Martha B. Bokee is an education program specialist with various responsibilities in the Division of Personnel Preparation (DPP), Office of Special Education Programs (OSEP), Office of Special Education and Rehabilitative Services (OSERS), U.S. Department of Education. Bokee directs the Preparation of Related Services Personnel program priority. She is also the area coordinator and advocate for the areas of special/adapted physical education and therapeutic recreation. This interview was given by Bokee in her private capacity. No official endorsement of the U.S. Department of Education is intended or should be inferred.

1. How do you view your role as the OSEP advocate in the area of special/adapted physical education?

As area coordinator for adapted physical education, I function as liaison, facilitator, and spokesperson with the intent of improving programs for infants, toddlers, children, and youth with disabilities. I view the role of area coordinator for adapted physical education with a sense of dual responsibility to the professionals in the field who direct such programs, and to the federal government that financially supports the development of personnel preparation programs across the nation. This role, in part, affords me the opportunity to meet with numerous individuals who maintain varying perspectives with regard to the educational needs of infants, toddlers, children, and youth with disabilities, and who are committed to specific approaches to the development of personnel training programs. As area coordinator for adapted physical education, my responsibility is to accurately represent the concerns and issues raised by those professionals, while at the same time, effectively conveying to them the intent of the governing legislation, accompanying rules and regulations, as well as the division's program priorities.

In this capacity, it is important to fully understand the often divergent viewpoints that may reflect programmatic variances, geographic considerations, or ideological differences. This information needs to be accurately synthesized in order to facilitate the match between those ideas and an effective program design that will ultimately respond to established guidelines for federal sources of financial support. To some extent, this is a role of a broker for ideas.

As area coordinator, it is not only important to facilitate and encourage communication between university representatives and administrators of federal programs, but it is equally as important to foster the sharing of programmatic information, research findings, and current educational strategies among members of the academic community. My involvement with professional organizations, especially the National Consortium on Physical

Education and Recreation for Individuals with Disabilities, blends these roles.

2. *How can special/adapted physical educators functioning at different levels assist you in your role as their OSEP advocate?*

Primarily, adapted physical educators can best assist me, and hopefully themselves as well, through open communication, on a regular basis. There is a wealth of information at every juncture of the education process; from service delivery to the development of university programs. Child-oriented experiences are often catalytic for research concepts. University-based discussions frequently yield functional changes in service delivery models. Although somewhat of a cliché, the need for effective networking or linkages still persists. The research papers that are not written, the speeches that are not given, and the successes and failures that are not shared create a void in the collective professional knowledge base.

The greater the participation adapted physical educators have in addressing the full spectrum of educational needs of infants, toddlers, children, and youth with disabilities, the more involved they are with the work of other professionals who are meeting these needs, the broader their impact. As the general educational and related services communities become increasingly aware of the value of adapted physical education and the skills of adapted physical educators, my role as area coordinator is greatly facilitated.

Adapted physical educators may also assist me as area coordinator through their written responses to proposed regulations, program priorities, and other OSEP initiatives. Their consistent professional participation firmly establishes their voice in the federal forum.

3. *What are your present and future perspectives on the quantity and type of preservice OSEP-funded training projects in special/adapted physical education?*

Since 1982, I have completed and widely disseminated an annual analysis of DPP's efforts toward the development of personnel preparation programs in adapted physical education and therapeutic recreation. This ongoing analysis is intended to serve as a data base and reference for future program development in these two training areas.

Using data from this document, it may be helpful to consider the division's past financial support of programs in adapted physical education as a means of putting current funding and future directions into perspective. From fiscal year 1982 through fiscal year 1993, DPP allocated more than $23.5 million to support 403 personnel preparation programs in adapted physical education. A majority of the states and the District of Columbia have sponsored these projects. More than 17,000 students have participated in these training programs and have received financial assistance. Yearly funding levels have grown from almost $800,000 in fiscal year 1982, to more than $2 million in fiscal year 1993. The highest level of funding in this area was in fiscal year 1988 ($2,453,058). In fiscal year 1982, the average grant award was $26,000; while in fiscal year 1993 the average award was $80,805. In addition, 313 students will be financially supported for these programs during fiscal year 1993. This is a respectable overall fiscal commitment when one considers that there are more than 20 areas of programming that we support through 10 program priorities, or grant competitions. Projects now focus upon preservice programming, that which leads to a degree or certification, rather than in-service activities, which may have consisted of only a six-hour workshop. The majority of the projects train students at the masters degree level.

Although it is difficult to predict, in all likelihood, DPP's appropriated budget for the next two years should remain near the $90 million level. If the quality of training grant applications remains constant or improves, then a slight increase in the number of projects and funds allocated could be anticipated. It has been my experience that the quality of such applications in adapted physical education has steadily improved. Applicants appear to respond well to published evaluation criteria and effectively relate their programs to federal priorities (I should also mention that this holds true for the special project and field-initiated research grant applications submitted by adapted physical educators).

Future program priorities, specifically in DPP, will continue to stress the importance of applicants to be able to quantify critical present and projected personnel needs. Personnel preparation programs will be encouraged to substantiate to what extent

the graduates of those training programs can be expected to have an impact on that need. Such an impact strengthens the university's linkage with state and local education agencies.

Under the Training Personnel for the Education of Individuals with Disabilities Program, DPP financially supports personnel training programs that represent one of the following types of projects: (1) development of new programs to establish expanded capacity for quality preservice training, (2) improvement of existing programs designed to increase the capacity for quality perservice training, or (3) special projects. Once the type of project is established, then the program should focus on meeting the specific personnel needs in adapted physical education. The first two types of projects need to emphasize utilizing innovative recruitment and retention strategies as well as promoting full qualification for personnel serving children with disabilities. Such emphases highlight the need for proactive strategies to prepare and retain highly qualified individuals in adapted physical education.

The OSEP Division of Innovation and Development and Division of Educational Services grant money to encourage research and demonstration activity related to the education of infants, toddlers, children, and youth with disabilities. Physical educators are entitled to apply for these funds on a competitive basis. However, to date, the record of special physical educators in receiving funds has, at best, only been fair.

Individuals with Disabilities. Those with disabilities also have been effective lobbyists. As direct consumers or receivers of direct services, individuals with disabilities are often in the best position to know what they

specifically need relative to all facets of their lives. Thus their input has been received and used to advance special physical education services. Formal groups have been established, such as the American Coalition of Citizens with Disabilities and the consumer affairs section of the United Cerebral Palsy Association.

Litigation

Although it can be powerful, leverage alone, or even in combination with the dissemination of literature, cannot accomplish all of its goals. Advocates of the rights of individuals with disabilities have realized that a potentially more powerful tactic is available, if needed. This tactic is litigation, which involves arguing a cause in a court.

A class action suit filed by the Pennsylvania Association for Retarded Citizens in 1971 and the 1972 Waddy Decree in the District of Columbia both resulted in court orders for the provision of free public appropriate education for children with disabilities. These are two classic examples of the use of litigation for educational change. More recent famous pro–special education cases include the 1979 *Armstrong* vs. *Kline* case, which argued the right of a child with severe disabilities to have summer educational programs, the 1981 *Roncker* vs. *Walter* case, which dealt with educating a child in the least restrictive environment, and the 1984 *Smith* vs. *Robinson* case, which allowed the award of legal fees to parents or guardians who successfully argued placement grievances in court.

In the field of athletics for individuals with disabilities, a number of classic cases of litigation have also been publicized (Questions and answers, 1977). In Michigan, a high school pupil with a prosthetic device was finally permitted to play football when a judge overruled the local school district's denial. At Ohio University, a basketball player with one functional eye was eventually granted the right to decide for himself whether or not basketball participation was safe and, subsequently, whether or not to try out for the university's team. Before the judge's decision in this case was rendered, officials at the university had consistently denied him any right to compete.

Legislation

The separate forces of literature, leverage, and litigation have often joined to change the laws of the land. Since the 1970s, the movement for civil rights, especially educational

rights, of individuals with disabilities has been in clear evidence by the passage of vital legislation and the approval of related rules and regulations. The legislation most important to special physical educators includes P.L. 93–112, the Rehabilitation Act of 1973; P.L. 101–336, the Americans with Disabilities Act of 1990; P.L. 94–142, the Education for All Handicapped Children Act of 1975; P.L. 99–457, the Education of the Handicapped Act Amendments of 1986; P.L. 101–476, the Individuals with Disabilities Education Act of 1991; and P.L. 97–35, the Education Consolidation and Improvement Act of 1981.

P.L. 93–112. The Rehabilitation Act of 1973 represented the major civil rights act to date for those with disabilities in America. P.L. 93–112 is based on the Fifth (due process) and Fourteenth (equal protection) Amendments to the U.S. Constitution. Of specific interest is Title V, Section 504 (September 26, 1973):

> No otherwise qualified handicapped individual in the United States . . . shall, solely by reason of his handicap, be excluded from participation in, be denied the benefits of, or be subjected to discrimination under any program or activity receiving Federal financial assistance.

The broad coverage of the law's thrust against discrimination in all programs or activities that receive federal funds is clearly indicated. Public schools are an obvious example of such a program.

Section 504 and the Rules and Regulations that implement it contain two major requirements with which schools must comply in order to receive continued federal funding. First, a pupil with a disability cannot be discriminated against by being excluded from participation in a school program provided in the least restrictive environment or more normal setting. This implies barrier-free physical accessibility to programs. June 1980 was the deadline for all structural and non-structural changes that would permit total accessibility to any program (including educational programs) receiving federal financial assistance.

Second, once admitted into a school program, a pupil with a disability cannot be discriminated against by being denied benefits of participation in those programs conducted in a least restrictive environment. For a physical education teacher this essentially means that such a pupil must receive appropriate accommodations so that he or she may be provided with a program as effective as those for nondisabled peers. Accommodations in physical education could include flexible scheduling (in which a pupil is provided with an alternative program when he or she cannot participate safely and successfully in satisfying activities), use of adapted equipment, use of interpreters, use of specialized auxiliary aids, use of rule modifications, or use of a buddy system. Note that the provision of appropriate accommodations and equally effective instruction does not connote treatment and results equal to those of the nondisabled. Similar treatment and results are not expected, according to interpretations of Section 504; instead, an equal opportunity to achieve equal results is the expectation and intention of the 504 guidelines.

P.L. 101–336. The Americans with Disabilities Act of 1990 strongly fortified the mandates of P.L. 93–112 by extending the civil rights of those with disabilities to all programs, school- or nonschool-related, irrespective of the receipt of federal financial assistance. This law's regulations (January 27, 1992) affect employment, transportation, public accommodations, state and local governments, telecommunications, and education. Applied examples of how this law directly affects schools include the following:

1. Administrators cannot discriminate against a teacher or potential employer who is qualified to teach.

2. Reasonable accommodations need to be made in order for a teacher to teach and for a pupil to learn.

3. Physical barriers in existing schools must be removed or alternative methods of providing educational services must be offered.

4. All new construction and renovations must be accessible.

The U.S. Department of Justice's Civil Rights Division is responsible for enforcing the requirements of this law. Of most relevance, monetary fines can now be applied for noncompliance with a $50,000 fine for the first offense.

P.L. 94–142. The Education for All Handicapped Children Act of 1975, most recently amended by the passage of the Individuals with Disabilities Education Act (P.L. 101–476), is recognized as blockbuster legislation that not only addresses specific mandates with respect to the education of children and youth with disabilities but also provides considerable financial support to fulfill those mandates. It affects only educational programs. Some of the major components of this law include the following:

1. All pupils with disabilities between the chronological ages of 3–21, no matter how severe their disability, are to receive a free appropriate public education. This is also known as the full service mandate.

2. All children with disabilities are to be educated in the least restrictive or most normal environment. This process also includes mainstreaming (discussed in Chapter 4).

3. A pupil with a disability (where appropriate) and the pupil's parent(s), guardian(s), or surrogate parent(s) must be actively

involved in the educational team that makes placement decisions and develops an individualized educational program (IEP) for each child on an ongoing basis.

4. States are under a mandate to locate all children in need of special educational services so that their educational needs can be properly addressed. This is referred to in this law as the child find mandate.

5. Each state must develop a comprehensive system of personnel development that impacts on the in-service and preservice training of regular and special educators and support personnel. All individuals, including physical educators, who are teaching or plan to teach children with disabilities in any capacity must be shown to be competent.

6. The federal government will provide funds to SEAs and LEAs in order to assist them in meeting the full service goal.

7. Parents have been afforded specific due process rights under P.L. 94–142. They can appeal special education–related decisions via local to state hearings and then, if still not satisfied, from the state to the U.S. Supreme Court.

The law's definitions of special education and related services, as amended by P.L. 101–476, are of particular interest to physical educators. The term *special education* for pupils age 3 through 21 is defined as "specially designed instruction, at no cost to parents or guardians, to meet the unique needs of a child with a disability, including—(A) instruction conducted in the classroom, in the home, in hospitals and institutions, and in other settings; and (B) instruction in physical education" (P.L. 101–476 Rules, *Federal Register*, September 29, 1992, p. 44804). Physical education is the only curriculum area specified in this definition of special education and, therefore, is a primary ser-

vice. The implications of this are discussed in the next section.

The term *related services* for pupils age 3 through 21 means "transportation, and such developmental, corrective, and other supportive services as are required to assist a child with a disability to benefit from special education, and includes speech pathology and audiology, psychological services, physical and occupational therapy, recreation, including therapeutic recreation, early identification and assessment of disabilities in children, counseling services, including rehabilitation counseling, and medical services for diagnostic or evaluation purposes. The term also includes school health services, social work services in schools, and parent counseling and training" (P.L. 101–476 Rules, *Federal Register*, September 29, 1992, p. 44803).

Physical education is not a related service and the federal government and all the states, therefore, cannot treat physical education as a related service. Further, implications can be drawn by all physical educators from the way the term *physical education* has been defined in the Rules and Regulations that implement P.L. 94–142.* Physical education is defined as the development of physical and motor fitness; fundamental motor skills and patterns; and skills in aquatics, dance, and individual and group games and sports (including intramural and lifetime sports). The term includes special physical education, adapted physical education, movement education, and motor development.

Physical education service delivery guidelines also are offered in the Rules and Regulations of this law. To quote:

---

*Rules and Regulations are written to implement a law, which is a separate document. For example, P.L. 94–142 was signed in November 1975; its Rules and Regulations were finally approved and signed in August 1977.

(a) *General.* Physical education services, specially designed if necessary, must be made available to every child with a disability receiving FAPE (free appropriate public education).

(b) *Regular physical education.* Each child with a disability must be afforded the opportunity to participate in the regular physical education program available to nondisabled children unless (1) The child is enrolled full time in a separate facility, or (2) The child needs specially designed physical education, as prescribed in the child's IEP (individualized education program).

(c) *Special physical education.* If specially designed physical education is prescribed in a child's IEP, the public agency responsible for the education of that child shall provide the services directly, or make arrangements for those services to be provided through other public or private programs.

(d) *Education in separate facilities.* The public agency responsible for the education of a child with a disability who is enrolled in a separate facility shall ensure that the child receives appropriate physical education services in compliance with paragraphs (a) and (c) of this section (P.L. 101–476 Rules, *Federal Register,* September 29, 1992, p. 44813).

With this type of specification, P.L. 94–142 (see Figure 2.8) has accorded special physical educators a prominent place on the educational team. Congress reinforces this in a key House report that states:

> The Committee expects the Commissioner of Education to take whatever action is necessary to assure that physical education services are available to all handicapped children, and has specifically included physical education within the definition of special education to make clear that the Committee expects such services, specially designed where necessary, to be provided as an integral part of the educational program of every handicapped child (House Report No. 94–332, p. 9, 1975).

Public Law 94-142
94th Congress, S. 6
November 29, 1975

An Act

To amend the Education of the Handicapped Act to provide educational assistance to all handicapped children, and for other purposes.

Be it enacted by the Senate and House of Representatives of the United States of America in Congress assembled, That this Act may be cited as the "Education for All Handicapped Children Act of 1975".

Education for All Handicapped Children Act of 1975. 20 USC 1401 note.

EXTENSION OF EXISTING LAW

Sec. 2. (a)(1)(A) Section 611(b)(2) of the Education of the Handicapped Act (20 U.S.C. 1411(b)(2)) (hereinafter in this Act referred to as the "Act"), in effect during the fiscal years 1976 and 1977, is amended by striking out "the Commonwealth of Puerto Rico,".

(B) Section 611(c)(1) of the Act (20 U.S.C. 1411(c)(1)), as in effect during the fiscal years 1976 and 1977, is amended by striking out "the Commonwealth of Puerto Rico,".

(2) Section 611(c)(2) of the Act (20 U.S.C. 1411(c)(2)), as in effect during the fiscal years 1976 and 1977, is amended by striking out "year ending June 30, 1975" and inserting in lieu thereof the following: "years ending June 30, 1975, and 1976, and for the fiscal year ending September 30, 1977", and by striking out "2 per centum" each place it appears therein and inserting in lieu thereof "1 per centum".

(3) Section 611(d) of the Act (20 U.S.C. 1411(d)), as in effect during the fiscal years 1976 and 1977, is amended by striking out "year ending June 30, 1975" and inserting in lieu thereof the following: "years ending June 30, 1975, and 1976, and for the fiscal year ending September 30, 1977".

(4) Section 612(a) of the Act (20 U.S.C. 1412(a)), as in effect during the fiscal years 1976 and 1977, is amended—

(A) by striking out "year ending June 30, 1975" and inserting in lieu thereof "years ending June 30, 1975, and 1976, for the period beginning July 1, 1976, and ending September 30, 1976, and for the fiscal year ending September 30, 1977"; and

(B) by striking out "fiscal year 1974" and inserting in lieu thereof "preceding fiscal year".

(b)(1) Section 614(a) of the Education Amendments of 1974 (Public Law 93–380; 88 Stat. 580) is amended by striking out "fiscal year 1975" and inserting in lieu thereof the following: "the fiscal years ending June 30, 1975, and 1976, for the period beginning July 1, 1976, and ending September 30, 1976, and for the fiscal year ending September 30, 1977,".

20 USC 1411 note.

(2) Section 614(b) of the Education Amendments of 1974 (Public Law 93–380; 88 Stat. 580) is amended by striking out "fiscal year 1974" and inserting in lieu thereof the following: "the fiscal years ending June 30, 1975, and 1976, for the period beginning July 1, 1976, and ending September 30, 1976, and for the fiscal year ending September 30, 1977,".

20 USC 1411 note.

89 STAT. 773

FIGURE 2.8   P.L. 94–142.

P.L. 99–457. The Education of the Handicapped Act Amendments of 1986 extended P.L. 94–142's preschool thrust and established a new federal educational initiative for infants and toddlers having an identified disability or determined to be at risk of developing a disability. The specific major components of this legislation are having an immediate positive effect on the targeted children. More specifically:

1. P.L. 99–457 mandates, and partially funds, P.L. 94–142 services down to age 3. Originally, the goal was to have programs available for the estimated one-third million preschoolers (ages 3–5) with disabilities by school year 1990–91.

2. P.L. 99–457 creates a new state grant program for infants and toddlers with disabilities (birth through age 2) with comprehensive family services planning. This component is not under P.L. 94–142 and, therefore, is not necessarily monitored by each state's department of education. In fact, the P.L. 99–457 program for infants and toddlers in Ohio is under its Department of Health.

3. P.L. 99–457 strengthens interagency provisions, stresses parent education, and mandates individualized family service plans (IFSPs) for those infants and toddlers who are served. This emphasis on parents and the family unit in constructing IFSPs contrasts with P.L. 94–142's child-centered approach in constructing individualized education plans (IEPs).

4. P.L. 99–457 establishes expanded authority as it relates to technology, media, and materials for infants, toddlers, and school-age children who have a disability, and this law, importantly, creates a National Center of Recruitment and Employment in Special Education.

With this federal and state commitment to early intervention, optimistic educators hope that all youngsters with disabilities will be mainstreamed more into regular classrooms and taunted less often over the years just for being different. And, as a potential long-range outcome, children without disabilities may find it easier to accept their peers who have differences and maintain this attitude throughout life.

P.L. 101–476. The Individuals with Disabilities Education Act of 1990, popularly known as IDEA, amended the entire Education of the Handicapped Act (P.L. 93–380), including P.L. 94–142 (Part B) and P.L. 99–457 (Part H). Key highlights of this law, and its accompanying Regulations (September 29, 1992), which impact all educators, include the following:

1. A new emphasis on person-first, disability-second language is clear (e.g., "pupil with a disability" is preferred over the phrase "handicapped pupil").

2. A transition services plan must also be included as part of the IEP at least by age 16. This relates to such areas as transition from school to work and transition from school to the community so that linkages can be established for a pupil with a disability before the pupil leaves the school setting.

3. Two new categories of disability have been added—autism and traumatic brain injury. Pupils with these disabilities now must be located and provided with an IEP and appropriate services, and can be counted by school districts for purposes of federal financial assistance.

P.L. 97–35. In the early 1980s there was a concerted effort by the Reagan administration to provide less federal special education monies to the states, to use a block-grant approach, and to place special education responsibilities primarily with each state. One major example of this is the Elementary and Secondary Education Block Grant Program mandated as a part of P.L. 97–35 and entitled The Education Consolidation and Improvement Act of 1981. This act essentially grouped, or "blocked," numerous programs from prior educational legislation into two major chapters.

Chapter 1 provides partial financial assistance to public and private nonprofit schools and their agencies to meet the special education needs of educationally deprived children, children in local institutions for neglected or delinquent children, youngsters in correctional institutions, migratory children, and Indian children. Among the institutions assisted are state-supported schools such as schools for the deaf and schools for the blind.

Chapter 2 allows the partial funding of state educational agencies and public and private nonprofit schools in order to impact on the education of both children with and without disabilities. Chapter 2 funds can specifically be used for basic skill development, support services, varied special projects, and a few discretionary programs, including those available through the National Diffusion Network. A few of these National Diffusion Network discretionary programs relate specifically to special physical education and are discussed in Chapter 3 of this text.

No set percentage of Chapter 2 money is allotted for use with pupils who are disabled; however, special physical educators have an opportunity to document their needs each year when school districts apply for Chapter 2 funds. While each state's education department administers P.L. 97–35 funds, the responsibility for the design and implementation of funded projects rests with school administrators, classroom teachers, support personnel, and others having the most direct contact with pupils and being most responsible to parents. Further, each state has a Chapter 1 and Chapter 2 coordinator who can assist teachers, administrators, or others in their quest for educational funding under P.L. 97–35.

Implications of Federal Laws for Physical Educators

Physical educators who have pupils with disabilities in their classes and directors of physical education in local school districts have a responsibility to become and remain knowledgeable about the six laws discussed, their amendments, and their associated regulations. By so doing, they will not only be well informed about legal mandates but also will be aware of resources to tap to improve programs and ultimately positively affect the pupils in their charge. Physical educators

should also know the appropriate state legislation. Each state must have an education law tailored to meet its needs and appropriately address the mandates of federal law. For example, in Ohio the P.L. 94–142 sequel legislation is House Bill 455; New York has Chapters 853 and 241. Physical educators and directors of physical education will be better able to enhance their programs with a knowledge of resources available through key state and federal legislation. In fact, there are over 100 federal sources of funds related to educating those who are disabled; major resources are available through P.L. 97–35 and P.L. 101–476.

In addition, it stands to reason that, because physical education is the only curricular area mentioned in the definition of special education in P.L. 94–142, it deserves a reasonable piece of the "funding pie" in order to provide full service programs of physical education for all children with disabling conditions. Physical education's prominence in this law should entitle physical educators to such benefits as adapted equipment and auxiliary aids, increased special staff, elimination of accessibility barriers, money for in-service training, and interpreters for the deaf. The resources potentially available to physical educators through federal legislation must not overshadow the serious mandates with which school personnel must comply. Real issues related to these mandates include the following:

1. Because P.L. 101–476 and P.L. 93–112 mandate education of all pupils with disabilities in the least restrictive environment, regular physical educators will have an increasing number of these pupils in their classes. The "out of sight, out of mind" attitude will be increasingly challenged at the grass-roots level.

2. Because placement of a pupil with a disability in a physical education class should stem

from the IEP, physical educators should be involved in the process from its origination so that they can best plan for the pupil and themselves.

3. Because SEAs and LEAs are under a child find mandate, and because physical educators have a unique opportunity to observe pupils in the gymnasium, pool, playground, locker room, showers, and a variety of community settings, they have an obligation to help identify additional pupils in need of special education and perhaps related services.

4. Because physical education is the only curricular area mentioned in P.L. 94–142's definition of special education, physical educators deserve a prominent place on the educational team within a school and all IEPs, including their content related to transitional services, should address physical education. Physical educators cannot sit back and allow others on the team to make all the pertinent decisions regarding the provision of educational services for a pupil who is disabled.

5. P.L. 94–142 clearly differentiates and mandates physical education as a primary service; physical therapy, occupational therapy, and recreation are examples of related services. These related services cannot, therefore, be considered a substitute for a program of required physical education; they are not synonymous with physical education. However, unfortunately, physical therapy, occupational therapy, and recreation programs often supplant the physical education requirement. As a rule, related services should be considered supplementary and should be offered only when they will benefit or enhance the provision of primary services, including physical education.

6. Since 1975, federal funding of special physical education has been inadequate compared to the funding of special education programs. This is one reason why fewer qualified special physical educators are being trained and employed and fewer

needy pupils are being served in special physical education. Public law 94–142, therefore, is not living up to its expectations entirely (Churton, 1987). For instance, each year the federal government publishes its Annual Report to Congress on the Implementation of Public Law 101–476. This document has been, and will continue to be, a primary source of data on this law's effectiveness over time. Special physical educators should consult it to justify documented needs in special physical education. In addition, quality control concerning the delivery of special physical education services can and should be monitored at the local school district level, the state department of education level, and at the federal Department of Education level. Such monitoring should be centered around the inclusion of physical education in individualized education programs.

7. Title II of P.L. 99–457 extends the P.L. 94–142 age down to 3 years. This significant preschool mandate carries with it the prominence of physical education within P.L. 94–142's definition of special education. Physical educators will, therefore, need more formal and informal preservice and in-service experiences in order to develop and refine their teacher competencies as they relate to children at the preschool level.

8. In addition, Title I of P.L. 99–457 stresses the physical development of targeted infants and toddlers (0–2 years) in the development, implementation, and evaluation of its IEP variation known as the individualized family service plan. Special physical educators are potential team members in this law's interagency, cross-disciplinary thrust. Our influence can now extend beyond the traditional school-age years and has spawned a growing emphasis on pediatric special physical education (Cowden & Eason, 1991).

9. The 1990 amendments to the Education of the Handicapped Act impact special physical educators and regular physical educa-

tors in a few significant ways. The Individuals with Disabilities Education Act (P.L. 101–476) now replaces the Education of the Handicapped Act and, in so doing, directly affects P.L. 94–142 and P.L. 99–457. Aside from such changes as new attention to pupils with autism, traumatic brain injury, attention deficit disorders, and drug-related disabilities, there is also a fundamental change in terminology suggested for use by all educators. As noted in the title of this new legislation, the person is now emphasized first and the disability is noted second as a characteristic of the person. This change is also reflected in the Americans with Disabilities Act of 1990 (P.L. 101–336). The new terminology, considerably more humane in nature, should be used by us and is, in fact, generally employed throughout this text.

10. Last, the Americans with Disabilities Act (P.L. 101–336) now provides physical educators with more ammunition toward the elimination of architectural and attitudinal barriers in schools. In this regard, an increased number of qualified physical educators, with disabilities themselves, can now

be employed in schools throughout the United States, and pupils with disabilities are further assured a guaranteed equal opportunity to participate successfully in least restrictive and safe physical activities, sports, and recreation programs with personal satisfaction.

International Perspectives

Developments in special education and special physical education are going on throughout the world. Rather than a list of bare-bone facts, we present a series of short interviews by experts in the field from selected countries that span five continents. They chiefly address the following question: "What is the status of special physical education in your country in terms of direct services for pupils with disabilities and professional preparation?" For additional information on European adapted physical activity (special physical education, therapeutic recreation, and sports for those with disabilities), see the 1989 issue of the *Adapted Physical Activity Quarterly* (vol. 6).

Sheila E. Henderson and David Sugden, on The Status of Special Physical Education in the United Kingdom

Dr. Sheila Henderson is a professor at the University of London's Institute of Education in the Department of Educational Psychology and Special Education Needs, London, England. Dr. David Sugden is a professor in the School of Education at the University of Leeds, Leeds, England.

Since the late 1970s, there have been some major changes in the way educators in the United Kingdom have conceptualized special education and the implementation of its provisions. Physical education for children with special educational needs is viewed within that context.

In 1978, a special committee, known as the Warnock Committee, made its report to the government on the state of special edu-

cation in the United Kingdom. Some of the recommendations of this committee were then embodied in law in the 1981 Education Act. Three components of this act affected the physical education profession directly. First, the category system for classifying children with disabilities was replaced by the generic concept of a continuum of special *educational* need. This, accompanied by the acknowledgment that one in six children are likely to require special help at some point in their school career, has led to a much broader view of who has to be served in schools. Second, a recommendation was made that, wherever possible, children should be educated in mainstreamed schools. And third, tighter regulations in the act concerning the identification and ongoing assessment of learning difficulties meant that children's needs had to be more accurately specified and monitored. The changes brought about by this act have led to much upheaval within the physical education profession—basic aims and objectives have been reconsidered, training courses have been revised, and individual school programs have been completely reorganized.

Within our schools, it must be said that current practice is variable. There are some superb examples of programs which meet the needs of even the most disabled of children, often extending right into community involvement in sports centers, clubs, etc. However, there are examples where active participation is minimal and children's physical and social needs are not well met. To be realistic, 10 years is a short time when it comes to implementing the sorts of radical

changes required to really do justice to the ideals of the Warnock Committee. As in many other countries, there is still much debate about the best way to ensure that *all* children with special needs in the motor domain are adequately educated.

And, just when the education profession as a whole was beginning to adjust to the changes arising from the 1981 act, a new and possibly even more difficult directive to respond to was received. In 1988, the Education Reform Act was passed, heralding the greatest changes in the British educational system for half a century. All levels of educ-tion are included, with a profound effect coming from the introduction of a national curriculum. When this new curriculum is fully enforced, *all* children (with few exceptions) will have to follow a recommended course of work in physical education and attempt to meet specified criteria at ages 7, 11, 14, and 16. The question of how this will affect children still in special schools, children with severe disabilities integrated into mainstreamed schools, or simply the less able child who has always been in a mainstreamed school remains unclear.

Nava Zwi-Isseroff, on the Status of Special Physical Education in Israel

Nava Zwi-Isseroff is a special physical educator in Tel-Aviv, Israel.

Sport for those with disabilities has been developing in Israel almost since the state's establishment (1948) and that is mainly due to the many young men who were injured in the different wars. Special physical education in the schools has had a much slower development and this subdiscipline is still undergoing changes and improvements.

A national committee appointed by the board of education in 1971 to investigate

the subject of physical education in the special education school system stated that the objective of physical education in the special education school system is identical to that of regular physical education, which is "to help the pupil to realize potential to the maximum in all domains of development— the psychomotor, the affective, and the cognitive." The committee also stated its recommendations in detail regarding stan dards related to hours and personnel in teaching, teachers' preparation, curriculum, facilities, and equipment.

On July 12, 1988 a Special Education Law was enacted in the Israeli parliament. The law defines special education as "systematic teaching, learning, and treatment including physiotherapy, speech therapy, occupational therapy, and other professional treatments that will be determined, including related services, according to the needs of the exceptional child." The new law prescribes free and appropriate public education for all children with disabilities aged 3 to 21. It outlines in detail the need for an individualized education program for every such child, the need for qualified personnel, placement committees, etc. The law is still under study by all professionals concerned. It is the hope of special physical educators that its implications will bring about an improvement in the quality and the quantity of physical education to which each child is entitled.

Professional preparation programs in special physical education have existed for some years in most of the teachers' colleges that offer physical education teaching certificates. Different programs continue to develop and improve as the awareness of the need of these specialists grows. Two specialization programs are offered, both at the undergraduate level. One is for those who study for a teaching certificate only (three years) or for a teaching certificate and an undergraduate degree (four years). The other is a one-year program for physical educators who wish to be certified in special physical education. The coursework offered in these programs includes areas such as psychology of the exceptional child, assessment and evaluation, movement as a developmental tool, and the human nervous system. All programs include fundamental course-work, observations at different institutions, and practical experience with various populations characterized as disabled. Unfortunately, graduate programs in special physical education are not yet available.

Harald von Selzam, on the Status of Special Physical Education in the Federal Republic of Germany (former West Germany)

Harald von Selzam is a special physical educator from Berlin, Germany.

The school system of the Federal Republic of Germany is divided into the regular schools and 10 different types of special schools. The following types of special schools exist: special schools for pupils who are learning disabled, intellectually disabled, physically disabled, hearing impaired, deaf, visually impaired, blind, behaviorally disordered, and chronically health impaired, as well as schools in hospitals and institutions. In general, special schools are well funded and well equipped by the states' governments. The idea of integrating pupils with disabilities in regular classes has become more popular recently.

However, there is no law that requires education in the least restrictive environment (LRE). LRE-based programming predominantly rests on the individual initiatives of certain school faculties or individual teachers or is practiced in so-called model schools. As with all regular schools, physical education is part of the curriculum of special schools. Three hours of physical education per week are required for most pupils; pupils who are mentally retarded receive four hours.

As an extension, sport activities are normally not offered by the schools but by sport clubs. Children, nondisabled and disabled, interested in sports can attend sport clubs in the afternoon when they do not have to be in school. Special sport clubs as well as special community-based organizations also serve the needs of pupils with disabilities in the afternoon.

The universities of Cologne and Frankfurt are the only schools in Germany that offer a degree in physical education with specialization in sport and physical activity for those with disabilities. This degree, however, does not qualify graduates to teach in public schools. In order to teach in regular or special schools, a teaching certificate is needed. The requirements for a teaching certificate to date do not include mandatory classes in special physical education. This is true for both the special education and physical education teacher.

Students interested in studying about special physical education can also voluntarily attend some classes which are offered on the initiative of individual teachers in almost all universities. Credit received in these classes may count toward the special education or physical education degree.

As an extension, certification for teaching/coaching athletes with disabilities in sport clubs can be obtained after attending a 20-week class offered by the German Disabled Sport Organization, or additional education through in-service programs and evening schools.

Katie Chaput Jarvis, on the Status of Special Education in Canada

Katie Chaput Jarvis is an elementary school principal in Ottawa, Ontario, Canada.

Probably due to its proximity, the development of special education in Canada parallels to a great extent its development in the United States. In many respects Canadians have had the unique opportunity to critically assess the American education system before fashioning their own education system.

It must be noted that in Canada legislation pertinent to education is governed by each province and territory. In fact, the only federal legislation governing the rights of individuals with disabilities is the Declaration of Human Rights. As a result, no federal money is allocated directly to education. Funding is provided through a combination of provincial grants and municipal taxes.

All ten provinces, as well as the two territories (Yukon and Northwest Territories), have legislation specific to the education of pupils who are disabled. The breadth of services varies and is more than likely a function of the wealth of the province or territory.

Throughout Canada, legislation is premised on the basic concepts of equal opportunity and free public education. Special education is considered a vital component of public education. Access to a free public education in the most normal setting is mandated. Assessment, diagnosis, remediation, and follow-up are components of the legislation and must be identified and monitored in school district policy. A cascade model of services, such as the Reynold's (1962) model, is suggested.

The Education Amendment Act of the province of Ontario in many ways parallels

P.L.94–142. This act is based on universal access; free public education; the right to appeal; and early ongoing identification, assessment, and review.

Concerns faced by most provinces include the lack of sufficient funding and professional development of teachers. Presently, Canada is experiencing a period of economic restraint. This has directly affected funding for special education services and programs and is probably a main factor in limiting integration. Total integration, or deinstitutionalization, from a philosophical point of view, is not considered to be beneficial to every pupil and, therefore, not the intent.

With respect to professional development, the responsibility of in-service of teachers lies with the school boards. Approximately five days of the school year are designated as professional development days. Program priorities are set by the school districts and monitored by provincial ministries.

Preservice education is under the auspices of the Ministries of Universities and Colleges. Unfortunately, a program to indoctrinate all teachers in the pedagogical methods necessary to meet the needs of pupils who are disabled is not a component of the general education program. As a result, only those interested in teaching this type of pupil follow the special education courses. Furthermore, graduate programs and research related to the education and integration of such populations are limited. The Ontario University education programs are under review. Hopefully, several courses with respect to the education of special populations will be mandatory for all education majors.

Barrie Gordon, on the Status of Special Physical Education in New Zealand

Barrie Gordon is a special physical educator in Hamilton, New Zealand.

At present, special physical education has limited status in New Zealand. It has limited scope; and that which exists is due to the enthusiasm of individuals rather than the result of Education Department policy or initiative. As one indication of this, New Zealand's Special Education Service, the agency responsible for supplying all schools with expertise and support in the overall area of special education, does not employ any physical educationists at present.

However, New Zealand's education system is now undergoing a few fundamental changes. These changes, under the heading "Tomorrow's Schools," open up the possibility of an improvement in status. A key policy change which will affect special physical education is the government commitment to mainstreaming. This policy has meant that, for the first time, numbers of pupils with disabilities are appearing in the classes of the regular physical education teacher. A second policy change affecting special physical education is the decentralization of school control. Under "Tomorrow's Schools," individual school administrators will have control over all aspects of education occurring within their school building. This will allow them to employ special physical educators if they consider it necessary. As another related indication of change, the Hillary Commission, a government body charged with providing sport and recreation for the nation, has recognized the importance of special physical education and has established a national commission to promote the integration of pupils with disabilities into physical education, sport, and recreation in the New Zealand education system.

In the arena of professional preparation, the School of Physical Education at the University of Otago has offered a specialization in special physical education for many years. Relatedly, in order to teach in the public school system, graduates must also attend a teachers training college; yet, it is not mandatory at any of the teachers colleges to study special physical education. Some teachers colleges offer the option of study in this area, others do not.

Outside the education system there are many groups offering programs of adapted sports and recreation. Such groups as the Crippled Children's Society, the Special Olympics, and the Paralympics help fill any void in the education system.

Thus through collective initiatives spearheaded by the Hillary Commission, teachers colleges, and sport/recreational groups, special physical education is establishing a stronger position in New Zealand. The past situation appears to be changing; a positive and building wave of momentum appears to be in our future.

Tora Grindberg, on the Status of Special Physical Education in Norway

Tora Grindberg is a professor in the college of Early Childhood Education, Queen Maud's Memorial, Trondheim, Norway.

The educational system in Norway is directed by the state and the local governments. One of their main aims is to ensure that all pupils receive equal opportunities for education and training which is mandated by current laws. In addition, within these laws, there are equal opportunities ensured for leisure sport and recreation that are the responsibilities of the Ministry of Culture and Scientific Affairs and the Norwegian Confederation of Sports.

As early as the 1880s, laws were enacted for school-age children and youth who were mildly and moderately mentally retarded, hearing impaired, or visually impaired giving them the right to public education. At this time several residential schools were built. From this time, various laws were implemented to educate other school-age children and youth with other disabling conditions. In 1951, all the different laws that relate to special education were consolidated into one law. In 1969, another law was enacted in primary education which states that all pupils (ages 7–16 years) shall have nine years of elementary education and/or training. This law and the consolidated special education law of 1951 became one law in 1976. Based on this law a curriculum was implemented in 1987 (Monsterplanen of 1987) which included programming for all pupils, including those with disabilities and addressing physical education. A key phrase in this curriculum is "adapted education." This phrase denotes a form of individualization.

The Norwegian Sport Association for the Disabled is a part of the Norwegian Confederation of Sports that, in cooperation with the Ministry of Culture and Scientific Affairs, set the regulations for leisure sport and recreation. Among other aims, effort is put on education of coaches for participants who are disabled and building accessible sport facilities. In fact, it was experiences in connection with the Second World War that created the development of one common sport association, and this association's cooperation with the government.

The Ministry of Culture and Scientific Affairs also has the role as a bridge builder between the school system and the sport association, and one of the results of this is the "day-around-use" of all types of sport arenas and buildings, for all individuals including the individual who is disabled.

David Jones, on the Status of Special Physical Education in Australia

Dr. David Jones is a professor in physical education at the Queensland University of Technology, Kelvin Grove Campus, Queensland, Australia.

The schools for individuals who are disabled provide quality special physical education programs with appropriately trained staff. Many primary (elementary) schools have effective motor experience programs conducted by both physical education specialists and classroom teachers. Remediation at the primary and secondary levels is limited, as there are few physical education specialists with appropriate training in these schools, particularly away from the major city centers.

All universities offering preparation of physical education teachers include units in special physical education; however, all these courses are electives. Those students who wish to pursue postgraduate studies in special physical education can do it in the areas of education or applied sciences at most universities. A graduate diploma is offered specifically in the field of special physical education.

Although this may indicate an indifference to the area, this is incorrect. Surveys of teacher needs in four Australian states have identified special physical education as an area of high concern in primary and secondary schools; universities are in the process of responding to these findings. The major limitation for the provision of additional professionals in special physical education and expanded university offerings, is the lack of government funding. This is due to the depressed state of the national economy rather than a lack of enthusiasm or desire of the training institutions of school systems.

Ana Luisa Pizzaro, on the Status of Special Physical Education in Costa Rica

Ana Luisa Pizzaro is a special physical educator from San Jose, Costa Rica.

Services for individuals with disabilities have been offered for 50 years in Costa Rica; however, it has only been within the last 20 years that these services have expanded. Based on the constitution of Costa Rica and recent national legislation, there must now be equal opportunities provided for all school-age children to receive an education. It is the responsibility of the minister of education to provide these educational opportunities.

The Office of Special Education, which is under the direct auspices of the Ministry of Education, has had the responsibility to supervise these services in both segregated and integrated public school settings since 1973. The five sections within this office are specifically designated for the education of pupils who are deaf, blind, mentally retarded, emotionally disturbed, and multiply disabled. The personnel within this office work closely with those in the Office of Elementary and Secondary Education to provide appropriate programming for those pupils who are disabled in an integrated setting and to prepare other pupils to move from a segregated to an integrated school setting.

Physical education programs in Costa Rica are offered in both segregated and integrated settings. Most children in elementary school receive at least one class lesson (60 minutes) per week, and at the secondary level two hours of lessons per week (120 minutes). Children with mild disabling conditions are increasingly being integrated into the regular physical education classes; however, the philosophy and training of the personnel in each school district are determinants of whether or not integration will occur.

In 1982, the University of Costa Rica initiated a minor program for those interested in special physical education. Some of these students are now employed at institutions such as hospitals for individuals with emotional disorders, segregated schools, and integrated public school settings. Interestingly, as of 1990, there were 12 special physical educators employed in the country's 22 segregated schools.

The faculty at the University of Costa Rica also supervise students in the last year of their bachelor's program in public physical education programs for pupils with disabilities. These faculty have developed physical education practica in both segregated and integrated settings. In addition, the university faculty and staff have implemented a recreational swimming program for children who have cerebral palsy through the summer sport programs in the schools. Through this program, and other practica, the students who are preparing for careers in special physical education apply their knowledge learned in the classroom with pupils who are disabled.

In April 1990, the University of Costa Rica, in conjunction with the Rehabilitation Council, sponsored the VIII Inter-Americana Conference for Persons with Disabilities. This conference was attended by several professionals from the United States. Doctors Jean Pyfer, Jim Mastro, and Karen Depauw sharedseveral principles in the area of assessment, motor development, and sports for those who have disabilities with educators, students, physicians, and parents from the Caribbean and Central and South America. The impact of this conference was very important because many of the participants came to a better understanding of the physical and motor needs of those who aredisabled. With this information, hopefully, Costa Rica will continue toward promoting better education and physical recreation opportunities for individuals who are disabled, enabling them to become a more integral part of our society than in the past.

Yi-Ning "Michael" An, on the Status of Special Physical Education in Taiwan

Michael An is a special physical education doctoral student at Ohio State University. He is from Taiwan, Republic of China.

In Taiwan, segregated institutions for pupils with hearing and visual impairments were the earliest sites for the provision of special education services. Later, catalyzed by increasing knowledge and legislation, the public schools began to provide more services to pupils with other types of special needs related to mental retardation, physical disabilities, and emotional disturbance.

In December 1984, the Special Education Law, which included services for the gifted, was passed and its regulations were enacted in March 1987. This law defines which special education services should be provided, where they should be provided, and by whom. It also provides standards for the categorical classification of pupils and the professional preparation of service providers (teachers). As a result, preschool and nine years of public education are available to all pupils with special needs at no charge. These pupils are placed in either special schools, special classes within a regular school, or mainstreamed into regular classrooms depending on their abilities.

Special physical education is very new in Taiwan and, as a result, not much of this type of direct service is being offered to pupils with special needs. In fact, physical therapists typically work with those pupils who have physical disabilities. Yet, in a 1990 report by the Department of Education, special physical education has been discussed and the importance of it has been recognized. As evidence of this, the professional preparation of special physical educators has been specifically addressed in this report. It emphasizes the delivery of rehabilitation-related in-service and associated preservice courses to give current and future physical educators more competence for the teaching of pupils with special needs.

As a related promotion of special physical education in Taiwan, the Republic of China Sports Organization for the Disabled, founded in 1984, provides sports training to those with disabilities and selects top athletes to participate in international competitions. It is a member of the Far East and South Pacific Games Federation for the Disabled, and the Foundation for the Benefit of Citizens with Mental Retardation.

In general, therefore, special physical education can be considered a new but emerging field of education in Taiwan. The challenge will be to integrate the knowledge and expertise of this country's special educators, regular physical educators, physical therapists, teacher educators, and related sport organization leaders in order to further the future development of special physical education.

Keys
to the
Noncategorical
Approach

This chapter and Chapter 4 make up the second part of this book, on the noncategorical approach in teaching special physical education. This system, to which we strongly adhere, emphasizes a pupil's educational needs, not his or her categorical label. Keys to the noncategorical approach, discussed in this chapter include adjustment to a disability, the developmental and functional concepts, the concept of individualization, and individualization in practice. Analyzed in Chapter 4 are such topics as rationales for mainstreaming, teacher attitudes, selected pedagogical (teaching) considerations, mainstreaming principles, and mainstreaming models in physical education. It is especially important to note that the noncategorical approach can and should be applied in physical education programs for preschool, school-aged, and adult individuals with disabilities.

LABELS

There are labels in my shirts; they tell me front from back, My P. F. Flyers make me run faster on the track. Billie the Kid made my pants and Bonnie Doon my socks. Momma says Mattel made my brightly colored blocks. There are labels on most all things, and that is plain to see. But Momma, why's there a label on me?
> Jean Caywood
> Physical Education Instructor
> Plano, Texas

All people are individuals first and members of groups second. Some happen to have unique needs or disabilities and are categorically labeled (e. g., mentally retarded, emotionally disordered) to reflect those differences. Labeling is often beneficial for administrative purposes because funding can then be available for specialized services. However, labels are not very useful for educational programming. The physical education teacher who has a pupil with a disability in class needs to know much more than the categorical label. More specifically, a teacher needs information related to the pupil's exact present level of performance or development in educationally related physical education tasks. With this type of information, the teacher can proceed with the instruction of a pupil who "marches to a different drummer."

Categorical labels tend to stigmatize people and to reinforce stereotypes and negative expectations. Too many physical educators assume that if an individual has a particular label, certain behaviors automatically follow. Stereotypic reactions are commonly observed when nondisabled individuals interact with or refer to individuals who have a disability (Rosenthal & Jacobson, 1968).

To deemphasize traditional categories and their negative connotations, other "labeling" systems have been proposed. One suggestion (Stein, 1980) is that a specific disabling condition be grouped according to how it affects sensation, integration, and motor responses. Thus all individuals who are vision or hearing impaired are sensation impaired, all those with learning problems are integration impaired, all neurological and physical disabilities are primarily response impaired, and most multiple disabilities are some combination of the other three. Another noncategorical system emphasizes functional levels when programming psychomotor activities. Geddes (1978) specifically stresses levels of deficit within a classification that uses the terms "mild," "moderate," "severe," or "profound." Under this system a child with a mild deficit would be viewed as more functionally able than a child with a severe

deficit. This approach allows learning and functioning to be viewed as a developmental process across the psychomotor, affective, and cognitive domains of development.

The federal government has also attempted to combat the negative effects of specific labels. In P.L. 98-527 (the Developmental Disabilities Act of 1984) all disabilities are grouped under the term "developmental disabilities." This system highlights the individual's functional ability, not a categorical label, as being the sole criterion for the provision of special education and rehabilitation services.

The central thrust of these efforts—and the emphasis of this chapter—is on an individual's level of function, not category of disability. We discuss the noncategorical approach to teaching with an emphasis on the concepts of developmental skills, functional skills, and individualization. These concepts are, however, closely related to how an individual adjusts to a disability and how others adjust to or treat an individual who is disabled. Poor adjustment will most likely preclude maximal learning, and vice versa. Our discussion, therefore, logically begins at this point.

ADJUSTMENT TO A DISABILITY

Whether or not an individual will adjust to a disability involves complex interactions among the individual, family, school, and community. Based on these interactions, such an individual may react positively or negatively. There are numerous examples of people who have positively adjusted to a disability. Some most relevant to this text are highlighted in Table 3.1. Unhealthy reactions to a disability may be evidenced by anger, denial, depression, or withdrawal. These

TABLE 3.1   THE PHYSICAL ACTIVITY ACCOMPLISHMENTS OF SELECTED INDIVIDUALS

NAME	ACTIVITY	DISABILITY
Jim Abbott	Pitched for the University of Michigan and the 1987 Pan American Games baseball team. In 1987, he won the Sullivan Award, which recognizes the top U.S. amateur athlete. Threw a no-hitter for the New York Yankees in 1993.	Single arm amputee
Terry Fox	Ran across half of Canada in 1980 before his cancer spread to his lungs, resulting in death.	Single leg amputee and had cancer
James Mastro (see Figure 3.1)	Doctorate in special physical education and former accomplished wrestler.	Visually impaired
Harry Cordellos	A water skier, marathon runner, Ironman triathlete, and skilled cross-country skier.	Visually impaired
Kenny Walker	Started as defensive tackle for the Denver Broncos.	Hearing impaired
Tom Dempsey	Former field goal kicker for the New Orleans Saints; his 63 yarder still stands as an NFL record.	Born with half a right foot and no use of the right arm
George Murray	First wheelchair athlete to break the 4-minute mile.	Paraplegic
Mark Wieland	Using arms to propel his body 3 feet per step, he locomoted across the United States.	Lost his legs in Vietnam
Rick Hansen	Between 1980 and 1984, he won 19 international marathons in England, Australia, Japan, Canada, and the United States. Shared Athlete of the Year Award in Canada with NHL hockey legend Wayne Gretzky.	Paraplegic
Jean Driscoll	In 1993, completed the Boston marathon in 1 hour, 34 minutes, 50 seconds.	Spina Bifida (wheelchair)
Jim MacLaren	Pronounced dead in 1985, he is now a leading triathlete.	Single leg amputee

reactions could be directed toward self, family, friends, others, or the physical environment.

The family is a major factor in a successful adjustment. Parents and siblings must be able to accept the condition and the limitation(s) it may impose on the family unit. They must be able to emphasize the positive attributes of the affected individual as a contributing member of the family. Family members must avoid solicitousness, rejection, isolation, fear, sympathy, pity, being patronizing, overreacting, overprotection, dependence, and being overly demanding.

After the home, children spend the greatest amount of time in the school environment. Teachers, including physical educators, play a major role in the lives of their pupils.

FIGURE 3.1   James Mastro, Ph.D.

To interact successfully with children who are disabled and assist them in their adjustment to the school environment, teachers must be able to cope with their own fears and preconceptions and anxieties about pupils who are disabled. They must acknowledge the fact that one of their responsibilities is to serve *all* pupils in their classes, disabled and nondisabled. Like family members, the physical educator can help pupils with disabilities by accepting the disability and the limitations it may impose, stressing abilities that the pupil possesses, avoiding comparisons with other pupils, setting and maintaining realistic expectations for the pupil with a disability, providing opportunities and independent

activities at school and in the community, providing opportunities to develop areas of weakness while maintaining areas of strength, using a fair and consistent approach to behavior management, and involving the pupil maximally in all class activities.

The teacher must also accept the responsibility to affect positively the attitudes of other pupils toward their peers who are disabled. For pupils who have negative attitudes toward people with special needs, affirmative steps must be taken to reshape such pupils' behavior in order to help them accept and understand individuals who may be different in some way. The most opportune time to affect nondisabled pupils' attitudes is during the preschool and elementary school years.

Historically the attitude of the community toward those with disabilities has been one of rejection, repression, fear, pity, and curiosity (see Chapter 2). To a large extent, such negative social attitudes have developed because of a lack of understanding, which is often coupled with limited experience with people who have a disability. Because of the recent emphasis on involving those with disabilities in more normal or less restrictive environments, people with disabilities are now more visible and active in their communities. This not only allows them to function partly or fully in society, but it also enhances the possibility for normal and healthy interactions with the nondisabled. These interactions have the potential to decrease significantly the stereotyping of individuals with a disability.

In addition, mass communication has influenced community attitudes. Through the mass media, an emphasis has been placed on strengths related to the ability of persons with a disability to adapt to a variety of conditions. Reports in the media on the Special Olympics, the National Wheelchair Games, the Paralympics, and the World Games for the Deaf reveal how competent those with disabilities can be. The times of wheelchair athletes in the Boston Marathon are often reported along with the times achieved by the able-bodied winners.

At this point, and in light of this discussion, we offer a number of tips for use in dealing with persons who are disabled. A more complete listing of suggestions is available from the National Easter Seal Society for Crippled Children and Adults and from Stein (1978).

Remember that a person who has a disability is a person like anyone else. For someone who has problems with an arm or leg, it is just that, not a problem with the whole person. Actually, it could be argued that we all have disabilities, only on some of us they are more visible or adversely affect us more.

Be yourself when in the presence of someone who has a disability. If you are hesitant to say anything, allow the person who has a disability to help make you more comfortable. In this connection, explore your mutual interests. The other person probably has a number of interests that have nothing to do with his or her disability. Without prying, you can talk about the disability if it comes up during the normal course of a conversation. Basically, be guided by the wishes of the person with the disability.

Appreciate what the individual is capable of doing. The problems that the person has may originate more from society's attitudes than from the disability itself. When a person with a disability does have a problem, it usually is not a big issue. As one example, we need to be considerate of the extra time it might take a person with a disability to say something or to communicate in some other way. In this case and when necessary, ask questions that require only short answers or a nod or shake of the head; speak calmly, slowly, and distinctly to a person who has a hearing problem or other difficulty understanding; stand in front of the person and use gestures to aid communication; and when full understanding is doubtful, write the messages. Above all communicate directly with a person who has a disability and do not permit a companion to become a conversational go-between. As a second example, if a person has a problem with movement, he or she may prefer resolving the problem independently. Thus do not move a wheelchair or appliance out of the reach of a person who needs it; never start to push a wheelchair without first asking the occupant if you should do so; do not hover over the person for any apparent reason; and when pushing a wheelchair up or down steps, ramps, curbs, or other obstructions, ask the person how he or she wants it done. Let the individual with a disability set the pace in communicating and moving. If this person does need assistance in any manner, he or she will tell you which is the easiest way.

Be alert to architectural barriers; doorways, stalls, curbs, aisles, and stairs. Barriers can exist in other forms as well, such as inadequate lighting.

In summary, let common sense and consideration be your guide and you will not err seriously.

Lastly, here are some important principles regarding adjustment to a disability:

1. There is no common adjustment reaction to a disability. Just as in the "normal" population, no two people with similar disabilities are alike.

2. Difficulty in adjusting to a disability is highly correlated to type of disability, age of onset, and severity of disability. An individual who has both legs amputated at 21 years of age would probably have a more difficult adjustment than a person born with a below-knee amputation.

3. Obvious disabilities are frowned on by society. Society's first impression of an individ-

ual with an observable physical disability would probably be more negative than the first impression of a person with a learning problem.

4. Adjustment to a disability involves the whole person. A child with cerebral palsy needs to adjust not only to motor awkwardness but also to the social, psychological, and intellectual implications of motor awkwardness.

5. The labeling of an individual with a disability often produces negative self-fulfilling prophecies by the nondisabled. A negative self-fulfilling prophecy lowers expectations of performance based on the incorrect perceptions of others.

To a large extent, the ability of a person to adjust to a disability depends on the acquisition and maintenance of a positive attitude that cannot be fostered and nurtured in isolation. It depends on positive feedback from many incidents and many people. In the end, though, acceptance of a disability must come from within the individual. In turn, acceptance will enhance overall development, including progress in acquiring physical education skills.

THE DEVELOPMENTAL CONCEPT

Typically, nondisabled pupils have a match between their developmental age (DA) and chronological age (CA), and therefore, their physical educators can stress keeping pupils at grade level. In working with many types of pupils with disabilities, however, there is often no match between their DA and CA; their DA is commonly below their CA. In working with these pupils, therefore, a developmental approach to teaching independent mature skills is generally indicated. Through such an approach, a teacher can track improved performance in physical education

skills, using each pupil's previous motor behavior or DA as the basis for analysis, rather than group scores or scores expected at a certain CA. To evaluate such a pupil's performance on the basis of group scores or scores expected at a certain CA would be grossly unfair to the child.

In physical education, all skills can be placed on a developmental continuum from easy to difficult. As a person moves along the continuum, progress occurs. This developmental process is applicable to all persons, whether disabled or nondisabled. If a person is highly skilled on a specific task, his or her performance would be viewed as high on the developmental scale for that task; if another person has limited ability in the same physical skill area, performance would be viewed as low on the developmental scale for that task.

A continuum of development can be ordered for the broad areas of physical education defined in P.L. 94–142—fitness, fundamental motor skills, aquatics, dance, and individual and group activities. In this regard, we consider play to be within the area of individual and group activities. The following is a brief overview of sequential development in each of these areas.

Fitness

Strength development (with implications for developing *flexibility*) has been viewed on a continuum of progressive resistance that includes four stages: passive, assistive, active, and resistive (DeLorme & Watkins, 1951). In the passive stage, the teacher or therapist takes the individual through a range of motion because the person is totally dependent. In the assistive stage, the individual can assume some part of the effort required to move one or more joints and is viewed as semi-independent. In the active stage, the individual has enough strength to move independently through some range of motion on a cue. These first three stages are most critical to individuals who are developmentally low in strength. When an individual has reached the active stage, enough strength and flexibility have developed for independent function in many everyday activities.

When a surplus of strength is desired or required, the resistive stage logically becomes the focus of attention. At this stage, the individual must independently exert force against an external resistance, whether it is movable or not. Exerting force against movable external resistance is called *isotonic* strength training. Exerting force against immovable external resistance, where muscles work against each other, is called *isometric* strength training. And exerting dynamic force against mechanized near-maximum resistance through an entire range of movement at variable preset speeds is called *isokinetic* strength training. When the exertion requirement is systematically increased for an individual, strength will increase over time for those muscles involved and across the entire range of motion. This, in essence, is strength training in a developmental sense. Continued progress in a developmental strength training program depends on adherence to the overload principle: If further strength is desired, greater efforts are constantly demanded of select muscle groups over time.

Cardiorespiratory endurance can also be viewed from a developmental perspective. Physical fitness specialists commonly espouse walking, walk-runs, and continuous running at increasing distances and at increasing speeds up to some optimal point. Physiological indices, such as decreased heart rate, decreased respiration rate, and increased aerobic capacity (ability to use oxygen), have typically been stressed in programs geared for the development of heart–lung endurance. A recommended plan for average adult heart–lung performance emphasizes rhythmic and aerobic exercise for at least 20 minutes three times a week at approximately 50 percent aerobic capacity. Heart–lung performances for adults above or below these parameters represent other points along the developmental continuum of cardiorespiratory capacity. Children and adults of both sexes can all be placed somewhere on this scale.

Fundamental Motor Skills

There are milestones in the development of all gross motor skills. For example, in the orderly development of locomotion skills there are at least 13 milestones: rolling, crawling (stomach touches ground), creeping (four points of support), cruising (one hand on object), walking, jumping, running, hopping, climbing, sliding, galloping, dodging, and skipping. Each of these milestones can be broken down further into other developmental subskills. For example, jumping subskills include a combination of integrated upper and lower body coordination, static and dynamic balance, and lower body power. These fundamental motor skills and patterns provide a set of expected achievements against which a teacher can assess a given child's movement competence. If these skills and patterns do not emerge on time developmentally, a child could be adversely affected throughout the school years and beyond (e.g., being generally excluded from participation in traditional games and sports).

For a stage of development to be fully set for the emergence of developmental voluntary motor milestones, a youngster needs to inhibit all primitive reflexes, differentiate mass random bodily movements, process incoming stimuli, and possess at least minimum fitness (strength, heart–lung endurance, flexibility) to respond motorically to environmental demands voluntarily. It is only when these goals have been attained that body awareness can be achieved. Body awareness includes both an awareness of self (body image) and space (spatial orientation). In time and with considerable practice, the development of body awareness leads to skilled performance in fundamental large muscle skills, which include locomotor, non-locomotor (balancing, turning, twisting), and gross object control skills (striking, kicking, catching). The development of these fundamental large muscle skills is, in turn, accompanied or followed by the development of precision fine motor skills. Finally, the development of all of these prerequisite skills can eventually lead to competence in individual activities and group games. To assist the reader further, a 60-month chronology of major gross motor skill milestones is presented. These normal developmental sequences form a yardstick against which the special physical educator can measure potential delays in a pupil's development.

Months	Milestones
3	Sits with head erect, but thrusts forward and is unsteady
	While supported, bears small fraction of weight momentarily
4	Sits with head set forward
	On the verge of rolling over, front to back or back to front
5	Rests weight on hands with chest off ground surface
6	Rolls from back to stomach
7	Maintains an erect sitting position
8	Stands and maintains balance briefly
10	Uses rail of crib to pull self to a standing position
	Creeps on hands and knees
12	Steps off low platform
	Walks forward and backward
15	Creeps up two steps
18	Walks and seldom falls
	Walks upstairs with one hand held
	Seats self in small chair
	Throws a ball
21	Walks downstairs with one hand held
	Squats while playing
	Kicks a large ball after demonstration
24	Runs well without falling (still not fast)
30	Walks on tiptoes after demonstration
	Jumps up with both feet off the floor after demonstration
33	Jumps off low platform (12 inches)
36	Alternates feet when going upstairs in adult fashion
	Jumps from bottom stair, landing erect
	Rides a tricycle using pedals
42	Walks on a walking board
	Ascends ladder with limb alternation
48	Jumps while running
	Skips with one foot forward
	Throws overhand
	Walks a low balance beam
	One-foot balance
54	Hops on one foot
57	Descends ladder with limb alternation
60	Skips alternating lead foot
	Catches

Aquatics

The orderly development of water adjustment activities, survival skills, swim stroke lead-ups, and traditional swim strokes with combinations can all be specifically sequenced from easiest to most challenging. These include, but are not limited to, the developmental progressions on the accompanying lists. Water depth can also be varied, taking into account safety and developmental levels.

Water Adjustment	**Survival Skills**
• Approaching water	• Front float
• Handling water	• Back float
• Sitting on pool side	• Treading water
• Entering pool	• Turning over
• Walking in shallow water	• Changing direction
• Walking in water of increasing depth	• Recovery to vertical
• Face in water	
• Towing	
• Bubble blowing	
• Rhythmic breathing	
• Bobbing	
• Retrieving objects under water	

Swim Stroke Lead-ups and Traditional Swim Strokes With Combinations

- Kick variations
- Arm variations
- Glides (front and back)
- Dog paddle
- Backstroke variations
- Crawl stroke variations
- Sidestroke variations
- Breaststroke variations
- Dive and stroke varitions

Two thirds of the earth's surface is water. Thus it is reasonable to assume that over an individual's lifetime, there is a chance that he or she will be in water that is deep. We believe that all individuals should learn how to survive in water. This, then, becomes the first and primary objective of aquatics instruction for all trainees, with or without disabilities. Any technique is acceptable at first, any stroke—survival is the key! Water possesses three essential properties that make aquatics a high priority activity for all individuals. First, buoyancy pushes the swimmer up, especially in salt water. Second, viscosity pushes a swimmer in from all sides. Third, gravity pushes a swimmer down. Collectively, these three properties permit a person with limited movement ability on dry land to move more efficiently and effectively in water.

In addition, according to Doremus (1992), the assessment and instructional programming of developmental aquatics for all swimmers (including those with serious disabilities) should sequentially take into account mental and physical adjustment to water, entering and exiting the pool safely, range of motion in water, balance and flotation, breath control–respiratory function, and increasingly active movement by a learner through the water.

Dance

All forms of dance (mixers, square, folk, social, aerobic, tap, disco) have simple to complex variations. Moran and Kalakian (1977) list a series of developmentally sequenced folk dances, grouping them according to level from easiest (Level 1) to most difficult (Level 5).

Level 1	**Level 2**
• Shoemaker's Dance	• The Wheat
• Chimes of Dunkirk	• Kinderpolka
• Dance of greeting	• Broom Dance
• Bleking	• Seven Jumps
	• Carousel

Level 3

- I See You
- Come Let Us
  Be Joyful
- Bunny hop
- Tropanka
- Glowworm Mixer

Level 4

- Seven Steps
- Teton Mountain
  Stomp
- Virginia Reel
- Oh, Susanna
- Pop Goes the
  Weasel

Level 5

- La Raspa
- Troika
- Buggy Schottische
- Hora

Individual and Group Activities

A child's need for play is no less important than the need for food, love, and shelter. We also recognize, and urge others to recognize, that play is the work of children and that toys are the tools of play. To learn by doing is the way to a child's growth and development. Thus children should be engaged in appropriate play every day.

Children without disabilities usually acquire most play skills on their own, in the backyard or playground. They use their imagination and natural enthusiasm to explore cause–effect relationships, formal rules, and problem-solving strategies. Specific types of natural play in a child's repertoire include animal play, water play, sand play, noise play, mud play, fantasy play, mirror play, toy play, and play on equipment.

Children with disabilities can be identified not only by type of play involvement but also by stage of play involvement. If the types and stages of play are delayed according to common expectations, a child may be disabled.

We can identify at least seven common developmental stages of play:

- Stage 1. Not even watching behavior—the child is not interested in playing and will not even learn passively by watching.

- Stage 2. Onlooker—the child spends most of the time watching other children play. He or she may talk to the children, give suggestions, and ask questions but does not overtly enter into play.

- Stage 3. Solitary or isolate play predominates—the child is oblivious to other children in the environment.

- Stage 4. Parallel play is evident—the child will play in the presence of peers, but the play is still solitary. The stage is characterized also by conflict if a child attempts to take away another's toy or invades another's territory.

- Stage 5. Associative play begins—the child is involved in movement activities and, at times, shares with other children in the same play area.

- Stage 6. Cooperative play begins—the child is actively involved in movement activities with continuous involvement with other players. Cooperative play has many levels, ranging from one to one, to small group, to large group. No competition exists. Participation in low organized games in small groups is possible. A child at this stage will take turns.

- Stage 7. Competitive play begins—development of cooperative play continues and there is active involvement in movement activities with continuous involvement with other participants. Win–lose elements are introduced. There are also different levels of competitive play that exist, from dual to large group and from organized to informal. At this stage a child shows more patience in waiting for one's turn and still enjoys play activities characteristic of lower stages.

The interview with Louis Bowers provides insight into the importance of play, playground design, and playground accessibility. Bowers is a world authority in the area of play, especially as it impacts players with disabilities.

Louis Bowers

Dr. Louis Bowers is a professor in special physical education at the University of South Florida, Tampa, Florida.

1. How important is play for the young child, particularly the preschooler who has a disability? What are the implications of P.L. 99–457 here?

The play of children around the world is characterized by spontaneity, enjoyment, creativity, discovery, and freedom of choice. Children do not wait for a specified time, but initiate a variety of unique play activities whenever they can. Play is a mirror of a child's development and thus is unique and individual to each child.

The play of children takes many forms in making contributions to their physical, psychological, and social development. Its most obvious form is the readily observable movement of children engaged in play. All young children need and desire to engage their bodies in activities requiring forceful contraction of muscles in order to facilitate growth and maintain the size and strength of both the muscular and skeletal systems.

Play additionally provides an opportunity for the testing of personal limits through selected physical challenges in which the body is moved up, over, down, under, and through a variety of challenges in the environment. Thus, movements such as rolling, crawling, climbing, walking, jumping, leaping, running, and sliding are natural and important expressions in the natural play of children.

Play is often referred to as the "child's most important business" as it serves such an important role for the child in experiencing and discovering life. The process of play contributes to the expertise and confidence of the player which is then transferred to the nonplay world.

The process of play also stimulates the player's senses of taste, smell, touch, hearing, seeing, and feeling movement. The player responds and alters the continuing play experience which involves the perceptual motor process. The development of this process through play is essential to the control of voluntary movement, and later, to acquiring motor skills.

Relatedly, P.L. 99–457 should provide an excellent opportunity for the involvement of parents in related early prevention/intervention programs for their children. Such programs can make a significant difference in the development of infants born prematurely or with disabilities or illness. As parents come to understand more about the abilities and developmental needs of their children and discover ways to stimulate their growth and development with the assistance of a professional child development specialist, an understanding of play will be very important.

2. What are your thoughts related to the future of playground design and accessibility with a particular stress on the preschool level?

Parents and teachers should remind themselves that a child with a disability is first of all a child, the disability is secondary. The need and desire to play exist among all children; therefore play equipment must be designed to accommodate all the players in an environment which is accessible, safe, and stimulates creativity. In this regard, findings from survey research indicate that much improvement needs to be made in play environments of children. In too many instances play equipment is inaccessible, poorly maintained, inappropriately positioned on the playground, allows for falls

from high levels, and has questionable surfaces under equipment.

While such conditions of existing playground equipment must be improved, we also must look toward alternative designs for play structures which go beyond the single use design of traditional play equipment. These developmental play centers of the future may be as varied as the ways in which young children will play on them; however, in my opinion, these play centers should adhere to the following basic principles of design in order to provide for safe, accessible, and creative developmental play:

a. Accessibility should be provided to and on equipment for all children by means of pathways, gently sloping ramps and stairs with handrails, as well as incline climbers and multilevel platforms.

b. Distances between levels should facilitate climbing to reasonable heights on equipment and yet minimize, through a multilevel design, the distance children can fall from one level to the next and to the ground.

c. A variety of inclines of not more than 35 degrees should be incorporated in the design in the form of ramps, flat and circular slides, carpeted inclines, stairs, and block and rope climbers to provide a variety of climbing opportunities.

d. Partially enclosed spaces through which children can move freely and safely, such as through tube slides, tunnels, and covered areas should be part of the design.

e. Placement of the play structure should provide ample, safe distances from other structures and take best advantage of shade trees and the surrounding natural environment.

f. The play center should present novelty to children through variation in size, shape, color, texture, and type of material which make up the play structure, and through manipulative accessories such as blocks, balls, sand, and water.

g. The overall design of the play center should interconnect each play component so that children can select alternative easy or difficult avenues to travel throughout the developmental play center at their own level of ability.

h. A sound structural design should be combined with strong, durable, nontoxic materials, and quality construction to provide a safe and lasting play environment.

It is time for a new beginning for the importance of play and playground equipment for all children. As electronic technology increases the sedentary aspects of the lives of young children, the need for large muscle activities and the experiences of moving, feeling, and interacting directly with other humans through play will become increasingly more important to good health and quality life. Young children need and desire quality playgrounds which in-

---

The rules and movement requirements of individual and group activities that require play skills can also be progressively sequenced from fundamental to complex (see Figure 3.2). In developmental order, these basically include movement education activities, drills/relays, low organized games, lead-up games, and high organized games.

Movement education is generally defined as an indirect, child-centered approach to the teaching of fundamental movement skills and concepts. This level of instruction is characterized by an emphasis on pupil choice, lack of competition, active learning, and pupils' experiencing movement based on challenging questions from the instructor ("How low. . . .?" "How many different ways. . .?" etc.).

Drills are physical activities dominated by direct instructor commands and fixed procedures. In a drill in which half the class is at each end of a gymnasium, each pupil might be required to kick a soccer ball under control between a series of cones to another play-er at the opposite end. In turn, that player weaves it through the cones back to the original starting point to the next player. In order not to overwork this noncompetitive level of teaching, an instructor could choose to divide the class into two or more teams and add a competitive element, using the same rules. In this case, the first team that successfully completes the coned course would be the victor. In using this level of instruction (relays), the activity might be more enjoyable to the class as a whole, but winning should not be overemphasized. One disadvantage to using relays is that quality of movement might be sacrificed.

Games of low organization incorporate the skills learned in movement education, drills, and relays. They are different, however, in their emphasis on multiple skills, greater activity flexibility, a generally increased emphasis on social skills and cooperation, the beginning of leadership responsibilities, and a beginning emphasis on game rules and strategies. Games commonly offered during

FIGURE 3.2 Developmental games hierarchy.

the early elementary years can be classified as low organized games. One example is Call Ball.

Lead-up games, as the name indicates, lead to successful participation in traditional games of high organization. That is, lead-up games involve transitional activities between games of low and high organization. A lead-up game such as kickball incorporates multiple skills and rules, is keenly competitive, and is very similar to baseball.

Finally, *high organized games* are the traditional sports. They involve a high level of skill, cooperation, and competition, plus the most complex rules and strategies. Some of the most common high organized games are

football, basketball, baseball, tennis, and volleyball.

Throughout this discussion of the developmental concept and its application to play and varied physical education activities, we have intentionally not considered chronological age. A person's developmental needs must be addressed first. A focus on developmental age is more relevant when attempting to teach to specific needs when a pupil is below grade level. This is the case for most pupils with disabilities.

Considerable information on the developmental approach to teaching specific individual and group activities within an educational and recreational context is available in the literature. A few key references follow.

Gallahue, D. L. (1987). *Developmental physical education for today's elementary school children*. New York: Macmillan.

Kamiya, A. (1985). *Elementary teacher's handbook of indoor and outdoor games*. West Nyack, NY: Parker.

Kirchner, G. (1992). *Physical education for elementary school children*, 8th ed. Duguque, IA: W. C. Brown.

Pangrazi, R., & Dauer, V. (1991). *Dynamic physical education for elementary school children*, 10th ed. New York: Macmillan.

Wisconsin Association for Health, Physical Education, Recreation and Dance. (nd). *The idea book*. Waldorf, MD: American Alliance for Health, Physical Education, Recreation and Dance.

THE FUNCTIONAL CONCEPT

Sometimes a pupil's independent skill development is so low that the difference between his or her developmental age and chronological age is very large. For example, Johnny may have trouble balancing on a balance beam while his peers have little trouble mastering this skill. Johnny also demonstrates real trouble in generalizing balancing from one type of gymnastics apparatus to another while his same-aged schoolmates show minimal or no difficulty with such skill generalization. As Johnny becomes older, the balancing problem still exists, yet balancing on different gymnastics apparatus becomes less and less important to his everyday life. For him a different instructional strategy in physical education is warranted. This new teaching strategy is known as the functional skills curriculum approach.

The functional skills curriculum approach has several key elements. First, it is community based and stresses only those skills that are most critical and important in a pupil's everyday environment, both in school and in the community. Visibility is also an integral aspect of the functional skills curriculum. The less visible an individual's disability is to others, the greater are the chances that the pupil will "make it out there" because he or she does not look too different. A third essential key is that the activities learned must be age appropriate. Too often elementary-level games and children's toys are used to instruct older pupils, an age-inappropriate and dehumanizing practice. In applying these elements, if balancing is a critical skill needed for Johnny's present and projected situation, it should become a target for functional training in the school and, more importantly, in natural settings within Johnny's home community. Further, it should be taught using age-appropriate functional obstacles on which to balance and taught so that his balancing technique does not look too different from that of his peers. Johnny should also want this training and have a choice in the matter. Certainly choice can be considered a fourth essential key in implementing a functional skills curriculum.

A specific scenario that builds on the skill of balancing might be: "Johnny was not able to demonstrate independent balance on a low balance beam in class. His efforts at forward,

sideways, and backward movements on the beam were continuously unsuccessful. After considering Johnny's needs in both school and nonschool settings, his teachers (including the physical educator) decided to put away the balance beam and substitute it with balancing skills on lower portions of gymnasium bleachers, on fallen tree trunks in outdoor fields, and on curbs in the school parking lots" (see Figure 3.3).

In this scenario Johnny's needs are more appropriately met by switching balance beam walking to everyday functional balance tasks (bleachers, fallen trees, curbs). On the other hand, because his peers have no difficulties in balance across different gymnastics apparatus, the traditional forms of training are justified for them. Again, if any pupil is falling significantly behind in acquiring physical skills, only those skills that are most important to his or her present and future school and nonschool environments should become targets for instruction. Time is probably wasted if a developmental approach to instruction continues; a change to a functional skills curriculum approach is indicated for this type of pupil.

An area from which numerous common functional skills can be drawn includes physical education. The following list provides some examples of what we believe are functional gross and fine motor skills, in contrast to related skills that we consider to be less useful.

- Lifting cinder blocks, tools, milk containers vs. lifting barbells
- Pitching sand bags vs. throwing a large ball
- Walking, jumping, running vs. skipping, hopping, leaping
- Shaking hands, turning doorknobs, vs. squeezing a dynamometer for grip strength

Nonfunctional

Functional

FIGURE 3.3 Pupils performing nonfunctional and functional balance tasks.

- Matching wood/lumber to slots vs. matching pegs to a peg board
- Painting furniture or walls vs. finger painting or painting by numbers
- Applying snaps on shoes or pants vs. using a board or cushion with various snaps
- Zipping a zipper on pants vs. zipping on a zipper board.

Special physical educators commonly use accommodations when they adapt physical activities so that a pupil with a disability can have a safe, successful, and satisfying experience in the gymnasium, pool, or playground. They do not, however, usually provide such instruction in the pupil's natural everyday environments. In other words, they do not take their instruction into the community. Some arguments can be made to provide numerous physical education activities in the community for all pupils, but at least everyone can agree that community-based func-

tional physical education instruction is critical for the pupil who is seriously disabled like Johnny. It simply makes more sense to have Johnny balance on natural obstacles rather than on a balance beam; lift cinder blocks, tools, and milk containers rather than barbells; and turn screwdrivers and door-knobs rather than squeezing a dynamometer.

In using the functional skills curriculum strategy, special physical educators also need to recognize that the everyday environments for any two people probably will not be the same. Therefore, the characteristics of Johnny's everyday environments must be assessed in order to determine those specific skills that will be most functional for him. Then programs are implemented in these environments.

The procedure for determining the most functional skills for Johnny involves conducting an ecological inventory. First, the educational team needs to agree on those environments in which Johnny probably will be functioning now and in the future. Then pupils without disabilities are observed in those environments in order to pinpoint the inventory of activities and specific skills required. Next, Johnny is given training in those same everyday environments both at school and in the community. This training involves progression from easy to difficult, with an emphasis on learning any functional alternatives, if needed. Because independence is a vital issue, too, functional alternatives for pupil skill accomplishment must also be determined and made available. These alternatives would then specifically be taught rather than the mature pattern, as failure would no doubt result otherwise.

Figure 3.4 provides examples of the use of the functional skills curriculum strategy with functional alternatives for each physical education area as specified in P.L. 94–142. The examples in the figure assume training in a variety of school and nonschool settings.

Such total environmental instruction will also require the assistance of nonschool individuals, the most important being Johnny's parents.

To summarize, the functional skills curriculum strategy involves

1. Skills of immediate usefulness to the pupil
2. Skills that probably will be frequently demanded in the pupil's natural environments
3. Skills that influence a pupil's ability to perform as independently as possible in the home, school, and community
4. Skills that are necessary for future functioning
5. Skills that are chronologically age-appropriate when acquired and have longitudinal age-appropriate implications
6. Skills that will permit the pupil to interact successfully and productively with the environment at some future time
7. The gathering of objective data from ecological inventories

FIGURE 3.4 Use of a functional curriculum in physical education.

AREA	SKILL	FUNCTIONAL ALTERNATIVES				
Fitness	Lifting	Push or pull	Disassemble, move, reassemble	Lift with partner	Operate robot	Watch someone lift object
Motor	Walking	Cane	Walker	Wheelchair unassisted	Wheelchair assisted	Be carried
Aquatics	Survival stroke	Dog paddle	Same-side propulsion	Single limb propulsion	Use of flotation device	Human assistance required
Dance	Square dancing	Cane	Walker	Wheelchair unassisted	Wheelchair assisted	Watch dancing
Games	Bowling	Two-step approach	One-step approach	Standing roll	Portable ramp	Watch bowling

← ← ← ←
Least visible (restrictive)   *Most visible* (restrictive)

8. Skills that make the pupil as invisible as possible when compared to same-age peers without disabilities

9. Skills that have functional alternatives to focus on in training, if necessary

10. Skills that are not only acquired but also maintained and generalized

11. Skills important to the pupil

12. Skills that substitute as completely as possible for "normal" skills

13. Skills that use the exact skills, materials, criteria, and personnel similar to those that are real (i.e., they will be encountered "out there")

14. Skills that are important to society

15. The educational team approach

16. Parent (guardian, surrogate) interest and training as critical to the acquisition, maintenance, and generalization of a pupil's functional skills in "real" environments

Information on functional skills curricula that relate to physical education and recreation is available in the literature. Some examples follow.

Certo, N., Schleien, S., & Hunter, D. (1983). An ecological assessment inventory to facilitate community recreation participation by severely disabled individuals. *Therapeutic Recreation Journal, 17*(3), 29–38.

Freagon, S., Wheeler, J., McDannen, K., Brankin, G., & Costello, D. (1983). *The individual student life skill profile system for severely handicapped students.* De Kalb: Northern Illinois University and De Kalb County Special Education Association.

Jansma, P., McCubbin, J., Combs, S., Decker, J., & Ersing, W. (1987). *Fitness and hygiene programming for the severely handicapped: A curriculum-embedded assessment guide.* Worthington, OH: Moody's Printers.

Maurer, S. (1983) *Project AMES.* Des Moines: Iowa State Department of Public Instruction, Division of Special Education.

Voeltz, L., & Wuerch, B. (1981). A comprehensive approach to leisure education and leisure counseling for the severely handicapped person. *Therapeutic Recreation Journal, 15*(4), 24–35.

Wright, J. (1986). *CREOLE: Leisure and recreation curriculum for severely handicapped secondary students.* Gretna, LA: Jefferson Parish Public Schools.

THE CONCEPT OF INDIVIDUALIZATION

Application of either the developmental or functional skills approach to teaching should lead directly to individualization of instruction—that is, instruction that addresses individual, not group, needs. In short, physical education teachers must individualize. Aside from legal requirements, researchers have shown that individualized educational approaches yield more proficient learning by pupils at all different levels than group approaches. Individualization works; individualization is teaching. Furthermore, "failure to provide for differences. . . is perhaps the greatest single source of inefficiency in education" (Skinner, 1968, p. 242).

Individualization is essentially pupil centered. The concept as a whole may involve many variables, not all of which an instructor must apply in dealing with every pupil. These variables include one or more teachers; playing different roles; teaching different things; to different individuals; on a one-to-one, small, or large group basis; at different times; by different methods; where individuals practice differently; at different paces; using different materials or support personnel; for different lengths of time; subject to different standards and different criteria for evaluating success; in different settings.

Individualization requires a multitiered hierarchy of instructional steps (see Figure 3.5). This hierarchy could be considered a closed loop; once one instructional goal is reached, based on evaluation and follow-up, the entire process is reinitiated toward the accomplishment of new short-term instructional objectives and annual goals. Notice in

Figure 3.5 that actual instruction cannot begin until a number of prerequisite tasks or steps are completed. Physical educators should not expect to provide individualized instruction until they first manage behavior, test and assess related skills, and appropriately plan activities to be taught.

When planning, a teacher must be able to task-analyze skills, that is, to break a skill

FIGURE 3.5   Individualized instruction hierarchy.

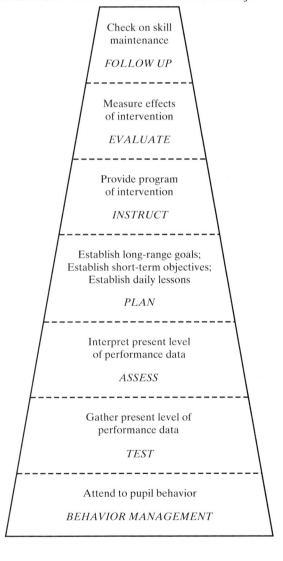

down into a logical progression. All good teaching involves the use of progressions. A *general task analysis* is the same as a developmental progression of behaviors related to a mature skill. Progressions that can be used with both nondisabled learners and learners with disabilities can be found in most texts on motor development and motor learning. A general task analysis or progression for mature hopping might include the following subbehaviors or tasks:

- Step 1: Two feet stand
- Step 2: One foot stand; toes from other foot touch ground
- Step 3: One foot stand
- Step 4: One foot stance; swing body upward; only toes of support foot touch ground
- Step 5: One foot stance: swing body upward; elevation of both feet and only lower half of body off ground
- Step 6: One foot stance; swing body upward; elevation of whole body; no use of arms
- Step 7: Mature hopping

A more detailed general task analysis or progression for roller skating is provided in Table 3.2. Before beginning this progression, the pupil must be taught the proper way of falling to both the right and left sides, as well as forward and backward. Here is progression to use when teaching safe falling : (a) relax like melting snow, (b) tuck hands, elbows, and arms close to the body, and (c) bend the knees and turn to the side before meeting the floor. This technique could first be taught without skates, then with skates but on a mat before being taught on a floor or pavement.

When planning for one specific individual, however, a more individualized approach to task analysis is often required, particularly for someone with significant disabilities.

TABLE 3.2   ROLLER SKATING PROGRESSION

A. Railing and Rug
  1. Two hands and both skates
  2. One hand and both skates
B. Railing and No Rug
  1. Two hands and preferred foot
  2. Two hands and nonpreferred foot
  3. One hand and preferred foot
  4. One hand and nonpreferred foot
  5. Two hands and both skates
  6. One hand and both skates
C. No Railing
  1. Preferred foot
  2. Nonpreferred foot
  3. Both skates
D. No Railing and No Rug
  1. Preferred foot
  2. Nonpreferred foot
  3. Both skates and 2 hand assist
  4. Both skates and 1 hand assist
E. Side of Person
  1. Twenty feet, wrist touch
  2. Twenty feet, elbow touch
  3. Twenty feet, shoulder touch
F. Back of Person
  1. Twenty feet, waist touch
  2. Twenty feet, shoulder touch
  3. Twenty feet, neck touch
G. Solo
  1. Twenty feet one way
  2. Thirty feet one way
  3. Forty feet one way

With permission. *Palaestra* (1989), *5*(2), 13–15, 46. *Palaestra* is a publication of Challenge Publications, Ltd., P.O. Box 508, Macolm, Il 61455.

Individualized task analysis involves a sequencing of skills outside the repertoire of a specific learner, based on the person's developmental-functional level, developmental-functional needs, and learning characteristics. Developmental-functional level is synonymous with present level of performance (the point at which there currently is function). Developmental-functional needs represent unique priority instructional areas that should be addressed in a person's individualized program. And learning characteristics are those attributes and deficits that an individual brings to the learning environment. For example, if a child has impaired mobility or vision loss, the physical educator must be able to modify instructional procedures in order to maximize the child's learning potential. In addition, teaching approaches must be adjusted according to the pupil's needs and characteristics; pupils should not be forced to adjust to an instructor's particular teaching approach.

When designing an individualized task analysis, each instructional task in the progression should be written behaviorally. This means it should include the audience (A), the precise observable behavior expected (B), the precise conditions under which a target behavior is to occur (C), and the measurable degree of expected success (D). For example, one instructional phase might require Johnny (A) to jump (B) over a 2-foot-high stick (C) on three out of three attempts (D). In short, an individualized task analysis involves a developmental or progressive ABCD approach for any skill to be taught to any specific individual. In practice, when the learner has accomplished any step in an individually designed movement sequence, the skill requirement should be made more independent and challenging by varying the complexity of behavior, condition, and/or degree. Table 3.3 gives further examples of this ABCD approach to teaching. Using the information contained in the Table 3.3, a teacher could mix any combination of behavior, condition, and degree in offering progressively more independent and challenging movement tasks related to one skill for a specific learner. All good teaching involves the use of progressions or task analysis.

TABLE 3.3 ANALYSIS OF SELECTED BEHAVIORS, CONDITIONS, AND DEGREE VARIATIONS

COMPONENTS	APPLIED EXAMPLES
Behaviors	
Any complete task	Mature throw
Any portion of a task	Stepping pattern of mature throw
Conditions	
Equipment, target, or area size	11-inch playground ball (yellow)
Level of equipment	Low balance beam
Equipment weight	10-pound weight
Speed dimension	Pitch with 6-foot arch
Degree of assistance	1 hand teacher support at mid-spine
Sensory condition	Eyes closed
Combinations	Eyes closed; low balance beam
Degrees	
Success ratio	4 out of 5 kicks
Length of time	Float 15 seconds
Performance distance	Throw 20 feet
Repetitions	5 sit-ups twice
Combinations	20 sit-ups in 50 seconds

INDIVIDUALIZATION IN PRACTICE

The Individualized Education Program

Those who teach physical education to pupils with disabilities are bound by the mandates of P.L. 101–476, P.L. 94–142, and P.L. 99–457, which require written individualized educational programs (IEPs) for all pupils who are directly affected by these laws: all identified school-aged children with disabilities from ages 3 through 21. This written program is a blueprint of the pupil's entire educational curriculum; each specific curricular area is only a part. The IEP must include the following components, which specifically address the issue of "individualization in practice."

1. A statement of the child's present level of educational performance
2. A statement of annual goals, including short-term instructional objectives
3. A statement of the specific media, materials, and special education and related services to be provided to the child
4. The projected dates for initiation of services and the anticipated duration of the services
5. The extent to which the child will be able to participate in regular educational programs
6. Appropriate objective criteria and evaluation procedures and schedules for determining, on at least an annual basis, whether the short-term instructional objectives are being achieved

The first of these mandated components, present level of educational performance information, refers to a behavioral statement of objective test results. These data are the foundation of a pupil's overall individualized educational program. All other components of the program flow from the precise knowledge of the level at which the pupil is currently functioning. Further, by law, the measurement of current level of performance must involve the use of more than one test understandable to the pupil.

By using behaviorally stated present level of performance test information, an IEP developer should be able to project a number of reasonable goals to be reached during the year in key curricular areas, including physical education. These general or broadly stated annual goals must not only be specified in the IEP but also be accompanied by a list of intermediate short-term instructional objectives that, when combined, address the gradual accomplishment of annual goals. Short-term instructional objectives, which should be precise, sequential, and measurable statements, are, in other words, behaviorally written. Examples of related present level of performance, annual goal, and short-term instructional objective statements are given in Table 3.4.

Often the obtainment of annual goals and short-term objectives will require education services in the form of media, materials, and/or supportive personnel. A pupil with a hearing impairment might need supplementary visual aids in the pool (media); a pupil who is visually impaired might require an audible goal locator and beeper ball in order to perform in kickball (materials); ongoing consultation from a school psychologist (supportive personnel) might be advisable in the case of a pupil who is emotionally disordered. The duration of needed educational services should also be specified on the IEP. If the physical educator thinks ahead in specifying these needs on the IEP, the possibility of receiving help for the pupil will be enhanced. (However, there are no guarantees of assistance.)

An IEP statement of participation in regular educational programs is also mandatory.

TABLE 3.4 IEP STATEMENT EXAMPLES

PRESENT LEVEL OF PERFORMANCE	ANNUAL GOALS	SHORT-TERM INSTRUCTIONAL OBJECTIVES
1. Linda can swim the modified dog paddle 50 feet independently in 5 feet of water, no scissors kick, verbal request only, head above surface	1. Learn mature crawl stroke.	1a. Linda will independently swim the modified dog paddle, holding breath for 20 seconds with face in 5 feet of water, 2/2 trials, verbal request only 1b. Same as 1a, plus add scissors kick. 1c. Same as 1b, plus add rhythmic breathing.
2. Linda can float on back for 2 minutes in 5 feet of water with verbal request.	2. Float on back in deep water for an extended time.	2a. Linda will independently float on back for 5 minutes in 5 feet of water with verbal request. 2b. Same as 2a, plus 10 feet of water.
3. Linda can maneuver wheelchair around basketball court 3 times in 5 1/2 minutes, verbal request only.	3. Improve maneuverability in wheel chair in different environments.	3a. Linda will maneuver wheelchair around basketball court 5 times in 6 minutes, verbal request only. 3b. Same as 3a, plus around the playground (500 feet), 3 times. 3c. Same as 3a, plus around neighborhood block (700 yards) in 8 minutes.
4. Linda can ascend 2 bleacher steps with 2 person assistance under the armpits, using braces and crutches, verbal prompt also.	4. Independently ascend and descend bleachers using braces and crutches.	4a. Linda will ascend 2 bleacher steps with 1 person assistance under the armpits, using braces and crutches, verbal prompts too. 4b. Same as 4a, plus 4 bleacher steps, one person assistance for any 2 steps. 4c. Same as 4a descending. 4d. Same as 4b descending. 4e. Combine 4b and 4d. 4f. Same as 4e independently.

When such a statement is included, physical education is quite often specified as one area in which a pupil with a disability can successfully participate with nondisabled peers. Physical educators need to be alert to this possibility and plan effectively for that eventuality.

The last required section to be completed at least annually in an IEP is a strategy for evaluating progress toward the accomplishment of the annual goals and short-term instructional objectives. Criteria, procedures, and scheduling of evaluation must all be laid out. A *criterion* refers to a measurable degree of success (e.g., 75 percent or 2 out of 3), *procedures* refers to the type(s) of evaluation format (e.g., oral test or fitness test), and *scheduling* refers to how often during the school year evaluation will occur (perhaps quarterly).

Physical educators should be aware of the following specific factors regarding IEPs:

1. By law, physical education must be included within a pupil's special education program. Therefore, physical education has a rightful place as a permanent section on all IEP forms.

2. The physical education portion of an IEP can appear in four different ways according to P.L. 101–476's regulations. First, because the large majority of pupils with IEPs attend regular physical education with no accommodations required, this fact only needs to be noted under the participation in regular programs section within the IEP. Second, some pupils will need only selected accommodations in order to participate safely, successfully, and with satisfaction in the regular physical education class. These specific accommodations only need to be stated on the IEP form. Third, when a pupil has unique physical education needs, all mandated components of the IEP have to be addressed for physical education service delivery itself. Fourth, pupils receiving all services at a separate facility would have their physical education content noted on their IEP by specifying, as examples, the relevant section(s) from the agency's physical education curriculum applicable to each pupil's needs or by following any one of the other three formats described above (American Alliance for Health, Physical Education, Recreation and Dance, 1980a).

3. If a pupil has special education needs in the psychomotor domain (posture, motor, fitness, or play), the physical educator should have direct input into the formulation of the IEP. This is, in fact, a physical educator's obligation.

4. IEPs are not legally binding contracts for a teacher. If a physical education teacher writes reasonable goals and objectives and makes a valid attempt to reach them during the school year, the IEP cannot be effectively attacked in court if goals and objectives are not reached.

5. The format of the IEP has been left to the discretion of LEAs. Therefore, from school district to school district, the total program form will vary.

6. IEPs can replace the traditional report card for pupils with identified disabilities. The pupil's periodic reports are then contained on the actual IEP form used in the school district.

7. An IEP must be constructed within 30 days after the school district's multifactored assessment team determines that a certain child will benefit from special education. Further, the IEP must be approved before any new services can begin for a pupil.

8. IEP meetings should involve the parent, the primary teacher, and LEA special education representative, and the child (where appropriate). If any other teachers (such as physical educators) are to be directly involved in an IEP, it is important that their input be sought before implementation of the IEP. Physical educators should not be in the vulnerable position of accepting a pupil with a disability when no preparation or input has occurred.

9. Finally, IEPs are not lesson plans. They are to be viewed as a program that covers a marking period or some longer time frame.

The overall IEP process sets the occasion for individualized accountability-based instruction. Keeping in mind the individualized instruction hierarchy (see Figure 3.5) when drawing up an IEP, educators should be aware that (1) behavior management is required before a present level of performance can be ascertained, (2) a statement of present level of performance necessitates both the gathering of data (testing) and their analysis (assessing), (3) planning can be either for a short period (short-term instructional objective) or over a long term (annual goals, and (4) instruction implies both proper class placement in a least restrictive environment and the use of media, materials, and supportive personnel, if needed. Any program should conclude with evaluation and follow-up.

An example of a completed IEP for a child's educational program is provided in Figure 3.6. The IEP exemplar from the Heartland (Iowa) Education Agency meets the standards set in the rules for P.L. 101–476 and provides actual details with which physical educators will have to cope. Motor skills, physical fitness, and games-oriented skills were addressed for the pupil on this IEP because those were the areas of weakness that needed unique attention. For other children, aquatics and dance could have been addressed; for still others, perhaps less would be necessary. In other words, the number of areas and extent of the information provided depend on the specific needs of each child. Related forms may also include those which the Heartland Education Agency uses, such as the following:

- Pre-Evaluation Conference/Referral Form
- Parent Consent for Evaluation Form
- Parent Notice of Special Education Re-Evaluation and/or Review of Records
- Parent Request for Special Education Services

Copies of these forms are contained in Appendix A1.

In a related area, some special physical educators may be working with infants and toddlers who are at risk of disability or who already have been determined to have a developmental disability. Such a possibility has been catalyzed by the passage of P.L. 99–457, as amended by P.L. 101–476, which has spawned a new field within physical education: pediatric special physical education. Of particular interest to special physical educators, these laws mandate attention to the "physical development" of targeted infants and toddlers. Of additional relevance, P.L. 99–457 requires that special needs infants and toddlers be offered special education, medical, and other habilitative services based on a team-written individualized family services plan (IFSP) that includes attention to a child's physical development.

IFSPs are the same conceptually as IEPs, but their content and focus do differ in at least two important ways. First, given the fact that 0–2 year olds typically spend most of their time at home, the IFSP's emphasis is on family involvement. The entire family, not just the targeted child, is viewed as instrumental in an IFSP's implementation. Second, IFSPs extend their sphere of involvement well beyond schools themselves. Social service agencies, health-oriented organizations, and other agencies (not typically associated with schools) are all targeted entities and interagency collaboration among key personnel across these agencies is especially emphasized within this law. We mention these critical specifics about P.L. 99–457 and this law's emphasis on the physical development of infants and toddlers with special needs

HEARTLAND EDUCATION AGENCY

PART III — EDUCATIONAL STAFFING REPORT/INDIVIDUALIZED EDUCATION PROGRAM
(Parts: III, IV, V constitute the IEP, Attach all evaluation reports)

Page 1 of 2

TYPE OF STAFFING

	A	B	C	D	
	A	B	C	D	

Original
Re-staffing
Three-year
Addendum

Speech Original
Speech Re-staffing
Speech Three-year

Pupil: Jenny Rogers B.D. 04/02/81 Sex: F Race: ___

Grade/Level: Grade 2 Language: ___ Teacher's Name: Detweiler

Referred by: L. Rust Position: Principal

Legal Parent: M/M Jim Rogers Address: 8000 NW Oakland, Ankland, Ankeny, IA 50021 Phone H: 292-5555 W: 294-5515

Foster Parent: ___ Address: ___ Phone H: ___ W: ___

Legal Parent's School District: Ankeny District/Building Student Attends: Northwest Elementary

Parent Notification of Staffing: Method letter Date: (M) 9 (D)15 (Y) 90 By: Detweiler

Date of this staffing: (M) 10 (D) 5 (Y) 90 Date of parent consent for evaluation/notice: (M) 8 (D) 29 (Y) 90

EVALUATIONS CONDUCTED:

	By	Date
Educational History	M. Grace	9-90
Speech-Language	J. Gray	9-90
*Hearing	L. Martin	10-90
Intellect	R. Schull	9-90
Academic Status	Detweiler	9-90
*Behavioral Observation	R. Schull	9-90
Motor Functioning	B. Knipe	9-90

EVALUATIONS CONDUCTED:

	By	Date
Health History	L. Lombard	9-90
Vision	L. Lombard	9-90
*Social Functioning	M. Grace	9-90

Adaptive Behavior is assessed as a component of: Speech-Language, Academic Status, Behavioral Observation, Intellect, and Social Functioning. Evaluations denoted above by an (*) indicates an area of functioning within the normal range.

PRIMARY DISABILITY: Mental Disability

LEAST RESTRICTIVE PROGRAM RECOMMENDATIONS:

Instructional Program: self-contained (1:8) Transportation: regular

Integration/Time: PE, lunch, guidance Adjusted Program Request: ___

**Support Services: APE, Speech Other: ___

Physical Education: regular PE with assistance from associate when necessary Other: ___

Date of Parent Consent for Placement/Termination: (M) 5 (D) 20 (Y) 87 (D) 1

Placement: (M) 10 (D) 5 (Y) 90 Date of estimated termination: (M) ___ (D) ___ (Y) ___ Reviewed by: team Date: (M) ___ (D) 5 (Y) 91

IEP TEAM: Receiving Teacher/Provider: L. Detweiler Consultant: D. Bach

Parent: Jim & Betty Rogers

PERSONS PRESENT AT STAFFING:

Name	Position	Initials
Chairperson:		
Parent: Betty Rogers, Parent		
Parent:	APE	
Student:	Psychologist	
Recorder:		

WEIGHING:

For Office Use
P R

APPROVAL: Principal (signature): ___ Date: 10/5/90

For the Director of Special Education Date: 10/9/90
by Zone Coordinator

** Support Services - Part IV short term objective sequence will be with the provider if not in the student file.

DISTRIBUTION: (1) AEA - white (2) School - yellow (3) Parent - pink

812-091A

FIGURE 3.6 Actual IEP that includes physical education.

HEARTLAND EDUCATION AGENCY

PART III — EDUCATIONAL STAFFING REPORT/INDIVIDUALIZED EDUCATION PROGRAM
(Parts: III, IV, V constitute the IEP, Attach all evaluation reports)

Page 2 of 2

Pupil: __Jenny Rogers__   B.D.: __04/02/81__   Date of Staffing: (MM) __10__ (DD) __05__ (YY) __90__

Reason for Referral: __three-year reevaluation__

CURRENT LEVEL OF FUNCTIONING: Document results of the evaluations and level of functioning that justify the recommended program. Indicate any adaptive behavior deficits requiring interventions.

Identifies about 100 functional words. Can sequence pictures and activities. Identifies numbers 1-25 out

of sequence. Good size and quantity concepts. Is strong willed. Overall behavior has improved. Some attending

difficulties. Enjoys physical education and is making good progress. Can balance on right leg for 10 seconds; 3

seconds on left leg. Hops 3 times on right leg. Broad jumps 18". Slides and gallops with either side leading.

Overhand throws a tennis ball 16 feet using a homolateral pattern. Catches a playground ball that is bounced to

her using her arms and body. Vocabulary development is a good area for Jenny. Articulation difficulties. Gives

up easily at times. Behavior interferes with overall school performance. Improvements seen in behavior.

_____

_____

_____

_____

PLACEMENT ALTERNATIVES DISCUSSED: __self-contained (1:5)__

ANNUAL GOALS (List by IEP goals)

	Goal Codes
Develop and improve functional academic skills: math, reading, written language	MAS, REH, LAL
Improve fine motor skills	_____
Improve domestice living skills	_____
Improve compliance with directions and activities	_____
Improve articulation and language skills (sentence structure)	_____
Improve balance and locomotor skills	GMBS, GMLS
Improve eye-hand and eye-foot coordination	GMEH, GMEF
Improve game skills	GMSG
Improve strength	GMDS

DISTRIBUTION: (1) AEA - white   (2) School - yellow   (3) Parent - pink   USE THE REVERSE SIDE FOR ADDITIONAL COMMENTS   812-0918

FIGURE 3.6 *(continued)*

School District __Ankeny__   Building __Northwest Elementary__

Pupil __Jenny Rogers__   Teacher/Provider __Detweiler__   Consultant __Grace__

Parent Attending 1.* __Betty Rogers__ Date __10-5-90__ Parent Attending 1.* _____ Date _____

(First Conference)   (Second Conference)

Goal No. __1-3__   Goal Code __GMBS__   Goal Description __Improve balance skills__

Goal No. __4-7__   Goal Code __GMLS__   Goal Description __Improve locomotor skills__

Goal No. __8-11__   Goal Code __GMEH__   Goal Description __Improve eye-hand coordination__

Goal No.	Date Initiated Month/Year	Objectives Sequence	Date Achieved Month/Year	Strategies Special Materials & Media COMMENTS (See explanation sheet)	Meeting Participants 2.* Name Date
1.	10/90	Balance on left leg for 5 seconds 3/4 times.		*demonstration and physical prompting	B.K. Rogers
2.	10/90	Walk forward heel-toe on a line for 12' 3/4 times.			
3.	10/90	Stand heel-toe and maintain balance for 5 seconds 3/4 times.			
4.	1/91	Skip a distance of 15 feet using an alternating leg pattern 4/5 times.		*use of music for rhythm	
5.	10/90	Hop three times on left leg 6/8 times.			
6.	10/90	Hop a distance of 4 feet 6/8 trials.			
7.	10/90	Jump rope that is twirled by others 3, then 5, consecutive times at least 4 times.		*16' jump rope with verbal cues	
8.	10/90	Overhand throw tennis ball with opposition 8/10 times.		*demonstration, verbal cue	
9.	10/90	Using her hands, catch a playground ball that is bounced to her, then tossed to her, 5/6 trials.		*begin with distance of 5 feet, then increase to 10 feet.	
10.	10/90	Bounce-catch a 9" ball to herself 10 times in a row.		*begin in sitting position, then standing.	
11.	1/91	Strike a balloon with her right hand keeping it in the air 5-10 times, then use short light racket.			

*1. If parent does not attend, indicate date and method of notification, recorder must initial.

*2. Participants date and sign by objectives added since last meeting. Indicate agreement after signature. Attach any statement of non-concurrence.

710-261

PARENT NOTIFIED:
Date __10-5-90__ BY __Rogers__
Phone _____
Note _____
Letter _____
Other _____

Copies:
School - (white copy)
Parent - 2nd conference (yellow copy)
Parent - 1st conference (pink copy)

FIGURE 3.6 (continued)

School District __Ankeny__

Pupil __Jenny Rogers__   Teacher/Provider __Detweiler__   Building __Northwest Elementary__   Consultant __Grace__

Parent Attending 1.* __Betty Rogers__   Date __10-5-90__   Parent Attending 1.* _____   Date _____
(First Conference)   (Second Conference)

Goal No. __12__   Goal Code __GMEF__   Goal Description __Improve eye-foot coordination__

Goal No. __13-14__ Goal Code __GMSG__   Goal Description __Improve game skills__

Goal No. __15-16__ Goal Code __GMDS__   Goal Description __Improve development of strength__

Goal No.	Date Initiated Month/Year	Objectives Sequence	Date Achieved Month/Year	Strategies Special Materials & Media COMMENTS (See explanation sheet)	Meeting Participants 2.* Name Date
12.	10/90	Kick a 9" ball that is rolled to her (no approach necessary) 3/4 times while maintaining balance.			_JB Rogers_
13.	10/90	Perform motor directions to tag games 2/3 times correctly.		*have person who is "it" wear bright colored pinney or belt	
14.	10/90	Perform motor directions of relay activities with 100% accuracy for 3 consecutive sessions.			
15.	10/90	Perform bent-knee sit-ups (ankles held; arms crossed over chest) 15 times on three consecutive sessions.			
16.	10/90	Perform modified push-ups (on hands and knees; flexion at elbows) 15 times on three consecutive sessions.			

*1. If parent does not attend, indicate date and method of notification, recorder must initial.

*2. Participants date and sign by objectives added since last meeting. Indicate agreement after signature. Attach any statement of non-concurrence.

710-761

PARENT NOTIFIED:
Date __10-5-90__   BY: __La Jyet__
Phone _____
Note _____
Letter _____
Other _____

Copies:
School - (white copy)
Parent - 2nd conference (yellow copy)
Parent - 1st conference (pink copy)

FIGURE 3.6   (continued)

HEARTLAND EDUCATION AGENCY

PART V — PROGRAM REVIEW/INDIVIDUALIZED EDUCATION PROGRAM

(Parts III, IV and V constitute the IEP)

PUPIL: (Last) Rogers   (First) Jenny   (MI)   (AKA)   Birthdate: (M)04 (D) 02 (Y) 81

Grade/Level: Grade 1   Teacher(s): Detweiler
Legal Parent(s): Jim & Betty Rogers   Address/City/State 8000 NW Oakland, Ankeny, IA   Zip 50021
Legal Parent(s) Phone: (Home) 292-5555   (Work) 294-5515   Foster Parent(s) Phone: (Home)   (Work)
Foster Parent(s):   Address/City/State: Zip
Legal Parent's School District: Ankeny   District/Building Student Attends: Ankeny Northwest Elementary
Date of Review: (M)10 (D) 20 (Y) 89

PARTICIPANTS: Name/Position

_____ , Teacher E.D.

_____ / P.E.

_____

"PARENTAL RIGHTS IN SPECIAL EDUCATION" on reverse side.

Name/Position	
M Grace Consultant	MG.
*Parent Betty Rogers	B.L.

Parent Notified:
Date: (M)10 (D) 1 (Y) 89
Phone:
Note:
Letter: X Detweiler
Other:

RESULTS OF REVIEW

Months in Program: 27 months   Should the child be re-evaluated: yes   Should the child be re-staffed: no

Is the child meeting program objectives: yes   Should the program be continued: yes   Estimated duration:

CURRENT LEVEL OF FUNCTIONING: Jenny is currently able to identify 60-65 functional sight words. She is able to identify all the letters of the alphabet. Jenny is able to identify the numbers 1-30; sequence numbers 1-15. Handwriting has improved and she is able to write the numbers 1-10 and the letter of the alphabet with a model. She is able to state her personal information. She is able to identify/categorize food pictures/groups. She is able to participate in domestic living activities and enjoys doing so. Jenny has difficulty at times completing directions and changing activities. She can be quite stubborn and at times will punch and scream. Many behavior management programs have been tried, however none haveconsistently been effective. She has learned to hop on her right leg and catch a ball that is bounced to her. Her balance continues to improve.

PRIMARY DISABILITY: mental disability

ANNUAL GOALS (List by IEP Goals)
Improve and increase functional reading skills
Improve and increase functional math skills
Improve and increase domestic living skills
Improve and increase social and behavioral skills
Improve balance and locomotor skills
Improve eye-hand coordination
Improve game skills

INSTRUCTIONAL PROGRAM PROVIDED: self-contained (3:6)

PROGRAM RECOMMENDATIONS
(a) Integration Plans: lunch, recess, guidance

(b) Support Services: adapted physical education; speech

702-032

DISTRIBUTION: (1) AEA (white)   (2) School (yellow)   (3) Parent (pink)   (4) Photo copy to resident district if different

FIGURE 3.6 (continued)

77

because there will, no doubt, be a need for increased preservice and in-service training in pediatric special physical education and thus more jobs available at this level for special physical educators. Moreover, special physical educators should look for continuing developments in this new area.

Individualized Approaches for Daily Instruction

Individualization in special physical education is most easily accomplished in activities that do not necessitate pupil interaction and dependence in group activity. Each pupil can then progress at his or her own rate without worrying about others in class. Common movement approaches and activities of this type that can be offered to pupils with and without disabilities include the following:

Selected General Approaches

- Circuit training
- Movement exploration
- Stunts
- Story plays/creative drama
- Self-testing activities
- Individual sports/activities
- Obstacle courses (confidence courses)
- Mimetics (imitating movements of objects and people)

Selected Specific Activities

- Gymnastics
- Archery
- Calisthenics
- Bowling
- Golf
- Diving
- Shuffleboard
- Horseshoes
- Rhythms
- Track and field
- Swimming
- Hopscotch
- Relaxation
- Fly casting
- Rope jumping
- Beanbag toss
- Hoop activities

When planning one of these lessons, a teacher should consistently teach to a pupil's individualized needs. In doing this, the teacher needs to base lesson plan content on each child's present level of performance. Daily lesson objectives can then be projected along with movement skill progressions. If lessons are not actually written for each pupil (hardly to be expected of any teacher), at least the thinking process of a superior teacher should be in tune to individualized present levels of performance, lesson objectives, and related progressions. Illustrating the use of present level of performance information, progressions, and lesson objectives, Figure 3.7 contains a 25-minute lesson plan that addresses Mac's needs within a gymnasium context, and Figure 3.8 contains a 30-minute lesson plan that addresses Sally's needs within a pool context. Notice that the first step in each progression is more challenging than the preestablished present level of performance and that the last step in each progression is less challenging than the related lesson objective that is projected. Also notice that each statement is written behaviorally.

Individualization Strategies. A number of specific individualizing strategies can be used in teaching physical education. These include the use of task cards and learning packets, peer tutoring, team teaching, learn-

Name of Teacher   *D. Rogers*   Name of Pupil   *Mac*   Date   *4/15*

Present Level of Performance: Mac uses a same-sided throw pattern (verbal request).

Lesson Objective: Given verbal cue, Mac will throw a tennis ball using overhand opposition to instructor 20 feet away, 3/3.

(Time)
8 min.   Progression:

1. Using footprints in opposition, when given a verbal request Mac will step and over hand throw a tennis ball toward a 3' x 3' target 10' away with instructor physical prompt at stepping leg, 2/3.
2. Repeat #1, from physical to only verbal prompt; 3/3.
3. Repeat #2, fade footprints.
4. Repeat #3, stress "hard" throw, target at 15'.

Present Level of Performance: Mac can independently balance on right foot for 1 sec., arms folded, eyes open, 2/3 (verbal request).

Lesson Objective: Will independently hold a right foot stand position, arms folded and eyes open, for 5 sec., 3/3 (verbal request).

(Time)
8 min.   Progression.

1. Independently stand on a 2" wide floor line for 15 sec., eyes opened, arms folded, 3/3 (verbal request).
2. Independently stand on right foot, with left foot on 8" high step, hands out to sides for balance, 5 sec., eyes opened, 2/3.
3. Repeat #2, place raised foot on beach ball.
4. Repeat #3, no left foot support, 2/3.

Present Level of Performance: Mac can do 6 squat thrusts in 20 sec. (verbal request).

Lesson Objective; 10 squat thrusts in 20 sec., with only a verbal request.

(Time)
9 min.   Progression:

1. Independently hold full body extension position for 30 sec., 2/2 (verbal request).
2. Independently complete 8 squat thrusts within 30 sec., 2/2 (verbal request).
3. Same as #2, 8 in 25 sec.
4. Same as #2, 8 full squats in 20 sec.

Figure 3.7   Gymnasium lesson plan model.

ing stations, resource centers, and contract teaching. Some of these are covered in more depth in Chapter 4. Here we take a brief look at each of these strategies.

The use of *task cards*, which could be part of an overall individualized learning packet, requires the child to read words or interpret symbols and then engage in appropriate physical education activities. The individually prescribed instructional (IPI) system es-

poused by David Auxter (1971) when he was at Slippery Rock State College (Pennsylvania), is a prime example of the use of a task card system with pupils who are disabled. Specifically, IPI, which has been successfully used with pupils labeled moderately retarded, has a coding system of symbols. Code language on each task card yields information on such variables as the nature of the response to be performed, equipment

Name of Teacher	*S. Hodge*	Name of Pupil	*Sally*	Date	*5/2*

Present Level of Performance: When pushing off wall with feet, Sally can prone glide 6 feet in 4 feet of water, 2/2 (verbal request).

Lesson Objective: When in 4-feet-deep water and pushing off wall with feet, Sally will prone glide to the instructor 15 feet away, 2/2 (verbal request).

(Time)
10 min.   Progression:

1. Sally will put face under water standing at 4-foot depth and, holding instructor's left hand, walk 10 feet, then 12 feet, 2/2 each (verbal request).
2. Same as #1, independently walk to instructor.
3. Sally will assume prone float position as instructor supports at hip level and walks forward 10 feet, then 15 feet, 2/2 each (verbal request).
4. Sally will independently push off side, prone gliding to instructor 8 feet, then 10 feet, then 12 feet away, 2/2 (verbal request).

Present Level of Performance: Sally can kick her legs rhythmically on dry land on command for 30 secs., 1/1.

Lesson Objective: In a prone position and using a kickboard, Sally will flutter kick for 25 feet, 2/2, 4-foot water depth (verbal request).

(Time)
13 min.   Progression:

1. Demonstrate and then upon verbal prompt, Sally will flutter kick with legs extended over bench, 30 sec., 2/2.
2. Will enter water and prone flutter kick while holding onto pool side, 30 sec., 3/3, 4 foot water depth (verbal request).
3. Flutter kick in 4 feet of water while holding onto kickboard with instructor holding at hips, 25 feet, 3/3 (verbal prompts).
4. Flutter kick 10, then 15 feet, kickboard alone, 2/2, 4 feet of water (verbal request).

Present Level of Performance: Sally independently submerges body under water when in 8 feet of water for 4 sec., 2/2 (verbal prompt).

Lesson Objective; 10 sec. full body submersion at 8 foot depth, 2/2 (verbal prompt).

(Time)
7 min.   Progression:

1. From side of pool at 8-foot depth level, Sally and instructor submerged together with both hands held for 5 sec., 2/2 (verbal prompt).
2. Same as #1, one hand held.
3. Same as #1, independently each submerges; watch each other.
4. Same as #1, independently, only Sally submerges; 6 sec., then 8 sec.

Figure 3.8   Pool lesson plan model.

required, direction of action, and time constraints.

Project EXPLORE (Brannan, 1979), another movement-oriented program that uses task cards, is a competency based, skill-oriented curriculum. One of the few major curricular areas is sports, games, and physical development. Within this area appropriate subcontent topics and related goals and objectives are provided on task cards, with pupil learning steps and teaching suggestions.

Peer tutoring involves the use of a responsible assistant who is approximately the same age as the individual needing personalized instruction. Even pupils in elementary grades have been known to be effective peer tutors. Older pupils (crossed-aged tutors), volunteers (parents or retirees), or student teachers from colleges of education can also be used.

Team teaching involves the use of more than one teacher in a class at the same time. One teacher could serve as the overall leader and the other could roam the instructional setting, offering individual assistance where needed. Assigned duties can be rotated on a predetermined basis.

Physical educators can also use *learning stations* to enhance individualized instruction. Predetermined activity stations are designed according to the individual's instructional needs. During class, participants are assigned to those learning stations most clearly related to their developmental needs. Learning stations can be set up in a gymnasium, playground, pool, or recreation center.

Resource centers are becoming popular throughout the field of special education, and physical educators can take good advantage of them. A resource center is a setting (usually a room) where a pupil is sent for supplementary individualized instruction. A resource center could conceivably contain materials and tutorial/therapeutic expertise associated with such physical education-related areas as occupational therapy and physical therapy.

Finally, *contract teaching* is an individualizing approach in which a teacher and pupil agree in writing on instructional goals and the steps and methods to reach these goals. Contract teaching could involve physical education homework, supplementary instruction at an activity center (such as a school), or self-teaching on the pupil's part. In effect, contract teaching is similar in many ways to independent studies offered in colleges and universities.

Physical Education Curriculum Models. A number of noncategorical or cross-categorical physical education curriculum models have been developed to aid a teacher in individualizing instruction for all types of pupils, including those with disabilities. Some of these projects have been approved by the Department of Education's National Diffusion Network (NDN) as validated, exemplary, and exportable.

In the NDN-approved *I CAN Model* (Wessel, 1976a, 1976b, 1976c, 1976d, 1979), also known as the *Achievement Based Curriculum (ABC) Model* (Wessel & Kelly, 1985), different skill levels of performance and focal points for activity are pinpointed in the context of attaining performance objectives within broad areas of instruction. This curriculum model offers individualized programming in three broad areas: preprimary skills, primary skills, and sport, leisure, and recreation skills. Specific modules of instruction include body management, fundamental skills, health/fitness, play participation, aquatics, outdoor activities, dance and individual sports, and team sports.

Project ACTIVE (Vodola, 1976; Karp & Adler, 1991) is an NDN-validated project that offers direct programming information for personalized-individualized instruction in physical education. The ACTIVE curriculum is primarily applicable to individuals from age 6 into postsecondary age across all primary categories of disability. Programming components specifically target those with low motor ability, low physical vitality, nutritional deficiencies, postural abnormalities, communication disorders, and breathing problems.

The *Data-Based Gymnasium System* (Dunn, Morehouse, & Fredericks, 1986), developed at Oregon State University and the Monmouth, Oregon, Teaching Research Division, focuses on a noncategorical teaching approach geared toward those with more serious disabilities. Its curriculum is task analytic, stresses the application of behavioral principles, employs frequent charting of 24-hour data on pupils' individualized clipboards, and depends on participation by trained parents and volunteers in order to accomplish one-to-one and small-group instruction. The curriculum emphasizes basic movement concepts, elementary games skills, physical fitness, and lifetime leisure skills.

The *Physical Best Program* (American Alliance for Health, Physical Education, Recreation and Dance, 1988) is a health-related fitness program for all pupils age 5 to 18. Awards are available for reaching specified norm-referenced standards. In addition, this program stresses recognition by means of participation awards and personal goals awards applicable to pupils who are gifted, normal, and motorically at a disadvantage. Importantly, its educational component teaches pupils the basics of healthful living by integrating fitness into their daily lives.

The *Every Child a Winner Project* is also NDN approved (National Dissemination Study Group, 1992). This project provides individualized movement experiences for all types of children centered on themes of space awareness, body awareness, quality of body movement, and body relationships through creative games, creative dance, and educational gymnastics. Competition is found in the program only when child-designed. The project slogan, "Every Child a Winner," finds meaning through the discovery learning approach to teaching movement. Pupils are encouraged to reach their personal potential, and "winning" occurs as each child does his or her best with movement challenges.

Project PEOPEL (Long, Irmer, Burkett, Glassenapp, & Odenkirk, 1980) was developed to meet the needs of pupils with and without disabilities through one-to-one peer tutoring in a success-oriented physical education experience. PEOPEL is for pupils who

because of some physical, mental, social, or emotional condition will benefit more from an individualized program than from general physical education. Through this individualized learning, pupils develop abilities at their own pace. The emphasis on the individualized learning of a variety of physical activities is possible by using peer tutors, called PEOPEL Student Aides, who have completed a special orientation class and are under the direct supervision of the physical education teacher. Project PEOPEL is NDN-approved.

A related, non-NDN-approved peer tutoring system is available through the *Peer-Mediated Aerobic Conditioning Program* (Halle, Gabler-Halle, McKee, Bane, & Boyer, 1991). This peer tutoring program matches elementary-aged pupils who have moderate and severe disabilities with pretrained nondisabled peers. The aerobic training program emphasizes weight, body fat percentage, and heart rate monitoring. Further field testing is warranted before any widespread use of this new program is indicated.

The *CREOLE Project* (Wright, 1986) also emphasizes peer tutoring and has developed curriculum guides and peer tutoring training manuals. These address a functional skills curriculum approach and task analysis in teaching physical education and leisure skills to secondary-level pupils with serious disabilities. The project emphasizes a meaningful and functional utilization of leisure time, age-appropriate interests, improved physical and emotional health, increased socialization with peers, an improved community delivery system and increased participation in home and community recreation activity. One example of a specific training area that impacts school and nonschool environments is appropriate use of a wheelchair—wheelchair exploration, wheelchair safety, wheelchair etiquette, transfers, mobility, and problem solving. Interaction of school personnel, parents, and community recreation agency personnel is a vital part of the CREOLE system.

The *Individualized Education Program in Physical Education* (IEP/PE) Project (National Dissemination Study Group, 1992) is approved by the NDN for special education and physical education teachers of preschool to high school pupils with disabilities of any type or degree. This project trains teachers to increase their proficiency levels in teaching both physical education and recreation skills. Objective-referenced materials range from basic motor skill acquisition to high-level sport skills.

The *Project MOBILITEE Model* (Hopewell Special Education Regional Resource Center, 1981) consists of a related series of tests, a cross-indexed curriculum guide, and implementing materials that address physical education instruction for pupils with moderate and severe disabilities. The tests are criterion referenced and stress a qualitative developmental approach to gathering accurate data on motor, fitness, and posture status. Evidence of the needs of nonambulatory pupils is found in such test items as striking and throwing from a wheelchair, a wheelchair run, wheelchair mobility, and alternative modes of movement. A unique emphasis is the testing and programming of games participation skills that emphasize social and emotional elements (e.g., complying with rules and directions).

Project UNIQUE (Winnick & Short, 1985) is a cross-categorical norm-referenced resource to the extent that it addresses the physical fitness testing and associated curriculum needs of pupils who are not disabled, pupils who are sensory impaired, and pupils who are physically disabled. The inventory of key test/instructional items covers body composition, muscular strength, muscular endurance, cardiorespiratory endurance, and flexibility. Project UNIQUE also relates the

physical fitness needs of its targeted pupils to severity of disability, onset of disability, age, sex, educational environment, sport modifications, and methods of ambulation. Additional research has been conducted to extend the project's applicability to pupils who are both mentally retarded and cerebral palsied (Winnick & Short, 1986).

The *I'M SPECIAL Project* is directed by Louis Bowers and Steven Klesius at the University of South Florida. Their products, including state-of-the-art interactive microcomputer laser videodiscs, cover a broad range of topics aimed at changing attitudes and increasing the knowledge of regular physical educators. Fifteen instructional modules collectively demonstrate a program of individualized physical education for a variety of children with disabilities.

The *Ohio State Motor Program* (Loovis & Ersing, 1979) emphasizes individualized instruction of children in fundamental motor skills. Qualitative test data and programming elements of this program are linked by means of the Ohio State University criterion-referenced Scale of Intra Gross Motor Assessment (SIGMA) and its Performance-Based Curriculum. Its 11 motor skills developmentally cover the ages of 3 to 9. This research-based program has been field-tested with success for a decade, some results of which are reported in the literature (Ersing, Loovis, & Ryan, 1982).

The *AIMS Program* focuses on the testing and teaching of selected motor skills common to early childhood (Strauss & DeOreo, 1979). Its materials have been developed for use by the nonspecialist and specialist alike in physical education so that the individualized motor needs of all types of children and youth can be appropriately met. Four motor areas are specifically emphasized: posture and body integration, body awareness, locomotor skills, and visual-motor skills. Both screening and more comprehensive testing tactics are available to teachers, along with correlated lesson activities matched to a child's present level of performance deficits. Both norm- and criterion-referenced approaches are incorporated within the program.

Body Skills: A Motor Development Curriculum for Children (Werder & Bruininks, 1988) is a comprehensive program for motor skill development of children from 2 to 12 years of age. *Body Skills* provides a systematic means to assess, plan, and teach gross motor skills in the areas of body management, locomotion, body fitness, object movement, and fine motor skills. A feature of *Body Skills* is that it is linked to the *Bruininks-Oseretsky Test of Motor Proficiency* (Bruininks, 1978), a test that provides an overall view of a child's motor development. The *Body Skills* curriculum is designed for use by regular and special physical educators, special educators, and early childhood and elementary education teachers.

The *Motor Activities Training Program* (Block, 1989), sanctioned by Special Olympics International, is designed for pupils with serious disabilities who perform at a level that precludes their participation in official Special Olympics sports. The program provides an easy-to-understand motor activity and recreation training curriculum with an emphasis on partial participation by involved pupils. It emphasizes use by a variety of trainers, deemphasizes competition, and uses goals, short-term objectives, task analysis, ongoing assessment, and teaching ideas for individualizing instruction. Activities are both school and community based and have undergone numerous revisions.

Mainstreaming in Physical Education

Putting individuals in programs or activities for which they are not ready is cruel; to keep them out of these same programs and activities when they are ready and can participate is criminal (Stein, 1978, p. 4).

Mainstreaming in physical education refers to the safe, successful, and satisfying physical and social inclusion of pupils with disabilities into regular physical education classes and may require the use of support personnel and accommodations. Since the 1970s (Stein, 1979), it has been the most widely used method for the inclusion of pupils with disabilities in regular physical education (Jansma & Decker, 1990). Thus, today, education outside the regular physical education class is the exception, not the rule. In fact, according to the U.S. Department of Education (1992), 69.1 percent of all pupils with disabilities age 6–21 were served during 1989–90 in a regular class environment for all or most of their educational programming, not too surprising inasmuch as most pupils with a disability are only mildly disabled. As a result, regular physical educators at the K–12 levels are increasingly finding pupils with disabilities assigned to them, the least restrictive environment placement in physical education, so that special physical educators can devote more of their direct service efforts toward pupils who are placed in more restrictive environments due to their very challenging special needs.

This movement of an increasing number of pupils who have disabilities into a regular class, referred to in the mid 1980s as the "regular education initiative" and now popularly termed "inclusion," met with much resistance at first and is quite controversial across the field of special education (Council for Exceptional Children, 1987; Reynolds, 1988; Lilly, 1988). Its proponents have gained considerable ground, however, and the inclusion movement is now sweeping the country with its full adoption seeming imminent (Stainback & Stainback, 1990; National Association of State Boards of Education, 1992). With little question, gone are the days when regular physical education teachers functioned with an "out of sight, out of mind" philosophy. They will have more and more pupils with disabilities in their classes. As a result, the need for related in-service and preservice training for these physical educators is keen and will continue to be for some time.

One source of information for physical educators is the Block–Krebs Model of inclusion, which involves a continuum of support for regular physical education in educating pupils with disabilities (Block & Krebs, 1992) with a particular focus on community-based programming (Krebs & Block, 1992). This model's continuum of support, in contrast to a continuum of least restrictive environment options (Aufsesser, 1991; Jansma & Decker, 1990), emphasizes how much and what type of assistance need to be provided to a particular pupil that will enable him or her to succeed in regular physical education. Level 1 in the model is full-time regular physical education (RPE) with no support; Level 2 is full-time RPE with special physical education (SPE) consultation; Level 3 involves SPE personnel co-teaching within an RPE context; Level 4 involves part-time SPE and part-time RPE in which nondisabled pupils are reverse-mainstreamed into the SPE sessions; and Level 5 involves full-time reverse-mainstreaming experiences exclusively in varied environments from integrated to segregated and from school to community. Built within Levels 2–5 is an emphasis on community-based instruction, peer tutors, cross-aged tutors, volunteers, and paraprofessionals. This inclusion-based model still needs considerable field-testing and validation before widespread adoption is warranted.

This chapter discusses a series of critical topics that must be addressed before a mainstreamed program can be offered in physical education. Our aim is to help answer such questions as: Why should we have mainstreaming in physical education classes? How important is the attitude of those involved in a mainstreamed physical education program? What are some attitude-change strategies? Where can I obtain more help to mainstream pupils appropriately in physical education? What specific types of physical activities and teaching methods are particularly suited to a mainstreamed physical education class? And are there any field-tested mainstreaming principles and models that can be applied in the gymnasium and pool and on the playground?

WHY MAINSTREAM?

There are important commonalities between regular and special physical education. The overall objectives of special physical education are similar for learners with all types of disabilities. Yet, more significantly, general objectives of special physical education for learners with disabilities are no different than are physical education objectives for the nondisabled. Everyone has common psychomotor needs, including the need for structured and unstructured play; for a variety of experiences in motor, fitness, games, dance, and aquatic activities; and for movement throughout all areas of life.

Teachers of physical education (regular and special) can make use of common instructional methodologies and strategies in teaching all different types of persons in a mainstreamed class. Some of these include the following:

- Delivering reinforcement in various forms
- Employing a multisensory approach to teaching

- Using the educational team as a resource
- Teaching within a medical margin of safety (i.e., using activity progressions that do not overly strain a participant)
- Using tutors (assistants) from among a school's pupil population, volunteers from the community, and student teachers from local colleges/universities
- Breaking skills down into component parts
- Stressing that trying is more important than succeeding
- Emphasizing ability, not inability
- Employing varied teaching approaches (Mosston, 1981), ranging from command (teacher directed) to discovery (pupil centered)

Even much of the equipment and materials that teachers of physical education typically use has applicability to all levels of individuals—for example, low and high balance beams, bats of different weights and sizes, a parachute, various flotation devices, music that stimulates interpretive movement, mats of various dimensions, utility balls of various sizes, and weight machines with adjustable loads for various types of lifts. In short, common objectives, individual needs, teaching methodologies, and equipment and materials enable the integration of pupils with differences into a mainstream class.

Many individuals with disabilities want to be in mainstreamed classes and believe that it is the proper and moral path to follow. Furthermore most people with disabilities are not that different from the norm. In fact, the vast majority are only mildly affected by their disability in physical education. As a result, it is often difficult to pick those individuals with disabilities out of a mixed group, especially in physical education (see Figure 4.1). We also believe that all individuals have limitations and deficits in performance. It's just that most are not given a disability label.

Another reason for mainstreaming is that it is humanitarian. All children have a right to be educated with their peers and to receive services geared to their individual needs.

FIGURE 4.1 Can you see obvious differences in this group?

Beyond being the proper, moral, and humane path to follow, mainstreaming is a mechanism to implement the least restrictive environment concept, which is legally mandated in both the U.S. Constitution and in federal and state laws. Constitutionally, it is a civil right guaranteed by the due process provisions of the Fifth Amendment and the equal opportunity declarations of the Fourteenth Amendment. When analyzed together, both P.L. 93–112 (the Rehabilitation Act of 1973) and P.L. 101–476 (the Individuals with Disabilities Education Act of 1990) require least restrictive environment placements in school (including in a regular class), extracurricular activities, work, and social services, as appropriate. Most states, in turn, have legislation to coincide with their circumstances, including court orders, as exemplified by House Bill 455 in Ohio in connection with P.L. 94–142 and Senate Bill 336 in Ohio in connection with P.L. 93–112.

Proponents also contend that mainstreaming enhances the preparation of individuals with disabilities for the real world—the goal of all education and training. If those with disabilities are overprotected and sheltered from their real-world community, society will pay for such treatment throughout each individual's lifetime through a drain on tax dollars. The next point, therefore, is that mainstreaming is more cost-effective than are segregated classes (disabled/nondisabled). It has been demonstrated by both the federal government and the Council for Exceptional Children that mainstreaming, with its emphasis on supportive personnel, will probably cost more at the outset of programming, not less as first thought by the experts. However, in the long run, if pupils are in fact prepared for the real world, they attain the potential to become taxpaying citizens and not a drain on tax dollars. (This is the strongest appeal to opponents of mainstreaming.)

One last reason, and one specific to physical educators, is that mainstreaming can work. Not only experience but also research supports the statement that pupils who have disabilities can be successfully mainstreamed into regular physical education classes (Rarick & Beuter, 1985; Karper & Martinek, 1985). It particularly works at the elementary level because young children are less aware and less critical of individual differences, less peer pressure is exerted at the elementary level, there is less emphasis on competition and winning at the elementary level, and elementary-level teachers tend to believe that mainstreaming will work. Conversely, at the junior and senior high levels there tends to be less interest in mainstreaming, accompanied by concerns mostly in the areas of discipline and legal aspects of educating pupils who are disabled (Minner & Knutson, 1982). Mainstreaming can still be successful at the upper-grade levels if pupils are given elective or selective options dealing with the content of their physical education classes.

There are many reasons for mainstreaming, whether one reason is better than another is not the issue. Rather, the provision of more normalized experiences for those who are disabled is the key. There is little question that mainstreaming is an appropriate philosophy for a physical education setting. In sum, we concur with Greer (1988) that

exceptional children cannot succeed as well if they are required to learn with their noses pressed to the glass, from the outside looking in. The history of special education reveals that nose-to-the-glass education does not do the job. Indiscriminantly educating exceptional children apart has proven to be bad educational practice, bad social policy, and, in the end, bad fiscal stewardship (p. 295).

Whether for or against it, mainstreaming is upon us and all around us. Our only charge is to find ways to appropriately integrate individuals with differences and then to begin teaching.

TEACHER ATTITUDES AND MAINSTREAMING

In Chapter 3 attitude was stressed as a key part of a successful adjustment to a disability—the attitude of the pupil with a disability, the attitudes of his or her nondisabled peers, and the attitudes of community members. There is at least one other individual who must have an appropriate attitude, the teacher. It is absolutely critical that those who teach mainstreamed physical education programs have positive feelings about all of the pupils in their classes. In reality, though, regular physical educators often think that their "hands are full" with the pupils they already have and, therefore, may be apprehensive about mainstreaming pupils with disabilities. They view mainstreaming as a problem, sometimes resulting in resistance, fear, and even anger. Yet the success or failure of a mainstreamed physical education class is largely determined by this same teacher's attitude. Attitudes cannot be legislated, but they can be changed, for attitudes involve learned behavior.

Successful attitude-change strategies for teachers (and others) come in numerous forms. One strategy, perhaps the most successful, involves some type of active interaction between those who are disabled and those who are not. Regular physical educators might visit a special physical education class and become actively involved by assisting in the actual teaching; work directly with (co-teach with) another regular physical educator who is teaching a mainstreamed class;

play in a game or engage in some other movement experience directly with a pupil who is disabled (e.g., wheelchair basketball); volunteer for Special Olympics, Wheelchair Games, or some other event for athletes with disabilities; or have a direct dialogue with pupils who have disabilities about their physical education experiences in a mainstreamed setting.

Another attitude-change strategy is less interactive and involves teacher observation of pupils with disabilities in a physical education class or listening to these pupils discuss their experiences in physical education. The regular physical educator could observe a special physical education class that has one or more pupils soon to be mainstreamed, talk with other regular physical educators who have already mainstreamed pupils with disabilities into their classes, listen to a speaker who has a disabling condition talk about successful movement experiences in school and nonschool environments, or watch sports events in which athletes with disabilities successfully compete.

Still another change tactic involves active simulation of disabilities by regular physical educators. Regular physical educators may simulate a number of disabling conditions while demonstrating selected physical education skills. The participants could be given the opportunity to use a wheelchair or a set of crutches (orthopedically disabled); participate in a physical activity with a sterile sponge in their mouths or with a rule that no speech is permitted (speech impaired); use earplugs while engaged in activity (hearing impaired); have a splint placed on one or both legs (orthopedically disabled); have a weighted knapsack on their back during activity or with a pillow stuffed inside their shirt maneuver through small obstacles (obese); or have one or both eyes blindfolded (visually impaired). When doing some of these simulations, however, limited movement is strongly advised at the beginning due to the participants' unfamiliarity with the imposed conditions. Blindfolding combined with movement is a prime example. In addition, such simulations should be followed with sufficient time for discussion of the experiences.

Other attitude-change strategies cannot be easily categorized into groups. Some examples follow.

1. Reading and talking about notable accounts in the literature that focus on individuals with disabilities and their movement-related accomplishments. Some recommended books include those below.

   Bleier, R., & O'Neil, T. (1975) *Fighting back*. Briarcliff Manor, NY: Stein & Day. Rocky Bleier overcomes his Vietnam injuries and discouraging advice from so-called experts in becoming a star running back for the Pittsburgh Steelers.

   Cordellos, H. (1981). *Breaking through*. Mountain View, CA: Anderson World. An autobiographical account of Harry Cordellos's adjustment to blindness. His physical prowess in distance running, water sports, and a number of other activities is highlighted.

   Buchanan, W. (1978). *A shining season*. New York: Bantam. The story of John Baker, who was stricken with cancer during the period of his best track performances. He coped with this disability by coaching young children at an elementary school. After his death, the school was renamed after him.

   Miller, R., & Conn, C. (1980). *Kathy*. New York: Berkeley. A biography about a girl who, despite brain damage, won the International Award for Valor in Sport in 1978.

   Strudwick, P., & Rutz, J. (1979). *Come run with me*. Hicksville, NY: Exposition Press. An account of Peter Strudwick, who had severely disabled hands and feet, yet became well known for his running ability. His training for the Pike's Peak Marathon is specifically documented.

   Jones, R. (1977). *The acorn people*. New York: Bantam. The story of a camp counselor's first experience with campers who were disabled. His attitude change from fear and negativism to positive adjustment occurs as he sees the physical capabilities of these "different" campers.

2. Talking with knowledgeable school personnel about pupils with disabilities. This could be considered as initial orientation to the educational team process by the regular physical educator. Such support persons might include the special education classroom teacher, the special physical educator, the director of special education, the school psychologist, or the physical therapist. (See Chapter 14, where the educational team approach is addressed.) Jim DePaepe's interview sheds more light on this and other strategies.

3. Taking a course or workshop related to special physical education or, better yet, receiving instruction at a school where mainstreaming in physical education is occurring. In the authors' experience, the topical areas requested most by regular physical educators during such experiences include behavior management, testing, adaptations, combining a broad mixture of pupils in the same physical activities (e.g., games), IEP development, special education law and physical education, and available curriculum packages in special physical education.

4. Viewing and discussing movies that feature individuals with disabilities performing at a high skill level in various physical activities.

It should be stressed that the successful use of any attitude-change strategy is not easily accomplished and will take time. Regular physical educators should not be expected to adjust immediately to a "new" pupil in class, nor should the pupils already in the class be

Jim DePaepe

Dr. Jim DePaepe was an associate professor in special physical education and an associate dean in the College of Education at the University of New Mexico, Albuquerque. He is now dean of the College of Education at Idaho State University, Pocatello.

1. *How important is it for regular physical educators to interact with other school professionals when programming for pupils who are disabled in a mainstreamed physical education class?*

This is perhaps the most critical first step in a physical educator's responsibilities. In order for children with disabilities to receive appropriate physical education services in the least restrictive environment for them, regular physical educators must systematically seek out all direct and related service providers, including staff. This means the special education teacher, special physical educator, teachers' aides, physical and occupational therapists, psychologists, social workers, speech and language pathologists, or any other member of the school system who somehow come in contact with an identified child. Some others include the school nurse, director of special education, principal, and school physician. An attempt should also be made to contact all physicians in the immediate vicinity. This is easier in rural areas, but in any case the school physician can help give you names and addresses of others. It is critical to your

future efforts to establish a good relationship with each of the aforementioned professionals. Ask the special education teachers and special physical educator (if available) in your building to help. This will begin an immediate relationship of working together, which is going to be critical to your success, and ultimately the success of the children taught. The initial contact should first be in written form as a way of introducing yourself and describing what physical education is. You probably should describe exactly what type of physical education you will be providing. Then ask each person you contact to either meet you individually or come to an open forum where you can present in detail your plans, and how these other professionals can assist you in the process of providing appropriate educational opportunities. These interactions will get you started. It is also up to you to keep the relationships going by perhaps establishing a small newsletter informing each of them of your progress with the children, problems you are encountering (after all, none of us know it all) and perhaps some anecdotal story they will appreciate

By taking these extra steps in the beginning and maintaining a good rapport with your contacts, you will be saving yourself a lot of time and energy later on, because when the school year starts and you jump on the merry-go-round of education it does not stop spinning until summer vacation. So be prepared and have an interaction plan in place before you begin.

2. *What professional personnel would generally give the regular physical educator who teaches in a mainstream setting the most assistance?*

The special educator is undeniably the best resource a regular physical educator has relative to working with children classified as disabled. Because all special educators are program managers as well as teachers, they can provide the regular physical educator with information about the children's skills and behaviors no one else can. Most of the success of a mainstreamed setting is governed by knowing the children whom you are teaching. By knowing in advance their skills, behaviors, and difficulties you can establish a safe and rewarding least restrictive environment within a mainstreamed class. As a bonus, if you are af-

forded the opportunity of consulting with a special physical educator, then the two professionals together can make your life as a teacher much easier.

3. *How important is it for regular physical educators to attend IEP meetings?*

Providing there is no special physical educator assigned to the building, it should be a mandatory responsibility in regard to all pupils with unique psychomotor domain needs. To avoid any misrepresentation of service and inappropriate placements of children, it is critical that someone from physical education attend each meeting. It certainly beats bus and hall duty, and in the long run it will be time well spent. Placement and program decisions will be made relative to the child's physical education needs in an IEP meeting irrespective of whether a physical educator is present or not. A typical complaint of physical educators is that they were not warned about having a child with a disability in class. Being informed is getting involved in the process, so you'll know in advance and can plan ahead for the children you'll inevitably be teaching anyway.

---

expected to accept peers with special needs, and vise-versa, without some adjustment time and training. Similarly, both pupils with and without disabilities need appropriate orientation beforehand to a new situation, just as the regular physical educator does. One idea for the benefit of younger pupils is to present the "Kids on the Block" puppet troupe. This show is probably the most popular in the United States to teach pupils about disabilities. Each of the puppets has a different disability. The dialogue and the

puppets' appearance typically generate useful conversation among viewers, and attitude change or initial attitude development commonly results. Information about the program can be obtained from any state education agency, local education agency, special education resource center, or "Kids on the Block," 1712 I Street N.W., Washington, D.C. 20006.

Other parties to influence include school administrators and, of course, parents of pupils with disabilities. Parents' influencing administrators, and vice versa, is an everyday event, and positive public relation efforts by physical educators in this regard can pay large dividends, including desirable attitude changes. Besides, without administrative and parental support, any mainstreaming effort is doomed to failure.

MISCELLANEOUS PEDAGOGICAL CONSIDERATIONS

There are numerous pedagogical considerations in combining pupils who are disabled and nondisabled to equalize ability levels. One way is to use *handicapping*, a technique applicable to those who are nondisabled, too. We have "handicaps" that we take for granted in golf, bowling, and horse racing, so why not use the term to include an expanded menu of activities? Physical educators can, in fact, determine handicaps for any physical activity. It is no big thing, and should not be considered as such. Activity leaders themselves can be given handicaps, too. Younger children are particularly amenable to such a teaching strategy.

When such handicaps are given to pupils in physical education, another important factor must be considered: Handicaps should be applied to the least extent, so that differences among participants are not that visibly apparent. This idea also holds in the use of adaptations and accommodations. Using the least amount of modification in order to appropriately combine pupils with differences is a crucial guideline. The whole idea of mainstreaming involves programming for less and less difference while maintaining successful performance. And even if successful performance is not attained at times, all pupils need to learn that mistakes are OK. In this regard pupils can see that even you, the teacher, can make skill performance mistakes, too. It takes courage to try and fail. Just the attempt is considered valuable as a step in the learning process.

One of the best ways to give handicaps is to ask the participants themselves about changes. What better way to figure out how to do it than to ask those directly involved? Along these same lines, physical educators in mainstreamed programs are advised to sit back at judicious moments and let the participants conduct class. A true story comes to mind: A well-known professor in special physical education was attempting to teach striking to a young pupil who was hyperactive and mentally retarded. The pupil kept missing a slowly thrown large ball. The fact that the pupil kept his bat in constant movement while waiting for each pitch was the key. One of his peers inquired if he could lend a hand. The professor wisely stood back and let the new pupil teach not only his peer but the professor as well. All this peer tutor did was to suggest to the batter that he stick the tip of his thumb in his corresponding ear while waiting for each pitch. The preliminary random movements ceased and the boy started hitting some pitches, with great satisfaction. The professor no doubt added this prompt variation to his teaching repertoire.

Consulting those with disabilities with reference to individual movement skills can be expanded to include their ideas in group activities and games. Traditional rules of games do not have to be followed if leaders and participants choose to do otherwise. All games and activities do not have to stress competition. Nothing forbids participants from deciding to change the rules, boundaries, or equipment of a game. As described in the section on models, the Games Analysis Model, New Games Model, and a physical activity mainstreaming model incorporate this concept by focusing on flexibility, full participation, and performer choices.

When deciding to use activities and games, without changing traditional formats, individual sports, games, and activities might be the best choice. Obstacle courses, with different levels of difficulty (Winnick, 1979, p. 22), cargo nets, stegels, circuit training stations, archery, bowling, mimetics (imitating leader movements or movement ideas), and creative or exploratory movement challenges are prime examples. All these activities have one fundamental common element: No one else or no other team members are depending on you and, therefore, the pressure is off. Further, with many of these individually oriented activities, the performer is encouraged to do his or her own thing. No performance can be a failure because no criteria for success are set or need to be set.

Most pupils mainstreamed into regular physical education programs can be motivated to a level that they can teach some physical activities to themselves. The use of task cards and contract teaching are two examples of self-pacing and self-teaching strategies.

Task cards involve individualized written activity assignments. Each activity is broken down into progressive steps, from easiest to most difficult, with each step written on one card. The pupil then works on his or her own, at school or at home, in an attempt to self-teach a target physical skill. The teacher acts as a consultant, as needed. Card packets for individual physical skills are commercially available, so teachers do not have to make their own. A typical task card is shown below.

A few published resources dealing with task cards include the following:

Educational Research Council of America. (1969). *Educational Research Council of American physical education program.* Columbus, OH: Merrill.

Mosston, M. (1981). *Teaching physical education.* Columbus, OH: Merrill.

For nonreaders, task cards could involve the use of human figures (see Figure 4.2), stick figures, or symbols portraying each desired step in the progression. This system has been used effectively with pupils labeled moderately mentally retarded.

Contract teaching is related to task cards but has a few unique features. In one form of contract teaching, the teacher and participant (and possibly others) agree on what is to be learned, to what degree of proficiency, over what time period, and for what reward. This information is written in contract form to be signed by at least the two parties, teacher and pupil, and a copy is retained by both. The principal, parent, or others could also be signatories of the contract, making it increasingly important. A physical activity contract might look like the sample shown page 96. Other types of contracts are discussed in Chapter 13.

Physical activity instruction formats can be varied beyond the traditional pedagogical approaches. Instead of the commonly used solo instructor–led activities during usual school time frames, three options may be considered: team teaching, preteaching, and assigned physical education homework. Such

---

"COFFEE GRINDER"

Assume regular push-up with arms extended. Move whole body around in full circle, keeping hands at the center, legs extended, and shuffling the feet in one direction. No resting allowed until full circle has been completed.

TASK CARD

FIGURE 4.2 "Windshield wipers."

Contract

By 12/1, John will perform the following activities at the levels indicated:
1. Push-ups = 10
2. Bent-knee sit-ups = 19
3. 95-lb. bench press = 5 repetitions
4. 100 meter run = 14.9 sec.

Award System

If 4 completed = Physical Education Gold Star
If 3 completed = Physical Education Silver Star
If 2 completed = Physical Education Bronze Star
If 1 completed = Physical Education Recognition Star

Signing Parties

Teacher _____   Date _____

Pupil _____   Date _____

Parent _____   Date _____

Other _____   Date _____

---

techniques are meant to keep a pupil at a mentally and physically competitive level with his or her peers.

Team teaching involves the use of multiple instructors in the same class. The advantage of this approach is that the strengths of each teacher can be used at appropriate times. No instructor can be an expert in all physical activity areas, and therefore, with access to different specialists, a better program can be offered. This applies to the use of teaching assistants and their expertise areas, too.

Preteaching is the provision of instruction prior to the actual time set for group instruction. Some pupils are far enough behind in the development of their physical skills that they require supplementary instruction in target areas but not that far behind that an alternate, more restrictive, physical education placement is indicated. Supplementary instruction at school can take place before

school, at the noon hour, or after school. What specifically occurs in preteaching is one-on-one or small-group instruction by regular physical educators (or designees, including peer or cross-aged tutors), and the skills emphasized are those that will actually be used in scheduled large-group activity. For example, if the large-group activity is softball, selected pupils who have trouble hitting a ball are provided preteaching instruction in this skill. It may be best if pupils with skills deficiencies be given systematic preinstruction and prepractice in those skills that are unique to a unit of instruction yet to be offered, even before their nondisabled peers begin this unit of instruction. Pupils needing more assistance will then have a planned "jump start" toward success.

Homework is another interesting concept that is being used more and more in physical education (see Figure 4.3). Other areas of the school curriculum commonly utilize a homework approach, so why can't physical education? If a pupil needs supplementary work in physical skills, those targeted skills can be assigned as homework and monitored by parents or guardians and followed up by the teacher.

Another concept should guide physical educators in providing a mainstreamed program: All participants should successfully be engaged in physical activity as much as possible (Vogler, van der Mars, Darst & Cusimano, 1992; Siedentop, 1991). This concept is known as academic learning time (ALT) and could also be called active learning time within the context of physical education.

It has been suggested that less than one third of class time is taken up by active learning in selected regular physical education classes (Siedentop, Mand, Taggart, 1986). If

FIGURE 4.3 Parent and child doing homework. *(Laimute Druskis)*

this low level of ALT exists in regular physical education programs across the country, there is little justification to continue them. Further, if such levels are reported for regular physical activity programs, percentages of ALT actually might even be lower in mainstreamed physical education classes, as shown by Vogler, et al. (1990). Such a concern might be valid because some activities in a mainstreamed context may require the nondisabled pupil to wait longer for turns or sacrifice maximal effort when performing with lower skilled peers. How, then, can active learning time be increased or maintained at a higher level in mainstreamed physical education programs? A few activity-related ideas are mentioned here:

1. In relays, drills, and gymnastics, make waiting lines shorter by increasing the number of teams or squads.
2. After a performance is complete, keep performers moving with established "return activities" or "postturn activities." For example, after a tumbling routine, the performer might practice a few stunts while returning to the line and waiting for the next turn.
3. Provide a piece of equipment for each participant. Activities involving balls, hoops, wands, and tires would apply.
4. Individual activities, obstacle courses, circuit training courses, movement exploration, and mimetics give the performer an opportunity to practice without interruption with corresponding high levels of ALT.
5. Group activities that permit the blending in of individual differences can be ideal for the generation of high ALT. Such activities include parachute play, stretch rope play, and movement on cargo nets. See Figure 4.4 for examples of each.

One last pedagogical consideration involves timing. First, we believe (and others agree) that the early school years are the best

FIGURE 4.4   High ALT-related equipment.

time to initiate mainstreaming efforts. This is when mainstreaming should start in physical education, too, if at all possible. Young children are more accepting and understanding of their peers' differences during their early years, but as they move into adolescence, they often become more cliquish, judgmental, and downright cruel to peers with differences. On a different scale, it may also be best to start such instruction at the beginning of a school year, when so many things are new to all pupils. And related to this, we suggest that such efforts begin at the start of any instructional unit. Such tactics enhance the probability of success for all pupils.

Above all, physical educators have one great advantage: By their very nature, humans, disabled or not, not only have a developmental need to move but typically enjoy movement. This natural urge can be used to increase ALT and to develop physical education skills in all pupils.

MAINSTREAMING PRINCIPLES

The ultimate goal of a heterogeneous group in a physical activity situation is safe, successful, and satisfying participation. *Safety* is an obvious necessity when providing any type of activity for pupils with disabilities. *Successful* connotes achieving a reasonable degree of mastery of the major goals and objectives of physical education while participating in physical activities. And *satisfying* means that participants are truly enjoying their experience of activity involvement. When these three criteria are met, physical activity participation within a mainstreamed context reaches its highest level not only for the pupils, both disabled and nondisabled, but for the physical educator as well. Obviously, physical educators rarely, if ever, find themselves in such an ideal situation where all three criteria are optimally met. A more realistic subgoal may entail an attempt to offer a mainstreamed program that, at an increasing level, approximates the ideal ultimate goal of safe, successful, and satisfying participation.

The aim of this section is to offer practice-oriented principles that can be directly applied to conducting a mainstreamed physical education program. Within this context, it is recognized that only occasionally can all participants with differences be maximally combined in physical activities. At times, pupils who are nondisabled do have to make certain sacrifices in order for pupils with disabilities to be combined with them appropriately. It is also recognized that the environment itself can be a major factor in the success or failure of physical education classes.

Maximally Combining All Individuals

The most ideal way to combine pupils, both disabled and nondisabled, in physical education involves full participation by all (Winnick, 1978). When no one has to sacrifice and every participant receives a good workout, both the teacher and pupils are making efficient and effective use of their time. Numerous mainstreaming principles with proven applications in physical education exist. In order to involve all pupils successfully in a combined activity, physical educators can be guided by the following rules:

MODIFY MOVEMENT REQUIREMENTS OF PUPILS WITH SPECIAL NEEDS

APPLIED EXAMPLES

- In a relay, walk instead of run

- In ball games, throw underhand instead of overhand.

- In basketball drills, relays, or scrimmages, carry the ball instead of dribbling it.

- In an elementary-level group game, standing is permitted on a stop signal versus lying down in order to be free from "Its" tag.

- In swimming, a modified crawl stroke may be used instead of a breast stroke.

- In dance, a quarter twirl is used when the more able-bodied dancer is required to full twirl.

VARY POSITION PLAYED IN A GAME OR ACTIVITY

Applied Examples

- In a ball game, a pupil can pitch for both teams.
- In floor hockey, a player could play goalie if running continuously is difficult.
- In newcomb, badminton, or volleyball, a pupil may play only at the net. This same pupil might also be permitted to serve at midcourt and then move to assigned position at the net.
- In basketball, the pupil with low physical vitality could play within a modified zone or self-space on offense and defense.
- In water polo, the pupil who is obese could play goalie.
- In football, pupils with poor hearing could be offensive line players.

ADAPT EQUIPMENT AS NEEDED

Applied Examples

- In ball games, use a whiffle bat (see Figure 4.5).
- In badminton, tennis, or volleyball, lower the net.
- In game balls, place a beeper for pupils who are visually impaired.
- In bowling, use a spring-loaded handle on the bowling ball for individuals who need five fingers to bowl (see Figure 4.6).
- In bicycling, use a hand-driven bicycle for pupils who have loss of function in the lower body.
- In all activities, use bright colored equipment for easily distracted pupils.
- In ball games, us a sponge ball instead of a hard ball.
- In racquet games, use enlarged racquets.
- In archery, use a less powerful string.

FIGURE 4.5 Pupil has a choice of bats.

FIGURE 4.6 Use of spring-loaded bowling ball.

VARY DISTANCES AND BOUNDARIES

Applied Examples

• In relays, shorten distances for some pupils.

• In jogging, use inner circle for pupil in wheelchair and outer circle for able-bodied joggers.

• In golf, use red tee (ladies) versus the blue tee (pro).

• In tennis, widen the boundaries on one side to make it easier for the other side to score (i.e., less mobile side).

• In kickball, softball, or baseball, shorten the bases. Keep regulation bases for players who are not disabled.

• In archery, shorten the distance only for those who need such an adaptation.

• In a rope course, allow a pupil to traverse the lower of two options.

ALLOW EACH PUPIL EQUAL TURNS OR TIME

Applied Examples

• In baseball, softball, or kickball, each inning involves every player at bat once versus the three-out rule.

• In an obstacle course, each pupil goes through an equal number of times; pupils may pass each other.

• In circuit training, every pupil spends an equal amount of active time at each station.

• In hopscotch, have numerous grids to allow equal participation in terms of both time and turns.

• In calisthenics, all class members engage in each form of calisthenics offered, yet modified on an individual ized basis.

SPREAD TALENT FAIRLY AMONG TEAMS WHILE PRESERVING A PUPIL'S SELF-CONCEPT

Applied Examples

• Have players with disabilities be captains and choose teams.

• Have high-achieving captains choose entire team away from group.

• Have captains draw names from a hat.

• Have captains pick teams only in the presence of the teacher.

• Have players randomized and count off.

• Have the physical educator choose teams.

• Switch teams/partners often so that pupils experience each other and nobody gets "stuck."

SHARE OR INTERCHANGE DUTIES

Applied Examples

- One pupil bats while another peer runs bases (see Figure 4.7).
- One person brakes, another steers a sled or toboggan, depending on functional level.
- One pupil baits the fishing line, another casts the line, depending on functional level.
- One pupil shoots arrows and another retrieves them.
- One pupil bowls, another sets pins, and another keeps score.

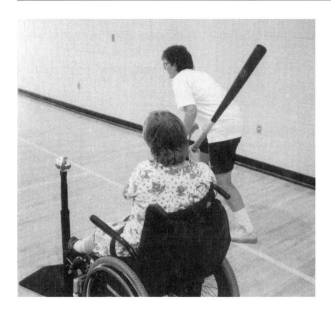

FIGURE 4.7   Pupil in wheelchair bats and peer runs.

EXECUTE ACTIVITIES WHILE TOUCHING

Applied Examples

- Place pupils who are visually impaired in middle of tug-of-war line for most tactile support (see Figure 4.8).
- Place pupil needing most physical and psychological support in the middle of a toboggan.
- Place weakest and smallest pupils nearer the top in pyramid building.
- Offer elementary group games that incorporate touching (e.g., multiple lines of 3–6 players each; last player in each line has flag attached to rear of pants; object is for the first player in each line to capture another line's flag.)
- Offer chain dancing such as The Thread Follows the Needle or Bunny Hop.
- Offer circle dances such as Here We Go Round the Mulberry Bush or Hokey Pokey.

FIGURE 4.8 Place pupil with vision problems in the middle.

ASSIGN ALL PUPILS TO RELATED DUTIES

Applied Examples

- A pupil could be assigned a referee's role for part of a class session.
- A pupil could be scorekeeper for part of a class session.
- A pupil could be the leader, teacher, or coach for part of a class session.
- A pupil could be in charge of equipment for part of a class session.

AVOID ELIMINATION-TYPE ACTIVITIES

(Remember, those needing activity most are usually knocked out first in traditional elimination games! See Figure 4.9).

Applied Examples

- Avoid Simon Says; instead, use reinforcement for correct responses only and judicious prompts to assist others.
- Use a modified form of battleball; instead of pupils being knocked out, they count points against their team.
- Regular Musical Chairs could be changed to a series of chair formations. If a pupil is eliminated from the A group, he moves to the next group of chairs. Chairs are added or subtracted from groups accordingly. Or try Musical Hoops in which pupils stand in hoops when music stops; progressively eliminate hoops, not pupils (see Figure 4.10).
- Standard single elimination mini tournaments should not be stressed; multi-chance mini tournaments are preferred.
- Tag games that eliminate pupils could be changed in such ways as making those tagged become taggers or blockers.

FIGURE 4.9   This pupil needs movement, not more sitting.

FIGURE 4.10   In musical hoops, all pupils stay in the game.

MAKE ACTIVITIES SAFER THAN USUAL

Applied Examples

- Use extra mats and/or protective clothing.
- Widen out-of-bounds areas.
- Use shallower end or add more lifeguards for pool games.
- Add cushions to sleds and toboggans.
- Cushion sticks more in field hockey, hockey, or lacrosse.
- Cushion arrow tips instead of using standard hard metal tips.
- Cushion the edges of entrances for crawl-through tunnels.
- Take additional types of directional finders when engaged in orienteering.

Above all, each pupil should be an active participant in the activities. This means that assigning a pupil to be an equipment manager, scorekeeper, referee, "go-fer," or towel monitor on a full-time basis would be inappropriate. Even more inappropriate and, in fact, dehumanizing would be such reported treatment of pupils as their acting as a boundary (e.g., left field pole) or as a piece of equipment (e.g., second base) because of a disability.

Maximally Combining Only Pupils Who Are Disabled

At times, a physical educator does have to make pupils who are not disabled sacrifice for the benefit of players with disabilities in mainstreamed physical activities. Admittedly not the best situation, when it does arise, follow the general rule of limiting participation by regular players the least amount possible while still permitting players with disabilities an equal opportunity to succeed. The following principles on activity limitation apply under this general category of circumstances, enabling those who are disabled to have potentially maximal or near-maximal success in mainstreamed physical activities.

Limit Play Areas. The boundaries of any traditional game involving considerable running (soccer, field hockey) can be brought in so that all participants do not have to move as much. This would impact negatively on those who enjoy maximum movement.

Move in Tandem. Mixed participants could be paired in tandem bicycling, which might limit a nondisabled pupil's ability to pick up and maintain speed. A runner who is visually impaired might need the physical guidance of a sighted runner. The latter would probable not be able to run as fast as usual.

Increase Number of Players. Instead of using the traditional number of players in a game (nine in softball), positions could be added so that players would have less territory to cover. This would make the activity less vigorous overall.

Shorten Time Periods. Standard time periods (eight-minute quarters in basketball) could be shortened in any robust physical education activity. Less continuous activity coupled with more rest would offset or delay fatigue in those participants with low vitality.

Freely Substitute Players. Larger teams and equal participation time for all team members would counter fatigue but precludes a full workout for some. An example would be floor hockey in which eight players are on the floor per team and after every two minutes of action, a new prearranged platoon of players enters the game for each team. Platoons then systematically rotate in and out of the game in order.

Decrease Points Required to Win. In volleyball, instead of 15 points, change the winning score to 10 points or whatever the teams agree upon. Games then would not last as long.

Have All Participants Experience Limitations. All players might be required, for example, to move on scooters in a given contest. This tactic would serve at least two purposes: (1) it would narrow any competitive edge between nondisabled pupils and pupils who are mobility impaired, and (2) it would sensitize nondisabled pupils to the challenges faced by those who are not ambulatory. Other examples of this strategy might involve blindfolding or plugging the ears or applying leg splints on all players. It is worth repeating that physical educators must exercise caution when implementing such simulation techniques. For example, sighted persons become very disoriented when blinders are required in an activity. These pupils probably have not had the opportunity nor were ever forced to cope with such adversity. In contrast, pupils who are visually impaired have had considerable practice in learning orientation and mobility skills and in developing their auditory sense. Therefore, when such a simulation is introduced, the pupil who is visually impaired will have an initial advantage over his or her sighted peers.

Helmets may be advisable for sighted players who are temporarily blinded.

These seven principles are applicable mainly when an individual or group initially becomes involved in a mainstreamed movement-oriented program. The goal would be, however, for the physical educator gradually to reduce these tactics and rely more and more on maximum participation techniques.

Environmental Considerations

Aside from modifications of activity equipment and adapting the movements of participants with disabilities, some environmental variables can be manipulated to increase maximum participation by pupils with and without disabilities. At least five factors can be identified.

Lighting. Bright lights (sun or bulbs) or dim lights can adversely affect the best of lesson plans. Constancy of illumination throughout the activity area is an important requisite. In addition, it is known that bright flickering lights can catalyze a seizure in a mainstreamed player who is seizure-prone, and lighting extremes can distract a pupil who is learning disabled or behavior disordered.

Acoustics. How noise travels in the environment is another concern. Some indoor swimming pools have poor acoustics, and noise reverberates throughout the setting to the detriment of instruction. Any time directions need to be repeated or signals need to be duplicated, physical activity is interrupted. This results in less than maximal ALT.

Temperature. Temperature is a critical factor. A pool temperature that is cold might cause some participants to resist going into the water; on the other hand, though, it might stimulate pupils who are depressed. Warm water might be appropriate to calm pupils who are tense or hyperactive, but may not be best for a pupil with multiple sclerosis. In any event, it is advised that air temperature be slightly warmer than pool temperature.

In the out-of-doors or in the gymnasium, if the air is too hot, vigorous movement will naturally lessen. This can be countered by decreasing the temperature in the gymnasium, moving to a shaded area outside, or changing the lesson to focus on limited movement activities. Cooler temperatures in these environments can be adapted to quite easily by, for example, adding clothing. A moderately cool environment is generally most advisable because this inherently stimulates movement.

Air Quality.   The quality of air must also be addressed. Proper ventilation in a gymnasium or pool cannot be assumed but must be monitored by the physical educator. Odors (e.g., body odors) can adversely affect ongoing physical activities, too. Polluted air in out-of-doors environments can be a major source of disruption. This could include pollutants from traffic, air inversions, or various allergens. Pupils probably will not as willingly, or might not be able to, engage in activity conducted in an environment with poor air. In such an event, the physical educator might consider switching the activity to a more comfortable controlled environment.

Architectural Barriers.   This environmental variable has received considerable attention. A chief reason is that federal law (P.L. 101–336 and P.L. 93–112) mandates that qualified participants may not be physically excluded from mainstreamed programs. Yet physical activity environments too often present architectural barriers. Some gymnasiums have steps for entrance and egress; some

playgrounds have nonaccessible play apparatus and are even difficult to get to; and some pools have steps, no ramps, and water that is too deep all the way around. Physical educators systematically need to eliminate these physical barriers if success in mainstreamed physical activity is to be realized (see Figure 4.11).

Other Distractions.   Extra lines on the floor, charts or figures on the walls, or bright colors in the environment that are not part of the activity are examples of other factors that have the potential to impact negatively a mainstreamed activity program. Such factors that are directly part of the activity could, however, work to the advantage of physical educators. For example, a brightly colored ball (e.g., bright yellow) could maintain the attention-to-task of players in ball games.

Physical educators also need to think preventively and be proactive when anticipating or confronting adverse environmental variables. Action needs to be taken before participants arrive for activity. If the action is delayed and modifications need to be made during activity time, chances are that learning will suffer.

MAINSTREAMING MODELS

Many of the principles and ideas presented in this chapter have been used as the basis for some recognized mainstreaming models in physical education. Such models have been discussed in the literature and have been successfully applied to a variety of pupils. These models include the New Games Model and the Games Analysis Model.* Each model is discussed and numerous applied examples

---

* The Project PEOPEL and Every Child a Winner models (see Chapter 3) also emphasize mainstreaming as an integral aspect of their curricula.

FIGURE 4.11 Architectural barriers in physical education.

are cited. Then a physical education mainstreaming model of our own is presented.

The New Games Model

The New Games Model originated out of the New Games Foundation, a nonprofit educational organization established in 1974. The New Games Model has all of the following elements, which ideally tie into a mainstreamed context: a deemphasis on competition, full participation, fairness, rule changes on the spot by the participants, games for small and large groups chosen by the participants themselves, hard and vigorous play, attention to safeguards, and mutual trust. Ideally, aggression is transformed into fun. For example, in a game such as cageball the name of the game is modified Earth Ball. It is played in a large space with a large group and the ball may even be painted as a globe. All standard rules of cageball are adhered to except that when the ball comes too close to a score, designated members of the team about to score change sides and the ball reverses direction. In making this type of an adjustment, a score may never be registered; how-

ever, all participants on both sides will have a vigorous and continuous workout. The key, again, is not to win but to play hard, have fun, play safely, be flexible, involve everyone, and to preserve the self-concept of all pupils. See a variation of Earth Ball in Figure 4.12.

Following are examples of other vigorous New Games from the literature (Fluegelman, 1976, 1981):

1. Knots. A group of eight or more participants form a circle and reach arms forward clasping the hands of two other players, neither one of whom is adjacent. The objective is for the group members to untie themselves without the need for a "knot-aid" (a required break of hands).

2. British Bulldog. One or more participants are "It." All others start behind lines opposite each other. When the pupils in the center give some creative signal, the others attempt to run or walk or roll or hop or the like to the opposite side without being caught. Being caught involves being grabbed and held (or lifted) for a set amount of time by one or more persons who are "It." If caught, that person joins the

FIGURE 4.12   A new game, Earth Ball. *(Reprinted with permission from* The New Games Book, *Copyright © 1976 by the Headlands Press, Inc., Doubleday Publishing.)*

center "team." The game continues until everyone is caught. Ganging up on elusive flee-ers is advised. This game is similar to a few games played in grade school, but is age appropriate for adults, too. A number of the New Games are characterized by this same cross-age feature.

3. Fraha. Obtain two paddleball racquets, a ball, and two pupils. Both players act as a team with no competition other than the elements (e.g., gravity). The objective of the game is to keep hitting the ball back and forth without catching it or allowing it to drop to the ground. Once a reasonable volley has been realized, other players can be added.

4. Monarch. A small or large group chooses a "monarch." The monarch is then confined to one spot for the entire event. From this spot the monarch throws a "royal Nerf" ball at any one of the "anarchists" moving within the designated boundaries. If hit, an anarchist becomes another monarch. The royal Nerf can then be thrown by either monarch from their chosen stationary positions. Other converts are obtained in the same manner. The royal Nerf can be passed from one monarch to another to more easily hit moving anarchists.

5. Swamp Chute. Using a large parachute, have all players except one sit around it, hold it with two hands, and slide half of their bodies under the chute. One player lies prone completely under the parachute anywhere near the center. He or she is the "alligator" or, as a variation, the "blob." While

those sitting around the chute ripple it as small waves in a swampland, the alligator attempts to approach someone's legs and pull him or her under the chute. If successful, two alligators then become free to roam for more victims. A grabbed player may release one hand from the chute and also use his or her legs to try to become free. Freedom from the alligator occurs only when an attacked player moves outside the chute without standing. All others remain fair game around the chute.

6. Human Spring. This game for two pupils starts with both participants standing, facing each other, and the palms of their hands flat against each other. From this position each player takes a half step back while momentarily releasing hand contact. The players then lean forward with stiff arms and body-"spring" back after contact with each other's palms. If successful, another half step back by one or both of the pupils is taken. The ultimate distance apart before balance is lost is a measure of cooperation, trust, and team work. For safety, the game can be played from the kneeling position or on a very soft surface (sand, thick mats, in 2 feet of water).

The New Games Foundation conducts workshops for New Games leaders, publishes New Games books and newsletters, provides related equipment and materials, and interacts with individuals in any possible manner in order to generate interest. Headquarter's address is New Games Foundation, P.O. Box 7901, San Francisco, California 94120.

The Games Analysis Model

The Games Analysis Model is based on the notion that the rules of traditional games can be changed to accommodate the varied skills of pupils, that pupils should be permitted to modify the structure of any games through problem solving by matching their physical performance levels with game requirements, and that participants with different levels of skill can be successfully combined in the same game (Marlowe, 1981; 1980a, & 1980b; Morris, 1980). Under such conditions, skill differences are accommodated and cooperation is promoted. Most importantly, no one is excluded from an equal opportunity to succeed in a group, even if competitive.

More specifically, the Game Analysis Model views games as containing six components and each can be adapted to meet the needs of pupils. These six components include players, equipment, movement pattern, organizational pattern, limitations, and purpose. The *players* component refers to a determination of number of pupils in a particular game. The *equipment* component connotes which equipment, adapted or regular, will be used in the game. *Movement pattern* refers to the bodily movements required for participation. *Organizational pattern* indicates the pattern of pupils "out in the field" relative to positions played. The *limitations* component is the specification of rules, regular or adapted, decided on for use in the game. And the *purpose* component is important in order to clearly make the goals and objectives of the game known to all pupils. It should be stressed that the determination of these six components by pupils and physical educators is based on a preevaluation of the pupils' skills. This formal or informal pretesting of pupils' physical skills will assist both pupils and physical educators in establishing realistic game expectations. Without knowing present skill level, the physical educator might establish rules that preclude success and encourage failure.

To make the Game Analysis process more understandable, we apply the model to kickball, battleball, and team bowling (see Tables 4.1–4.3). Using these three examples, a physical educator should be able to adapt any traditional game, whether intended for use with

TABLE 4.1 KICKBALL GAMES ANALYSIS

PLAYERS	EQUIPMENT	MOVEMENTS	ORGANIZATIONAL PATTERN	PURPOSE
Equal number per team	Ball of choice	Kicking Catching Running Ball rolling	Fielders in nomal kickball positions (varied if not 9 players).* Kicking team divided into four equal units. Bases are twice the distance apart from the traditional arrangement, and bases are each chalked/lined squares with 8' diameter.	To develop and refine targeted game movements. To develop judgement and coooperation

Limitations

1. Pupils in each kicking unit are numbered consecutively and each player bats once per inning.
2. All members of each kicking unit advance only one box forward per kick; kickers are only selected from home plate box player (in numbered rotation).
3. Inning begins with only the home plate box occupied by unit 1 players and kicker 1 in that unit kicks. When the fourth kicker's (unit 4, kicker 1) turn arrives, all boxes will then be filled until the inning is over.
4. How to score: Only the defense scores. When the ball is "live", a score is made by rolling the ball and hitting a runner below the waist while outside a box. Once a particular player is hit, no more points can be scored against that player in the same inning. Hit offensive runners can become blockers for their unit's unhit runners still in "live" territory.
5. Any extra kicker (odd/even numbered units) kicks at the end of the inning regardless of base occupied.

*More than nine pupils per side is desirable since units should consist of more than two pupils each.

TABLE 4.2 BATTLEBALL GAMES ANALYSIS

PLAYERS	EQUIPMENT	MOVEMENTS	ORGANIZATIONAL PATTERN	PURPOSE
Equal number of players per team	Nerf balls One blue hoop per player (offense). One red hoop per player (defense) Cones	Dodging Catching Throwing	Activity area divided in half by cones Each team's half divided in individualized player zones. Each player has offensive hoop and defensive hoop placed according to that player's ability (i.e., If throwing is hard and accurate, player's offensive hoop would be set back; If player's dodging and catching abilities are poor, player's defensive hoop would be set back).	Develop and refine targeted movement skills

Limitations

1. Pupils in each kicking unit are numbered consecutively and each player bats once per inning.
   a. Hitting a player in that player's defensive hoop. The thower must me in his or her own offensive hoop.
   b. Catching a ball in his or her own defensive hoop.
2. No player is eliminated throughout any game.
3. Two referees serve as counters, one per side. Referees are rotated per game.
4. Twenty-one points comprise a game, or a 5-minute time limit per game is established if 21 points are not reached by any one team.

TABLE 4.3 TEAM BOWLING GAMES ANALYSIS

PLAYERS	EQUIPMENT	MOVEMENTS	ORGANIZATIONAL PATTERN	PURPOSE
Equal number per team up to 5 players	Bowling ramps (to accommodate mobility impaired players). Different weighted balls (to accommodate smaller and physically weaker players). Bowling ball with spring-loaded handle (to accommodate player with poor finger strength). Bowling rail (to accomodate the visually impaired).	Rolling	Use traditional lanes.	Improve bowling accuracy.

Limitations

1. Each bowler rolls 10 frames.
2. Scoring is adapted:
   a. Zero to 4 pins = 1 point
   b. Five to 9 pins = 2 points
      Ten pins = 3 points
   c. Only one ball is rolled per player per frame.
   d. Maximum score per player per game is 30.

younger or older pupils. The key ingredient, remember, is direct pupil input about the format and function of the game to be played.

One last word of caution about the use of the Games Analysis Mainstreaming Model: Whenever traditional games are modified, they should be structured in such a way so as to approximate the traditional or original activity or game as closely as possible and still provide success for all participants. Our goal in using any model is eventually to introduce players to situations they will face in the real world. Adaptation should not be an end in itself but only a temporary adjustment to be faded when realistically possible.

Physical Education Mainstreaming Model

In Box 4.1, the two cluster variables of independence-cooperation-competition and

individual-dual-group can be viewed together along a mainstreaming continuum of physical education participation. The least anxiety would probably be created in a pupil who is disabled when only individual activities are provided. These establish no success criteria and eliminate competition with others. Greatest anxiety would probably be imposed in the situation of competitive physical activity participation in a large group in which teammates depend on each other.

The goal in this proposed model is to move pupils to the point that maximizes their successful participation closest to real-world realities for them. Initially, pupils begin on the continuum at that stage most suitable for them. It is not assumed that all individuals in mainstreamed physical education will always start at any one stage within the model. An individualized approach is advocated from the outset, with the further understanding that not all pupils can reach the highest stage.

More specifically, the model proposes seven stages of training:

- Stage 1 involves independent participation in individual activities such as swimming and archery. At this stage expectations are individualized and based on the performer, with social sanctioning by others downplayed if not altogether eliminated.
- Stage 2 adds the element of another performer, but competition is not involved. Cooperation is the key. Dancing as partners is a classic example of an activity engaged in for the purposes of motor skill learning, movement enjoyment, and social development.
- Stage 3 adds a competitive element; however, only two participants are involved. Appropriate matching of contestants in an activity such as wrestling is a key to programming at this level.
- Stage 4 deemphasizes competition again but requires the addition of more players.

An activity such as pyramid building requires at least four participants, and the cooperative team element, by the very nature of the activity, far outweighs any competitive overtones.

- Stage 5 joins both the small-group and competition elements. For many pupils with disabilities, this could be the most challenging and difficult stage to pursue. If successfully accomplished, however, the pupil is well on the way to involvement in traditional games played within an everyday context. Success at Stage 5 is considered the major milestone in this model. The elements of competition and group are merged at this level in such activities as hopscotch and bowling.
- Building on this milestone, Stage 6 emphasizes an increased number of players, even to the point of mass participation. To make success of this stage more possible, the element of competition is faded. For example, in any of the New Games discussed earlier, all pupils are required to be involved with numerous others on a cooperative basis. This, admittedly is a difficult task for a

BOX 4.1   A Physical Education Mainstreaming Model

- *STAGE 7*: Large-Group Competitive Activities (e.g., regular games and sports)
- *STAGE 6*: Large-Group Cooperative Activities (e.g., New Games, parachute and stretch-rope play)
- *STAGE 5*: Small-Group Competitive Activities ($N = 4 - 8$) (e.g., hopscotch, track and field, doubles racquet games, bowling, golf)
- *STAGE 4*: Small-Group Cooperative Activities ($N = 4 - 8$) (e.g., pyramid building, rope jumping, trampoline)
- *STAGE 3*: Dual Competitive Activities (e.g., handball, badminton, wrestling, combatives)
- *STAGE 2*: Dual Cooperative Activities (e.g., partner stunts, ball toss, rope climbing, dancing)
- *STAGE 1*: Individual/Independent Activities (e.g., relaxation, weight training, swimming, calisthenics, archery, circuit training, obstacle courses, cargo net play)

pupil with a disability. Yet, if that pupil has competence at Stage 5, a higher probability of Stage 6 success is ensured.

- Finally, at Stage 7, the challenging elements of both competition and large groups are faced. At first, a traditional game could be modified at this level. Such modifications might involve use of the Games Analysis Model or selected simple modifications created on the spot.

Eventually, however, the ultimate goal is successful participation in traditional physical education with all adaptations or modifications faded. At this point we have arrived. And having successfully arrived not only increases the probability of pupil satisfaction in traditional physical education activities but also has implications for carryover benefits in other areas involving competition and groups.

Mental
Retardation

All children and youth, including those who happen to be disabled, must be served in schools. What is especially significant to regular and special education teachers is that, generally, most disabilities interfere with pupils' abilities to learn appropriately within any educational environment, including physical education.

In this third part of the book (Chapters 5–12), we discuss the 13 disabilities covered by P.L. 101–476, plus a variety of other, less common, disabilities found among pupils in physical education classes. Although the information is organized in a disability-specific format—the categorical approach in teaching physical education—teachers must always remember to design educational programs around each pupil's instructional needs and not be influenced by the label a pupil happens to have. The information relates to groups of individuals with specific

disabilities (e.g., all those with mental retardation), not necessarily to the special needs of a specific person within one of these groups. In addition, many pupils are multiply disabled. A pupil's primary disability could be a learning disability, but there could also be a secondary emotional problem because of an inability to cope with the frustrations associated with learning. Thus, in some cases, the physical educator must combine information related to more than one condition, based on the multiple educational needs of each child.

DEFINITION, CAUSES, AND SCOPE

Definition

There are currently two accepted definitions of mental retardation. The most recent definition approved by the American Association on Mental Retardation (AAMR) is as follows:

> Mental retardation refers to substantial limitations in present functioning. It is characterized by significantly subaverage intellectual functioning, existing concurrently with related limitations in two or more of the following applicable adaptive skill areas: communication, self-care, home living, social skills, community use, self-direction, health and safety, functional academics, leisure, and work. Mental retardation manifests before age 18 (Luckasson et al., 1992, p. 1).

This definition reflects a major change in the way people with mental retardation have been viewed in education and in other spheres, and has the potential to be universally accepted in the not too distant future. What distinguishes this definition are its deemphasis on intelligence quotient (IQ) score and level of disability and its emphasis on such factors as support needed, ability, and the natural environment. A classification of mental retardation depends on an IQ measurement of 75 or below (using 90–110 as a norm range), onset before age 18, and significant needs in two or more adaptive skill areas. In turn, the identification of any support required for a classified person can range from intermittent, limited, extensive, to pervasive. Moreover, a profile of any required support is derived from among four dimensions: intellectual functioning and adaptive skills, psychological and emotional considerations, health and physical considerations, and environmental considerations.

School personnel, however, do not use the 1992 AAMR definition. Instead, they follow the definition of mental retardation as contained within the Rules for implementing the Individuals with Disabilities Education Act (P.L. 101–476). This definition states:

> Mental retardation means significantly subaverage general intellectual functioning existing concurrently with deficits in adaptive behavior and manifested during the developmental period that adversely affects a child's educational performance (P.L. 101–476 Rules, *Federal Register*, September 29, 1992, p. 44801).

This definition involves three criteria: significantly subaverage general intellectual functioning, existing together with deficits in adaptive behavior, and originating during the developmental period. All three must be met before a pupil can be classified as mentally retarded even though intelligence score is the most crucial factor.

Significantly subaverage general intellectual functioning specifically refers to a poor performance score (two or more standard deviations below the norm) on a standardized IQ test. Such tests typically have a scoring range from 0 to 200, with 100 as the mean, and a standard deviation of 15. The most common standardized IQ tests are the Stanford Binet Scale of Intelligence (Terman & Merrill, 1973), the Wechsler Intelligence Scale for Children—Revised (Wechsler, 1974), and the more recent Kaufman Assessment Battery for Children (Kaufman & Kaufman, 1983).

The severity of an individual's mental retardation is described by levels. The most common levels are mild, moderate, severe, and profound. These levels and associated IQ ranges, with some room for variability depending on the test administered, are approximately:

- Mild mental retardation = 55–70
- Moderate mental retardation = 40–54
- Severe mental retardation = 25–39
- Profound mental retardation = below 25

Deficits in adaptive behavior must accompany significantly subaverage IQ performance. Adaptive behaviors generally encompass the areas of maturation, learning, and social adjustment. Maturation includes effective self-help skills (e.g., feeding, dressing, and toileting), communication, and psychomotor development (e.g., gross motor and manipulative skills); learning skills include such variables as language acquisition and an understanding of number concepts; and social adjustment connotes level of appropriate behavior and abilities related to self-direction and socialization. According to Grossman (1983), adaptive behavior expectations in our society are related to chronological age (CA). Major emphases for specific CA ranges include:

Infancy and Early Childhood

- Sensorimotor skills
- Communication skills
- Self-help skills
- Socialization skills

Childhood and Early Adolescence

- Application of basic academic skills in daily life activities
- Application of appropriate reasoning and judgment in mastery of the environment
- Social skills

Late Adolescence and Adulthood

- Vocational and social responsibilities and performance

Expected adaptive behaviors by level of retardation can be estimated. The individual who is mildly retarded typically has few if any significant psychomotor problems, can usually learn the academic content expected of a sixth grader, and can often learn sufficient social and vocational skills to live and work in society. The individual who is moderately retarded can learn fundamental motor skills and communication skills, can usually learn the academic content expected of a second grader, and can learn semi-independent skills related to living and working. The individual who is severely retarded often shows marked problems with psychomotor and communication skills. Although simple tasks can be learned, independence in work and other living environments is not to be expected and supervision will be required. The individual who is profoundly retarded will show evidence of serious problems across the psychomotor, cognitive, and affective domains very early in life and beyond. This person may respond to basic training, but intensive and ongoing intervention will be required.

Tests have been developed to measure these adaptive behaviors. The most popular are AAMR's Adaptive Behavior Scales (e.g., Nihira, Foster, Shellhaas, & Leland, 1974), the Revised Vineland Adaptive Behavior Scales (Sparrow, Balla, & Cicchetti, 1984), and the Comprehensive Test of Adaptive Behavior (Adams, 1984). Professional judgment is used in interpreting performance on these tests.

According to the law, the developmental period is that time from birth up to 22 years of age. However, by medical standards, the developmental period ranges from 6 months before conception up to 22 years of life, reflecting the critical importance of the mother's health before and during pregnancy. If a person is to be diagnosed as mentally retarded and best served, clear evidence of the condition must surface before he or she reaches the age of 22. In fact, such a diagnosis is usually made before a child reaches the first grade of school. Our laws provide for far fewer education and training services for these individuals after their school-age years.

A few additional points relative to the definition of mental retardation need to be stated:

- Mental retardation is not a disease in itself; it could be the result of a disease.
- Mental retardation does not automatically imply actual brain damage.
- The term *mentally handicapped* is sometimes used to refer specifically to a person who is mentally retarded. However, because of its association with mental functioning overall, mentally handicapped has also included those who are emotionally disordered or learning disabled; therefore, the term could mislabel a person. It is best to use specific terms, such as "mentally retarded," if labels are needed.
- Given the three-criteria definition of mental retardation in P.L. 101–476, it is possible for a person to have different scores from test to test (IQ or adaptive behavior test), which might change the retardation level or, conceivably, make a person who is labeled "normal." Reasons for test score variability could include mistakes in administering a test or a variety of environmental factors. For whatever reason, scores have been known to change over very short periods even without known intervention and pupil maturation. A person could, therefore, be mentally retarded at one point in life and not at another.
- The term *6-hour retardate* has been used (and is still being used inappropriately) to describe the child who shows evidence of retardation in school but not out of school (President's Committee on Mental Retardation, 1969). Such a term is applied to the situation when a pupil's IQ and related academic performance are very deficient in school, but adaptive responses outside of school approach or are "normal." Outside of school, this child is not retarded. And, in fact, if the child's adaptive behaviors in school are "normal," the child technically

is not "retarded," no matter how low the IQ test score.

- Mild mental retardation is often diagnosed when a child begins formal schooling and IQ testing is stressed. This is when a child's academic abilities are evaluated for the first time, and intellectual deficits may surface under these conditions. The lower functioning child, on the other hand, typically is diagnosed earlier because deficits are more obvious. The children who are most profoundly retarded, who often have physical or sensory problems as well, are typically diagnosed at birth or shortly after.

Causes

How mental retardation originates is not easily explained. There are well over 100 documented causes, including some organic (e.g., brain damage) and some nonorganic (i.e., no known physical cause). Causes can relate to heredity or environment. The causes of most cases of mental retardation are not known and are, therefore, said to be idiopathic. Table 5.1 presents an overview of the causes of mental retardation, organized by time of occurrence. The table lists only the major causes of mental retardation and, therefore, is not all-inclusive. A discussion of the causes follows.

Prenatal period. The chromosomal anomaly that causes the greatest number of cases of mental retardation is Down syndrome. In the most common form of this syndrome, the child has an extra chromosome, resulting in moderate mental retardation and numerous other developmental complications. Specific characteristics include eyes that look slanted and crossed, obesity, protruding tongue, maloccluded teeth, pronated and flat feet with spread toes, short stature, deficient speech, heart defects, hyperflexible joints, small

TABLE 5.1   MENTAL RETARDATION CAUSES

Prenatal (before birth)
1. Chromosomal anomaly (e.g., Down syndrome)
2. Hydrocephalus, microcephalus
3. Disorder of metabolism (e.g., phenylketonuria, PKU)
4. Maternal disease (e.g., rubella)
5. Parental blood incompatibility (e.g., Rh factor)
6. Maternal self-abuse (e.g., smoking, alcoholism, other drug addiction)

Perinatal (at birth)
1. Premature birth, postmature birth
2. Low birth weight
3. Diffucult labor and delivery

Postnatal (after birth)
1. Disease (e.g., menigitis, encephalitis)
2. Developmental retardation, environmental deprivation
3. Poisoning (e.g., intake of lead-based paint)
4. Disorders of metabolism (e.g., galactosemia)

Combined occurrence before, during, or after birth
1. Accident
2. Cerebral anoxia
3. Tumors
4. Syphilis
5. Idiopathic conditions

hands, less than normal muscle tone, and susceptibility to respiratory infections (see Figure 5.1). In large measure, these characteristics explain Down syndrome children's notable deficiencies in motor development (Share & French, 1993; Block, 1991) and physical fitness (Eichstaedt, Polacek, Wang, & Dohrmann, 1991). The older the mother at the time of conception, the greater the chance the child will have Down syndrome.

Hydrocephalus is a condition where the fluid that bathes the brain (cerebrospinal fluid) cannot be eliminated normally, is overproduced, or is obstructed within the head. This causes the cranium to expand (see Figure 5.2), which affects cells in the brain, resulting in various degrees of mental retardation. Medical personnel have developed a technique to circuitously shunt the fluid into the heart or intestines. Early detection followed by shunt surgery can prevent the negative effects of fluid buildup. As the child grows physically, the shunt must be lengthened periodically. (See the discussion of spina bifida in Chapter 10 for additional information.) In contrast, microcephalus is characterized by a head that is too small. The maximal

FIGURE 5.1   Two young men with Down syndrome.

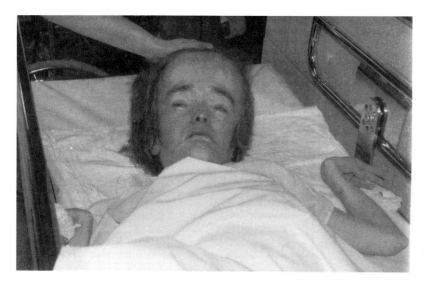

FIGURE 5.2 Severe hydrocephaly.

growth of brain cells or actual number of brain cells is consequently limited, resulting in mental retardation.

Certain inherited metabolic disorders such as phenylketonuria (PKU) are associated with mental retardation. PKU results from the lack of a special metabolic enzyme, which causes a buildup of a damaging acid in the body. This acid prevents the proper metabolism of the amino acid phenylalanine in protein, which results in damaged brain cells. Early, strict dietary control of phenylalanine intake (e.g., milk-free diet) is essential to prevent retardation.

Rubella, or German measles, can inflict considerable damage to the developing embryo when contracted by a woman during the first trimester of pregnancy. The first trimester (first three months of pregnancy) is the most critical period of human development and also the most vulnerable. A rubella virus invasion during this period is most damaging to the cerebral cortex, the eyes, and the ears. The introduction of rubella vaccine has helped lower the number of cases of

mental retardation and other disabilities attributed to this cause.

The effect of parental blood incompatibility can be devastating to an unborn child. One type of blood incompatibility associated with mental retardation is Rh factor. Most humans (approximately 85 percent) have a factor in their blood that is also contained in the blood of rhesus monkeys. When a mother's blood does not contain this factor and the father's blood does, the unborn child is at high risk of being Rh positive and having blood incompatible with the mother's. Blood testing of couples before the woman becomes pregnant is critical. Drugs are available to mothers that will allow for normal birth; these drugs need to be taken before each conception after the first child.

A last prenatal consideration is maternal care. It has been documented that maternal intake of nicotine, alcohol, cocaine, and certain other toxic substances can damage the developing child. Pregnant women should limit or totally eliminate the ingestion of these substances in order to lower risk to the embryo. Other prenatal care considerations, such as calorie intake, should be discussed with an obstetrician.

Perinatal Period. Prematurity and post-maturity can cause mental retardation because the child does not have sufficient time or has too much time to develop within the womb. In addition, if the predicted date of birth is accurate, yet the infant is low in birth weight (less than 5 1/2 pounds), the same concern exists as if the child were born prematurely. Another unfortunate cause of mental retardation is rough delivery, whether due to inappropriate hand, instrument, or surface contact. Difficult deliveries also include breech births (head delivered last) and caesarian section (abdominal incision to allow delivery).

Postnatal Period. Any disease that affects brain cells or prevents an adequate flow of oxygen to brain cells can cause mental retardation. Infection of the soft protective layers of the cranium (meningitis), infection of the brain (encephalitis), scarlet fever, and pneumonia are among these diseases.

Developmental retardation specifically refers to lack of environmental stimulation, which results in underuse of brain cells. All body cells need use or the "law of atrophy" prevails—that is, the cells will waste away—and mental atrophy is the unfortunate result. Parental neglect or sensory loss at birth are the two major causes of developmental retardation.

Infant or toddler poisoning is another major concern. Many cases of poisoning are caused by lead-based paints. If a child ingests a significant amount of this paint, the lead could reach a toxic level and adversely affect the child's brain cells. Even though current paints are not lead-based, parents should take appropriate precautionary measures because many old objects and structures are still covered with lead-based paints.

A child can also be born with a metabolism disorder, such as one that does not permit normal digestion of a mother's natural milk. This condition, known as galactosemia, specifically involves difficulty with the lactose in milk. As with PKU, mental retardation can be prevented by diet under the careful supervision of a physician.

Combined Periods. At any time before, during, or after birth mental retardation could be caused by trauma, deprivation, abnormal growth, disease, or other variables. Accidents involving the head, cerebral anoxia (lack of oxygen to the brain), tumors or lesions, syphilis, and numerous idiopathic causes fall within this broad category.

Prevention of mental retardation has become a major concern in the United States. In the 1970s, the President's Committee on Mental Retardation projected the reduction of mental retardation by 50 percent by the year 2000. Toward this end, genetic counseling is strongly encouraged for couples who have reason to believe that their child would be at a greater than normal risk (because of parents' ages, blood incompatibility, parental drug use). Two prenatal tests, analysis of the amniotic fluid within the placenta (amniocentesis) and intrauterine analysis of the fetus as a whole (sonogram), are strongly recommended for an unborn child at abnormal risk. These tests give objective data that could be used in the decision to abort a pregnancy. In addition, after conception, prenatal and perinatal care and a stimulating postnatal environment are critical.

Scope

By definition, approximately 3 percent of the U.S. population is mentally retarded, or approximately 7.5 million people. This statistic, however, takes into account only IQ scores. If the criterion of adaptive behavior or adaptive skill deficiency is also used in determining the scope of mental retardation, the percentage decreases. The actual scope of mental retardation seems more realistically to be somewhere between 1 and 3 percent of the population. In light of these figures, it has been determined that every 5 to 6 minutes a child is born in the United States who will be labeled MR at some point in life (approximately 9,000 per month). In fact, according to the *Fourteenth Annual Report to Congress on the Implementation of The Individuals with Disabilities Education Act* (U.S. Department of Education, 1992), 0.97 percent of all pupils aged 6–21 (N = 552,658) were labeled mentally retarded during the 1990–91 school year— a percentage surpassed only by those labeled learning disabled and speech impaired.

The scope of mental retardation also varies considerably when severity is considered. Approximately 89 percent of all individuals who are mentally retarded are mildly affected; 6 percent are moderately affected; and only 5 percent or less are severely or profoundly affected. A physical educator who has a pupil who is mentally retarded in class will probably have a child who is only mildly mentally retarded. Parental socioeconomic status also affects the scope of MR. Specifically, many children who are mildly mentally retarded have parents from low socioeconomic classes. Whether the mental retardation is physically or environmentally based is a matter of considerable debate; in any case, these children need to be watched and taught carefully with the goal of eliminating or reducing their "retarded" behaviors.

One last factor related to the prevalence of MR is that medical science has developed techniques to prolong life, which particularly affects those who are severely and profoundly mentally retarded. Individuals who are mildly retarded now tend to live as long as "normal" people. Moreover, whereas the average age of death for persons with Down syndrome was 9 years in 1929, it now is almost 50 years.

CHARACTERISTICS AND INSTRUCTIONAL STRATEGIES

Common psychomotor, cognitive, and affective characteristics of pupils who are mentally retarded should be considered by physical educators in educational programming. We emphasize instructional strategies (including general methods, instructional goals, and placement-related information) that are particularly important in teaching these pupils. The discussion includes both general and specific guidelines for pupils who are mildly, moderately, or severely/profoundly retarded. The reader is referred to the following resource for more comprehensive information on physical activity and mental retardation at all levels of severity across the life span:

Eichstaedt, C. B., & Lavay, B. W. (1992). *Physical activity for individuals with mental retardation.* Champaign, IL: Human Kinetics.

Two resources for information at the severe/profound level are:

Jansma, P., Ed. (1993). *Psychomotor domain training and serious disabilities*, 4th ed. Washington, DC: University Press of America.

Joseph P. Kennedy, Jr., Foundation (1989). *Special Olympics motor activities training program.* Washington, DC.

We particularly want to guard against rigid teacher expectations of pupils who are mentally retarded based on these guidelines. Our statements need to be interpreted as tendencies for this population as a whole, with each pupil unique unto himself or herself. In conducting actual classroom activities, therefore, teachers should gear their strategies to individual, not group, needs.

Developmental age (DA) needs to be stressed in programming rather than chronological age (CA) for most pupils who are mentally retarded. DA refers to the present level of overall functioning, whereas CA simply refers to biological age. DA should be used to determine teaching approaches in physical education; yet care must be taken not to insult pupils' intelligence. The DA/CA differential should be minimal during the elementary years but may later extend to three years for pupils who are mildly mentally retarded. This range can be extended for those labeled moderately or severely/profoundly retarded. After physical maturity, chronological age is a more significant factor in consistent provision of age-appropriate activities that are important in the pupils' present and future school and nonschool environments. In this case, a functional curriculum may be the best to offer (see Chapter 3).

Across Levels of Retardation	
CHARACTERISTICS	INSTRUCTIONAL STRATEGIES
Psychomotor	
1. Pupils who are mentally retarded follow the same developmental patterns as normal pupils but at a slower pace.	1. Teach to developmental psychomotor needs. This includes attention to human growth and development principles, such as proximodistal development (trunk develops before extremities) and cephalocaudal development (development moves from head toward feet).
2. Physical fitness and motor proficiency are below normal. The fitness level gap between pupils who are mentally retarded and the nondisabled increases with CA.	2. Provide a wll-rounded program of fitness and motor activities based on each pupil's present level of performance.
3. Proficiency in cardiorespiratory endurance is a deficient performance area among pupils who are mentally retarded.	3. Allow for intermittent periods of rest during instruction; mix exertion-oriented and quiet activities (i.e., fast-slow-fast-slow).
4. Pupils probably will be most successful in skills involving some type of physical ability.	4. Teach leisure time functional skills for use during nonschool time, particularly for use after graduation. They will no doubt be using their bodies more than their minds when time is their own. Avoid assignment of physical activities that require considerable planning.
Cognitive	
1. Individuals who are mentally retarded function best in concrete, noncomplicated activities; abstractions and complexities tend to "lose" them. They acquire skills best by doing.	1. Simplify, positively reinforce, demonstrate, and use multisensory approaches (e.g., verbalize and manually assist). Use numerous activities but only one or two per class. Expect that many skills will need to be taught from the beginning step. Use developmental progressions in teaching all activities, teach from part to whole. Best test results will come by using simple test items.
2. Little maintenance of skills can be expected without intervention.	2. Spot-check often for skill retention. Once a specific skill has been acquired, it may be wise to check for skill maintenance the next day, the next week, the next month, and even six months later, depending on retardation level.
3. Generalization of skills cannot be expected without intervention.	3. As part of the overall educational team, systematically program for generalization of skills around different people with varied equipment (e.g., chang-

ing color, size, or hardness of a ball), in different environments, and at different times. Generalize to natural community-based settings whenever possible.

4. Never assume that incidental learning will occur with this population.

4. You cannot assume good hygiene practices when shower, soap, and deodorant are made available within the context of physical education class. Cause-effect (e.g., if you run around a pool, you may slip and be hurt) and safety assumptions cannot be made.

5. Memory and attention span are deficient.

5. Offer activities with few rules to memorize. Instructional periods should be short. Teach in small groups and stress skill repetition. Expect delayed pupil responses; wait patiently for responses, particularly if the pupil is seriously retarded. Highlight activity-related stimuli (bright color, music, rewards) and be enthusiastic about teaching. Pupils who are retarded tend to do best initially when attempting any skills. Concentrate on distributed practice.

6. Vocabulary is limited.

6. Use few and simple words and maximize demonstrations. Encourage but do not force improvements in expressive and receptive language.

7. The thinking ability of pupils who are mentally retarded can be underestimated by an instructor. Above all, these pupils *can learn.*

7. Make no assumptions about level of performance. Approach teaching with the attitude that progress is possible. Stess cause-effect understandings (e.g., safety).

Affective

1. Pupils with mental retardation are easily frustrated, often have an inadequate self-image, and may often lack motivation and aggressiveness.

1. Offer activities that provide initial success. When teachable moments fade, change the activity. Ask for ideas or observe the child's choices of class activities. Help pupils understand that some activities are difficult for others too.

2. Pupils who are mentally retarded tend to be followers and imitators.

2. Do not force into leadership roles.

3. They, at times, have difficulty exhibiting appropriate behavior.

3. Systematically attempt to ignore inappropriate behaviors. Be a model of appropriate behavior in your teaching. Praise appropriate responses.

4. Often they are easily upset with changes in routine.

4. Offer continuity from class to class, particularly stressing similar or identical activities at the beginning and end of each class. Consistently structure the instructional setting with regard to equipment, signals, and lesson plan flow.

General

1. Pupils who are mentally retarded have the same basic needs as do the nondisabled.

1. Approach teaching these pupils as persons who happen to be disabled, yet have typical basic needs in all domains of development. Initial instruction should emphasize psychomotor and social objectives, followed, in order, by vocational and academic objectives.

2. A range of needs among pupils who are mentally retarded often becomes evident relatively early in their lives.

2. Early intervention is crucial for a pupil who is mentally retarded; the critical formative years are birth to age 5. Early intervention might lessen and even pre-

3. Young children who are mentally retarded often are not self-motivated, do not have healthy play experiences, and may show little interest in play.

vent secondary problems, such as posture, motor, fitness, and play deficiencies.

3. Structure play experiences systematically. Teach these children how to play from the noninvolved through, if possible, competitive stages. Provide age-appropriate play experiences for older pupils; no "baby games."

Mildly Mentally Retarded

CHARACTERISTICS	INSTRUCTIONAL STRATEGIES
Psychomotor	
1. Pupils who are mildly mentally retarded are significantly behind their "normal" peers in physical fitness (Eichstaedt et al., 1991), and boys perform fitness skills better than girls who are mildly mentally retarded. (Rarick, Dobbins, & Broadhead, 1976).	1. Systematically offer a broad menu of fitness activities based on each pupil's present level of performance. Use physical education homework and chart progress for instruction and motivation.
2. These pupils tend to be more overweight than nondisabled pupils.	2. A milieu (24-hour environment) approach to proper diet and regular exercise is advised. Ongoing cooperation between school and home is necessary.
3. Performance of these pupils in motor development skills, such as balance, locomotion, and manual dexterity, is significantly below the norm when compared with nondisabled peers (Cratty, 1974; Drew, Logan, & Hardman, 1990; Eichstaedt et al., 1991; Rarick et al., 1976).	3. Same as guideline 1 for motor activities; stress motor development deficits reported in the literature cited and each pupil's present level of motor performance.
Cognitive	
1. Pupils who are mildly retarded can reach a level of education at least equal to the upper primary level. These pupils often develop mentally at one half to three quarters the level of their "normal" peers.	1. Instructions should be geared to developmental level. When dealing with chronologically older pupils, do not insult their mental age.
2. These pupils can usually acquire vocational skills at some level.	2. Psychomotor elements with vocational relevance (endurance, locomotion, strength) are high priority and should be a frequent focus of training.
Affective	
1. The pupil who is mildly retarded can learn acceptable socialization and communication skills.	1. Encourage the use of language and socialization skills in physical education class; stress activities that involve group interaction.
2. This pupil will probably need guidance under unusual stress.	2. Do not put these pupils in the position of frequently making decisions for a group (e.g., captain, quarterback).
3. Many of these individuals obtain jobs, marry, and live close to ordinary lives.	3. In many respects, the pupil who is mildly retarded should be treated like his or her nondisabled classmates.
General	
1. The child labeled mildly retarded is much more like the normal child than different in all areas of development, particularly in the psychomotor domain.	1. Stress ability rather than disability in teaching physical education. Performance by this child above the median can be expected in psychomotor activities. Expect the child to do well. Encourage acceptance of these pupils by nondisabled peers.

Moderately Mentally Retarded

CHARACTERISTICS	INSTRUCTIONAL STRATEGIES

Psychomotor

1. The fitness level of the 6- to 19-year old pupil who is moderately retarded is typically below that of the pupil who is mildly retarded (Londeree & Johnson, 1974). Deficiencies are shown in static strength (grip strength), dynamic strength (sit-ups), explosive strength (standing long jump), speed, cardiovascular endurance, and agility (Rarick and McQuillan, 1977). Flexibility scores of pupils who are moderately retarded are typically superior to the scores of those labeled mildly retarded.

1. Offer daily programs of fitness instruction, based on the child's individual needs. Encourage calendar-year program continuity through homework and parental cooperation in an attempt to help the child catch up.

2. The child who is moderately retarded tends to be more overweight and obese than the child who is mildly retarded (Eichstaedt et al., 1991).

2. Use a calendar-yaer milieu approach to proper diet and regular exercise in cooperation with the pupil's parents.

3. Performances in the motor areas of static balance, dynamic balance, body perception, gross agility, locomotor agility, throwing, and tracking are inferior to those labeled mildly retarded (Cratty, 1974; Rarick & McQuillan, 1977).

3. Same as guideline 1 for motor activities; stress motor development deficits reported by researchers and each pupil's present level of motor developement.

4. Approximately one third of all children who are moderately retarded have Down syndrome, which is associated with the following most notable psycho-motor characteristics:

4. Become acquainted with strategies related to the unique needs of pupils who have Down syndrome

a. Susceptibility to respiratory infection.

a. Ensure that pupils are well dried after acquatics activities and showering. Play on dry surfaces and consider how cold it is before conducting class outside.

b. Susceptability to nonalignment of upper cervical vertebrae (atlantoaxial dislocation syndrome).

b. Activities that forcibly afftect the neck must be avoided, such as dive rolls in gymnastics and the butterfly stroke in swimming. X-rays of the upper spine must be taken as a prerequisite to approved activity participation.

c. Hyperflexibility in major joints.

c. Hyperflexed joints should be strengthened, not stretched.

d. They have a tendency toward a small mouth and normal tongue size.

d. Mouth breathing probably will be evident along with related labored breathing. Cardiorespiratory activities should not be bunched together over long periods and should be offered within a medical margin of safety.

e. These pupils have a tendency toward having small hands.

e. Throwing and catching activities will need to be made easier during intial instruction.

f. Their growth is generally stunted along with pronated and/or flat feet and crossed eyes.

f. Numerous functional balancing activities should be offered.

g. Older pupils with Down syndrome are typically overweight (DePauw, 1984).

g. Sustained programs emphasizing diet and exercise programs are vital with this group. Individualized motivational techniques must be used at home and at school throughout the year.

h. Heart conditions are more common.

h. Avoid overexertion. Look for open mouth breathing and blueness of lips and fingernails.

Cognitive

1. Children who are moderately retarded usually develop mentally at one quarter to one half the level

1. Directions must be simple, using a minimum of different words. Repeat if necessary. As the child grows

of "normal" children. Education at approximately a second-grade level is possible.

2. These pupils can learn fundamental communication skills.

Affective

1. Children who are moderately retarded often need assistance when under mild stress.

2. These pupils often have a low tolerance for frustration, which can lead to aggressive behavior.

General

1. The pupil who is moderately retarded is more like the nondisabled pupil than different, especially in they psychomotor domain.

older, offer functional age-appropriate activities modified to match mental age in school and non-school environments.

2. Encourage appropriate verbalizations in physical education class. Never assume that a single direction is understood. Sometimes have pupil repeat instructions. Use clear, varied stimuli. Permit pupils to keep their own scores (see Figure 5.3).

1. Do not force decisions or a leadership role on these pupils.

2. Teach appropriate outlets for aggression. Reward pupils for not displaying frustration-caused behaviors.

1. Encourage acceptance of this pupil by pupils who are not disabled and mildly retarded. Likenesses should be stressed.

Severely/Profoundly (S/P) Retarded

CHARACTERISTICS	INSTRUCTIONAL STRATEGIES

Psychomotor

1. Among all children who are mentally retarded, the psychomotor competence of those labeled S/P retarded is the lowest. Yet the pupil who is the most profoundly retarded still has a developmental need to move.

1. Encourage any type of range of movement that is purposive and that provides, where possible for exploration of the environment. Allow freedom of the hands for the child who is nonambulatory by using a scooter or any other functional alternative.

FIGURE 5.3   Pupil who is moderately retarded recording her own performance.

2. The retention of primitive reflexes, including postural reflexes, is one reason for their poor psychomotor performance.

3. Most of the needs of this type of individual are physical and motor. The more serious the mental retardation, the more significant are the psychomotor needs.

Cognitive

1. Pupils who are S/P retarded are grossly intellectually deficient and usually develop mentally at no more than one quarter the level of "normal" children. They can learn some fundamental skills, but many never develop competence even in self-help skills (dressing, eating, toileting).

2. These individuals are often nonverbal.

3. Often the child who is S/P retarded needs to be taught how to imitate and lacks the ability to attend to obvious stimuli independently.

Affective

1. Individuals at this level of mental retardation lack play skills and, therefore, usually cannot share in the social benefits of play. Yet this individual will have considerable leisure time available.

2. These pupils are a genuine challenge to motivate.

General

1. Pupils who are S/P retarded often are muliply disabled with concomitant physical defects and widely differing needs. Many of these individuals are institutionalized.

Passive stimulation should be followed by activities in which the child actively participates with large muscles as soon as possible. Sensorimotor awareness is a high-priority objective for those most profoundly involved (Jansma, 1993; Webb, 1969).

2. Instuctors should have knowledge of and practice basic reflex inhibition and facilitation techniques with assistance from occupational and physical therapists, if appropriate (Jansma, 1993; Finnie, 1975).

3. Systematically stimulae key senses. Nonambulatory pupils should experience many positions every hour. Eventually teach skill clusters that enhance functional development.

1. Be patient. Be encouraged by small gains as compared to expectations for nondisabled pupils. Break skills down to their most rudimentary components and begin at that level. Instruction should be given often and over short periods.

2. A few common words can serve as directions. Hand signing, sounds, touch, smells, and colored signs or articles of clothing are effective avenues of communication.

3. The intensity of environmental stimuli (e.g., colors) must be carefully monitored so as to enhance rather than distract from instruction. One-on-one instruction is the rule rather than the exception. Touching and physically manipulating children who are S/P retarded encourages imitation.

1. Assume no play skill acquisition without instruction. Teach age-appropriate functional play skills in multiple environments.

2. Electrical response devices can be used to motivate pupils who are profoundly retarded and nonambulatory (Jansma, 1993; French, Folsom-Meek, Cook, & Smith, 1987). When a pupil moves appropriately, an electrical impulse could allow music to play, a bright light to turn on, or other type of instant reinforcer.

3. Consult with physical and occupational therapists with regard to the treatment of physical disabilities. Do not accept a program of custodial care; it does not foster education and training. All individuals *can learn.*

We also want to emphasize that if such appropriate strategies are systematically used with these pupils, no matter what the level of retardation, the chances for success are enhanced. Proof of such success has been noted in numerous writings—in particular, see Campbell (1978), Dresen (1985), Hsu and Dunn (1984), Lavay, Reid, and Cressler-Chaviz (1990), McCubbin and Jansma (1987), Mulholland and McNeill (1985), and Skrobak-Kaczynski and Vavik (1980). From our own and colleagues' experiences, we know that these techniques work.

INDICATED AND NONINDICATED ACTIVITIES

In this section we suggest specific physical education activities and related methods that we have found to be successful or were recommended by others (Eichstaedt & Lavay, 1992; Finholdt, Peterson, & Colvin, 1987). In addition, we note activities and related methods that are generally not advised. These suggestions should serve only as guidelines; again, there are exceptions to every rule. This section includes information on developing fitness, motor, swimming, dance skills and games. Most of the information centers on the pupil who is mildly or moderately retarded, followed by programming ideas for those labeled severely/profoundly retarded, where appropriate. Remember, in the actual selection of activities and methods for a specific lesson plan, recommended activities for groups of pupils should be considered only in the light of individual pupil need. And as important, also remember that psychomotor competence can be improved in pupils who are retarded as a result of planned and systematic programs of physical education.

Physical and Motor Fitness

Development of physical and motor skills is very important for pupils who are mildly or moderately retarded, and the differences among them are often a matter of fewer repetitions completed or small adaptations rather than radical change in activity. In contrast, pupils who are severely/profoundly retarded should generally not be given activities that stress only traditional fitness develop-

ment, but rather should be given rudimentary fitness activities that are associated with and help develop physical and motor skills. For example, when postural muscles are strengthened by using resistance exercises, the pupil's postural experience and walking body alignment may be monitored at the same time, as postural muscle tone directly affects the development of locomotion. As pupils with serious retardation grow older, however, traditional fitness activities, per se, are more important.

Only three 15-minute fitness training sessions per week over six weeks has been found to be sufficient to increase significantly the strength of adolescents with Down syndrome. Such gains can be made with the use of a weight machine program or an exercise program (Weber & French, 1988). Further, three 20-minute activity sessions each week can be effective in improving strength, cardiovascular endurance, flexibility, and other fitness components in the pupil who is mildly or moderately retarded. Rarick and colleagues (Rarick et al., 1976; Rarick & McQuillan, 1977) recommend that approximately 30 percent of physical education programming for these pupils should be devoted to strength and power activities. In addition, they recommend that stress be placed on activities that emphasize the efficient use of oxygen (i.e., aerobic activities). Here are some specific safe activities and methods that address fitness for these pupils:

1. Use a Universal weight training device or a modified one to cover all strength areas without fear of weights dropping and subsequent injury or equipment breakage.

2. Simple combative strength and power activities, such as wrist wrestling, leg wrestling, human tug-of-war (one-on-one) are recommended.

3. Use self-testing fitness activities that directly improve performance scores on standard-

ized fitness tests, such as the standing broad jump (power) and bent-knee sit-up (abdominal strength). Bent-knee sit-ups or adaptations (such as roll-ups with hand push) are particularly good for pupils with Down syndrome, some of whom may have weak abdominal muscles, which predisposes them to hernia.

4. Supervised performance in fitness activities incorporated in standardized tests of fitness should be stressed for pupils who are retarded: 50-yard dash (speed), 600-yard run-walk (cardiovascular endurance), softball throw (power), full or flexed chin-ups (strength), shuttle run (agility), modified burpees in which there is no standing (flexibility, strength). See Figure 5.4 for shuttle run participation.

5. Medicine ball throwing is effective (power, strength).

6. Stationary rowing machines (flexibility, strength) and stationary bicycles (cardiovascular endurance) are effective.

7. Group tug-of-war with a strong rope is fun and fitness oriented (strength, power, cardiovascular endurance).

8. Jogging under supervision is highly encouraged (cardiovascular endurance).

9. Teach individual or partner isometrics using bike tires or towels (strength). Force can be applied against most body parts.

10. Isotonics are recommended using chairs, small logs, and weighted or stuffed animals (strength) depending on the pupil's chronological age.

11. Under supervision, isokinetic exercises can give pupils a kinesthetic awareness of controlled movement and force.

In a prescribed fitness-oriented activity with pupils who are mildly or moderately retarded, the instructor always has the option to adapt. For example, pull-ups can be changed to a measure of hang-time; 90-degree flexed arm hangs can be 45-degree hangs, or the grip can be changed from over- to underhanded. Sit-ups and push-ups can be made easier by partially to totally eliminating the force of gravity—for instance, push-ups off the wall and sit-ups from an inclined surface. In addition, the pupils themselves can monitor instruction and progress in fitness activities using notebooks with developmental progressions in stick figure form. The pupils can be taught the meaning of a stick figure drawing and can independently progress to more advanced levels of performance. (See the discussion of task cards in Chapter 3.)

In testing and instructing fitness-oriented activities with older pupils and adults who are severely and profoundly retarded, the materials from Project TRANSITION at the Ohio State University can be used (Jansma et al., 1986, 1987). Project TRANSITION products include a series of five curriculum-embedded fitness test items that have leisure time and vocational value for those who are seriously retarded and of adolescent or

FIGURE 5.4 Pupil who is moderately retarded on shuttle run course.

postschool age. These items include a modified bench press (see Figure 5.5) to test upper body strength and muscular endurance, a sit and reach item (see Figure 5.6) to test lower back and hamstring flexibility, a grip strength dynamometer test, a 300-yard run/walk item to test cardiorespiratory endurance, and a sit-up item (see Figure 5.7) to test abdominal strength and endurance. Numerous additional teaching ideas are provided in its user manual (Jansma et al., 1987), which focuses on functional fitness in the community. A few examples of these functional curriculum ideas include cinder blocks being carried from one outside location to another, laundry and garbage bags being loaded onto a truck, pulling out drawers of cabinets and desks, learning a firm handshake, and hammering.

Also of importance to the physical education teacher is that test item scoring in Project TRANSITION places an emphasis on both skill performance and level of independence (prompts needed by pupils). More information on the Project TRANSITION test scoring system is provided in Chapter 15.

Fundamental Motor Skills and Patterns

As we continue to stress, pupils who are mildly retarded have many deficiencies in fundamental motor skills and patterns as compared to nondisabled pupils; yet their physical education activities can and often should involve interaction and involvement with their "normal" peers. Most pupils who are mildly and moderately retarded can attain at least minimal motor skills and patterns related to everyday activities such as walking, climbing, avoiding objects, jumping, running, moving objects, throwing, catching, and kicking. Again, as mentioned, performances of pupils who are mildly retarded are likely to be superior to those of pupils characterized as moderately retarded.

FIGURE 5.5   Project TRANSITION bench press equipment.

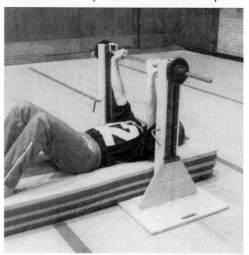

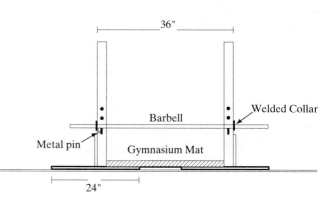

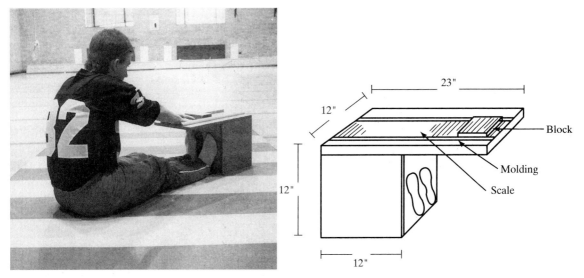

FIGURE 5.6   Project TRANSITION sit and reach equipment.

FIGURE 5.7   Project TRANSITION sit-up equipment.

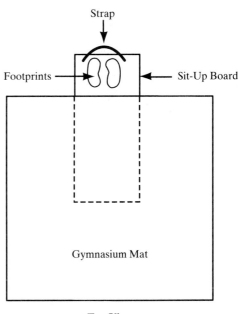

Approximately 20 percent of physical education programming for pupils who are mildly or moderately retarded should be devoted to gross motor limb–body coordination activities (Rarick et al., 1976; Rarick & McQuillan, 1977). When programming any motor activities, more adaptations will be necessary for pupils who are moderately retarded than for those who are mildly retarded. Some related activities used successfully for pupils who are mildly or moderately retarded include the following:

1. Initially emphasize modified rope jumping skills. Instead of a full-swing technique, a stationary or pendulum swing could be employed.

2. Time, force, and spatial concepts can be taught using adapted movement education. Activities can be generated that focus on the concept of time for an entire class period. The next class period might start with a review of the time concept and then be primarily devoted to the development of one other concept, force or space. The third class might be totally devoted to an integration of any two of these concepts.

3. Throwing can be greatly enhanced by having pupils throw at motivating targets— clowns, figures, and peers. (Soft missiles should be used if a classmate is the target.) Pupils who are moderately mentally retarded often have particular difficulty with mature throwing patterns and other fundamental motor skills that require crosslateral (opposition or reciprocal action) patterns, because the brain hemispheres must function together.

4. Static and dynamic balance can be enhanced by using graduated balance beams, standing on tires or inner tubes, or using a mini trampoline or air mattress.

5. Creeping and crawling can be practiced on mats or through chairs, tunnels, boxes, or the instructor's legs. Scooter boards can be used to stimulate crawling and creeping patterns.

6. Trampolining activities should be offered that are minimally difficult and are done under careful supervision. We recommend one-to-one supervision of simple bounces taken from a prone, supine, sitting, kneeling, or standing position. See in Figure 5.8 how a rope can be used to assure safety using one of these bounces. Although the use of trampolines is restricted and, in some cases, altogether forbidden in schools, these recommended activities not only involve minimum risk but have been found very useful for assessment and program planning with pupils. In the interest of safety and to avoid more common trampoline-related injuries, we recommend the elimination of flips, back bounces, and knee bounces.

7. Independent walking can be stimulated using movement exploration, games such as Follow the Leader, and walking within designated boundaries.

8. Solo running can be improved with the use of simplified chase and flee games, even on a one-to-one level, and simplified relays.

9. Walking, hopping, jumping, and sliding can be taught to a group using two bamboo poles or ropes between which the pupils move. Galloping, jumping, hopping, skipping, and leaping can be successfully offered using music and a model leader, a jumping rope, or water or some other obstacle to jump over.

10. Throwing and tracking patterns can be defined with the use of brightly colored, soft, large, or deflated balls, beanbags, and balloons.

11. Many psychomotor objectives can be met with obstacle courses, circuit training courses, mimetics, or story plays. Encourage various levels of independent play from solo to interactive play.

a

b

c

FIGURE 5.8   This pupil is safely engaged in trampoline challenges.

The needs of the pupil who is severely/profoundly retarded are fundamentally psychomotor. The development of common motor skills and patterns, such as walking, running, and jumping, is based on many postural, reflexive, and more refined motor building blocks. These prerequisites are typically the focus of psychomotor intervention for those who are severely and profoundly retarded. For this population, any activities that stimulate purposive movement are desirable. The only sure way of becoming acquainted with the body and its parts is to use it. Movement stimulation activities that arouse interest and activities that relate pupils to the environment and inhibit primitive reflexes are high priority. Specific fundamental multisensory activities for pupils who are severely/profoundly retarded include the following:

1. Visual stimulation with the use of mirrors, visual aids, flashlights, and brightly colored toys, cribs, clothes, and walls.

2. Tactile stimulation with temperature changes (air, water), passive brush, hand, and towel stroking, ice play, water play, sand play, and tapping.

3. Medically approved kinesthetic stimulation through passive (dependent), assistive (semi-independent), and active (independent) grasp/release, flex/extend, rolling, restraining, rocking, swinging, bouncing, or positioning activities. These activities can be designed to inhibit primitive reflexes with the assistance of an allied medical specialist. The individual who is profoundly retarded will often require considerable manual stimulation.

4. Auditory stimulation through passive or active clapping, the use of drums or records, audiotape recordings, and voice modifications.

5. Olfactory stimulation with the use of incense, flowers, and perfumes.

6. Gustatory stimulation with the use of various liquids and solids (obtain approval from parents).

When attempting to teach fundamental motor skills and patterns to the pupil who is severely/profoundly retarded, be careful not to overstimulate him or her. With one sense being stimulated too much or many senses being bombarded over too short a time period, neurological overload is more likely in an underdeveloped central nervous system. Thus overstimulation counteracts the original intention of the stimulation. In dealing with these pupils, physical educators should seek support and expertise from others on the educational team, including occupational and physical therapists.

Pupils who are severely/profoundly retarded should, over time, be encouraged to engage successfully in many motor development activities: including crawling, creeping, reaching, grasping, holding, releasing, tracking, bending, extending, bouncing, twisting, balancing, pushing, pulling, rolling, lifting, standing, sitting. For those pupils who are nonambulatory, movement from a lying or sitting position should be encouraged. For example, rolling or using the hands and buttocks to move to a reinforcing object can be required of a pupil. If one body part is immobile, those body parts that are mobile should be active. Again, these pupils can learn, and their achievements should not be limited by the instructor's expectations.

Aquatics

As a general rule, pupils who are mildly retarded can become proficient swimmers, use a variety of quality stroking techniques, and learn basic rescue skills. Pupils who are moderately retarded can be expected to learn safety around water and learn some strokes at a lower level. Pupils who are severely/profoundly retarded can learn some water orientation, which includes safety around water and perhaps some water survival skills. In our view, survival in water is the initial key for all pupils, no matter how the technique looks.

Instruction in the pool should follow a sequential pattern, with safety considerations being foremost. Here is a general hierarchy of instructional priorities:

1. Physical and psychological adjustment to the water

- Elimination of apprehensions associated with water
- Awareness of safety considerations (critical if pupil will eventually function independently in the water)

2. Attention to survival skills

- Supine floating (on back)
- Prone floating (on stomach)
- Rhythmic breathing
- Turning over
- Changing direction

3. Attention to specific strokes

- Dog paddle
- Crawl
- Elementary backstroke
- More advanced strokes

During such instruction, personal flotation devices (PFDs) need to be used wisely. Such devices can range from float boards (see Figure 5.9) to those that can be attached to the swimmer's body. When using such devices on a pupil's body, use simple attachments to secure them. It is our view that PFDs should be considered "crutches," to be

FIGURE 5.9 Learning to glide using a flotation device.

faded as soon as possible. We would not be serving our pupils well if we made them depend on PFDs on an ongoing basis.

In working with pupils who are mildly or moderately retarded on safety awareness or actual swimming skills, an instructor should not assume the child is competent, even if he or she claims ability at a certain level. All pupils should be tested for present level of performance in and around water before instruction and before free swim periods. Instructors and more advanced pupils should act as appropriate models.

As a method of instruction, movement education is advocated for pupils who are mildly or moderately retarded. Using this approach, the teacher can incorporate motivating materials like rubber bricks that pupils retrieve at varying depths, inflatable objects that pupils accompany into deeper water under guidance, hoops that can be passed through under water, and weighted objects (puck, coins, keys) that pupils can retrieve from the bottom of the pool. With the use of materials like these, pupils can be challenged to explore and solve problems while becoming acclimated to the water. Another effective method is the use of intriguing names for movements in the water. For example, the "torpedo" could refer to push and glide movements with or without instructor support; the "steamboat" could refer to a glide accompanied by a flutter kick (see Figure 5.10). As a supplement to such activity, instructors will probably find even more success in teaching swimming to pupils (including preschoolers) with mild or moderate retardation by using gentle persuasion within the context of routine, repetition, relaxation, and systematic reinforcement (Bundschuh et al., 1972). Instructors can work on fitness, motor, dance, and games objectives while teaching swimming skills, too.

Aquatic activities have much to offer the pupil who happens to be severely/profoundly retarded. Many movements that these pupils cannot do on land can be accom-plished in the water. Any type of safe movement is desirable. The buoyancy (pushes up), gravity (pushes down), and viscosity (pushes into the sides) of the water can be used to improve range of motion, to experience semi-independent ambulation, or to teach how to survive in water temporarily. And aside from the assistance of inherent water properties, instructor physical assistance is a key to swim skill acquisition by those who are seriously retarded. The Halliwick method from England is a specific example of the graduated use of physical hands-on assistance to teach these children individually or in a group (Grosse & Gildersleeve, 1984). Many other fundamental instructional objectives can be realized in the medium of water, whether or not directly related to traditional aquatics instruction.

For additional information relating to aquatics, consult the following references:

YMCA of the USA. (1987). *Aquatics for special populations*. Champaign, IL: Human Kinetics.

American National Red Cross. (1977). *Adapted aquatics*. Garden City, NY: Doubleday.

FIGURE 5.10 A modified "steamboat" using a flotation device and instructor assistance.

Dance

Many pupils who are mentally retarded particularly enjoy music, dance, and rhythmic activities. These activities, therefore, can be used very effectively as media through which to accomplish all kinds of physical education objectives. Higher functioning pupils can be quite successful with all types of dances, including the most current fad dances. Pupils who are moderately retarded can be successful in simplified ballroom, folk, singing, modern, square, and tap dances, particularly those performed alone or in very small groups. Pupils who are severely and profoundly retarded can enjoy music, even if they are nonambulatory. The whole body or selected body parts can be used in dance-related movement sequences. The pupil who is severely/profoundly retarded should be permitted to watch others in dance activities and encouraged to keep time to the music in whatever way is possible and appropriate. Remember, they also have a developmental need to move.

The following factors are important to successful dance experiences. The more pronounced the level of retardation, the more attention needs to be paid to these factors.

1. Music beats and lyrics should be clearly audible.
2. Even rhythms and beats should be used, especially at the outset of a new learning experience.
3. Initially use slow tempos; gradually increase the music speed.
4. Substitute swaying, swinging, walking, or sliding movement for complex dance steps, particularly at the beginning of the activity. Perhaps this adaptation will need to be permanent, but it will probably not decrease the level of enjoyment experienced by the participants.
5. Teach new dances using a part-to-whole method. Portions of a dance gradually build on each other to the level of the participants' ability. Again, if a complete dance is not taught, the dancers will still probably be engaging in a satisfying experience.
6. Timing, force, body level, and use of space can be analyzed.
7. With the pupil functioning at a lower level, it is often effective to give each dancer a piece of engaging equipment or material. Examples include a scarf, drum, towel, bell, and tamborine.
8. The lower the level of cognitive functioning, the smaller the number of participants in a dance group.

The following action songs, singing games, folk dances, and square dances represent just a sampling of recommended dance-related activities matched to increasing mental age (MA) (Moran & Kalakian, 1977):

- I'm a Little Teapot (MA 3–4)
- One Finger, One Thumb (MA 3–4)
- Heads, Shoulders, Knees, and Toes (MA 3–4)
- Oats, Peas, Beans, and Barley Grow (MA 4–6)
- The Thread Follows the Needle (MA 4–6)
- Farmer in the Dell (MA 4–6)
- Twinkle, Twinkle, Little Star (MA 4–6)
- Pop Goes the Weasel (MA 7–8)
- Virginia Reel (MA 7–8)
- Oh, Susanna (MA 7–8)
- Troika (MA 8–9)

Aerobic dance has become especially popular and it has direct implications for use with pupils who are mentally retarded. Barton (1982) provides an example of a successful aerobic dance program that consists of warm-ups, sit-ups, a systematic workout, and a cool-down with pupils labeled mildly retarded. Her program was offered three times per week, 45 minutes per session, over an eight-week period. Importantly, it permitted the pupils to work at their own intensity level, and the pupils were trained to monitor their own heart rates. Other elements included pupils working in pairs and various forms of positive reinforcement, including verbal encouragement, pats on the back, handshakes, and tokens to be traded on a delayed basis. Barton's program significantly increased both the pupils' physical fitness and their self-concept.

Creative dance has applicability for pupils who are mentally retarded at all levels (Boswell, 1989). Strengths of this dance type are attributed to such factors as its occurrence in a relaxed environment and it not requiring technical skills. Therefore, success is more easily realized. "Vocabulary development, long- and short-term memory, concentration, attention span, and choice making are only a few of the intellectual skills which can be developed through creative dance" (Riordan, 1980, p. 15). Creative dance allows verbal expression through body movements and, therefore, can be a great approach to teaching a child with poor language skills, the case with many pupils who are mentally retarded. The enjoyment of movement is important in itself, even if no specific instructional objectives exist.

During creative dance instruction, a variety of sensory stimulation and movement stimulation techniques should be used. For visual stimulation, employ different colors, sizes, and shapes; for auditory stimulation, bells, sirens, noisemakers, musical instruments, and records/tapes. Perform movements that have different directions, sizes, shapes, spaces, levels, tempos, and weights that collectively impact all the senses and enhance the goal of active movement. For example, in a creative dance lesson that

focuses on the concept of weight, a scarf could be given to a pupil so that lightness can be felt and a padded brick could be given so that heaviness can be experienced. The pupil can then try to dance as "light" as a scarf or as "heavy" as a brick. Light movements can be felt as the body moves like a scarf, and vice versa. The loud sound of the body can be heard as the body lands hard on the floor as a brick would. Partners can then be added in order to experience lightness and heaviness together. After all movements have been experienced, the pupils could be asked how they felt about selected movements. Music via records, tape, or the use of actual instruments could be used. Adaptations for pupils who are more seriously retarded could include passive physical manipulation, the use of ankle weights for "heavy," and their removal for them to experience "light."

Individual and Group Activities

Involvement in individual and group games requires prerequisite skills that include minimal motor skills and patterns and physical and motor fitness skills. In addition, successful participation in traditional individual and group sports is based on previous success in related adapted and lead-up activities, including drills, relays, and graded group games (see Figure 5.11).

The whole gamut of traditional individual, dual, and group sports can be realistically considered in programming for more advanced pupils who are mentally retarded. Pupils who are moderately retarded can be successful in traditional sports, but tend to have more success in activities requiring fewer participants. This relates to a large extent to developmental stages of play and chronological age. For example, an 8- to 9-year-old pupil who is moderately retarded may be at the same developmental stage of play as a nondisabled preschooler. Team

FIGURE 5.11 Pupil with Down syndrome foul shooting.

games, therefore, would not be indicated for this pupil.

For pupils who are mildly retarded or moderately retarded, those activities with applicability after formal school years should be high priority. Many of these pupils will have considerably more leisure time as adults than nondisabled individuals. Bicycling and bowling are examples of enjoyable skills that can be carried over into adulthood.

Most pupils who are severely/profoundly retarded should be engaged primarily in fundamental activities that enhance motor skills and patterns. At times, some games at a developmentally low level can be appropriately modified for their use and enjoyment.

Here are some specific activities and methods for use with pupils who are mentally retarded:

1. Class members should be observed in a free play situation in order to determine group interactions. Future instructional content could then be geared to developmental needs and interactional level.

2. Simple rules and only those rules that are essential should apply for all individual group activities. The most simplified game for the pupil who is at a very low level might have only one rule or cue.

3. Initially stress simplified games such as Red Light, Red Rover, Midnight, Keep Away, and Hide and Seek. For the pupil who is severely/profoundly retarded, tetherball (which traditionally involves hitting a ball tied to the end of a rope attached at the top of a vertical pole) might be modified by using a softer, lighter, and more colorful ball on a string within confined quarters. For the pupil who is nonambulatory this could be between two beds, wheelchairs, or chairs. This might be called "bat ball."

4. Story plays and mimetic activities should be simplified and short.

5. When simplifying games, fade simplifications where possible over time in order to approach real game conditions as soon as feasible.

6. The progression used by an instructor should generally be from individual to dual to group activities; from games of low organization to games of high organization; and, if in a group, from cooperative to competitive. Activities commonly used successfully with these pupils are individual and include, among others, stunts, tumbling, and performing on elementary gymnastics apparatus.

7. Environmental stimuli must be arranged wisely. The judicious use of circles, lines, whistles, colors, and so on can greatly aid successful individual and group games for pupils who are retarded.

8. Allow participants enough time to become thoroughly familiar with all equipment. Increased time requirements for this preliminary activity will be a direct function of the level of retardation.

9. Participants should be identified clearly ("shirts and skins," different colors, use pennies).

10. Participants should engage in trial runs before the actual activity commences. Pupils should not only see a demonstration; they might be much more successful if initially allowed to walk or run through the activity.

11. Some pupils who are mildly retarded can be given responsibility, but decisions and leadership imposed on such a pupil should be tempered with good judgment on the part of the teacher.

In concluding this chapter, we wish to mention one program of physical activity that addresses all levels of retardation. This is the Let's Play to Grow Program, which was field-tested, revised, and expanded by the Joseph P. Kennedy, Jr., Foundation (1977) over a number of years. This program is geared not only for the school but also for the home and parental participation. Let's Play to Grow (family) clubs have been formed around the world. In Let's Play to Grow, physical activities stress development in all five dimensions of physical education as defined in the Rules of P.L. 101–476—the same five dimensions stressed in this text. The program can be obtained at minimal cost from the foundation.

An expanded curriculum of numerous "recipes" for fun (Rappaport, 1986) has been adapted for use by families (and teachers) with the Let's Play to Grow Program. This resource's recipes are for use by children aged 0–8 who are mentally retarded and disabled in other ways. Stress is on exploring the world of the senses; movement; outdoors, waterplay, and make-believe; arts and crafts; music and rhythms; and group activities. According to Rappaport: "Everyone should be a winner in Let's Play to Grow. The emphasis is not on winning, but rather on the physical activity and social interaction.

The most important rule is to have FUN" (p. 93). A few excerpts from the *Recipes for Fun's* section on exploring the world of movement are given as examples for use at school or in the home.

Mountain Climbing, Rolling
(Rappaport, 1986, p. 33)

To increase body awareness by rolling and crawling up and down an incline.

- Mattress
- Target objects such as plastic bowling pins, plastic milk cartons, or empty shoe boxes.

1. Slant a mattress off the side of a bed, forming a ramp. Begin "mountain climbing" by crawling up the slope. Encourage your child to follow closely behind. (You may need to buffer the space below the mattress with a bolster.) Talk to your child about climbing the mountain. When he reaches the top, help him roll back down, huffing and puffing as you go, saying "Down the mountain we go." Repeat several times.

2. Body Bowl. Place target objects at the bottom of the mattress. Make a game by rolling down the ramp and knocking over targets with your body. Your child will soon join in the fun. You can demonstrate how much fun this can be. Allow your child to freely explore various ways he can move up and down the incline.

The Creeping/Crawling Trail
(Rappaport, 1986, p. 35)

To help your child develop the ability to vary motor patterns and encourage motor planning; to understand how objects are related to oneself and others in space.

- Yarn, rope (40 or 60 feet long) or masking tape
- Mats, open floor space or grassy area

Using colored yarn or plain rope, outline a winding trail on the floor or a grassy area.

Have your child crawl along the trail on his hands and knees. You might want to demonstrate the game first. Crawl next to your child and demonstrate the various ways to creep and crawl—follow the trail using a "commando style" crawl (lying on the tummy and using arms in an arm-over-arm pulling motion); or follow the trail by knee walking—everyone is in a kneeling position with upper body upright while walking on knees. Arrange the trail so that you can creep beside a reluctant child if necessary. Arrange the trail around, under, over, and between objects. Talk to your child about his movements around, under, or over objects.

Adaptation for Physical Impairment: Use a scooter board for the child who is unable to crawl and encourage him to use his arms and/or legs to propel himself. A brother or sister can pull him through the trail on a wagon or scooter board if he cannot push himself.

This chapter ends with an interview with a colleague, Dwan Bridges, that centers on the whole question of physical activity program relevance for individuals who are mentally retarded.

DWAN BRIDGES

Dr. Dwan Bridges is an assistant professor of special physical education at California State University, Los Angeles.

1. *What are your views on the importance of physical education for the pupil who is mentally retarded?*

In my opinion, physical education may be the most important curriculum area for the pupil who is mentally retarded. I believe this since most individuals who are mentally retarded reach their highest level of achievement in the psychomotor domain. Such achievement has implications for employment, social integration, and independence generally. The values which are associated with psychomotor domain training do not need to be justified for it is commonly known that without competence in this domain of development, it is most difficult for this type of individual to acquire and maintain independent living skills such as mobility, body management, fitness, and even self-help skills which require gross motor control. The ability of anyone to initiate and maintain such skill then precludes dependence on others, as it should.

The least restrictive environment principle is also applicable to every phase of this pupil's life. In this connection, I believe that physical education can be and should be a critical curriculum area through which the least restrictive environment principle can be realized and maximized in schools. As a pupil develops psychomotor skills, the least restrictive environment should change and ability levels should continue to expand. The ultimate goal of physical education is to mainstream this pupil who is mentally retarded into classes with nondisabled peers, when appropriate. Mainstreaming then becomes one of the first steps towards normalization for life.

Last but not least, physical education must be taught as defined by law. Public Law 94–142, The Education for All Handicapped Children Act, identifies physical education as a direct service related to the educational instruction of pupils with disabilities in all schools. Further, according to P.L. 94–142, the components of each physical education program shall include physical and motor fitness, fundamental motor skills, aquatics, dance, and games and sports. In my view, we have fallen far short in providing appropriate direct physical education services to all pupils with identified disabilities, including those who are mentally retarded. We must address this overall issue. It drives at the heart of the exact question which you asked above.

2. *Should the role of the special physical educator change as this type of youngster approaches graduation? If so, how?*

Yes, as the pupil with mental retardation approaches graduation, the special physical educator's role should change in regards to effective programming. Such programming should have two basic components, which include training which is age appropriate and skill training which is functional. Age-appropriate programming examines levels of physical skill in relationship to a person's chronological age. This area requires a thorough assessment of the present level of functioning. Based upon these data, the second component, functional skills programming, comes into focus. The focal point of this type of programming centers on attaining skills which are of value for everyday living. As one example, a programming idea may involve jumping over puddles of water to avoid wet feet as opposed to vertical jumping 10 times which has negligible functional value as a daily living skill. Another central theme of a functional skills program is to capitalize and expand upon the skills which are already present in the pupil's repertoire. There is no need to completely "reinvent the wheel" if present skills are functional, even in part.

Related to all of this, lifetime leisure skill training is a vital component of the physical education curriculum as the youngster with mental retardation approaches graduation. One of the goals of physical education should be to provide this pupil with skills that can be used throughout life. This youngster should be aware, for example, of his or her role as a spectator and participant in leisure lifetime physical activities. In addition, successful participation in lifetime leisure skills can enhance other areas of life which are important to the overall growth of any individual. These other areas include, but are not limited to, problem solving, peer interaction, maintenance of skills, and generalization of trained skills into additional community-related activities. In short, the special physical educator must be aware that the age-appropriate and functional teaching of leisure lifetime skills to this type of youngster just prior to graduation is one of the most important phases of his or her educational program because of the lifetime implications of such programming.

Learning Disabilities

DEFINITION, CAUSES, AND SCOPE

Definition

The federal government defines specific learning disabilities in the Rules and Regulations of P.L. 101–476 as:

A disorder in one or more of the basic psychological processes involved in understanding or in using language, spoken or written, that may manifest itself in an imperfect ability to listen, think, speak, read, write, spell, or to do mathematical calculations. The term includes such conditions as perceptual disabilities, brain injury, minimal brain dysfunction, dyslexia, and developmental aphasia. The term does not apply to children who have learning problems that are primarily the result of visual, hearing, or motor disabilities, of mental retardation, of emotional disturbance, or of environmental, cultural, or economic disadvantage.

According to this definition, learning disabilities is a disorder related to language and academic areas that cannot be attributed to other defined disabling conditions, such as mental retardation or sensory impairments. In other words, learning disabilities is an umbrella term that encompasses all disabilities not included among traditional categories. Beyond this, there is a specific reference to a significant discrepancy between a pupil's actual and potential achievement. It implies that special educational methods must be used in order for the pupil to progress. Not all professionals and parents of children who are learning disabled are satisfied with the government's current definition of learning disabilities, which is the culmina-

145

tion of numerous other efforts to define the condition, beginning with the early work of Strauss and Lehtinen in 1947. For example, some authorities feel that other characteristics should be included in a formal definition and that the expression "significant discrepancy" needs an operational definition. Others want to exclude terms from the definition. For instance, the National Joint Committee for Learning Disabilities in 1981 recommended the removal of "basic psychological process" in order to recognize the existence of the medical disorder aspects of this condition. As a result, the search for a more acceptable definition goes on, and the federal Office of Special Education Programs has been charged with the task of formulating a final definition.

Confusion over the definition appears to center around the fact that a learning disability is a hidden disability. A child who is learning disabled has normal or above-normal intelligence, is not blind or deaf, and appears in no other way to be different to the casual or even intense observer. The child (and adult) who is learning disabled looks perfectly normal: "He may have a robust body, good eyes, sound ears, and a normal intelligence. He has a disability of function, however, which is just as real as a crippled leg" (Anderson, 1970, p. 1). For reasons that are complicated and difficult to pinpoint, these children have one or more significant problems in learning.

An additional problem in defining learning disabilities is that there is no consensus among professionals on the standard use of the term. In fact, so many terms are used that confusion rather than clarity is the typical result—minimally brain damaged, educationally disabled, attention deficit disordered, neurologically impaired, hyperkinetic, perceptually disabled, dyslexic, and developmental aphasia are all in use. One author has suggested, clearly in jest, that the do-it-yourself terminology generator shown in

TABLE 6.1 TERMINOLOGY GENERATOR

QUALIFIER	AREA OF INVOLVEMENT	PROBLEM
Minimal	Brain	Dysfunction
Mild	Cerebral	Damage
Minor	Neurological	Disorder
Chronic	Neuroligic	Dissynchronization
Diffuse	CNS (central nervous system)	Handicap
Specific	Language	Disability
Primary	Reading	Retardation
Disorganized	Perceptual	Impairment
Organic	Impulse	Pathology
Clumsy	Behavior	Syndrome

Source: E. Fry, "Do It Yourself Terminology Generator," *Journal of Reading*, 11 (1968), 428. Copyright © 1968 the International Reading Association. Used with permission of Edward Fry and the International Reading Association.

Table 6.1 could be used in reference to learning disabilities by any professional or parent (Fry, 1968, p. 428). He encourages you to mix and match one word from each of three columns to arrive at an acceptable term. This system will yield more than 1,000 combinations. The most commonly accepted term, however, is learning disabilities, which reflects the federal government's preference.

A number of special educators view learning disabilities as encompassing numerous other critical characteristics beyond the federal government's restrictive definition related exclusively to disorders of language, reading, writing, and arithmetic. Nonacademic, related disabilities can contribute to specific significant academic deficiencies. The 10 most frequently cited characteristics of the child with learning disabilities are:

- *Hyperactivity*: excessive motion at the wrong time
- *Perceptual-motor impairments*: difficulties with discriminating among and identifying sounds, shapes, symbols, and various sensations

- *Emotional lability*: illogical shifts in affect and social immaturity
- *General coordination deficits*: clumsy and awkward
- *Disorders of attention*: easily distracted by people or objects; opposite problems related to shifting attention (perseveration)
- *Impulsivity*: instant reactions without thought of consequences
- *Disorders of memory and thinking*: difficulty in conceptualizing and deficits in short-term or long-term memory (usually related to visual or auditory events)
- *Specific academic learning disabilities*: deficiencies in one or more academic areas
- *Disorders of language*: word-flow deficits in a broad language/speech context
- *Equivocal neurological signs*: "hard" or "soft" signs of neurological dysfunction, including brain damage

As with emotional disorders (see Chapter 7), all pupils show some characteristics and behaviors that contribute to learning problems at some time during their school experience. Only when a child shows consistent and significant discrepancy between actual and potential academic ability, not attribut-able to any other recognized disability, can a learning disability be validly suspected.

Causes

Rarely can the specific cause of a learning disability be pinpointed. When the condition was first described, brain damage was thought to be the cause. A commonly accepted notion today is that learning disabilities are neurologically derived, that there is a neurological breakdown somewhere within the central nervous system's processing mechanism (see Figure 6.1). Sensory information is taken into the body through the visual, auditory, and/or other sensory avenue, but the information is processed inappropriately. Some examples follow:

- *Dyslexia*: an inability to comprehend what is read. There are distinct types of dyslexia. One type is dysphonetic dyslexia, which involves interpreting and integrating written symbols with their corresponding sound. It should be noted that many educators and psychologists prefer the term *developmental reading disorders* instead of dyslexia unless describing a reading disability presumed to be of neurological origin.

FIGURE 6.1 Sensory information processing, if functioning efficiently, leads to normal learning; if this is not working correctly at any level, learning disabilities may arise.

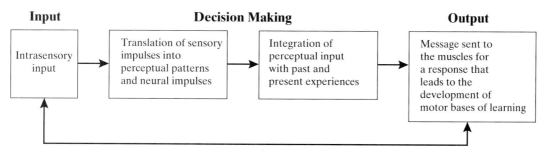

Continuous Feedback to Input

- *Sensory aphasia*: an inability to comprehend the spoken or written word.
- *Tactile agnosia*: a difficulty in tactile recognition of objects, specifically the analysis and synthesis of tactile and kinesthetic stimuli.

Somewhere within the central nervous system, interference of some sort affects the ability to learn and perform maximally. Exactly where this interference takes place is difficult or impossible to determine, and only "soft" neurological signs might be evident. At other times, "hard" signs are conclusively found by using techniques such as the EEG (electroencephalogram). In these cases evidence of actual brain damage can be confirmed, clarifying the origin of the learning disability.

There has been movement away from relating learning disabilities to a neurological dysfunction and toward other specific possible causes (Feingold, 1974, 1976; Kavale, Forness, & Bender, 1987; Mercer, 1987):

1. Chemical neurotransmitters break down at one or more of a neuron's synaptic gaps, which prevents a smooth flow of sensory messages.
2. Low blood sugar (hypoglycemia) causes learning disabilities.
3. Artificial food additives cause learning problems.
4. A vitamin synthesis deficiency may result in learning disabilities.
5. The process of myelinization occurs prematurely within the nervous system.
6. There is some evidence available that certain cases are genetically determined.

In addition, it has been suggested that environmental deprivation could be at the core of these children's learning problems. Both limited environmental stimulation and malnutrition stem primarily from parental behaviors. Teacher neglect is reflected in poor teaching strategies. Perhaps a child needs to be taught by nontraditional teaching methods and teachers fail to perceive this need. The negative effects of a child's environment can adversely influence his or her emotional development and motivation to learn.

Whether the cause is neurological, biochemical, genetic, or environmental, the physical educator's challenge is the same: The teacher must recognize that, even if other factors may adversely affect children with learning disabilities, part of such pupils' problems could be due to lack of relevant teacher training and the inability of school personnel to recognize that instructors need to adapt to pupils' unique characteristics.

Scope

Estimates of the scope of learning disabilities differ, owing to various definitions, diagnostic techniques, and categorical terminology. When P.L. 94-142 became law in 1975, the U.S. Office of Education estimated 2 percent as the approximate extent of learning disabilities in schools throughout the country, and today that figure is approximately 49 percent of all pupils with disabilities (U.S. Department of Education, 1992). Other estimates range from 4 to 50 percent of school-aged children, with considerably more boys affected than girls.

Given the scope of learning disabilities and the reasonable chance that a teacher (including those who teach physical education) might have one or more pupils with significant learning problems in class, sources of professional assistance are necessary and do exist. A few of the major sources are the following:

- National Association for Children with Learning Disabilities (Pittsburgh, Pennsylvania). This is the largest learning disabilities organization in the country. Founded in 1963, it includes both parents and educators.

- Division for Children with Learning Disabilities, Council for Exceptional Children (CEC), Reston, VA. This is the largest division within CEC. Founded in 1968, it is made up primarily of professionals.

CHARACTERISTICS AND INSTRUCTIONAL STRATEGIES

Pupils who are learning disabled need more than the essentials of a basic physical educa-tion program. Because physical education is one of the best settings in which the characteristics of pupils who are learning disabled can be observed and addressed, physical educators not only have the opportunity but also the obligation to serve as important members of the educational team for these pupils. The interview with April Tripp, currently a special physical education consultant in Maryland, addresses the placement in physical education of pupils with learning disabilities, as well as instructional issues.

April Tripp

Dr. April Tripp has served as professor, direct care provider, and consultant in special physical education. She has a keen interest in the field of learning disabilities.

1. *In which type of physical education environment are most pupils with learning disabilities placed?*

Most pupils who have learning disabilities are integrated into regular physical education classes without any support personnel providing assistance to the teacher and/or pupil. Most of these pupils are placed in this environment without assess-ment of their physical and motor abilities. In this regard, some are unfit and/or motorically awkward and need additional assistance for regular physical education to be an appropriate placement. One reason for this dilemma is that, often times, regular physical educators are not aware of the types of support services available and, as an unfortunate result, physical education becomes a negative experience for these teachers and pupils. Therefore, while pupils with learning disabilities are most commonly placed in regular physical education classes, it must be remembered that this may not be the most appropriate placement unless the proper support services are provided.

2. *What do you consider to be an appropriate ratio between pupils who are learning disabled and those who are nondisabled in a regular physical education setting?*

In order to obtain a truly integrated physical education class, the ratio of pupils who are nondisabled to those with learning disabilities should be approximately 8 to 1. This 12 percent figure matches the government's estimate of the percentage of pupils with disabilities being served in our schools. Beyond this statistical ceiling, a higher proportionate number of pupils with learning disabilities placed in a regular physical education setting appears to promote separate social groups that may inhibit effective integration. Further, the total number of pupils in such a physical education class must be within a range (less than 30) that makes individualized teaching possible for all pupils, including those with learning disabilities.

3. *What models could be used by regular physical educators to assist them in including pupils with learning disabilities into their classes?*

There are three such teaching models that I would recommend to regular physical educators that would assist them to effectively teach an integrated physical education program:

Hellison, D. R. (1985). *Goals and strategies for teaching physical education.* Champaign, IL:

Human Kinetics. Hellison's developmental self-responsibility model places pupils' self-concept, self-actualization, and interpersonal relation at the center of the physical education teaching process. Pupils participate at appropriate developmental levels and reflect on feelings, goals, and behaviors through the use of written journals. Physical educators who have used the self-responsibility model have demonstrated affective, behavioral, and knowledge changes in pupils.

Morris, G. S., & Stiehl, J. (1989). *Changing kid's games.* Champaign, IL: Human Kinetics. The emphasis of Morris and Stiehl's Purposes Implementation Evaluation Model is on games that assist pupils in achieving maximum cognitive, social, emotional, and physical potential. This model has been used extensively in elementary public school programs and has also demonstrated considerable promise when used with pupils who have learning disabilities.

Mosston, M. (1981). *Teaching physical education,* 2nd ed. Columbus, OH: Merrill. Mosston presents seven alternative teaching styles that can enhance the learning environment for all pupils in physical education. Using these alternatives, successful physical educators can vary their teaching style on the spot to match the needs of their pupils.

A lot of pupils with learning disabilities have difficulty learning in traditional ways. Therefore, teachers who have a repertoire of proven styles to teach from may be more effective in teaching new skills to pupils with learning disabilities. Further, all regular physical educators must under-stand behavior management techniques that allow pupils to enhance their ability to more effectively understand both themselves and how their environment impacts on their behavior.

4. *What competencies should be developed when preparing regular physical educators to teach pupils who have learning disabilities in their classes? How should these competencies be developed?*

Some of the competencies that must be developed by regular physical educators teaching pupils who are learning disabled are (a) an understanding of how attitudes toward individuals with learning disabilities are formed and changed; (b) knowledge of the laws that mandate an education for pupils with a learning disability and which specifically spell out equal opportunity provisions and access to public physical education, intramurals, and competitive sports;

and (c) ability to obtain assistance and support services that will contribute to safe, successful and satisfying physical education experiences for pupils with learning disabilities.

These competencies cannot be developed solely through lectures. There must be hands-on experiences provided with pupils who have learning disabilities in both segregated and integrated model program settings.

Instructional intervention with pupils who are learning disabled is often based on a theoretical orientation, and numerous approaches to remediate learning disabilities are employed. These include perceptual-motor, medical (drugs, neurological), psychoeducational, language (linguistics), and ecological (environmental) approaches.

The perceptual-motor and neurological approaches to remediation of learning disabilities have gained considerable attention in the field of physical education since the 1960s. These approaches are based on a presumed organic cause originating somewhere within the central nervous system (CNS). Programmed movements purportedly affect the CNS in a positive way, and therefore the movements somehow "help" or may "help" learning. Physical educators can draw from the work of these theorists, many of whom, ironically, have limited or no background in formal physical education training. Table 6.2 summarizes the key theories describing learning disabilities. Refer to the original writings of these theorists for a complete account of the approaches.

As with other disabling conditions, we prefer to take an eclectic approach to learning disabilities and match relevant characteristics

to recommended instructional strategies. Again, our recommendations are based on our experience and literature review. This information should help physical educators begin to understand the complexity of learning disabilities, the problems of the pupil with a learning disability, and how movement may be used to assist such a pupil.

Many of the characteristics of learning disabilities have recently been grouped under the terms *attention deficit disorder (ADD)* and *attention deficit hyperactivity disorder (ADHD)*. Earlier terms used were hyperkinesis, minimal brain damage, and even learning disabled. The reason for the change in terminology was due to research findings that revealed there were children who exhibited the same characteristics as children with hyperactivity but who were not overly active (Kirby & Grimley, 1986). These children have problems concentrating, have short attention spans, and perform poorly in their schoolwork, but they do not "bounce off the wall" (Hunsucker, 1988, p. 7). Thus there are two major categories: with hyperactivity (ADHD) and without hyperactivity (ADD). Approximately 3 to 10 percent of the school-aged population have ADD, considered to be neurological problems in the brain.

TABLE 6.2   LEARNING DISABILITY THEORIES

THEORETICAL BASIS FOR LEARNING	NAME	KEY REFERENCE(S)	POSITION
Perceptual-motor basis	Newell Kephart	*The Slow Learner in the Classroom* (1971) *The Purdue Perceptual Motor Survey* (Roach & Kephart, 1966)	Movement is the basis of the intellect. Motor bases and generalizations (balance and posture, body image, laterality, directionality, locomotion, contact, receipt, and propulsion) affect efficient higher thought proccesses.
	Raymond Barsch	*Achieving Perceptual Motor Efficiency* (1968)	Learning problems are remediated by learning to move efficiently in order to survive in space and its stress-producing energy surround. Barsch originated the Movigenics Curriculum.
Neurological basis	Glen Doman & Carl Delacato	*The Diagnosis and Treatment of Speech and Reading Problems* (Delacato, 1964)	Development of an individual follows the development of a species or race. Thus the "theory of neurological organization" suggests that treatment for LD (and other problems) consists of patterning the nervous system starting at the lowest level at which evidence of a developmental lag exists.
Sensory integration basis	Jean Ayres	*Sensory Integration and Learning Disorders* (1972) *Southern California Perceptual-Motor Tests* (1969)	All senses must be integrated for complete development. Tactile and vestibular forms of stimulation are most basic. Defects in the brain stem may be the key to LD etiology.
Visual basis	Gerald Getman	*The Physiology of Readiness* (Getman & Kane, 1964)	80% of learning is visual. Physiologic readiness is visual; perceptual readiness means academic success.
	Marianne Frostig	*Movement Education: Theory and Practice* (1970) *Development Test of Visual Perception* (Frostig, Lefever, & Whittlesey, 1966)	Learning is mostly affected by the ability to perceive visually.
Movement may be one basis	Bryant Cratty	*Perceptual and Motor Development in Infants and Young Children* (1979) (Numerous other books)	Movement activities may enhance the intellect; they are not necessarily the foundation of intelligence. Natural and synthetic bonds within and between domains enhance overall development.

CHARACTERISTICS	INSTRUCTIONAL STRATEGIES
Psychomotor	
1. Pupils who are learning disabled often have attentional deficit behavioral disorders which include pupils with hyperactivity or hypoactivity.	1. Offer activities that channel extremes. For the child who is hyperactive, this might involve slow activities (including relaxation) or activities with a "tight" structure (Brandon, Eason, & Smith, 1986). Relax pupils who are hyperactive with a rest period before sending them back to their classroom. Jogging (Allen, 1980) and swimming (Cole, 1978) are also reported to reduce hyperactivity. Fast-tempo activities might be best for the pupil who is hypoactive.
2. Clumsiness is often exhibited (Arnheim & Sinclair, 1979).	2. Determine whether clumsiness is the result of auditory, visual, and/or other sensory misperceptions. After this determination (perhaps with the assistance of others), focus instruction on best learning mode for each pupil. In addition to offering a basic physical education program, focus attention on the correction of perceptual dysfunction through supplementary perceptual-motor training sessions. Early intervention programs of gross movement and sensory stimulation are strongly recommended for young pupils who are noticeable clumsy for their chronological age.
3. Body awareness and kinesthetic sense perceptions are sometimes faulty.	3. Train body part identification on self and others, give vestibular stimulation activities (balancing and positioning), and train laterality (internal awareness of sides) and directionality (orientation to all directions in space). Teach internal followed by external awareness. Offer both earthbound and off-ground activities. Pupils should be barefooted for tactile stimulation in activities not requiring sneakers or another type of shoe.
4. Pupils often are unable to maintain a rhythmic motor pattern.	4. Practice activities using a metronome or music with a strong beat.
5. Problems crossing midline are sometimes noticeable.	5. Practice activities requiring the pupils to cross their midline. One example is the "windmill" exercise, which involves crossing the midline with an arm and touching the toes on the opposite foot.
6. Pupils may generate too much force in skills requiring control (e.g., hopscotch).	6. Practice activities by performing them slowly or by a teacher's sequenced and spaced verbal commands.
7. Pupils may demonstrate inconsistent performance.	7. Have pupils repeat the instructions for a motor act before actually performing the skill. A behavior management system could also be initiated in an attempt to increase the pupil's attention related to performing skills.
8. Level of health-related physical fitness may be low. Mestre (1986) reported that these pupils were lower than their normal peers in the following areas: subscapular skinfold, sit-ups, 50-yard dash, softball throw, and 1.5-mile run for distance and for time.	8. Develop a long-term physical fitness program that involves numerous reinforcers that can be earned.
9. Pupils may have visual discrimination difficulties.	9. Give many opportunities to experience the size, shape, color, and textural characteristics of objects,

10. They may have other visual perception problems related to discriminating a figure from its background (see Figure 6.2), recognizing objects from different distances and angles, and ocular tracking.

10. Program for obvious to more subtle visual perceptual skills with respect to figure-ground, depth perception, and object constancy (view from different angles) problems. Practice must be given in watching still and moving objects. Advice from an optometrist or ophthalmologist will be useful. Keep the activity area clear of distractions.

11. Pupils may have auditory perception difficulties reflected in problems of discriminating the pitch, rhythm, loudness, and direction of sounds.

11. Program systematically for obvious to more subtle auditory perception skills in a movement context with respect to differentiating the attributes of sounds. Sounds such as music must be clearly audible.

12. They may have abnormal reflexes that could interfere with their motor performance.

12. If a pupil is suspected of having abnormal reflexes that may be causing poor motor performace, work closely with an allied medicine therapist (PT, OT) for an in-depth evaluation and seek reflex inhibition suggestions.

FIGURE 6.2   Can you decipher this figure/ground illusion?

Cognitive

1. There may be problems in right-left discrimination.

2. Children with learning disabilities often learn best through modes other than the visual.

3. Language concepts are often difficult for the individual with learning disabilities to comprehend.

4. Many pupils with learning disabilities have expressive or receptive language deficits.

5. They may concentrate on only selected parts or a part of a task rather than the task as a whole (dissociation).

6. These pupils' short- or long-term memory is sometimes faulty.

7. Pupils may be unable to plan a complex sequence of activities.

Affective

1. Pupils may think of themselves as failures because of a long history of being unsuccessful.

2. Pupils may perseverate during instruction. This is associated with an inability to switch activity focus comfortably.

3. They may be easily distracted (opposite of perseveration) due to perceptual problems.

4. Learning problems may lead to social immaturity and rejection (Geuze & Borger, 1993).

5. A learning disability can be very frustrating to a child.

---

1. Incorporate activities into program that involve knowing right and left such as Mother May I. Also, cues could be provided to the pupils to initially help in learning right and left discrimination, for example, wearing an armband on the left hand or putting a water tattoo on the right hand.

2. Determine (perhaps from another professional) which learning mode is best for each pupil. Then teach new material through this dominant mode. In addition, offer activities and stress techniques that will aid in the remediation of a deficient learning mode.

3. Offer verbal directions in a fun, movement context, moving from simple to complex. The use of a few words that are easily understood should be eventually followed by instruction that incorporates multiple words and more advanced terminology. Address language difficulties in the physical education context with the educational team.

4. Problems in receiving communication (written or spoken) and expressing oneself can be addressed in physical education. Language reportedly is based on experiences that initially are concrete.

5. Introduce a whole skill first through demonstration and practice. Then analyze and teach parts of the whole activity and eventually put the parts together.

6. Train for memory in any movement-oriented activity. Short-term memory skill should be stressed before long-term memory. Memory sequences should be from very short to lengthy.

7. Separate complex activity into smaller components; gradually add additional components.

1. Avoid solo nonchoice activities in which failure is more likely and highly competitive group activities.

2. Use activities that emphasize nonrepetition and change; avoid those that stress repetition in movement. Do not assume that a child is intentionally misbehaving. Use clear pretested signals for transition.

3. Structure the environment: space reduction, equipment selection, equipment placement, pupil location, number of pupils in class, controlled eye contact, elimination of interferences from outside the activity area (e.g., lights, noise), lesson plan activities, limited pupil opportunity for choice, and lines on the activity surface all can be varied. Choose activities such as ladder climbing that filter and screen attention.

4. When prerequisite skills permit, offer dual and group physical activities. Ability can be highlighted and attended to by others in this context.

5. Determine whether a pupil's reactions to frustration are due to inability or unwillingness to perform. Switch activities before the frustration tolerance level

6. Sometimes these pupils prefer to play with younger children whom they can dominate.

7. Pupils with learning disabilities may be impulsive.

is reached; however, go back to the activity so that the pupil cannot intentionally avoid it.

6. Provide numerous opportunities to play with pupils their own age. Reinforce this behavior when it occurs.

7. Have these pupils repeat the instructions back to the teacher before they can start the activity. A signal could be determined and no one could start the activity until the signal is given (e.g., whistle blown). Have these pupils take the time to understand consequences as they relate to their behavior.

General

1. Learners with learning disabilities are different from each other. Multiple characteristics make up this group of learners with disabilities.

1. Observe the numerous behaviors exhibited by pupils who are learning disabled. Avoid the notion that these pupils come out of a similar mold. There is no one method to employ in teaching the pupil who is learning disabled. Behavior management and instructional content must be individually designed. With a group, use a multisensory approach to direction giving (e.g., show and tell). In addition, when grouping, try to avoid placing all pupils with similar behavioral characteristics in the same squad or group.

2. Pupils who are learning disabled are often inconsistent.

3. They typically have a history of failure in one or more domains of development.

2. Expect the unexpected from day to day. Tolerance on an instructor's part is a must.

3. Stress having fun, and provide activities in which the pupils can be successful. Success will then build on itself. Fun-oriented activities will not only cause pupils to look forward to the next session but will also motivate them to attempt more difficult tasks.

4. Medication is often prescribed for children with learning disabilities. Drugs can affect one or more behavioral domains.

4. Become familiar with the most common medications and their impact, particularly as they affect movement (French & Jansmal, 1981). If necessary, adapt lesson plan activities on the basis of this knowledge.

INDICATED AND NONINDICATED ACTIVITIES

Physical and Motor Fitness

Environmental considerations are often most critical in providing physical and motor fitness activities for pupils with learning disabilities. The activities themselves can be the same as those provided in any well-balanced program of physical education for any child. These would include standard exercises to enhance strength, flexibility, and endurance. For those pupils who are easily distracted

and need a highly structured environment, the following activity modifications might be appropriate. Calisthenics can include standard exercises, but should be conducted every day with pupils in the same spot, in the same room, in the same direction, at the same point in class, and usually led by the same individual. If partner exercises are used, the same duo should work together each day. If a fitness training circuit is used, set up the same stations for several days, in the same sequence, in the same direction, and using the same rotation signal. In any other fitness-oriented approach, similar constants are advised. Intermittent rest periods are particularly important for the child who is hyperactive.

In addition, specific activities can be offered that not only enhance fitness but also address specific concerns about learning disabilities. For example, fitness-oriented movement education activities can be provided to improve body part awareness and kinesthesis. An instructor might use isotonic or isometric training not only to improve strength but to focus on a specific body part, using pushing, pulling, and squeezing actions. Fitness activities can also be systematically provided to improve a child's midline crossing efficiency and awareness of body sides (laterality). Opposite-hand-to-opposite-foot flexibility exercises, sit-ups that require elbow to opposite knee, and trunk rotation exercises force pupils to cross their midlines and attend to both sides. Clear signals are necessary for pupils who have a tendency to perseverate in their movements.

Jump roping is an excellent way to increase the level of cardiorespiratory fitness and also coordination skills. Rhythms can be added to help the pupil coordinate the tempo, a crucial element in rope jumping. The following are some appropriate rhymes to use:

1. Not last night but the night before

   Twenty-four rabbits came knocking at my door

   As I ran out they ran in

   And that's the way my story begins

   Spanish dancer turn around (child turns around)

   Spanish dancer touch the ground (touch the ground)

   Spanish dancer get out of town (get out of rope).

2. Lollipop, lollipop makes me sick

   Now it's time for arithmetic

   One plus one equals two

   Two plus two equals four

   Four plus four equals eight

   Now it's time for spelling

   R-a-t spells rat

   C-a-t spells cat

   M-a-t spells mat.

3. I had a little brother

   His name was Tiny Tim

   I put him in the bathtub

   To teach him how to swim

   He drank up all the water

   Ate up all the soap

   And now my baby brother

   Has a belly ache.

At first, these rhymes are sung by the other pupils, to give the pupil the tempo. Once the skill level is achieved, the jumper can begin to sing the rhyme, too.

Fundamental Motor Skills and Patterns

Of foremost concern for the pupil who is learning disabled is the domino effect of perpetual clumsiness: A child who is always clumsy is apt to fall farther and farther behind in physical education. The habilitation and remediation of deficient fundamental motor skills and patterns involve perceptual-motor training, generally in a gross motor context. The ideas of perceptual-motor theorists (see Table 6.2) have value in this respect, and their suggestions are reflected in the activities and methods discussed here.

One of the most fundamental motor skills is body awareness, including the subcomponents of body image and spatial orientation. Body image involves knowledge of the body itself, without regard to space. Spatial orientation is internal and external awareness of movements, which includes the mature development of laterality (internal awareness of sides) and directionality (external awareness in all directions). Another ability that directly influences specific motor skills and patterns is balance (static and dynamic). Movement skills also require keen sensory perception, particularly in the areas of vision and audition. The following activities address the development of these areas as they relate to the emergence of fundamental motor skills and patterns.

Body Image. Passive to active movements should be used when teaching children about their body parts. In addition, knowledge of one's body parts usually precedes knowledge of body parts of others. At first, pupils can watch, listen, and sense as an instructor speaks, touches, and moves one child's primary body parts. Based on the child's perceptual and learning skills, instruction should then proceed with the child's active involvement. The pupil can touch a body part on command or can use foot- and handprints on the floor. In addition, body parts or the whole body can be traced on paper with the child lying down. Use of a mirror is also very effective for body image orientation. Where feasible, the child can watch videotapes and review them for multiple purposes, including body image orientation.

Spatial Orientation. Awareness of self precedes awareness of others and objects in space. Laterality, therefore, should be emphasized before directionality. For those pupils for whom it is high priority, laterality training should initially stress static or limited movement. One side of the body should be distinguished from the other using, for exam-

ple, color or weights only on one side. Over time, the child will associate differences from side to side. When movement is introduced, devices like rocking boards on which a child is prone/supine lying or sitting can be used. With these devices, children are challenged to exercise their reflex-righting and equilibrium reactions. This enhances body awareness as a whole. Next, a child should be encouraged to stand and move freely in progressively more difficult tasks (varying speed, directions, etc.). At first, equilibrium requirements should be minimal (standing, sliding, walking), followed by more difficult movements that require greater awareness of both sides of the body and space.

Spatial orientation can be developed further with the systematic use of such activities as crawling through a cloth and wire tunnel without touching the sides. This can be made more difficult by placing an obstacle to be avoided at the beginning or end of the tunnel. Another challenging activity requires the pupil to traverse an obstacle course consisting of objects of varying sizes placed at varying distances. An obstacle course of this type could include chairs, tables, apparatus, sticks, hoops, and other common items in the classroom or gymnasium. The design of any obstacle course is wide open to ideas and modifications from the class members or instructor, but should present an array of fundamental movement challenges. Pupils enjoy designing and conquering these obstacle courses. Eventually they can be encouraged to move in a group among each other in the environment, even with additional obstacles, in order to refine body awareness as a whole.

Balance. Even when body awareness is adequate, a pupil may need specific training in balance skills while immobile (static), while moving (dynamic), and perhaps while performing rotating movements (rotary balance). The best piece of equipment, the human body, can and should be trained in all three types of balance. Numerous activities can be suggested for each type of balance; we discuss only a few here.

Auxter (1976) provides a useful static balance progression that manipulates three primary body parts—the eyes, arms, and feet. Their interaction to make balance progressively more difficult is illustrated in Table 6.3. Auxter's progression involves contact with a stable surface, with the heel 2 inches from the ground for at least 5 seconds. An unstable surface such as a rocking board, balance board, mattress, moonwalk, or trampoline can be added to make the task more difficult.

Dynamic and rotary balance can also be stimulated using the moonwalk and trampoline. In addition, spinning boards and balance beams of graduated widths and heights are very useful in training for balance while in motion.

Visual Ability. Short- and long-term visual memory, plus such other visual abilities as tracking, form and color discrimina-

tion, depth and speed perception, and figure–ground and object constancy discrimination, can be enhanced in a physical education setting.

A short then eventually longer list of written directions related to fundamental movement tasks not only engages pupils in basic movements but also increasingly taxes their memory skills. When working on memory skills in movement, the pupil should be allowed only one view of any list of directions. Reinforcement should be offered, even if a child can remember only some of the directions on a given list.

Almost all activities in physical education require one type of visual perception or another. Some activities that are particularly useful in educating a pupil in fundamental movement and, at the same time, emphasize visual perception ability include the following:

1. Throwing balls, beanbags, or other objects at targets of different shapes, backgrounds, sizes, and colors; throwing from varying distances
2. Tracking a ball when catching
3. Jumping rope
4. Jumping on trampoline
5. Kicking stationary or moving balls
6. Manipulating cutout forms, moving through forms, or using the body to make shapes, including letters (see Figure 6.3)
7. Completing a fundamental movement circuit training, obstacle, or confidence course that requires reading by all participants (directions could pertain to some fundamental motor skill or pattern)

Auditory Perception. Teachers can program for auditory abilities in a basic movement context. Short- and long-term auditory memory, as well as distinguishing pitch, rhythm, loudness, and the direction of

TABLE 6.3 STATIC BALANCE BEHAVIOR OBJECTIVES

Eyes	Arms	Foot
Anywhere	Side	Foot
Anywhere	Front	Foot
Up	Side	Foot
Up	Front	Foot
Anywhere	Side	Toe
Anywhere	Front	Toe
Closed	Side	Foot
Up	Side	Toe
Up	Front	Toe
Closed	Front	Foot
Closed	Side	Toe
Closed	Front	Toe

Source: D. Auxter, "Diagnostic Prescriptive Individualized Programming," paper presented at meeting of the American Association of Health, Physical Education and Recreation, Milwaukee, 1976. Used by permission.

FIGURE 6.3 Shape recognition training through gross motor movement.
Reprinted by permission of © J. A. Preston Corporation, 1981.

sounds, can be worked on in physical education class.

Verbal commands or gestures can be systematically combined in increasingly longer series to train auditory memory while also engaging in a series of fundamental movements. Numerous manipulations of sound can effectively train auditory skills while pupils are blindfolded and participating in activities requiring body image, spatial orientation, and balance. Different sounds can also be given concurrently while the pupil must make forced choice decisions. Successful decisions would indicate auditory figure–ground discrimination, distance perception, and differentiation of pitch. At the outset of combined auditory and fundamental movement training, distinctively novel sounds that require only limited auditory sophistication can act as cues to move. These novel sounds can then be progressively blended with other sounds or faded from novel to familiar to signal specific required actions. A particularly useful activity in training locomotion patterns and rhythms associated with sounds is marching. The auditory cues in marching can be manipulated by the instructor at will in order to stimulate certain deficient auditory skills. Here are some other ideas:

1. Divide the class into partners and assign them to be a particular animal. Blindfold

one partner and have the pupils spread out. The child who is blindfolded attempts to locate his or her partner by listening for the appropriate animal sound from the partner.

2. Divide class into partners and blindfold one partner. Place numerous beanbags in front of blindfolded partners to represent mines in a minefield. The seeing child attempts to guide the blindfolded partner through the minefield by the use of verbal cues.

For pupils with perceptual-motor problems, the following concepts are important:

1. Perceptual-motor habilitation or remediation activities are most effectively offered while a child is in an early intervention program or in the early elementary grades. Early intervention will help ensure beneficial cumulative effects later in a child's life.

2. At times, certain senses may be masked in order to concentrate on a key sense (e.g., use a blindfold, earplugs).

3. The ability not to move (i.e., to relax) is a perceptual-motor activity. A child's kinesthetic sense must be finely tuned in order to control tension in large and small voluntary muscles. One of the greatest needs of children who are hyperactive is to learn how not to move. Relaxation training is, therefore, an important part of their educational program (see Chapter 13 for a more in-depth discussion of relaxation methods).

4. Pupils with learning disabilities, who are presumed to have a neurological deficit, especially need developmental activities on a daily basis. Fundamental gross motor activities should progress developmentally from bilateral (legs or arms) to unilateral (one part) to homolateral (one side) and finally to cross-lateral (opposition). This progression complements normal neurological development. As another example, locomotion progressions should start with crawling, then (in order of normal se-quence) creeping, walking, running, jumping, hopping, galloping, leaping, and finally skipping.

Aquatics

The aquatics environment is another area in which the deficits of pupils who are learning disabled can be addressed. Even academic concepts can be taught in a pool setting. Swimming pools can be designed in such a way that figures (such as letters) and symbols (such as numbers) are incorporated as permanent fixtures. The systematic use of these figures and symbols in a movement context can enhance the learning of preacademic and academic tasks. Note, though, that this setting would probably not be appropriate for a highly distractible pupil.

Motor skills training can also be emphasized in aquatics. The use of and awareness of both sides and the crossing of the midline can be accomplished with the use of selected fundamental swimming strokes, whether practiced on dry land or actually in the water. Body part identification and function can be emphasized in the water through movement education. Certain questions stimulate thought about the function and value of certain body parts. For example, What body parts help you to float? What do you use to move through water? How many ways can I take a breath? Body awareness can also be significantly enhanced with the use of obstacles in the water. Pupils can be urged to move over, through (see Figure 6.4), under, and around hoops, a sunken table, or another person's legs.

Teachers should be alert to certain characteristics exhibited by pupils who are learning disabled. Pupils with kinesthetic deficits should be initially oriented to the water vertically and then horizontally, as vertical positions are usually more familiar to these pupils. Pupils with spatial orientation problems might have problems with water depth and distance from others. Close supervision is indicated here. Easily distracted pupils also need close supervision in aquatics. Even with

FIGURE 6.4 Body awareness training in aquatics. *(From* Adapted Aquatics, *copyright © 1977 by The American Red Cross. Used by permission.)*

a one-to-one pupil–teacher ratio, a third person is needed for demonstrations. Last, instructors should be alert to the fact that warm water may calm the pupil who is hyperactive and cooler water tends to stimulate the pupil who is hypoactive. Some research data, however, refute this latter guideline (Cole, 1978).

Dance

Dance is an exciting and enjoyable activity that can be used to improve the gross motor skills of pupils who are learning disabled. All types of dance can be incorporated into a physical education program for each pupil. Here are some activity ideas:

1. Folk, square, social (including disco), and other types of dance can develop social maturity. As an added motivator, a teacher might use records brought to class by the pupils.
2. Dances with an irregular and nonrepetitive beat are best for those pupils with a history of perseveration.

3. Body part identification and memory can be enhanced by asking pupils to touch certain body parts in response to specific musical cues.
4. A bell placed on only one side of the body can establish laterality. Consistent rotation to one side (as in many square dances) can also enhance awareness of sides.
5. Auditory perception is perhaps the most obvious deficiency that can be remediated through dance activities. Teachers can systematically manipulate pitch, loudness, background noises, and the distance and direction from which music originates.
6. Pupils who are hyperactive can be calmed with soothing music; slowly moving pupils might need a fast tempo.
7. Spatial orientation is improved when dancers must move in restricted areas. The limbo (leaning backward and moving under a horizontal pole) is an ideal dance for training in body awareness.

Individual and Group Activities

Pupils labeled learning disabled can benefit from participation in both individual and group activities. Graded group games and low organized games are beneficial not only for their value in preparing for participation in high organized games but, importantly for pupils who are learning disabled, also for their positive social thrust and inherent emphasis on structure with rules, boundaries, and limits. The concepts of win–lose and follow–lead can also be gradually and systematically introduced in beginning and intermediate game participation.

Movement education, a group activity, with an emphasis on such concepts as force, size, distance, flow, tempo, space, and weight, addresses many of the characteristic deficits of pupils who are learning disabled. With its stress on individuality, choice, and success, movement education stands out among recommended approaches to instruction for pupils who are learning disabled (remember, however, that it is not recommended for pupils who are easily distracted).

The specific characteristics of learning disabilities suggest certain additional considerations for individual and group activities.

- *Hyperactivity*: gymnastics and other activities that emphasize controlled movement are important.
- *Distractibility*: equipment should be placed in the same location every day. It should be approached and mounted from the same direction.
- *Perseveration*: routines on a piece of apparatus or tumbling mat and rhythmic routines using contrasting movements should be offered. Graded group games and low and high organized games that employ frequent changes and "attention-getters" are also beneficial (e.g., Red Light, Midnight, Bombardment, Volleyball).
- *Auditory memory*: story plays allow considerable opportunity for practice in auditory memory; the rules of any lead-up or high organized game also enhance memory.
- *Body part identification*: the game Simon Says is particularly valuable for a pupil who needs assistance with the development of body image.
- *Visual perception*: most individual and group games require visual perception. A few activities include striking in tetherball, catching in a variety of games, punching in cageball games and controlled boxing, hitting in softball and baseball, and kicking in kickball and soccer.
- *Academic and language deficiencies*: numerous gross motor activities have been designed to incorporate academic skills (Cratty, 1971a, 1972, 1973; Humphrey, 1965; Humphrey & Sullivan, 1970). These activities can be used if the purpose of the activity is related to psychomotor domain development and the academic component does not take away from this primary purpose.

Physical educators can also recommend gross motor/academic skill activities to regular classroom and special educators to increase the amount of physical and motor activity pupils receive. As a supplement to classroom activities that are used to teach the same academic skills, the physical education activities may be even more effective for their pupils' learning because gross motor activities are generally highly motivating, involve additional sensory input, and give pupils immediate feedback that they did the activity correctly. The following are some examples of gross motor activities that also involve academic learning:

1. Numerous *language concepts* or general action words can be inherent in physical education activities. They just need to be targeted during the activity. See the following lists for some space concepts and action words:

Space Concepts	Action Words	
High–low	Bend	Reach
Front–back	Bounce	Rotate
Up–down	Carry	Run
Over–under	Catch	Shake
Left–right	Dismount	Slide
On–over	Extend	Slow
In–out	Fall	Sprint
Inside–outside	Fast	Stand
Above–below	Flex	Step
Behind–in front	Hang	Stoop
Around–over	Hold	Straddle
Away–near	Invert	Stretch
	Kick	Stride
	Land	Sway
	Lean	Swing
	Leap	Throw
	Lift	Turn
	Move	Twist
	Push	Walk
	Pull	

Language type games can also be played. Three examples are Spelling Relay, Crows and Cranes, and Alphabet Bowling. In

Spelling Relay, the class is divided into squads with an even number of pupils. Each squad is given space on a chalkboard and one piece of chalk. The teacher identifies a motor skill that each squad member must perform going to and from the chalkboard. The classroom teacher also gives the pupils two or more key spelling words that must be included in a sentence that they are to form. On the teacher's cue of "go," each pupil, one at a time in each squad, goes to the board and writes one word and then gives the chalk to the next squad member. The first team that writes a complete sentence that incorporates the words specifically identified by the teacher wins. Between the relays, the teacher changes the motor skill that must be performed while going to and from the chalkboard.

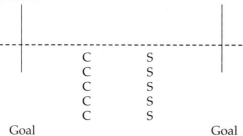

As shown in the illustration in this adaptation of Crows and Cranes, the pupils are divided equally into two groups, the Cs and the Ss, who line up facing each other, with their lines about 5 feet apart. A goal line is drawn a given distance behind each group. The teacher calls out a word that is spelled with either a *c* or an *s*. If the word requires a *c*, all the Cs run to their goal before being tagged by a member of the S group. All of those tagged become members of the opposite group. The groups then return to their respective line, and the same procedure is followed with another word. The group having the greater number of players on its side at the end of a specified playing time wins.

Word examples	Ceiling	Sand
	Cedar	Sun
	Cell	Saw
	Cease	Save
	Cemetery	Scissors

In Alphabet Bowling, the teacher makes 26 cards, at least 8 inches wide and 10 inches long, on thick paper. Each card is folded over 3 inches from the bottom of the length side so that it can stand on its own. On each card a different upper- and lowercase letter is written. Pupils verbally identify a letter and then attempt to roll it over using a tennis ball. If successful, the pupil keeps the card and then tries for another. If unsuccessful, it is another pupil's turn.

2. The following are two active *science games*. In Oxygen and Fuel, one pupil is selected to be oxygen (air) and another fuel (trees in the forest). The rest of the class (preventers of fire) join hands and form a circle with the pupil representing fuel in the center. The pupils in the circle attempt to keep the pupil representing oxygen from entering the circle and touching the fuel and causing a fire.

   In Eclipse Tag, pupils are paired and face each other around the playing areas. Two pupils who are not paired, are identified as the runner (earth) and the chaser, who tries to tag earth. Earth is safe from being tagged when he or she runs between the paired pupils and calls out "eclipse." If earth is tagged he or she becomes the chaser. The moon is represented by the pupil earth faces and the pupil at earth's back represents the sun. The pupils need to know also that the earth's shadow covers the moon.

3. Number line and number and letter grids can be used to teach *math concepts* using the active academic games concept. A number line (rocket space) can be drawn or painted on the playground and numerous math activities can be performed. As examples, a pupil could jump each numbered square calling out the number when it is landed on, perform the same activity on the pre-

ferred and nonpreferred foot, or jump or hop only on the even or odd numbers.

Also, a number grid (6 feet × 6 feet square; 36 letters, 1 foot × 1 foot) could be painted on the playground. Some math activities to use with such a grid are to jump/hop on the numbers 1 through 9; jump/hop on your phone number or street address; and depending on academic skill level, jump/hop all steps related to a math problem given verbally or written on a chalkboard.

Similar to a number grid, a letter grid can be painted on the playground and numerous language arts activities can be per-formed. Some of these activities are jump/hop to specific letters; spell words; and play Twister.

4. A map of the United States could be painted on the playground to be used in a *social studies* unit. Pupils can identify the location of each state and the location of each state's capital. Also, pupils can be asked to jump/hop to a specific state or capital. They could move to states or capitals that begin with a specific letter, jump/hop to or around states that fought for the confederacy during the Civil War, or jump/hop to or around the states that were included in the Louisiana Purchase. Imagination is the only limiting factor in the determination of any gross motor/academic skills game.

7

Emotional Disorders

DEFINITION, CAUSES, AND SCOPE

Definition

Individuals who are emotionally disordered are considered as having perhaps the most mysterious and unsettling type of disabling condition. This is due, in part, to the fact that the term *emotionally disordered* has never had a universally accepted definition. Add to this the fact that a *severe* emotional condition, one that impacts a pupil's ability to learn, must exist before this label can be given to any pupil and before federal funding is permitted. This is in contrast to all of the other 12 disability categories specified in P.L. 101-476. As an example, a child with mild mental retardation can be labeled for special education and federal funding purposes.

More specifically, according to the Rules of P.L. 101-476, the child who is emotionally disordered or disturbed is defined as an individual who exhibits one or more of the following characteristics over a long period of time and to a marked degree that adversely affects a child's educational performance:

- An inability to learn that cannot be explained by intellectual, sensory, or health factors;
- An inability to build or maintain satisfactory interpersonal relationships with peers and teachers;
- Inappropriate types of behavior or feelings under normal circumstances;
- A general pervasive mood of unhappiness or depression; or
- A tendency to develop physical symptoms or fears associated with personal or school problems.

The term includes schizophrenia. The term does not apply to children who are socially maladjusted, unless it is determined that they have a serious emotional disturbance (P.L. 101-476 Rules, *Federal Register*, September 29, 1992, p. 44802).

Social maladjustment refers to varying emotional problems related to the effects of environmental deprivation (poverty, malnourishment, ghetto living, gang involvement, parental neglect or abuse, living as a migrant) that are associated with emotionally disordered behavior. Because of marked environmental plight, many of those who are socially maladjusted tend to dwell on failure, which can directly affect their feelings of self-worth and perpetuate an unhealthy self-concept. This syndrome is often reflected in behavioral extremes over time. Children and youth who are socially maladjusted are commonly referred to as juvenile delinquents, and adults who are socially maladjusted sometimes become criminals. In this chapter we address only those individuals with extreme social maladjustment. This condition can be subsumed under the terms *emotionally disordered* or *emotionally disturbed*.*

Emotionally disordered essentially describes any individual who chronically has noticeable problems in coping with everyday events and who acts inappropriately. The term connotes the consistent inability to live within social mores. Both temporary and permanent emotional disorders may be viewed along a behavior continuum from normal, to some degree of neurosis (within reality), and finally to some degree of psychosis (out of touch with reality). This continuum, with arbitrary cutoff points that are meant to represent degrees of disordered behavior, is presented in Figure 7.1. The graph takes into account intensity (magnitude and extremity) and occurrence (frequency, rate, duration) of inappropriate behavior. On this continuum a person who emits inappropriate behavior within the 0 to 50 percent range on the intensity or occurrence dimension would probably be regarded as "normal." Someone who displays more than 50 percent and less than 80 percent inappropriate behavior would probably be perceived as slightly to markedly "neurotic," and a person disturbed more than 80 percent on either dimension would be labeled "psychotic."

Each of us can all be placed on this continuum at any given moment because it represents the complete range of human emotional behavior. In addition, everyone tends to move up or down on both dimensions of the continuum as a function of varying life events from moment to moment. In this regard, emotional disorders may be situational (even for a moment in time), and when the situation or event ends, the disorder goes into remission and behavior becomes "normal." The emotional disorder continuum, therefore, should be viewed as both all-inclusive and flexible.

Within a life span, we each have the chance of being free of problems or being dominated by them for a short or lengthy period. The worst situation is when an individual emits intense inappropriate behavior all of the time. Most school-aged children who function at this level are institutionalized or, at best, placed in segregated special classrooms. Fortunately, most of us are generally in control and are responsible for

*In this chapter we use the terms *emotionally disordered* and *emotionally disturbed* interchangeably, instead of the traditional *mental illness*. Mental illness connotes a medical cure with an accompanying deemphasis on personal responsibility. Other terms used in the literature and among professionals include, but are not limited to, behaviorally disordered, behaviorally disabled, emotionally handicapped, psychologically disordered, behaviorally disoriented, and mentally ill.

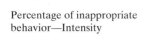

Percentage of inappropriate
behavior—Intensity

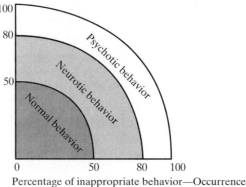

Percentage of inappropriate behavior—Occurrence

FIGURE 7.1 Emotional
disorder continuum.

determining our own positions on this emotional disorder continuum almost all of the time.

In physical education, standards for behavior include both intensity and occurrence. When a pupil behaves inappropriately, the teacher might consider it a temporary condition. If, however, a trend of intense or frequent disordered behavior persists over time, physical educators have an obligation to intervene systematically with outside professional assistance because there might be an emotional disorder. Physical education is different from other curricular areas because gross motor movement is encouraged in a less structured and larger environment with a greater teacher—pupil ratio. We see the wide range of behaviors of many pupils every schoolday. Under these conditions, those who teach physical education have a unique opportunity to observe, identify, counsel, and refer pupils who may be emotionally disordered.

Children who are labeled emotionally disordered display a number of inappropriate behaviors that have direct relevance to the teaching of physical education. These behaviors include, but are not limited to, distractibility, inappropriate peer interaction, excessive poking and teasing other pupils, odd mannerisms, not standing in line, diffi-

culty in handling independent tasks, temper outbursts, inability to accept direction, inaccessibility, short attention span, disrupting class routine, defying the teacher, disruptions, destructiveness, unpredictability, variability in performance, "go-go" jet propulsion, impulsive hitting out, breaking or taking other children's possessions, running away, surprising streaks of information, excitability, silly laugh, disorientation, and imaginary tales. Their behavior can also be at the opposite pole: withdrawal, tuning out, blank expression, frozen silence, ghostly appearance, lack of communication, distance from teachers and classmates, averted look, backing away if a friendly hand is placed on the shoulder, a wall of silence, a separate island.

Later in this chapter many of these specific characteristics will be matched with instructional strategies. At this point it is essential to note that all children may occasionally emit one or more of these behaviors in school, and no child will emit them all. The key to emotional disorder is chronic occurrence or intense evidence of abnormal or inappropriate behavior.

Emotional disorders are also defined, classified, and diagnosed according to the American Psychiatric Association's 1987 Diagnostic and Statistical Manual of Mental

Disorders (DSM-III revised). DSM-III revised stresses the individual first ("an individual with schizophrenia" instead of "a schizophrenic") and also assumes that each listed mental disorder is not a discrete entity (they can overlap). In addition, the manual offers specific diagnostic criteria for each of literally hundreds of mental disorders listed to facilitate agreement of diagnoses among clinicians. DSM-III revised is not used frequently, however, in schools.

Traditionally, the major diagnostic categories in psychiatric diagnosis have included mental retardation (see Chapter 5), organic brain syndrome (physical insult to the brain), and numerous functional disorders—neurotic behavior (nonoffensive bizarre behavior emitted by a person in touch with reality), personality disorders (nonpsychotic antisocial behavior that seriously offends other people, such as sexual perversion and drug addiction), psychosomatic manifestations (incessant problems of the mind that cause physical complications), and psychotic behavior (bizarre behavior by a person not in touch with reality). Schizophrenia is a common diagnostic category. Individuals with schizophrenia are seriously psychotic and commonly engage in extreme obsessive, compulsive, delusionary, and hallucinatory behaviors. They appear to be "split" from the world and within themselves. A few major types of schizophrenia can be differentiated:

- *Paranoid*: extremely defensive, the individual perceives that he or she is the object of attack from many sources; also associated with delusions of grandeur
- *Catatonic*: totally withdrawn from reality physically and psychologically, as expressed by varying degrees of immobility
- *Hebephrenic*: inappropriately attaching humor, babbling, or emitting hyperactive movement in response to common mundane events

Some young children are autistic. Autism is now a separate category of disability in P.L. 101-476 and is defined within this law's rules as

a developmental disability significantly affecting verbal and nonverbal communication and social interaction, generally evident before age 3, that adversely affects a child's educational performance. Other characteristics often associated with autism are engagement in repetitive activities and stereotyped movements, resistance to environmental change or change in daily routines, and unusual responses to sensory experiences (P.L. 101-476 Rules, *Federal Register*, September 29, 1992, p. 44801).

As this definition indicates, autism is generally characterized by severe problems in communication and an inability to relate to people normally.

Further, children who are labeled autistic display one or more of the following specific characteristics to an extreme extent:

- Difficulty with speech and language
- Withdrawn, apathetic, and unresponsive
- Resistant to change; perseveration of sameness
- Disinterested in people and surroundings
- Unusually interested in inanimate objects (often spinning or twirling them)
- Hyperactive (often engaged in self-stimulating acts such as rocking or head banging)
- Sleeping and feeding difficulties

Autism can be suspected as early as a few weeks or months after birth or not until about 2 years of age. Because of its rarity, as well as for other reasons, little is known about causes or conditions preceding or accompanying autism. There is no cure; but a growing body of research points to a biochemical error, and some treatments seem promising. Autism affects boys more than girls. Because of the severity of their condition, children who are autistic-like sometimes are not served in regular schools, even though they can be healthy and intelligent.

The central problem with all of these classification systems and all of this labeling for those who are emotionally or otherwise disabled is that a label or classification does not provide specific information to assist a teacher in actual teaching. In fact, labeling a child without also programming appropriate intervention strategies might do more harm than good. Labels or classifications are only useful as aids in the procurement of funds in pupil placement. Once a pupil is placed, however, a physical educator will need to match correctly behavioral, descriptive, and objective identifying data to instructional strategies in order to teach on a day-to-day basis. In addition, behavioral data should be kept current in order to address the ongoing specific needs of those who happen to be classified as emotionally disordered.

Causes

Heredity, organic, and functional causes of emotional disorders appear to exist. Those associated with heredity are difficult to pinpoint directly. Organic causes, which are infrequent, include such insults as glandular imbalance, disease, neurological degeneration (old age), neurological trauma or brain damage, poor nutrition, abnormal somatotype (body type), and chemical imbalances (e.g., effects of drugs). Functionally related disorders, that is, disorders that result from experiences, are in the majority. They are often associated with real or imagined pressures from peers, parents, teachers, or other authority figures, or the environment. The specific cause of functional disorders is usually unknown. Authorities claim that most behavioral disorders are first discovered when a child enrolls in school.

The cause of behavior disorders can be largely traced to family and school. Meyen (1978) also recognizes the importance of both predisposing factors (a condition that may cause disturbance, such as neglect) and precipitating factors (a specific condition, such as a scary moment, that triggers the disturbance) as they relate to the cause of emotional disorders.

Scope

Estimates of how many pupils are emotionally disordered vary. The U.S. Department of Education (1992) has estimated that only 0.69 percent of all American pupils aged 6–21 (N = 392,559) were labeled seriously emotionally disturbed during the 1990–91 school year. Yet survey reports of the incidence of emotional disturbance in American children have ranged from 2 to 69 percent (Reinert, 1980). Such higher estimates tend to include children with short-term and long-term behavior disturbances of varying extremes. The number of pupils with extreme and chronic or long-term emotional problems is considerably lower, and the 0.69 percent level calculated by the federal government, therefore, seems somewhat reasonable. Further, autism occurs in about 5 in every 10,000 births, usually firstborn males (National Society for Autistic Children, 1977). Add to this number a yearly estimate of approximately 3 percent of youngsters of school age who are labeled juvenile delinquents. In 1988, there were actually more than 1.6 million children arrested under the age of 18 (U.S. Department of Commerce, 1990). In all, perhaps 5 percent of all pupils may be emotionally disordered or juvenile delinquents.

Most important, only a minority of these

children and youth appear to be receiving appropriate specialized services (Heward & Orlansky, 1992). Thus regular and special physical educators may well have to teach pupils who have identified abnormal behavior, whether they are labeled or not. It is also likely that the number of pupils with emotional disorders will grow with increasing peer pressure, mainstreaming, parental overemphasis on child achievement, premature assumption of major responsibilities by children, rampaging inflation, and overpopulation. (Interestingly enough, many writers refer to our times as the "age of anxiety.")

Teachers should keep in mind the following considerations:

1. Individuals who were emotionally disordered or socially maladjusted as children tend to exhibit similar behavior as adults.
2. More individuals (children and adults) at lower socioeconomic levels are prone toward acting inappropriately (e.g., aggressively) than persons at middle and upper socioeconomic levels.
3. More males than females are categorized as emotionally disordered. A common ratio given in the literature is 6:1 (Reinert, 1980). Yet it is unclear whether there actually is a greater number of boys with emotional disturbances or whether girls are socialized to exhibit less disruptive behaviors and, therefore, are not so labeled.

4. About half of all hospital beds in the United States are occupied by individuals who are labeled emotionally disordered.
5. About half of those who are hospitalized for an emotional disorder have schizophrenia.
6. We all have some chance of being so seriously emotionally disordered as to require hospitalization at some point. No one is automatically immune to this possibility.

CHARACTERISTICS AND INSTRUCTIONAL STRATEGIES

Many of the specific characteristics of emotional disorders can impede learning in a physical education setting. Therefore, teaching these pupils can be physically exhausting and emotionally draining for the instructor. Those discussed here do not represent all common characteristics in all environments, but those that the physical educator should consider. Refer also to Chapter 13 for additional relevant information on behavior management and also to the following book for more comprehensive information specifically on physical education and the child with autism:

Davis, K. (1990). *Adapted physical education for students with autism*. Springfield, IL: Charles C Thomas.

CHARACTERISTICS	INSTRUCTIONAL STRATEGIES
Psychomotor 1. School-aged children who are emotionally disordered usually attain physiological and anatomical growth without equal affective development (social, emotional, psychological).	1. Select people-oriented physical activities with a view toward affective development. Give pupils time to reflect on their behavior.
2. The greater the emotional disorder, the less perceptually keen and physically fit an individual tends to be. This is particularly true for those who are extremely antisocial such as the pupil who is autistic-like (Reid, Collier, & Morin, 1983).	2. Use all resources of the mental health team, including the school psychologist. Find reinforcing activities and use them often for motor, fitness, play, and social skills development. Haptic cues are best for skill acquisition for pupils who are autistic-

3. Individuals who are emotionally disordered often have heightened emotions that directly affect their physiological parameters (e.g., increased flow of gastric juices, increased heart rate), which can lead to inappropriate outbursts.

4. Children and youth who are emotionally disordered exhibit a wide range in motor and fitness function.

5. Specific behavioral disturbances of any kind (nonattending, aggression, withdrawal) inhibit motor learning and fitness progress over time.

6. Psychomotor performance may vary from time to time.

7. These pupils tend to be action oriented.

8. Pupils who are both socially maladjusted and emotionally disordered often attain superior ability in sports and games.

9. Some youth who are maladjusted or delinquent tend to shy away from sport with its inherent win-lose emphasis.

Cognitive

1. Pupils who are behavior disordered usually score somewhat below normal in IQ tests, their school achievement is even lower than their scores would predict, and many have learning problems (Knitzer, Steinber, & Fleisch, 1990; Heward & Orlansky, 1992).

2. Pupils who are disturbed and disordered often misperceive the reactions and intentions of others, including authority figures.

3. Some pupils who are severely disordered have a total lack of understanding and disregard for safety.

4. Many pupils who are disordered have short attention spans.

5. These pupils often communicate their needs nonverbally.

like (Collier & Reid, 1987). Such cues should be applied with light pressure while varying the contact point over time. However, if such a child shows a sensory preference, use that sense (and gradual varied stimulation of that sense) in teaching (Connor, 1990).

3. A systematically paced program of physical education activities will tend to stimulate more natural physiological reactions and, in addition, will permit appropriate channeling of outbursts. Allow pupils to take time-outs, as needed.

4. Individualize physical education programming as much as possible.

5. Managing behavior and establishing rapport are necessary prerequisites to psychomotor learning. A number of behavioral strategies are detailed in Chapter 13.

6. Gather evaluative data on a test of posture, motor, fitness, or play proficiency more than once. An average of scores would be most useful and revealing.

7. Structured action-oriented physical education activities of all types can be offered with success.

8. Emphasize sports and games; however, the physical educator also has an obligation to impress on pupils that physical prowess should not be pursued at the expense of academic ability.

9. Never force competitive sports activities on reluctant pupils. Gradually introduce these activities with an initial emphasis on spectatorship and then self-improvement through noncompetitive participation.

1. One traditionally strong incentive to achieve in all areas is the privilege of participating in interscholastic sports and intramurals. A system that incorporates a written contract between teachers, parents, the principal, and the pupil could be used to clearly specify contingencies involving sports or intramural participation and school achievement in all subjects.

2. Be honest with pupils; directly address their concerns in a caring and timely fashion.

3. Set up a structured environment in which limits and essential rules are strictly adhered to by the teacher and pupil. Teach safety.

4. Plan several activities in each physical education lesson. If pupils assist in planning, their attention tends to improve.

5. Observe pupils' eyes and body language accurately. (e.g., Is there eye contact? Are their bodies turned toward and in the proximity of classmates and the instructor? Are they smiling?) Be empathetic when eventually reacting to disturbing behaviors. (See Figure 7.2.)

FIGURE 7.2 Body language showing potential problem.

6. Some pupils who are emotionally disturbed and are members of a minority group (probably also labeled maladjusted) have a low frustration level, especially related to others' perception of the language they speak. These pupils are not well versed in English.

Affective

1. As a population, individuals labeled emotionally disordered are heterogeneous, particularly in affect.

2. Pupils who are behaviorally disordered are, at times, sensitive to touch.

3. A pupil who is labeled emotionally disordered may be easily distracted.

6. Locate resources that can bridge the bilingual gap. This could involve the use of sign language during physical education instruction. Help pupils to have pride in their ethnic backgrounds. Slowness and impatience with language should not be associated with stupidity.

1. Get to know pupils and conscientiously and consistently plan individualized structured programs. No one recommended plan can be given for all of these pupils.

2. Establish rapport with pupils before using kinesthetic and tactile manipulation.

3. All environmental stimuli need to be under the teacher's control in a structured setting. Highlight relevant stimuli (e.g., bright yellow ball) and reduce or eliminate distracting stimuli (e.g., doors open to busy hallway). Pupils' waiting time should be minimized. As examples, avoid equipment setup while pupils are forced to wait, avoid giving too many verbal directions while pupils are standing or sitting, and avoid having long waiting lines for activity such as tumbling or relays. All directions should be precise and to the point. A child's head could be gently physically diverted for eye contact (see Figure 7.3).

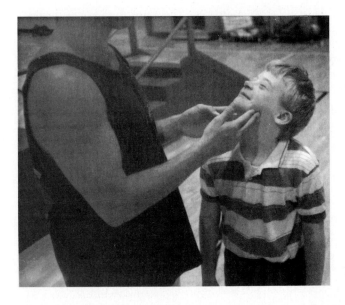

FIGURE 7.3 Cupping child's head for eye contact.

4. Pupils who are emotionally disordered are often easily upset or agitated.

4. Be calm and patient. Intersperse active and quiet activities. Know pupils well enough so that their first signs of agitation can be detected and countered before the blowup occurs. This "psychological margin of safety" approach needs to be used consistently.

5. Some pupils tend to exhibit extroverted behavior, such as aggressiveness.

5. Offer physical activities (e.g., noncontact, noncompetitive) that not only address psychomotor needs but also counteract or are incompatible with behavioral extremes. Aggressiveness, anger, and tantrums sometimes need to be handled with restraint; reasoning probably will be fruitless. Tasteful humor on the spot may diffuse aggression.

6. Other pupils tend to exhibit introverted behaviors, such as shyness and withdrawal.

6. Foster attention to healthy relationships through activities that lend themselves to interaction. One-to-one, small-group, and large-group activities should be offered in progression. Such a progression should also move from cooperative to competitive.

7. Pupils who are emotionally disordered will, at times, verbally or physically challenge the specific authority of teachers.

7. Apply firm and consistent discipline coupled with concern. Above all, remain calm, be an active listener, and use physical restraint when a child is a danger to self, others, or property. Do not shy away from such challenges and avoid threats.

8. Children and youth who are disturbed may be preoccupied with personal thoughts, sometimes morbid in nature. They may engage in hallucinatory or delusional fantasies.

8. Offer lesson plans that not only address developmental needs but also "flow" without abrupt or hesitating moments. Resist reinforcing a child's abnormal thoughts; for example, do not engage in fantasy talk at the child's level in order to reach the child; show disapproval of abnormal thoughts by confronting their abnormality.

9. Disturbed behavior sometimes evidences itself in self-abuse, such as overeating, undereating, or drug abuse.

9. Show concern, counsel pupils, and seek assistance from others on the educational team with more knowledge in dealing with psychological disturbances and maladjustment reactions.

10. Polar behaviors or behavioral opposites such as hyperactivity and hypoactivity may characterize these pupils.

10. Use relaxation and noncompetitive activities for hyperactive pupils; active games and activities are most appropriate for pupils who are hypoactive.

11. Many pupils who are emotionally disordered have poor self-concepts.

11. Offer systematic programs of physical education in which pupils receive instant quantifiable feedback on improvement and, therefore, experience success soon. Examples of activities may include weight lifting and "confidence" obstacle courses. Fitness activities may improve appearance, which in turn may improve body image and feelings of self-worth. Use pupils' first names when addressing them.

12. Pupils who are emotionally disturbed are often suspicious of others.

12. Build rapport before expecting pupil effort. Provide a nonthreatening and secure environment.

13. Problems in relating to people appropriately are common. Reactions range from fight to flight.

13. Dual and group physical activities with a leisure time focus are of high priority for older pupils. Young children need numerous play experiences with consistent attention to developmental stages of play. If pupils will not relate to peers or the teacher initially, encourage them to attend to an object and finally to interact with increasing numbers of peers and adults.

14. Pupils with noticeable adjustment and behavior problems typically cannot direct themselves.

14. These pupils need a teacher-directed, structured environment. Initially make choices for these pupils, then offer a few choices only, and finally offer open-ended choices once responsible behavior has been demonstrated. Rules, boundaries, and rest areas need to be fully agreed upon by pupils and teacher before activity begins. A pupil may need his or her own spot (e.g., see Figure 7.4) to sit or stand on for all beginning and closing class activities.

15. Pupils with behavior problems often have difficulty accepting change, criticism, and limitations.

15. Through positive communication, strive to instill in these pupils an appreciation of the differences in everybody and a capacity to accept limitations and change without withdrawing or attacking people. Introduce change in the middle of a lesson and stress constants at the beginning (e.g., always start with teacher-led exercises) and at the end of a lesson (e.g., always conclude a lesson with relaxation exercises).

16. These pupils tend to be easily threatened and often fear real or imagined social sanctioning.

16. Begin by engaging the pupil in non-threatening and no win-lose activities such as New Games (see Chapter 4); allow pupils to save face in actual or potentially threatening situations. Dressing room behavior may need to be monitored.

17. Pupils who are emotionally disordered often seek attention in any form.

17. If possible, do not reinforce inappropriate behavior with attention. Give earned leadership roles (e.g., squad leader, captain) at different levels to appropriately behaving pupils. The responsibility and attention implicit in a leadership role will tend to decrease inappropriate behavior.

FIGURE 7.4 Pupils standing on designated marks for control.

18. Emotional reactions to new activities in the form of excessive fear and over-anxiousness are common.

19. Willful defiance of rules is characteristic.

20. Pupils who are emotionally disturbed may have a very noticeable nervous behavior (e.g., twitches or tics) or some obsessive-compulsive habit (e.g., not stepping on any floor crack).

21. These pupils may have additional problems, as compared to the norm, in relating to those of the other sex.

General

1. Children who are emotionally disordered tend toward extremes of inappropriate behavior.

2. They can act unpredictably and irrationally.

18. Do not force activities on pupils. Gradually introduce novel activities in a familiar environment.

19. Participation in a team sport (intramural or interscholastic) and in games can instill respect for rules and authorities who enforce them (teacher, coach, referee).

20. Use incompatible activities to offset such behavior. As examples, twitches of the hand may be countered by pupil holding heavy equipment; twitches of the head may be offset by using "freeze" activities that require concentrated and conscious stillness of a pupil's body parts; and crack avoidance may be approached by having all classmates stand on a crack to prevent becoming "It" in a game.

21. Some activities in physical education are naturals for appropriate coeducational involvement. Examples include social dancing, volleyball, relays, and cooperative games.

1. Model appropriate behavior. Accompany teaching/intervening with the measurement of behavioral extremes to determine teacher effectiveness (Cooper, Heron, & Heward, 1987). Use the resources of behavior specialists on the educational team. Not all children with similar problems should be placed in the same class.

2. Expect the unexpected from these pupils, and counter it with appropriate predictable behavior.

	Pupils should know what consequences will follow unpredictable, inappropriate behavior.
3. A lifetime of disordered behavior and maladjustment tends to "harden" an individual's lifestyle.	3. Early intervention and exposure to appropriate behavior and physical education activities in school are critical.
4. Many pupils who are maladjusted and disadvantaged and who emit disturbing behaviors happen to be minorities.	4. Middle-class white teachers need exposure to readings, in-service training, and numerous hands-on experiences with children and youth who are minorities and disadvantaged.
5. Pupils who are emotionally disturbed may be taking prescribed medications.	5. Physical educators need to be familiar with common medications and their effect(s) on movement (see Chapter 13). For example, a tranquilizer may prevent a pupil from engaging in rope climbing activities. Avoid administering prescribed medications to pupils.

Many of the characteristics and instructional strategies suggested for pupils characterized as socially maladjusted, disadvantaged, and at risk are addressed within Hellison's four-tiered value-based model, which has been successfully field-tested in the Chicago city school system (Georgiadis, 1990; Hellison, 1990a, 1990b, 1990c; Lifka, 1990). This model specifically deemphasizes bodies and winning but, instead, teaches self and social responsibility through stages of awareness, practice, decision making, and self-reflection. The four levels essentially address self-control, inclusion of everyone, setting individualized goals, and cooperating as a group/team. Other related physical activity programs can be cited for their actual impact on delinquency rates (Greenwood & Turner, 1983; Winther & Currie, 1987). We especially recommend a thorough review of these programs by those physical educators who are particularly challenged by this type of pupil.

INDICATED AND NONINDICATED ACTIVITIES

Physical and Motor Fitness

Researchers claim that the level of fitness among children and youth who are emotionally disordered tends to be below normal. Researchers also support the notion that the body image and self-concept of these youngsters tend to be poor. Thus pupils with emotional disorders need physical education programs that emphasize physical and motor fitness, and are offered in a teacher-directed, structured, nonthreatening environment. Gains in fitness may not only improve body image and self-concept but may also enable greater successful participation in games and sports, which has direct implications for positive social experiences. In addition, increased strength and endurance may enable these children to cope better with increased physical demands. Finally, and especially important for those who are emotionally disturbed, participation in a sustained program of physical fitness has proven to reduce maladaptive behavior—as when physical activity has been used as an initial stimulus (Jansma & Combs, 1987; Santarcangelo, Dyer, & Luce, 1987) and as a reinforcer (Jansma, 1978b; Pierce & Risley, 1974; Vogler, 1981).

We recommend that body building (not with free weights) and heart–lung endurance programs be stressed in a physical education class that includes pupils who are emotionally disordered. One of the first such programs was Temple University's Buttonwood Farms Project, a combined weekend and summer experience for children labeled emotionally disordered and mentally retarded. It included a systematic, structured variety of movement experiences emphasizing fitness (Hilsendager, Jack, & Mann, 1968). Combining some ideas generated from this project, Figure 7.5 shows a fitness or confidence course. It is designed to enhance central fitness (strength, cardiorespiratory endurance, flexibility) in a structured, individualized, nonthreatening manner where failure need not occur. Notice that the teacher is physically elevated on a centrally located platform, movable partitions are used at most stations to reduce distractions, rest areas are provided, and all entrances to exercise areas are visible to the instructor. In this system the number of mats available, lesson plan objectives, and degree of inappropriate behavior by pupils will determine the number and type

FIGURE 7.5 An engineered fitness setting. The teacher may also rotate to individual stations for individualized attention. Dotted lines indicate partition placements. Portable folding mats are placed sideways end-to-end. All doors are locked.

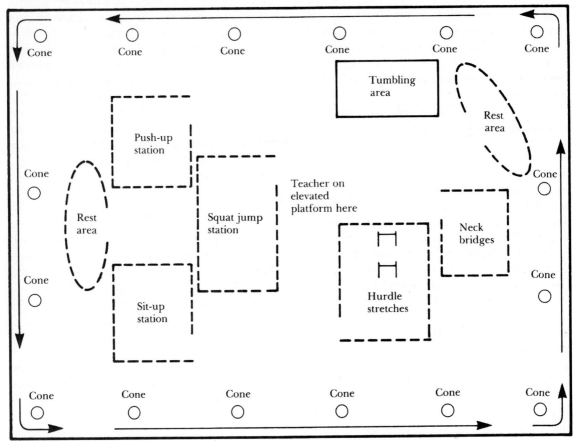

of stations. Also, pupils are encouraged to aid the instructor in setting up and storing equipment.

Fitness activities can also be provided in an open setting if equipment that inherently limits random movement is used, for example, a stretch rope for group calisthenics (see Figure 7.6). All individuals, including the instructor, hold the rope with both hands from the inside or outside. The instructor holds both loose ends for controlling purposes. In this position, pupils can be doing group sit-ups, group stretching, and one-way circle running all at the same time. A durable parachute (see Figure 7.7) can be used in the same manner as a stretch rope. Other examples: Pupils can be given a hoop with which they engage in fitness activities (see Figure 7.8); and tires can be used to limit movement to one area (see Figure 7.9). Extended jumping on the tires (endurance) and supine-lying tire lifting in various ways (strength and flexibility) can be used for fitness activities.

Fundamental Motor Skills and Patterns

Deficits below the norm in fundamental motor skills and patterns are evident with pupils who are emotionally disordered. Therefore younger children should be given a steady diet of activities that enhance spatial orientation, body image, locomotion, eye–limb coordination, balance, and rhythm. Older pupils should regularly perform skill drills designed to improve coordination, balance, and motor planning. One other basic concern for this type of pupil is the ability to relax under different conditions (see Chapter 13 for relaxation activities). Furthermore, all pupils who are emotionally disordered need confidence in working individually with nonthreatening equipment and objects to enhance fundamental movement patterns.

These prerequisites eventually combine to permit successful games participation, in which the much-needed social element is stressed.

Activities for a number of pupils who are emotionally disordered can be planned simultaneously within a structured, teacher-controlled environment such as that illustrated in Figure 7.5. In such an environment activities that enhance basic motor patterns would replace those related to fitness. Equipment that forces attention on the learner is ideal. For example, a tunnel station (cloth and wire or mats over chairs) for spatial orientation, a combined walking-hopping-jumping-running-leaping-galloping-skipping station around the coned periphery for locomotion, a graduated low balance beam station (beams with gradually increasing height and decreasing width), relaxation stations, and a pitch-back or wall rebound station for eye–limb coordination could be used in a basic movement confidence course. Again, an elevated teacher platform and movable partitions might be advisable, particularly at the outset. Finally, group fundamental motor activities using tires, parachutes, and stretch ropes, similar for fitness enhancement, might also be encouraged.

Aquatics

The medium of water is uniquely beneficial for the pupil who is emotionally disordered. Killian, Joyce-Petrovich, Menna, and Arena (1984) maintain that aquatic programs are especially appropriate for pupils who are autistic-like. Aside from the movement experiences, which are recommended for all pupils, disabled and nondisabled, the temperature of water can directly affect pupils' behavior. For example, the pupil who is overanxious, aggressive, and hyperactive may be calmed in water that is 85° to 95°F. Conversely, colder water will stimulate

FIGURE 7.6 A stretch rope is used for control during exercise.

FIGURE 7.7 A parachute is used to manage pupils' movements.

movement in pupils who are withdrawn. Here are some other techniques and activities the teacher can use that are especially helpful for pupils with noticeable emotional problems:

1. For the pupil sensitive to touch, provide "personal space" within a psychological margin of safety. A calm demeanor and gradual use of closer proximity, which eventually results in teacher–pupil physical contact, are essential.

2. At times, pupils are abnormally fearful of water to the point of being aquaphobic. Such pupils require the assistance of members of the educational team, including the swim instructor, school psychologist, classroom teacher, and behavior modification specialist. The overall objective of their

intervention would be the desensitization of this abnormal fear. Desensitization steps such as the following might decrease the abnormal fear of water over time:

a. Talk about water.

b. With audiovisual aids, show the pupil how others enjoy the water.

c. Play splash games in the shower.

d. Have the child observe pupils in the water from afar.

e. Encourage the child to move closer to the pool while observing (50 feet, 40 feet, 30 feet, 20 feet).

f. Have the pupil dangle feet in water.

g. Have the pupil stand in water with instructor with an accompanying motivational device such as a beachball.

FIGURE 7.8 A hoop limits random movement.

FIGURE 7.9 A tire limits random movement.

Splashing from any source is not indicated at first.

h. Use a game approach to water orientation.

The instructor fades more and more as various stages of advanced water awareness activities are presented. Success in these activities might take years.

3. These pupils may require one-to-one attention in the water.

4. Pupils who are emotionally disordered may relate appropriately to inanimate objects first and then to a person. In aquatics, a youngster might first be encouraged to associate with a ball, a toy, or a flotation device while in the presence of a teacher. Eventually the toy or other inanimate nonthreatening object can be faded and replaced exclusively with a peer or teacher.

5. For this type of pupil, pushing, kicking, stroking, dunking, punching, and splashing water are actions that might release overly pent-up emotions.

Dance

All types of dance can be incorporated into a physical education program for the pupil who is emotionally disordered. Specific advantages of dance include the natural socialization element and emotional effect of many types of music. Slow, peaceful music tends to calm; fast, loud music tends to make pupils more active. Such music may be intentionally used as part of the lesson directly or as background music for activities.

Some youngsters communicate through movement and can be reached only through movement in order to learn appropriate behavior. This is the thrust of Costonis's volume of readings entitled *Therapy in Motion* (1977), which also contains a bibliography of approximately 400 references on dance therapy or movement therapy. According to the American Dance Therapy Association (circa 1974):

Dance therapy is the psychotherapeutic use of movement as a process which furthers the emotional and physical integration of the individual. Dance therapy is distinguished from other utilizations of dance (for example, dance education) by its focus on the nonverbal aspects of behavior and its use of movement as the process for intervention. Adaptive, expressive, and communicative behaviors are all considered in treatment, with the expressed goal of integrating these behaviors with psychological aspects of the person. Dance therapy can function as a primary treatment modality or as an integral part of an overall treatment program (p. 1).

In essence, dance therapy is nonverbal, movement-oriented psychotherapy. Within this context, we believe that when movement of any type fosters affective development, it can be thought of as therapeutic.

The potential benefits of some specific dance-oriented methods and activities include the following:

1. With the use of any dance form (ballroom, folk, square, disco, creative), appropriate language, movement, and interactions can all be systematically addressed.

2. Excessive repressed emotion can often be adequately released in the context of interpretive or creative dance. Those who teach physical education are encouraged to use others on the educational team in this context.

3. Disco and aerobic dancing are healthy outlets for energy. Aggressive and destructive urges may be productively channeled while fitness is enhanced or maintained.

4. Pupils who are emotionally disordered are, at times, socially or touch defensive. A desensitization schema, similar to the one

proposed for aquatics, could be appropriate for use in a dance context. For example, observation would precede actual participation and noncontact dancing would precede contact dancing. In addition, pupil-preferred music may be more appropriate than teacher-preferred music, quiet and slower music may be best initially, and practice at home may be highly beneficial before participation at school. Again, therapeutic effects might take a considerable amount of time. Teachers, therefore, should not expect immediate results but should be satisfied with small gains.

5. Nodding, clapping, stomping, swaying, rocking, swinging, and other movements are energy releasers, and many of these movements can be engaged in by the pupil who is most severely emotionally disordered and nonambulatory. As a cautionary note, those activities associated directly with a particular pupil's emotional problem should not be encouraged. For example, body rockers should not be instructed to nod, sway, and rock.

6. Soothing music and movements should be used just prior to the change of classes in an effort to calm the pupil.

Individual and Group Activities

Participation in individual, dual, and group activities not only provides needed psychomotor benefits but also a context in which disordered and maladjusted behavior can be modified. For example, low organized games such as Midnight and Squirrels in Trees are excellent for impulse control because they teach the child to remain still until some cue is given. Individual and group activities also inherently allow for appropriate release of aggression and pent-up energy in a socially appropriate manner. In addition, the inherently reinforcing or enjoyable aspects of games and sports will tend to involve pupils who are antisocial in

small and finally larger groups. It is safe to say that everyone has at least one activity that he or she enjoys and that could encourage interaction.

Physical educators must determine reinforcing social activities and incorporate them systematically into their physical education programs. When determining a progression of individual and group activities, a physical educator should generally offer first individual, then dual, and eventually team or group activities starting with a cooperative and then moving to a competitive focus. The Physical Education Mainstreaming Model (see Chapter 4) ties directly into this progression.

The gradual introduction of new participants and activities is essential in working with the pupil who is emotionally disordered. Sometimes the activity chosen is not as critical as participation itself. In a larger sense, children need to learn how to function appropriately within a group before leaving school. Morris and Stiehl (1989) provide numerous examples for designing and modifying games that would enhance overall pupil participation and thus appropriate for pupils with emotional disturbances. In their system designing appropriate games requires three steps: understanding the basic structure underlying all games, modifying the basic game structure, and managing the resultant game's degree of difficulty.

Pupils who are severely frustrated and distracted or disoriented should, at first, be taught one-on-one or with only a few others in the class. With this population, Sherrill (1986) states: "Small class size in physical education, as in special education, is probably the single most important criterion for success" (p. 490). In addition, activities in which success can be achieved with little effort should be offered at the outset, rules should initially be simple and few in number, environmental distractions should be carefully monitored, emphasis on competition should be limited (see the New Games Model in Chapter 4), and activities in which pupils contact each other physically should not be stressed. Over the course of a school session, one or more of these variables should intentionally be modified toward natural conditions in order to increase very gradually the pupil's tolerance for frustration and distraction.

Special Considerations

Play Therapy. As with dance, some youngsters communicate through play and can be reached only through play to begin and further the process of learning appropriate behavior (Axline, 1947). Certain professionals do use movement intentionally as a medium to encourage emotional change in pupils; the average physical educator is not trained in this specialized area and thus should seek support from play therapists, when indicated.

Movement Education. A pupil who is easily distracted at first might not be able to benefit from open unstructured movement education as it is traditionally presented because randomly moving peers naturally interfere with order. On the other hand, highly structured story plays, creative drama, and mimetics might be used to address specific behavior characteristics. For example, pretending that you are a lumberjack (mimetics), sawing and chopping in a limited space can release tension and aggression. Imagining that the class is attending Disneyland (story play) using a small multipurpose room will enhance socialization for the pupil who is withdrawn.

When the physical educator thinks that a pupil can tolerate less structure, more traditional movement education activities can be increasingly emphasized. Movement education aims to promote inner experience and

the experience of interacting with the environment (including interaction with pupils in the environment) as it deals with the three factors that influence these feelings: movement, perception, and emotion. All pupils are encouraged to explore the possibilities of the elements of movement: force, time, and space. For example, these pupils can experience their own body weight (force) as they work with or against gravity. Then they can utilize that as a reference point for applying force in different situations. Time can be the pupil's perception of what is fast or slow, which determines perception of external speeds. Activities involving rhythm also can promote awareness of time. Space gives meaning to time and force and can be experienced by moving in certain paths, directions, and levels. The central point of focus and judgment is the pupil's own body. From there each pupil learns about objects outside the body or the environment.

Coping with Fear. Some pupils are overly fearful of heights and loss of equilibrium. These fears might originate in such activities as work on certain gymnastics apparatus (parallel bars, balance beam, trampoline), ladders, and ropes. The desensitization approach suggested in the aquatics and dance sections would again be useful here. Similarly, the physical educator could use a desensitizing strategy for the pupil who has excessive fear of undressing in the locker room, fear of enclosures, fear of people, fear of open spaces, fear of losing, or fear of falling. Collaboration with behavior specialists on the educational team cannot be stressed enough.

Grouping Pupils. The instructor of physical education should pay consistent attention to the grouping of pupils and its effect on interpersonal dynamics. The instructor should ask such questions as: Are pupil X and pupil Y ready for this activity together, not only in a psychomotor and cognitive but also an affective sense? Has the environment been appropriately structured? Will pupil X and pupil Y be able to relate appropriately?

Choosing Teams. Careful attention needs to be paid to the manner of choosing teams and a captain. One technique that appears to have considerable merit involves random selection of captains, followed by the selection of only half a team by the captains. The teacher selects the other half to each team by moving half of those remaining as a group to Team A and the remaining half to Team B. Other variations on this technique (discussed in Chapter 4) include drawing a team from a hat (blind draw), teacher preposting team members for review by pupils when first entering the class, separation of pupils by assignment of colors, team selection by using an alphabetical schema (e.g., all pupils with last names from A to M on one team and N to Z names on the other), squads competing against each other with squad membership varied each term, or pairing pupils as buddies who are then chosen as a twosome to be members of a team. In these systems the child with deficient skills and low self-esteem is not always chosen last and social sanctioning may be kept to a minimum if not eliminated altogether.

Modifying Rules. The rules of a game can, at times, be modified initially to enhance success by all participants. This is a major aspect of the Games Analysis Model reviewed in Chapter 4. Attention to this factor is especially important for pupils who are emotionally disordered. During teachable moments, rules of a game could be extrapolated to rules for living.

Precise Signals. Once an activity begins, pupils who are emotionally disordered particularly need precise "stop" signals. With-

out clear agreement on signals, behaviors can quickly deteriorate. Whistles, horns, voices, lights, and other stimuli are commonly used in physical education. Pupils need to practice the stop signals on a regular basis.

Controlled Aggression. Pupils who are overly aggressive and enjoy competition can be given activities in which they are encouraged to push, pull, beat, strike, kick, blow, or punch objects in a controlled environment. Teachers must be alert for teachable moments that allow a distinction to be made between appropriate and inappropriate behavior. One responsibility of teachers is to show pupils how to control aggression in acceptable ways. This is especially true for children characterized as emotionally disordered. Some activities that naturally incorporate controlled aggression include handball (kill shot), squash (kill shot), racquetball (kill shot), tennis (smash shot), badminton (smash shot), volleyball (spiking), golf (drive off the tee), cageball (push or punch), bag punching (punch), tetherball (hit), and kickball (kick). These activities are not indicated for the pupil who has no control over aggressive tendencies and who is noncompetitive.

Individualizing Instruction. We have stressed that pupils who are classified as emotionally disturbed will often require individualized instruction. However, we wish to emphasize that most of these pupils' physical education programs should be based on the same general objectives as are those for nondisabled pupils. Within this context, most activities in regular physical education classes are appropriate for pupils who are disturbed; only the teaching methods might vary. The interview with John Furst reinforces these points as well as others that we have espoused in this chapter.

JOHN FURST

John Furst is a classroom teacher of pupils who are emotionally disturbed in the Independent School District of Austin, Texas.

1. *How important is physical education to pupils who are emotionally disordered?*

Physical education for pupils who are emotionally disordered is very important. Historically the major problem in providing physical education to this population has been the inability of the teacher to manage their behavior. And because of this inability, instructional physical education programs were either eliminated or became a physical recreation program and given as a reward for appropriate classroom behavior. However, careful planning can drastically reduce the behavior problems of these pupils and improve their physical education programs.

2. *In your experience, are there any specific activities that you recommend that can be effectively used with this population?*

No, the manner in which the activity is presented is more important than the type or nature of the activity. In my judgment, the effectiveness of a physical education class with pupils who are emotionally disordered is often determined by the ability of the instructor to manage behavior effectively in, for example, controlling pupil frustration. Related to this, whatever the activity, the teacher must first build the subskills necessary to be effective in a particular activity before actually playing the actual game. Furthermore, the teacher must consider in selecting an activity, the varying levels of competitiveness of their pupils that may range from extremely competitive to not competitive at all.

3. *Can you suggest any behavior management techniques that can be used in physical education classes for pupils who are emotionally disordered?*

Behavior management techniques that have proven effective in classroom settings for pupils who are emotionally disordered can and should be borrowed and adapted by physical educators to meet the needs of these pupils. Behavioral expectations should be clear, concise, and consistently followed. Consequences for appropriate, as well as inappropriate behavior, should be preplanned. Attention must be given to early signs of misbehavior before the behavior escalates; don't ignore too much, hoping the problem will extinguish itself. Finally, special discipline problems may require special solutions if your current system of managing behavior is failing.

4. *Do you see a need for the physical educator to interact with a pupil's special education teacher?*

Regular communication between the special educator and the special physical educator benefits everyone. Information concerning special characteristics, idiosyncrasies, interests, warning signs, etc., can be shared. A simple note or verbal communication concerning a significant behavioral problem that may have just occurred prior to the pupil arriving in a classroom or gymnasium can prepare the physical educator. Lack of this type of information may lead to further escalation and potentially dangerous results.

Pupils who are emotionally disordered in my self-contained class bring back a daily evaluation form from the regular physical education class they attended. The pupils self-evaluate their behavior (from "zero"—very inappropriate—to "four"—very appropriate). The regular physical educator, using the same form, also evaluates the pupils' picture of the previous class period and alerts me to significant progress or problems. I, in turn, walk to the physical education class with my pupils and share pertinent information with the teacher. This type of system is quick, easy, and effective.

Deafness and Hearing Impairment

DEFINITION, CAUSES, AND SCOPE

Definition

Those who have significant problems with their hearing include individuals with a hearing impairment and individuals with deafness. With regard to the education of pupils who have such problems, the U.S. Department of Education has defined these two groups in the Rules of P.L. 101-476 as follows:

"Hearing impairment" means an impairment in hearing, whether permanent or fluctuating, that adversely affects a child's educational performance but that is not included under the definition of deafness in this section.

"Deaf" means a hearing impairment that is so severe that the child is impaired in processing linguistic information through hearing, with or without amplification, that adversely affects a child's educational performance (*Federal Register*, September 29, 1992, p. 44801).

As implied in these definitions, hearing problems can range from slight to severe. Only when a person is classified as profoundly hearing impaired is the word *deaf* justified and properly used. All educators need to understand that only a few pupils are deaf; most pupils who are hearing impaired have some residual hearing that can and should be used in the instructional environment.

Two primary characteristics of any sound are loudness and pitch. *Loudness*, or intensity of sound, is measured on an arbitrary scale called the decibel (dB) scale. The point of first audible sound for people with normal hearing is 0 dB; normal hearing ranges from 0 to 25 dB loss in the best ear without the assistance of any artificial aid (hearing aid). The hearing losses associated with commonly used levels of hearing impairment and deafness include

- Slight   = 25–40 dB loss
- Mild   = 41–55 dB loss
- Marked   = 56–70 dB loss
- Severe   = 71–90 dB loss
- Profound = 91 dB or greater loss

To clarify, normal speech 10 feet away is approximately 45 to 65 dB loud, whereas a freight train passing 10 feet away is approximately 90 to 120 dB loud. Thus a person who cannot hear the train is deaf.

The *pitch* of the sound, or the frequency of the sound wave, is expressed in hertz (Hz), or cycles per second. Humans with normal hearing can usually perceive any sound within the range of 500 to 2,000 Hz, which is also the frequency range generally used in hearing tests. To get a better perspective, consider that 500 to 2,000 Hz is the range of normal speech, whereas a piano's frequency range is approximately 30 (lowest note) to 4,000 Hz (highest note).

The impact of a hearing loss is not only determined by dB and Hz acuity loss but also by the age at which a person experiences the loss. We live in a communications-oriented world that depends heavily on hearing. The earlier in life a child loses this precious sense, the graver is the circumstance. Problems multiply for a child who is not only totally deaf but is born deaf (congenital loss). Congenital hearing loss significantly interferes with language development, which primarily occurs during the first five years of life. The greater the hearing loss at birth, the more severe this interference. The most serious cases of hearing loss are usually diag-

nosed at birth or within the first year, as the infant obviously does not respond motorically or orally to auditory stimuli. On the other hand, a hearing loss acquired after language and communication skills have already developed will usually not interfere as much with ongoing language learning, although it often brings difficult emotional adjustments. Problems of adjustment to a hearing loss are similar in many respects to those for any other disability.

The effects of a hearing problem are also related to the type and site of hearing loss. Four types are commonly cited: conductive, sensorineural, central, and psychogenic. A specific person's hearing loss can be a combination of two or more of these types.

A *conductive* hearing loss originates in the outer or middle ear or the eustachian tube (see Figure 8.1). Most acquired (adventitious) losses are conductive. In a conductive hearing loss, air-conducted (versus bone-conducted) vibrations to the inner ear are obstructed because of wax accumulation, infection (otitis media), or fluid buildup. Because sound waves comprising speech travel through air waves, an individual with a conductive hearing loss will have some receptive language hearing loss. On the other hand, because people with conductive hearing loss retain bone conduction, they tend to speak softly, because their own voices reverberate in their ears. This type of hearing loss is often correctable by such means as draining, medication, surgery, or use of a hearing aid.

Sensorineural hearing losses are generally more serious. A sensorineural loss is an inner ear complication that can involve damage to the auditory nerve (eighth cranial nerve), nerve fibers, or one of the structures of the inner ear (e.g., cochlea). Hearing aids are helpful in only some cases. A sensorineural hearing loss is generally irreversible.

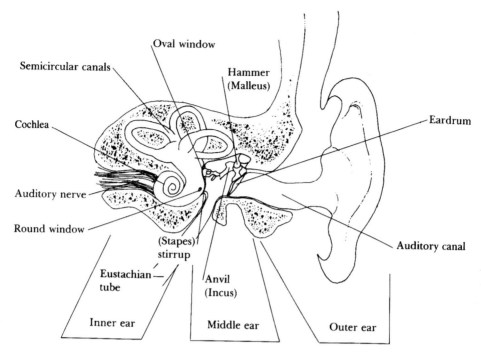

FIGURE 8.1   The human ear.   *(Reprinted with the permission of Macmillan College Publishing Company from* Exceptional Children: An Introductory Survey to Special Education *by William L. Heward and Michael D. Orlansky. Copyright © 1980 by Macmillan College Publishing Company, Inc.)*

Central hearing loss is a neurological hearing complication that originates somewhere between the eighth cranial nerve and the temporal lobe of the cerebral cortex, where auditory messages are interpreted. Central hearing loss is similar to sensorineural loss in that it is generally serious and irreversible.

The fourth type of hearing loss, *psychogenic*, is a psychological hearing disability with no known organic cause. Like the other types, it can range in severity from slight to profound; it may be reversible through appropriate counseling.

Teachers are not diagnosticians; however, they are in a position to observe pupils for evidence of hearing problems. If consistently observed in a pupil, the following signals might indicate a need for a referral to an audiologist:

- Poor speech
- Tilted head or leaning toward source of sound
- Asks too often that statements be repeated
- Recurring earaches
- Fluid drains from ear
- Daydreaming and inattention
- Balance problems

Teachers can use informal hearing assessment techniques—the watch tick, the whisper, and conversational tests—to verify suspicions of a hearing problem. In each of these, the tester varies the distance of a constant, steady sound. The sound is directed at the pupil being tested. If a hearing loss is still suspected, a test by an audiologist with a pure-tone audiometer is the next step. This instrument not only tests for dB and Hz acuity loss, but is also used to check for air and bone conduction in both ears.

Causes

Hearing problems can often be traced to specific genetic (hereditary) or environmental causes. However, some hearing problems cannot be specifically attributed to any cause. According to the National Information Center on Deafness (1984), approximately 50 percent of all cases of profound hearing loss have a probable genetic link. In addition, more than 50 genetic syndromes are associated with hearing impairment and deafness. This poses serious questions, particularly for prospective parents who have relatives classified as hearing impaired or deaf. Genetic counseling appears to be essential in this situation.

Environmental causes of hearing loss are also prominent. Major among them are the following: maternal rubella, premature birth, prolonged labor, meningitis, accidents, toxicity from drug use, mumps, measles, otitis media due to bacteria, cold, or allergy, real or imagined psychic stress (psychogenic), presbycusia (deafness linked to aging), Rh blood incompatibility, scarlet fever, influenza, encephalitis, diphtheria, whooping cough, typhoid fever, anoxia, pneumonia, glandular fever, chicken pox, brain tumors (could be genetic), outer or middle ear blockage due to wax or fluid accumulation, otosclerosis (bone transformation disease that obstructs the movement of the middle ear bones), and noise. Some of these conditions cause other disabilities as well; and hearing impairment or deafness can be accompanied by vision loss, motor problems, or retardation. Among these causes, otitis media is very prominent in elementary school-aged children. The eustachian tubes in children are short and wide, which permits foreign agents to move from the nose and throat to the middle ear. It is not uncommon for children to have recurring bouts of otitis media and accompanying temporary hearing losses.

Physical educators can help prevent the development of hearing problems by paying particular attention to certain pupil behaviors. For example, if a child complains of an earache, the instructor would be prudent in not allowing the child to swim, to participate in outdoor activities if the weather is cold or in the presence of key allergens, or to take part in particularly noisy games. Teachers should also pay keen attention to safety practices that help prevent injury to the hearing mechanism, such as requiring all pupils to wear regulation batting helmets in baseball.

Scope

Approximately 15 million people have hearing problems in the United States, and of this number about 3 million are of school age. This figure includes those with slight, mild, marked, severe, and profound hearing loss, with the scope decreasing as the severity of hearing loss increases. It is estimated that approximately 6 percent of all pupils have hearing problems, but only a small percentage of these require special education services. The federal government reports (U.S. Department of Education, 1992) that only 0.10 percent of all American pupils aged 6–21 ($N = 59{,}312$) were actually classified as either hearing impaired or deaf and were receiving special education services during the 1990–91 school year.

Children with slight and mild hearing losses are typically educated in regular classes, as are pupils with other slight and mild disabling conditions. In addition, more and more children with severe losses are being taught in the public schools, although many children classified as deaf are still attending separate day and residential schools. Interestingly, fewer than 10 percent of pupils enrolled in residential schools for the deaf have no residual hearing. In this connection, the National Information Center on Deafness (1984) reports that only one out of eight pupils with a hearing loss is deaf.

There are a few institutions of higher education geared for individuals with serious hearing problems. Gallaudet College, in Washington, D.C., is the only accredited liberal arts college for this population in the United States, offering programs through the doctoral level. The National Technical Institute for the Deaf (NTID) is part of the Rochester Institute of Technology in New York State. It provides vocational training for those who are hearing impaired and deaf. Both institutions are funded by the government. Gallaudet serves only those classified as hearing impaired and deaf, whereas NTID emphasizes the integration of college students who can hear with those students who have significant hearing challenges.

The number of people with hearing problems who need special services will probably increase, for several reasons: Auditory assessment methods are becoming more precise; people are living longer, which increases their susceptibility to hearing defects; more infants at risk are being saved at birth; and noise pollution is on the rise.

CHARACTERISTICS AND INSTRUCTIONAL STRATEGIES

Educating a child who is hearing impaired or deaf requires perhaps more technical skills than does teaching a child with any other type of disability, with the exception of multi-

ple and severe/profound disabilities. In this regard it is almost universally agreed that the greatest challenge to teachers (including physical educators) of pupils with hearing problems is effective and efficient communication. In fact, the communication problems can be so great that some experts argue that this type of pupil should probably not be placed in regular physical education and sport programs (Butterfield, 1991).

All educators can improve their instructional abilities by learning to communicate in a variety of contexts with all types of pupils. Manual communication through gross signing (hand signals that signify words or phrases) might enhance instruction with both hearing pupils and pupils with hearing problems in the physical education setting, which commonly involves a large space. In addition, use of gross signs might help hearing pupils to communicate better with their peers who have hearing deficits. Further, Birch (1975) strongly suggests in-service training in rudimentary gross signing and fingerspelling for teachers who have one or more pupils with hearing problems in class.

Physical educators can use both traditional and nontraditional techniques for communicating with pupils, whether they have hearing problems or not. Traditional sign language, however, may have greater acceptance among the members of the typical educational team and individuals who are hearing impaired or deaf. Traditional signs can be learned from the following recommended books:

O'Rourke, T. J. (1973). *A basic course in manual communication.* Silver Spring, MD: National Association of the Deaf.

Riekenhof, L. L. (1985). *The joy of signing.* Springfield, MO: Gospel Printing House.

Figure 8.2 shows the traditional fingerspelling alphabet and numeral system. Figure 8.3 shows some gross signs from American Sign Language (ASL)—a widely used

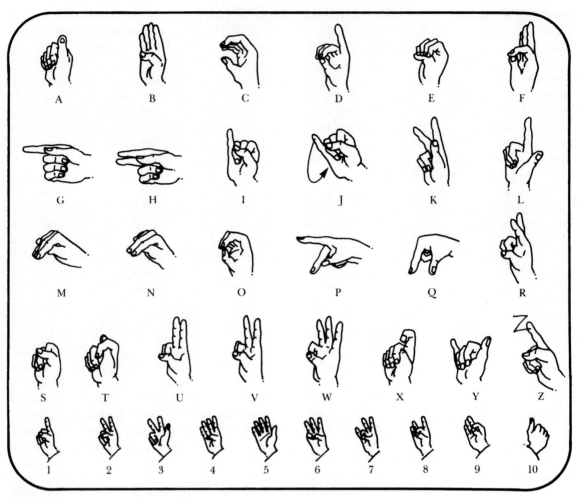

FIGURE 8.2 Standard fingerspelling and number signs.

sign language—relevant to physical education.

On the nontraditional side, Schmidt and Dunn (1980) suggest using novel, yet easily understood, signs displayed on poster boards. The signs can be varied from concrete to more abstract to signify concepts of body awareness, spatial awareness, and quality of movement. For example, a picture of hands might signify the use of only hands in a movement task, arrows might connote direction of movement, and a steady wavy line with many peaks and valleys might indicate a regular, quick movement flow.

Whichever approach to language education is decided upon, all members of the educational team (including the physical educator) should consistently use the same communication approach in dealing with a pupil. Further, it is important to use commu-

FIGURE 8.3   Selected signs important to physical educators. (Source: *26 captioned signs provided by Steve Butterfield, Ph.D., University of Maine at Orono*)

"IMPROVE"
Place little finger side of open palmed right hand on lower portion of extended left hand. Walk hand up the arm toward shoulder.

"GOOD"
Place fingertips of open hand at mouth. Move hand out and away from mouth, ending with palm of hand fading upward.

"SOCCER"
Bring right hand upward in an arc striking the index finger against the left downturned palm twice, i.e. pantomime kicking a soccer ball.

"TRY, ATTEMPT"
Starting with hands in "e" position, palms facing up in front of the waist, move the hands in an arc, turning the wrists over while moving.

"SLOW, SLOWLY"
Drag the fingers of the right open hand back toward the body over the left open hand, both palms are down with fingers forward.

"SIT"
With hands in "h" position, lay the fingers of the right hand across the fingers of the left hand both palms facing down.

FIGURE 8.3 (continued)

"HOCKEY"
With the index finger of one hand curved in the shape of a hockey stick, pantomime a sticking motion on the open palm of the other hand.

"HURRY"
Place hands in "h" position, palms facing each other and fingers pointing forward; move hands in a bouncing pattern while moving forward.

"GAME"
Make fists with both hands, thumbs sticking up, move fists toward each other, knuckles bumping and moving upward.

"CATCH"
Make a closed fist with one hand. With the other hand open, pantomime catching a small object, ending with closed fist on top of the other hand.

"DIFFICULT, HARD, PROBLEM"
Strike the knuckles of both bent "V" hands, palms toward the body, as they pass each other in alternating up and down movements.

"RUN"
Hook right index finger into notch of left thumb; point left index finger; move hands forward quickly.

FIGURE 8.3 (continued)

"STOP"
Little finger side of open-palmed right hand comes down on horizontally held open-palmed left hand.

"ATTENTION, PAY ATTENTION, CONCENTRATE
Move both open hands from the side of the face, palms facing inward, keeping the fingers pointing upward.

"BALL"
Pantomime an imaginary ball with both hands.

"LINE UP"
Hold the right hand in front of the chest, palm facing left. Place the left hand in line near the right little finger, palm facing right. Move hands apart. Pantomime people standing in line.

"CIRCLE AROUND ME"
Place hands in front of body, fingers pointing down and index fingers touching; move hands away from each other describing a circle or semi circle.

"JUMP"
Place first two fingers of one hand ("V" shape) in standing position on palm of the other hand. Bend fingers and move upward, pantomiming a jumping movement.

FIGURE 8.3 (continued)

"EXERCISE"
Place both arms at right angles; flex and return to 90°
position several times as if pantomiming calesthenics.

"SWIM"
Place both hands in front of body, palms facing down.
Pantomime swimming motion.

"TERRIFIC, WONDERFUL, GREAT, FANTASTIC"
Pat the air repeatedly with both hands in "five position.

"STRONG"
Make fists with both hands. Raise arms to "muscle man"
posture.

FIGURE 8.3 (continued)

"WALK"
Alternately swing both hands back and forth
from in front of the body, palms facing down,
back to the sides, palms facing back. Pantomime
movement of the legs while walking.

"DIVE"
With fingertips touching, pantomime
diving motion.

"TENNIS"
With right hand, pantomime a forehand striking pattern.

"BASEBALL"
Pantomime the baseball batting
motion.

nication techniques that this type of pupil can use not only during the school years but also later in life.

Let us now turn to other primary characteristics that commonly describe pupils who have hearing problems. As in the other categorical chapters, instructional strategies that are pertinent to the work of physical educators with this type of pupil are highlighted.

Hearing Impairment and Deafness

CHARACTERISTICS	INSTRUCTIONAL STRATEGIES
Psychomotor	
1. By definition, the pupil who has a hearing problem has a partial or full hearing loss. Few children are totally deaf.	1. Use other senses for instructional purposes. Pay particular attention to the use of visual aids, such as bulletin boards, slides, chalkboards, videotapes, captioned films, overhead transparencies, mirrors, and demonstrations. Use manual guidance and encourage the use of residual hearing ability.
2. Pupils with hearing problems are prone to ear infections.	2. When a pupil has an infection, avoid activities in a setting with excessive changes in temperature (e.g., cold), dampness (e.g., swimming), or dust.
3. Some pupils have perpetual ringing in their ears (tinnitus).	3. Avoid excessive noise in the gymnasium, pool, or playground.
4. Loss of hearing ability eliminates auditory background feedback, which adversely affects the ability to relate to space and motion.	4. Teach pupils to differentiate spatial relations via gross movement using either movement education or structured free play. These activities are particularly important during the early elementary years.
5. Pupils with hearing problems have a tendency toward faulty posture.	5. Model good static and dynamic postures. Use mirrors and other types of visual feedback and reinforce proper postures.
6. At times, these pupils will demonstrate purposeless movement ("deafisms").	6. Directly intervene to extinguish inappropriate mannerisms, because they will not disappear by themselves. They will probably become more evident if not attended to. Use operant conditioning techniques (see Chapter 13).
7. Some individuals classified as hearing impaired or deaf have a shuffling gait. This problem relates to their inability to hear movement and to feel the security of continual contact with the ground.	7. Use pupils who can hear and yourself as models. Use audiovisual feedback and a mirror as techniques. Physically prompt a child to lift his or her feet by gently tapping legs. Reinforce any nonshuffling walking.
8. The motor development of pupils with hearing problems is typically behind the norm (Cratty, Cratty & Cornell, 1986; Butterfield, 1987; Myklebust, 1964).	8. The whole range of developmental motor activities is especially important for these children. Stress efficient walking, running, climbing, and jumping along with eye-limb coordination skills because they will be used throughout life. Mirror and videotape feedback can be effectively used to improve motor patterns.
9. Overall, these pupils appear to be less physically fit than pupils who can hear. Abdominal strength is especially inferior for 10- to 17-year-olds with hearing problems (Winnick & Short, 1986). Their tendency to be sedentary is one reason. Another reason is that they spend their psychological and physical energy in struggling to communicate most of the time.	9. Offer strength (especially abdominal), cardiovascular, and flexibility activities at least three times weekly. Make maximal use of visual aids. Chart each pupil's progress and encourage participation in fitness-oriented activities at home. Use individualized motivational techniques as often as possible.

10. Balance (static and dynamic) and agility are usually deficient in pupils with inner ear complications.

Cognitive
1. Most pupils who have hearing problems have normal intelligence, but they are typically well behind their "normal" peers in school achievement due to their communication problems. The ability to comprehend abstractions is usually affected. Overall achievement decreases with increases in hearing loss.
2. Deficits in communication present the greatest challenge to pupils who are hearing impaired or deaf.

3. Language skills of the pupil with a hearing problem are often enhanced through the use of hearing aids that amplify sound. Hearing aids may be placed on the chest, behind the ear, or on glasses. However, hearing aids will not eliminate the distortion caused by a sensorineural defect. Most pupils who need an aid wear a one-ear (monaural) type. See Figure 8.4 for an example.

10. Avoid altitude work (ropes, apparatus, ladders). Agility drills that involve other randomly moving bodies are also usually not advised.

1. Do not treat these pupils as though they are mentally retarded. Physical educators (and all others on the educational team) need to focus conscientiously on this pupil's auditory problem as the primary cause of poor achievement.

2. Lip- or speechreading and speech training, auditory training, signing, total communication (combination of the previous three systems), reading, and writing are the receptive and expressive communication methods used by these pupils. Imitating demonstrated actions of the teacher or a peer and kinesthesis are other communication modes especially important for those who teach physical education.

   Use only essential words or actions to transmit any message in a well-lighted area. Prevent glare from being in the pupil's eyes. Repeat oral messages differently if communication breaks down. Do not exaggerate lip movements for speech readers. Speak slightly slower than your normal pace so that more lipreading is possible. Remain in a stationary position and have the child close to, at the same level, and face-to-face with you. Use a paper and pencil if absolutely necessary. Avoid circle formations; opt for staggered formations.

   Demonstrate physical skills with your back to the pupil to avoid mirror-image confusion, but do not speak unless you are facing the pupil. Physically guide pupils through desired movements when necessary, and use essential manual signs where and when appropriate. Funds from P.L. 101-476 can be used to provide an interpreter, if necessary.

   A portable communication board could be used in a movement context. Pictures on the board could represent specific motor skills, essential people, and selected self-help signs (e.g., toilet). The number of items per board would depend on the pupil.

3. Find out how a pupil's hearing aid is put on, removed, and maintained, because some activities require removal of the aid and some permit its use. Also note the fact that sweat is not good for the aid. Have the pupil keep a spare battery for the aid. The pupil should not wear starched clothes or any clothing made of crisp fabric that could be a source of auditory static. Remember that, once the hearing aid is removed, audition becomes much more limited. Encourage the child to wear the aid whenever possible to stimulate language development. When talking to a person with a hearing aid, do not talk into the earpiece or lean so close that he or she cannot watch your mouth.

FIGURE 8.4 The most common hearing aid used in physical education.

4. Aside from using hearing aids and residual hearing ability, pupils with hearing problems compensate for auditory loss primarily by using vision. They observe signs, gestures, and body language, and decipher environmental cues. The tactile sense is a secondary mode used for communication.

5. The most competent lipreader may determine only one third to one half of another's speech. Only a minority of speech sounds can be visibly deciphered.

Affective

1. Pupils with hearing problems tend to be lonely and shut out from the world. They tend to associate mainly with others who have auditory losses.

2. Young children who have hearing deficits are most prone to social deficits because they have few natural play opportunities.

3. Pupils with severe hearing problems are generally silent. They seldom laugh.

4. Pupils with hearing problems tend to be overly anxious and fearful, partially because they cannot be easily warned of dangers.

5. Those who have acquired significant hearing loss later in life may be prone to depression.

4. Use attention-getters of various kinds, such as raised hands, foot stomping, remote control devices, flashing lights, low tones, and colored flags. Highlight important stimuli and eliminate distractions. Make sure that the teaching environment has adequate lighting and that bright background light (e.g., the sun) does not interfere with communication.

5. Make sure that major directions are understood through repetition or use of a buddy system before beginning an activity. Directions are much more difficult to transmit of a pupil is already moving.

1. Give social activities the highest priority. Show peers who can hear the effects of hearing loss through stimulation and actual use of signs.

2. Early intervention is critical for youngsters with congenital hearing loss. Assist these children by providing opportunities for play. Expose young children who can hear to pupils' with hearing problems. Reinforce their interaction.

3. Offer a wide variety of physical activities that involve others. Robust movement experiences stimulate the emotions.

4. Classes in which these pupils are placed should be small, from seven to ten pupils. Orientation to facilities and equipment must precede any activity. Teach pupils how to fall. Complete all essential directives before the movement starts, and use visual and tactile signals.

5. Be optimistic and positive; it might become contagious. Highlight fun experiences in any movement context.

INDICATED AND NONINDICATED ACTIVITIES

Almost all activities offered in a regular physical education program are appropriate for pupils who are hearing impaired or deaf. However, the increased danger caused by auditory loss is of special concern for physical educators. Guidelines for compliance with P.L. 101-476 in physical education with these pupils follow.

Physical and Motor Fitness

Owing to their tendency to be sedentary, most pupils who are hearing impaired or deaf need programs that stress fitness. There is a wide array of appropriate activities requiring strength, cardiovascular endurance, and flexibility that need little or no adaptation. Many fitness exercises that can be conducted without equipment or materials can be performed close to or on the ground. Bent-knee sit-ups is one example of a needed exercise (particularly for this population) that can be done on the floor.

For exercises when the body is normally erect, pupils with significant balance problems should be permitted to take a position with a lower center of gravity. Pupils without balance problems do not need that adaptation and should be allowed to participate fully in all fitness-related activities, including

- Weight lifting with portable weights
- Weight lifting with a universal system
- Isometric strength training
- Calisthenics
- Middle distance and long distance runs
- Fitness tests
- Fitness-oriented circuit training courses
- Fitness-oriented obstacle courses
- Self-testing activities that enhance fitness
- Home programs of fitness training

One idea for fitness instruction is to project slides of planned progressive activities that automatically change every few minutes. Slides of stretching activities, strength-building activities, aerobic activities, and others could be incorporated. The teacher is then free to help individual pupils. For younger pupils, popular cartoon characters could be portrayed doing the exercises on slides that pupils then imitate. This concept could also

be useful in other areas of instruction in the physical education program.

Fitness training that includes a social element is even more valuable for a person (young or old) who has hearing deficits. A group committed to fitness training within a social context is the Aerobics and Fitness Training Institute of the Deaf at Gallaudet University in Washington, D.C. The mission of the institute is to provide state-of-the-art fitness opportunities for mixed groups of persons, with and without hearing deficits, in communicatively accessible environments. These opportunities are further enhanced through the institute's ongoing research projects, consultation with outside groups (including schools) and individuals, and the preparation of fitness instructors who are hearing impaired or deaf.

Fundamental Motor Skills and Patterns

Aside from the standard forms of motor development skill that should be taught to all pupils, pupils who are hearing impaired or deaf particularly need activities that enhance spatial orientation, rhythm, posture, and balance. One nonthreatening method to develop these fundamental skills is movement education (see Chapter 3). The guided discovery and experimentation with new and familiar movements that this approach promotes aid in reducing overall anxiety concerning movement in general. In addition, after engaging in a variety of movements, the pupil will probably be less apprehensive when a novel movement is required in the future. Finally, quality of movement should be stressed after fear of random movement subsides.

Balance activities are one of the greatest needs of those pupils who have equilibrium deficits. Even though the equilibrium centers may be irreversibly damaged, purportedly balancing can be improved by refining the other senses (especially kinesthetic and visual). Simple balance-oriented tasks with limited danger are those that can be performed on the floor in a bent or standing position or involve limited nonsupport in a well-padded or cushioned area. Balance activities that involve height (ladders, ropes, high balance beams) generally should be avoided. Spinning activities are also not indicated for those with balance problems. Simple trampolining activities are very useful for the development of balance and coordination. When planning activities, remember that signing will not be effective when a pupil is bouncing.

Rhythm can be effectively taught using vision, residual hearing, and the haptic (tactile and kinesthetic) sense. Many movements (such as marching) can be taught successfully through imitation of others. Cymbals, low tone drums, bells, low tone whistles, phonographs, microphones, and megaphones can create vibrations and auditory sensations that pupils with hearing deficits can feel.

In the course of teaching fundamental motor skills and patterns, other perceptual abilities can also be addressed. In turn, the use of such stimuli as various shapes, sizes, and colors in physical education can affect the development of concepts, divergent thinking, and abstractions.

Aquatics

Pupils with hearing deficits can participate in most swimming activities. A few precautions, however, are to be noted: Hearing aids should be removed before the pupil enters the water. In consequence, the instructor will need to adjust his or her teaching techniques because the pupil will not be able to hear as well, if at all. Also, otitis media, ear surgery, ventilation tubes, or medicine in the ear might temporarily prevent participation in aquatics. If a child's parents and physician indicate that he or she can swim, earplugs or cotton and a tight swim cap should be worn.

For activities in deep water and during free swim periods, instructors should design a buddy system for pupils with hearing deficits. This pupil's buddy should be able to hear and be a competent swimmer. The buddy should be required always to face the partner (see Figure 8.5).

A swim stroke that allows the swimmer's head to remain above the water will be needed for the pupil who either becomes disoriented under water or who medically should not have water in the ear(s). Underwater swimming is not generally indicated, and diving is sometimes not recommended.

FIGURE 8.5   A pupil with hearing deficits swims with guidance from a buddy.

Diving not only necessitates underwater activity but also involves an impact between the hearing mechanisms and the water surface.

For those pupils who can tolerate some underwater activity, teaching the concepts and mechanics of inhaling and exhaling might take longer than usual. This difficulty relates not only to communication problems in general but also to an inability, at times, to comprehend cause-and-effect relationships. The use of instructional progressions is, therefore, indicated; the instructor should make no assumptions about pupil competence.

Dance

Dance offers numerous benefits to pupils who are hearing impaired or deaf. The movements associated with any structured or unstructured dance directly affect psychomotor development. Perhaps more importantly, the environment created is conducive to socialization, which is so necessary for these pupils. In addition, dance can act as therapy; it can address emotional needs by prompting creative outlets, providing opportunities for nonverbal communication, and encouraging emotional release. Some say that for pupils with hearing problems, dance can especially be viewed as communication through movement. In fact, "some deaf people think in terms of motion. Consequently the area of the dance may have relatively more importance in the lives of the deaf than of the hearing" (Wisher, 1969, p. 81). Finally, dance is particularly valuable for the pupil who has hearing deficits because it provides a natural environment for auditory training to encourage use of residual hearing. In this regard, hearing aids should be worn consistently during dance activities, further increasing the chance for social interactions.

Specific dance-related activities and methods have proven effective with these pupils. The use of percussion instruments, such as a tamborine, can be quite effective. Such instruments are highly motivating because they allow the child to feel the music. As another example, vibrations from the floor (stamping) or from the surface of an instrument (touching) can serve as cues. Instructors can also use percussion instruments (such as the low tone drum) and amplified music. Low tones are usually better deciphered than high tones; amplified music encourages the use of residual hearing. The teacher of physical education should also encourage pupils to take off their shoes and use their bare or socked feet to pick up vibrations better. Related to this, because bone is a good conductor of sound, allow pupils to touch the source of music (if possible) in order to feel the vibrations. Place the music source on the floor to enhance floor vibrations, and allow pupils to dance as close as possible to the machine. It is a good idea to move from the out-of-doors or gymnasium to a room with a low ceiling. This way the sound of the music will be better contained.

In teaching a new dance pattern, the instructor can use obvious clapping by others, slight physical prompts, an oversized metronome, and modeling. In addition, pupils who are hearing impaired or deaf can learn tempo and rhythm as they relate to a dance through the tactile sensations of the palms of their own hands (clapping) or the soles of their own feet (stamping). Further, particularly with more complex dances, these pupils can sometimes walk through related movements or learn dances using the part–whole approach. As with other activities, when demonstrating an element of a dance, the instructor's back should be turned to the pupils in order to avoid mirror-image confusion.

Individual and Group Activities

Pupils who are hearing impaired or deaf can be successful in all types of individual, dual, and group games. Here are some suggested adaptations and guidelines for a program consisting of individual and group activities.

1. Games with few rules, no fouling, and minimal boundaries promote immediate success. Any traditional game can be modified by the teacher, at times with the assistance of the pupils, in order to facilitate success.

2. When the rules of a game need to be rigorously enforced, physical educators must use visual aids throughout the class and make sure that the basic rules and signals are fully understood by all participants before the activity starts.

3. Pupils who are hearing impaired or deaf (especially the deaf) can be given written materials to supplement instruction. These materials could repeat the rules and strategy of a game already introduced in class.

4. For activities in which the head contacts an object or another person, all hearing aids should be removed. These activities are completely inappropriate for those pupils prone to further hearing mechanism dam-

age. Activities such as boxing, battleball, and football are included in this category.

5. Games such as Blind Man's Bluff and relays in which the eyes are covered are generally not indicated for all pupils without adequate hearing ability.

6. Use hand signals for relays and drills. In graded group games such as Call Ball, have "It" point to or gently tag participants while calling out numbers for those pupils who have some residual hearing ability. Use pennies in games to identify players more easily. Also, use flashing lights, raised hands, or colored flags as signals.

7. Use low tone drums and whistles. Not all whistles and drums are set at a constant pitch.

8. Golf requires a partner who can hear to respond to such auditory warnings as "fore."

The social element of games is at least as important as the physical skills acquired and maintained. Competencies in leisure time activities are valuable after a pupil who is hearing impaired or deaf leaves school.

We conclude this chapter with an interview of a physical educator who has taught pupils with hearing problems for a number of years.

Steve Butterfield

Dr. Steven Butterfield is an associate professor of special physical education and coordinator of the Department of Physical Education at the University of Maine at Orono.

1. *What are some of the myths about pupils with hearing impairments that have implications for the physical educator?*

First is the uninformed notion that these pupils are less intelligent than so-called normal people. Nothing could be further from the truth. In fact, when the cognitive abilities of pupils with a hearing impairment (HI) are measured by appropriately trained examiners, the results show a normal pattern of IQ scores. Another myth is that they are somehow motor deficient. With the exception of those who have balance problems due to vestibular dysfunction, most children who have a HI perform at levels comparable to the general population in motor and physical fitness. The many successes of those who are athletes at the national and international levels lend further testimony to the fact that individuals labeled with a HI can perform very well in physical education and sport. The implications are obvious: Have high expectations and make every effort to facilitate two-way communication.

2. *How do you feel about the mainstreaming of pupils with hearing impairments?*

This is a tough one. But one must keep in mind that the inclusion/mainstreaming movement was initiated by special education generalists and not by leaders in deaf education or by prominent people who are deaf. Consequently, the residential school population has declined, and placement decisions are frequently made by individuals who are unfamiliar with the needs of these pupils. An even greater concern perhaps is that the education of children who have a HI is often in the hands of sign language interpreters as opposed to trained educators of this population. What I'm leading up to is that the residential school for these pupils should continue to be a viable placement option for them. I also believe that these schools should expand their outreach and consultant functions and work cooperatively with school districts, especially in isolated rural communities. Bottom line: This type of pupil should be placed in the least restrictive environment. For them, a restrictive environment is usually one where communication is limited. Consequently, we must remind ourselves that for many children who are deaf, the residential school *is* less restrictive.

3. *What are the most effective and efficient communication techniques that physical educators can use with the pupil who has a hearing impairment?*

First, if a child communicates manually, the teacher should learn some sign language. Although it may take years to master sign language, basic skills can be acquired in a relatively short time. Perhaps the best way is to enroll in a sign language course and practice communicating as much as possible with individuals who are HI. Communicating verbal information to the very young child can be especially difficult. So, whenever possible, let the environment help you. Cutout footprints can be used to prompt correct foot position; carefully designed obstacles can tell where to climb, how high to jump, or how low to crawl. A little imagination can go a long way. Of course, there is also common sense. Teachers should remember to provide these pupils with a direct view of their face. Lipreading is difficult when the face is viewed from a sharp angle. When outdoors, the sun and wind should not be in the pupil's eyes when the instructor is speaking.

4. *Do you have any advice for the physical educator when initially being oriented to a new pupil who happens to be hearing impaired?*

Number 1—Don't panic! Chances are the kid is a pretty skillful mover. I believe the first goal should be the acceptance of this type of child by his or her peers. This can be accomplished partially by the enthusiastic acceptance of the pupil by the physical education teacher. You won't need to adapt any activity or make many overt changes in rules or procedures, so stress communication and conduct business as usual.

Visual
Impairment

DEFINITION, CAUSES, AND SCOPE

Definition

Visual impairment has both educational and legal definitions. Based on the implementing Rules of P.L. 101-476, the educational definition is: "'Visual impairment including blindness' means an impairment in vision that, even with correction, adversely affects a child's educational performance. The term includes both partial sight and blindness" (*Federal Register*, September 29, 1992, p. 44802). The terms *partial vision* and *legally blind* have more precise legal definitions for use in educational placements, employment, and other purposes. Ten percent of normal vision in the best eye after correction is considered legal blindness, and visual acuity equal to approximately 30 percent of normal vision under the same conditions is consid-

ered partial vision. Partial vision also includes those individuals who fall somewhere between 10 and 30 percent of normal vision. In addition, legal blindness is defined according to field of vision. If a person can perceive sight in only a 20-degree (180 degrees is normal) field of vision, he or she is considered legally blind, even if visual acuity within that range is normal.

The most common method used to determine visual acuity at different distances is the Snellen Test. For this test, the subject is seated 20 feet from a chart that contains block letters in rows. (Another version of the Snellen Test places the subject only 14 inches from the chart.) All letters in a row are the same size, and the rows decrease in size going down the chart. The most common criterion for normal vision not requiring correction is the ability to read a certain row of symbols from a distance of 20 feet. This is called 20/20 vision. As vision decreases, the denominator increases. For example, the individual who is partially sighted would have a Snellen score of 20/70 at best. In other words, at 20 feet, that person can first read letters that a person with normal vision could read at 70 feet. Similarly, for the person who is legally blind, the Snellen score would be at best 20/200, indicating that this individual must be 20 feet away to read what a person with normal visual acuity could read at 200 feet.

It is critical to understand that a person with legal blindness can still have some residual vision. Thus more specific terminology is needed to describe visual impairments. Three other classifications have come into common use. From least to most restrictive, these terms include *travel motion*, in which an individual has less than 20/200 visual acuity, yet can still perceive objects well enough to move around safely; *light perception*, in which an individual cannot determine objects, yet can perceive a bright light shown directly into the eyes; and *total blindness*, in which there exists negligible or no light perception whatsoever. We use the term *visual impairment* to include all classifications of visual difficulty, from partially sighted to totally blind. Note that we speak of "vision" instead of "sight," because the former connotes the ability to interpret what is seen, whereas the latter refers only to the physiological ability to see or receive visual stimuli.

Physical educators are being increasingly challenged to integrate pupils with some degree of visual impairment in their regular classes. This new population of pupils usually includes those with some functional or residual vision. Physical educators also have pupils who have never been diagnosed as having significant visual impairment but have compensated in various ways to offset their visual limitations. In fact, a pupil might not even perceive an existing visual problem.

Such pupils have no frame of reference related to their disability. Teachers, therefore, need to be keen observers in order to detect those who show vision problems that indicate the need for referral to a vision specialist. Some of the signals that teachers should watch out for include squinting, eye sensitivity (excessive blinking, complaints, itching, avoidance of increased light, sties), frequent tripping, stooped posture, and studying objects up close.

Causes

Many specific types of visual impairments can be directly attributed to a specific cause, and each type is directly associated with functional vision problems. The major causes of visual impairment include defects within the ocular mechanism, diseases of the eye, and accidents affecting the eye. Some visual disabilities are of unknown origin, or idiopathic.

With only a basic knowledge of the human eye (see Figure 9.1), most major types of visual impairment can be understood. The human eye can be considered a camera for the brain. Light rays enter the eye through the outer covering (cornea) and pass through the eye's pupil. The size of the pupillary opening is regulated by the iris and is determined by the intensity of visual stimulation. Those stimuli that are permitted to pass through the eye's pupil next enter the lens, which is a transparent biconvex structure that appropriately focuses light rays onto the back wall of the eyeball (retina). The retina contains visual reception cells (rods and cones) that collectively pass messages about color and light imagery to the rear opening of the eyeball, which is the optic nerve. In effect, the retina is an extension of the optic nerve. This nerve, in turn, transmits visual messages to the occipital lobe of the brain, where visual stimuli are interpreted. It is essential that both eyes have coordinated neural activity so

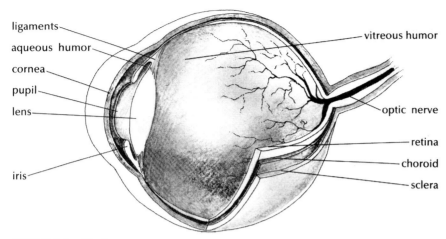

FIGURE 9.1 The human eye. *(Reprinted with the permission of Macmillan College Publishing Company from* Exceptional Children: An Introductory Survey to Special Education *by William L. Heward and Michael D. Orlansky. Copyright © 1980 by Macmillan College Publishing Company, Inc.)*

that clear binocular vision results. It is also critical that the fluid that bathes the inner and outer portions of each eyeball remains clean and clear of infection and that the six muscles that move each eyeball remain strong and in balance for best eye function. Given this background, let us look at the most common visual impairments.

The configuration of the eye as a whole, including the lens and corneal surface, can cause common defects of refraction, including myopia, hyperopia, and astigmatism. Myopia is the most common refractive error; it refers to nearsightedness, or the ability to see well only up close. In myopia, the eye is too long from front to back, which causes the focus of light rays to fall in front of the retina. Hyperopia is the opposite of myopia in all characteristics; thus it involves farsightedness. Astigmatism is a condition in which visual perception is somewhat distorted or blurred due to an irregularity of the lens or corneal surface.

Other defects primarily affect the lens, retina, choroid, iris, optic nerve, and muscles of the eye. Cataracts involve the progressive clouding of the lens, which blurs vision. They are more common in older individuals. Retinitis pigmentosa is a condition in which there is a progressive retinal rod detachment. Albinism is a hereditary condition in which there is an absence of pigment in the body, including choroid and iris, which yields sensitivity to light and refractive errors. Atrophy of the optic nerve is another hereditary condition that keeps visual messages from reaching the brain in whole or in part. Tumors can also cause visual problems by forming in the eye itself, as well as along the optic nerve or within the visual integration center in the brain.

Three common visual problems are caused by ocular muscle imbalance. Strabismus involves crossing of the eyes and foreshortened internal rotators or abnormal outward separation of the eyes due to foreshortened external rotators. Nystagmus is a condition that causes the eyeball to jump as though the ocular muscles were twitching. Heterophoria is a visual complication in which the muscles of the eye do not coordinate so as to allow efficient binocular vision.

A number of diseases can have direct or indirect effects on vision. Glaucoma is a progressive increase in pressure of the eyeball fluid (vitreous humor), which causes the eyeball to expand. Structures within it are squeezed, up to the point of destruction. Conjunctivitis (pinkeye) and keratitis are two direct inflammatory diseases that involve the infection of the conjunctiva and of the cornea, respectively. Diseases that can adversely affect the eyes as well as other parts of the body are venereal diseases, diabetes (mostly in adults), mumps, maternal rubella, and meningitis.

Accidents are a more common cause of visual problems for children than for adults. Technically, an accident could involve injury to the mother while the unborn infant is still in the womb, injury during delivery, and injury later in life. The eyeball is padded with soft tissue and coverings to allow a certain degree of trauma or shock. A sharp object or quickly moving blunt object can, however, penetrate the eye under certain conditions. Shock to the eye can also cause retinal detachment and lens dislocation. In the case of retinal detachment particularly, the detached portion must be reattached as soon as possible if full vision is to be restored. Finally, one "man-made" accident involved the treatment of premature infants during the 1950s and 1960s. At that time, premature infants were often placed in incubators and given pure oxygen to help them breathe. The oxygen adversely affected their eyes, and scar tissue typically formed behind the lens, causing blindness. This condition is called retrolental fibroplasia. Fortunately, the extent of this tragedy has significantly decreased now that the problem has been pinpointed.

Whatever the cause of a specific visual problem, the full impact on the individual also needs to be analyzed in terms of age of onset and degree of visual loss. Generally speaking, the younger an individual is when visual loss occurs and the greater the loss, the more difficult will normal cognitive, affec-

tive, and psychomotor development be. Total congenital blindness is the most serious of all conditions. Conversely, visual loss acquired after the age of 6 is not as detrimental to educational performance and development in other areas as is visual loss from birth. However, negative emotional effects tend to be greater when visual loss occurs later in life.

Scope

Visual impairments are a low-incidence disability, with only the classification of deaf-blind being lower. Nearly 2 million Americans (children and adults) have serious visual problems, and only about 20 percent of them are blind. Most of those who are blind are over 40 years of age. It has also been estimated that approximately 20 percent of all pupils have some visual impairment; however, the large majority of these defects are correctable by means of eyeglasses, contact lenses, and eye muscle exercises. Considerably less than 1 percent of all K–12 pupils are, in fact, visually impaired to the extent that they require special education services. The federal government reports (U.S. Department of Education, 1992) that only 0.04 percent of all American pupils aged 6–21 ($N = 23,686$) were labeled visually impaired and were receiving special education services during the 1990–91 school year. Of all pupils, only 1 out of every 2,500 is legally blind. Since 1950, when the cause of retrolental fibroplasia was discovered and a vaccine for rubella was developed, the extent of blindness in young children has decreased by about half.

Most pupils who are visually impaired attend regular schools, and vision specialists are increasingly being employed in these settings. There are also about 50 residential schools for the blind in the United States. A small minority of the pupils who attend these schools are totally blind; however, they all are at least legally blind (20/200) and increasingly are being admitted only if they have one or more additional disabilities. Those employed at residential schools for the blind are needed more than ever before as an essential resource in day schools for ongoing consultation and, in some cases, direct teaching services.

Given the increasing numbers of pupils labeled visually impaired being educated in the public schools, physical educators especially need the services of vision specialists, whether they are employed by the school system on a full-time basis or they consult and are chiefly employed by residential schools. Some districts employ a professional to act as an itinerant teacher, traveling among a few schools; others coordinate a resource room in one school. Other districts employ a full-time specialist in education for pupils who are visually impaired to run a self-contained classroom housed in a regular school. In this situation, pupils who are visually impaired are integrated with their sighted peers during nonacademic situations, perhaps including physical education. Still other schools practice a cooperative plan where the pupil with visual impairment attends any regular class where an equal opportunity for success can be reasonably expected.

In addition to human resource assistance from inside or outside the school, the physical educator has at least four other sources of outside assistance: audio materials, print materials, the support of numerous organizations dedicated to those who are visually impaired, and medical specialists.

There is a great variety of audio and print materials related to visual impairment. Records ("talking books"), record players, and tapes are available from the Library of Congress. Print materials are available (usually free) from the American Printing House for the Blind in Louisville, Kentucky. In addition to providing print materials, the American Foundation for the Blind in New York City has compiled more than 1,000 names and addresses of organizations that serve those who are visually impaired. For a listing of all of these addresses and other comprehensive information on a variety of services for this population, the latest edition of the foundation's *Directory of Services for Blind and Visually Impaired Persons in the United States* is recommended (approximately $40).

Books are also available to physical educators. Listed here are three sources of comprehensive information on physical education for pupils who are visually impaired:

Buell, C. (1982). *Physical education and recreation for the visually handicapped*, 2nd ed. Washington, DC: American Alliance for Health, Physical Education, Recreation and Dance.

Buell, C. (1984). *Physical education for blind children*, 2nd ed. Springfield, IL: Charles C Thomas.

Kratz, L. E., Tutt, L.M., & Black, D. A. (1987). *Movement and fundamental motor skills for sensory deprived children*. Springfield, IL: Charles C Thomas.

Two other resources provide easy-to-understand guidelines for the "person on the street" relative to the child with a visual impairment. These guideline manuals cover all areas of living, with an emphasis on play. *Move It* is a sequel to *Get a Wiggle On*. Their citation follows:

Drouillard, R., & Raynor, S. (1977). *Move it: A guide for helping visually handicapped children grow*. Reston, VA: American Alliance for Health, Physical Education, Recreation and Dance.

Raynor, S., & Drouillard, R. (1975). *Get a wiggle on: A guide for helping visually impaired children grow*. Reston, VA: American Alliance for Health, Physical Education, Recreation and Dance.

Four types of medical specialists serve the needs of those requiring visual care. The oculist or ophthalmologist is a physician trained to diagnose and treat diseases of the eye with drugs or surgery. Optometrists are trained to give complete eye examinations and prescribe corrective measures, including glasses, lenses, and ocular muscle exercises. They do not perform surgery and generally do not administer drugs. An optician is a medical specialists who grinds lenses according to the prescription determined by an optometrist or ophthalmologist. An orthoptist is a specialist in eye muscle exercise who works closely with ophthalmologists.

CHARACTERISTICS AND INSTRUCTIONAL STRATEGIES

As stated, age of visual loss onset and degree of loss are critical determinants of the need for specialized instruction. The most serious consequences face the child who is afflicted when younger than 6 years of age. However, experts on blindness urge that even the most profound visual loss at a very early age does not preclude growth and development in all areas. Charles Buell, a leader in the field of physical education for the visually impaired, has stated that "blindness is not a tragedy; rather it is a nuisance that can be compensated for or overcome" (1973, p. 9). His positive attitude has permeated many years of valuable direct service in physical education to pupils who are visually impaired.

A most essential prerequisite in instruction is an appropriate attitude. One factor is knowing how to address and interact with those who have visual problems. As an aid, Buell (1973, p. 11) offers a list of pertinent suggestions that have been adapted for use in physical education:

1. Please address me directly and not through my guide or companion.
2. I can walk more easily with you than with a dog or cane. But don't grab my arm or try to propel me; let me take yours. I'll keep a half step behind, to anticipate curbs and steps. Going down stairs I may prefer to hold a railing. When giving me directions, make it plain whether you mean your right or my right. (See Figure 9.2).
3. Speak to me when you enter the room and tell me who you are—don't play guessing games. Introduce me to the others, including children. Guide my hand to the arm or back of a chair.
4. For me, doors should be completely closed or wide open—a half-open door is a hazard; so are toys on the floor.
5. Don't avoid words like "see"—I use them too! I'm always glad to see you.
6. I don't want pity. But don't talk about the "wonderful compensations" of blindness—whatever I've learned has been by hard work.
7. I'll discuss blindness with you if you're curious, but it's an old story to me. I have as many other interests as you do.
8. Don't think of me as a blind man. I am a man who happens to be blind.

With a proper outlook, physical educators can objectively begin to match instructional strategies to the specific needs and characteristics of the pupil who has a visual impairment.

FIGURE 9.2 Guiding technique for use with individual who is visually impaired.

CHARACTERISTICS	INSTRUCTIONAL STRATEGIES

Psychomotor

1. By definition, the individual who is visually impaired has a significant sensory problem, but there is a wide variation of useful vision among those who are visually impaired. The greater the visual limitation, the more significant is the hindrance to overall psychomotor development.

1. Prepare for physical activity instruction by initially assuring that the pupil receives orientation and mobility (O & M) instruction* indoors and outdoors at the earliest possible time. Make sure the pupil is shown the dressing room, showers, toilet, and all activity areas. Opt for a keyed lock versus a combination lock. Take advantage of the skills of a certified O & M instructor. Talk to each pupil who has low vision before physical education classes begin to determine accurately the true extent of residual vision, if any. Then try the pupil out on a few movement challenges one-on-one to verify the pupil's verbal account.

    With attention given to environmental constants and orientation to each new activity (including reference or anchor points in the environment), proceed by using the pupil's auditory, tactile, and kinesthetic senses, plus residual vision. Those pupils with more residual vision can help those with less residual vision. If appropriate, use large printed charts, contrasting colors (orange, yellow, lime), and intense light. Use figure–ground contrasts when there is some residual vision. Lighting contrasts are critical, too (Gardner, 1985). This has implications for walls, floors, and light bulb types. Fluorescent fixtures are a good source of light. Use words, whistles, hand clapping, "talking" targets, and other sound sources. A continual or frequent sound is the best and it should be directed in front of or behind a pupil, not to the side or at an angle. The location of any sound and the meaning (discrimination) of sounds are important when teaching movement. Teaching through the haptic approach (tactile and kinesthetic) can be accomplished by manually guiding a pupil through motion, having a pupil touch the instructor, or exploring a model of some kind (doll, mannequin, small replication of setting). See Figure 9.3 for an idea with use of a mannequin. Movements can also be Brailled.

2. Significant movement and fitness problems show up in complicated movement patterns and with most visual losses originating at an early age.

2. "The blind come nearer to the norms of the normally sighted in uncomplicated activities performed in place. Examples include the flexed arm hang, sit-ups, pull-ups, and the standing broad jump" (Winnick, 1979, p. 307). Activities should be sequenced from simple to complex and from static to dynamic. The most difficult are those that involve multiple movements all at once and are not earth-bound.

3. Pupils who are visually impaired follow the normal sequence of motor development but at a slower pace, primarily because of a lack of movement

3. Pupils with low vision should be permitted to attend a regular class with older or younger pupils or to attend a remedial or segregated class, depend-

---

* O & M is a system of instruction specially devised for individuals who are visually impaired. Its purpose is not only to orient the pupil to different environments (mild and harsh) but also to teach him or her how to move safely in these environments. Cane (the most popular), dog, cat, peer assisted, and unassisted travel are O & M techniques.

FIGURE 9.3 Brailling a mannequin to develop body image.

experiences, poor mobility, and spatial orientation difficulties. The motor differences between those labeled blind and normally seeing youngsters tend to decrease with increasing age.

4. Physical fitness scores for pupils labeled visually impaired are generally below those of sighted peers (Seelye, 1983; Hopkins, Gaeta, Thomas & Hill, 1987). Scores worsen as visual problems increase, and girls score lower than boys (except in flexibility). Fitness scores of pupils who are visually impaired improve with age, and differences between them and the nondisabled decrease with increasing age, with the exception of teenaged girls (Winnick & Short, 1982).

5. The balance ability of pupils who are visually impaired is below the norm (Ribaldi, Rider, & Toole, 1987).

6. Children who are visually impaired tend to have faulty posture. Rigidity, round shoulders, forward bending to feel for objects, and swaying backward to protect the head are common.

7. Running and throwing are particularly poor in pupils who are visually impaired, largely because of poor body image.

8. The overall body image of pupils who are visually impaired tends to be deficient.

ing on the pupil's needs. When young, they should practice basic motor development activities such as those requiring spatial orientation, balance, locomotion, and eye–limb coordination not only in physical education class but also in other classes and at home.

4. Pupils who are visually impaired need a steady regimen of weekly and even daily fitness activities. When fitness test scores are needed, modify tests that involve mobility, complex movement (such as shuttle run, throwing a softball), and cardiovascular endurance to reflect the best performance of these pupils.

5. While stressing body image, offer static and dynamic balance activities that progress from low to higher body level. Teach pupils how to fall.

6. Provide exercises that increase tone and strength in relaxed postural muscles. Stretch tight muscles. Teach relaxation in different static and dynamic positions. Have pupils tactually inspect a model for postural cues.

7. Permit pupils to touch your arms and legs when you are throwing and running. Allow the pupil to run between two runners and feel the hip action of adjacent runners. Verbally instruct and manually move the pupil through desired motions.

8. The body image of these children can be measured objectively (Cratty, 1971b). Once body image deficiencies are known, offer sequential activities that address body part identification, understanding the

9. Pupils who are visually impaired have a tendency to be overweight.

10. Glasses, contact lenses, or hand-held magnifying devices are commonly used by individuals who are visually limited.

Cognitive

1. The intelligence of individuals who are visually impaired varies as widely as that of their sighted peers.
2. Because academic achievement is based largely on the ability to read, it is hampered because of partial or complete loss of vision.

3. The range of overall cognitive awareness tends to be limited in comparison with normally sighted persons. Most of their object world is only perceived when small and close. Perceiving the relationships between objects and differentiating parts of a whole are difficult. Dealing with the abstract can be vague and frustrating.

relationship of various body parts, and being able to identify selected body parts on others.

9. Confidence gained by participation in a variety of vigorous physical activities will help prevent further weight gain and get rid of sedentary habits. Offer activities that the pupils can do after school.

10. Allow pupils to use any device that will enable better comprehension of any written instructions or hasten dressing or undressing. Remove glasses for contact activities, or reinforce the stems with tape and have the pupil wear glass protectors.

1. Do not have low expectations; do not automatically treat these pupils as if they were mentally retarded.

2. Large-print letters and numbers can be perceived by many pupils who are partially sighted. Those who are labeled blind can learn Braille, * a shorthand form of tactile reading. (See the Braille alphabet in Figure 9.4.) However, reading Braille typically takes much longer than visual reading. More recent technology advances include the optacon, which converts printed material into impulses that can be read tactually, and the Kurzweil Reading Machine, which converts printed material into oral messages. Although both devices have applicability to physical education instruction, they are too costly for general use.

3. Pupils who are visually impaired need visual efficiency training. Visual blurs can become meaningful with training. Some individuals make better use of their limited vision than others. Listening skills also need to be practiced.

    In physical education, the whole-part-whole approach is most effective when it uses auditory and haptic senses. Where possible, encourage the use of residual vision. Scaled-down models of equipment, facilities, and human figures (dolls) can be used in teaching primarily through touch. Task feedback on every trial is critical because normal

* In Braille, letters are derived from six-dot cells. Dots in each cell are raised to indicate letters, numbers, punctuation, abbreviations, and other specific symbols.

FIGURE 9.4   Standard English Braille alphabet.

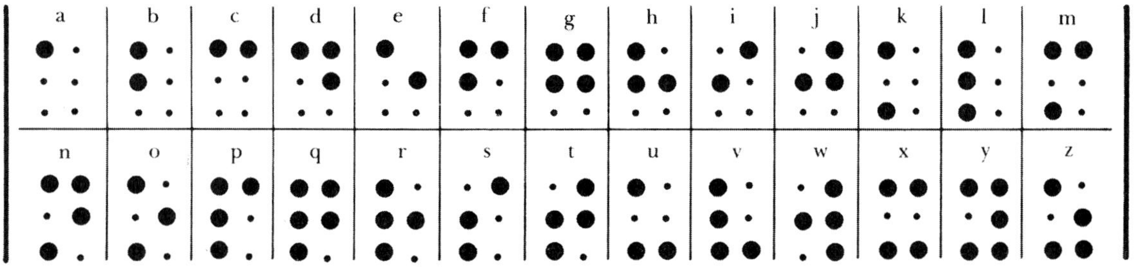

Affective

1. Many people who are visually impaired lack self-confidence and feelings of value.

2. Many pupils who are visually impaired lack initiative in engaging in gross motor activities. This directly relates to poor vision and not being able to see consequences.

3. Structured and spontaneous play experiences are often limited for young children who are visually impaired. Their social development tends to be delayed.

4. Being fearful of movement and overly dependent on others are characteristic of pupils who are visually impaired.

5. These children tend to be highly verbal because they cannot attend to or easily send nonverbal cues.

6. Blindisms may be characteristic of the pupil who is visually impaired. These inappropriate movements may include rocking, digging at the eyes, and general overflow of unused limbs. Blindisms appear to be a reaction to frustration resulting from the inability to move as desired; they may also fulfill a need for gross movement.

7. Some individuals who are partially sighted might pretend to have more vision than they actually do in order to give the impression that they are fully normal.

8. Some individuals who are visually impaired downplay their disability and take pride in acquired independent skills.

feedback from the pupil's visual mechanism is lacking.

At times, avoid concepts acquired through vision when giving verbal directions (e.g., Do not say "Chop here as though you were splitting firewood." The pupil might not know the word firewood or the action you mean).

1. Keep your attitude toward those who are visually impaired positive and encourage positive attitudes in normally sighted peers. Still training in a vast array of movement experiences will improve confidence.

2. Thoroughly orient those pupils to new environments and equipment. Allow them to handle equipment before using it. Once orientation is completed, encourage the pupils to move alone or with others. Directions could be recorded onto tapes in order to individualize training. Incentives could also prompt their initiative.

3. Isolation of these individuals has no place. Systematically provide young children with frequent play experiences with others. Normal bumps and bruises are to be expected. Gradually fade instructor initiative.

4. Have pupils do things independently once they are oriented to the environment and have mastered prerequisite skills. Demand maximal efforts from pupils who are visually impaired.

5. Address these pupils by first name. Allow them to express themselves fully. Extinguish the habit of repeating statements. Tell the pupil when you are leaving the immediate environment.

6. Do not ignore blindisms, especially if obvious; they will probably not disappear on their own. Provide a variety of vigorous movement experiences to encourage appropriate movements and to replace blindisms.

7. Assign a sighted peer to the pupil who is visually impaired. Have pupils face their limitations, yet emphasize their strengths in teaching.

8. Good deeds for this type of individual have their limits. Make sure that the individual who is visually limited wants and needs your assistance. In class, use as few adaptations as possible within a margin of safety.

INDICATED AND NONINDICATED ACTIVITIES

In the past, most pupils with visual impairment in public schools were not provided with well-rounded vigorous programs of physical education. In fact, one common practice, which is still done to some degree, was to excuse them from physical activity. Reasons included fear on the part of teachers and administrators, ignorance concerning effective teaching approaches in physical education for those who are visually impaired, negative attitudes toward having a pupil with low vision in one's class, overemphasis on vocational objectives, overprotectiveness by parents or guardians, and overwillingness of physicians to write temporary or blanket excuses from physical activity. But, as Helen Keller once said, "The curse of blindness is not blindness, but idleness." As for all children, physical activity for the child who is visually impaired is crucial for total development (Kratz, Tutt, & Black, 1987).

Physical and Motor Fitness

Children who are visually impaired need to be even more fit than the normally sighted because ordinary movement requires more effort for them (Buell, 1973). Movement without vision is less energy efficient than movement with vision. Uncomplicated activities that emphasize the development of strength and cardiorespiratory endurance are, therefore, particularly critical.

Strength can be developed safely in these pupils through pushing, pulling, and lifting activities, such as:

- Weight lifting using a Universal gym (start with no weight in order to master the mechanics of lifting; then introduce weights)
- Isometric exercises
- Hand walking a horizontal ladder
- Climbing cargo nets and ropes
- Hand walking a vertical pegboard

Especially worthy of mention is that very heavy weight lifting might be dangerous for those children with glaucoma, as the activity may increase pressure on the eyeball.

The following are key cardiorespiratory activities that can be successfully employed with the pupil who is visually impaired:

- Stationary running
- Use of an exercise bicycle (stationary)
- Running over a distance (there have been marathon runners who were blind)
- Rowing machine exercises
- Bench stepping

There are numerous techniques to assist a pupil in distance running. The runner who is visually impaired could listen to a sighted caller (make sure that other noises do not interfere with the caller's signal). An older pupil could hold the back of the upper arm just above the elbow of a sighted assistant, running a half pace to the side and a half pace behind the sighted runner. A 1983 film that clearly depicts these first two techniques, featuring the long distance running ability of Harry Cordellos, is highly recommended. Entitled *Survival Run*, the film is available from Media Marketing, W-STAD, Brigham Young University, Provo, UT 84602.

As another example, a young pupil with vision problems could hold a sighted helper's wrist or hold a wand, rope, or wire also held by a sighted runner (see Figure 9.5). A runner

FIGURE 9.5 Runner who is blind using guide rope. *(Courtesy of the American Alliance for Health, Physical Education, Recreation, and Dance).*

with residual vision could follow a yellow, orange, or lime line or hold a rope or wire that slides along an overhead or adjacent wire or rope. In the latter case, appropriately spaced knots or changes in running surface are needed to indicate the end of the course. However, any device that must be held by a runner prevents the normal arm swing characteristic of efficient locomotion. An alternative is to have a sighted partner ride a bicycle beside the runner who is visually impaired. The sighted partner could talk; a device (like a piece of cardboard) could be attached to the bike wheel to make noise as it touches the wheel spokes; or a transmitter that emits directional signals could be strapped on the runner (Gallagher, 1977).

As visual loss increases, more obvious physical or body mechanic deviances tend to appear. One technique for body mechanic training is to have the pupil tactually inspect a mannequin or doll with movable joints. Another technique involves a fan. Air directed from a large fan to the front of a body can stimulate awareness of body parts; for example, a pupil can be told to straighten a drooped head to face the air.

Fundamental Motor Skills and Patterns

Pupils who are visually impaired usually lack a sound body image and spatial orientation; thus awareness of the body and its relationship to space are two of their most basic needs. The physical education class should include a variety of uncomplicated activities that begin to develop these skills, along with balance, more completely. Some appropriate activities are the following:

- Naming body parts
- Moving parts separately
- Moving on different parts
- Coordinating movements of more than one part
- Balancing on certain parts or number of parts
- Moving objects with various body parts
- Balancing on a low balance beam
- Feeling the size of different body parts
- Identifying the body parts of others
- Balancing on a Lind climber (also known as a Stegel)

Pupils with visual limitations are often behind in developing proficient locomotor skills. Some of them walk with their feet wide apart and toeing out. This habit provides an increased base of support and is probably related to lack of self-confidence in movement and to balance deficiencies. These pupils also tend to take large, high steps, as if to step over obstacles. Often these same faults generalize to other skills, such as running. Pupils who have these habits should be made aware of their problems and practice moving correctly so that they perceive appropriate kinesthetic feedback and form new patterns. To correct toeing out and walking with spread feet, have the pupil walk on a board of limited width or between two boards, sticks, or ropes placed on the floor, just wide enough apart to accommodate two straight feet. Learning to walk in a straight path is also essential for this pupil. For the pupil who shuffles the feet, walking on something soft (e.g., sand, soft mat) encourages him or her to lift the feet and prevents shuffling.

Other specific fundamental movement skills can be taught to pupils who are visually impaired. Throwing is often one of their most deficient motor skills. When analyzed closely, mature throwing is a very complex skill, even for those who can benefit from demonstrations. While pupils who have serious vision problems can develop a mature throwing pattern by means of frequent auditory and haptic prompts, the energy and time spent might justifiably be better used in training other motor skills that have a lifelong utility in day-to-day living.

Kicking, jumping, hopping, skipping, galloping, leaping, and running can be taught with slight adaptations. Practice in kicking is enhanced by kicking a small can or milk carton—a can makes a good sound on a hard surface—and retrieval distance for both is minimal. Jumping and hopping can be taught on a trampoline that has a bell taped to the center of the bed. And skipping, galloping, leaping, and running can be taught by initially linking both arms of the pupil to instructors on each side (perhaps peers) who move, thus transmitting continuous kinesthetic messages. These techniques can be employed along with auditory and haptic cues.

Fundamental motor skills and patterns can also be developed by encouraging pupils to experiment with basic movements. With pupils who are visually impaired, space equates with their imagination to a large extent, because what has never been seen can only be imagined. Assuming that the area is free of obstacles and that pupils have lost their inhibitions to move, you have a variety of options, including experimentation with all forms of fundamental movement, sound localization, and the introduction of such concepts as "big" and "slow."

Because children who are visually impaired are unable or only partly able to receive visual input, they must rely on less exact information from other sensory sources. This information does not lend itself as readily to the imitation of fundamental movement skills. Basic movement training may, therefore, have to be continued over longer periods of time. These classes should promote refining of these skills as well as extensive use and practice.

Aquatics

Swimming is not only important for psychomotor development, but it is also a valuable activity that can be pursued for socialization and health maintenance later in life (Cordellos, 1987). Physical educators need to consider a number of guidelines, however.

Related to equipment and materials, racing lines and distinct localized sounds enhance straight-line swimming. Turns at the end of the pool require a preparatory auditory cue from a machine or person. Dividers in the water and Braille guides out of the water should provide information on water depth. Instructors must make sure that swim caps do not prevent pupils from hearing instructions. Flotation device fasteners need to be simple because the pupil will use the tactile sense primarily in putting on, adjusting, and taking off such equipment.

Related to teaching techniques, orientation and mobility training in and around the pool are especially important, as safety is such a high priority in this setting. A buddy system is indicated for swimmers who have serious visual limitations. An assigned sighted buddy who is a competent swimmer should always be near and face-to-face with a swimmer who is blind. Such proximity will increase feelings of security, too. When entering a pool from the edge, the pupil who is visually impaired should "see" the edge with the feet, then sit down, cross one leg over the other, and slide down facing the edge. The instructor can teach strokes by moving the pupil's limbs while breathing audibly so that a coordination of movement and breathing can be realized. At first, teach skills in which the pupil's head remains above water.

Be aware that diving and deep water swimming are not indicated for pupils with glaucoma, and diving may be forbidden for those with detached retina. In addition, free time jumping or diving into pools for pupils who are blind is not advised. And, of course, pupils with limited or no vision should never be subjected to objects being thrown around the pool environment.

Dance

Like swimming, dancing has social and leisure time values. Fun and success in dance can be enjoyed by everyone. Here are some guidelines for teaching dance to pupils who are visually impaired.

1. Dances in which pupils continuously touch are most successful with those who are visually limited. Many social, square, folk, and tap dances meet this criterion.
2. Partner dances naturally lend themselves to the pairing of a pupil who is visually impaired and one who is sighted. A natural buddy system exists and is obviously desirable.
3. As noted, pupils who are visually impaired have a tendency to be overly verbal. Creative dances can emphasize the awareness and meaning of facial expressions that sighted people take for granted. Even if a pupil who is blind cannot perceive the facial expressions of another person, he or she can learn to express some messages nonverbally, which may reduce the urge to overexpress verbally.
4. Choose music that is free of auditory distortion. The environment should also be relatively free of noise pollution.
5. Records with accompanying verbal instructions are effective. They permit the instructor to attend to pupils' movements.
6. Simple forward, backward, sideways, and in-place steps can be substituted for any complex dance steps as the need arises.
7. Participants who are blind can use a hands-on-hips approach when learning a new dance; they can also be provided with valuable haptic sensory information if an instructor (perhaps a peer) moves their fin-

gers on the floor just as the legs would move. The pupil with a visual impairment can also follow the movements of a rag doll or mannequin.

Individual and Group Activities

Pupils who are visually impaired can safely participate in almost all individual and group activities. There is no evidence that these pupils experience more accidents than usual in physical education. Here are some guidelines for adapting individual and group activities and games for safe, successful, and satisfying participation.

1. Place audio devices inside balls, on bases, by goals, and in bean bags.
2. Use chain formations (touching).
3. Participate from a stationary position.
4. Participate while on the floor (e.g., on scooters).
5. Manipulate the playing surface texture (different grass heights, sand, dirt, asphalt) to indicate sections of the play area and the out-of-bounds areas.
6. Modify the texture of equipment.
7. Use soft outer restrainers such as padded walls or bushes around play areas.
8. Use brightly colored activity objects and boundaries.
9. Use naming, calling, and whistling. Use a megaphone for amplification.
10. Limit the play area.
11. Limit the number of participants on each side.
12. Play in slow motion when introducing a new game.
13. Use odors as signals in selected situations.
14. Notify the sightless player(s) when a key person leaves the field or area.
15. Always keep playing areas uncluttered.

The most desirable activities to offer pupils who are visually impaired are those that require the least adaptation and are uncomplicated. Any activity that depends on continuous contact among participants (e.g., Tug-of-War or Auto-Tire-Tug) or does not require vision (e.g., Blind Man's Bluff) is ideal. In the latter, the leader should be particularly careful when blindfolding sighted pupils. Their initial adjustment will, at best, be tentative and extremely guarded.

Here are some basic activities to use with young pupils who are visually impaired.

1. When the children are constantly in contact with a parachute, no major modifications are necessary. The child can engage in numerous gross motor movements, including all types of locomotion.

2. The language concepts required in story plays, movement exploration, and mimetics and the many movements practiced in these activities are needed by pupils who are visually impaired. However, some words or phrases spoken by the leader could easily confuse a child who has never been able to know their meaning visually—a certain animal and how it moves, for example. Space and the function of things in it are often not clear to children with no vision; they are largely figments of the imagination.

3. Participation in relays such as the over-under relay, wheelbarrow races, sack races, and three-legged races is enhanced by either direct contact with a sighted partner or by participants remaining stationary. Familiar starting and finishing lines must be used.

4. Traditional graded group games such as Call Ball, Jump the Torpedo, and Bull in the Ring can be offered. In Call Ball, a pupil's number is called by "It." A ball with a beeper inside is tossed straight up and must bounce no more than twice before being caught by the called player. In Jump the Torpedo, "It" rotates a flat piece of metal attached to a rope from the center of a circle composed of other players. As the metal piece scrapes along, it warns each player in the outer circle when to jump and clear the object and avoid being the new "It." In both of these games, an auditory adaptation is employed (a bounced beeper ball, a scraped piece of metal). Bull in the Ring is successful because of the pupils' close contact. The players stand in a circle with hands grasped. One player, the bull, must try to break out of the circle. In Team Bull in the Ring, two or more players as a team try to break out.

5. Graded group games especially designed for pupils with low vision have proven successful. A few are listed and described here.

   Scoop Ball. Use plastic scoops and a whiffle softball with bells. There are two teams, and goals are ends of the wrestling room or gymnasium. Players may hit or throw the ball with a scoop, trying to hit the wall at the opposite end. The ball must bounce at least twice or roll before hitting the wall. No body contact is allowed (penalties may be assessed if contact does occur) and players may go anywhere in the room. Helmets are advised in case of contact. Two sighted referees are used to guard against collisions.

   Area Ball. Four teams are assigned, each to one quarter of the gymnasium. Use a noise-making cageball or rubber playground ball. Players kick or throw the ball, trying to always keep it out of their quarter. At the end of 1 minute, a whistle blows and the team whose quarter the ball is in gets a point. The team with the least points wins. Players may move anywhere in their quarter. Mats are placed along all boundaries.

   Find Your Partner. Each pupil chooses a partner and stands with that partner. A command is given, "run" (the locomotor movement changes each time), and players run away from their chosen partner. On a signal of "find," partners run to find each other and sit down. The last pair together gets a point. The low point group wins when the game ends. Or the first couple together gains a "Champion Rest" for one turn. This is a good game for learning to listen for verbal cues from another person (one partner calling another to find him). The game could employ only walking at first.

Cageball Push.   One person sits on either side of a 36-inch canvas cageball with back to the ball. On the start signal, players try to get the ball to the opposite goal line. They may push, pull, kick, or throw the ball. This may also be done with partners or teams with different starting positions.

Hold the Fort.   A mat placed at one end of the gymnasium represents a fort. One team is designated "Defenders" and the other "Attackers."   After 2 minutes of attacking, each attacker in the fort scores one point for her team. The teams then reverse positions and the game is repeated.

Red Hot.   One or more balls are passed around a circle. If several balls are used, one of them should be distinctly different and designated the Hot Ball. At the command "stop," the person with the Hot Ball gets a point. The pupil with fewest points wins.

6. In lead-up games such as kickball, the ball can have beads or an audible beeper in it, the runner might have a sighted substitute runner, a fielder with limited vision might only have to stop and pick up a kicked ball for the batter to be out, a kicker might run to a base or cone that emits an audible sound or to a human voice or whistle sound, the bat or ball can be enlarged, and contrasting colors can be used with the equipment and on the playing field.

7. When playing dodgeball, a sighted partner should assist the pupil with a visual impairment to dodge the ball, and when this pupil becomes the thrower, the other players should clap or shout to help the thrower "see" the targets.

The following modified activities can be used with older pupils who are visually impaired.

1. In wrestling, touch must be maintained throughout the match. Pupils who are blind have been known to excel in interscholastic wrestling.

2. Combative activities in which continual contact is maintained include wrist wrestling, wand pull and push, arm wrestling, and leg wrestling. As an adaptation, in wrestle ball, two or more players kneel around a basketball or volleyball. When the signal "go" is given, each player or team attempts to pull the ball away and one player must stand up with the ball at full arm's length overhead. Two or 3 minutes' duration constitutes a draw. With well-timed rest periods, the entire class has a chance to "wrestle," rest, "wrestle," and rest. As another adaptation, in Tractor Pull, two players represent tractors and are back to back. Two other players are tractor riders and reach back, grasping wrists. Then the tractors PULL!

3. Tandem bike riding can be successful if the pupil who is blind sits in the rear seat.

4. In bowling, a hand guide rail can be used. Portable guide rails are weighted with bowling balls at each end and need no wall or floor attachments to hold them down (see Figure 9.6). The guide rail could be made less restrictive by using carpet pieces as "stepping stones."   Bowlers also can learn directional cues and paces from the foul line. A sighted helper can inform the bowler about pin count and placement, and Braille score sheets can be used.

5. Many adaptations are possible in archery, including audio signals emitted from targets; Braille directions; foot-positioning restraints; contrasting colors on target, pathway to target, and arrows; change in textured surfaces to the target; and a guide rope to the target (Jansma, 1978a).

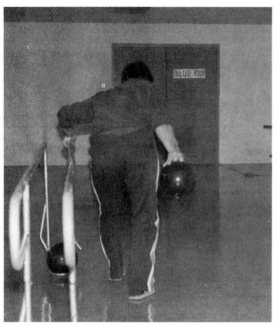

FIGURE 9.6 Bowling rail in use.

FIGURE 9.7 An audible basketball goal locator.

6. Snow skiing requires a sighted guide along with some type of auditory cue.

7. In football, more success is obtained by narrowing the field and reducing the number of players. Participants who are blind should play on the line of scrimmage, perhaps as center.

8. In basketball, the basket should have an audible goal locator attached to it (see Figure 9.7). Sighted players should call the pupil's name before passing and use bounce passes. Sighted players should call for passes from participants who are visually impaired.

9. In softball, the ball can be struck from a tee; use similar adaptations as in kickball. Beep baseball is a closely related activity that could be played in physical education classes with pupils who are visually limited. (See a pupil running to a beep baseball base in Figure 9.8.) More information on beep baseball is provided in Chapter 17.

FIGURE 9.8 A player quickly running by a base in beep baseball.

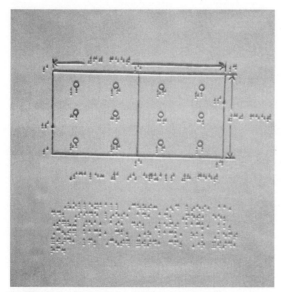

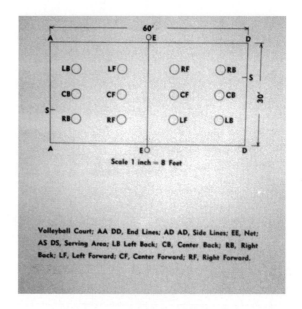

Volleyball Court; AA DD, End Lines; AD AD, Side Lines; EE, Net; AS DS, Serving Area; LB Left Back; CB, Center Back; RB, Right Back; LF, Left Forward; CF, Center Forward; RF, Right Forward.

FIGURE 9.9   A tactile model for volleyball.

10. In whiffleball, bells can be placed inside the ball; use adaptations listed for softball and kickball.

11. In volleyball, the surroundings and ball should incorporate contrasting colors and audio cues. Rules might require the ball to bounce once before a return is made. Perhaps the pupil with very little vision could serve for both teams. Tactile models can be made for a variety of group games, including volleyball (see Figure 9.9).

12. Pupils who are blind can succeed in track and field events, including the shot put, discus throw, standing and running broad jump, high jump, and running events (excluding hurdles). In the shot put and discus, a sighted companion must properly position the athlete before each throw. In the running broad jump and high jump, surface textural changes can indicate a "warning" area and a distinct takeoff spot. When running on a track, a sighted peer could run in tandem and call out lane numbers in order to keep the runner who has low vision positioned properly. Tandem running or running in which a sighted

buddy runs in front needs to be accompanied by multiple and continuous verbal cues when running in open areas.

13. Golf requires a sighted person to locate the ball, protect the partner who is visually impaired from errant shots, and give directional cues with regard to pin placement.

14. Goal ball (discussed in Chapter 17) can also be played with success. In this game, all players (visually impaired and sighted with blindfolds) must lie on the ground somewhere on their half of the playing court. They roll a large beeper ball to the opposite court trying to hit their opponents' back wall (or some other marker) in order to score a point.

15. Gymnastics and tumbling activities that are earth-bound and noncomplicated will be most successful with this type of pupil. Consistent attention to spotting is a must.

Some individual and group activities are generally not indicated for pupils with low vision. Among these are regulation racquet games (e.g., tennis, racquetball, squash) and handball; activities in which agility is involved, particularly around others; activities in which pupils run by each other from opposite directions; midair activities such as tumbling flips and moves involving noncontact with gymnastic apparatus; tumbling for pupils with glaucoma; and activities (e.g., football, boxing, wrestling, judo) in which a person or an object (e.g., battleball) makes contact with a pupil who has an easily detached retina.

High school pupils who are visually impaired should be taught to enjoy spectator sports. They should be given information— whether verbal, in large print, or in Braille— that explains the strategy and rules of games in which they seem interested. These pupils can also be provided with pointers relating to the use of equipment and facilities.

We finish this chapter with an interview of James Mastro, an expert wrestler who is blind.

James Mastro

Dr. James Mastro is the director of the Braille Sports Foundation and an instructor of physical education at the University of Minnesota.

1. *How important is physical activity for pupils who are visually impaired?*

Physical activity is probably more important for individuals labeled blind and visually impaired than for pupils who are sighted. By 5 or 6 years of age, 46 percent of children who are blind and 22 percent of children who are visually impaired cannot pass at the minimal level on physical fitness tests compared to just 5 percent of their peers who are sighted. Infants with blindness begin to show differences in motor performance early in life. They do not physically explore their environment because of fear and/or lack of visual motivation to move. Two additional factors that may contribute to this discrepancy are parents, teachers, and significant others who are overprotective and, relatedly, many times these children lack the opportunity for vigorous exercise in their environment.

2. *What do you think about mainstreaming pupils who are visually impaired?*

In many cases, mainstreaming is great for these pupils. It really depends on each pupil's strengths, weaknesses, and margin of safety. However, educators must take into consideration the amount of functional vision of a pupil. If a pupil does not have enough vision to participate without requiring major game modifications that impact on the other pupils, it probably is an inappropriate activity and a "token placement." For instance, a pupil who is blind generally does not belong in traditional team games such as football, basketball, and volleyball. These pupils should, however, learn the rules, strategies, and jargon specific to these games so they can socially interact with their peers who are sighted. Pupils who are blind and visually impaired generally do best in individual activities such as movement education, swimming, track and field, weight lifting, judo, wrestling, and many forms of dance.

3. *What is your opinion of adapted equipment designed for use by pupils who are visually impaired in physical education?*

A major consideration for pupils who are visually impaired is the use of equipment that is of contrasting colors. For instance, a white kickball against a green background is easier to see than a kickball that is white against a light background. Another adaptation is equipment that makes noise. Bell balls are adequate, but once they stop, these pupils can not locate them. It is best, although more expensive, to use battery-powered noise equipment such as beep baseballs, sponge balls, and goal locators.

4. *What would you like to say to regular and special physical educators who teach pupils who are visually impaired or blind?*

Physical education teachers of pupils who are visually impaired or blind have to treat them as individuals. Consideration must be focused on the potential of these pupils and the determination of their physical and motor capabilities. Programs which involve vigorous activity and the learning of basic fundamental skills must be started very early in life. Also, any activity taught should be functional. There is no point in teaching the overhand throw to pupils who are blind when the activities in which they will participate in the future, such as goal ball, beep baseball, and bowling, involve different motor patterns.

Physical educators must also know if there are any activities not indicated based on the pupil's medical condition such as contact sports for a pupil with a detached retina or headstands for a pupil with glaucoma. Medical reasons such as these may keep such pupils from participating in vigorous physical activities, but still must always be considered in programming.

Neurological and Muscular Disabilities

Numerous neurological and muscular disabilities directly affect the ability of an individual to benefit from a regular physical education program. The *neurological system*, an elaborate network of nerve cells, is composed of the spinal cord, brain, ganglia, and nerves. Through this network information is transmitted from an individual's environment to the brain. The brain reacts to the information by sending messages to various muscles through other pathways to enable the body to respond to the information. The nervous system also regulates internal functions, such as heartbeat and breathing. All thought, emotions, sensations, and movement are products of a person's nervous system. The major neurological disorders that adversely affect the reception or transmission of these impulses and in turn influence motor per-formance are cerebral palsy, traumatic brain injury, spinal cord injuries, seizure disorders, spina bifida, and multiple sclerosis.

The *muscular system* consists of a number of types of tissue that not only enable us to move from place to place but permit movement within the body for the function of internal and external organs. An example of an internal organ is the stomach, in contrast to an external organ, such as the eye. The muscular system is subject to damage in numerous ways, including disease, congenital defects, physical injury, tumors, infection, and poor nutrition. The most common muscular disease is muscular dystrophy.

We begin our discussion with an interview of Peter Aufsesser.

Peter Aufsesser

Dr. Peter Aufsesser is a professor in special physical education at San Diego State University.

1. *Is physical education programming any more important for the child who has a neurological or muscular disability than for a nondisabled pupil?*

The physical education needs of a child with a neurological or muscular disability are more important than they are for a child who is not disabled. The reasons for this include such a child's unique need to maintain physical abilities (fitness and motor) as well as overall health. A child with cerebral palsy (a stable neuromuscular condition) needs to continue to exercise to improve or maintain range of motion, strength, muscular endurance, etc. On the other hand, a child with muscular dystrophy (in many cases a progressive neuromuscular condition) needs a regular exercise program to maintain physical abilities or to hopefully slow down the progression of the condition. In either case, the exercise program can assist the child to be more independent in the execution of daily living skills and assist in developing fitness and motor capabilities needed for vocational training. Finally, due to the generally more sedentary lifestyle characteristic of children who have a neurological or muscular disability, a good cardiovascular component is needed in each exercise program to prevent secondary health problems (heart and lung).

2. *Are there any stories which you could share which indicate the success of a special physical education program for a child who has a neurological or muscular disability?*

Bob was an 18-year-old quadriplegic injured in a sandlot football accident. When he entered our Fitness Clinic for the Physically Disabled, he had no arm movement and a small degree of shoulder elevation. Bob was put on a basic motor program which stressed gross movements of the shoulders, arms, and wrist. In addition, through the use of an upper body exercise unit (at that time a Monarch bike bolted to a table) and taping his hands to the bike pedals, we started a cardiovascular exercise program. Over a period of years Bob developed almost total movement of the shoulders and some gross movements of the arms. The most amazing aspect or outcome of the program was Bob's ability to use the hand crank (Monarch rehabilitation trainer) for 50 minutes. In May 1988 we were able to stress test Bob in our Adult Fitness Program using a modification of the American College of Sports Medicine protocol. Bob is currently employed as a marriage and family counselor for the U.S. Navy. He was married in June 1989.

CEREBRAL PALSY

Definition, Causes, and Scope

Cerebral palsy is a medical term that refers to one of a series of motor disorders that stem from brain malfunction. It is specifically related to "hard" neurological signs, which include either the identifiable absence of cranial structures or, more typically, damage to the brain's motor centers, such as the motor cortex, basal ganglia, brain stem, or cerebellum. Damage is commonly associated with the retention of primitive reflexes (Bobath & Bobath, 1975).

Primary reflexes should be integrated and postural reactions should emerge as an infant develops during the first year of life. In this connection it has been suggested by many authorities that before postural responses can occur, the primitive reflexes must be integrated (Bobath, 1971). Others, though, believe that these two sets of reflexes are independent (Bailey & Wolery, 1984; Peterson, 1987).

The initial movement of normal infants is dominated by a considerable number of reflexes that trigger responses to specific stimuli. If reflexes never appear, appear late, or last longer than normal, these are signs of possible abnormal motor development. For instance, children with cerebral palsy generally show markedly abnormal reflexes that interfere with efficient movement.

Numerous primitive reflexes are important for an understanding of motor development of individuals with cerebral palsy. The following is a brief description of some of those that are pertinent for physical education.

1. *Grasping reflex*: contact with the palm of the hand causes a sustained grasping reaction (see Figure 10.1). This reflex, if sustained, will inhibit the child from properly playing with and exploring objects and using eating utensils. This reflex is generally present at birth to 6 months.

2. *Moro reflex*: reaction caused by sudden noise or loss of support. Under either stimulus condition, a newborn will reflexively abduct the legs and arms (move them away from the body) and immediately adduct both sets of limbs (move them toward the body). This prohibits feeding and all forms of quadripedal (four points of support) and bipedal (two points of support) behavior (see Figure 10.2). This reflex is generally present from birth to 7 months.

3. *Asymmetrical tonic neck reflex (ATNR)*: reaction caused by head rotation to the side. In this important reaction, the limbs on the face side extend and the limbs on the skull side flex. Retention of the ATNR will prohibit the development of such motor milestones as creeping, rolling, and all forms of bipedal behavior (see Figure 10.3). This reflex is generally present from birth to 6 months.

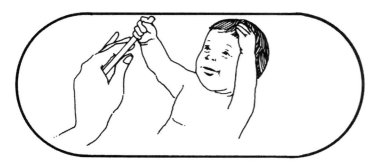

FIGURE 10.1 Palmer grasp reaction.

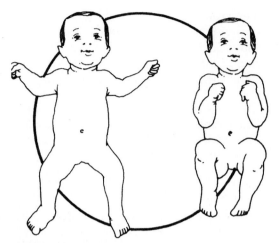

FIGURE 10.2   (a) Moro reflex, first phase; (b) Moro reflex, second phase.

4. *Symmetrical tonic neck reflex (STNR)*: reaction elicited by either flexion or extension of the head. When a newborn's head is flexed, the arms also flex and the legs extend; when the head is extended, the arms extend, and the legs flex. If this primitive reflex is not inhibited, the infant will not be able to push the chest and head off the ground with the arms (prone prop) or engage in bipedal activity (see Figure 10.4). This reflex is generally present from birth to 6 months.

5. *Tonic labyrinthine reflex (TLR)*: reaction elicited when a newborn is placed in either a prone (on stomach) or supine (on back) position. When prone, the TLR causes excessive flexor tone throughout the body. When supine, the TLR causes a predominance of extensor tone throughout the body (see Figure 10.5). Retention of this reflex precludes such motor milestones as head raising, rolling, maintaining an all-fours position, or bringing hands to the midline. It appears in normal infants up to 4 months.

Cerebral palsy appears in various forms and many levels of severity. A precise description for a given individual necessitates classification by degree of involvement, motor disability type, anatomical involvement, and possible associated disabilities. We consider each of these four parameters.

The broadest classification is by degree of motor involvement. In a *mild* case of cerebral palsy, the individual can walk unassisted, and little or no treatment is needed. *Moderate*

FIGURE 10.3   (a) ATNR left; (b) ATNR right.

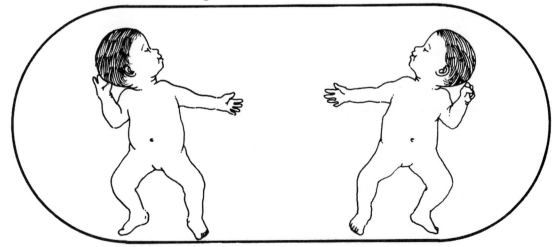

FIGURE 10.4 (a) STNR flexion response; (b) STNR extension response.

cerebral palsy usually connotes the need for motoric assistance, perhaps from crutches or braces, and ongoing intervention programs. In the case of *severe* cerebral palsy, the prognosis for independent motor function is poor; the individual functions on the ground (apedal) or uses a wheelchair.

Classification based on motor disability type includes spastic, athetoid, ataxic, tremor, rigidity, and mixed cerebral palsy. In each one there is some type of abnormal muscle tone that hampers gross and fine motor development.

1. *Spastic* cerebral palsy is characterized by increased muscle tone (hypertonus), primarily in the antigravity muscles, which makes free movement difficult. Primary or agonist muscles are commonly strongly flexed; the opposite or antagonist muscles are usually stretched. In addition, tendon reflexes are easily excitable, and stretch reflexes are exaggerated. Because of these muscle and reflex reactions, individuals

with spastic cerebral palsy often develop contractures in major and minor joints, and the joints gradually lose their range of motion. In addition, a child with spastic cerebral palsy who has all limbs involved typically exhibits a scissors gait (see Figure 10.6). In a complete scissors gait, the person walks on the toes with feet turned in, knees flexed and adducted, hips, trunk, elbows, and wrists flexed, and forearms pronated (turned under). A moderate or severe case of contractures (see Figure 10.7) or scissors gait calls for a specialized program of physical education. Aside from motor considerations, individuals with spastic cerebral palsy are often mentally retarded, have crossed eyes (strabismus), and have a tendency toward being underweight.

2. *Athetoid* cerebral palsy is characterized by an overflow of purposeless, involuntary, writhing movements. In contrast to the spastic form, affected individuals move too much and have too little muscle tone (hypotonus). Such individuals also have a tendency toward drooling, a hollow back

FIGURE 10.5 (a) TLR prone; (b) TLR supine.

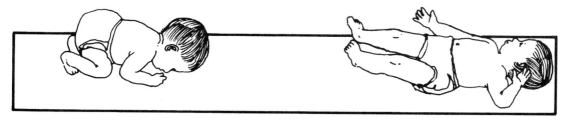

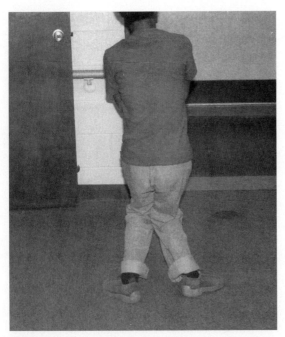

FIGURE 10.6   Front and back views of a child with a scissors gait.

FIGURE 10.7   A child with severe contractures.

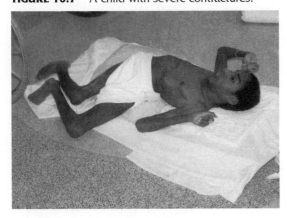

(lordosis), and all four limbs affected. They are not often overweight.

3. *Ataxia* involves a deficient sense of balance and kinesthesis. Spatial awareness is limited, and movement simulates inebriation. Ataxia is usually acquired postnatally.

4. *Tremor* cerebral palsy involves uncontrolled, regular, and strong movements that could be described as pendular (in contrast to the movement of individuals with the athetoid form of cerebral palsy). The person generally has less overall difficulty in movement than those with other cerebral palsy types.

5. *Rigidity* involves increased muscle tone in both agonist and antagonist muscles, which tends to freeze movement. In contrast to people with spasticity, these individuals have little or no stretch reflex, and their

muscles have minimal elasticity. As a result of these muscle and reflex conditions, these persons either involuntarily resist total movement in joints (lead pipe resistance) or allow slight shifts in joint action (cogwheel phenomenon). The rigidity form of cerebral palsy is often associated with mental retardation.

6. People with cerebral palsy are often primarily classified according to one type of motor disability, yet show some evidence of *mixed types*. A combination of spastic and athetoid characteristics is most common. If signs of two types are equally evident, a mixed classification is given.

Because cerebral palsy can affect one or more body parts, an anatomical or topographical classification system is often used:

- *Hemiplegia*: paralysis on one side of the body; arm and leg
- *Paraplegia*: paralysis in the legs
- *Diplegia*: paralysis primarily in the legs; some paralysis in the arms
- *Quadriplegia*: paralysis in all limbs
- *Triplegia*: paralysis in three limbs
- *Monoplegia*: paralysis in one limb

Cerebral palsy is associated with other disabilities more frequently than any other disabling condition. Commonly an individual with cerebral palsy may also have speech problems, mental retardation, seizures, visual problems, hearing deficits, or perceptual-motor difficulties. A certain child might be comprehensively described having moderate, spastic, hemiplegic cerebral palsy, with speech and hearing problems. Another child might have severe, rigid, quadriplegic cerebral palsy with moderate mental retardation, visual impairment, and a seizure disorder. A physical educator needs to know and understand this terminology in order to best address a pupil's programming needs and contribute to the school's educational team.

Cerebral palsy can be either congenital (prenatal or natal) or acquired (postnatal); there is little consensus that it is linked to heredity. The most common causes are listed in Table 10.1 according to onset.

Pupils with cerebral palsy represent the largest group of pupils with physical disabilities who receive special education services. According to Sherrill (1986) there are 3.5 cases of cerebral palsy per 1,000 births. Data reveal there are somewhere between 500,000

TABLE 10.1   CAUSES OF CEREBRAL PALSY

PRENATAL	NATAL	POSTNATAL	COMBINED
Rubella	Premature birth	Measles	Anoxia (brain oxygen
Poor maternal care	Rough delivery (including	Mumps	starvation)
Poor maternal health	forceps trauma)	Whooping cough	Accident/trauma
habits	Breech birth	Chicken pox	Hemorrhaging
Rh factor incompatibility	Prolonged labor	Influenza	Decreased level of vitamin K
Maternal diabetes	Meningitis	Encephalitis	
Maternal high blood	Child abuse	Brain lesion	
pressure		Vascular diseases	
Maternal kidney disease			
Excessive radiation (x-rays)			
Maternal venereal disease			

to 750,000 people with cerebral palsy in the United States, many of whom are of school age. In addition, 30 percent of cerebral palsy cases originate prenatally, 60 percent natally, and only 10 percent postnatally. It is interesting to note that child abuse is the cause of 75 percent of the postnatal cerebral palsy.

Of those children with cerebral palsy, about 10 percent are mild cases and are typically placed in regular classes. Approximately 80 percent have moderate cerebral palsy; they are usually placed in special day school classes. The 10 percent classified as severely afflicted are commonly institutionalized in residential facilities. This group is also typically beset with other complicating disabilities. These percentages are currently in flux because of P.L. 94-142. More pupils with cerebral palsy are being placed in regular classes every year.

In regard to motor disability type, approximately half or more of those with cerebral palsy have the spastic type; one fourth are athetoid; and less than one fourth represents the total of the ataxic, tremor, and rigidity types (Morris, 1973). Ataxia is the third most common type; the tremor classification is uncommon among children. The most common specific label is spastic hemiplegia.

Characteristics and Instructional Strategies

Because a majority of pupils with confirmed cerebral palsy have moderate or severe involvement, as well as other disabilities, the physical educator will need assistance from other professionals. Cerebral palsy is a medical condition amenable to treatment and training; however, it is not curable. The effectiveness of intervention is related to the age when intervention is begun, the nature and degree of the condition, the mental alertness and motivation of the pupil, support from the home, and the expertise of the professionals involved, including physical educators.

The therapy provided by the medical habilitation or rehabilitation team is usually spearheaded by physical and occupational therapists. A team thrust is also vital among educators deciding which positive effects of a physical education program are possible and most desirable. It is important that pupils with moderate to severe cerebral palsy receive a regimen of both *physical education* and *medical therapy*. One should never supplant the other; they should complement one another. In consequence, physical educators need to be aware of the work of medical therapists, and vice versa.

Physical therapy and occupational therapy are universally recommended therapies in the treatment of cerebral palsy. Therapists in these areas are specialists who understand abnormal movement, the use of adaptive devices (e.g., bolsters, prone boards, wedges), and reflexology. There are a few neurophysiological approaches used by these therapists. For example, Bobath neurodevelopmental treatment techniques are commonly used by physical therapists (Bobath & Bobath, 1964; Bobath & Bobath, 1975). The Bobath approach concentrates on the inhibition of abnormal reflexes, facilitation of normal motor and postural actions, and normalization of muscle tone. Key anatomical points of reference from which to facilitate movement in children who are afflicted by retained primitive reflexes are central to the body and include the neck, shoulder girdle, trunk, and hips.

One of the major considerations for people who work with a child who is passive and nonambulatory is attention to the proper techniques of lifting, carrying, transferring, and positioning of the child and objects for an activity. The fact is that too many special physical educators sustain back injuries directly related to one of these activities.

When lifting, carrying, and transferring children and objects, the teacher must use good body mechanics. We list some of the key body mechanics in performing these activities.

1. Plan the task in advance.
2. As a general rule, if the child or object weighs more than one third of your weight or is awkward, get help.
3. Always tell the child what you are going to do, step by step as you proceed.
4. Keep the child or object close to your body and be well balanced. One foot should be ahead of the other with the front foot usually pointed in the direction you are going. Keep your feet flat on the floor and about the width of your shoulders apart. The key is to keep the child or object as close as possible to one's center of gravity.
5. Avoid leaning and stretching.
6. Bend knees and hips when lifting. Keep the back straight. The body should be lowered near the level of the child or object. When possible, do not lift but roll, slide, pull, or push.
7. Do not twist the trunk when carrying or lifting. If there must be a change in direction during a lift, step around and turn your whole body without twisting at the waist or lower back.
8. Lift one end of the child or object slightly, if necessary, so one hand can be placed underneath in order to get a firm grasp.
9. Have the shoulders directly over the knees so the hands reach straight downward toward the child or object.

It is very important that children be placed in the correct position and be provided the type of support to enable them to participate effectively in a physical activity. Proper position can also help reduce abnormal muscle tone and counteract retained primitive reflexes. If improper positioning is allowed to continue, it can increase incorrect movement patterns, increase deformities, or tire the child.

Although positioning techniques should be individualized, there are important general principles that need to be heeded. One is that the child needs to be provided support at key points—the neck, shoulders, hips, and spine—to enable him or her to relax and normalize muscle tone. This allows the child the freedom to attempt voluntary limb movement. Another principle is that the child should be placed in a position to inhibit primitive reflexes from interfering with planned activity. For example, if a child has an abnormal ATNR, the physical educator would have activities performed in front of the child, or the child should be placed on his or her side to perform activities. Laying a child on his or her back is generally not the best position because it tends to increase muscle stiffness; rather, placement on the stomach on a wedge or bolster is generally recommended. A third guideline is that force should not be used when manipulating a child's limbs, as force may elicit unwanted reflexes and counter any teaching effort.

Another major consideration for preschool-aged children, as well as older individuals, who are nonambulatory is the proper use of a wheelchair during physical education to ensure successful participation, safety, and comfort. No matter what type of wheelchair is used, all have common parts (see Figure 10.8).

1. Handgrips
2. Back upholstery
3. Armrests
4. Seat upholstery
5. Front rigging
6. Footplate
7. Casters
8. Crossbraces
9. Wheel locks
10. Wheel and handrim
11. Tipping lever

Wheelchair safety considerations in a physical education class include the following.

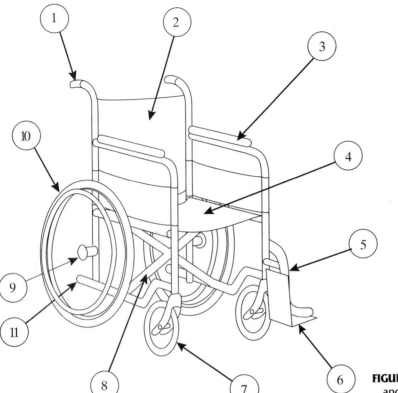

FIGURE 10.8 Traditional wheelchair and its parts.

1. Lock chair when pupil gets in and out; lock the chair at all times when the child is unattended if the child cannot propel the wheelchair alone.

2. When appropriate, require the child to wear a seat belt.

3. Only allow pupils to push a child in a wheelchair at a walking speed, to prevent loss of control.

4. Always back down a wheelchair when descending a ramp or hill.

5. When going up steps, turn the chair around backward, tip the chair way back and pull up the steps using the back wheels.

6. When going down steps, face the chair frontwards, tip the chair way back, and go down the steps on the back wheel.

Sport wheelchairs (see Chapter 17 and Appendix C) are now being utilized by individuals even though they may not be involved in sports. The chairs are lightweight and increase the user's independence at home, in school, and in the community. It is the opinion of many that the traditional wheelchair was designed for durability and for the convenience of the person who may push the wheelchair; it was not designed with the functional ability of the person in the wheelchair in mind.

Ambulatory aids can be used to assist individuals with balance and strength problems. These aids are used singly or in combination to assist in weight bearing. The following is a brief discussion of some of these aids. Canes are made from a variety of materials such as aluminum or wood (see Figure 10.9). Some canes even have four legs. When a cane is used for walking, it is placed on the strong side; the user steps forward with the weak leg and then the strong leg. The individual should always stand as straight as possible and look forward.

Crutches are common ambulatory aids (see Figure 10.10). Different gait patterns are used based on an individual's needs. In the two-point pattern the right crutch and left foot simultaneously move forward, then the left crutch and right foot simultaneously are moved. In the three-point pattern both crutches and the weaker leg simultaneously move forward, then the stronger leg is moved forward. In the four-point pattern the right crutch is moved, then the left foot, next the left crutch, and then the right foot.

There are two types of basic walkers (see Figure 10.11). There is the standard type with a four-legged rigid frame and the reciprocal walker, which has hinges, allowing each side to move forward independently. The standard walker is moved forward followed by the right and then the left foot. In contrast, with the reciprocal walker, the right side of the walker is moved forward followed by the left foot, then the left side of the walker and right foot are moved forward. Another pattern used with the reciprocal walker is to move the right side of the walker and the right foot.

Several types of braces can be used to stabilize the legs to assist in movement (see Figure 10.12). The double bar short leg brace with the shoe attached is used by individuals who have a problem with the ankle joint. The double-bar long-leg brace is used by people with problems with the knee joint.

Physical educators, occupational therapists, physical therapists, and parents all collaborate to offer appropriate activities and to

FIGURE 10.9 Types of canes.

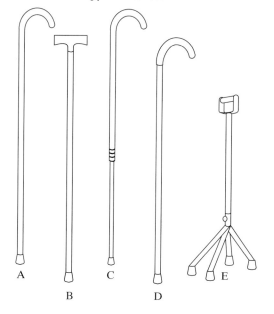

A - Standard wooden single-axis cane

B - T-top or J-line cane

C - Adjustable aluminum cane

D - Non-adjustable aluminum cane with rubberized handle

E - Four-legged or Quad-cane

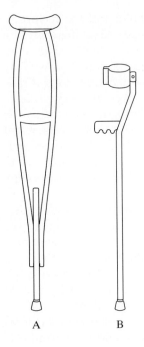

A - Adjustable underarm
    or axillary crutch
    with double uprights
    and hand bar

B - Forearm aluminum crutch

A   B

FIGURE 10.10   Types of crutches.

avoid the use of inappropriate, nonindicated activities at school and in the home. Physical educators need to individualize their programs for pupils with cerebral palsy because their characteristics and needs are so varied. The characteristics discussed here are not all-inclusive but are the most relevant to the physical educator's work.

1. Cerebral palsy often affects language and speech development, so speech and communication skills should be practiced in all classes. Physical educators can use supplementary aids for expressive language, including hand signs, pointing to meaningful symbols on a communication board, and modeling.

Standard

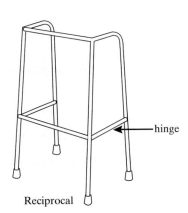

Reciprocal

— hinge

FIGURE 10.11   Types of walkers.

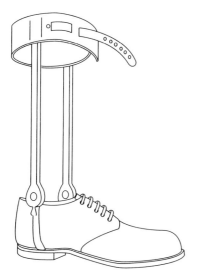

Double-bar short-leg brace with shoe attachment. Indicated for problems associated with the ankle joint.

Double-bar long-leg brace used when lower extremity problems involve the knee joint.

FIGURE 10.12 Types of braces.

2. Many people with cerebral palsy, especially those with numerous physical anomalies, have few valuable social contacts. Play can be enhanced for young pupils when the action is confined to the floor, where there is less concern for balance. Frequent integrated playtimes should be scheduled. Nondisabled pupils should be informed about cerebral palsy, with stress on ability and strength rather than disability. Physical educators should also encourage group play experiences at home through parental contact and support.

3. Involuntary motions must be controlled in people with cerebral palsy. Control can be enhanced by normalizing muscle tone and inhibiting abnormal reflexes. Symmetry inhibits abnormal involuntary movements. Individuals with athetoid and ataxic characteristics should work on holding a position, whereas those with spasticity and those with rigidity need flowing motion. Once

movement begins, those with spasticity perform best in activities that are repetitive, simple, and slow; individuals with athetoid cerebral palsy need to stop (relax) and start frequently to succeed in gross movement. Children with all types of cerebral palsy must stop before becoming fatigued or their motor patterns will deteriorate.

4. Extra time should be provided for relaxation training before, during, and after any activity. Then concentrate on single joint action, followed by movements involving several joints. Expect developmental patterns to evolve slowly and do not require quality movement. For fitness training, use progressive resistance exercises. Extra training at home is highly recommended. Avoid habitual flexed positions and flexion-oriented activities that reinforce contractures. Use stretching exercises under the guidance of medical personnel.

5. Extra handrails in the dressing room, show-

ers, and toilet might be needed. A bench for dressing and showering is also recommended.

6. Physical educators need to be familiar with any relaxants or anticonvulsants that pupils may be taking and their effects on mental alertness and gross movement.

7. Physical education programs should be augmented through after-school sports and homework to assist in developing higher levels of motor and physical development.

Indicated and Nonindicated Activities

Individuals with cerebral palsy can participate in most physical activities. However, it is essential that any activity offered is medically safe. Do not expect perfect skills; high-quality movement efficiency is less important than independent function in a variety of activities. Certain activities are particularly important and others are definitely nonindicated for pupils with cerebral palsy.

Physical and Motor Fitness. Individuals with cerebral palsy generally need to be more fit than the norm to accomplish everyday movements because of their overall mechanical and muscular inefficiency. Physical educators, therefore, need to provide frequent experiences that enhance strength, flexibility, and cardiorespiratory endurance through such activities as cycling (see Figure 10.13), swimming, running, or wheelchair pushing. Because the symptoms of cerebral palsy vary so widely, all activities should be individualized for each pupil. Pupils who are spastic need to have their flexor muscle groups stretched and extensors strengthened; individuals with the rigidity form of cerebral palsy require stretch and strengthening exercises for both agonist and antagonist muscle groups. Individuals with athetoid and ataxic forms of cerebral palsy need relaxation and

FIGURE 10.13 A woman with mild hemiplegia builds muscle strength and cardiovascular endurance through cycling.

stabilization between fitness-oriented gross motor activities.

For all types of cerebral palsy, most pupils can tolerate intense activity for 15 to 20 minutes two times a week with less intense activity for longer periods of time (Bar-Or, Inbar, & Spira, 1976). Cardiovascular activities should be used to push pupils to a safe level of exertion just below the maximum possible. Strength activities should be guided by the progressive resistance principle. Specific activities particularly suited to the fitness needs of these pupils include hanging activities using a pull-up bar or stall bar (stretch producing and strength developing); lifting weights through a range of motion using the Universal gymnasium; and medicine ball activities, which encourage socialization and strength building. (An advantage of the use of the medicine ball is that it does not usually have to be retrieved from any great distance.)

Another priority is body mechanics training. The better the body is aligned, the greater the chance that gross intentional movements will be efficient and abnormal movement reactions will be inhibited. Body symmetry enhances efficient overall movement.

Fundamental Motor Skills and Patterns. A three-phase approach, "muscle education," is usually recommended in teaching fundamental motor skills and patterns to pupils with cerebral palsy. Phase 1 consists of relaxation training, especially important for those with rigid or spastic forms of cerebral palsy. During this phase, tight muscles are stretched or massaged with medical approval in an attempt to normalize muscle tone. Appropriate positioning and handling procedures also help to inhibit abnormal reflex reactions. In addition, whenever fatigue is reached or patterns noticeably deteriorate, relaxation should be practiced. Pupils with cerebral palsy might need relaxation minisessions 10 or more times in a 30-minute session.

In phase 2 the major focus is on voluntary muscle training of single joint action. Primary actions like flex/extend and grasp/release are the major concern. Sherrill (1986) suggests a series of release activities to inhibit the grasp reflex. Phase 3 is implemented after single joint actions are mastered. In this phase developmental and multiple joint patterns are trained against gravity. Crawling, creeping, walking, running, and jumping are examples of developmental, multiple joint movement patterns. Throughout the stages of muscle education, slow deliberate movements are emphasized and a high-quality multiple joint movement pattern is not required; best approximations of these patterns and independent mobility are the essential goals.

As a group, pupils with cerebral palsy need body image activities because defective body parts are not easily related to fully functional parts. Some pupils seem to prefer to ignore the existence of less than adequate body parts. Movement exploration activities under the guidance of a physical educator are ideal to develop body awareness. In this approach all sincere effort is acceptable and all children with all levels of cerebral palsy can participate. Even pupils who are apedal (earth-bound) can explore the environment and relate body parts with their legs in constant contact with the ground. A large diet of sensorimotor and eye–limb coordination activities is also highly recommended because of the typical deficiencies in these areas of development.

For gross coordinated movement, a progression from lying to sitting to standing to locomoting is advised. Before bipedal (two points of support) activities are offered, pupils with cerebral palsy should learn how to fall. Teachers should keep in mind that loss of balance, excitement, distraction, anxiety, and sudden fast movements often elicit pathological reflexes and abnormal movement reactions.

Individuals with ataxia, who often lack kinesthetic awareness, require training in spatial orientation, perhaps more than children with any other type of cerebral palsy. During spatial orientation training, a mirror can be used to provide instant visual feedback. Pupils with the hemiplegic form of cerebral palsy, should "know" their defective side as well as their more functional one. They should not ignore their palsied side. Laterality training is a high priority for them.

One preschool program for children who are cerebral palsied in New York City has made physical education an integral component (Ruhlig, 1987). The physical education element is designed to provide new and different motor experiences that are not generally available to children who are disabled in the areas of body image, body awareness, self-confidence, play skills, and basic gross motor skills. Based on sound program objectives, a few examples of some of the equipment and activities in the program are

- *To promote balance, endurance, strength, and body awareness.* Using stairs, ladders, wooden climbing castles, balance beams, slides, tunnels, and nets, pupils walk, crawl, run, creep, roll, jump, climb, and lower themselves to the floor as they go through, across, around, over, and under the equipment.
- *To enhance eye–hand and eye–foot skills.* Using hoops, cube chairs or mats, and Pillow Polo sticks suspended from the ceiling by hooks, pupils kick, push, or hit one stick away and catch it by using both hands while lying down, sitting, or standing.

For both the elementary and secondary levels, Miller and Schaumberg (1988) suggest some fundamental motor activities that pupils with cerebral palsy enjoy that can improve their skill level and self-confidence. Three specific activities are:

- *Four-Pin Stretch.* A pupil is placed on his or her back on a mat. On each corner of the mat a plastic bowling pin is placed, and when the signal is given, the pupil tries to knock all the pins down using the hands and/or feet. The pupil must remain on the mat at all times. Some modifications of this activity are to increase or decrease the size of the mat or the distance from the pins, require that the pins must not roll off the mat, require that the pins be grasped and held in the air with a straight arm instead of knocking them down, and allow an assistant to be a co-player to ensure success.
- *Wheelchair Knockdown.* While in a manual or motorized wheelchair, the pupil must move around the room and knock creatively placed pins over with a hand. The pins cannot be knocked down by the wheelchair.
- *Tetherball.* In a sitting position, the pupil hits a pole-suspended ball using a plastic bat. Whenever possible, the pupil should use both hands. If holding the bat is a problem, an Ace bandage can hold the hand(s) onto the bat.

Aquatics. Swimming is especially beneficial for individuals with cerebral palsy. Because of the interaction of water's natural buoyancy, viscosity, and gravity, many pupils with mobility impairment can do more in this medium than on dry land (Peganoff, 1984). The following are a series of suggested activities and specific guidelines that are particularly relevant for this population.

1. As with all nonswimmers, pupils with cerebral palsy should be kept in water that is not over their heads until they can handle deep water swimming. Many individuals with spasticity have an exaggerated fear of the water (Adams & McCubbin, 1991).
2. Head control and any involuntary bodily reactions to head movement must be fully understood before prone position or underwater activities are offered.
3. Breath control and rhythmic breathing should be emphasized because many pupils have abnormal tone in the respiratory muscles and the vocal muscles.
4. Rest is easiest while in a standing (vertical) position; sitting on the edge of a sunken table or dock is also a relaxation tactic.
5. Supine floating should be emphasized initially to decrease fear of underwater activity.
6. Survival strokes that are performed slowly and emphasize maximum range of motion (ROM) are most advisable; yet, if the pupil has contractures and limited ROM, modified strokes should be encouraged. Free

movements in water can be expected, but quality stroking motions are not to be demanded.

7. Flotation devices are recommended, along with one-to-one instruction, for those pupils who are more severely impaired with cerebral palsy. Both techniques, however, should be gradually faded when possible.

8. Swimming the length of the pool, which requires fitness, should begin at the deep end, in case a pupil with cerebral palsy tires just before reaching the opposite end.

9. Recommended water temperature is 85°F or higher. Warm water promotes relaxation, which allows the swimmer to remain in the water longer. If the water temperature cannot be manipulated, the pupil should wear tight-fitting clothing, which acts as an additional layer of skin to warm the body and maintain body temperature.

10. Splashing is generally not indicated. It tends to excite the pupil, which, in turn, causes adverse central nervous system reactions.

11 A system of hand signals or visual aids can be used for better communication.

12. Training in basic motor skills and patterns is more effective in water. The properties of water may let the pupil walk, jump, and perform other developmental patterns in water before they can be done on land.

One technique of teaching swimming, developed by James McMillan in England, that is very appropriate for pupils with cerebral palsy is the Halliwick Method (Martin, 1981). It is designed to improve muscle power, circulation, and breathing patterns, as well as to increase personality and character development.

There are four basic phases in the method, which leads to water safety and independent movement in the water environment. The first phase involves mental adjustment to the water and development of the ability to move freely in the water in an upright position. In the second phase, individuals learn to move from a vertical to a horizontal and back to vertical position. Lateral body rotations are also part of this phase. An individual moves the arm and leg (or both) across the body and rotates the head in the water from one side to the other; then learns to roll the body 360 degrees. In addition, individuals learn to enter the water independently (when possible) using the skills they have attained in this phase.

In the third phase the individuals learn movement control in the water, learn a balance floating position (for some, it might not be in a horizontal position), and begin to open the eyes and explore underwater using games that may involve the retrieval of objects. Turbulent gliding is also part of this phase. This involves the individual's floating while the teacher creates turbulence with hand or leg action under the head of the pupil. This motion by the instructor prompts the individual to move through the water.

In the fourth phase, the pupil learns to move in the water by sculling, using small hand movements at the center of balance, followed by a moving action of both arms when both are lifted over the water. The last movement in the phase is a simple back crawl in which the arms are moved in a rhythmical pattern.

Some individuals with cerebral palsy will need little or no skill modification in order to participate in swimming. One such person is Sue Moucha (see Figure 10.14), who has a mild case of hemiplegia. Moucha successfully competes in international and national swimming events in sports programs for individuals with cerebral palsy.

Dance. When pupils with cerebral palsy are allowed choices, have rest periods, intermittently move in place, and move slowly,

FIGURE 10.14   Sue Moucha, who has a mild form of hemiplegia, swims competitively throughout the world.

they can greatly benefit from many forms of dance. For example, in creative dance, pupils can experiment with various movement choices, and all gross motor efforts can have value to the performer. No one can fail in creative dance, unless he or she refuses to perform. Simplified folk, square, and social dances, in which some movement from a stationary posture is permitted, are ideal. In addition, dances such as square dances provide natural rest periods, which are important.

Music in itself can act as a relaxant. The tempo and loudness of the music can be manipulated. Slow, quiet music is generally ideal.

Individual and Group Activities. Pupils with cerebral palsy are often unsuccessful in physical activities that involve competition, fast movement, fine motor movements, movement of long duration without opportunities for rest, considerable noise and outside distraction, and limited boundaries. In addition, competition between pupils with different types of cerebral palsy is usually unfair. A person with the athetoid form has less labored gross movements than one who is

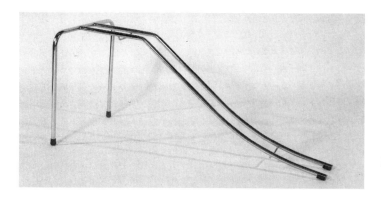

FIGURE 10.15 A bowling ball ramp can allow participation from a wheelchair. Courtesy of Flaghouse, Inc.

spastic; the rigid type presents the greatest obstacle to free movement. Given these constraints, the following guidelines and adaptations are recommended for offering individual and group activities to pupils with cerebral palsy.

1. Games where individuals compete against best personal records or in which opponents are equated by functional ability are most highly recommended. Competing teams should be made up of performers at different levels of functional ability, with each team equated overall.

2. When individuals of the same age and sex do compete against each other, pretested functional ability should be the criterion for matching competitors.

3. Any activity that results in overstimulation, overfatigue, and excess tension is not indicated.

4. Games that have carryover value and can be performed partially or totally in place are recommended. Examples include bowling (see Figure 10.15) and shuffleboard.

5. Games that have strictly limited boundaries are less well suited for participants with cerebral palsy; they should be adapted to use more open space.

6. Archery and riflery are generally not indicated for pupils with cerebral palsy.

7. In games, use soft-textured and slow-moving objects such as yarnballs, balloons, fluff balls, and partially deflated balls.

8. Substitute walking for running, bouncing for throwing, gross for fine movements, slow for fast activities, and kicking or striking stationary rather than moving objects. In addition, programming should take into account the fact that throwing is generally easier than catching for these pupils, but their throwing accuracy is usually marginal.

Common group activities like softball, soccer, football, basketball, and volleyball can be offered to pupils with cerebral palsy if certain constraints and recommendations are followed. For example, in volleyball the ball could be replaced by a beachball or balloon; and the pupil with cerebral palsy could be permitted to catch and throw, or catch and bat or hit, after one bounce.

Above all, the physical educator needs to use common sense and should strive to be imaginative in providing activities in which all pupils can have a safe, successful, and satisfying movement experience. Ideas from the pupils themselves will be very valuable; they are sometimes more aware of their personal limitations and understand their own and their playmates' needs at least as well as the instructor.

TRAUMATIC BRAIN INJURY

Everything that is experienced, thought, planned, and felt is achieved through and depends on the functions of the brain (Eames & Wood, 1989). Because of this, the destruction resulting from traumatic brain injury may cause complex problems (Bontke, 1990).

Traumatic brain injury (TBI) refers to an acquired injury to the brain caused by some external force that results in a partial or total disability and/or psychological impairment that negatively affects a pupil's educational performance. The term applies to both open or closed head injuries that result in deficiencies in one or more of the following functions: cognition; language; memory; attention; reasoning; abstract thinking; sensory, perceptual, and motor abilities; judgment; problem-solving; psychosocial behavior; physical functions; information processing; and speech. TBI does not apply to congenital or degenerative brain problems, or brain injuries induced by birth trauma (P.L. 101-476 Rules, *Federal Register*, September 29, 1992, 44802).

Traumatic brain injuries generally occur between 15 and 24 years of age and are most often caused by automobile and motorcycle accidents (Talbott, 1989). A significant number of individuals who are injured have a history of substance abuse. For instance, in most motor vehicle accidents, where there is screening for blood-alcohol level, more than 50 percent have alcohol in their blood (Rimel & Jane, 1983). It is estimated that 500,000 to 1.5 million individuals in the United States sustain a traumatic brain injury. Of these, 50,000 to 70,000 injuries are classified as moderate to severe. These individuals will live the rest of their life with a combination of cognitive, physical, behavioral, and/or social deficiencies and require rehabilitation services (Bontke, 1990).

Most researchers have suggested that overall recovery from a traumatic brain injury is better in preschool or school-aged children as compared to young infants and adults (Cockrell, Chase, & Cobb, 1990; Savage, 1987). In one investigation, 73 percent of 344 individuals who were younger than 18 years of age and severely brain-injured regained their physical independence (Brink, Imbus, & Woo-Sam, 1980).

There is a major classification system for individuals with traumatic brain injury based on the severity of the injuries (Talbott, 1989).

1. Individuals who make a rapid or nearly complete or complete recovery. Individuals within this classification generally are medically treated for weeks or months to recover from the condition. Usually the symptoms that are treated are headaches, dizziness, disturbances in behavior, and subtle cognitive disabilities such as attentional deficits.

2. Individuals with significant physical or communication disabilities that are slow to rehabilitate. Individuals in this group require lengthy physical and cognitive rehabilitation. This treatment needs to be provided in a medical facility with a rehabilitation unit that specializes in head injuries.

3. Individuals who made reasonably good and rapid physical recovery but who have severe socially unacceptable changes. Individuals in this category require extensive cognitive, social, life skills management, and occupational training.

4. Individuals who suffer from diffuse brain insults. Many of these individuals are not head injured but suffer from superimposed secondary complications such as respiratory or cardiac arrest. Behavior problems of these individuals generally cannot be effectively managed by traditional behavior management techniques and require long-care psychiatric care.

5. Individuals with head injuries that are so severe that they will never recover. These individuals suffer from a persistent vegetative state and require "coma care" treatment.

Because of the complexity of traumatic brain injury, there are numerous programming considerations that a physical educator must take into account when dealing with a pupil with a traumatic brain injury. First, different types of injuries produce different patterns of disabilities and rate of improvement in performing physical and motor activities. Therefore the physical educator must work closely with medical professionals such as physical and occupational therapists for those who have a physical and motor deficiency and the school psychologist for assistance in rehabilitating any social-emotional problems. Specially related to physical activity, the teacher can use their assistance to design a program around the following components: muscle performance, flexibility, balance development, and physical condition (Tomberlin, 1990). When medically appropriate, sports can be incorporated into the rehabilitation program and extended after rehabilitation is completed (see Chapter 17 for more information).

Second, the physical educator must be aware of any medication the pupil may be taking. Many can negatively impact on physical and motor performance. The following is a brief discussion of some medications and their effects.

1. *Antidepressants.* Generally these medications are used to control or reduce symptoms of depression, such as disorders of sleep continuity, anorexia, diarrhea, variation in mood, psychomotor retardation, and concentration impairments. Some possible side effects include fatigue, increased heart rate, blurred vision, and lightheadedness.

2. *Antipsychotics.* These medications are used to control severe symptoms of schizophrenia, such as auditory hallucinations and delusions. Some possible side effects are changes in the smoothness of voluntary muscle activities—for example, tremors, difficulty initiating or stopping movement, drowsiness, and potential to decrease cognitive capacity.

3. *Antianxiety agents.* These medications are used to decrease preoperative anxiety, muscle spasms, and some types of tremors. Some major side effects are drug dependency, forgetfulness, drowsiness, and less coordinated than usual.

4. *Mood stabilizers.* These medications are used to reduce an antidepressant, aggressive behavior, and behavior disturbances that may occur between seizures. Some side effects are increased thirst, increased urination, and mild tremors. If the individual perspires, mood stabilizers will increase the possibility of dizziness, irritability, lethargy, and even death due to interaction effects.

5. *Stimulants.* This type of medication is used primarily with individuals who are lethargic and have impaired concentration and attention. A few short-term side effects are irritability, insomnia, and aggressive behavior. Long-term side effects may be delusions, hypertension, and addiction.

6. *Anticonvulsant medications.* These medications are used to suppress posttraumatic seizures. Some common side effects are irritability, headaches, dizziness, vertigo, ataxia, and drowsiness. Chronic use of anticonvulsants may cause behavioral disturbances, hyperactivity, and impaired ability to learn.

7. *Antispasticity medications.* These medications are generally used to manage spasticity. Some side effects are negative influence on cognitive functioning and such motoric side effects as general muscle weakening.

Obtain information about the influence of specific medications on safe participation in physical education from the pupil's physician.

Third, various behavioral management techniques may be required to deal with possible adverse social-emotional behavior exhibited by a pupil with traumatic brain injury and should be designed around the individual needs of the specific pupil. In severe cases the behavior problems will not be able to be managed in a public school setting and long-term psychiatric care may be required. Numerous techniques that could be effectively used are presented in Chapter 13. All these techniques are based on the same premise: to promote the teaching of specific appropriate responses; to provide opportunities for the pupil to demonstrate the new responses and have them reinforced; and to provide a monitoring system for both the teacher(s) and staff regarding the pupil's progress (Cockrell, Chase, & Cobb, 1990).

Fourth, most schools have limited experience with the special needs of pupils with head injury. Thus such a school should request a series of in-service programs for teachers about traumatic head injury, and have knowledgeable, experienced rehabilitation professionals assist in developing an appropriate IEP (Kreutzer, Zasler, Camplair, & Leininger, 1990).

SPINAL CORD INJURIES

Definition, Causes, and Scope

The spinal cord consists of 31 pairs of spinal nerves and extends the length of the neck and torso. It is protected by the vertebra column which consists of 24 movable (7 cervical, 12 thoracic, and 5 lumbar) and numerous fixed vertebrae (5 sacral and several coccygeal bones). (A three-sided view of the vertebral column is provided in Chapter 11, Figure 11.7.) The major function of the spinal cord and nerves is to conduct nerve impulses between the brain and other parts of the body. Insult to the spine, by automobile accident, a gunshot, or fall, could have serious consequences to the lifestyle of an individual, for once soft neural tissue is destroyed, nerve cells cannot be replaced.

Traumatic spinal cord injuries are among the most catastrophic of all disabling conditions because of the decrease in independence of the individual and the secondary problems associated with this type of injury. The extent of the injury is generally described using a five-point grading system: complete, incomplete with sensation only, incomplete with nonfunctional motor ability, incomplete with motor function, and complete recovery.

The level of the spinal cord lesion is also an important consideration. Generally, the higher the lesion, the greater the paralysis and/or loss of sensation. The level of injury is described in relation to its location to the vertebra where the damage to the spine occurred and the lowest level where normal motor and sensory function exists. Level of injury is a major factor in determining the activities and physical education program for a pupil with a spinal cord injury (see Table 10.2).

The five major causes of traumatic spinal cord injuries are motor vehicle accidents (47.7 percent), falls or being struck by a falling object (20.8 percent), acts of violence such as gunshot wounds and stabbings (14.6 percent), sports/recreation activities such as diving and football (14.2 percent), and other injuries (2.7 percent). Spinal cord injuries affect mainly young adults between the ages of 16 to 30; approximately 82 percent of these individuals are males who were generally engaged in high-risk activities.

Characteristics and Instructional Strategies

Numerous general characteristics of pupils with traumatic spinal cord injuries must be considered when programming for these individuals. In the psychomotor domain, for example, factors that must be taken into account range from a high incidence of soft tissue injuries, blisters, abrasions/lacerations/

TABLE 10.2 LEVEL OF INJURY AND FUNCTIONAL ABILITY LEVEL

LOCATION OF LESION	FUNCTIONAL ABILITY
C–4	Has use of neck and diaphragm and will need total assistance to transfer to and from wheelchair.
C–7	Has ability to extend elbows and flex and extend the fingers. Can independently use wheelchair and make some transfer, and may be able to drive an automobile with assistive devices.
T 1–9	Can use upper limbs but little or no use of lower limbs. There is some control of the upper back, abdominal, and rib muscles. Generally can lift objects because of improved stability and ambulate with brace but mainly independent of the wheelchair.
T 10–12	Has complete control of upper back, abdominal, and rib muscles. Uses wheelchair for conveniences but mainly ambulates with the use of long leg braces and sometimes with the assistance of crutches.
L 1–3	Has hip joint flexibility and ability to flex the thigh. Can independently walk with short leg braces, cane, or crutches.
S–1	Has ability to bend knee and lift feet. Can walk with crutches but may require ankle braces and/or orthopedic shoes.

C = cervical, T = thoracic, L = lumbar, S = sacral.

cuts, decubitus ulcers, to temperature regulation. Physical educators must try to prevent or reduce these problems in order to provide pupils a chance for healthy participation in physical activities (Millikan, Morse, & Hedrick, 1991). Table 10.3 provides a useful listing of injury causes and their prevention.

Another problem is waste elimination. Many pupils with severe spinal cord injuries lack the ability to feel when their bladder is full and becomes distended. This condition requires catheterization to stop urine from being retained in the bladder and backing up into the kidneys. Because of this problem, these individuals tend to get kidney and urinary tract infections. Infection can result from many causes: faulty catheterization techniques, poor hygiene, and inadequate cleaning of the urinary equipment. One sign of infection is a flushed face. If this sign or others appear, activity should be terminated.

Many individuals with spinal cord injuries, however, can be catheter-free. For these individuals, an external urine-collection system can be used. All drainage devices basically consist of a condom attached to a 2-inch connector that is inserted into a leg bag made of disposable plastic or rubber. Women with quadriplegia who are incontinent may require indwelling catheters to provide unobstructed drainage to avoid infection and urethra and bladder trauma.

Bowel control may also be lost, causing constipation and incontinence. This control can generally be achieved through diet and the use of mild laxatives. In extreme cases ileostomy is a recommended surgical procedure used to eliminate stools coming from the small intestine. This procedure involves connecting the illium directly with a targeted portion of the small bowel, which permits the drainage of fecal matter through the abdominal wall. The initial opening on the surface of

---

TABLE 10.3   INJURY CAUSES AND PREVENTIONS

Soft Tissue Injuries
Causes
1. Tearing and overstretching of ligaments (falls, physical contact)
2. Chronic overuse of muscles and tendons
3. Overexertion without proper warm-up

Prevention
1. Routinely stretch, warm-up, and cool-down for each workout
2. Slow progression in a strengthening conditioning program; do not jump into it all at once
3. Use preventive taping or splinting for better stabilization of old injuries

Blisters
Causes
1. Traction or irritation of skin in contact with wheelchair rim
2. Irritation of skin at top of seat post on back of wheelchair

Prevention
1. Encourage callous formation as initial protection
2. Tape fingers
3. Wear gloves
4. Apply padding over seat post area
5. Wear shirt between skin and wheelchair back

Abrasions/Lacerations/Cuts
Causes
1. Fingers, thumbs contact brakes or metal edges on empty socket for armrests or push rims
2. Inner arms come in contact with larger tires of track chairs on downstroke
3. Chair contact with fingers trapped between wheels (e.g., basketball)

Prevention
1. Remove brakes
2. Use armrests or file off sockets for armrests
3. Wear clothing or protective covering of upper arms
4. Camber wheels for basketball chairs

Decubitus Ulcers/Pressure Sores
Causes
1. Shear forces (mainly a problem for those without sensation) and pressure over sacrum and buttocks with friction on chair
2. Track wheelchair design with knees higher than buttocks may conribute to problem
3. Sweat, moisture in combination with shear forces

Prevention
1. Adequate cushioning and padding for buttocks
2. Frequent skin checks over buttocks region
3. Shifting weight to relieve pressure intermittently
4. Good nutrition and hygiene
5. Clothing that absorbs moisture

Temperature Regulation
Causes
1. Exposure to hot/heat or cold, especially a problem for spinal injured without temperature control or sweating mechanisms
2. Inadequate fluid intake/excessive water loss

Prevention
1. Wear adequate clothing for protection in hot and cold weather (insulation)
2. Replace fluids, drink water
3. Assist with heat convection; cool towels over body
4. Minimize exposure; seek shade and cover

Source: Curtis (1982, pp. 23–24).

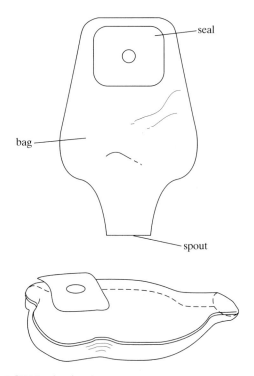

FIGURE 10.16   Ileostomy appliance

the abdomen, referred to as a stoma bud, cannot control the flow of elimination, so a secure appliance (see Figure 10.16) must be worn at all times. In general, the appliance has a seal that adheres it to the body and provides protection for the stoma bud. The appliance has a collection bag for the storage of stools that can be emptied via the bag spout. The appliance can be disposable or reusable. A similar operation in which a section of the colon is redirected to the stomach is called a colostomy.

Pupils who have had bowel-related surgery may have very low cardiovascular fitness and poor lower back, hamstring musculoskeletal function, which will require a structured and systematic exercise program (Vogler, 1990). Such pupils should be allowed to go to the restroom as needed. Further, they should be permitted to shower

and dress earlier or later than the other pupils or dress in a different aisle in the locker room.

Abnormal reflexes could impact programming in physical education. Just after a spinal injury, the spine is typically in shock, during which time there is an absence of reflexes below the level of injury. Usually, within a few months, most if not all of these reflexes return. In some individuals, however, there may be residual exaggerated reflexive action that will lead to involuntary muscle activity. In addition, most individuals with cervical and thoracic spinal injuries have intermittent muscle spasms. In some instances, individuals may have such severe and frequent muscle spasms that they may require surgical or chemotherapeutic intervention. These spasms could be at such an intensity to propel an individual from a wheelchair. The physical educator must be aware of safety and programming considerations, such as making sure the individual is strapped into the wheelchair and that the physical environment near the wheelchair is free of obstacles and padded.

Other problems in the psychomotor domain that could impact programming in physical education can be identified:

1. There may be a tendency toward permanent shortening of the muscles (contractures) caused by remaining in a stationary position for an extended period of time. What is needed is active and passive flexibility exercise in order to maintain normal muscular length.

2. Postural deficiencies may also occur, especially scoliosis. As with contractures, an exercise program is indicated. This program would involve strengthening weak muscle groups and stretching those muscle groups that are tight.

3. Because of lack of or restricted physical activity, many pupils with spinal cord injuries may become overweight or obese.

They need physical education programs that include sustained vigorous activities and dietary management.

There can also be problems in the affective domain, such as depression, anger, feeling the lack of support from family and friends, and fear of rejection. Wheelchair sports is one medium that has been tapped to improve the psychological well-being of individuals in wheelchairs (Greenwood, Dzewaltowski, & French, 1990; Paulsen, French, & Sherrill, 1991; Silliman & Sherrill, 1989). (For a discussion of wheelchair sports, see Chapter 17). In extreme instances, extensive counseling or psychotherapy may be required.

Indicated and Nonindicated Activities

Physical and Motor Fitness. Most exercises performed by able bodied individuals can be used for pupils with spinal cord injuries who are in a wheelchair.* Specific activities will depend on the severity and level of neurological impairment. The following are just a few examples of flexibility, strength, and aerobic exercises that can be performed by a pupil in a wheelchair.

Flexibility Exercises

1. *Neck Circles.* Slowly move the head through a complete circle. Repeat in the opposite direction (see Figure 10.17).
2. *Arm Circles.* Slowly move both arms through full circles. Repeat in the opposite direction (see Figure 10.18).
3. *Arm Cross.* Place one hand on the opposite shoulder so that the elbow points forward. Pull the elbow toward the body with the other hand and hold. Repeat on the opposite side (see Figure 10.19).

*Refer to Appendix C for manufacturers that design and distribute lightweight wheelchairs that are appropriate for use in physical education settings.

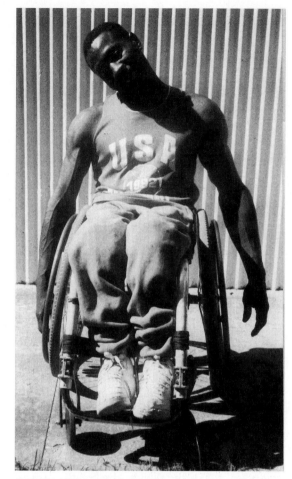

FIGURE 10.17   Neck circles.

4. *Side Stretch.* With one arm overhead and the other hanging beside the chair, lean as far as possible in the direction of the hanging arm (do not lift the buttocks off the chair). Note: If balance is poor, hold on to the side of the chair (see Figure 10.20).
5. *Trunk Twist.* Hold both arms on opposite side of the chair. Gently twist the trunk to one side while bringing the opposite arm across the chest. Hold. Repeat to the other side (see Figure 10.21).

FIGURE 10.18   Arm circles.

FIGURE 10.19   Arm cross.

FIGURE 10.20   Side stretch.

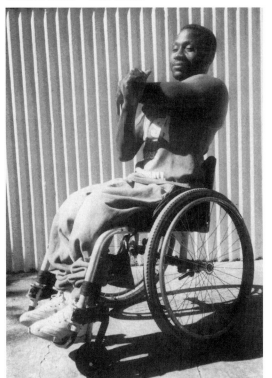

FIGURE 10.21   Trunk twist.

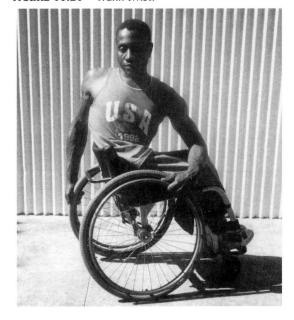

Muscular Strength Exercises

1. *Side Arm Raises.* In a sitting position, with the arms hanging on either side of the chair, hold dumbbells with the palms facing in. Lift the arms to the side until they are horizontal (exhale), then slowly return them to the starting position (inhale) (see Figure 10.22).

2. *Seat Dips.* Sitting in a chair with armrests, place one hand on each armrest. Lift the buttocks off the chair by straightening the elbows (exhale), then slowly return to the starting position (inhale) (see Figure 10.23).

3. *Shoulder Shrug.* In a sitting position with the arms hanging on either side of the chair, hold dumbbells with the palms facing in. Shrug the shoulders as high as possible (exhale), then slowly return to the starting position (inhale) (see Figure 10.24).

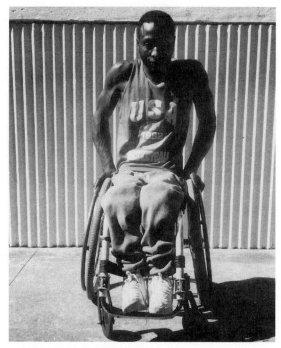

FIGURE 10.23   Seat dips.

FIGURE 10.22   Side arm raises.

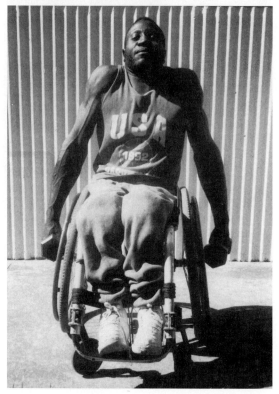

4. *Bend Over Lateral Raise.* In a sitting position, lean forward until your chest is resting on thighs. Allow the arms to hang on either side of the chair and hold dumbbells with the palms facing in. With the arms slightly bent, raise the arms to the sides until they are at shoulder height (exhale). Slowly lower to the starting position (inhale) (see Figure 10.25).

5. *Arm Curl.* In a sitting position, with the elbow bent at 90 degrees, hold a barbell in an underhand grip. Curl the weight to shoulder height (exhale), then return to the starting position (inhale) (see Figure 10.26).

6. *Triceps Press.* In a sitting position, with the arms directly above the head, hold dumbbells with the palms facing each other. Slowly lower the dumbbells behind the head by bending the elbows (inhale). Push back to the starting position (exhale), keeping the elbows directly above the shoulders (see Figure 10.27).

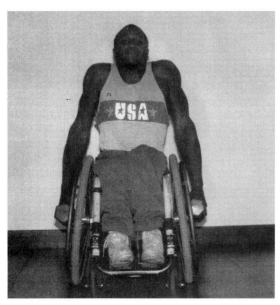

FIGURE 10.24   Shoulder shrug.

FIGURE 10.25   Bend over lateral raise.

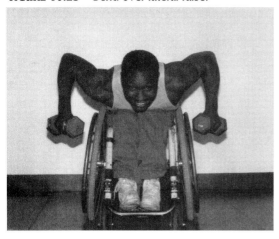

FIGURE 10.26   Arm curl.

FIGURE 10.27   Triceps press.

Aerobic Exercises

1. *Wheeling.* See Figure 10.28.
2. *Quad-Stationary Cycling.* See Figure 10.29.
3. *Stationary Arm Cycle.* See Figure 10.30.

The use of different sized and weighted medicine balls has been recommended to develop short-term endurance, throwing velocity, hand speed, and sitting stability (Morse, Hedrick, & Hart, 1992). Wheelchair fitness centers have been developed in the United States. One center is the Bilkare Wheelchair Center, located outdoors at an elementary school for pupils who are physically disabled. It was designed to increase the independence of the pupils through strength and endurance development and improved

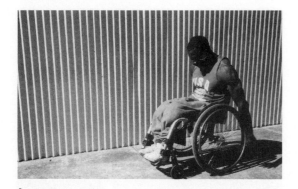

a

b

FIGURE 10.28 a and b   Wheeling.

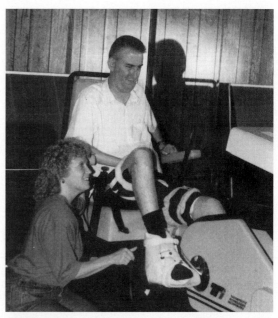

FIGURE 10.29   Quad-stationary cycling.

FIGURE 10.30   Stationary arm cycle.

wheelchair mobility. In developing the center, these basic factors were emphasized:

1. Accessible self-directed and independent use of physical fitness workouts or skill practice

2. Appropriate challenging design to maximize functional use to primarily improve muscular strength, endurance, and wheelchair movement skills

3. Progressive development opportunities in a tabletop mat area surrounded by improvement stations with various levels of performance challenges

4. Designed to minimize the possibility of injury at each station involving the use of material

5. Construction material of the center specifically selected and treated for use in the outdoors.

There are numerous activity stations in the tabletop area (see Figure 10.31). These stations and functions are:

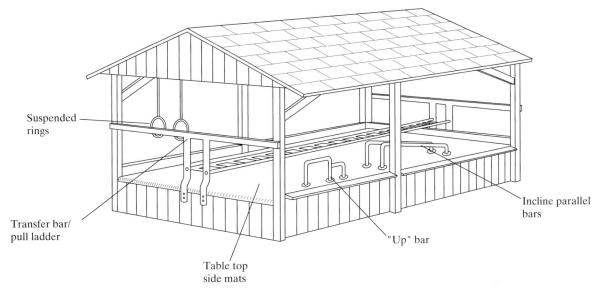

FIGURE 10.31 Tabletop Mat Area. *(With permission, Bill Price, Department of Physical Education, University of South Florida, Tampa; and Karen Jacobs, Tampa General Hospital Rehabilitation Center, Tampa, Florida.)*

1. Transfer bar/pull ladder, horizontal pipes attached to the roof uprights, to give user access to areas on the mat

2. Suspended rings, for pull-ups and arm and trunk flexibility activities.

3. "Up" bar, for learning pull-ups and for push-ups

4. Incline parallel bars, to learn push-ups and dips in a sitting position

5. Table top side mats at different heights, to support legs when performing exercises such as curl-ups, sit-ups, and neck raises

6. "The mat," a padded area for relaxation exercises, body flexibility, body crawls, and push-ups.

There are also wheelchair mobility improvement stations at the school (see Figure 10.32) that are generally used to develop wheelchair management skills that are involved in activities of daily living:

1. Two-wheel lean ramp is designed to provide experience in leaning, which involves weight distribution practice.

2. Post maze is used to learn how to maneuver a wheelchair in a coordinated manner against time.

3. Pipe tunnel offers experience in ducking obstacles while moving forward and backward.

4. Corner ramps are used to develop such factors as weight distribution, body lean, arm strength, and endurance.

5. Stretch and reach is used to develop flexibility as well as the ability to distribute and balance body weight.

6. Wheelchair-pull bars provide experience in learning to control a wheelchair in tight spaces.

7. Pop-over path is designed to provide experience going over small obstacles.

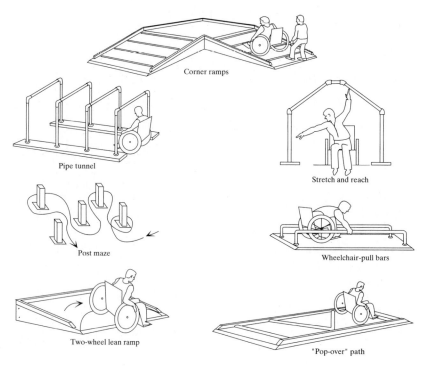

Corner ramps

Pipe tunnel

Stretch and reach

Post maze

Wheelchair-pull bars

Two-wheel lean ramp

"Pop-over" path

FIGURE 10.32 Wheelchair Mobility Improvement Stations. *(With permission, Bill Price, Department of Physical Education, University of South Florida, Tampa; and Karen Jacobs, Tampa General Hospital Rehabilitation Center, Tampa, Florida.)*

Fundamental Motor Skills. Most pupils with spinal cord injuries can participate in traditional motor skills training with very minor modifications. For instance, a pupil in a wheelchair can push it instead of hopping, running, or galloping. Throwing and catching activities may not require any modification, except the distance of the throws might be reduced. For those activities which require major adaptation, refer to Chapter 4, on mainstreaming for numerous techniques to individualize for and combine pupils who use crutches, braces, and/or wheelchairs in motor skill activities.

Aquatics. Swimming activities are often used in the rehabilitation process of individuals with a spinal cord injury. Again, each individual will require an individualized swimming program to meet his or her specific needs. This program is generally developed in cooperation with an occupational

therapist, physical therapist, and/or physician. In general, though, swimming is an excellent activity for physical fitness development for pupils with at least partial shoulder and bicep control (C-5). Further, those with functional abdominal and thoracic muscles can compete in numerous swimming events, including those sponsored by the National Wheelchair Athletic Association.

Dance. As with able-bodied individuals, there are numerous benefits in dance for individuals with a neurological impairment that causes them to use crutches or a wheelchair. The physiological benefits can be the maximization of muscular strength, muscular endurance, cardiorespiratory endurance, and flexibility. The psychological-sociological benefits can be the enhancement of the ability to express emotions, interact socially, communicate with others, increase self-concept, and relax (Hill, 1976).

The three major types of social dance are square dance, ballroom, and folk dance, and all three types can generally be modified for individuals with spinal cord injury. A major key to teaching social dance is to practice the steps without the music initially until the steps are mastered.

Some square dance movements can be easily modified for use in a segregated or integrated setting.

1. *Honor Your Partner or Bow to Your Partner.* Partner and person in a wheelchair side by side, the latter just pulls backward on wheels and then moves to a position facing partner. The dancers nod their heads and return to the original position.

2. *Allemande Left.* Roll to corner and each partner grasps other's left vertical armrest support, and then turn 180 degrees and return to original position.

3. *Ring-Hang Swing.* Roll toward partner and grasp right vertical armrest, then push with left hand and rotate 180 degrees. Next, dancers return to home position and face partner.

4. *Grand Right and Left.* Roll toward partner, pass partner on right side, pass next dancer on the left side, and so on, until facing partner.

There are many forms of ballroom dances—waltz, fox-trot, polka, and rumba. It is interesting to note that most of these dance steps were derived from dances performed over a century or more ago, such as the minuet. The basic steps to perform the waltz box step for individuals in a wheelchair or using crutches are illustrated in Table 10.4.

The easiest form of dance to teach is folk dance, which involves skill motor patterns. Instructions for the hora are presented in Table 10.5. In this folk dance, the males and

---

TABLE 10.4 THE WALTZ

The waltz is of middle European origin. Its style is very smooth and gliding, and it is executed to dreamy and romantic melodies. Timing for this dance is 3/4 with various tempos or speeds; the American tempo is slow whereas the Viennese tempo is faster. Timing should be adjusted according to abilities of the dancers, or individual steps may be altered so as to keep better time with the music.

Waltz—Wheelchairs

COUNTS	MAN	WOMAN
Basic		
1,2,3	F	B
1,2,3	B	F
Box step (see diagram)		
1	F	B
2,3	Turn R 90°	Turn L 90°
1	F	F
2,3	Turn L 90°	Turn R 90°
1	B	F
2,3	Turn L 90°	Turn R 90°
1	F	F
2,3	Turn R 90°	Turn L 90°

Lady's turn: As the man does balances, the woman takes 12 counts to turn all the way around to her right; she may repeat this move turning to the left.

Double turn: The man and woman make complete turns in 12 counts, the man to his left, the woman to her right; it may be repeated in opposite directions.

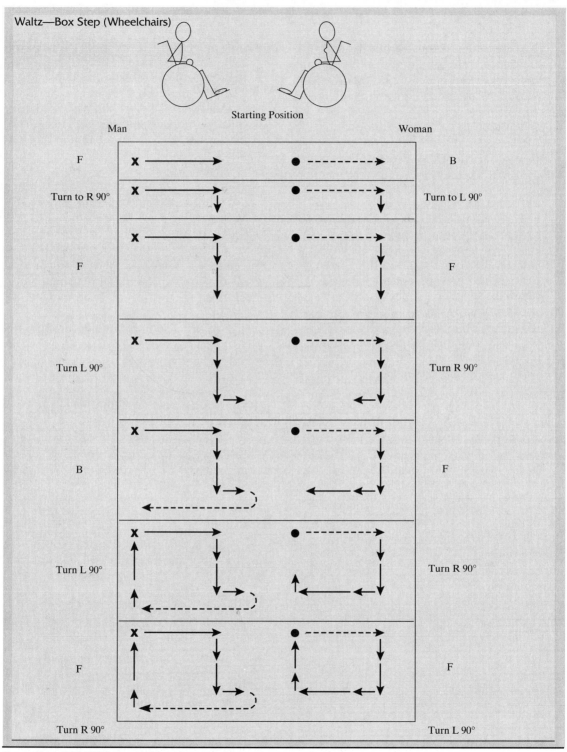

Waltz—Box Step (Wheelchairs)

Starting Position

Man

Woman

F

B

Turn to R 90°

Turn to L 90°

F

F

Turn L 90°

Turn R 90°

B

F

Turn L 90°

Turn R 90°

F

F

Turn R 90°

Turn L 90°

Source: From Hill (1976), pp. 11–12, with permission.

TABLE 10.5   THE HORA

The Hora is often considered the Jewish national dance. The circle in which it is performed symbolizes unity for the Jewish people. Dancers, all of whom do the same steps, move in a counterclockwise direction and in half-time.

	Basic	
	1	Turn L 45°
		Turn R 45°
	2	Turn R 45°
		Turn L 45°
	3	F
	4	F
	About Face	
	1	Turn L 45°
	2	Turn L 45°
	3	Turn L 45°
	4	Turn L 45°

The basic step is then continued in this clockwise direction until another about face is called.

Circle left

All dancers turn to the left completely around in place. This takes four or eight counts, depending on the ability of the participants; they then continue the basic step.

Hora – Crutches

	COUNTS	DANCERS
Basic		
	1	Crutches L
	2	Swing – to
	3	Crutches R
	4	Swing – to
	5	Crutches R
	6	Swing – to
	7	Crutches L
	8	Swing – to
	1,2	Crutches F
	3,4	Swing – through
	5,6	Crutches F
	7,8	Swing – through

Turn in place

Take 16 counts to run completely around in place, either to the right or to the left.

Source: From Hill (1976), pp. 70-71, with permission.

females perform the same steps in a straight line. Instructions for other ballroom dances and full dances are presented in a manual by Hill (1976).

SEIZURE DISORDERS

Definition, Causes, and Scope

Seizure disorders, also referred to as *convulsive disorders* or *epilepsy*, are one of the oldest known disabling conditions. They are also one of the least understood and, to this day, are considered by some to signify magical powers. More typically they are erroneously associated with mental retardation or emotional disturbance.

A *seizure disorder* is a neurological condition triggered by an irregular series of excessive electrochemical brain waves* which usually produce major or minor body convulsions. During a convulsion, the voluntary muscles of a portion or the entire body usually react to brain wave irregularity by tensing and contracting involuntarily. There are six common types of seizures.

1. A *grand mal*, the most common and severe, is a generalized motor seizure in which a massive isometric episode occurs in all voluntary muscles at different times during an unconscious state. This type of seizure is often preceded by a warning signal (an aura), such as a ringing in the ears, a tingling sensation, or a distinct smell. The actual seizure is characterized by a tensing or static contraction phase (tonic phase), usually for a few seconds, followed by a muscular spasmodic jerking phase (clonic phase), which usually lasts for a few minutes. During the clonic phase, the tongue might be bitten and the bladder or bowel might empty. Perhaps due to its dramatic manifestations, the grand mal is the type of seizure most often associated with seizure disorders.

2. A *petit mal* is a short seizure (approximately 1 to 30 seconds) characterized by a generally dazed appearance, no falling to the ground, a cessation of mental processes and amnesia, minor twitching, and eye jerking or staring. A pupil will usually proceed with the previous activity when the seizure ends. Petit mal attacks do not particularly tire the victim; they can occur many times during one day.

3. During a *psychomotor seizure*, the individual appears to be conscious and engaged in purposeless and sometimes antisocial behavior (such as aggressiveness) without remembering it afterwards (amnesia). Psychomotor attacks do not usually last long.

4. A *Jacksonian seizure* is a focal point seizure, during which muscle contractions occur in only one portion of the body. It usually lasts less than 1 minute. This type typically involves only a clonic phase with no aura and only rarely is there a loss of consciousness. Consciousness can be lost, though, if the seizure contractions cross the body midline. Jacksonian seizures often can be observed to originate at the edge of the mouth, at the thumb of one hand, or the big toe of one foot.

5. A *minor motor seizure*, as the name implies, is a short, minor seizure that involves a sudden major contraction of one or more muscle groups. Rarely does unconsciousness result.

6. An *autonomic seizure* is one in which the rate of involuntary physiological functions is temporarily heightened. Such symptoms as pallor, increased perspiration, blood pressure, and heart rate, and gagging are possible.

An individual can have a mixture of different types of seizures or can conceivably

---

*Brain waves are minute electric currents essential to the function of the brain. They are measured by an electroencephalograph (EEG).

switch from one type to another during a lifetime. According to Sherrill (1986), approximately 40 percent of all individuals who have a seizure disorder are in this category.

Not all seizure disorders have known causes. In fact, a surprising 60 to 70 percent have unknown (idiopathic) etiology; no structural or organic damage can be located by medical experts. Hereditary links, however, are often implied in idiopathic seizure disorders, particularly when both parents have seizures. Known causes include various types of infections, accidents, and other types of environmental insult, including encephalitis (inflammation of the brain), meningitis (inflammation of the soft tissue in the brain or spinal cord cover), allergies, malnutrition, anoxia, high blood pressure, brain tumors, and head injuries (before, during, and after birth).

Physical educators need to be alert to those factors that trigger a seizure over which they might have some control. Seizures are more likely to occur under the following conditions:

1. Low blood sugar
2. Heightened emotional state or stress
3. Physical fatigue
4. Alcohol consumption
5. Just after intense concentration
6. During menstruation period
7. High alkalinity of the blood
8. Excessive noise or bright flashing lights
9. Lack of sleep
10. Constipation
11. Improperly used medications

With a knowledge of these specific mitigating factors, physical educators can derive clues that will allow them to directly influence the point of the seizure threshold (that time just before a seizure occurs). Further, physical educators are in a unique position to offer activities and advice to help pupils themselves control their seizures.

Because of the stigma attached to seizures, their concealment by parents and affected pupils distorts the true picture of the extent of the disability, and a precise accounting of its scope is impossible. According to the Epilepsy Foundation of America, there are about 4 million people with seizure disorders.

Seizure disorders appear to be primarily a "disorder of youth." Approximately 70 percent of all individuals with seizure disorders first display evidence of seizures before the age of 20; most of these appear during or near pubescence, when many metabolic and chemical changes affect the body. Important to all teachers is the fact that approximately 80 percent of all children with seizure disorders can control their seizures with proper medications. Major anticonvulsant drugs include mysoline, dilantin, phenobarbital, and depakene. Surgery is another treatment that can eliminate or cure epilepsy in some cases (such as seizures caused by tumors). When the cause is idiopathic, however, medical treatment cannot cure the condition; it can only control it with drugs. Fortunately, with or without drugs, seizures tend to decrease naturally in frequency and intensity with increased age.

Characteristics and Instructional Strategies

Convulsions, unconsciousness accompanied by falling, and the possibility of injury are characteristic of grand mal seizures. Other seizure types have little or no potential for injury. Given the possibility that pupils with grand mal seizures will be in their classes, physical educators need to know how to administer first aid when such a seizure occurs during class. The following measures should be taken:

1. Remain calm. A grand mal seizure *cannot* be stopped by shaking, administering fluids, or restraining the pupil. A seizure must be allowed to run its course.

2. Assist the unconscious pupil when collapsing onto the ground. Lower the body gradually, preferably to a cushioned spot (grass, mat, a coat), and clear obstacles to prevent bodily injury during clonic phase thrashing.

3. Tilt the head to the side to prevent the possibility of swallowing the tongue and to release saliva.

4. Observe the pupil throughout the seizure in order to be able to report the incident fully on school forms. Call medical help *only* if the seizure lasts more than 10 minutes, one seizure immediately follows another, or if it is the first known seizure.

5. After the seizure, allow the pupil to rest, as the pupil's voluntary muscles have just had a real "workout." Give the conscious pupil energizing foods (such as soft drinks or orange juice), if available. Usually there is no need to send a pupil home to recuperate.

Physical educators also need to know various instructional strategies for pupils with seizure disorders. For instance, a seizure disorder is more a social than a medical disability. During a seizure, the instructor must have poise and the class should continue if at all possible. Class members should be told what a seizure is in order to dispel myths and to develop empathy. Physical educators also have the obligation to emphasize the pupils' abilities. Success for these pupils in social activities is especially vital, so many social activities should be provided.

Heavy doses of anticonvulsant drugs tend to affect adversely overall coordination and mental alertness. The instructor needs to monitor the effect of medication on movement. Abnormal side effects need to be reported to the physician in order to help determine the dosage that would control the seizures but allow maximum learning. Further, if seizures commonly cause the pupil to fall unconscious to the ground, protective helmets are advised. Type of helmet could range from football helmets to bicycle racer helmets to those that are custom-made.

Indicated and Nonindicated Activities

Pupils with seizure disorders usually can participate in all of the activities offered in a regular physical education class. However, a few priorities need to be considered.

Physical and Motor Fitness. Individuals with seizure disorders are inclined toward sedentary habits. In addition, reaching the point of physical fatigue increases the chance of having a seizure. Cardiovascular endurance activities that gradually increase the fatigue threshold, therefore, are desirable. If the fatigue threshold increases and seizures decrease in frequency, duration, and intensity, the need for prescribed medication may also decrease.

Activities such as long distance runs and in-place running are ideally suited for increasing the fatigue threshold. However, the physical educator must operate within a medical margin of safety when programming the activity. That is, the teacher should provide activities under a physician's advice that do not cause the pupil to reach the point of extreme fatigue but, rather, only gradually tax the body's energy. If this individualized fatigue point is then reached from day to day, it will tend to rise, enabling cardiovascular loads to be progressively and safely increased. Another consideration is stress. There is evidence of an association between stress and seizures. For some pupils, certain sports might produce high levels of stress and may not be psychologically appropriate for them.

As with other pupils, muscular endurance and strength are important fitness indices for pupils with seizures. Certain precautions are, however, important. Any activity that would become dangerous if a seizure occurred would be nonindicated. Hanging on stall bars, vertical wall peg climbing, and rope or ladder climbing are examples.

Fundamental Motor Skills and Patterns. All fundamental motor skills and patterns should be acquired by pupils who are seizure-prone. Most attention should perhaps be given to the development and maintenance of overall eye–limb coordination, due to the possible adverse effects of anticonvulsant drugs on motor coordination.

Activities that are dangerous to pupils whose seizures are not well controlled are nonindicated or need to be judiciously supervised. In some cases a helmet needs to be worn for protection. Activities that involve significant height, swings, monkey bars, merry-go-rounds, trampolines, and the like are certainly nonindicated for those pupils who have uncontrolled grand mal seizures without an accompanying aura. Cycling is another activity that some authorities caution pupils with seizure disorders not to engage in and never do on the streets.

Aquatics. Swimming is an excellent activity for pupils with a seizure disorder, particularly for its social, leisure time, and cardiovascular values. Only a few precautions need to be followed with these children. Pupils who are seizure-prone should have a buddy who is not disabled assigned to them in the water. This strategy provides additional supervision for the pupil with a disability and an ongoing social contact, and it also allows the instructor to attend to the class as a whole. Hyperventilation (breathing in and out quickly) activities at rest tend to be non-

indicated because they raise the alkalinity of the blood, which may trigger a seizure. Diving and underwater swimming are not recommended because they could be life threatening if a seizure occurred while the pupil was engaging in them.

Contrary to popular belief, water can be a safe medium in which to experience a seizure. However, this is true only if the seizure occurs while the pupil is on the surface of the water and in the presence of an assistant who is nonseizure disordered. When a seizure does occur under these conditions, the buddy only needs to rotate the pupil to a supine position, keep the head tilted back and out of the water, and stay away from the pool edge. The thrashing during the clonic phase will then be safe and noninjurious. Once the seizure is over, the buddy should get assistance to lift the pupil to a dry, warm location. A few towels or a blanket should be placed under and on top of the pupil, and the pupil should rest.

Dance. A child with a seizure disorder should participate in all forms of dance. The social benefits derived from involvement in dance activities are vital. Again, the instructor and the classmates should be aware of the disorder and prepared for any seizures. If a seizure occurs during dance class, it is strongly advised to continue the dance while addressing the pupil's needs in an appropriate spot as inconspicuously as possible. The embarrassment associated with a seizure, especially during adolescence, is at least as important as most medical considerations.

Individual and Group Activities. Games that increase fitness are highly desirable because collectively they have the potential to lessen the duration, frequency, and intensity of seizures. Games can also increase social and emotional growth.

In the past, the common practice in physical education for pupils who were seizure-prone was to deemphasize competitive activities because of the heightened emotion and stress inherent in competition. Head contact activities were also generally nonindicated, because it was believed that brain waves might be adversely affected.

Based on research data and clinical observations, this philosophy has now changed. All these activities are being increasingly recommended, particularly if a pupil's seizures have been controlled for more than one year and prerequisite skills have been mastered. Activities such as football, heading in soccer, boxing, judo, battleball, and the group game Bull in the Ring are now acceptable. Many educators and medical personnel feel that the social benefits of participation in group activities are at least as important as the slight possibility of a seizure.

Certain precautions need to be practiced, however. Pupils who do not have their seizures well controlled need to be carefully supervised in activities that could be dangerous in case of a seizure. Fitted with helmets, some of these pupils could safely play in many activities such as volleyball (see Figure 10.33) and softball. Participation in archery, riflery, and bicycling, as well as on parallel bars, rings, and the high bar, are in most instances ill-advised. In addition, long involvement in very vigorous activities, such as basketball or soccer, need to be closely monitored and adjusted for each person's exercise tolerance.

SPINA BIFIDA

Definition, Causes, and Scope

Spina bifida is a malformation of the spinal structure caused by improper closure of one or more vertebrae (see Figure 10.34). Spina bifida without serious consequence is

FIGURE 10.33 By wearing a helmet, this child can safely play volleyball.

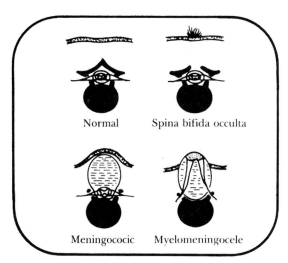

FIGURE 10.34   Forms of spina bifida. (From G. D. Stark, *Spina Bifida: Problems and Management.* London: Blackwell Scientific Publications, 1977, p. 5. Used by permission.)

called *spina bifida occulta. Spina bifida cystica* is an extension of this condition where the covering of the spinal cord, with or without spinal cord and nerve roots, protrudes from the spinal canal through the abnormal vertebral opening. When the covering of the spinal cord protrudes, the condition is referred to as *meningococic*; if the spinal covering, spinal cord, and nerve roots protrude, it is called *myelomeningocele.*

It is estimated that 1 out of 350 infants is born with some form of spina bifida and that there are approximately 50,000 school-aged children in the United States with some form of the condition. An estimated 80 percent of the children with this impairment have the myelomeningocele form. The specific cause of spina bifida is unknown. It appears that there is a combination of genetic and environmental factors that may increase the risk of spina bifida, but no one factor can be directly identified.

There is usually no damaging effect on the body in spina bifida occulta. In fact, the condition may not even be detected until a child's spinal column is x-rayed. In other cases, there may be an abnormal hair tuft, mole, or dimple in the skin above the impaired vertebra. If the meningococic form accompanies the vertebra deformity, a sac filled with cerebrospinal fluid protrudes from the defect on the surface of the skin. The spinal cord remains in the spinal canal and generally remains intact. In most cases, surgery is required to close the lesion. This operation protects the infant from infection and may prevent a possible future neurological impairment.

The most severe form of spina bifida is the myelomeningocele, which involves mild to severe irreversible neurological damage. This hinders or stops critical function of organs or muscle groups of the lower body. As with the meningococic form, surgery is performed as early in the infant's life as possible. An infant with this condition may be multiply disabled, with lower limb paralysis and urinary and bowel incontinence. Some musculoskeletal anomalies may be apparent at birth. The ribs and pelvis may be deformed, with associated scoliosis or kyphosis. Some infants may also have a congenital hip dislocation. Usually corrective casting, remedial positioning, and bracing are used to correct these conditions. If this form of treatment is ineffective, surgery is indicated.

About 90 percent of infants born with the myelomeningocele either have or soon develop hydrocephaly. This condition is characterized by an imbalance between the production of cerebrospinal fluid within the cranial vault and its drainage into the circulatory system through the surface of the brain. If this condition is not corrected, the head will become larger because of the pressure caused by the excessive accumulation of fluid. The pressure can cause varying degrees of mental retardation or even death.

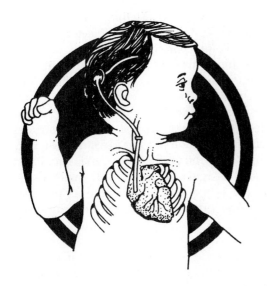

FIGURE 10.35   Ventricular-atrial shunt. (From G. D. Stark, *Spina Bifida: Problems and Management.* London: Blackwell Scientific Publications, 1977, p. 92. Used by permission.)

The treatment for hydrocephaly is the insertion of a shunt to divert the excess fluid, the ventricular-atrial shunt being the most widely used (see Figure 10.35). The shunt involves a one-way valve, implanted behind the right ear, which pumps fluid from a catheter inserted in the right side of the brain to a catheter running under the skin in the neck and entering the venous blood system, terminating in the right atrium of the heart.

Characteristics and Instructional Strategies

Specialized programming is not usually required for pupils with spina bifida occulta or pupils who had the meningococic form repaired during infancy. We focus here on pupils with the myelomeningocele form of spina bifida.

Children with spina bifida are often embarrassed by their condition in the pres-

ence of peers, and their school social life is usually limited. Individual counseling should be provided. A locker could be assigned in a vacant aisle, if necessary, and the child should be allowed to dress earlier or later than others. The pupil should also be encouraged to participate not only in class but in extracurricular activities. Further, many children with spina bifida are fearful of injuries from gross movement since their paralysis makes them awkward movers. Physical activities must be matched to each pupil's present psychomotor skill level; then gradually the difficulty of physical and motor tasks can be increased.

Physically and motorically, children with spina bifida with lower body paralysis may have postural deficiencies, and development delays are very common. There is a large incidence of scoliosis and kyphosis among this group. A physician or allied medicine specialist (physical therapist, occupational therapist) should be consulted and a corrective exercise program initiated. During the first year of life, medical personnel and parents should initiate an exercise program (see Figure 10.36). When the child enters school, the physical educator should then assume a major role in this training.

Some other characteristics and teaching suggestions include the following:

1. Provide programming at the same time each day to establish a consistent routine. Consistency should help the pupil develop self-help skills, such as toileting routines. The physical educator should get medical advice on using collecting bags and catheters during participation in physical activities.

2. Pupils with shunts must take precautions to protect the area where a shunt has been implanted.

3. Care must be taken to eliminate possible friction of the skin against hard surfaces, as

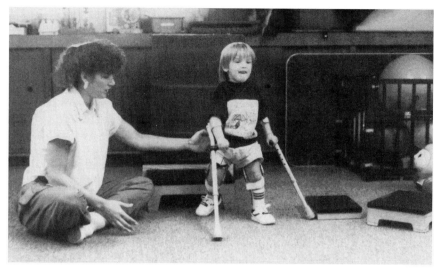

FIGURE 10.36 Physical therapist exercising a child with spina bifida.

some pupils cannot sense an insult to the lower body. After activities, pupils with braces should always check their skin for irritations. Left unattended, irritations could lead to decubitus ulcers.

4. The pupil may need crutches, braces, or a wheelchair to perform physical activities. Modifications of the rules, strategies, and equipment of games may be required.

5. The physical education program should be scheduled prior to recess, study hall, or lunch to allow more time for dressing, undressing, showering, and toileting.

Indicated and Nonindicated Activities

Because of the heterogeneity of pupils with myelomeningocele, no one physical activity program can be planned. Each pupil must be considered individually by physical educators with the assistance of a physician and, whenever possible, an occupational or physical therapist.

With contractures developing in the lower limbs and a higher than normal incidence of postural deviations, physical and motor fitness is very important. A light punching bag is one piece of equipment that can be used as a general body conditioner. The development of upper body coordination and rhythm also benefits from a punching bag. Many problems can be habilitated with close coordination with an allied medicine therapist and supplementary work at home.

Many basic fundamental motor skills and patterns, such as running, jumping, or hopping, cannot be performed in the traditional manner. The skills must be modified or alternate skills provided. In running activities, for example, pupils in wheelchairs should be allowed to participate. The distance can be shortened, and occasionally the ambulatory pupils can be placed in wheelchairs for the activity.

Many pupils with the myelomeningocele form of spina bifida have visual-motor problems, which may hinder their catching, hitting, or throwing a ball. Consultation with the classroom teacher and support personnel may be required for strategies that can be adapted to teach visual-motor skills needed for physical education.

The aquatic environment provides an opportunity for movement that cannot be experienced out of the water by pupils on crutches, in braces, or in wheelchairs. Water is also an excellent environment in which to stretch and strengthen the lower limbs to prevent contractures. An aquatic program for this type of pupil has three major goals (Adams & McCubbin, 1991):

1. *Weight control and increased endurance.* It is one of the few vigorous physical activities suitable for children with spina bifida.
2. *Outlet for emotional and social development.* A sense of independence is achieved in the water because the child can have more freedom of movement without the restrictions of braces, crutches, or wheelchairs.

3. *Overcoming fear.* Overcoming the fear of water may help a child overcome other fears. Most children with spina bifida have a fear of water and look to others for support to the point of complete dependency. The beginning stages of learning to swim must focus on adjusting psychologically as well as physically to the water and on developing confidence in the instructor.

No special urinary appliance is required for swimming. If the pupil is wearing a collection bag under the swimsuit, the catheter should be detached from the bag and clamped. The bag should also be emptied before swimming.

Whenever possible, pupils with the myelomeningocele form of spina bifida should be allowed to participate in a regular physical education program. Activities that require little or no modifications in which these pupils can excel include archery, bowling (see Figure 10.37), weight lifting, and fencing. Several techniques can be used to adapt

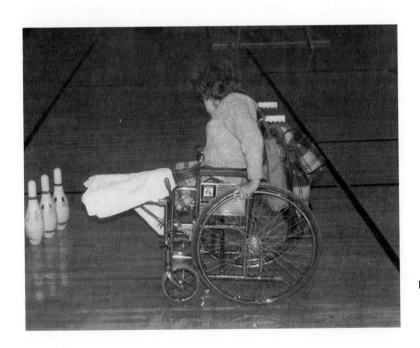

FIGURE 10.37   Many modifications can be made to allow pupils with spina bifida to learn common games.

activities to enable these pupils to participate in a regular program (Seaman, 1976).

1. Modify the time needed for the pupil to complete an activity. More time can be provided to complete circuit training or extra time given before or after school to complete a task.
2. Place the pupil in a physical activity where he or she can succeed. In volleyball or softball, select the position that requires the least movement (e.g., server or first base player). Two pupils can combine in a position traditionally designed for one.
3. Modify the equipment and facilities. Make the distances shorter and the targets larger. Balls can be bigger and bats lighter than those ordinarily used.
4. Substitutes can run bases or kick a ball.
5. Adaptation of rules may be necessary—for instance, four strikes instead of three.

The same techniques can be used to modify traditional physical activities in segregated environments. Tackle or flag football can be transformed into wheelchair football with a few modifications. Touching the player or the player's wheelchair can replace tackling or flag pulling. Blocking can be limited to the line of scrimmage to minimize the danger of injury, and the playing area can be changed to a hard surface (such as asphalt or cement) with reduced boundaries. Otherwise, where safety permits, the usual rules and regulations of a game may be followed.

MULTIPLE SCLEROSIS

Definition, Causes, and Scope

Multiple sclerosis is a noncontagious, progressive neurological disease of the central nervous system. The nerves of the body are covered by a sheath that contains myelin. In multiple sclerosis, segments of the myelin sheath disintegrate and are replaced by scar tissue. When scarring occurs, the transmission of nerve impulses that control gross and fine muscle control are distorted or blocked.

Multiple sclerosis is characterized by a series of attacks, usually causing increased disability and periods of remission. Some individuals with multiple sclerosis may suffer only mild symptoms, which could disappear for several years. Generally, attacks are approximately six weeks in duration and remission periods are of a few months. Many older adults with multiple sclerosis may become incapacitated and be confined to a wheelchair; others will be able to move with varying degrees of difficulty. There is no set pattern of development, but we list some of the general symptoms:

1. Partial or complete paralysis of part of the body
2. Double or other defective vision
3. Loss of bladder or bowel control
4. Extreme weakness
5. Tremors of the hand
6. Numbness in parts of the body
7. Dragging of one or both feet
8. Slurring of speech
9. Loss of balance
10. Prickling sensation in parts of the body
11. Loss of coordination

A combination of three or more of these symptoms could be warning signals of multiple sclerosis.

The cause and effective treatment of multiple sclerosis are unknown. Some possible causes of the demyelination process are heredity, injury, exposure to heat, cold or viruses, and vitamin deficiencies. Typical forms of treatment include building up a general resistance to respiratory and other infections, avoiding extreme temperature, performing moderate exercise, diet, and rest. Bracing is also utilized to stabilize affected limbs.

Of all the neurological diseases, multiple sclerosis is the leading cause of permanent disability and the third cause of death in the United States. It usually attacks individuals between 18 and 45 years of age. There are more than 500,000 persons in the United States with multiple sclerosis. Its extent is slightly higher among women, and occurs five to ten times more often in the northern than in the southern states.

Characteristics and Instructional Strategies

Physical activities must be designed for each person with multiple sclerosis based on the severity of the condition. The program should be determined by the physical educator in consultation with a physician and the individual, particularly during an active period of the disease. A scale has been devised that indicates degree of motor disability (Kurtzke, 1965):

0 = Normal neurological examination

1 = Minimal signs (diminished ability to touch finger to nose, diminished vibration sense)

2 = Minimal dysfunction (slight weakness or stiffness, awkwardness, mild visual-motor disturbance)

3 = Moderate dysfunction (mild hemiplegia, moderate urinary or visual problems)

4 = Relatively severe dysfunction (still able to work and carry out normal activities)

5 = Severe dysfunction (with maximal effort can walk without assistance several blocks; the ability to work normally is hindered)

6 = Assistance required for walking (braces, canes, crutches)

7 = Restricted to wheelchair (able to move chair by self)

8 = Restricted to bed, but can use the arms effectively

9 = Totally dependent

10 = Death due to multiple sclerosis

Because multiple sclerosis is progressive and unpredictable, the emotional state of the individual is often adversely affected. A well-designed physical education program not only assists the individual in psychomotor development but also provides opportunities for positive psychological and social development.

Indicated and Nonindicated Activities

Two of the major needs of such a person are flexibility and range of motion exercises. Contractures can be minimized by ensuring full range of motion of all involved muscle groups. Exercise sessions should progress slowly. A weakened muscle can be further injured and the disability increased if the individual is overexerted. Periods of inactivity will rapidly cause atrophy, a loss of motor coordination, and decreased balance abilities. Physical activity programs during periods of remission must stress restoration of muscles.

Cool water stimulates circulation and warm water tends to induce fatigue at a faster rate in individuals with multiple sclerosis. The water cannot be too cold, though, or it will cause undue body tension. Further, as the disease progresses, consult with the individual's physician to determine if swimming is a suitable physical activity. Various aquatic exercises can be provided for persons with multiple sclerosis, depending on the state of the disease (Lewis, 1985; Ponichtera-Mulcare, Glaser, Mathews, & Camaione, 1993).

In the early stage of multiple sclerosis emphasis is on strengthening the arms and trunk to assist those individuals who are in wheelchairs. Leg exercises are introduced to enable persons to walk, climb stairs, stand, and sit. Swimming is also a very good activity. Begin swimming on the back at first, then progress to swimming with the face down.

In the advanced stage, individuals may be in pain from contractures that have developed from spasticity and muscle imbalance; they may be unable to walk. The lessening of weight due to water's buoyancy may relieve the pain and provide some degree of movement freedom. Relaxation is encouraged by completely supporting the individual, either by a flotation device or manual assistance.

MUSCULAR DYSTROPHY

Definition, Causes, and Scope

Muscular dystrophy is a group of chronic diseases that are characterized by degeneration and atrophy of skeletal or voluntary musculature occurring after a latent period of apparently normal development. These disorders usually affect the muscles on both sides of the body, which causes symmetrical weakening. The diseases vary in age of onset, initial muscles attacked, and rate of progress (see Table 10.6).

Muscular dystrophy is generally considered an inherited condition. However, it has a high spontaneous mutation rate, so some victims have no previous family history of muscular dystrophy. The specific cause of the genetic error is unknown, though it is speculated that it may be a muscle metabolic defect. The liver and the hormonal system have been identified as possible sites of the problem, because both produce substances involved in the metabolic process. More than 250,000 people in the United States are estimated to have some form of muscular dystrophy.

Especially in regard to the Duchenne type, there is no known treatment to correct or arrest the progression of this disease. Medical management generally involves the prevention of secondary symptoms through physical therapy and the use of orthopedic devices. The muscles simply progressively deteriorate, and the child becomes weaker and more dependent until unable to perform self-help activities or to combat infections. Death usually results from respiratory fail-

TABLE 10.6   COMMON TYPES OF MUSCULAR DYSTOPHY

TYPE	
Pseudohypertrophic (Duchenne)	The onset is in early childhood and progress is rapid, involving all voluntary muscles. Death generally occurs within 10 to 15 years of the onset of the disease. The initial symptoms are swayback, waddling gait, and difficulty in standing.
Facio-scapulo-humeral	The onset is generally in early adolescence and progress is very slow. The average life span is rarely shortened. The initial symptoms are lack of facial mobility, difficulty in raising hands over the head, and forward shoulders.
Limb-girdle	The onset is between 10 to 30 years of life and progress is variable. The disease may not become severe and some individuals have an average life span. The initial symptoms are muscle weakness in both the pelvic and shoulder girdles.

ure, and in some cases is precipitated by deterioration of the heart muscle.

Characteristics and Instructional Strategies

The pupil with Duchenne muscular dystrophy generally progresses through at least seven motor function ability stages.

1. Walks with a mild waddling gait with accompanying lordosis. Demonstrates some problems in activities that require lifting the legs, such as stair climbing.
2. Walks with a moderate waddling gait with accompanying lordosis. Supportive assistance is required in activities that require the legs to be lifted.
3. Walks with a severe waddling gait and accompanying lordosis. Cannot climb stairs, even with assistive devices, and cannot rise from a chair.
4. Can move independently in the environment using a wheelchair.
5. Can move in the environment using a wheelchair but requires assistance for most wheelchair activities and in getting to and from the wheelchair.
6. Can only roll the wheelchair a short distance and requires a back brace to sit upright in the chair.
7. Is confined to bed, with assistance required to perform basic self-help activities.

At all stages of the disease, prolonged physical activity is detrimental. The child should be encouraged to perform as many activities as possible while standing. In the early stages, a general goal is at least 3 hours of standing and ambulation each day to maintain strength and inhibit or slow down the development of contractures (Ziter & Allsop, 1976). Activities must be selected with the advice of a physician. In the latter stages, the physical educator should also work closely with physical and occupational

therapists, not only in designing activities but in learning the correct techniques of positioning, handling, lifting, and carrying a pupil with muscular dystrophy. Care must be taken in lifting the pupil, as the muscles are weakened, and improper lifting techniques may injure the pupil or the teacher.

Because activities should be designed not to overtire the pupil with muscular dystrophy, periodic rest periods may be required. The environment where the activities will be performed should not be damp or expose the pupil to extreme changes in temperature, as that may lead to a respiratory infection that can progress quickly to pneumonia.

Many children with muscular dystrophy are emotionally immature, as demonstrated by a lack of independence and confidence, lack of physical activity and association with friends of their own age, temper tantrums, and excessive withdrawal from social activities. The major cause of the emotional immaturity has been traced to parental overprotectiveness and, in a few cases, rejection. The physical education environment can be used not only for skill learning but as a medium in which to help these children develop emotionally through appropriate social and physical interaction with other pupils.

Indicated and Nonindicated Activities

Range of motion exercises are necessary to stretch or prevent contractures. These exercises should be done daily on all tight or contracted muscle groups. Each stretch generally should be for 10 seconds to (not beyond) the point of pain and repeated two to three times. Postural exercises involving the trunk and pelvis are also recommended to help delay the onset of lordosis and scoliosis. Exercise may be important to reduce excessive weight, which places an additional burden on the body. Dietary and nutritional counseling should be used to complement the physical activity program to help slow down the process from independence to dependence.

Exercises should develop weak antagonistic muscles with the minimum contraction of stronger agonists. Residual, unaffected muscle tissue is trainable, and strength and endurance can be maintained or improved. Again, strength exercises may be of value, but some authorities suggest that strength exercises may accelerate the degenerative process. Factors that must be considered are the degree and rate of the muscle weakness, degree and intensity of the exercise, and the type of exercise (Croce, 1987). Written consent from a physician should be obtained before any exercise program is initiated.

Physical activities designed to improve locomotor skills may delay bracing or confinement to a wheelchair. Static and dynamic balance activities may also help delay the progress of the disease.

Water provides such a pupil with the opportunity to feel "normal," and, through appropriately designed activities, may forestall the effects of the disease on ambulation. Activities should emphasize body mechanics and the development of strength and endurance. Flotation devices can be effectively used to support one part of the body while another part is being exercised. The major precaution in aquatic activities is to avoid chilling in order to decrease the probability of muscle cramping and respiratory infections. Temperature differences between the air and water should not be extreme, and damp locker rooms should be avoided.

The pupil with muscular dystrophy should remain in a regular physical education program until he or she cannot safely or successfully benefit with satisfaction. The focus of the physical education program should be on a variety of leisure skills including those that can be performed during the nonambulatory phase of the disease. Adaptations may be required to enable participation by the pupil in modified individual or group activities, such as using a larger ball in a smaller playing area for individual activities, lowering the net in basketball, using a bowling ball ramp, or using a large ball in group activity (see Figure 10.38). This will require at least part-time placement in a special physical education class; eventually full-time placement may be required.

FIGURE 10.38 A large ball can be used for modified kickball.

Physical Deviations

This chapter addresses weight problems, several relatively common orthopedic disabilities, and body mechanics deviations, all of which could directly influence physical education programming. The interview with G. William Gayle on page 279 relates to physical education programming for pupils with physical and neurological deviations and serves to highlight the content of this chapter and Chapter 10.

WEIGHT DISORDERS

Overweight and obesity, anorexia nervosa, and bulimia are addressed in this section. The major focus is on overweight and obesity, the number one nutritional problem in the United States.

Overweight and Obesity

Definition, Causes, and Scope. There is no one completely satisfactory definition of overweight and obesity. A common component of most definitions, however, is that excessive calories are stored either by increasing the amount of triglyceride in existing adipose tissue (which increases the cell size) or by the formation of new adipose cells. In the early part of life, an increase in the number of adipose cells is the major factor responsible for growth of fatty tissue. By approximately age 20, being too heavy is usually associated with an enlargement of the adipose cells.

Functional definitions that can be used easily in schools relate to expected weight for height and body frame size. A pupil who is

G. William Gayle

Dr. G. William Gayle is an associate professor of special physical education at Wright State University in Dayton, Ohio.

1. *Is physical education programming any more important for the child who has a physical deviation than for a child who is not disabled?*

Physical education occupies a unique position in the general education curriculum by impacting the affective, cognitive, and psychomotor domains of all pupils. However, physical education programming is even more important in the special education curriculum, as Congress recognized when it cited physical education as the only curriculum area in the definition of Special Education within P.L. 94-142.

Prior to 1975, pupils with disabilities (including physical deviations) did not receive adequate physical education programming. Some professionals felt it was not a priority, not worth the expense, or it posed a health hazard. Luckily, these philosophies have not stood the test of time, and those who teach physical education, and the Congress, are promoting physical education for all pupils with disabilities.

Able-bodied children have the opportunity to enhance their psychomotor development through participation in unrestricted physical education, community recreation, and neighborhood free play. If not afforded these opportunities, sedentary individuals with physical disabilities exhibit a higher incidence of cardiorespiratory, circulatory, and skeletal disorders. Unlike their ambulatory peers, individuals with physical deviations often fatigue before physiological benefits or skill acquisition occurs due to energy-inefficient mobility aids requiring mostly small muscle group usage.

Children with physcial abnormalities also may exhibit delayed motor and social skills because of central nervous system problems, postural irregularities, and surgical procedures. As these children grow older, the use of mobility aids (e.g., prosthetic and orthotic devices) and architectural and attitudinal barriers may further delay motor skill acquisition, resulting in fewer chances for participation in normal motor activity. Finally, as the child moves through adolescence into adulthood, motor skill obsolescnece, obesity, and depression may result in a passive observer of phys- ical activity rather than an active partici- pant.

For individuals with physical deviations, appropriate physical education provides a foundation upon which recreational and vocational independence can be constructed. For these individuals, possessing knowledge and techincal skills alone is not sufficient if the fitness level is not commensurate with the rigors of an entire play or work session.

2. *Are there any stories you could share which indicate the success of a special*

physical education program for an individual who has a physical deviation?

When I met Jim he was wandering aimlessly through his sophmore year in college, searching for an exercise outlet that had eluded him since an accident resulting in a C5-6 spinal cord lesion. Aquatics appeared to offer the greatest possibility of immediate success. This proved to be the turning point in his life as he became more focused. The time once used for partying was now reserved for career preparation and physical education skill courses, which led to training for competitive sport participation. He soon met with regional and national success in NWAA aquatics competitions and after a challenge from another athlete he expanded into wheelchair track and road racing. He eventually became the first individual in his classification (1-A) to complete the Boston Marathon. Today, Jim is an accountant and is competing in regional, national, and international track and road racing.

10 percent above the expected weight for height and body frame size is classified as overweight. A female is considered obese if she is 30 to 35 percent above the expected weight for her height and body frame size; a male is considered obese if he is 20 to 25 percent above his expected weight. Any pupil who is 50 percent over the expected weight is classified as superobese. These percentages are rough estimates and will not identify some pupils who are too heavy; and others may be incorrectly classified as overweight, obese, or superobese. For instance, using this functional definition, a pupil with a small skeletal structure and excessively frail mus-

cles may have too high a percentage of body fat, but might not be considered to have a weight problem. On the other hand, some football players and weight lifters could be categorized as overweight because of their increased muscle mass, not body fat.

Obesity in the United States is considered a major epidemic, and the problem is increasing. At least 15 to 20 percent of all children are obese (Bender, 1992), with high incidence among children from low-income families. Since 1970, the prevalence has increased more than 50 percent for children aged 6 to 11 and by approximately 40 percent in adolescents aged 12 to 17 years. In the adult population over 40 years of age, 30 percent of all males and 40 percent of all females are at least 20 percent above their ideal weight. In the adult population, the accumulation of excessive weight is typically due to increased food consumption. If you consume 10 extra calories each day, in 1 year you would gain 1 pound; in 10 years you would gain 10 pounds.

Numerous fallacies about obesity in our society have, in some instances, perpetuated this weight problem. Here we list a few.

Fallacy	Fact
• Primary cause of creeping obesity is increased caloric intake.	• Lack of or reduced amount of physical activity is the primary factor.
• Increased physical activity increases the appetite.	Only excessive exercise increases the appetite.
• Crash diets are an effective way to lose weight	• Crash dieting frequently causes deficiencies in essential food substances.
• Children who have an overweight disorder outgrow their tendency to be heavy.	• Such children generally become adults who are too heavy. At least 80 percent of the children who are obese in the United States are destined to remain obese (Plimpton,1987).
• Children who are obese are well adjusted.	• These children have emotional problems.

Our society is very sedentary, caused, in part, by television. The average family in the United States watches television more than 7 hours a day. Most children spend more time each year watching television than they spend in school (Tucker, 1986). Not only are these children physically inactive, but there are other dimensions of health that are negatively impacted by watching television. The average child watches 22,000 commercials each year with 5,000 being related to high-calorie, high-sugar, low-nutrition food products. Very few commercials promote fruits, vegetables, and dairy products. In addition, television characters, many of whom serve as role models, rarely eat balanced meals or give adequate attention to what they eat. Also, because very few television characters are obese, children believe it is appropriate to eat foods that are not adequate for a healthful diet.

There is, though, no single cause of weight problems. Most often several factors function interdependently to cause the problem (see Figure 11.1). A combination of constitutional and environmental factors is the most frequent general cause.

The offspring of mothers who are obese have significantly more subcutaneous fat than those infants whose mothers are not obese. A child of parents without weight problems has less than a 10 percent chance of being obese. When one parent is obese, there is a 40 to 50 percent chance; if both parents are obese, the chance increases to over 80 percent.

Endocrine disorders can also cause excessive weight gains, but only 10 percent of all cases of obesity can be attributed to endocrine problems. The hypothalamus, located in the brain, regulates neural input for signs of hunger and satisfaction. If there is a dysfunction in the neural input for food satisfaction, there will be an overactive internal signal for hunger. This causes a neural message to eat more, even when more calories are not

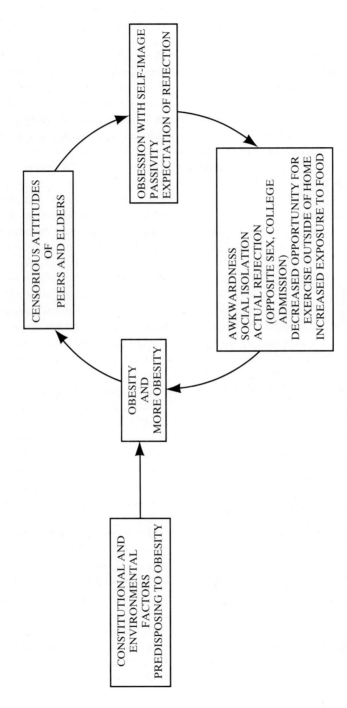

FIGURE 11.1 Obesity in adolescence: a vicious circle. (*From Overweight: Causes, Cost, and Control by Jean Mayer © 1968. Used by permission of the publisher, Prentice Hall/A Division of Simon & Schuster, Englewood Cliffs, N.J.*)

required. Malfunctioning of the thyroid and pituitary glands can also cause abnormal weight gain.

Certain emotional factors can cause abnormal weight gain. Children may overeat to alleviate anxieties, tensions, and frustrations brought about internally or through pressures from home, school, or peers. With increased weight, the problem becomes worse, and a vicious cycle is established. The child who may have been socially ridiculed (which caused the problem) is now further ridiculed because of even more weight, and his or her self-image keeps plummeting. Physical activity also decreases, often because the child is socially isolated and spends more time at home. This provides additional opportunity to eat and the problem compounds itself.

The one factor considered to be the major cause of obesity in children is lack of physical activity (Seltzer & Mayer, 1970). With parents driving their children everywhere and children constantly sitting and watching television, the average child's daily physical activity has decreased over the years. Even in the schools the number of physical education classes has decreased and the class period itself has been shortened. The number of pupils within a class has also drastically increased; it is common to see a physical education class of 60 pupils. All this leads to decreased opportunities for optimal physical activity experiences and adequate instruction.

Treatment generally is determined by the causes of the condition. It usually involves a combination of diet management, physical exercise, appetite suppressants or metabolic stimulants, and counseling. For individuals with endocrine disorders, additional medication is required. A number of other treatments, including surgery to wire the jaw almost closed, obstruct the intestines, or remove a portion of the body fat (i.e., liposuction); short-term starvation; hypnosis; crash dieting; and psychotherapy are used occasionally. In most cases, these techniques have little long-term effect. Whatever the treatment, the prime ingredient is attitude. The person must want to lose weight and must be willing to modify his or her lifestyle; otherwise, treatment effects will not last.

Characteristics and Instructional Strategies. The basis for weight management is caloric balance, which means that the total caloric intake is the same as the total caloric expenditure for a 24-hour period. In a weight loss program, the total caloric intake must be reduced below the total caloric expenditure. With a negative caloric imbalance, stored fat is converted and used for energy. This, in turn, reduces body weight.

One good way to create a negative caloric imbalance is to exercise. Not only can excess calories be used, but physical activity may actually depress the feeding signal in the brain. Any successful school-based obesity program, one that will have long-term effects, must include physical activity.

Two disadvantages of weight reduction through physical activity are that it is inconvenient and slow. A caloric deficit of about 3,500 calories is required to lose 1 pound of fat, and weight should be lost at a rate of 2 pounds or less per week. Table 11.1 shows the estimated caloric expenditure of a 150-pound person in 1 hour of certain activities. Clearly, you cannot lose 2 pounds (7,000 calories) without a lot of exercise each week. Another difficulty is maintaining a balanced diet that includes approximately 15 percent protein, 30 percent fat, and 55 percent carbohydrates.

TABLE 11.1 ESTIMATED CALORIC EXPENDITURES PER HOUR FOR SELECTED ACTIVITIES (150 lb. PERSON)

ACTIVITY	CALORIES
Backpacking (without load)	490
Cycling	400
Jumping rope at 70 per min.	660
Rowing (race)	800
Running (9 min. mile)	800
Swimming (slow crawl)	520
Tennis (recreational)	440
Walking (slow to fast)	130-550

Here are some general rules to follow when programming for pupils who are overweight or obese.

1. Work with a physician, parents, and other teachers to develop a program. One effective strategy is a home-based activity to supplement the physical education program at school (Bishop & Donnelly, 1987). For this strategy to work over the long term, there must be (a) a good parent–teacher relationship, (b) printed material on how to implement the program for the parents and the pupil, (c) regular follow-up consultation by the physical educator by telephoning or having an in-person meeting, and (d) preset contingencies for pupil and parents.

2. Organize a school weight management club to enable pupils to work together. This club could meet during part of the lunch period to reduce the opportunity to eat or to encourage controlled eating; physical activities could be incorporated into the meetings.

3. Implement a behavior management system in order to provide a consequence for successful or unsuccessful attainment of weight loss goals. In one program pupils were taught how to modify their personal social and physical environments to reduce food input and increase energy expenditures. As part of this program, elementary-aged pupils were reinforced for positive changes in their eating habits and exercise behaviors through the use of con- tracts with the teacher and parents. At the end of the program, 95 percent of the pupils lost weight (Brownell & Kaye, 1982).

4. Create progress charts to enable the pupils to monitor their weight change (see Figure 11.2). In the example shown, no more than 2 pounds a week are lost, the optimum recommended loss.

5. Frequent rest periods may be required, particularly on hot days, because body fat acts as an insulator. Obese pupils will perspire excessively and require fluid replacement and rest.

6. During the same activity there is more strain on the heart of a pupil with excess weight than on that of the nonobese pupil. Thus strenuous physical activity must be monitored closely.

7. Avoid activities that involve quick movements that require momentum and sudden stops, which might damage knee and ankle joints.

8. Because the inner thighs constantly rub against each other, chafing may occur, causing discomfort during some activities. The pupil should be aware of this problem and apply an ointment or stop the activity.

9. Schedule the physical education program before snack or lunch periods.

10. The notion that an intense, fast start in an exercise program is a more effective method to increase weight loss when compared to a gradual, slow start method is not necessarily true.

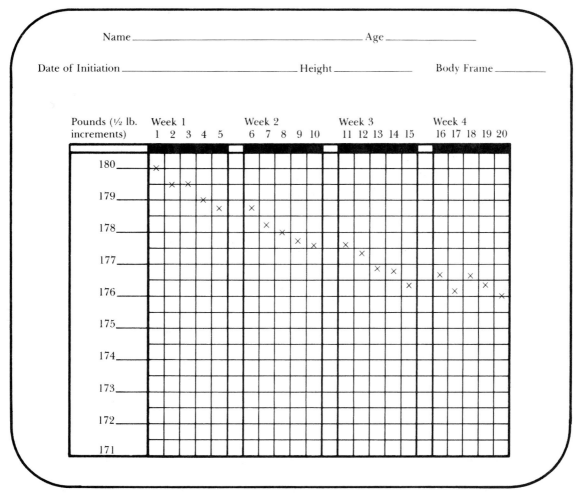

FIGURE 11.2 Weight-management progress chart.

Most school-based programs incorporate many of these programming rules (Emes, Velde, Moreau, Murdoch, & Trussell, 1990). One such program is the Lose to Win Program (Marin, 1985). Lose to Win is a team approach, where the members of the program are generally referred to the guidance counselor by parents or teachers and some are self-referred. The goals of the program are to help pupils learn about good nutrition and how the body uses food, better understand their own weight problems, and bring about some change in their eating and exercising habits. In the program, school lunches are frequently studied, systems to increase or decrease recipe portions are taught, and group exercises are incorporated into the program with the assistance of a physical educator. Members are expected to commit to a daily routine of strenuous exercise. There are also tasting parties to introduce new foods and to try simple recipes that the pupils can make themselves. Pupils are continually weighed, and if there is a weight loss, they are immediately rewarded with such items as balloons, stamps, stars, jack sets, and the like.

Most of the school staff and faculty are involved in the program, including the school nurse and lunchroom supervisor. A vital key to the success of the program is parents. They support their child's efforts to-ward weight control and improved health at home.

Another program is one offered by The American Alliance for Health, Physical Education, Recreation and Dance for school-aged pupils (Malone, 1989). The program meets two to three times a week for 60 minutes each session and is divided into exercise and nutritional components. It is suggested that the program continue for a minimum of 24 weeks and be conducted ideally by a physical educator, a school nurse, a classroom teacher, and the school psychologist. Information is provided on selecting participants, inviting participants to the program, providing informal meetings with parents and/or participants, obtaining parental and medical permission forms, testing procedures, and reporting progress.

An excellent weight control program has been adopted by the National Diffusion Network supported by the federal government. The purpose of this program is to give overweight students in grades 10 through 12 the knowledge and opportunity to interrupt the cycle of obesity and inactivity that prevents a healthy and effective lifestyle. The curriculum includes behavior change, physical conditioning, nutrition education, and positive image building. Additional information on the program can be obtained from Eileen Solberg, Project Director, Physical Management Project, P. O. Box 891, Billings, MT 59103.

Indicated and Nonindicated Activities. Exercise programs for pupils who are overweight and obese should be designed around aerobic endurance activities that are slow and rhythmical. Jogging, swimming, and cycling are good examples. Any endurance activity requiring heavy lifting must be implemented gradually because of the possibility of cardiac problems or developing a hernia.

When one exercises, body fat is lost from areas where fat is most heavily deposited, no matter what exercise is performed. Exercising a specific part of the body to lose weight there may be very ineffective.

Pupils who are too heavy at any age may not have acquired basic motor skills and patterns because of a fear of falling, awkwardness, or lack of opportunity to participate in activities. In a structured developmental physical education class, these skills can be progressively acquired. If these skills are not acquired, the pupils will be un-able to participate adequately in traditional games and leisure time activities with their peers. This could lead to serious social and emotional problems in school and after graduation.

Paced aerobic, rhythmic swimming and water exercises are excellent activities for this type of pupil. The water provides support for the body, which relieves strain on the joints and the skeletal structure.

Here are some aquatic activities appropriate for pupils with obesity:

1. Walking/jogging in chest- or waist-high water, to improve cardiorespiratory endurance.

2. Increasing the speed of movement through the water or placing the limbs and trunk in a nonstreamlined position, to improve strength. Nonstreamlined positions are obtained by pushing the arms through the water with the palms perpendicular to the direction of the movement or using various equipment to create similar resistance (e.g., sea hands, kickboards, Dyna-Bands).

Besides developing motor ability and physical fitness, dance provides opportunity for social interaction with peers. Slow and moderate dances that do not require maximal range of motion should be used at first. Faster, more vigorous dances should be incorporated gradually into the program. Aerobic dancing is an appropriate and popular programming choice (Ellis, 1980).

Pupils who are too heavy can benefit from most individual and group activities as long as they are offered within a medical margin of safety. Appropriately programmed activities also provide the opportunity for positive peer interaction. Further, it has been suggested that participation in a wide variety of games and activities provides greater and more sustained weight losses than aerobic exercises.

Activities that may require adaptations because of pupils' lack of gross motor ability, flexibility, speed, and endurance include flag football, soccer, diving, basketball, tumbling, skiing, boxing, and gymnastics activities requiring body support. The appropriateness of these activities must be determined jointly by the teacher, parents, physician, and pupil. Recommended individual activities are those in which the pupil competes against his or her previous performance for self-improvement. Activities that require competition with peers may cause or add to emotional and/or social problems and may be medically unsafe.

Anorexia Nervosa

Anorexia nervosa is an eating disorder characterized by severe weight loss, which is defined as a loss of 25 percent of appropriate body weight, due to deliberate self-starvation. A person with anorexia carries the principles of exercise and dieting to a dangerous extreme, and in some cases even death. Such individuals have an intense fear of gaining weight and of becoming fat. They also (Nagel & Jones, 1991):

1. Have a body image disturbance.
2. Have a weight loss of more than 25 percent of their original body weight. If the person is below 18 years of age, weight loss from original body weight in addition to projected weight gain expected from growth charts can be combined to make the 25 percent.
3. Refuse to maintain body weight over a minimal normal weight for age and height.
4. Have no known physical illness that would account for the weight loss.

The excessive weight loss often results in medical disorders such as, slowness of heartbeat, hypotension, cardiac arrest, dehydration, dryness of skin, hypothermia, hyperactivity or lethargy, amenorrhea, and abdominal stress.

Ninety-five percent of the victims of this disorder are females. It is estimated that as many as 1 per 250 adolescent females in the United States are anorexic. One investigation (Nagel-Murray, 1989) reported that more than 62 percent of high school teacher surveys stated that eating disorders were a pupil problem. Of the two thirds of adolescent females who eventually diet, about 1 or 2 percent will be diagnosed with an eating disorder (Mallick, Whipple, & Huerta, 1987). The most alarming statistic is the 5 to 20 percent mortality rate associated with anorexia nervosa (Ogden & Germinario, 1988).

There are a few theories to explain why an individual will become anorexic (Muss, 1985):

- *Social theory.* Society emphasizes being fit, dainty, and slim as positive attributes.
- *Family systems theory.* Individuals with anorexia come from families where problems are not discussed, which means problems are not defined or resolved.
- *Biological theory.* It has been suggested that there is a disturbance in hypothalamic functioning that is associated with anorexia.
- *Psychobiological regression hypothesis.* The person with anorexia produces a psychobiological regression back to a prepubertal stage of development. This could be caused by an inability to cope with the stresses of adolescence.

In connection with these theories about the cause of anorexia, there are several treatments frequently recommended. Some of these treatments are:

- *Psychotherapy.* Focus is on eliminating incorrect and irrational attitudes and beliefs about nutrition, exercise, and body image.
- *Family therapy.* Purpose is to restore average weight and change the family structure by developing clearer psychological relationship boundaries between family members. This therapy is generally used with adolescents who are under 16 years of age and live with their parents.
- *Behavior management.* Contingent relationships are determined between certain desirable behaviors (consumption of appropriate amounts of food) and specific reinforcers (e.g., money, privileges).

Physical educators are in a unique position, not to diagnose or treat but to recognize and attempt to prevent eating problems through teaching principles related to physical fitness, weight control, and nutrition (Lindsey & Janz, 1985). If now knowledgeable about this disorder, the physical educator could unknowingly reinforce a pupil's pathological eating problem. It is important in any program planning for a pupil with anorexia that the physical educator work closely with other members of an education team. Further, it has been recommended by Charest-Lilly, Sherrill, and Rosentswieg (1987) that special physical educators who teach pupils with eating disorders take training in body composition.

Bulimia

Bulimia is a Greek word which means "ox" and "hunger." This disorder was so named because the affected individual eats like a hungry ox. Individuals with this disorder repeatedly binge eat, which can go on for hours. A minor binge would be eating a half gallon of ice cream in one sitting and then vomiting. A major binge (5,000–15,000 calories) would be eating a box of cookies, a quart of milk, a loaf of bread, three candy bars, a dozen cupcakes, four containers of yogurt, and two sandwiches. At the end of the binge the bulimic feels physically sick and purges the food. The purge is generally accomplished by vomiting, laxatives, compulsive exercising, or weight-reducing drugs.

Some of the characteristics of this disorder are the following (American Psychiatric Association, 1987):

1. Excessive concern with weight gain and body image

2. Strict periods of dieting followed by eating binges
3. Frequent overeating, particularly when distressed
4. Feeling out of control in regard to eating patterns
5. Guilt or shame following binges and purges
6. Disappearing after a meal for the purpose of purging
7. Self-defeating thoughts and feelings of hopelessness and depression
8. Resistance to seeking professional assistance

It is estimated that 15 to 20 percent of college-aged women exhibit bulimia characteristics and 40 percent of the total female population experience at least one bulimic episode. A concern in the male population is young athletes whose weight is a problem, in particular wrestlers, who must meet a weight requirement.

As for anorexia nervosa, biological, psychological, and social factors have been suggested to play a role in bulimia. Bulimia occurs with personality and behavioral deficits, as well as with ineffective coping strategies. Some personality characteristics of bulimics are overidentification with the feminine stereotype and difficulties in heterosexual relationships; victims hold irrational beliefs, such as an excessively high need for approval and perfectionist standards, and have a poor body image and tendencies toward depression (Weiss, Katzman, & Wolchik, 1985).

Little research has been done on the effectiveness of treatments for bulimia. The major treatments are similar to those for individuals with anorexia.

1. *Hospitalization.* If the individual vomits 10 or more times a day, this approach is used.

2. *Individual therapy.* This involves an attempt to change beliefs related to inaccurate nutritional information, unrealistic goal setting, perfectionistic thinking, and unfounded beliefs and superstitions particularly related to the need for social recognition.

3. *Group therapy.* Sharing and seeing that others have the same problem.

4. *Behavior therapy.* This involves the use of behavior modification techniques to regulate a person's eating habits.

5. *Drug therapy.* In some cases antidepressant drugs are used because bulimia is closely associated with depression.

As with anorexia nervosa, physical educators need to know that cultural attitudes influence the behavior of children and youth (e.g., the standard that emphasizes thin body shapes). Athletes, cheerleaders, and dancers often attempt to achieve a specific weight, and this could lead to weight loss methods that are used by bulimics. The key for physical educators is to educate their pupils and be alert to any abnormal behavior that may be symptomatic of bulimic behaviors.

ORTHOPEDIC DISABILITIES

Disorders of the musculoskeletal system, especially in the joints and spine, are orthopedic disabilities. They include acute as well as permanent and chronic conditions. Common acute conditions are sprains, strains, and fractures that have a short and severe course. Amputation is classified as a permanent condition, and Legg-Calve-Perthes and Osgood-Schlatter conditions are considered chronic, as they persist over a long period of time.

Pupils with any one of these conditions should not be totally excluded from physical education. In most cases, the orthopedic problem is localized in one portion of the body. Activities can be modified to enable the pupils to participate by using other parts of the body, or alternative activities can be provided. Nothing is more upsetting to a special physical educator than to walk into a regular physical education class and observe a pupil with an orthopedic problem sitting on the sidelines because the teacher does not have the skill or inclination to program for the pupil. Classroom teachers do not stop programming cognitive activities for pupils if they are mentally retarded; they design activities to meet each pupil's functional level. The same philosophy holds when programming physical activities for pupils who are orthopedically disabled.

Amputation

An amputation is the removal of part or all of a limb. Congenital amputations are the result of improper or total lack of development of a limb during fetal growth. With the exception of the effects produced by thalidomide taken by pregnant women, the cause of congenital limb deficiencies is obscure. Some related factors include the following:

1. Nutritional factors, such as extreme increases or deficiencies in amino acid production or iodine deficiency.
2. Mechanical factors, including the amount of amniotic fluid, fetal position, and partial separation of the placenta.
3. Other factors, including chemical or drug toxins, endocrine disorders (particularly diabetes), anoxia, Rh incompatibility, and rubella.

Surgical amputations are usually performed to remove malignant or benign tumors, to counteract serious infections that will not heal with the use of medication, or to combat vascular disease. There is always an attempt in this surgery to cut below joints in order to provide more functional ability of the limb or fingers or toes, as well as to save the thumb. The major causes of amputation due to injury are motor vehicle, industrial, and farm machinery-related accidents.

It is estimated that the number of individuals with amputations in the United States is over 300,000; 32 percent have upper and 68 percent lower limb amputations. About 7 percent are under 21 years of age, 58 percent between 21 and 65 years of age, and 35 percent over 65 years old. It is also estimated that there are twice as many congenital amputees as acquired amputees (Adams & McCubbin, 1991).

One general classification of amputations relates to the site of occurrence, and there is specific terminology used for lower and upper extremity types. The abbreviations and terms used in Figure 11.3 include:

- *Hemipelvectomy:* an amputation through half of the pelvic bone
- *Disarticulation:* an amputation at a joint
- *Styloid:* the long slender pointed body processes on the ulna and the radius
- *Acromion:* the lateral extension of the scapula that projects over the shoulder joint
  - A: Above
  - E: Elbow
  - B: Below
  - K: Knee

Most school-aged pupils with amputations elect to wear a prosthetic device. The prosthesis comfortably replaces the function and cosmetically compensates for the appearance of an absent limb. Most prostheses are made of plastics, which are moisture-resistant, durable, and cosmetically very appealing. The type of prosthesis is selected according to the growth of each patient. A school-aged child may require a new prosthesis every 12 to 18 months and teenagers about every 18 to 24 months.

The physical educator must consider the capabilities of the pupil when using and car-

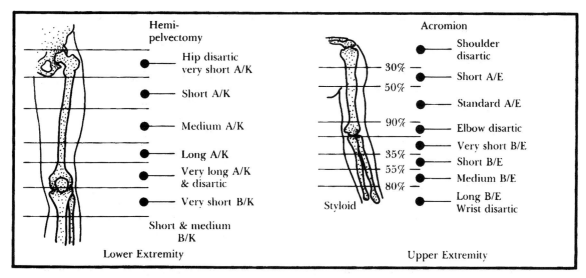

FIGURE 11.3 Classification of amputation by site of occurrence. *(From A.B. Wilson, "Limb Prosthetics Today," Artificial Limbs, 1963, 7, 7. Used by permission.)*

ing for a prosthesis. The stump and section of the prosthesis covering the stump must be cleaned and ventilated often to decrease the probability of cysts and abrasions developing. The stump should be cleaned and aired after strenuous physical activity. In addition, peer reaction to the child using a prosthesis is too often overlooked. A physical educator has the obligation to make pupils who are nondisabled aware of disabling conditions, including the use of a prosthesis, so that they do not have inappropriate reactions to differences.

In planning a physical education program for a pupil with an amputation, medically safe activities must be selected within each pupil's functional capacity. This major consideration must be addressed by a physician and, if possible, by occupational and physical therapists, along with the physical educator.

Physical educators themselves need specific instructional guidelines in their work with pupils who are amputees. These include the following:

1. Provide activities in which pupils can succeed or can perform equal to or better than other pupils, as many pupils who are amputees feel inferior.

2. Shame is characteristic of many individuals with amputations, so individual counseling by support personnel (such as a school psychologist or school counselor) may be needed. Showering may be a problem. If absolutely necessary, the pupil could be allowed to shower before or after other pupils. The pupil could also be allowed to wear sweat clothes and be given a locker in an isolated aisle.

3. Individuals with amputations are often dependent on others, so they need opportunities for independent work. Obstacle courses and circuit training are two techniques that can be used.

4. The teacher should attempt to help pupils with amputations, who lead very sedentary lives, become actively involved in school functions. Physical education instruction should be supplemented with extracurricular activities that involve gross motor movement.

5. Teach the appropriate techniques for falling. Children who are not used to a lower limb prosthesis may be fearful of falling. The falling height should be gradually increased from kneeling to standing positions. The falling surface should shift from soft to hard.

6. A major emphasis for pupils with lower limb involvement should be the development of static and dynamic balance.

7. An individual with an amputation requires training in the external awareness of the body in relationship to objects in space. Dodgeball and catching skills are excellent activities here.

8. Children with lower limb problems may use an inappropriate swing-through gait. Teachers and peers need to serve as models of correct walking. Individuals with amputations may use a mirror for visual feedback in practicing a normal gait. Teachers should spot-check for normal gait and reward children when they walk correctly.

9. Physical educators must work closely with other professionals and parents in planning robust activities for a pupil with a prosthesis because mobility problems contribute to weight gain.

10. General physical fitness exercise programming may be required because of the sedentary lifestyle adopted by many pupils with amputations. Homework is encouraged.

11. Care must be taken to ensure that a prosthesis does not adversely affect the safety of peers (and pupil with an amputation) in gross movement. In some activities, such as swimming, the prosthesis must be removed; in other activities involving catching or hitting a ball, prosthesis removal may be optional.

The variations in location, number of limbs involved, and functions provided by the prosthesis make it impossible to provide specific indicated or nonindicated activities for all individuals with amputations. Thus we focus on four of the more frequently occurring types of amputations: unilateral above knee (A/K), below knee (B/K), above elbow (A/E), and below elbow (B/E).

A pupil with a B/K unilateral amputation, while hindered in the normal performance of physical activities involving the lower body, is more proficient than an A/K unilateral amputee in speed and general coordination. Some generally recommended activities that do not require any modifications for single lower limb amputees are presented in Table 11.2. An example of a specific activity is the shot put (see Figure 11.4).

Pupils with upper limb deficiencies usually can perform more activities than lower limb amputees because of their superior ability to move effectively in the environment. Some activities in which A/E and B/E pupils can participate without modifications are listed in Table 11.3. Remember that the information in the table provides only general recommendations and should not place unnecessary, inflexible restrictions on a pupil. With a little creativity on the part of the instructor, activities in which normal participation is questionable or difficult can be adapted.

Pupils with bilateral amputations can also participate in many physical education activities. For instance, pupils with upper limb bilateral amputations can swim, perform on the trampoline, play soccer (see Figure 11.5), skate, and become actively involved in track and cross-country runs. In football these pupils could be blockers; they would have difficulty in basketball, softball, and racquet games.

Most activities that can be performed by children with unilateral lower limb deficiency can also be performed by those with a bilateral lower limb deficiency using a wheelchair or crutches, when necessary. The major difference is that the speed of the activity should be reduced along with the game boundaries. Various wheelchair sport organizations in the United States have individuals

TABLE 11.2 SUGGESTED PHYSICAL ACTIVITIES FOR INDIVIDUALS WITH A UNILATERAL LOWER LIMB AMPUTATION

ACTIVITY	Participation Encouraged		Participation Questionable		Participation Difficult/ Impossible	
	A/K	B/K	A/K	B/K	A/K	B/K
Archery	x	x				
Badminton		x			x	
Basketball				x	x	
Bowling	x	x				
Dancing	x	x				
Diving	x	x				
Field Events	x			x		
Fencing		x			x	
Football		x			x	
Golf		x	x			
Gymnastics			x	x		
Handball		x	x			
Racquetball		x	x			
Skiing		x	x			
Soccer		x			x	
Softball		x			x	
Swimming	x	x				
Tennis		x	x			
Track					x	x
Volleyball		x			x	
Weight lifting	x	x				
Wrestling		x	x			

FIGURE 11.4 The shot put is an activity that does not require modifications for single limb amputees.

with amputations as members. In wheelchairs, they compete in activities such as archery, basketball, table tennis, weight lifting, tennis, and track and field events. Several of these activities involve only minor modifications in their rules and regulations.

A few individuals with amputations cannot perform most physical activities without the use of specifically designed equipment; yet they, too, should be provided with a physical education program. Individuals with lower limb amputations can ski with the use of special skis and poles (outriggers). They may be able to swim by using some type of flotation device or by attaching fins to the body or stumps to provide needed support. An inflatable swimming suit is also commercially available. One-armed swimmers may need these assistive devices. For these swimmers, the sidestroke with the

ACTIVITY	Participation Encouraged		Participation Questionable		Particpation Difficult/ Impossible	
	A/E	B/E	A/E	B/E	A/E	B/E
Archery	x	x				
Badminton	x	x				
Basketball		x	x			
Bowling	x	x				
Dancing	x	x				
Diving	x	x				
Fencing		x	x			
Football	x	x				
Golf	x	x				
Gymnastics			x	x		
Handball	x	x				
Skiing	x	x				
Soccer	x	x				
Softball		x	x			
Swimming	x	x				
Tennis	x	x				
Track	x	x				
Volleyball	x	x				
Weight lifting			x	x		
Wrestling		x			x	

TABLE 11.3 SUGGESTED PHYSICAL ACTIVITIES FOR INDIVIDUALS WITH A UNILATERAL UPPER LIMB AMPUTATION

functional extremity under the body is most efficient.

Rules for individualized and group activities can also be modified. For instance, a pupil with a unilateral lower limb amputation should be allowed to touch the table for support when playing table tennis. The distance to be covered in an activity can also be reduced for activities such as badminton or tennis (see Chapter 4 for principles of adaptation and applied examples).

Finally, general program considerations should include postural exercises and balance activities. Because pupils with a unilateral amputation are forced to use one side of the body continually, they may need posture exercises. Pupils with lower limb deficiencies often have balance problems, particularly if the amputation has been very recent.

Legg-Calvé-Perthes Condition

The Legg-Calvé-Perthes condition is a hip disorder in which the head of the femur degenerates (see Figure 11.6). This condition is usually reversible, and affects only one hip in 85 to 90 percent of the cases. Complete regeneration usually occurs one to three years after the onset of the condition. The cause of the Legg-Calvé-Perthes condition is unknown, although vascular disturbance and physical trauma are possible causative factors. This condition occurs mainly in children between the age of 4 and 8 years, but the full range is 3 to 12 years. In the past, this condition occurred mainly in very physically active boys; but with girls becoming more actively involved in competitive sports, the number of girls with this condition is increasing.

FIGURE 11.5 Bilateral upper limb
amputee kicking and heading a ball.
*(Courtesy of the Department of
Photography & Cinema, The Ohio State
University.)*

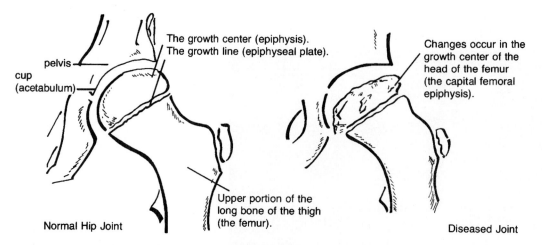

FIGURE 11.6 Normal hip joint; Legg-Calvé-Perthes disease. *(From J. L. Bigge, ed., Teaching Individuals with Physical and Multiple Disabilities, 2nd Ed. Columbus, Ohio; Charles E. Merrill, 1982, p. 6. Copyright © 1982 by Macmillan College Publishing Company. Used by permission.)*

Treatment consists of a variety of techniques to prevent the collapse of the femoral head by limiting undue weight-bearing pressure. Two of the basic techniques are:

1. The use of a leg sling and crutches removes the pressure from the head of the femur and allows the pupil to walk with crutches. Some physicians have suggested that this treatment may be ineffective.
2. Weight bearing has been recommended by some physicians as long as the leg(s) is abducted through bracing so that the femoral head is protected. In extensive femoral degeneration, surgery is required to replace the femoral head.

All physical education programming during the progression of this condition and the recovery period must be done with the approval of a physician. In general, after onset of the condition the physical education program should not be terminated because the majority of the large muscle groups are not involved. Weight training for the upper body and the other leg (if not affected) is per-missible. Almost all physical activities can be modified to enable the pupil to participate.

Osgood-Schlatter's Condition

The Osgood-Schlatter's condition is a knee disorder caused by the incomplete separation of the quadriceps tendon at its attachment on the tubercle of the tibia. This is caused by a disturbance of the ossification center of the bone. The individual with this condition generally feels "pain in the anterior aspect of the knee, tenderness and swelling of the patellar tendon and excessive enlargement of the tibial tubercle" (Adams & McCubbin, 1991, p. 110). This condition occurs generally in boys between the age of 10 and 15 who participate in vigorous games and sports where the knee is subject to trauma. With girls participating in more activities that involve jumping and running, such as certain track and field events, the number of girls with this condition is increasing.

Usually six to nine months is required for healing. Depending on the severity of the condition, the knee may be immobilized with a cast during the first month of treatment. Corticoid injections may be given in the knee region, and surgery may be recommended when traditional treatment is not successful. In the acute stages of the disorder, physical activity will aggravate the condition. This is especially true of locomotor activities performed on hard surfaces or activities involving significant absorption of shock. Explosive knee movements, as in jumping and kicking, would, therefore, not be indicated. Although activities are limited in the affected limb, activities involving the other limbs should be continued. After recovery, specific exercises are required to rehabilitate the affected leg. This will involve increasing the range of mo-tion of the knee and ankle and strengthening the quadriceps in both the affected and un-affected legs resulting in the child's ability to ambulate without favoring the affected limb.

BODY MECHANICS DEVIATIONS

At one time, the major focus of special physical educators was postural correction to develop proper body mechanics. Today the emphasis has moved to developing skills and knowledge to participate in games and sports. However, the trend away from postural training toward games and sports may have shifted too far. In the schools there are now thousands of pupils with postural deviations who are not being given appropriate exercises to remediate the problem. If not corrected, these deviations could lead to back strains and lowered muscle tone, which, in turn, could lead to body image problems: "As one's body sags, so one's spirits sag" (Lee & Wagner, 1949, p. 155).

Efficient body mechanics is the ability of a person to assume and maintain proper positions in all movements. A specific definition of body mechanics was developed at the White House Conference on Child Health and Protection (1932, p. 5):

Body mechanics may be defined as the mechanical correlation of the various systems of the body with special reference to the skeletal, muscular, and visceral systems and their neurological associations. Normal body mechanics may be said to be obtained when this mechanical correlation is most favorable to the function of these systems.

Maintenance of good body mechanics, particularly proper static posture, is considered to be a sign of physical and mental health. Improper body mechanics can cause greater expenditure of energy, back strain, muscle soreness, menstruation difficulties, and lowered muscle tone.

Improper body mechanics have numerous causes:

1. Poor nutrition
2. Weak musculature
3. Physical inactivity
4. Constant use of one side of the body
5. Improperly fitted clothing and shoes
6. Hearing or vision deficiencies
7. Chronic illnesses
8. Sagging bed mattresses
9. Poorly designed furniture
10. Injuries and congenital deformities

The general rule for correct body mechanics is that the body segments must support each other in a vertical alignment directly over the base of support. One key to such support is the spine (see Figure 11.7).* For a better understanding of the application of this rule, we briefly analyze four common

*All figures in this section of the text were taken, unless otherwise stated, from *Corrective Physical Education*, Publication No. SC-566, Los Angeles City Schools, Division of Instructional Materials, 1958. Used by permission.

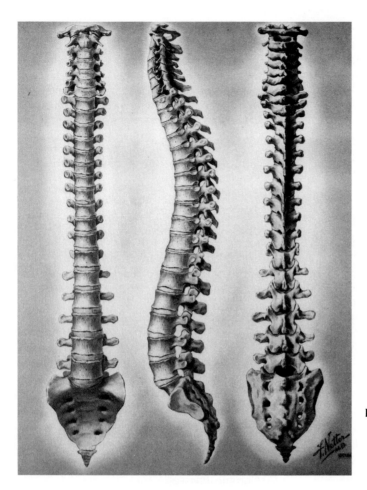

FIGURE 11.7 Three views of the spine. *(© Copyright 1953, 1972 CIBA Pharmaceutical Company, Division of CIBA-GEIGY Corporation. Reprinted with permission from The CIBA Collection of Medical Illustrations by Frank H. Netter, M.D. All rights reserved.)*

movement patterns: sitting, standing, walking, and running.

The correct *sitting* posture (see Figure 11.8) depends to a large extent on the design of the chair. The ideal chair should have an upright back and a firm, flat seat. The height of the seat must allow the person to rest the feet on the floor with the toes pointed forward. The head should be erect, and the shoulders and pelvis should be relaxed and braced against the chair (lower back slightly curved inward), with the thighs and buttocks resting level on the chair seat. Armrests, if any, should be at the height of the elbows when the arms are relaxed. This position will allow the person to relax and to conserve energy because the body segments are aligned and properly supported.

Standing is basically an extension of the sitting posture (see Figure 11.9). A correct standing position involves an erect posture without strain or tension, with the eyes forward, head and chin up, neck flat, chest high, hips straight and abdomen and lower back slightly curved, knees slightly flexed, and feet parallel pointing forward about 2 to 4 inches apart. When this posture is assumed, a straight imaginary line can be drawn down the side view of the body through the top of the head, the ear, the center of the shoulder,

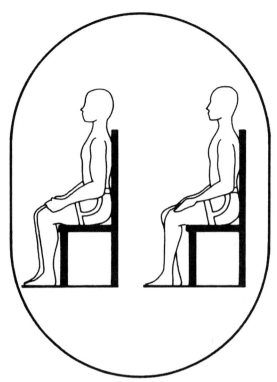

the center of the hip joint, the back of the kneecap, and slightly behind the ankle.

Here are some general techniques to maintain the correct standing posture:

1. Keep relaxed.
2. Stand tall and light as a feather.
3. Keep chin in and up.
4. Let the shoulders hang wide.
5. Keep buttocks tucked under.
6. Keep the abdomen pulled in.
7. Keep the knees loose.
8. Keep the chest up.
9. Keep toes pressed to floor with thighs rotat-outward slightly.
10. For short periods, keep feet together, weight equally distributed on both feet.
11. For long periods of standing, keep one foot forward and carrying the weight.

Walking is a dynamic extension of the standing position that involves propelling the body from one base to another without

FIGURE 11.8   Correct sitting position.

FIGURE 11.9   Correct standing posture.

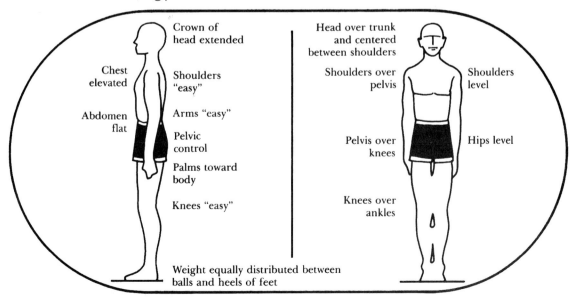

Crown of head extended

Chest elevated

Abdomen flat

Shoulders "easy"

Arms "easy"

Pelvic control

Palms toward body

Knees "easy"

Weight equally distributed between balls and heels of feet

Head over trunk and centered between shoulders

Shoulders over pelvis

Shoulders level

Pelvis over knees

Hips level

Knees over ankles

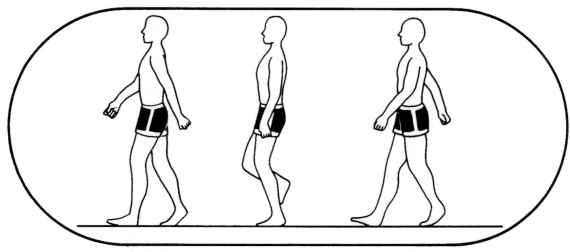

FIGURE 11.10 Correct walking posture.

loss of ground support (see Figure 11.10). The emphasis in walking is on an erect head and back, chin up, arms hanging freely from the shoulders, and legs swinging freely from the hips. The feet should alternately swing forward with first the heels and then the balls of the feet touching the ground. There is also a cross-extension pattern between the arms and the legs.

Here are some techniques to maintain correct walking posture:

1. Stand erect.
2. Keep knees close together.
3. Move slowly and smoothly.
4. Keep toes forward.
5. Keep knees relaxed.
6. Glide.

The *running* posture is similar to the walking posture, except that there is a forward body lean, the feet alternate position more rapidly, and there is a phase in which the body is completely airborne (see Figure 11.11). The arms also are bent more at the elbows and swing in opposition.

Here are some techniques to maintain a correct running posture:

1. Keep trunk erect.
2. Swing leg from hip joint.
3. Keep knees and ankles relaxed.
4. Lean forward a little from the hips.
5. Keep eyes looking straight forward.

Remember that there is no one correct way to describe proper body mechanics. We have presented only general guidelines. In analyzing a pupil's posture, you must also consider individual differences. The age of the child, for instance, is of prime importance. A pupil just entering school may demonstrate a slightly protruding abdomen and an inward curve in the lower spine. This is a normal posture for a young child, but it is a postural deficiency for young adults.

People with certain body types are more prone to postural deviations and are inclined to assume different postures because of their body types. Sheldon, Dupertius, and McDermott (1954) described predominate body types (see Figure 11.12). A person with a

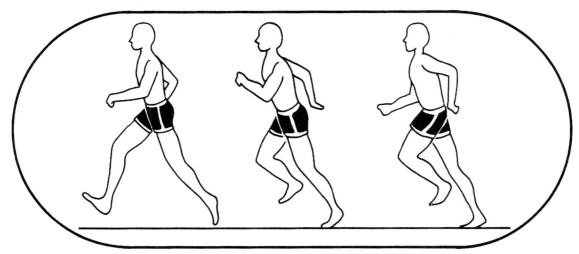

FIGURE 11.11 Correct running pattern. *(Figures 11.8–11.1 reprinted from Corrective Physical Education, 1958, by permission of Los Angeles Unified School District.)*

FIGURE 11.12 Traditional body types.

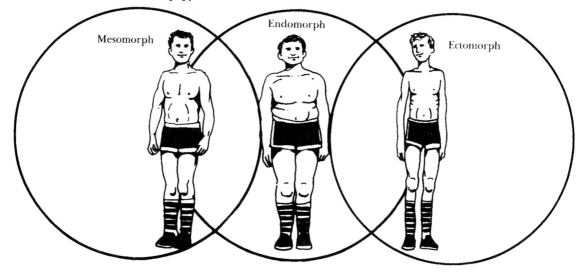

mesomorphic body type is usually well equipped structurally, physiologically, and neurologically to meet the stresses of life. Most athletes are mesomorphs. The *ectomorphic* body build is characterized by the lanky, slender person, sometimes described as "skin and bones." An ectomorph may be prone to fatigue easily and to slump. The *endomorphic* body type is exemplified by a stout, flabby person who is prone to lower back problems caused by a protruding abdomen. Both ectomorphic and endomorphic children do not usually reach as high a level of physical and motor fitness as do mesomorphic children, yet some improvement can be achieved through proper physical education and diet.

Approximately 70 to 80 percent of all children in the United States have some diagnosable postural deviance that interferes with proper body mechanics. This is often evidenced after high school. As an example, in recent studies, 387 university students registered in health and wellness classes were evaluated for posture problems (Althoff, Heyden, & Robertson, 1989). Almost 60 percent of these students had slight asymmetrical shoulders, and 2.4 percent were marked. Fifty-four percent of the students had held their head slightly forward. Other problems noted were that 28 percent had uneven hips, 27 percent had lordosis, 26 percent had protruding abdomens, 24 percent had rounded upper backs, and 19 percent had scoliosis. In addition, more males than females had postural deficiencies. One major contributing cause for such widespread problems is that, biomechanically, the human body seems best designed for a quadruped (four-footed), not a biped (two-footed), posture.

An uncorrected postural deviation can lead to other deviations. The body compensates when out of alignment. For example, a child with scoliosis may develop a simple C curve of the spine; but if the problem is not remediated, the body develops an S curve to compensate for the spine being out of alignment. (See the section on scoliosis for more detailed information.) Once a postural problem is identified and a physician's consent is given, the physical educator and parents should begin an exercise program for the pupil. Exercises can correct functional deviations, that is, those that disappear when the pupil assumes the correct posture. Postural deviations that do not disappear because the pupil cannot assume the correct posture are called structural. If the skeleton has been structurally modified, surgery, braces, or casting is required to straighten it; only then

will exercise be effective. We now look at a few common postural deviations.

Neck Postural Deviation

Torticollis is a deformity of the neck in which the head tilts toward the shoulder on one side and the chin is tilted upward toward the opposite side. This condition is caused by a shortening of the muscle (sternocleidomastoid) that is attached just behind the ear and inserts into the upper border of the collarbone and sternum. Exercises started at a young age will usually correct congenital torticollis. If exercise is not effective, surgery may be required. Acquired torticollis is caused by an inflammatory process resulting from strains or wounds. Head rotation, isometric neck, and neck bridging exercises will correct the problem if cervical vertebrae have not already realigned.

Trunk Postural Deviations

Kyphosis involves an abnormal increase in the cervical curvature of the upper back (see Figure 11.13). Usually round shoulders and forward head accompany the condition. In some cases a flat chest and lordosis may develop. The upper back extensors and the trapezius are weakened, and the pectoral and intercostal muscles are shortened. In extreme cases the shoulder joint movement is restricted and the flexibility of the rib cage is limited.

Here are some common exercises to remediate functional kyphosis:

1. Lie on stomach with hands behind the neck. Pinch the shoulder blades together and lift head and chest slightly above the floor. Repeat.

2. Sit with legs crossed, back erect, and hands on the knees. Raise arms slowly to the side and turn palms up. Clasp hands together

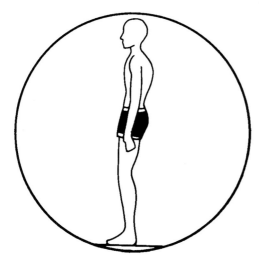

FIGURE 11.13   Kyphosis.

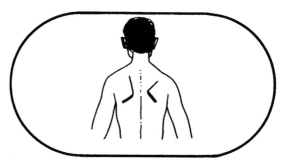

FIGURE 11.14   Winged scapula.

behind the head. Press elbows and head back, extending the spine; slowly extend arms upward and slowly lower hands to the knees. Repeat.

3. Lie on stomach with arms extended sideways. Lift arms while keeping the head, trunk, and legs in contact with the floor. Then slowly lower the arms to the floor. Repeat.

Clearly nonindicated for kyphosis are traditional push-ups and the "chain breaker" performed against resistance.

The term *winged scapula* refers to a postural deficiency in which one or both shoulder blades are farther than normal from the spinal column (see Figure 11.14). This condition may be caused by weakened rhomboids and trapezius and tightened pectorals.

Here are some exercises that may correct this postural condition:

1. Lie on back with knees bent and feet on the floor, while holding a medicine ball with the hands. Raise the ball vertically toward the ceiling, keeping feet together, body in correct alignment, and back as flat as possible. Repeat.

2. Lie on back with knees bent, feet on the floor, arms out to side, and elbows bent. Pinch shoulder blades together and concurrently press arms, wrists, neck, and lower back to the floor. Repeat.

An abnormal lateral curvature of the vertebral column is referred to as *scoliosis* (see Figure 11.15). In this postural deviancy, numerous muscles may be involved. Scoliosis is a common postural deviation, affecting almost 20 percent of the U.S. school-aged population to some degree. Females are more susceptible to idiopathic (unknown cause) scoliosis than males. The ratio is almost six females to one male. The incidence is also higher than would be expected in pupils with other disabling conditions. For instance, in one study approximately 50 percent of individuals with cerebral palsy also had scoliosis and 15 percent had a structural deficiency (Robson, 1968). The incidence in pupils with mental retardation in another study was 36 percent of the population (Stoker, 1977), and the incidence increased with age (Kudlac, 1978). A person with scoliosis could also be susceptible to cardiopulmonary deficiencies. The more severe the lateral curvature of the spine, the more severe the dysfunction, particularly in reduced lung volume, deficient

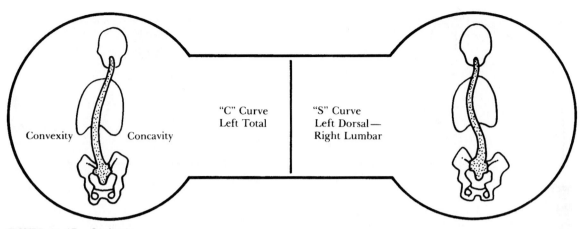

"C" Curve
Left Total

Convexity   Concavity

"S" Curve
Left Dorsal—
Right Lumbar

FIGURE 11.15   Scoliosis.

oxygenation of the blood, and pulmonary hypertension (DiRocco, 1981).

There may be a single curve or a compound curve present in scoliosis (see Figure 11.16). The single curve, called total scoliosis, involves the entire spine and is known as a C curve or reverse C curve. Compound curves consist of two or more curves in different directions. This type of scoliosis develops as a result of the body's attempt to maintain balance. This double curve is usually shaped like the letter S and is known as the S curve.

Scoliosis may also be functional, transitional, or structural. Functional scoliosis is characterized by its disappearance on traction, stooping, and reclining. Short of surgery, bracing, or casting, it can be improved through exercise and/or electrical stimulation after prescription from an orthopedist. Here are some common exercises generally prescribed for scoliosis:

1. Lie on back with legs extended and arms stretched over head as far as possible.

2. Hang from a horizontal ladder.

3. Stand erect and extend arms above the head with palms forward. Bend down from the waist as far as possible, knees remaining extended; return to the erect position. Repeat.

4. Stand erect; take a deep breath, raise arms vertically above the head, then rise up on tiptoes. Then exhale, lower arms, and lower heels. Repeat.

5. Stand erect facing a wall with feet spread apart approximately 18 inches. Climb up the wall with fingers on the concave side of the scoliotic curve and down the wall on the opposite side. Repeat.

Transitional scoliosis is a postural state in which there is continuous or intermittent mild lateral rotation of the vertebrae. This curve will not straighten completely in a prone or recumbent position, and the individual may not be able to self-correct with exercises. In structural scoliosis, the vertebrae have significantly changed in the lateral contour. In general, the spine deviates from the midline to form a C or S curve; one illiac crest is more prominent; the ribs on one side project backward; a flank crease is visible; one arm hangs lower than the other; and the chest is asymmetric. Very little, if any, correction can be achieved through exercise because structural deviance may preclude it.

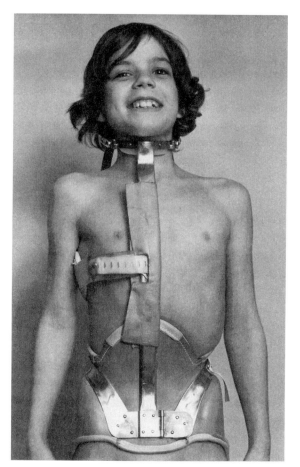 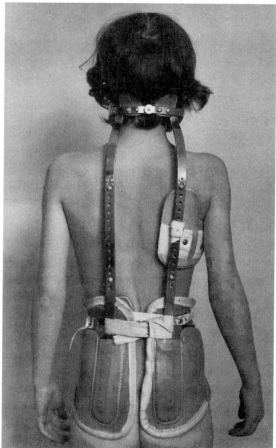

FIGURE 11.16   Milwaukee brace. *(Courtesy of Walter Blount, M.D.,
Blount Orthopedic Clinic, Milwaukee, Wisconsin.)*

In transitional and structural scoliosis, bracing, casting, or surgery is required to correct the postural problem. A Milwaukee brace is used for curves that are less than 40 degrees. The brace encases the body from the top of the neck to the pelvis; it is made of leather and two metal rods in the back and one in the front to straighten the spine (see Figure 11.16).

A pupil with a Milwaukee brace should be allowed to participate in almost all physical activities. In track events, only short dashes and relays are recommended. Gymnastic activities on the parallel bars, still rings, and horizontal bars are appropriate as long as the skills are sequenced and within the capabilities of the pupil. Trunk flexion, extension, and rotation exercises (e.g., windmills, sit-ups) are generally not indicated.

A Risser localizer cast is used when the curves are more than 50 degrees or after surgery (see Figure 11.17). The Risser is an

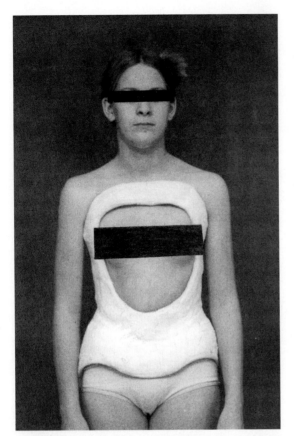 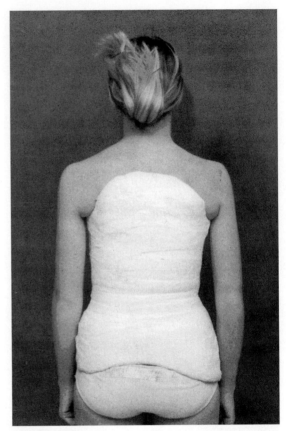

FIGURE 11.17   Risser localizer cast. *(Courtesy of J.K. Mayfield, M.D., Twin Cities Scoliosis Center, Minneapolis, Minnesota.)*

ambulatory plaster cast. With a Risser cast, noncontact physical activities are recommended. Vigorous activities and contact sports such as football, wrestling, climbing, and tumbling are not indicated.

The surgical procedure includes making an incision over the vertebrae to expose the spinal column. The spinal processes are then clipped off and an adjustable stainless steel rod, the Harrington rod, is attached above and below the abnormal curvature. The surgeon then tightens the device, which pulls the spine into the correct position. After the

operation, the patient spends approximately 10 days in the hospital and wears a Risser localizer cast for 7 to 10 months. When the cast is removed, as when a brace is removed, exercises and/or electrical stimulation are required to strengthen and stretch specific muscle groups.

The term *lumbar lordosis,* commonly called hollow back or saddleback, was derived from a Greek word meaning "to bend backward." In this type of lordosis (see Figure 11.18), there is an increase in the lumbar curve, which creates a strain on the abdomen, which

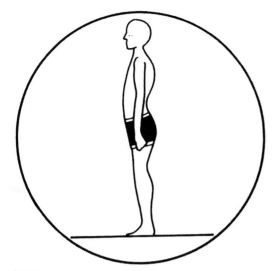

FIGURE 11.18 Lumbar lordosis.

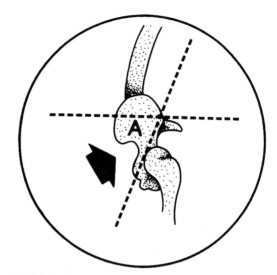

FIGURE 11.19 Anterior pelvic tilt. (The arrow points to the anterior spine.)

becomes weakened and usually prominent. The lower back muscles and hip flexors are shortened, the hamstrings and gluteal muscles may be weakened, and the knees are hyperextended. The pelvis may also be tilted forward and downward.

Here are some exercises to remediate lumbar lordosis:

1. Sit with legs crossed, hands on hips, and back erect. Relax trunk by leaning forward and extend arms forward. Hold trunk forward. Repeat.
2. Lie on stomach with a towel under the abdomen. Contract gluteal muscles and pinch buttock muscles toward the midline of the body. Repeat.
3. Sit erect with fingertips at the side of the neck. Bend forward, bringing the head closer to the floor. Repeat.
4. Stand erect with back against a wall with heels 4 inches from the wall. Contract abdominal muscles and push the lower back against the wall. Repeat.
5. Assume a creeping position (on all fours). Contract the gluteal and abdominal mus-

cles, and raise or hump the lower back (the "angry cat"). Repeat.

Exercises that are clearly nonindicated for pupils with lordosis include straight leg sit-ups and leg raises.

Hip Postural Deviation

The angle of the pelvic tilt is normally 50 to 60 degrees (angle A in Figure 11.19). Any further downward tilt at the front part of the pelvis results in a postural condition called *anterior pelvic tilt.* This condition involves tightened lower back muscles and hip flexors and weakened abdominal muscles and hamstring muscles. Depending on its severity, a pupil with this condition could also have prominent buttocks, lumbar lordosis, and protruding abdomen. This condition can develop because of muscular weakness or by chronically assuming incorrect postural positions.

Here are some exercises that can improve an anterior pelvic tilt:

1. Lie on the back with knees bent and feet flat on the floor. Contract abdominal muscles and concurrently flex the buttocks muscles together, raising the buttocks off the floor.
2. Perform Exercise 1 with the legs extended.
3. Stand erect; contract abdominals and concurrently pinch the buttocks muscles together.

Knee Postural Deviations

Two major postural deficiencies in the knee region are knock-knee and bowlegs. *Knock-knee* is a condition in which the knees are medially together or even overlap. When the feet are together (see Figure 11.20), usually one knee is more involved than the other. The medial ligaments of the knee are usually stretched, the external rotator muscles are weak, the tensor fascia latae are tight, and the feet are everted and flat.

Knock-knee is a common condition in infancy and is generally not considered a postural deficiency at that age. The condition almost always corrects itself without any treatment. However, knock-knee can be a congenital or an acquired deviation. If there is a congenital bone deficiency, exercise will not be effective, and bracing or surgery could be required. In children, knock-knee can be caused by weak muscles, sprains, fractures, improper diet, or other postural deficiency (e.g., feet). It is estimated that 20 percent of the U.S. school-aged population has knock-knee to some degree. There is an even greater incidence of knock-knee among children and youth who are obese.

Correction of this postural deficiency is possible if the condition is functional (correct postural position can be assumed), and more effective if the exercise program is initiated before the child is 12 years old. Some exercises that can be performed to improve functional knock-knee are the following:

1. Stand with feet parallel and knees relaxed. Attempt to turn the knees out and pull the thighs and calves inward. Repeat.
2. Stand with feet parallel and knees relaxed. Bend the knees and turn both outward. Repeat.
3. Stand erect with heels 3 to 4 inches apart and big toes together, while holding the back of a chair. Continuously rotate the knees outward and inward while supporting body weight on the outer surfaces of the feet that are flat on the floor. Repeat.

Bowlegs is a condition in which the knees are laterally separated when the feet are together (see Figure 11.21). Although it can be congenital, bowlegs is usually caused by an injury, poor diet, disease, or poor sleeping habits that create pressure on the inner parts of the legs. Mild bowlegs usually corrects itself in young children if disease or structural damage is not present. In more severe cases, braces may be required. In the case of poor sleeping habits, infants who chronically sleep in knee-chest position with the feet

FIGURE 11.20   Knock-knee.

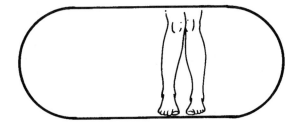

FIGURE 11.21   Bowlegs.

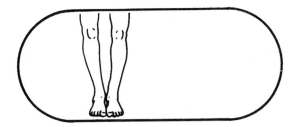

doubled up and turned under them could develop bowlegs. Infants should be placed in various sleeping positions to prevent this problem. On the side is the most suitable position. The cause of bowlegs in children and youth is generally faulty posture due to an outer rotation of the legs, accompanied by some degree of hyperextension of the knees. Bowlegs disappear when the hips are rotated inward.

Most pupils with mild bowlegs will not require special physical education. Only specific exercises should be regularly performed. In extreme cases of bowlegs, where there is structural damage with the knee and tibia forming a definite angle, violent physical contact should be avoided because of the possibility of dislocating the knees. Whereas most gymnastic activities are appropriate, trampolining is not indicated because of this factor. Swimming is an excellent activity, particularly for extreme cases of bowlegs.

Strange as it may seem, exercises for knock-knee are also effective for bowlegs. The purpose of these exercises for a pupil with bowlegs is to improve the pupil's posture in order to enable the body weight to be supported evenly on the bones, not only on the ligaments and muscles of the outer borders of the feet. Here are some additional exercises:

1. Sit on floor with legs extended supporting the back against a wall. Roll the legs inward and turn the feet outward. Repeat.
2. Lie in a supine position on the floor and place a pillow between the ankles. Spread straightened legs and rapidly bring them together against the pillow. Repeat.

Ankle and Foot Postural Deviations

The feet are the foundation of posture. Thus problems with the foundation can affect overall posture. The feet must be attended to with considerable care. The focus here on

FIGURE 11.22 Flat foot.

those conditions a physical educator may encounter in schools.

Flat foot is a congenital or acquired condition in which the longitudinal arch is lower than normal (see Figure 11.22). Congenital flat foot is rare, but when present is more severe than acquired flat foot. If there is structural damage (rigid flat foot), correction requires a series of plaster casts to change the convexity of the longitudinal arch. In some instances surgery is the mode of treatment. The results of either treatment are not always successful.

Usually the acquired flat foot develops in children because of poor functional posture. In flexible flat foot, and after cast removal or after surgery, exercise may have some remedial value. Some exercises performed barefooted that can be used to remediate this condition are the following:

1. Sit in a chair and try to pick up pencils, marbles, or thin pieces of rope with the toes and feet. Repeat.
2. Sit in a chair and then place a tennis ball between the feet. Roll the ball back and forth, using the soles of the feet. Repeat.
3. Stand erect and raise the longitudinal arch as high as possible; hold the position for a few seconds. Repeat.
4. Sit on the floor with legs extended forward; flex the toes and extend the foot as far as possible away from the body. Repeat.

Hollow foot is the opposite of flat foot. In this deviation the longitudinal arch is too high (see Figure 11.23). The muscles in the soles of the feet, and sometimes the heel cord, are tight. Hollow foot is usually an inherited or congenital defect. In mild cases, the condi-

FIGURE 11.23   Hollow foot.

tion can be successfully treated by properly fitted shoes with specific orthopedic modifications and with exercises. In extreme cases, surgery on soft tissue or a tendon transplant may be performed. Usually these treatments are not very successful. This condition is also difficult to correct by exercise.

Clubfoot is another orthopedic condition in which the foot is formed into an abnormal position. There are many types of clubfoot: talipes calcaneous, in which the heel is lower than the toes; talipes equinus, in which the toes are lower than the heel; talipes valgus, in which the toes and the sole of the foot are turned outward; and talipes varus, in which the toes and the sole of the foot are turned inward. Combinations of these types may also exist.

Clubfoot is predominantly a congenital deformity that can be caused by heredity, abnormal Achilles or tibial tendon insertion, intrauterine position, or muscle and ligament imbalance. Talipes equinovarus is the most common type, comprising 95 percent of all cases. It is also one of the most common orthopedic deformities, occurring in 1 out of every 700 live births. Furthermore, clubfoot may be acquired as part of various neuro-muscular diseases such as cerebral palsy.

Two other common foot conditions are toeing in and toeing out. In *toeing in,* which is sometimes referred to as pigeon toes, the feet are pointed inward when the person is standing or moving. A condition in which the feet are pointed outward when standing or moving is *toeing out,* sometimes referred to as duck walking. If either condition is a functional deviation, exercises can be used to correct it. For example:

1. Sit on floor with legs extended forward; slightly raise the leg from the floor, fully extend foot, and perform foot circles. Use the hands to elevate the leg. Repeat this exercise with the foot flexed. Repeat.

2. Sit in chair with feet on the floor, sideways to a wall; kick a large soft ball (e.g., beachball) repeatedly against a barrier with the outer part of the foot (for toeing in). Rotate chair 180 degrees and perform the exercise with the inner part of the same foot (for toeing out). Repeat.

3. Sit in chair with feet on the floor about 24 inches apart. Now rotate feet outward and inward without moving the heels. Repeat.

4. Roller skate.

In mild cases and if the treatment is initiated at a young age, corrective taping with adhesives, casts, splints, braces, or special corrective shoes (i.e., orthodics) may be the only necessary treatments. In severe cases, or if the treatment is not begun until later in life, surgery will probably be required to remove or reduce the physical deformity. Usually exercise programs are effective only in very mild cases. Exercise is used mainly to strengthen and stretch specific muscle groups after strapping, cast, splint, or brace is removed or after surgery. No matter when the exercise program is begun, it should be done with a physician's approval.

Other Disabling Conditions

In this chapter, several disabling conditions are discussed. These conditions may interfere with an individual's ability to participate safely and successfully in physical activities. According to the Rules and Regulations of P.L. 101–476, many of these conditions are subsumed under the category of other health impairment. The other health impaired category includes those individuals with limited strength, vitality, or alertness due to chronic or acute health problems that adversely affect their educational performance. We also address five conditions or disabilities that are not covered under the P.L. 101–476 category Other Health Impaired. These include menstrual problems, pregnancy, aging, speech or language impairments, and multiple disabilities.

Menstrual problems are covered here because more than 50 percent of all menstruating females have painful and sometimes even debilitating menstruation. Because increasing numbers of pregnant minors are enrolled in secondary schools across the country, a brief discussion of pregnancy is essential. Regular physical education classes must be modified to accommodate the later stages of pregnancy. Similarly, aging is not a disability in itself, but one phase of the normal life cycle. The process we call aging involves decline in physical appearance and health, at the cellular tissue, organ, and system levels of the body, and in physical performance.

Speech or language impairments and multiple disabilities are addressed in the Rules and Regulations of P.L. 101–476 in separate categories. The category of speech or language impairment is specifically defined as "... a communication disorder, such as stuttering, impaired articulation, a language impairment, or a voice impairment that adversely affects a child's educational performance" (*Federal Register*, September 29, 1992, p. 44802). The multiple disabilities category is defined as a combination of impairments (e.g., mental retardation and blindness) that cause such severe educational problems that the pupil cannot be accommodated in special education programs designed solely for one of the impairments.

Many misconceptions surround some of the conditions discussed in this chapter. For instance, even today there are educators who think there is a mystique about pupils with cardiac conditions. They may be hesitant about providing an appropriate program and believe that pupils with cardiac conditions cannot participate in any physical activity. Others believe that pregnant teenagers should be excused from physical education. It is our purpose to dispel many of these misconceptions by providing basic information about these conditions as they relate to physical education.

RESPIRATORY PROBLEMS

Two major *respiratory problems* in children are bronchial asthma and cystic fibrosis. *Bronchial asthma* is characterized by wheezing, constricted muscles in the shoulder girdle and neck region, coughing, and rapid breathing. An attack may last for a few minutes or several days. Asthma is the most common chronic childhood disease. It is estimated that 1 million children under 16 years of age have asthma; slightly more males than females have the disease (U.S. Department of Health, 1992).

Asthma is characterized by the narrowing of the air tubes of the lungs (bronchi, bronchioles, trachea) because of constricted muscles, excessive mucus production, and swollen tissue due to sensitivity to various stimuli. The stimuli, called *allergens*, include such substances as dust, animal fur, and plants. Nonallergenic factors, such as cold air, viral infections, and emotional stress, can also stimulate asthma. Another nonallergenic factor that is very important to the physical educator, is vigorous exercise. Although physical activity is highly recommended for pupils with asthma, it may trigger an attack referred to as exercise-induced asthma (EIA). This is due to the fact that the temperature entering the respiratory passages during exercise must be humidified and warmed. For the body to accomplish this, body heat from the lower respiratory tract must be used, which can lead to an attack. EIA also has a refractory period. If, within 40 minutes after the provoking exercise, the pupil exercises again at the same intensity, the exercise may elicit milder EIA responses. Rest intervals of 2 hours or more generally restore pulmonary function to its normal level.

Medications can be used to prevent or reduce the various forms of asthma, such as cromolyn sodium, theophyline, terbulaline, metaproteranol, and alupent. Inhalers (isproternol and isoetherine) and medihalers are used during wheezing to dilate bronchial passages (Hahn, 1985). Other methods to prevent or stop an asthmatic attack are avoidance of the allergens and relaxation. Techniques to remove excess mucus include drinking fluids, breathing moist air, infusing fluids into the veins, and postural drainage.

Cystic fibrosis is an incurable hereditary disorder, generally of the pancreas, which causes a dysfunction of the exocrine glands (mucus, salivary, and sweat glands). One in every 1,000 to 2,000 live births produces an infant with cystic fibrosis; the life expectancy of victims is 20 to 25 years.

Physical education programs for pupils with asthma and cystic fibrosis are similar. One reason to promote activity for children with these respiratory conditions rather than confining them to bed is that gross motor activities help to loosen mucus. It must be noted that though most researchers recommend physical activity for children with cystic fibrosis, their findings on cardiovascular and pulmonary functioning improvement are limited and inconsistent (Horvat & Carlile, 1991).

Some considerations in planning and implementing a physical education program include the following (Schneichkorn, 1977):

1. Be aware of the medical problems related to respiratory function by understanding the effects of medication, particularly antihistamines, on the performance of physical activities.
2. Encourage the pupil to participate in all appropriate activities.
3. Give due recognition to children when they excel.
4. Help other pupils to understand the problem.
5. Allow the pupil to leave an activity to take medication when required or during an attack.
6. Recognize those periods when the pupil may be medically forced to reduce involvement in gross motor activities.
7. Support the acceptance of a pupil with respiratory problems in the general activities of the school, home, and community.

Most pupils with asthma or cystic fibrosis can participate in physical activities with minimal difficulty. The physical educator must be aware, though, that some asthmatic attacks are induced by strenuous physical activity, and the child may need to take medication before beginning. In addition, pupils with cystic fibrosis have shortness of breath on exertion and decreased effort and tolerance with diminished pulmonary reserve. The program for any pupil with a respiratory problem must be determined individually in consultation with a physician. The pupil's tolerance level and the duration and intensity of the physical activity should be considered.

Breathing exercises can be performed to improve respiration and posture. Many children with respiratory conditions only use the accessory muscles of respiration, which results in inefficient breathing, fatigue, and poor posture. Some breathing exercises include ping-pong ball blow relay; balloon blow relay; blow out the candle game; ping-pong ball blow croquet; keeping a 1-inch square of tissue above the floor with the breath as long as possible; and timed breathing with maximal slow diaphragmatic expiration during an exercise such as stair climbing.

Children with asthma or cystic fibrosis have a high frequency of postural deficiencies. These specifically include kyphosis, barrel chest, round shoulders, and kypholordosis. Exercise programs should be designed to prevent or rehabilitate these conditions. Strengthening the abdominals, back, and shoulder girdle muscle groups is recommended, but exercises that strengthen already shortened muscles must be avoided.

Relaxation training is essential for those pupils whose asthmatic attacks are caused by stress and anxiety. Conscious relaxation can prevent or lessen extreme emotional states, which can precipitate an attack. Once relaxation skills have been developed, a warm-up period of mild exercise before more vigorous activities can help the pupil to use oxygen more efficiently.

Active play—running, skipping, hopping, and rope jumping—is very beneficial for the young pupil with asthma or cystic fibrosis. These activities loosen mucus, as well as provide opportunities to develop basic motor skills and patterns. Movement in aquatics activities can also loosen mucus, develop rhythm in breathing, and increase the respiratory capacity of lungs. As precautions, a nose clip should be worn to keep water from reaching the lungs, and water temperature should be controlled to reduce the possibility of chilling that could lead to respiratory infections.

Pupils with respiratory problems should participate in any individual and group activity in which they might be competent. Possibilities include gymnastics, tennis, golf, skiing, badminton, basketball, soccer, and football. Trampolining is an excellent individual activity not only because it develops coordination and physical fitness but because it loosens mucus. Other activities that require vigorous up-and-down motions are also therapeutic.

CARDIAC CONDITIONS

Any disease that affects the heart or the blood vessels is called a *cardiac condition*. The major cardiac conditions in children are hypertension, congenital heart disorders, and rheumatic heart disease.

Hypertension

Hypertension was largely overlooked in children until the late 1970s. An individual is considered hypertensive when diastolic pressure, normally 65–88 mm in a person 50 to 60 years of age, stays regularly at a level over 90 mm or so. In hypertension, the systolic pressure also rises above its normal range of 100–140 mm or so but without a rise in diastolic pressure. Researchers have reported hypertension in 2.3 to 11 percent of infants and children, with an average of 5 percent of the school-aged population. It is important to diagnose these children because hypertension is one of the five predictive factors in the development of adult heart disease and heart attack and it must be treated at any early age. Ninety percent of cases of childhood hypertension is caused by both genetic and environmental factors, only 10 percent are caused by disease, tumors, or defective cardiac development. Hypertensive adolescents most likely will become hypertensive adults. A chief concern is that the number of children with hypertension has increased over the past decade.

Children with borderline high blood pressure generally are not medicated, and physical activity is recommended. However, it is also suggested that these children control their weight, be on a diet in which salt is avoided and with a high potassium intake, and be involved in relaxation training. Dynamic exercises, such as swimming and running, are recommended. Static exercises, such as weight lifting, wrestling, and isometric exercises, which may place an unacceptable load on the heart, should be avoided (Task Force, 1977).

In cases where blood pressure is chronically elevated, medication probably is required. In severe cases, physical educators should use aerobic activities only with a physician's written consent because these activities could raise the systolic blood pressure. Some of the possible side effects of medication are dizziness, postural hypotension, drowsiness, headaches, visual problems, and abdominal pain.

Because hypertension is an important predictor of high blood pressure in adulthood, it is recommended that children 3 years and older should have their blood pressure checked annually. The ideal situation is to prevent hypertension. There are numerous techniques to prevent or manage high blood pressure caused in part or total by hypertension. Some of these techniques are the following (Silliman, French, & Ben Ezra, 1989):

1. Running or jogging seems to be the most widely used technique to maintain cardiorespiratory fitness. A major concern of physical educators is that pupils become bored and rebel when asked to run and jog. Some ideas to motivate pupils are:
   a. Encourage pupils to run/jog around playgrounds before participating in recess.

b. Develop imaginative obstacles courses.

c. Have physical education majors from a local university conduct physical fitness training during recess.

d. Place a large clock on the playground so the pupils can determine how long it will take to run/jog a specific distance.

2. Use aerobic dance activities that combine fundamental motor skills and patterns.

3. Use mini trampolines. They have been reported as effective as a stationary bicycle or treadmill.

4. Use jump rope activities.

5. Integrate cycling into the program. It can combine the same aerobic benefits as running/jogging. Cycling not only can involve the entire family, but it overcomes many of the possible orthopedic problems associated with running/jogging.

6. Use modified games that can be used to develop aerobic fitness. For instance, use relays where the pupils perform an activity while waiting in line (e.g., jogging in place).

Numerous health programs designed for the public schools can be utilized by the physical educator and other professionals responsible for teaching health to pupils about the prevention or reduction of hypertension. The Running for Life Program (Davis, 1982) is designed to increase the fitness levels of school-aged pupils and their knowledge of academic subjects. In this program pupils earn points for each lap run per day. The points for the total class are converted into a distance and plotted on a map of the United States. When the class reaches a specific state, lessons are given about the terrain or weather. Mathematics is incorporated in the program by having pupils determine the average speed or distance traveled.

Project Super Heart (Way, 1981) is a curriculum designed to develop knowledge about cardiorespiratory health. The physical fitness component involves aerobic activities (jogging, swimming, hiking, cross-country skiing, aerobic dancing) to raise the heart rate to a determined target level and then sustain the level for 15 minutes.

Project Hearty Heart (Harkins & Chrietzberg, 1983) provides guidelines for cardiorespiratory activities with school-aged pupils. The program presents numerous high-energy activities and movement experiences with which to develop and maintain the effects of body exercise, specifically on the heart; understand the influence of exercise on the body; improve cardiorespiratory fitness; and encourage lifestyle development based on cardiorespiratory fitness. The Circulatory System Fitness Model (Kern, 1987) teaches school-aged pupils about the functions of the circulatory system and how it is affected by exercise.

Congenital Heart Disorders

There are numerous forms of *congenital heart disorders* caused by abnormal or premature development. Figure 12.1 shows the normal heart and pinpoints the sites for the 10 most common operable heart defects. Following are brief descriptions of these defects (American Heart Association, 1982):

1. *Patent ductus arteriosus.* There is an open passage between the pulmonary artery and the aorta. Normally, this passageway closes after an infant is born. If this fails to happen, some of the blood that should go through the aorta is returned through the lungs. If the opening is large, the infant will tire easily and the growth process will be slow.

2. *Ventricular septal defects (VSD).* There is a large opening between the ventricles in which oxygen-enriched blood from the left side of the heart is forced through the opening into the right side of the heart, instead of being transported through the aorta to the body. Infants with this condition may not demonstrate a normal growth pattern and be undernourished.

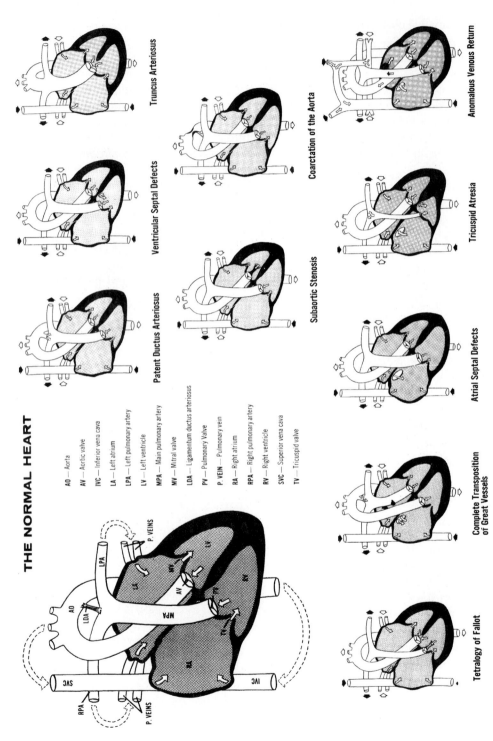

THE NORMAL HEART

AO — Aorta
AV — Aortic valve
IVC — Inferior vena cava
LA — Left atrium
LPA — Left pulmonary artery
LV — Left ventricle
MPA — Main pulmonary artery
MV — Mitral valve
LDA — Ligamentum ductus arteriosus
PV — Pulmonary Valve
P. VEIN — Pulmonary vein
RA — Right atrium
RPA — Right pulmonary artery
RV — Right ventricle
SVC — Superior vena cava
TV — Tricuspid valve

Tetralogy of Fallot

Complete Transposition of Great Vessels

Atrial Septal Defects

Patent Ductus Arteriosus

Subaortic Stenosis

Tricuspid Atresia

Ventricular Septal Defects

Coarctation of the Aorta

Anomalous Venous Return

Truncus Arteriosus

FIGURE 12.1 A normal heart; congenital heart abnormalities. *(From "Congenital Heart Abnormalities" [Clinical Education Aid No. 7], Ross Laboratories, Columbus, Ohio. Copyright 1970 Ross Laboratories. Used by permission.)*

3. *Truncus arteriosus.* This is a complex disorder where there is only one artery from the heart to form the aorta and pulmonary artery.

4. *Subaortic stenosis.* This deficiency involves the narrowing of the aortic valve, which makes it difficult to pump blood to the body. Children with this condition frequently do not display any symptoms; others have chest pain, unusual tiring, dizziness or fainting episodes.

5. *Coarctation of the aorta.* In this disorder the aorta is constricted, which reduces blood flow to the lower part of the body, and blood pressure is increased above the constriction. Symptoms generally do not occur at birth but can develop after the first week of life.

6. *Tetralogy of Fallot.* This deficiency is a combination of numerous disorders. The two major defects are a large hole between two ventricles and a constriction between the right ventricle through the pulmonary artery to the lungs. Symptoms of this condition are blueness of the lips and fingernails, which generally occurs soon after birth. During exercise a child with this condition may become short of breath and experience fainting spells.

7. *Complete transposition of great vessels.* In this deficiency the pulmonary artery and the aorta are reversed, which causes deoxygenated blood to go to the body and oxygenated blood to the lungs. Infants born with this condition will survive only if they have at least one passageway to allow oxygenated blood to reach the body. For this to occur, the infant must have an accompanying ventricular septal defect, atrial septal defect, or patent ductus arteriosus.

8. *Atrial septal defects.* This defect involves a large opening between the atria, which allows oxygenated blood from the left side of the heart to be returned back to the lungs with deoxygenated blood from the body instead of being transported through the left ventricle and out the aorta to the body.

Many infants and children with this deficiency display few if any symptoms.

9. *Tricuspid atresia.* In this deficiency there is no opening in the tricuspid valve through which blood in the right atrium can flow into the right ventricle. For the infant or child to survive there must be an accompanying atrial septal defect and a ventricular septal defect to allow blood to return to the right atrium.

10. *Anomalous venous return.* This defect involves the narrowing of the pulmonary valve, causing the right ventricle to pump harder to overcome the obstruction. In severe conditions there may be a bluish appearance under the fingernails.

More than 5,000 infants born each year in the United States require cardiac surgery before their first birthday. The survival rate of these children has increased dramatically in the past few years because of refined diagnostic and surgical techniques and improved understanding of abnormal physiology.

Rheumatic Heart Disease

Approximately 1 percent of the reported cases of streptococcal pharyngitis (strep throat) will develop into rheumatic fever. It is believed that this fever represents the body's overreaction to antibodies developed to fight the initial infection. During the acute phase of rheumatic fever, tiny wartlike nodules can develop along the line of closure of the valvular leaflets of the mitral valve and less often the aortic or tricuspid valves. This can cause improper closure of the leaflets, which in turn allows blood leakage. This condition is *rheumatic heart disease.* After congenital heart disease, rheumatic heart disease is the second most common cardiac condition in childhood. At one time more than 35 percent of all childhood heart disease was caused by rheumatic fever, which led to rheumatic heart disease. Today, with medical advances and treatment, this figure is diminishing: The incidence of rheumatic heart disease now ranges from 0.2 to 5 percent of the school aged population. Of those who have recovered from rheumatic fever, 95 percent will be able to lead basically normal lives, only 5 percent will require major daily activity restrictions.

In designing specific instructional strategies for individuals with cardiac conditions, the functional capacity of the pupil (as determined by the physician) must be considered. A therapeutic classification should be used as a guide to the management of the physical activities of a pupil with any cardiac problem (Criteria Committee, 1964).

- *Class A.* Patients whose physical activity need not be restricted in any way.
- *Class B.* Patients whose ordinary physical activity need not be restricted but who should be advised against severe or competitive efforts.
- *Class C.* Patients whose ordinary physical activity should be moderately restricted and whose more strenuous efforts should be discontinued.
- *Class D.* Patients whose ordinary physical activity should be markedly restricted.
- *Class E.* Patients who should be at complete rest, confined to bed or chair.

One of the biggest problems in providing an appropriate program is those school administrators and teachers who have unrealistic fears about physical education for a pupil with a heart condition, and therefore decrease the pupil's activity below that recommended by the physician. An excessively conservative attitude may be as harmful as overpermissiveness. In determining an appropriate level of physical activity, the approximate range of energy cost must be determined. Examples of the amount of ener-

gy required to perform traditional physical activities are presented in Table 12.1. The energy requirements during exercise are measured in METs (metabolic equivalents). Although there is individual variability, 1 MET is approximately equal to resting oxygen consumption, which is approximately 3.5 ml/kg of body weight per minute. To determine the METs during a physical activity, the work metabolic rate is divided by the resting metabolic rate.

The average intensity of exercise may be estimated by determining 70 percent of a pupil's functional capacity. For a pupil with cardiovascular disease, it may be only 40 to 50 percent. For example, if a pupil's maximum functional capacity is determined by a physician to be 5 METs, the average condition-

TABLE 12.1 AMOUNT OF ENERGY NEEDED TO PERFORM PHYSICAL ACTIVITIES

ACTIVITY	METs
Archery	3–4
Badminton	4–9
Basketball	7–12
Bed exercise	1–2
Bicycling	3–8
Bowling	2–4
Calisthenics	3–8
Dancing	3–7
Fencing	6–10
Touch football	6–10
Golf (walking)	4–7
Handball	8–12
Jogging	7–15
Racquetball	8–12
Skating	5–8
Snow skiing	5–12
Soccer	5–12
Softball	3–6
Swimming	4–8
Table tennis	3–5
Volleyball	3–6

Adapted from American College of Sports Medicine, *Guidelines for Graded Exercise Testing and Exercise Prescription.* Philadelphia: Lea & Febiger, 1975. Used by permission.

ing intensity equals 0.7 (functional capacity) X 5 (METs) = 3.5 METs. For the pupil with cardiac disease it would be 0.4 X 5 METs = 2.0 METs. A physical activity program at this level indicates adherence to the medical margin of safety principle.

Depending on the classification of the heart deficiency, other general instructional strategies must be considered.

1. Never force extreme physical exertion. Activities can be modified to reduce the level of intensity:
   a. Allow another pupil to run the bases.
   b. Reduce distance in a relay.
   c. Reduce speed of an activity by using balloons or beach balls.
   d. Play doubles.
   e. Reduce boundaries.
2. Include 5- to 7-minute warm-up and cooldown periods.
3. Physical activity must be decreased or stopped if there is:
   a. Chest pain.
   b. Dizziness.
   c. Shortness of breath.
   d. Increased heart rate over 120 beats per minute or the maximum number prescribed by a physician.
   e. Undue fatigue.
   f. A bluish tint to the lips.
   g. Poor recovery pulse rate following physical activity.
4. Pulse rates should be taken during the activity. There are commercially developed devices that can provide a pulse reading within seconds. Some of these devices are durable, portable, and weigh less than 2 pounds.
5. Avoid purposeless moving.
6. Provide opportunity for numerous rest periods.
7. Anaerobic (oxygen debt buildup) and arrhythmic activities can be dangerous or fatal, because there is a restriction placed on the circulatory system. Aerobic and rhythmic activities, which involve a great amount of constant circulation (walking, jogging, swimming, skating), are best.
8. Avoid extreme temperature variations.
9. Gradually increase the intensity, duration, and frequency of activities.
10. Encourage weight management to minimize additional stress on the heart. Some related guidelines are:
    a. Reduce red meat consumption and replace with poultry, fish, and vegetarian meals.
    b. Avoid food cooked in saturated fat.
    c. Eliminate butter and reduce consumption of margarine.
    d. Use low-fat and fat-free salad dressings and dairy products.
    e. Increase fiber intake.
    f. Use cereals without sugar and salt added.
    g. Avoid egg yolks and organ foods.
11. Be aware of the effects of medication on physical performance.
12. Long-term exercise compliance is important as with any lifestyle intervention. Refer to Chapter 13 for behavior management techniques that may be appropriate to use with specific pupils. Further, include a variety of activities to reduce boredom.
13. Incorporate relaxation training into the physical education class.
14. Reduce competitive or stressful activities.

ANEMIA

Anemia is a condition in which the number of red blood cells is reduced or the quality of the hemoglobin is reduced. Anemia is the most common blood disorder in children. Individuals with anemia can exhibit a wide range of symptoms. Some of the most common are pallor, little desire for physical activity, rapid pulse, shortness of breath, rashes, irritability, difficulty in concentrating, headache, dizziness, lack of endurance, nausea, decreased appetite, menstrual irregularities, heart murmurs, heart failure, delayed skeletal maturation, shortness of stature, lack of strength, apathy, and fragile and spoon-shaped fingernails.

Anemia can have numerous causes, both congenital and acquired. Congenital anemia includes abnormalities in the synthesis of hemoglobin, defects in red blood cell membrane function, deficiencies of red blood cell enzymes, and too few or immature blood cells in the bone marrow stem. Acquired anemia may be caused by nutritional deficiencies in iron, folic acid, and vitamin B_{12}; by acute hemorrhage; by bacterial infections and toxins and other infectious agents; by administration of high doses of medication, such as penicillin, sulfanomides, and aspirin; by ingestion of household solvents, dyes, paints, and glues; and by excessive x-ray or other radiation treatments.

The extent of anemia in children and youth varies markedly, from 3 to 22 percent, in different sections of the United States. This range is due to variations in the age, sex, race, and socioeconomic background of the subjects of the numerous studies in which these figures have been reported.

The severity and type of anemia will influence physical education programming. Written approval from a physician to determine the need for special programming and the extent of participation recommended is required. For instance, pupils with sickle cell anemia are prone to ulcers on the legs and ankles, and so certain activities that could irritate an ulcerated area must be avoided. Activities in which there is a high probability of receiving cuts and bruises must be avoided by some pupils with anemia because they heal slowly. Pupils with severe anemia tend

to withdraw from physical activity. The teacher must design the program based on a pupil's abilities, always considering the social implications if the pupil cannot succeed.

Pupils with anemia may be short and lack physical strength and muscle endurance when compared to their peers. Therefore, fitness exercises are highly recommended not only to develop their bodies, but because the increased oxygen required to perform these activities stimulates red blood cell production. At the same time, though, the heart must pump harder than the norm to meet the demands of the body of a pupil who is anemic. More blood must be circulated because of the presence of either oxygen-deficient cells or decreased cells. A pupil with severe anemia may risk heart failure by being highly active. Such pupils also may be unable to participate generally in physical activities, which delays the development of fundamental motor skills and patterns. This is particularly true for those with severe anemia, which may cause prolonged absences from school.

Motor exploration activities may enable pupils to progress at their own rate. These activities provide pupils with a basic understanding of the body and its relationship to the environment. An integral component of the physical education program should also be relaxation training to enable pupils to learn to use their energy resources effectively.

Aquatics activities are recommended because of the ease with which pupils can perform many activities in water. Not only can swimming skills be developed, but water can be used as a medium for fitness instruction.

Most types of dance activities are also appropriate if selected to meet the pupil's needs and abilities. Dances that permit rest periods, such as most square dances, are also beneficial because the pupil with anemia can stop and rest when needed without inconveniencing others.

Medically safe individual, dual, and group physical activities are encouraged not only for their physical and motor benefits but also for the social and emotional values derived from peer interaction, group enthusiasm, and competition. The playing time, area, and equipment may have to be modified to meet the pupil's needs and capabilities.

ACQUIRED IMMUNODEFICIENCY SYNDROME (AIDS)

The purpose of the body's immune system, specifically T and B white blood cells, is to act as a barrier against disease. Some T cells help B cells produce antibodies that fight organisms that cause disease. Other T cells function to suppress the fight against invading germs once the infection has been controlled. If there is a deficiency in the immune system, an individual can contact numerous diseases. A primary example is the AIDS virus. It does irreparable harm to the immune system by destroying the cells that produce antibodies that fight infections. The virus sends a false chemical message that the organisms causing the infections have been destroyed, which, in turn, increases the probability that a person will contact other diseases, such as pneumonia or cancer. The virus may also cause brain damage.

Today it is estimated that there are over 270,000 AIDS cases in the United States. The incidence of AIDS is approximately 1 in every 6,700 individuals.

The AIDS virus, referred to as the human immunodeficiency virus (HIV), can be transmitted by intimate contact with a person who is infected and by exchange of body fluids, as from mother to fetus, sexual intercourse, sharing a hypodermic needle, and blood transfusions (Ogden & Germinario, 1988). There is no evidence that the AIDS virus can be transmitted by casual contact, such as holding hands, hugging, coughing, or using the same toilet seat (Ohio AIDS Education Package, 1987).

Some of the symptoms of this disease are fatigue, change in activity level, weight loss, dyspnea, color change, and chronic diarrhea. It may take two to seven years before these symptoms appear after exposure to the AIDS virus.

Neurological impairments have been well documented in a substantial number of adults with AIDS (Britton & Miller, 1984). There are also neurological, as well as developmental, delays in infants and children with the disease. As a matter of fact, some infants and children lose motor abilities as the disease progresses (Ultmann, et al., 1985). With such concerns in mind, Surburg (1988) offers important guidelines to be carefully followed when serving such a pupil in physical education:

1. The pupil can attend school if any sores and skin eruptions are covered.

2. The pupil can attend school if diarrhea, fevers, coughs, or symptoms of respiratory illness are not evident.

3. If the pupil suffers an abrasion or cut or is bleeding from an injury in physical education, the physical education teacher should wear gloves when providing first-aid treatment. The material used to clean up the fluid should be disposed of in a leakproof bag.

4. Only ordinary hygiene practices are needed regarding towels unless the towels are contaminated with body fluid.

5. Showers and swimming facilities can be used by these pupils without any additional considerations.

6. Frequent rest periods may be required in severe cases. Pulse rates should be monitored.

Physical educators and other pupils should not demonstrate negative attitudes toward pupils with AIDS. These pupils should not be treated as a potential health problem but as pupils who deserve an appropriate physical education program (Surburg, 1988).

HEMOPHILIA

Hemophilia describes several inherited blood coagulation disorders. The most common and most serious is classic hemophilia or hemophilia A. A sex-linked recessive disorder of the clotting mechanism, it is believed to be caused most frequently by a clotting deficiency in one of the plasma proteins that function as clotting factors. When the mutant gene is carried on the single X chromosome of a male, he will be a hemophiliac. If the mutant gene is carried on one of the two X chromosomes of a female, she will not generally develop the hemorrhage symptoms but can transmit the mutant gene to her offspring. The actual distribution of offspring produced by the mating of hemophiliac males or female carriers is based on the laws of probability.

The severity of hemophilia corresponds roughly to the degree of the antihemophiliac factor deficiency (illustrated in Table 12.2). The scope of hemophilia is approximately 1 in 10,000 males and 1 in 100,00 females. About 35 to 90 percent of the cases are the classical form of hemophilia. Ninety percent of all hemophilia cases are diagnosed before 25 years of age; the average is 11.5 years.

TABLE 12.2 CLASSIFICATION OF HEMOPHILIA BY SEVERITY

CATEGORY	ANTIHHEMOPHILIAC FACTOR CONCENTRATION	APPROXIMATE VENOUS CLOTTING TIME	CHARACTERISTICS
Mild	5–25% of normal	Normal to 12 minutes	Few joints are involved, and functional impairments are infrequent. Bleeding problems are pronounced in physical trauma or surgery. Clotting is often normal. Usually not detected until the individual is between 8–13 years of age.
Moderate	1–4% of normal	12–25 minutes	Joint involvement may not appear until middle age. Spontaneous bleeding is observed, but uncommon. Renal and gastrointestinal swelling occurs. Usually symptoms appear before 8 years of age (mass blood clotting).
Severe	1% or less	Over 25 minutes	Symptoms usually become noticeable when the infant begins to crawl. There often is repeated bleeding with impaired joint function by 10 years of age in some individuals; by 20 years of age, there is usually moderate to severe joint disability. Hemorrhage from the urinary or intestinal tract is characteristic, and hospitalization is frequent. Swelling or a mass of clotted blood could also develop spontaneously in the area of the abdominal cavity.

Modified from T. Tarney, *Surgery in the Hemophiliac* (Springfield, Ill. Charles C. Thomas, 1968), p. 10. By permission.

The major treatment is a transfusion with blood serum containing the antihemophiliac factor. The antihemophiliac factor concentrate can be stored in a refrigerator. Some individuals with hemophilia keep an emergency supply at home and have been taught to self-administer the transfusion. Because the spleen may store and release the natural antihemophiliac factor in the body, a future treatment may be a spleen transplant.

The characteristics of individuals with hemophilia vary greatly depending on the severity of the condition. Generally problems include excess bleeding, rebleeding with surgery and trauma, joint deformity, muscle atrophy, contractures, and central nervous system bleeding.

One half of the pupils with hemophilia have poor school attendance. One third of these pupils attribute this to poor health. Chronic health problems also cause the parents to become overprotective, which could influence the type of activities in which the pupil is initially willing or allowed to participate. In the past, pupils with hemophilia were restricted from physical activity. Rest and/or immobilization were the major medical prescriptions. Because of the atrophy that occurs with these types of treatment, the joints often would become unstable and collapse. It was noted, though, that pupils who disregarded their physician's advice were in better physical condition and experienced less joint bleeding than those who rested or were placed in casts. Physical education is now recommended for pupils with hemophilia.

The program must be carefully designed with continuous input from a physician. Komp and Adams (1972) present some important considerations:

1. Morale may be very low in regard to participation in physical activities. Through a planned physical education program, activities can be designed to enable the pupil to participate successfully.

2. Because of lack of instruction and opportunity to participate, the motor coordination of pupils with hemophilia is below normal as a group. Motor coordination can be improved through a structured program of developmental physical education.

It must be remembered that each pupil should be judged on an individual basis. The degree of severity, as well as the pupil's adjustment to school and peers, must be considered. There are pupils with hemophilia who participate in contact sports. If injured, a booster shot of cryoprecipitate* will usually avert most serious bleeding. Extra padding may also be provided for use in contact physical activities and in the general physical education program.

An optimal level of physical and motor fitness is very important for a pupil with hemophilia. Developed muscles act as a protective barrier for joints after trauma and aids in the rehabilitation process, if needed, after long periods of bed rest or wheelchair confinement.

The development of a well-coordinated pupil is not only recommended but essential. Increased coordination may decrease the number of bleeding episodes caused by falling or running into objects. It is recommended that most preschoolers with hemophilia be permitted to participate in activities similar to their peers. Many of the children are ready for tricycles or hot wheels by their third or fourth birthday and can roller skate at about 6 years of age. It is generally recommended that shoe skates be used to provide better support and stability than skates that are clamped to the shoe.

Noncontact sports such as swimming are highly recommended. One caution would be diving; the impact with the water may cause

---

*A cryoprecipitate results from cooling cryoglobulin.

internal bleeding. If there is external oozing or bleeding, aquatic activities are not indicated until healed. In severe cases of hemophilia, prolonged periods of absenteeism create social isolation. As a counter to this, for adolescents with hemophilia in particular, all forms of dance activities provide an opportunity for social interaction and peer acceptance.

There are several general guidelines to consider when selecting physical education activities in which a pupil with hemophilia may participate. Most noncontact games are highly recommended, particularly such activities as jogging, cycling, table tennis, golf, and badminton. Some nonbody contact games that may involve forceful contact with objects such as a ball (e.g., battleball, dodgeball) may not be recommended. The reason for this relates to the major hemophiliac problem of internal bleeding around the bones, joints, stomach, intestines, throat, and nasal passages. Generally, direct contact activities such as basketball, soccer, and football are similarly not recommended. However, as stated earlier, care must be taken not to be overcautious, as some pupils do participate in Little League baseball and intramural sports such as soccer and basketball. Because pupils with hemophilia vary widely in their responses to physical activity, the decision must be individualized based on the severity of the condition and the frequency and type of bleeding episodes and in consultation with a physician.

The following are traditional physical activities that have been categorized by risk for a pupil who is hemophilic by the National Hemophilia Foundation and American Red Cross (n.d., p. 8):

- Category 1: activities recommended for most pupils with hemophilia.
- Category 2: games and sports in which the physical, social, and psychological benefits

may outweigh the risks. Most physical activities are in this category.
- Category 3: activities in which the risk outweighs the benefits for all pupils with hemophilia and are considered dangerous.

Activity	Category
Baseball	2
Basketball	2
Bicycling	2
Bowling	2
Boxing	3
Football	3
Frisbee	2
Golf	1
Gymnastics	2
Hockey	3
Horseback riding	2
Ice skating	2
Motorcycling	3
Racquetball	3
Roller skating	2
Running and jogging	2
Skateboarding	3
Skiing:	
Downhill	2
Cross-country	2
Soccer	2
Swimming	1
Tennis	2
Volleyball	2
Waterskiing	2
Weight lifting	2
Wrestling	3

DIABETES

Diabetes is a complex metabolic disorder. There are two major types of diabetes. Type 1 diabetes requires insulin injections because the pancreas produces little or no insulin. Individuals with this type of diabetes must adhere to a very strict diet and insulin injection schedule. If this condition is poorly controlled, it can lead to cardiovascular, renal, and visual complications, as well as a shortened life span. Type I represents 10 to 20 percent of the diabetic population and usually is diagnosed before 18 years of age.

In contrast, individuals with Type II diabetes have a functioning pancreas but have cells that are insulin resistant. This disease is controlled through diet and sometimes through the use of an oral sulfate-urea agent, which improves the body's sensitivity to its own insulin. Many authorities suggest that if individuals with this type of diabetes exercise regularly and maintain an appropriate weight level, their condition could reverse

and they would be symptom free (Rash & Rash, 1988). Type II represents 80 to 90 percent of individuals with this disease; most individuals are obese and the onset of this disease is usually after 40 years of age.

Figure 12.2 compares the utilization of food by a nondiabetic individual and an individual with diabetes.

Insulin is a hormone produced in the pancreas and secreted into the bloodstream. It regulates sugar metabolism and the rate at which glucose is either used or stored. The

FIGURE 12.2   The utilization of food by nondiabetic persons and persons who are diabetic. *(From "A Guide for the Diabetic." Indianapolis: Eli Lilly and Company, 1978. Used by permission.)*

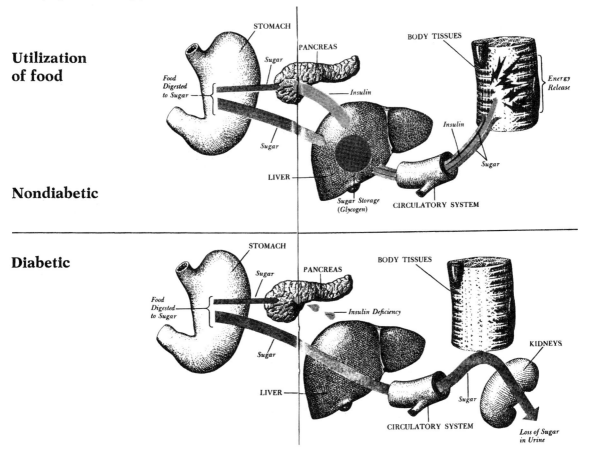

two major complications associated with diabetes are diabetic coma (acidosis or hyperglycemia) and insulin reaction (hypoglycemia). If the proper amount of insulin is not produced or cannot be used by the cells, glucose accumulates in the bloodstream and causes the level of blood sugar to rise above normal. The excess is eliminated by the kidneys and excreted in the urine. If this condition is not treated, the body must use fat as an energy source. This causes an excess of fatty acids, which could lead to acidosis, coma, and finally death. An insulin reaction is caused by too much insulin in the bloodstream. It can be caused by strenuous energy output or a lack of food supply to the cells. The warning signs of acidosis and insulin reaction are shown in Table 12.3.

The first-aid treatments for the two conditions are exactly opposite. In acidosis, a physician should be contacted to inject insulin; in an insulin reaction, the conscious pupil should ingest some form of sugar (candy bar, sugar cube) immediately. Diabetes cannot be cured, but some of its effects can be managed.

An estimated 10 million individuals in the United States have different diagnosable degrees of diabetes, and 4 million of these do not know they have the disease. Approximately 90,000 diagnosed diabetics are children under 18 years of age. It is estimated that every minute one individual in the United States is diagnosed as a diabetic. Diabetes is the seventh leading cause of death in the United States and a leading cause of blindness in adults under 70 years of age.

Most pupils who are diabetic can actively participate in physical activities. Consider the list of nationally known sports figures with diabetes:

Mike Pyle	Football
Ty Cobb	Baseball
Jackie Robinson	Baseball
Catfish Hunter	Baseball
Bobby Clarke	Ice hockey
Scott Verplank	Golf
Hamilton Richardson	Tennis

Some pupils, though, may require special attention. A physician's written consent and advice concerning participation should be obtained before the program is initiated for these pupils.

The teacher should know that the pupil may need to leave class for medication, to test the sugar content of his or her urine, or to eat some sugar if symptoms of an insulin reaction are developing. The physical educator may want to keep some sugar cubes at hand in case of an emergency. The teacher can help the pupil to schedule classes so that physical education falls immediately after a snack or lunch period. Physical education is a very important component of such a pupil's educational program, because sugar is used faster so there is less need for insulin or medication.

TABLE 12.3   WARNING SIGNS OF ACIDOSIS AND INSULIN REACTION

	ACIDOSIS (DIABETIC COMA)	INSULIN REACTION
Onset	Gradual	Sudden
Skin	Flushed, dry	Pale, moist
Behavior	Drowsy	Excited
Breath	Fruity odor	Normal
Breathing	Deep, labored	Normal to shallow
Vomiting	Present	Absent
Tongue	Dry	Moist
Hunger	Absent	Present
Thirst	Present	Absent
Sugar in urine	Large amounts	Absent or slight

From *About Diabetes* (New York: American Diabetes Association, Inc., 1979).

There are numerous guidelines for programming for a pupil with diabetes in physical education. First, physical activity tolerance levels must be determined through communication with the pupil's family and physician. Second, physical activity must be coordinated with food intake and insulin use. If the amount of activity will be significantly increased during a class period because of a physical fitness test or activities that require sudden bursts of energy, the amount of insulin or amount and type of food eaten before class may need to be adjusted.

Third, skin infections should be watched for and prevented,

> because infections may increase the need for insulin by increasing metabolism generally, interfering with the utilization of insulin, limiting the output of insulin by the pancreas, or increasing the poison or toxins absorbed by the blood stream and thus bringing about acidosis (Winnick, 1979, p. 392).

Pupils with diabetes can get skin infections easily, so cuts and bruises must be taken care of immediately. The recommended first-aid steps are to wash the area, apply antiseptic medication, and cover the area with a sterile pad. If the cut or bruise does not begin to heal by the next day, a physician should be contacted. Also, sunburn is a potential source of infection that should be avoided.

Foot care is particularly important, not only because cuts and bruises may occur on the feet but also because blisters may develop. Tennis shoes and socks must be properly fitted to prevent blisters. Athlete's foot, a common foot infection, may be contracted in the locker room. It can be combated with disinfection powder. It is also recommended that the pupil with diabetes avoid walking barefoot and wear thongs or sandals instead.

When showering, care must be taken to carefully clean with a mild soap to prevent infections. A soft, clean towel should be used. In severe cases of diabetes, the pupil should not rub but rather should pat-dry, to decrease the possibility of skin irritation.

Another source of infection could come from participating in water activities. Ear canal infections such as otitis externa can develop from contact with bacteria in the water (Coram & Mangum, 1986). To prevent such infection, earplugs should be worn while swimming.

Fourth, circulatory restrictions must be avoided. Tennis shoes must not be tight, and shorts and socks with tight elastic bands should not be worn. A pupil with diabetes may already have circulatory problems, as there is a tendency with diabetes for blood vessels to thicken and harden prematurely. Wearing too-tight clothes could further decrease the amount of oxygen and nutrients reaching the cells of the body. In severe cases, gangrene may result because the cells die of starvation. However, note that thickening and hardening of the arteries and gangrene usually occur in the adult, not in the juvenile, form of diabetes.

Fifth, proper body weight must be maintained. Excess weight increases the strain on the pancreas and liver, as well as on the heart and circulatory system. Proper diet and weight control are major components of managing diabetes.

Sixth, several social-emotional factors must be considered. The emotional and social development of pupils with diabetes should be in the normal range. Pupils with diabetes must take as much responsibility for the management of the disease as possible, including attention to the role of physical activity. The basic stages of self-management are (Malone & Rosenbloom, 1981):

- Ages 2–3: Can help plan snacks based on nutritious choices provided by parents.
- Ages 4–6: Recognizes that he or she is different from peers but focuses on similarities, not differences.
- Ages 7–8: Learns to initiate simple self-care, such as measuring or administering insulin, but generally does not understand the purpose for the treatment.
- Ages 9–11: Can manage urine testing and insulin injections. Begins to understand immediate reactions to behavior (e.g., an insulin reaction may occur unless he or she eats before exercising).
- Ages 12–15: Understands delayed consequences related to behavior (e.g., skipping insulin one day, may feel nauseated later).
- Ages 16–18: Manages self-care entirely. Wants to know the effects of marijuana and alcohol on diabetes and how sexual function is affected.

The physical educator must be cautious of those pupils who try to control other people or situations—for instance, a pupil saying that he cannot participate in physical education because he does not feel good, when actually he just does not care for the day's activities. Others may not want to exercise because they may be afraid of a hypoglycemia reaction (Fremion, Marrero, & Golden, 1987). To avoid exercise-induced hypoglycemia, pupils can, on the days of exercise, reduce insulin by 10 to 30 percent or add a piece of fruit to the diet for each 30 minutes of aerobic exercise and one item of protein for aerobic exercise longer than 1 hour. Further, psychological stress due to competitive activities or activities that create extreme excitement may influence metabolic rate, which in turn changes the blood sugar level.

Seventh are the techniques used in taking insulin. One way is to take insulin injections. These injections are generally taken in the outer area of the upper arm; above and below the waist, except the area around the navel; in the upper area of the buttock; and outside of the front of the thigh. The general rule in using such sites is to avoid repeated injects in the same spot over short periods of time and inject into areas that will maximize the effectiveness and minimize fluctuations in daily control of insulin since exercise affects the rate of insulin absorption. For instance, if a pupil with diabetes injects into the thigh and then goes on a bicycle ride, the exercise will increase the blood flow to the thigh, thus speeding up the rate of insulin absorption. Because of this, pupils with diabetes should not inject the skin over muscles that will be exercised.

Related to this, a new concern for physical educators are pupils with diabetes who use insulin pumps. Insulin pumps deliver insulin through a plastic tube attached to a needle that is inserted under the skin and is taped in place. While not a replacement for the pancreas, the pump can continuously provide a slow trickle of insulin through the day and night. Manually the pupil can also give an extra squirt of insulin before meals to counter the blood sugar increase that normally results from eating food. All pumps now in use have an alarm that sounds if the infusion line is blocked or the pump is about to run out of insulin. Pump users frequently are unwilling to reveal the pump, which makes exercise programming more risky. Presently, though, conventional subcutaneous injection is more appealing to children and adolescents.

MENSTRUAL PROBLEMS

Menstruation is the normal cyclic process of physiological uterine bleeding in healthy nonpregnant pubescent and postpubescent females (Weideger, 1976). It generally occurs approximately once a month in women between the ages of 12 and 50. About 3 ounces of blood are lost in each menstrual period. Common disorders that may occur during menstruation are dysmenorrhea, amenorrhea, and menorrhagia.

Dysmenorrhea describes painful menstruation, which occurs to some degree in 50 to 70 percent of all menstruating females. Described as one of the world's commonest conditions, its symptoms include tension, constipation, and pressure and pain in the pelvic region. These symptoms usually appear at the beginning of the menstrual cycle, sometimes referred to as *premenstrual syndrome (PMS)*. These physiological changes are linked to reproductive hormone activity, but lack of exercise, poor posture, and tight clothing aggravate the condition.

Amenorrhea means the absence of menstruation. It can be caused by anemia, emotional stress, hormonal disturbance, failure to develop, or abnormal organs. Amenorrhea is relatively common in females who are heavy exercisers. Some researchers have reported that up to 50 percent of female subjects who are heavy exercisers have irregular menses or amenorrhea. Thus it is very important that physical educators have knowledge about the seriousness of the condition (Brooks & Boatwright, 1992). Other factors, such as weight loss, obesity, and physical and emotional stress, also increase susceptibility to menstrual disturbance. The age at which the female begins physical training may provoke amenorrhea. Females who are involved in intense physical activity prior to menarche show a higher incidence of menstrual disorders than those who begin after menarche. Amenorrhea may not be permanent. In many cases menstruation begins after psychological conflicts have been eased or after the body has adapted to stress.

Menorrhagia refers to excessive blood loss during menstruation. This condition can be caused by an inflammation of the pelvic organs, tumors in the uterus, organ displacement, or circulatory disturbances leading to excessive blood in the abdominal and pelvic areas.

In the early part of the twentieth century, "the occurrence of the menstrual flow was often the excuse for adopting a semirecumbent position with a handkerchief in one hand and a bottle of smelling salts in the other" (Wilson & Rennie, 1976, p. 61). Today, there are generally no restrictions related to physical activity during a normal menstrual period. For those with severe discomfort and abnormally heavy bleeding, some activities may be restricted or modifications based on medical advice may be needed.

Special exercises to develop abdominal strength or to remove functional posture problems can be effective in reducing pain in many cases of menstrual problems, particularly dysmenorrhea. As early as 1914, Mosher recommended that, wearing loose clothing, the woman lie on her back with the knees bent, arms at the sides, and one hand on the abdominal wall. Then she lifts and lowers the hand on the abdomen by rhythmically extending and contracting the abdominal muscles. This exercise should be repeated 10 times, twice a day (see Figure 12.3). Through this exercise abdominal muscles and the diaphragm become active, which tends to decrease menstrual congestion.

Another exercise to relieve menstrual pain was developed by Billig (1943). The woman stands with her side 18 inches from a wall with her feet together. She elevates the elbow nearest the wall to shoulder height, with the forearm and hand resting on the wall. The other hand is placed in the hollow of the hip joint (see Figure 12.4). Her knees are completely extended. Then she forces her hips inward toward the wall far enough to stretch contracted ligamentous bands. This exercise should be performed 10 times on each side of the body, 3 times each day. When learning this exercise, a woman should be supervised to ensure correct performance. This exercise is a practical method to release abnormally contracted ligaments caused by postural deficiencies that irritate compressed nerves.

FIGURE 12.3   Mosher exercise.

FIGURE 12.4   Billig exercise.

An equally effective exercise developed by Golub (1959) has some advantages over the Mosher and Billig exercises. It requires no wall and little floor space and can be performed in street clothes with little or no supervision. There are two parts to this exercise. In the first part, the woman stands with the arms raised sideways at shoulder height. Her knees are straight and her feet are a few inches apart. She now bends and twists her trunk and attempts to touch the outside of her left foot with her right hand (see Figure 12.5a). The second part of the exercise involves standing with the arms at the sides of the body, feet next to each other and a few inches apart. She then simultaneously swings her arms forward and backward, rotating at the hips to the right side and raising the left leg backward as far as possible (see Figure 12.5b). Both parts of this exercise should be performed at least four times on each side of the body, three times daily. Gradually the number of exercise sets should be increased to 10.

Although historically swimming has been avoided during menstruation, with today's

FIGURE 12.5a Golub exercise–Part 1.

FIGURE 12.5b Golub exercise–Part 2.

use of tampons, aquatic activities should not be automatically precluded. However, chilling should be avoided, because the heat regulation mechanism of the body may be less stable during the menstrual period. Depending on severity and associated side effects, females with menorrhagia may have to be temporarily excused from swimming.

PREGNANCY

Pregnancy describes the period when an unborn child is carried in the body—from conception until birth, which usually lasts about 280 days, or 40 weeks. Each year approximately 10 percent of the teenaged girls, between 15 and 18 years of age, in the United States become pregnant, and most of these girls give birth. Teenagers in the United States are at least 15 times more likely to give birth than their peers in any other Western country. Approximately 40 percent of these pregnancies end in abortions. Teen births comprise almost one-eighth of all births recorded in the United States. In addition, one in four young women become pregnant before leaving high school (Ogden & Germinario, 1988).

In the past a great deal of hostility was directed toward adolescents who were pregnant. Today, though, there is a marked trend toward acceptance and inclusion of such teens with the rest of the school population. Not only do these young women need physical education for the same reasons as do their peers, but it can prepare young mothers for delivery and can also alleviate some of the complications associated with teenage pregnancy. Compared to women who are 20 to 40 years old, when pregnant, teenagers have a greater probability of developing complications, such as toxemia, anemia, and prolonged labor. In addition, problems for the child of low birth weight, mental retardation, seizure disorders, and spinal injury are more frequently associated with these births. Infants born to minors also have an increased probability of death during their first year of life.

Until recently, pregnancy was considered a disabling condition and teenagers who were pregnant may have received special physical education services. (See Figure 12.6). Such teenagers now generally attend regular physical education classes. No matter what the setting, however, a young woman who is pregnant needs to maintain a reasonable level of physical fitness while avoiding the potential hazards of inappropriate exercises. Solberg (1988) advises the following to physical educators:

1. Evaluate your attitude toward the pupil and her situation. Do not be judgmental and nonsupportive. The goal is to achieve an excellent relationship with the mother and child.

2. Encourage the pupil to seek prenatal medical care and determine any medical restriction that would have a negative impact on an exercise program. Some examples of pre-existing conditions are diabetes, heart disease, respiratory disease, and anemia.

3. Assist the pupil to understand the importance of a high level of physical fitness, some benefits of which are the following:

   a. Good posture will decrease lower back pain.

   b. Fewer extra pounds will remain after the infant is born.

   c. Labor and delivery may be easier if the mother has the muscular strength and endurance to assist in the efforts. Recovery time may also be shorter.

   d. Exercise could be an outlet for stress, as well as, giving the pupil a feeling that she is in control of her body.

There must be written medical consent in any physical education programming for pupils who are pregnant. This consent should be renewed at least once every two months, not only during the pregnancy but for two months after pregnancy as well. Related to pregnancy should be considered a period of intensive conditioning to enable the body to meet the demands of labor, delivery, and recovery.

Maternal exercise up to 70 percent of maximal capacity will not interfere with normal fetal growth and development (Collins & Curet, 1985). In this connection the American College of Obstetricians and Gynecologists in 1986 introduced exercise-related guidelines during pregnancy. Some of these guidelines are the following:

a

b

FIGURE 12.6   Minors who are pregnant exercising.

1. Regular exercise, three times per week, is preferable to intermittent activity.
2. Competitive activities are discouraged.
3. Vigorous exercise should not be performed in hot, humid weather or during an illness.
4. Exercises should be done on a wooden floor or a carpet to reduce shock and provide sure footing.
5. Activities that require jumping, jarring motions, or rapid directional changes should be avoided because of joint instability.

6. Vigorous exercise should be preceded by a 5-minute period of warm-up activities such as walking or stationary bicycle riding at low resistance.

7. Strenuous activities should not exceed 15 minutes.

8. Target heart rates and limits must be established with consultation with a physician. Maximum heart rate should never exceed 140 beats per minute.

9. Gradually rise from the floor in order to avoid orthostatic hypotension.

10. Although controversial, it is recommended that no exercise be performed in the supine position after the fourth month of gestation.

11. Liquids should be consumed before and after exercise to prevent dehydration. Fluids may be taken, if needed, during the activity period.

Remember that these are general guidelines and may be helpful to some women and not others (Gauthier, 1986). The physical educator must always individualize activity pro-

grams, and such programs should be monitored by a team that includes a physician. All exercise periods should begin with warm-up and end with cool-down. This will allow respiration, heart rate, and metabolism to gradually increase at the beginning of the exercise session and slowly normalize when the exercises are completed.

During pregnancy, overall fitness should be the primary goal. Special attention should be given to daily stretching of the calf, thigh, and perineal muscles. Exercise may decrease the frequency of leg cramps, which are common in pregnancy, and may limber those muscles used in labor and delivery. Here are some exercises found to be useful.

1. Kneel on one knee, extend the other leg to the side (knee faces forward), and stretch to that side; then perform the exercise on the other knee (see Figure 12.7).

2. Assume the same position as in Exercise 1, except turn the trunk and flex the foot so that the knee of the extended leg faces up;

FIGURE 12.7   Limbering-up exercise #1.

FIGURE 12.8 Limbering-up exercise #2.

Beals (1978) suggests these two exercises to relieve lower back discomfort:

1. Lie on back, resting on elbows, with knees bent and the soles of the feet on the floor. Elevate the head while bringing the bent left leg toward the chest as far as possible; then return the leg to the starting position and perform the same exercise with the right leg (see Figure 12.10).
2. Lie on the right side with the head resting on the bent right arm (legs slightly bent, neck straight). Hold the left leg with the left hand and pull the bent knee as near to the chest as possible, then return the left leg to the starting position. Do this several times; then perform the exercise lying on the left side using the right leg (see Figure 12.11).

then perform the exercise with the other leg extended (see Figure 12.8).

3. Sit with the soles of the feet together; push down on the knees with the elbows (see Figure 12.9).

Lordosis, which can lead to back pain, is caused by the forward shifting of the body's center of gravity because of additional weight in the abdominal area. This is a frequent complaint toward the end of pregnancy.

Be very selective in the exercises performed during the eighth and ninth months of pregnancy. All exercises that place considerable strain on the lower back or involve violent actions or sudden jolts should be avoided. Specific activities should be provided to develop awareness of the forward-shifting center of gravity. Training in these activities influences the ability to balance, which is one of the basic components of most physical

FIGURE 12.9 Limbering-up exercise #3.

a

b

FIGURE 12.10   Exercise #1 for back pain.

activities. This can also help minimize accidents that can occur because the young woman tries to perform activities that require balance similar to that needed before pregnancy.

After delivery, the young woman will need to return the abdomen to normal shape, firm the breasts, help the vaginal and rectal muscles to return to normal, and generally improve overall fitness levels. Here are two useful exercises.

1. In a creep position (on hands and knees), take a deep breath for 15 counts, sucking in the abdomen while pulling in on the hips and up on the rectal region (see Figure 12.12).

2. Clasp hands together with arms partially

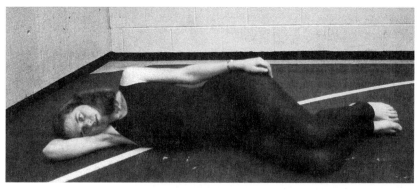

a

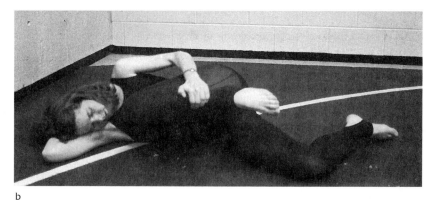

b

FIGURE 12.11   Exercise #2 for back pain.

outstretched; then push hands together and hold (see Figure 12.13).

These exercises should be repeated daily as often as possible.

Relaxation training is very important. Relaxation is a major component of childbirth classes because tension is the primary source of energy loss during labor and delivery. Through training, a woman can learn to manage labor contractions more effectively.

Swimming is no problem for women who are pregnant. Many feel clumsy because of the continuous shift forward of their center of gravity, and water eliminates this problem,

allowing them to maintain or develop a functional level of fitness. However, water skiing should be avoided because of the jolting involved and because water could be forced into the birth canal.

Generally, during the first few months of her pregnancy, a pupil should be able to participate in almost all types of individual and group activities, with the exception of contact sports such as football, basketball, soccer, and field hockey. Activities such as softball, tennis, bowling, race walking, fencing, archery, bicycling, and golf are preferred. Bicycling is an excellent way to inhibit the development of varicose veins because it

a

b

FIGURE 12.12   Muscle-toning exercise #1.

stimulates circulation in the legs. As the pregnancy progresses, the pupil may want to discontinue strenuous activities and concentrate on such sports as bowling and golf, which provide intermittent rest. During the last part of the pregnancy, activities in which the body is suddenly placed on one foot should be avoided in order to prevent balance difficulties and falling. Snow skiing may not be indicated because of stress caused by inclement weather and the possibility of balance loss. Also, climbing above 12,000 feet could present a risk to the mother and fetus.

FIGURE 12.13 Muscle-toning exercise #2.

CHILD ABUSE

The Child Abuse Prevention, Adoption, and Family Services Act of 1988 defines child abuse and neglect as physical or mental injury, sexual abuse or exploitation, negligent treatment, or maltreatment of a child by a person who is responsible for the welfare of the child. Physical abuse accounts for the greatest type of abuse incidences, followed by emotional neglect.

An estimated 2 million school-aged children in the United States are abused by caregivers each year (Select Committee, 1989). Further, children with disabilities may be at greater risk than their nondisabled peers. Types of abuse have three major forms: physical, emotional, and sexual.

Physical abuse involves nonaccidental physical injury to a child. Some of the overt signs are extensive bruises, (some in the shape of handprints or hanger marks), burns, frequent complaints of soreness, awkward movements that could be caused by pain, unexplained abdominal swelling, and ex-treme sensitivity to pain. A major problem is that there is little understanding of basic child-rearing practices by parents, and this problem is compounded because of the widespread social acceptance of the use of physical punishment with little positive reinforcement in homes.

Child abuse takes place not only in homes but also in schools. Many abused children misbehave in school because they bring their problems from home. Yet, instead of finding a supportive school environment where the problem is addressed with understanding, they may face further corporal punishment. While corporal punishment that is not used excessively and without malice is supported by the U.S. Supreme Court and the majority of parents, the physical educator should try to learn something about these pupils (i.e., family background) and use corporal punishment only as a last resort.

Emotional abuse involves rejecting or belittling a child. It is generally related to not providing a positive, loving, and emotional atmosphere in which the child can grow psychologically and socially. There are numerous characteristics of a child who is emotionally abused: withdrawal, extreme behavior such as overly happy or affectionate, bizarre behavior such as self-destruction or laughing when in pain, anorexia, substance abuse, delinquent behavior, and developing physical manifestations such as asthma, ulcers, or allergies.

Sexual abuse refers to sexual activity that is imposed on a child by an adult who has greater knowledge and authority. It has been suggested that between 60 and 75 percent of child abuse cases involve sexual abuse and 70 to 80 percent of the time the abuse is committed by someone who the child knows and often loves (Tower, 1987). Such a child may have more sexual knowledge than seems appropriate for the child's age, receive an inordinate number of gifts from questionable sources, display sexually promiscuous behavior, have nightmares or insomnia, cry seemingly without reason, complain of pain in the genital areas, frequently vomit, excessively bathe, excessively masturbate, or run away from home often.

The problem of child abuse is very complex, and a team approach in the school needs to be used for the betterment of these pupils. If physical educators attempt to solve the problem by themselves, they may be overwhelmed and this could impact on their mental health. Physical educators, classroom teachers, counselors, and social workers can pool their professional expertise and efforts in order to assist a pupil who is abused. Ersing and Huber (1992) state that "exposure to the issue of child abuse and neglect at some point in professional preparation of teachers in physical education is essential" (p. 41). There are numerous child abuse organizations in the Untied States to assist physical educators and other school personnel in dealing with the problem. We list three here.

American Association for Protecting
  Children
9725 East Hampden Avenue
Denver, CO 80231-4919
(303) 695-0811

National Child Abuse and Neglect Clinical
  Resource Center
University of Colorado Health Sciences
  Center
1205 Oneida Street
Denver, CO 80220
(303) 321-3963

National Resource Center for Child Sexual
  Abuse
11141 Georgia Avenue
Suite 310
Wheaton, MD 20901
(800) KIDS-006

PRENATAL EXPOSURE TO DRUGS AND ALCOHOL

A newly recognized form of child abuse for which there is mounting concern by educators is *prenatal exposure to drugs and/or alcohol*. It is estimated that in the United States alone more than 1 million women a year may be giving birth to at-risk infants because of maternal use of drugs or alcohol (Chasnoff & Burns, 1986). The National Institute for Drug Abuse has reported that 1 out of 10 women who are pregnant use cocaine. In one county in California, 400 to 500 infants each month test positive for the presence of abusive substances (Cratty, 1990).

There is no specific profile for a child who has been exposed to drugs and/or alcohol prenatally; however, some general characteristics can be cited (Sanders-Phillips, 1990):

1. Motor and Neurological
   a. Poor vision
   b. Tremor when reaching
   c. Decreased body awareness
   d. Periods of blackout
   e. Clumsiness
2. Emotional
   a. Depressed
   b. Rapid shifts in behavior

c. Irritable and explosive behavior

d. Noncompliant

e. Inability to regulate own behavior

3. Social

a. Limited eye contact to begin any social interaction

b. Indiscriminate attachment to strangers

c. Aggression toward peers

d. Decreased use of adults for comfort or recognition

4. Problem Solving

a. Attentional deficiency

b. Distractible

c. Impulsive

d. Easily gives up without trying

e. Decreased use of trial and error strategies and visual scanning in problem-solving situations

5. Play

a. Does not play spontaneously

b. Cannot organize own play materials and focus on an activity

c. Has difficulty with peers during unsupervised play

The process of identifying and programming for the motor problems of such children is only in its beginning stages. It is not clearly known how their early motor problems will progress. In addition, the motor development signs that are observed in infancy are not only unusual but unique (Little, Anderson, Ervin, Worthington-Roberts, & Clarren, 1989), requiring new research strategies and assessment techniques (Cratty, 1990). There are six major guidelines that should be an integral part of any physical education program, for both children prenatally exposed to alcohol and drugs as well as for other pupils in the program (Sanders-Phillips, 1990):

1. *Curricular*. The curriculum must be both functional and creative. Learning experi-

ences should be designed to involve exploration and play activities that are relevant to the child's developmental needs.

2. *Routines*. The environment must be structured so that it is very predictable. There will be times, though, when material and equipment may need to be added or reduced either to enrich or reduce the stimuli in the environment.

3. *Rules*. The rules should be concrete, clear, and concise. They should also be limited in number to no more than five to seven. Rules must be written to address the unique needs of these children.

4. *Assessment*. The evaluation and modification of such a child's program should involve a continuous process and be conducted when the child is engaged in observable activities such as play and self-help skills.

5. *Adult/child ratio*. There must be a sufficient number of adults in the environment to promote a child's attachment to at least one adult, promote predictability, nurture learning, and enable continual assistance. The adults should also be able to have enough time to provide a role model for the child to imitate.

CANCER

Cancer refers to the uncontrolled growth and spread of cells in body tissue, such as skin, muscle, or bone. More than 100 types of cancer have been identified in humans. There are three major types of cancer: Carcinoma is the most common type of cancer; some examples include cancer of the skin and cancer of the lining of the lungs, stomach, intestines, and glands. Sarcoma is cancer of the connective tissue in the bone, cartilage, and fat. The third is leukemia, cancer of the cells of the bloodstream, bone marrow, and lymphatic system. Almost 80 percent of all cancer is related to environment and lifestyle, and thus many can be prevented through adoption of healthier ways of living (*Diet and Cancer,* 1986).

In the United States, cancer is the second leading cause of death, second only to heart disease. More than 450,000 cancer deaths occur yearly, with almost 25 percent directly attributed to use of tobacco; other deaths are attributed to consumption of high fat, nitrite-cured foods, and large amounts of alcohol, which can cause cancer of the esophagus, stomach, and colon.

It is not known if there is a correlation between physical activity and risk of cancer. A concern, though, is that a person's past lifestyle may increase the risk of certain types of cancer. It is possible that some cancers may have a latency period of 20 years. Children whose lifestyle includes a balanced diet and exercise may have a protective factor in their favor (Gauthier, 1986). Some cancers are associated with obesity, specifically cancer of the breast, prostate, colon, and pancreas. Exercise may help to avoid weight gain and thus reduce the probability of these cancers.

It must be stressed that the association between exercise and certain types of cancer is only potentially important. Much more research is needed to determine if any specific relationship actually exists. It has been reported, though, that female athletes have a significantly lower risk than nonathletic females in regard to cancers of the reproductive system and breasts (Frisch, Wyshak, & Albright, 1985) and that patients undergoing chemotherapy for breast cancer reported decreased nausea as exercise sessions progressed (Winningham & MacVicar, 1985). Gauthier (1986, p. 178) states that "even though the effects of exercises are indirect, it still means they're worth something."

With more children and youth recovering from or surviving cancer for long periods of time, physical educators need to know how

to assist these pupils because their periods of immobilization can cause progressive deterioration in muscle strength and endurance. In designing an activity program, several concerns must be addressed (Winningham, MacVicar, & Burke, 1986):

1. The pathological effects of malignancy need to be understood.
2. Fever, weight loss, and fatigue have to be considered.
3. Chemotherapy or radiation patients may not respond normally to training. The reaction is very individual: One pupil with cancer may be very sensitive to the side effects and another may suffer very little and be able to carry on normal activities. Because of this, these pupils must be constantly monitored for possible irregular pulse, joint pain, shortness of breath, or excessive fatigue. If the pupil has hair loss, allow a cap to be worn. If there are dermatological side effects, allow the pupil to wear clothing to cover affected areas.
4. Develop an exercise program within the pupil's medical margin of safety. For instance, a pupil with lung cancer will have respiratory restrictions. A pupil with bone cancer (osteogenic sarcoma) may be at risk to jog because of possible fractures. A pupil with leukemia may well have similar problems as a pupil with anemia and may require the same activity modifications (Surburg, 1990).
5. Intense exercises should be used judiciously. Gradually increase intensity, as warranted. Remember that these pupils may be deconditioned because of surgery or prolonged therapy.
6. Psychological information is very important in programming. Many pupils with cancer may be depressed and be less physically active.

Pupils with cancer or recovering from cancer deserve and can benefit from physical activity. The physical educator must work carefully with school personnel (e.g., school counselor, psychologist, school physician, nurse) as well as with pupils, parents, and family physician(s).

ARTHRITIS

Arthritis describes diseases that mainly involve joint inflammation and are associated with pain. General symptoms are decreased range of motion, muscle atrophy, snapping sounds in the joints, and muscle tenderness. There are more than 100 known types of arthritis. The most frequent joint inflammation disease occurring in school-aged children is rheumatoid arthritis. It involves the recurring inflammation of the joints and sometimes other connective tissue. Muscle weakness and weight loss are symptoms of this disease. The disease has various stages (see Figure 12.14): normal joint with synovial lining one to three cells thick; early inflammatory disease with symmetrical cartilage reduction, including thickened synovium, increased synovial fluid, and fusiform swelling; and advanced inflammatory disease showing marked synovial hypertrophy with pannus formation, bone and cartilage erosion, and severely diminished cartilage.

Arthritis is the number one crippling disease in the United States. Thirty million Americans suffer from this disease, and four out of five of these people will have some form of arthritis that requires medical attention during their lifetime. Four million suffer from rheumatoid arthritis, and 250,000 have the juvenile form. The average age of onset is 6 years, and the disease affects more girls than boys. While most of these children will recover completely, 10 to 15 percent will be severely crippled and 30 percent will have mild or moderate crippling.

FIGURE 12.14 (a) A normal joint; (b) early inflammatory disease; (c) advanced inflammatory disease. (Source: *J. E. Melvin*, Rheumatic Disease: Occupational Therapy and Rehabilitation. *Philadelphia: Davis, 1977. By permission.*)

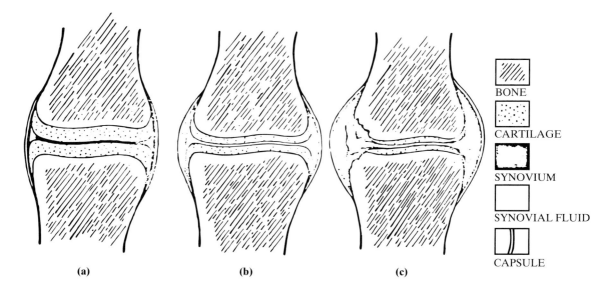

(a)   (b)   (c)

BONE

CARTILAGE

SYNOVIUM

SYNOVIAL FLUID

CAPSULE

Usually rheumatoid arthritis occurs in persons over 20 years of age and appears most often between 40 to 60 years. There is at least a 20 percent probability of recovery but the cartilage deterioration remains. The juvenile form of rheumatoid arthritis differs from the adult form in that it is usually limited to a few of the larger joints. The three major clinical types of juvenile rheumatoid arthritis are acute-onset arthritis, polyarticular, and monarticular and panciarticular arthritis.

Pupils with juvenile rheumatoid arthritis may develop personality problems, particularly if the disease extends over a long period of time. Common personality descriptors related to the disease include the following: lead quiet lives, shy and feelings of inadequacy or inferiority, self-sacrificing, overly conscientious, need to serve others, obsessive-compulsive, and tendency toward depression. There also may be a marked body image deficiency and peer adjustment problems because these children are frequently absent from school or unable to participate in school activities.

There is no specific treatment for juvenile rheumatoid arthritis. In general, a balance must be determined between exercise, diet, and medication. Some forms of treatment traditionally recommended are aspirin; cortisone and cortisone derivatives (may inhibit normal growth if used over an extended period); warm baths, physical therapy; posture training; correct-fitting shoes; or assistive devices such as splints, braces, and casts. In extreme cases, surgery may be performed to rebuild or replace joints, remove inflamed tissue, or fuse the disease joint.

Arthritis may be caused by physical trauma to the joints. Traumatic arthritis may be precipitated by participation in contact sports, such as football or ice hockey, or in sports where a joint may be overused or misused. Chronic improper weight bearing during locomotion causes excessive strain on ligaments and may also be a contributing factor to childhood traumatic arthritis.

To determine the extent of joint damage and the degree of irritation, the advice of a physician is required. Activities that place strain on afflicted joints should be eliminated. A physical therapist may be consulted to provide suitable physical activities. Regardless of the activities selected, frequent rest periods may be required. Because prolonged periods of rest may cause the muscles to atrophy, a brace or cast may be required. Exercise is needed to assist in the prevention of physical deformity, muscle weakness, and decreased range of motion. According to Sherrill (1986, p. 530):

> It is essential, therefore, that the physical educator plan exercise sequences which will strengthen the extensors, the abductors, the internal rotators and the pronators. Most authorities agree that flexion exercises are contraindicated. The activities of daily living provide adequate flexion, and there is no danger that the joints will stiffen in flexion.

The following are examples of range of motion exercises that could be incorporated into a physical education program for a pupil with arthritis. These exercises should be conducted smoothly and slowly, without the use of force or jerky movements and within a pain-free range. Stretching exercises should be held for 6 to 8 seconds or longer and performed two or three times for each muscle group.

Shoulders

1. Raise arms straight over the head, keeping them close to midline, and touch the palms together; then bring them back down. Repeat (see Figure 12.15).

2. Place arms behind the neck with elbows pointing forward. Slowly move the elbows back and hold in this position for 5 to 7 sec-

FIGURE 12.15   Exercise #1 for arthritic shoulders.

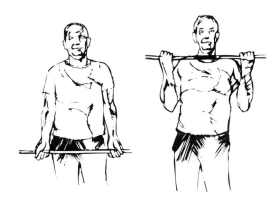

FIGURE 12.17   Exercise #1 for arthritic elbows.

onds. Then bring elbows forward and try to touch them. Hold this position for 5 to 7 seconds. Repeat (see Figure 12.16).

Elbows

1. With arms straight next to the body and at the side, place palms up and hold an object such as a broom handle. Raise forearms to vertical, then return to the starting position. Repeat (see Figure 12.17).
2. Rotate palms inward and outward. Repeat (see Figure 12.18).

Wrists

1. From the edge of a table, move wrists forward (palm down) and backward (palm up). Repeat (see Figure 12.19).

FIGURE 12.16   Exercise #2 for arthritic shoulders.

2. Place hands with palms down on a table. Now rotate them in a sideways manner. Repeat (see Figure 12.20).

Hands and Fingers

1. Place hands palm down toward the floor. Slowly curl and then open and extend fingers, then close the straightened fingers in. Repeat (see Figure 12.21).

Hips

1. While in supine lying bent-knee position, raise and lower a leg, bending it at the knee. There should be no rotation of the legs. Perform the exercise with the other leg. Repeat (see Figure 12.22 on p. 347).
2. With the legs straight and together and hands clasped behind the neck, raise one

FIGURE 12.18   Exercise #2 for arthritic elbows.

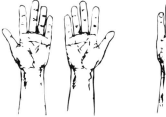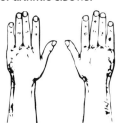

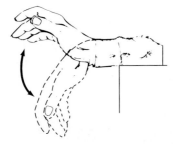

FIGURE 12.19   Exercise #1 for arthritic wrists.

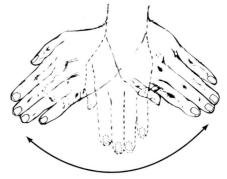

FIGURE 12.20   Exercise #2 for arthritic wrists.

leg and cross it over the ankle of the other just above the knee. Now bring this ankle up the leg and push the knee out slowly. The exercise should be performed with one leg, then the other. Repeat (see Figure 12.23).

Knees

1. In a supine lying bent-knee position, raise one foot toward the hip and grasp in front of the knee with both hands. Pull the leg back using the hands for 5 seconds. Perform the exercise on the other knee. Repeat (see Figure 12.24 on p. 348).

Ankles

1. With the legs and feet straight and keeping the heels on the floor, move foot upward (dorsiflex) and downward (plantarflex). Repeat (see Figure 12.25 on p. 348).

Toes

1. With the legs and feet straight, curl the toes downward, then raise them. Now pick up

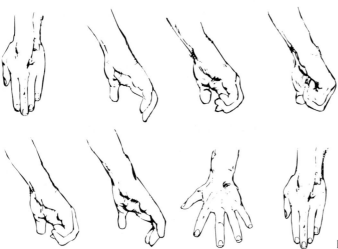

FIGURE 12.21   Exercise for arthritic hands.

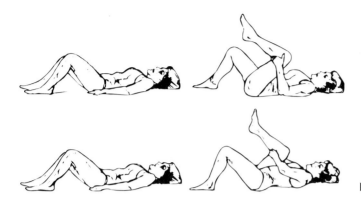

FIGURE 12.22 Exercise #1 for arthritic hips.

items such as a thin rope. Then release the item by spreading the toes and pointing the toes upward. Repeat (see Figure 12.26).

Music is one way to maintain pupils' interest in performing activities. Exercise periods should be conducted at least three times weekly and must be within the tolerance range of the pupil. Generally, exercise duration up to 35 minutes can be therapeutic, and as little as 15 minutes of exercise three times a week is sufficient to improve the aerobic capacity in pupils with severe limitations due to rheumatoid arthritis.

In severe cases of arthritis the aquatic environment is an excellent medium in which to perform strength, flexibility, and endurance activities because water buoyancy decreases the amount of body weight on diseased joints. The Twinges in the Hinges moderate water-exercise program, initiated at the Whittier YMCA in Whittier, California, is for individuals with arthritis (Wilson, n.d.). The basic rule in the program is, if it hurts—stop! Further, not all individuals with arthritis are allowed into the class. Each person is considered individually. The following are a few exercises used in the program.

1. Hold pool wall and flutter kick.
2. Turn to side of pool, hold edge of pool, and perform large leg circles from hip with leg straight.
3. Face wall and lift heels up and down.
4. While standing, perform the breaststroke arm motion with the palms always pressing the water.
5. Turn hands, thumbs up and down, while pulling arms back and forth.
6. Walk in place.
7. With back to wall, move legs in the bicycle motion.

Numerous activities can be incorporated into an aquatics program—walking and swimming relays, playing catch with beach

FIGURE 12.23 Exercise #2 for arthritic hips.

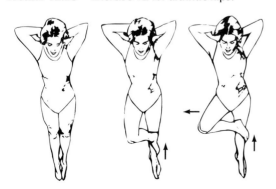

FIGURE 12.24   Exercise for arthritic knees.

balls, throwing beach balls at targets, (e.g., hula hoops), square dancing (Grand Right and Left and Do-see-do).

The air (78° to 82°F. with no drafts) and water temperature (86° to 88°F.) should be warm to prevent constriction of the blood vessels in the extremities around the diseased joints. The pool area must be accessible, clean, and uncluttered.

Creative dance experiences involving range of motion activities are very appropriate for pupils who are arthritic and can be designed to meet a pupil's functional level. Other forms of dance may be appropriate, depending on the severity of the condition and the joints involved. For instance, a modified, low-impact aerobic dance program conducted on a soft surface (e.g., mat) is a good way to improve cardiorespiratory endurance (Rimmer, 1989).

Through individual activities the quality of movement and quantity of activity can be

easily managed. Some suggested sports are archery and bowling. In both cases the distance and weight can be adjusted to accommodate individual needs. Some activities that may not be indicated because of the trauma on the affected joints are jumping rope, gymnastics, hopscotch, and trampolining.

Group activities that do not involve body contact (e.g., combatives) or a high risk of falling are excellent not only to develop basic motor and fitness skills but also to provide an opportunity for peer interaction. If the pupil with arthritis cannot safely participate in certain group games, the child can participate in lead-up activities that involve the requisite skills of the game. For instance, if other pupils are playing softball, pupils with arthritis can practice hitting a ball from a batting tee or catching the ball.

AGING

The complex process we call *aging* involves decline at the cellular, tissue, organ, and system levels of the body. Aging also involves a

FIGURE 12.25   Exercise for arthritic ankles.

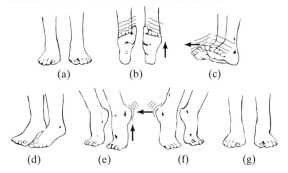

(a)   (b)   (c)

(d)   (e)   (f)   (g)

FIGURE 12.26   Exercise for arthritic toes.

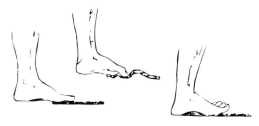

decline in physical performance and the onset of numerous diseases. Some researchers have suggested, though, that about half of such decline frequently attributed to physiological aging is really caused by inactivity in an industrialized society (Serfass, 1980).

Steady and gradual decline begins during middle age, but does not generally become a major concern until late adulthood. The specific time of onset of old age is variable. The World Health Organization has classified older individuals into four broad age groups: middle age, 45 to 59; elderly, 60 to 74; old, 75 to 90; and very old, over 90 years of age. Of individuals aged 60 or older, 95 percent live independently or with their families. It is projected that 22 percent of the U.S. population will be over age 65 by the year 2050 (Moore, 1988)—a shift related to societal attitudes, family size (lower birth rate), and medical and health practices that have lowered the mortality rate. Physical activity is another factor that may increase the life span. With the life span of people who are aged increasing, there is a greater demand for physical activities for these individuals.

Characteristics and Instructional Strategies

Personnel are being trained to teach physical education skills not only to preschool and school-aged children who are disabled but as well to adults with disabilities to help them reach appropriate psychomotor skill levels. The importance of some type of physical activity for such individuals is stressed in the interview with Charles Daniel.

Charles Daniel

Dr. Charles Daniel is a professor of special physical education at Western Kentucky University.

1. *What are your views on the importance of physical education in the lives of senior citizens?*

The development and maintenance of movement and fitness skills are critical to the quality of life for senior citizens. In this connection, physical education can play an important role in providing needed positive knowledge, skills, and behaviors necessary to improve and maintain the quality of life of our seniors.

Research has shown that the human

species biologically could live to be 120 years old. Having the ability to live to a "ripe old age" must be balanced with the quality of the extended life. In this regard, we know that physically active seniors maintain a higher quality of life for a much more extended period of time.

The term *physical education*, therefore, takes on a whole new and more important meaning when viewed as a lifelong learning experience and an active participation process, not just physical education in a school setting. Physical education is a lifelong process that can provide a quality and quantity of movement for all people at all ages.

2. *What role does the special physical educator have to play with this population of individuals?*

Since most special physical education programs concentrate on children and developmental physical education, the special physical educator needs training specifically in gerontology in order to work with this population. My experience has been that the special physical educator, with this additional training in the specific area of gerontology, has the knowledge and skills

to work directly with seniors, many of whom acquire disabilities due to accidents, disease, and the aging process. This training should also cover aspects of physical, mental, and emotional disabilities that are helpful in working with individuals who are disabled and in nursing homes.

The ability to individualize and adapt games and activities can be very helpful in fitness, leisure, and recreation programs for seniors. Yet seniors are not children, and just having the ability to adapt activities for school-aged pupils does not guarantee the special physical educator success with seniors. Another important difference between school-aged children and seniors is that the latter have had a long life of experiences; therefore, activities need to be age appropriate for them and based on each individual's needs. Also, seniors tend not to be a captive audience (as in schools). They will refuse to participate. The special physical educator with such understandings brought about by additional training of skills in gerontology can make major contributions to senior programs, especially in nursing homes and day and full-time institutions.

The following factors are related to the major biological systems of the body of a person who is aged. First, in the visual system, more light stimuli are required to stimulate the visual receptors and visual acuity. The ability to focus on a moving object is decreased. This correlates with an increase in the frequency of cataracts. Thus physical activities that are conducted at night or indoors must be well lit. Many of the techniques used for people with visual disabilities are also appropriate for this group.

Second, individuals who are aged lose sensitivity to high auditory frequencies. Many techniques are available for use with people whose hearing impairment hinders their participation in physical activities. They include developing alternative ways to communicate, such as using a blackboard to illustrate what is spoken, using visual demonstrations, using a buddy system, or using flash cards to signify fouls, substitutions, and the beginning or end of an activity. For those with residual hearing, reduce verbal input because this can overload and slow the information processing. Verbal cues in the form of a word or phrase can be used before and during physical performance.

Third, muscles begin to atrophy and lose elasticity with increasing age. This not only influences the ability to move but also to maintain correct posture. One major cause for this decline in the muscular system is physical inactivity. Physical and motor fitness and posture can be enhanced through appropriate physical activities. There is also a higher incidence of strains, sprains, and fractures because the bones have become brittle and the muscles weakened. The physical environment must be free of holes and dangerous obstacles. Warming up and cooling down are essential to reduce possible strains and sprains. Further, activities that involve physical contact should be modified to reduce contact.

Fourth, the efficiency of the cardiorespiratory system decreases. There is a decline in cardiac output, and a longer recover period is required after strenuous activity. The capacity of the heart to pump blood decreases approximately 8 percent during each decade of adulthood (Serfass, 1980). This is generally caused by the accumulation of fatty tissue in the arteries, diseased heart valves, and lessening of the elasticity in the arteries. Inactivity over the years creates many of the cardiac output and blood pressure problems reported in this population. In addition, this problem is many times compounded by obesity. Well-supervised physical activities can often reverse this process somewhat, if they are programmed within a medical margin of safety. Some traditional activities are cycling, dancing, fast walking, jogging, and swimming.

The decline in respiratory efficiency may be due to skeletal changes that limit the expansion of the rib cage, muscles involved in inhalation and exhalation become weakened, and the lungs lose elasticity. Further, diseases such as asthma and lung cancer can decrease the functional ability of the respiratory system. Numerous exercises can be performed to offset deteriorating postural conditions. If a person does have respiratory diseases, activities can be modified by reducing the size of the playing area or playing time.

Fifth, the nervous system is affected. Nerve cells, as are other cells in the body, are lost daily and are replaced at a slower rate or not at all. For instance, thousands of brain cells die each day and are not replaced. Transmission of messages throughout the nervous system also slows down, which in turn influences reaction time. Games may have to be modified; for instance, in volleyball, a beach ball can replace a regular volleyball to slow down the activity or the court size can be decreased. The ability to balance decreases progressively with age because the time required to recover equilibrium increases while proprioceptive sensitivity in the feet (which affects the sense of position and balance) decreases. This may be due to a nervous system deficiency. Postural changes may induce vertigo and loss of balance.

Static balance activities, such as standing on one foot with arms at sides with eyes closed, are generally not indicated. Fast swirling and whirling movements of the body are also poor choices. Activities should emphasize slow rotary and/or circumducting limb movements. On the other hand, dynamic balance activities such as walking down a balance beam with eyes focused at the end of the beam are beneficial. However, balancing on curbs, large stones, pieces of fallen wood, chunks of sod, or other more functional everyday items is advised. This type of activity improves functional balance in the upright position and uses vision to establish a point of reference.

Another system that ages is the skin. With

increasing age, the skin becomes thin, loose, wrinkled, and very sensitive to the sun. Thus contact activities and long periods of exposure to the sun should be avoided.

Short-term memory loss is more severe in those who are aged than is long-term memory loss. Thus, any instruction must be concrete, clear, presented slowly, and repeated as necessary.

Social and Emotional Characteristics

Motivation of participants who are aged is a critical factor in programming physical activity. Getting such individuals involved and keeping them involved is a major task of the physical educator. The most reliable technique for increasing physical activity in this population is the reassurance from an authority such as a physician. Further, for many people, aging is a threat to the ego. They may begin to withdraw from individual and group activities that in the past represented a significant portion of their daily routine. Therefore, structured group physical activities that are within the capacity of each participant can provide an opportunity for interaction and successful experiences. Some prime activities that involve interaction with members of the opposite sex are square and folk dancing and bowling. If social interaction does not work, other techniques, for instance, external motivators such as models and tangible object rewards, can be used.

A guest speaker who is a model for the group could be invited to give an inspirational lecture. Films and videotapes depicting individuals who are elderly performing physical activities could serve a similar purpose. Several local, state, and national organizations offer literature that encourages exercise for people who are aged. These organizations include the League of American Wheelman (Palatine, Illinois), Mile-a-Thon International (Long Beach, California),

and the National Jogging Association (Washington, D.C.).

Tournaments or contests where tangible objects such as trophies, plaques, or ribbons are awarded can be set up. The tournament must be designed so that each person competes against himself or herself, not against others. In group-oriented competition, the least skilled will constantly lose, and the individual may drop out after a short time.

Indicated and Nonindicated Activities

Almost all activities offered for young adult and middle-aged persons are also appropriate for individuals who are older. However, three major programming questions need to be asked about this population: Is the chosen activity within the ability level of the participant? Is the activity medically safe? And is it motivating?

For activities that are appropriate, the teacher should always remember that the ABCD approach to teaching will be required to meet the needs of each person. The teacher should also consider other individualization and combining techniques. It is important that participants not continually sit waiting for their turn. Volunteer schoolchildren or young adults can be used as teacher aides to increase activity time, providing social and emotional benefits for both the participant and volunteers. If there is a shortage of equipment, teachers can try to solicit funds or equipment from community groups and agencies looking for worthy projects to support.

Activities that may not be indicated are those that may involve violent effort and sudden twisting and hyperextension of the back muscles. Because of the limitation of vision, visual perception, and balance, caution must be taken in any activity where there is a possibility of collision or falling.

Extremes in temperature must also be considered. Hot and humid conditions could cause cardiac arrest, and cold and dry conditions may evoke angina. In addition, for individuals, playing the actual game may not be indicated. Fun team sports are good with just minor modifications such as reducing the pace. Last, consider the side effects of medication. Some prescribed medications have a negative impact on exercise and motor performance. For instance, beta-blocking medication that could be used by a person with angina may cause muscle fatigue.

Physical and Motor Fitness

No matter what the age, a structured and long-term physical fitness training program emphasizing the development of cardiorespiratory endurance, flexibility, and strength can be developed. As a first step, before a home or structured physical activity program is begun, level of health must be evaluated. One approach is to use the test designed by the Fitness Task Force of the American Alliance for Health, Physical Education, Recreation and Dance (Clark, 1989). The factors on this functional fitness test battery are agility/dynamic balance, en-durance (half-mile walk), flexibility, muscle strength/endurance, and fine motor coordination. Preliminary norms for this test have been developed based on age and gender.

The first session of a program should also include instruction on the major warning signals of overexertion and procedures for monitoring the heart (pulse) rate. Numerous danger signals alert the participant to overexertion: chest, arm, or throat pain; extreme breathlessness; abnormal heart rhythm; persistently high heart rate after exercise; trembling; and nausea. If any of these symptoms appear, the participant must tell the instructor so the physician can be informed and the program modified. It is essential that each participant be able to monitor his or her own heart rate.

As age increases, maximal heart rate that can be reached decreases. Endurance activities should be set at 80 percent of the maximal heart rate, if this percentage is not against the advice of a physician. In general, the approximate minimal heart rate reached in the program (maximum 80 percent) is 128 at 60 years of age; 124 at 65 years of age, and 120 or less at 70 years or older. If a participant is "unfit," the highest programming heart rate should be 70 percent of the maximal heart rate.

Once the program begins, the activity periods should be scheduled regularly at least three times weekly for a period of 20 to 40 minutes. These periods should be at least 1 hour before meals. A few excellent resources for activities that can be used for persons who are aged include the following:

Greninger, L., & Kinney, M. (1988). *Therapeutic exercises for older adults.* Dubuque, IA: Eddie Bowers.

Lasko, P., & Knopf, K. (1988). *Adapted exercises for the disabled adult: A training manual,* 2nd ed. Dubuque, IA: Eddie Bowers.

Leslie, D. K. (1989). *Mature stuff.* Reston, VA: American Alliance for Health, Physical Education, Recreation and Dance.

Rikkers, R. (1986). *Seniors on the move.* Champaign, IL: Human Kinetics.

Basic criteria for selecting activities are related to the needs and interests of the participants. The program should include exercises and recreational physical fitness activities. The President's Council on Physical Fitness and Sports and the Administration on Aging have developed three types of exercise programs, based on difficulty or the amount of stress involved. Exercises within each program should be performed in the order listed. See Table 12.4.

A comprehensive home activity program for individuals over the age of 50 has been published by the Fitness and Amateur Sport

TABLE 12.4 PHYSICAL FITNESS EXERCISE PROGRAMS

RED PROGRAM SEQUENCE (EASIEST)	WHITE PROGRAM SEQUENCE	BLUE PROGRAM SEQUENCE (HARDEST)
Walk 2 minutes	Walk 3 minutes	Alternate walk (50 steps)
Bend and stretch	Bend and stretch	Jog (50) 3 minutes
Rotate head	Rotate head	Bend and stretch
Body bender	Body bender	Rotate head
Wall press	Wall press	Body bender
Arm circles	Arm circles	Wall press
Wing stretcher	Half-knee bend	Arm circles
Walk 2–5 minutes	Wing stretcher	Half-knee bend
Lying leg bend	Wall push-away	Wing stretcher
Angel stretch	Walk 5 minutes	Alternate walk (50 steps)
Walk a straight line	Lying leg bend	Jog (50) 3 minutes
Half-knee bend	Angel stretch	Leg raise and bend
Wall push-away	Walk the beam	Angel stretch
	(2" x 6"beam)	Walk the beam
Side leg raise	Side leg raise	(2" x 4"beam)
Head and shoulder curl	Head and shoulder curl	Hop
	(arms crossed on chest)	Knee push-up
Alternate walk (50 steps)	Diver's stance	Side leg raise
Jog (10) 1–3 minutes	Alternative walk (50 steps)	Head and shoulder curl
Walk 1–3 minutes	Jog (25)	(hands clasped behind neck)
	Walk 1–3 minutes	Stork stand
		Alternate walk (50 steps)
		Jog (50) 5 minutes
		Gradually increasing walk
		100 steps, jog 100
		Walk 3 minutes

Source: The Fitness Challenge . . . in the Later Years, DHEW Publication No. (OHD) 75-20802. (Washington, D.C.: U.S. Department of Health, Education and Welfare, 1968), p. 9.

Secretary of State of Canada (1980). The philosophy of the program is that physical activity is highly related to health, aging, and well-being. How to begin a physical fitness home program is discussed, including a readiness questionnaire related to medical considerations and guidelines for participating in a program. The three stages of a program are discussed and illustrated:

- Stage 1 (warm-up): neck exercise, shoulder release, hand and finger exercises, ankle rotations, sitting stretches, hamstring stretch, and side bends.
- Stage 2 (endurance): shape-up, wall push-aways, abdominal curls, single knee tuck, and side leg raises.

Aerobic: walking, walk-jog, jogging, and other aerobics.

- Stage 3 (cool-down): easy walking, relaxation exercises, stretching.

Within each stage of the program the beginning and more advanced exercises are clearly identified.

Certain traditional physical fitness exercises must be prescribed with caution or completely eliminated because of the possibility of injury to a specific muscle group or the development of postural deficiencies over a period of time. Isometric exercises are not recommended because they cause an inappropriate increase in blood pressure and restriction of blood flow. All endurance activities should be rhythmic, particularly in working with participants with heart conditions. Walking and jogging are especially good because they provide sustained circulation. The following exercises are performed with a light nonfolding kitchen or auditorium chair:

Individual Exercises

1. Sit down and stand up.
2. Run around chair to the right; then to the left.
3. Raise chair by arms, with wrists and hands over the head or straight out in front.
4. Raise chair with one arm, with wrist or hand over the head, in front, or to the side.
5. Step on and off chair. Depending on skill level, some participants may hold the back of the chair when performing this exercise. A spotter is advised here.

Individual exercises can also be designed for people who are bedridden. These exercises are generally performed with fewer repetitions and with longer rest periods. Some exercises are (Leitner & Leitner, 1985):

- Neck: head raiser and head turns
- Shoulders: arm raises, overhead stretches, and elbow flexors
- Arms: arm circles, arm extensions, hand raises, hand circles, wrist rotations, and wrist raises
- Fingers: finger flex, finger spread, thumb rotations, and finger stretch
- Chest: straight arms crossed in front of chest and touching elbows in front of chest
- Abdominal: abdomen contractions and abdomen curls
- Lower Back: back press and knee to chest
- Legs: leg rotations, feet circles, and toe points

Group Exercises. One group exercise is to place chairs in rows and weave between them while fast walking, jogging, or running. Rocking chair exercises that can be performed while sewing or watching television have also been recommended (King & Herzig, 1968). Numerous group exercises can be performed using a parachute. When performing these exercises, each participant should constantly alternate from an overhand to underhand grip to develop different muscle groups in the arms and hands. Parachutes can be purchased in varying dimensions, depending on the size of the group. Some enjoyable activities are the following (French & Horvat, 1983):

1. Holding onto the edge of the chute with the right hand, walk, jog, or run clockwise in a circle. Try the same activity holding the chute with the left hand and moving counterclockwise. At the same time the leader could ask the participants to hold the chute at the waist, knees, legs, and so on.

2. Roll the chute up using the fingers until all the participants meet in the middle; then unroll it.

3. Shake the chute, making waves. Then put one or more balls in the middle and shake the chute, trying to get the balls to fall back onto the chute. To add a competitive element, have the participants on one side of the chute try to throw the balls by shaking them off the other side of the chute and the players on the other side do likewise. A score is kept on the number of balls that are thrown over each side.

4. Place a participant in the center of the chute. The other people raise the person up and *slowly* bring the person down. The leader could ask the participants holding the chute to walk clockwise or counterclockwise at the same time or hold the chute over the head, at the waist, knees, and so on. A mat should be placed beneath the parachute under the carried participant.

5. Sit on the floor and face the center of the chute with both hands grasping the edge of

the chute. The participants then pull and twist their trunks to the right and left.

6. Hold onto the edge of the chute with both hands, then pass the chute from hand to hand (releasing one hand from the chute at a time). In essence, the chute is passed clockwise (counterclockwise) from participant to participant. The group leader could also turn this activity into Hot Potato by designating a piece of the parachute as "hot."

Bicycling is a rhythmic activity to develop cardiovascular endurance and leg strength; however, it should be entered into carefully because the ability to balance decreases with age. Riding on a rough surface could cause an injury. In addition, the ability to react to an emergency situation, such as a car coming out of a driveway, could be decreased because reaction time also slows with increased age. Use of a stationary bicycle or a three-wheeled bicycle is highly recommended.

Equipment such as sponge balls, wands, bicycle inner tubes, Frisbees, and towels are recommended for the development and maintenance of positive vigor. Walking and jogging can be used in an activity program. Walking can be done throughout the year, at any time of the day, at no cost (see Figure 12.27). It is an excellent physical fitness activity if the person can walk at the rate of 3.5 miles per hour. To keep the participant motivated, activity leaders can form clubs where the participants go on group walks or hikes at local recreational facilities.

Fundamental Motor Skills and Patterns

Selected fundamental motor skills and patterns may have to be learned or relearned later in life in order to participate in physical fitness, aquatics, dance, and individual and group activities. A checklist has been devel-

FIGURE 12.27 Walking is a simple exercise enjoyed by most adults.

oped by Lasko and Knopf (1988) to evaluate the fundamental motor skills and patterns of adults who are disabled, specifically those with neurological impairments such as brain trauma, aphasia, cerebral palsy, or Parkinson's disease. Based on the results of the evaluation, a motor program is designed and implemented. The major focus of the program is related to improving static and dynamic balance, kinesthetic awareness (body awareness, laterality, and bilateral coordination) and fine motor skills.

Aquatics

Swimming is an excellent activity because it involves all the major muscle groups (see Figure 12.28). The two major obstacles in teaching swimming to those who are elderly are fear of the water and lack of confidence in their ability to learn. To counter these objections, the educator must offer continuous encouragement and sequence the instruction of each skill. Here are some examples of exercise activities for such individuals (Huettig, 1989):

FIGURE 12.28 Aquacise class for seniors.

- *Morning stretch*: In waist-high water, reach above head and stand on toes.
- *Stomach twister*: While holding onto the edge of the pool, let legs float to the surface. Then twist over to left then right hip.
- *Stomach tuck*: Place back against the side of the wall holding onto the wall with the hands. Bring the knees up toward the chest and flatten back against the wall. Then return the legs to the pool floor.
- *Kickboard press*: With hands flat on the kickboard, press the board underwater until arms are fully extended.
- *Floating stomach tuck*: While floating in the water, tuck body into a ball position.
- *Arm circles*: In upright position (sitting or standing) in shoulder-height water, hold

arms out to sides of the body and make large and then small arm circles.
- *Vertical arm sweep*: Place chin close to the water with palms and arms on the surface of the water. Press down on the water and move hands vertically forward and backward.
- *Leg circles*: Hold the side of the pool and move one leg in a circular fashion, alternating clockwise and counterclockwise motions.

Aquatic jogging provides partial body support, which enables the participation of some people who might otherwise not be able to enjoy the activity. Physicians are recommending this form of jogging even to those who are able to jog on land, because the water eliminates problems of injury to the hip, knee, and ankle that can occur on hard surfaces. Further, water can be used by those who are aged as a medium in which to enjoy aerobics, individual activities, and group games. The environment aids in maintaining and im-proving physical and motor fitness, particularly as it affects muscle tone, flexibility, and proprioceptive ability.

Dance

Dance has numerous physical, psychological, and social benefits for adults who are older. For instance, folk and square dances are not only excellent social activities but also maintain or develop physical and motor fitness and provide psychological benefits such as self-confidence, self-esteem, and sense of achievement. Many times, though, dance programs are difficult to initiate because the participants will not become involved. To stimulate reluctant participants, use seated rhythmic activities at first, with participants just moving different body parts to music. Mild forms of activities involving standing and moving can then be gradually introduced.

Cautions include avoiding vigorous dance activities immediately following a heavy meal, wearing restrictive clothing or jewelry that might interfere with circulation, and robust dance activities when the air quality is poor or when the room is hot (Leviton & Campanelli, 1980).

Individual and Group Activities

Most traditional physical activities are appropriate for individuals who are aged, and more of them are becoming actively involved. In performing these activities, avoid a lot of competition, or many participants may drop out of the program. In addition, consider the physical environment in terms of such variables as temperature, humidity, and sunshine. It is preferable to perform activities in air-conditioned environments.

One program that has increased the number of participants who are elderly in sports and games is the Senior Olympics, founded in 1969. At that time, approximately 200 male and female amateur athletes competed in Senior Olympic track and field, swimming, and diving events. Today the program has expanded throughout the United States and involves international championship competition. Events now include archery, badminton, basketball, bowling, boxing, canoeing, cycling, fencing, golf, gymnastics, ice skating, horseshoes, softball, walking, squash, table tennis, tennis (see Figure 12.29), volleyball, and wrestling.

Most of these activities, as well as other individual and group activities, can be performed with few, if any modifications, even if the participant is in a wheelchair. For example, tennis and badminton can be performed as doubles, and a beach ball can be

FIGURE 12.29   Sports such as tennis can be enjoyed by seniors on both a competitive and a recreational level.

substituted for a regulation ball in a volleyball game. The developmental games hierarchy (see Chapter 3) also should be used in selecting physical activities that are functionally within each individual's ability level.

SPEECH OR LANGUAGE IMPAIRMENTS

According to the U.S. Department of Education (1992), 22.7 percent of all pupils with disabilities age 6–21 had speech or language impairment during the 1990–91 school year. This represents the second highest incidence of disability in schools.

There are three major categories of *speech or language impairments* (National Institute, 1989). One is voice impairments that could involve partial or total loss of the voice. This type of impairment is generally caused by paralysis of the vocal folds, absence of vocal folds, and lesions or nodules on the vocal folds that makes normal sound production weak or impossible. Another category is articulation impairments that can range from problems with respiration, phonation, and articulation muscles to total absence of articulation. This type of condition could be caused by a number of neurological or neuromuscular disorders, such as cerebral palsy, muscular dystrophy, brain tumors, and trauma. The third category is language impairments. Language impairments are directly connected with learning difficulties, such as autism. Aphasia is thought to be caused by a lesion to the cerebral cortex or subcortical structures, which can lead to both receptive and expressive language problems. Pupils with learning difficulties (e.g., learning disabilities, mental retardation) that affect their ability to solve problems and to recognize relationships can have mild to severe speech impairments. Autism may also have a negative influence on the ability to develop speech and language skills for communicative purpose.

Implications for the physical educator teaching pupils with speech impairments are:

1. Consult with the classroom teacher to know more about such a pupil in order to make him or her more a part of the physical education class socially and emotionally.

2. Consult the speech therapist whenever a pupil has a speech impairment to develop an understanding of the impairment.

3. If the pupil has a severe speech impairment, a first priority is to develop a method with which the pupil can summon the teacher or a classmate in case of an emergency.

4. Do not avoid the pupil but use substitution communication devices such as pencil and paper, sign cards, chalkboard, or communication boards.

5. Do not think the pupil is mentally retarded simply because he or she cannot speak. One of the major keys for successful programming of a pupil with a speech or language impairment into physical education is the attitude of the physical educator.

MULTIPLE DISABILITIES

Approximately 2 percent of all children with disabilities have two or more disabilities that, in combination, cause severe educational problems (Eichstaedt & Kalakian, 1993; U.S. Department of Education, 1992). They cannot easily or appropriately be accommodated in a special class designed solely for children who are singly disabled. Some of the more common multiply disabling conditions are mental retardation–cerebral palsy, mental retardation–hearing impaired, and mental retardation–visually impaired.

Because of the wide variations represented within this classification, it is impossible to provide specific instructional strategies for use in physical education for the multiple disabled population as a whole. In general, though, programming involves combining appropriate instructional strategies related to the disabling conditions of each pupil. Refer to the following resources for additional information on individuals who are multidisabled:

Gaylord-Ross, R. J., & Holvoet, J. (1985). *Strategies for educating students with severe handicaps.* Boston: Little, Brown.

Goetz, L., Guess, D., & Stremel-Campbell, K. (1987). *Innovative program design for individuals with dual sensory impairments.* Baltimore: Brookes.

Horner, R. H., Meyer, L. H., & Fredericks, H. D. (Eds.) (1986). *Education of learners with severe handicaps: Exemplary service strategies.* Baltimore: Brookes.

Jansma, P. (Ed.) (1993). *Psychomotor domain training and serious disabilities*, 4th ed. Washington, DC: University Press of America.

Orelove, F. P., & Sobsey, D. (1987). *Educating children with multiple disabilities: A transdisciplinary approach.* Baltimore: Brookes.

Snell, M. E. (Ed.) (1989). *Systematic instruction of students with severe handicaps*, 3rd ed. Columbus, OH: Merrill.

One specific related condition in which some information on programming in physical education is available is deaf–blindness— a disability that is given its own definition by the U.S. Department of Education. "Deaf-blindness" means concomitant hearing and visual impairments, the combination of which causes such severe communication and other developmental and educational problems that they cannot be accommodated in special education programs solely for children with deafness or children with blindness (P.L. 101–476 Rules, *Federal Register*, September 29, 1992, p. 44801). Pupils with such a rare disability could be born with both an auditory and visual impairment (congenitally deaf–blind), could lose both sight and hearing in childhood (adventitiously deaf–blind), could be born with a hearing impairment but acquire a visual impairment later in life, or could be born with a visual impairment and acquire a hearing impairment later in life.

The age of onset of the hearing impairment is very important because it will influence a child's ability to communicate. Children who are prelingually hearing impaired lose their hearing before the establishment of childhood language skills; children who are postlingually hearing impaired lose their hearing after the establishment of language ability. If a child loses hearing after language has been established, there is a much better chance that he or she will understand and be able to communicate in physical education classes.

There are numerous causes associated with the onset of deaf–blindness. The most common is German measles. In addition, Usher's syndrome is a congenital hearing-related impairment that involves a progressive eye condition called retinitis pigmentosa.

Other possible causes are head injuries and high fevers. It is estimated that there are about 735,000 individuals in the United States who are deaf–blind. Of these, only about 1,500 children who have this condition are receiving some type of support through the U.S. Department of Education (1992).

Familiarity with the instructional environment is the essential prerequisite for teaching physical education to pupils who are deaf–blind. Feeling comfortable in any environment sets the stage for learning. Before activity for the first time in a gymnasium, playground, pool, or classroom, the child needs to be fully oriented to the immediate surroundings. On some occasions, further orientation may be appropriate, and any new object in an already familiar environment should be introduced when it is first used. Then, and only then, can activities be safely and successfully presented to this type of pupil.

Most pupils who are deaf–blind have significant psychomotor deficits. Activities can and should be offered in the areas of fitness, fundamental movement, swimming, dance, and games instruction. They need to have at least minimal physical fitness so that they can master fundamental movement skills. Adequate strength, range of movement, and cardiorespiratory endurance need to be acquired and maintained so that a child can more easily engage in body awareness, spatial orientation, balance, eye–limb coordination, and locomotion activities. Additional teaching techniques in physical education to guide pupils who are deaf–blind are the following (Sherrill, 1979):

1. Assessment should be continuous using different instruments. The use of videotaping will assist in analyzing the pupil's performance level.

2. Emphasis should be placed on motivating the pupil to become an active participant.

For some, food will not be reinforcing because they may have a feeding problem.

3. Programming should incorporate as many sense modalities as feasible.

4. Emphasis at the younger ages should be on developing play behaviors. It seems that many of these pupils are frozen at the isolated or solitary play stages.

5. Objectives should encompass the cognitive and affective domains with the use of specialists from different professions working as an integral team to improve the pupils' quality of life.

A combination of fitness and fundamental movement patterns can be addressed at the same time by using a haptic learning circuit training center, similar to one designed and constructed by Tymeson (1977) and Silberman and Tripodi (1979). Tymeson's center consists of eight stations—barrel creeper, stair climber, rope ladder, graduated balance beam, team exerciser, climbing tower, diagonal overhead ladder, and running course. Carpet squares are used to establish pathways between stations, and the outside running course uses a sighted assistant and the tactile grasp of a common stick at chest level while participants are running. Detailed progressions for each station and charted data to reflect daily performance are integral aspects of this learning center.

In the circuit used by Silberman and Tripodi (1979, pp. 273–276) generally six "I can" stations are used in a typical class period:

- Station 1, Trunk and leg flexibility. These activities improve sitting posture and strengthen the trunk and leg muscles, increase stamina, and help reduce low muscle tone, common in those children as a result of lack of physical activity.
- Station II, Dynamic balance. The development of moving balance helps improve

skills related to walking and gait and serves as a prerequisite for higher level games.

- Station III, Arm/shoulder/chest (strength and endurance). Upper body strength is an area of development that is frequently delayed in children who are blind or deaf–blind. Push and pull activities using the hands will improve midline (hand-over-hand motion) and fine motor skills, essential for many types of work-related skills.
- Station IV, Walking. Essential for mobility, the activities for this skill improve posture, gait, and body alignment and reduce the shuffling of feet commonly found in these children.
- Station V, Underhand roll. Besides being a fundamental skill basic to leisure sports and games, this objective develops socialization skills by helping a child who is deaf–blind attend to occurrences in the immediate environment and to become more aware of other children. It provides opportunities for parallel play and is a lead-up skill for recreation team sports.
- Station VI, Relaxation. A relaxation period is critical in helping the child who is deaf–blind calm down at the end of each physical education class. These activities reduce self-stimulatory behaviors such as flicking and rocking. Associated music provides sensory input in the form of sound vibrations.

The child who is deaf–blind needs considerable body awareness and spatial orientation activities at the earliest possible time. One-to-one instruction is generally advisable, emphasizing initial actions, including instructor-directed turning, rolling, pulling, pushing, bobbing, crawling, creeping, and balancing. Fundamental movement reactions can be stimulated by the use of gravity, an unstable piece of equipment (balance or rocking board), or an instructor's physical manipulation.

FIGURE 12.30   A person who is deaf-blind overcomes fear of the water.

Aquatics instruction (see Figure 12.30) should also begin as early as possible, partly because many uninitiated individuals who are deaf–blind have an extreme fear of water when they become older. There should be a physical communication system developed that directly relates to the aquatics tasks that will be taught. A set routine of tasks is necessary, and verbal praise should be given when there is compliance by the pupil (Grosse, 1985). Further, music, rhythms, dance, and games are important and can be enjoyed using various techniques that stress vibration. For example, sit together around a piano or large drum. As these instruments are played, the pupils can feel movement cues through their hands.

Behavior Management

Most people who select a career in education do so because of an interest in imparting knowledge and skills to pupils. This is a simplistic and ideal view. Thus our purpose in this fourth part of the book is to make the reader aware of the many other integral aspects of the teaching process.

How important is the management of pupils' behavior in the educational sphere? How can pupils' behavior be managed? What professionals are available to provide a team approach to assist pupils with disabilities? What testing and evaluating instruments and techniques are available to assess pupils' physical education skills and the quality of programs? How can a special physical education program be effectively

Note: Much of the material in this chapter is taken from R. French and P. Jansma, "Management of Behavior Problems," unpublished manuscript, 1981.

and efficiently administered? What are appropriate extracurricular activities for individuals with disabilities? Answers to these pertinent questions for those who teach physical education are provided in this and the next four chapters.

Behavior management, or discipline, is one of the major problems in American schools (French, Henderson, & Horvat, 1992). Although discipline seems to be a problem of contemporary times, in fact it has been chronic throughout the ages. More than 2,000 years ago Socrates stated:

> Our youth now love luxury, have bad manners and contempt for authority. They show disrespect for elders and they love to chatter instead of exercise. Children are now tyrants, not the servants of their household. They no longer rise when elders enter the room, they contradict their parents, chatter before company, gobble their food and terrorize their teachers.

Over the centuries, behavior problems have permeated schools. As evidence, in fourteenth-century England when teachers graduated they received both their diploma and a disciplining cane.

BEHAVIOR PROBLEMS

Behavior issues permeate all curriculum areas, particularly those that commonly involve large classes in relatively open, unstructured, and flexible environments such as physical education. Physical education is an integral part of a school's instructional program; yet many pupils with problem behaviors are provided physical education programs that resemble recess or are excused altogether from physical education. Unfortunately lack of a proper instructional program for such pupils is often due to the absence of expertise on the part of physical educators to manage behavior in the gymnasium, playground, and pool. Without this ability, efficient and effective instruction cannot occur and physical educators will be viewed as only baby sitters or protectors of life and limb. Teachers cannot teach a skill or game unless cooperative behavior is first established. That behavior must be managed before one can teach class management is *central* to the task of teaching (Luke, 1989).

Federal legislation mandates that even more pupils who exhibit behavior problems will be educated in least restrictive environments. All schools receiving federal support are directly affected by this legislation. It is of particular interest to note also that ancillary subjects, such as physical education, are often the first ones considered when mainstreaming pupils in need of special education and related services. Barry Lavay's interview applies here:

Barry Lavay

Dr. Barry Lavay is a professor of special physical education at California State University, Long Beach. Much of his research has been in the area of behavior management.

1. *What are the biggest problems facing regular physical educators today?*

In an education poll conducted each fall for the past 10 years by Phi Delta Kappan (educational fraternity) teachers and parents have cited a lack of pupil discipline as one of the major problems facing educators in the schools. Repeatedly, the majority of beginning teachers who leave the profession do so during the first three years, and a major reason often cited is an inability to manage pupil behavior. Behavior problems most often cited include challenging authority, acting aggressively toward other pupils, and nonattending to teacher instruction. A class that is unmanageable is unteachable!

Overcrowded classes and limited facilities are other major concerns regular physical educators face especially on the high school level. It would be unthinkable to place 50–60 pupils in an English class for individualized and group instruction while having them share one or two textbooks. However, many physical educators are placed daily in this difficult teaching situation. They are too often expected to teach their subject to 50–60 pupils outside (or best in a small gymnasium or cafeteria) with only a few pieces of equipment to share among the pupils.

2. Do you see a trend for more teacher preparation programs to place a greater emphasis on behavior management?

If teacher preparation programs are to survive and prosper in the 1990s they have a responsibility to graduate future teachers with the training necessary to effectively meet the needs of all pupils, especially those who lack discipline and/or are unmotivated. Too often students graduate from teacher preparation programs with a sound knowledge and training base in their subject area (e.g., physical education), but lack the knowledge and practice required to manage pupil behavior. It is merely not

enough for teacher preparation programs to graduate students with one or two theory courses in behavior management. Necessary is the infusion of management principles and practices into the majority of each major's teacher training coursework as well as realistic practicum experiences in applied settings. Examples of effective management procedures include the application of various reinforcement practices, modeling, group contingencies, self-talk, response cost, and time-out.

3. What behavior management techniques generally are the most appropriate to incorporate into mainstreamed physical education classes?

For many pupils who are disabled, mainstreaming has become a series of miserable and embarrassing failures such as being unable to keep up with classmates, being chosen last, and being laughed at for being clumsy. To assist these pupils the instructor must emphasize success by providing positive experiences such as organizing environmental and instructional strategies that are responsive to each individual's needs. Examples of strategies to consider are the use of a variety of teaching styles, learning stations, task cards, peer tutors, a buddy system, and cooperative games. Most importantly, the instructor must realize the application of these strategies will not occur by accident, but rather must be administered in a positive, systematic, and consistent manner. Finally, to determine if the administered strategy is effective, it must be periodically evaluated.

Pupils may exhibit numerous inappropriate behaviors that need to be managed in physical education. An inappropriate behavior is any action that is demonstrated where it is not wanted. The appropriateness of a behavior is more dependent on the tolerance of the physical educator than any characteristic of the behavior itself. The following are lists of behaviors, separated into three general categories, that most teachers consider inappropriate in an instructional setting.

Mild	Moderate	Severe
Selfishness	Swearing to	Stealing
Gum chew-	oneself	Fighting
ing	Withdrawal	Lying
Being a tattle-	Ring-leader	Truancy
tale	behavior	Smoking
Name calling	Slamming	Drinking
Domineering	lockers	Drug abuse
Malingering	Interrupting	Sex play
Impatience	Bullying	Vandalizing
Not wearing	Easily dis-	Bullying
uniform	couraged	Intimidating
	Laziness	Phobias
	Tardiness	(water,
	Inattention	height)
	Sloppiness	Direct dis-
	Crying (when	obedience
	you lose)	(noncom-
	Naughty fin-	pliance)
	ger	Snapping
	Impolite	towels
	Horseplay	Swearing at
	Trouble in	others
	lining up	
	Poor sports-	
	manship	

Traditionally, physical educators do not think of themselves as behavior managers. They are hired to teach and they expect pupils to behave in order to learn. In cases where teachers have taken a participatory role in behavior management, a haphazard "band-aid" approach has been used, to the detriment of the overall educational process.

Such tactics as the following are, unfortunately, still being used exclusively by some physical educators:

- Taking laps
- Writing repetitive statements
- Taking away a prized possession
- Suspending the pupil from school
- Sending the pupil to the principal
- Using ridicule
- Sending a negative note to parents

Numerous authors of physical education texts (e.g., Auxter, Pyfer, & Heuttig, 1993; Sherrill, 1986) state the importance and need for effective behavior management techniques in physical education to control inappropriate behaviors. Physical educators are often the first to be summoned to manage pupil behavior, and the physical educator as counselor of pupils is a common situation. This chapter, devoted to behavior management, is specifically tailored to meet the needs of physical educators in segregated, inclusive, mainstreamed, or regular instructional physical education settings.

The management of behavior obviously has no simple or singular solution. Just as no two pupils are alike, so, too, no two physical educators are identical in their specific or overall approach to effective behavior management. Individualization is a concept that should be applied not only for pupils but also for physical educators. Pupils have their own unique needs relative to behavior control and learning techniques. Physical educators have their individual styles and values with reference to teaching methods and behavior management approaches.

There are, however, a number of functional behavior management approaches that are traditionally utilized by physical educators. The major approach discussed in this chapter is operant conditioning. Other approaches, but not within the scope of this introductory text to discuss in detail, are the self-responsibility model, transactional analysis, reality therapy, the Foster approach, life space interviewing, assertive discipline, medication, relaxation training, and biofeedback. All approaches are designed to prevent undesirable behavior, to increase appropriate behaviors, and to decrease inappropriate behaviors already displayed. The emphasis is on pupils engaging in responsible and appropriate behavior. Physical educators should be instrumental in managing behavior, but only within the context and philosophy that eventually their managing roles will fade and pupils will eventually learn responsible, adaptive, and self-managing behavior with which to face the "real" world.

OPERANT CONDITIONING

It is maintained in operant conditioning (often referred to incorrectly as behavior modification) that all voluntary behavior is learned and, therefore, voluntary behavior can be managed (Skinner, 1968). Teachers, including physical educators, consciously or unconsciously manage voluntary behavior of their pupils throughout the total educational milieu on a daily basis. Operant conditioning techniques have direct application in physical education settings in managing behaviors. In physical education, operant behaviors include both social behaviors and physical, motor, fitness, and play skill behaviors. Each of these behaviors is generally described as one or a combination of overt, observable, and measurable responses emitted by pupils and *operating* on the immediate environment—therefore, the term *operant management*.

Operant management is based on a simple *A-B-C* paradigm. In this paradigm an *a*ntecedent stimulus precedes and occasions a

related *b*ehavior which is followed by an earned *c*onsequence or contingent reward. In other words, behavior is a function of stimulus and/or consequence control. Physical educators using this behavior management paradigm manipulate either the antecedent stimulus and/or the consequence. An example of stimulus management might involve the physical education teacher blowing a whistle, which immediately causes pupils to line up. On the other hand, consequence management might include increased free play contingent on the display of an appropriate behavior by the pupil(s). See Figure 13.1 for other examples of the A-B-C paradigm operating in physical education.

Numerous specific operant conditioning techniques are used in physical education. These techniques can be grouped into three categories:

I. Those that maintain, strengthen, or teach new behavior: reinforcement, fading, shaping, chaining, and prompting.

II. Those that eliminate or weaken behavior: time-out, overcorrection, extinction, satiation, deprivation, response cost, and corporal punishment.

III. Those that maintain, strengthen, eliminate, and weaken behavior: token economy, behavioral contract, group consequences, Premack principle, and modeling.

In using any of these reinforcement techniques, there are general guidelines that must be followed to maximize the probability of successful use.

Techniques That Maintain, Strengthen, or Teach New Behavior

Reinforcement is the critical operant management element typically used to increase the probability that pupils will maintain, increase, or learn new behaviors. A reinforcer

Antecedent Event	Behavior	Consequence
A	B	C
Gymnasium: Bell ringing	Lining up	Plus ("+") recorded in roll book

| Pool: Pool door left open | Pupil enters illegally | Pupil receives demerit, verbal and non-verbal admonishment |

FIGURE 13.1   ABCs of operant conditioning.

is systematically offered after the emission of an appropriate response in order to increase the future occurrence of the response. It is one form of consequence.

Reinforcement can be either positive or negative. The following is an example of the use of *positive reinforcement,* which involves providing the pupil something he or she values to increase the probability that a behavior will occur. If John has difficulty dressing for class because he is shy or withdrawn, the teacher can pat John on the back (positive reinforcement) and tell him, "John, your gym clothes look good on you" (positive reinforcement). The frequency of dressing behavior may then increase, and it is likely that John will continue to dress in the appropriate manner.

There is a hierarchy of positive reinforcers (see Figure 13.2) that can be used by the physical educator. The selection of the correct type of reinforcement is determined by discussion with and observation of pupils and discussions with other professionals and parents.

Tangible reinforcement (e.g., edibles) is considered the lowest and most artificial type of positive reinforcement. An example of a tangible reward is the use of a patch (object)

or allowing pupils to use the diving board for 5 minutes (activity) if they display appropriate behavior during stroke work. Here are other examples of object and activity reinforcers that have been used in physical education:

Objects

1. Award ribbons or patches
2. Trophies or plaques
3. Physical education shirts or trunks of different colors (each color representing the attainment of a specific behavioral goal)
4. Posted photograph of the pupil
5. Grades
6. Names placed in yearbook
7. Complimentary note or letter home

Activities

1. Pass out towels
2. Distribute soap
3. Keep score
4. Run an errand
5. Pupil picks activity of choice as a reward
6. Be a referee
7. Lead exercises

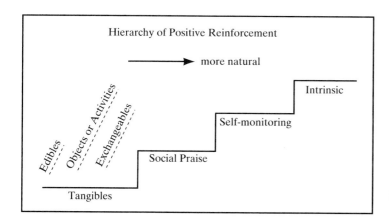

FIGURE 13.2 Types of positive reinforcement.

DENT SCHOOL DISTRICT

Physical Education Award

_____ has been chosen the most

improved pupil in physical education during the week

of _____ .

★

_____
Mr. Vinnick

_____
Date

FIGURE 13.3   Physical Education Award.

Another type of reinforcer is the use of formal certificates for good behavior or sportsmanship. This has proven to be very effective in many cases and is inexpensive. Figures 13.3 and 13.4 provide two examples of this type of tangible reward.

Farthest along the continuum of less restrictive or less artificial tangible rewards is the exchangeable or token system of rewards (expanded on later in this section). When earned objects (e.g., awarded tokens) can later be traded in or exchanged for something of more value, an exchangeable system or token economy is in effect. Many physical educators will not use tangibles, particularly edibles, in managing behavior. It must be remembered, though, that the major function of a physical educator is to teach. If a pupil's

---

Colombo School District

CERTIFICATE OF ACCOMPLISHMENT

FALL 1994

Presented to _____

for sportsmanship.

_____
Teacher

_____
Principal

FIGURE 13.4   Certificate of Accomplishment.

behavior is interfering with the learning process, teachers must develop a management system to enable learning to begin and progress. If raisins are most appropriate (make sure an edible is nutritionally safe), use it if all the other positive reinforcers have been used without success. Then, as soon as possible, gradually fade away from edibles toward object/activity reinforcers. The goal is to provide the most natural consequences possible so that eventually a pupil can be self-managed.

Social praise is a very successful approach to manage behavior. Some social reinforcers applicable in physical education are

1. Pat on the back
2. Gestures
   Grin
   Look of pleasure   High five
   Smile   Pumping the arm
3. Say
   "Better"   "Good"   "Right"
   "Correct"   "Great"   "Terrific"
   "Excellent" "I like that" "Well done"
   "Fine"   "Okay"   "Wow"

The effectiveness of these social reinforcers in managing behavior can be increased if the pupil is immediately informed why praise is being given. For instance, "I really like that, Joe. You quietly waited your turn until Jill finished her exercise." This ensures that pupils know the specific behavior required for social praise. If, on the other hand, a target behavior is not verbally tied to social praise, another behavior could be reinforced accidentally. For example, when the physical educator said, "I really like that, Joe," Joe was waiting for his turn, but was in fact not paying attention to instruction. In this example, physical educators might be reinforcing nonattending behavior.

Self-monitored reinforcement—the ability of pupils to monitor their own behavior—is an even more natural form of positive reinforcement. One of the major advantages of this technique is the fact that teachers can attend to other duties because behavior is monitored by pupils. Behavioral contracting (discussed later in this section) is an example of a self-monitoring procedure that is used in schools.

The most sophisticated type of positive reinforcement is intrinsic. This type does not require recognition from an outside source but rather is an internal, intangible feeling of accomplishment. One's maturity level has a direct correlation with one's ability to function at the intrinsic reinforcement level.

A behavior may also be maintained or strengthened by pupils emitting a response for which the consequence is the removal or avoidance of an aversive stimulus. This is termed *negative reinforcement*. Negative reinforcement should not be confused with punishment; they are distinctly different concepts. Punishment results in a decrease in the frequency of a response, whereas negative reinforcement produces the strengthening of a response because an aversive consequence is removed or avoided. A pupil has a choice, for example, to lose points (punishment) for an inappropriate behavior or to avoid losing points (negative reinforcement) by behaving. The only relationship between negative reinforcement and punishment is that an effective punishment must exist in order for negative reinforcement to be a reality.

Reinforcers are not only categorized as positive or negative but can also be separated into those that are primary or unconditioned and those that are secondary or conditioned. *Primary reinforcers* relate to physical life needs, such as foods and liquids. *Secondary reinforcers* are acquired (learned) in association with primary reinforcers or other strong secondary reinforcers. An object can also be both a primary and a secondary reinforcer.

For young pupils, the warmth and feel of a school sweater may be the most rewarding characteristics (primary). As pupils grow older, they quickly learn that these rewarding characteristics are not the most important, because the sweater becomes associated with social recognition and praise (secondary).

Learning is a function of immediacy or delay of reinforcement. There are different methods of *scheduling reinforcement*. The two basic patterns are continuous (immediate) and intermittent (delayed) reinforcement. If the pattern of reinforcement involves a one-to-one payoff contingency (one consequence for every one behavior), the pattern is referred to as *continuous*. Continuous patterns usually yield high rates of behavior but are not very resistant to extinction. If the pat-tern is one to two or greater, the term *intermittent* reinforcement is employed. Intermittent patterns usually yield behavior that does not extinguish quickly when reinforcement is removed and real-world consequences exist.

With regard to continuous and intermittent patterns of reinforcement, the time between the response and the consequences is the critical factor in influencing behavior change toward natural events. Most pupils can delay the need for reinforcement over some period of time. Obtaining first place in a fitness test is an example of delayed reinforcement. Pupils may not be reinforced for five weeks while conditioning and training for the test. After five weeks of training and successfully meeting the test criteria, recognition is finally given in the form of a patch from the President's Council on Physical Fitness and Sports.

While most pupils can function at this level, others need more immediate reinforcers to change or maintain their behavior. However, once continuous reinforcers manage a pupil's behavior, the delay between the response and reward should be increased to the natural response/reward time lag used for the other pupils in a class. Immediate reinforcement is more effective than delayed reinforcement when developing a new behavior because pupils can easily be motivated to emit a specific response (behavior) that is being reinforced frequently; yet intermittent reinforcement eventually should be used in order to condition the pupil to typical real-world delayed reinforcement.

Two types of intermittent reinforcement exist: ratio and interval (see Table 13.1). The ratio schedule involves reinforcement for a specified number of pupil responses, and is behavior based. If the ratio always involves a specific number of responses by the pupil before reinforcement, it is termed *fixed ratio.** If the ratio requires responses that vary around an average number of required responses, it is termed a *variable ratio* schedule of reinforcement. The interval type of schedule conversely focuses on a unit of time rather than on a specified number of pupil responses. Interval schedules are time based. If the interval involves a specific time after which the next appropriate response is reinforced, it is termed *fixed interval*. If the interval requires a response after an interval that varies around an average amount of time, it is termed a *variable interval* schedule of reinforcement. Variable intervals are most resistant to extinction. Table 13.1 illustrates these concepts in a physical education context.

In using any reinforcement technique, general guidelines must be followed to maximize the probability of successful use.

1. Physical educators must determine the target behavior to be changed. This behavior must be observable and measurable. Si-

---

*A fixed ratio of one reinforcer for one response is a continuous reinforcement pattern. Continuous reinforcement patterns are behavior based.

TABLE 13.1 REINFORCEMENT SCHEDULE TYPES FOR USE IN PHYSICAL EDUCATION

PATTERN/TYPE	DESCRIPTION
1. Fixed ratio (FR)	A pupil receives one reward for a fixed number of responses. For example, if a pupil completes the eight stations of a circuit without goofing off, he receives 5 minutes of free play.
2. Variable ratio (VR)	The ratio of reinforcement changes after each reinforcement. For example, a pupil is rewarded the first time she does not fight in the gymnasium, then the second time, the fourth, the seventh, etc.
3. Fixed interval (FI)	The pupil is rewarded for the first target behavior emitted after the lapse of a specific time period. For example, after a period of 5 minutes, the pupil is rewarded for engaging in cooperative play.
4. Variable interval (VI)	The presentation of a reinforcer varies with different time intervals. The pupil is reinforced for not cursing in the pool after 1 minute, 3 minutes, 5 minutes, 2 minutes, etc., have lapsed.

lently standing in line is an observable behavior that can be measured in terms of length of time. Other examples of operants that can be observed and measured in physical education include dressing time, showering time, number of tasks completed during class, number of inappropriate gestures during class, and number of reinforcers handed out in class by the teacher.

2. Baseline measurements of how often an observable target behavior is occurring must be collected. These baseline data provide an objective account and proof of the need for behavioral intervention. Baseline data are in contrast to intervention data. The former refers to the initial level of inappropriate behavior without the physical educator intervening and the latter refers to changing the behavior during the application of a specified intervention technique.

3. In most cases pupils must understand the specific response that is being reinforced. They should not have to use a trial and error approach to determine why a certain behavior is being reinforced. Telling a pupil that she is "being a good girl" is too general and could mean many different things. A more specific statement might be, "Joan,

you are acting like a good pupil by standing in that (physical education) circle for one minute." The latter statement may increase the probability that the standing or waiting response will occur again because Joan knows exactly what to do for the verbal reinforcement.

4. Select the appropriate antecedent event and reinforcing consequence. The initial stimulus must be clearly perceived and understood (e.g., a whistle) and the reward selected must possess a strong reinforcing quality to the pupil. Many educators will ask pupils what they enjoy in order to determine an appropriate consequence. Another approach is to observe pupils during recess, free play, or lunch to see what activities they engage in on a consistent basis. The latter approach may be more of an accurate assessment of the types of food, trinkets, or activities that are strongly reinforcing to pupils.

5. Determine an appropriate amount of reinforcement. Giving a junior high school pupil who is behaviorally disordered two M&M's for standing in line will probably be inappropriate. The physical educator may find them forcibly returned. Allowing pu-

pils to select the first exercise or earning two points toward a Frisbee (20 points) may be more appropriate and reinforcing.

6. A variety of reinforcers must also be identified for each pupil. It cannot be expected that the same reinforcer will be effective over a long period of time. See the accompanying list of reinforcers available for use by a physical educator on page 375.

7. It is also inappropriate to apply the "all or none" principle in which pupils either display or do not display target behaviors. Rather, pupils should be reinforced for exhibiting even some target behavior.

8. Reinforce immediately. The timing of reinforcement is critical in the use of operant management. Teachers should reinforce appropriate behavior as soon as pupils have earned the specified reward. If this guideline is not strictly adhered to and there is a delay between completion of task and the reward, the strength of the reinforcer could diminish. For example, pupils might hold a firm base of a pyramid for a specified time and expect an appropriate consequence for this behavior. However, if the reward is not given immediately, they could lose their motivation and allow the pyramid to collapse. Appropriately timed reinforcement could very well have maintained the pyramid for a longer period of time and eliminated the potential of injuries and class disruption with pupils falling on each other.

9. It is wise to continually measure and chart target behavior whether during baseline observations or during an intervention period. This recommendation applies to both behaviors that are a permanent product (e.g., amount of mess remaining around lockers) and/or behaviors that are transitory or fleeting (e.g., swearing).

10. It may be that the selected intervention technique(s) may not automatically result in target behavior change. Therefore, the teacher should possess the ability and patience to modify and replan so that appropriate levels of behavior can eventually be realized. The operant manager must be persistent, in tune with the class, set the right pace, manage time efficiently, set realistic goals, involve the entire class, use humor, be assertive but gentle, generate enthusiasm, be knowledgeable, be a good role model, and take responsibility for managing behavior (French, Henderson, & Horvat, 1992).

11. Be systematic and consistent. The implementation of the selected operant management technique must be systematically and consistently applied for the best results. This step is often the hardest.

Numerous physical educators have stated that operant conditioning techniques do not work! When we observe them actually applying a technique, however, it is often readily apparent that the teacher does not follow one or more of these guidelines. Successful teachers utilize these approaches fairly and consistently and change their techniques to accommodate the strengths and weaknesses of their pupils.

Fading, shaping, chaining, and prompting techniques can also be incorporated into any behavioral management approach to maintain, strengthen, or teach a new behavior.

Fading is a procedure in which an antecedent event (stimulus) and/or reinforcer is gradually shifted from artificial to natural at a rate that will not interfere with the production of a desirable target behavior. For example, physical educators can fade the amount of physical guidance of a pupil on the balance beam going from a situation where one finger is held to only physical proximity or standing beside the pupil as he walks the beam. In another example, pupils who do not dress for class are commonly given a failing grade for nondressing behavior. In this instance physical educators may develop a behavioral contract with pupils that indicates the criteria to achieve a passing grade such as dressing once for the total week. As soon as possible, the fading procedure should be initiated and a new contract negotiated with the number of dressing days

Privileges
1. Run errands
2. Record attendence
3. Be a teacher's aide
   a. Safety patrol
   b. Recess line
   c. Shower monitor
4. Help plan, decorate, and maintain bulletin boards
5. Tutor other pupils
6. Represent class in school activities
7. Get equipment
8. Supervise outside of class
9. Grade or check work
10. Pass out towels
11. Pass out equipment
12. Lead opening exercises
13. Have free time classes
14. Choose an activity
15. Answer questions
16. Plan special activities (e.g., sports day)
17. Conduct tours
    a. Parking lot tours
    b. Conducting tours of school
18. Participate in field trips
19. Compete against other person
20. Participate in a physical education demonstration
21. Use of playground equipment
22. Being visited by an athlete
23. Being dismissed early
24. Being exempt from specific assignments
25. Being captain

Nonconsumable Reinforcers
1. Trophy
2. Medal
3. Badge
4. Awards
5. Books
6. Records
7. Tickets to entertainment events
8. Grab bag objects
9. Toys
10. Pictures (of athletes)
11. Trading cards (e.g., baseball cards)
12. Ball
13. Inexpensive games
14. Models
15. Money

Food Reinforcers
1. Gum
2. Popcorn
3. Candy
4. Apples/bananas
5. Raisins
6. Orange or tangerine sections
7. Milk
8. Juices
9. Lemonade
10. Soda

Nonverbal Social Reinforcers
1. Nod
2. Wink
3. Praise
4. Proximity
5. Smile
6. Pat on back
7. Show approval
8. Laugh with
9. Provide opportunities for recognition
10. Hug

Verbal Reinforcers
1. "That's good"
2. "Right"
3. "Terrific"
4. "Wow!"
5. "Fantastic"
6. "I like it"
7. "I'm very proud of you"
8. "Excellent"
9. "Att-a-boy (-girl)"
10. "I think that's marvelous"
11. "Beautiful"
12. "Right on"
13. "Super"
14. "I'm very pleased"
15. "Good work, _____"
16. "Keep up the good work"
17. "That's much better"

Field Trips
1. Bowling
2. Movies
3. Historic places (e.g., a hall of fame)
4. Sports events
5. Track and field day
6. State fair
7. Swimming
8. Local university or college (to see athletic event)

reasonably increased in order to receive a weekly passing grade. Such fading techniques often evolve from a one-to-one contingency that is progressively changed or faded into a stretched (i.e., more than one-to-one) fixed ratio of reinforcement; then changing the reinforcement pattern to intermittent. As a final example of fading, physical educators can teach appropriate dressing by using a number of steps such as physically dressing pupils, then modeling, then telling the pupils to dress, and finally pupils dressing within school bell intervals. As each new step is reached, prior steps fade and the school bell eventually controls dressing behavior.

Shaping is the development of a new response through selectively reinforcing closer and closer approximations of the desired terminal response. The shaping procedure has three basic steps:

1. Develop a continuum of behavioral objectives that eventually leads to a planned terminal behavior.
2. Identify behaviors that are presently related to the desired response.
3. Select the reinforcing event to be used and the manner in which it will be administered.

An example of shaping can be applied to teaching safety related to a previously unlearned motor skill: If pupils do not know how to climb safely on the gymnasium ropes, they may swing and clown around while using the climbing ropes. A possible reason for this behavior is that they never have acquired a sense of safety related to rope climbing. By utilizing a behavior shaping procedure, the following sequential steps can be completed:

a. Teach safety related to climbing ropes and give an oral test to pass.
b. Hold the base of the rope while a pupil climbs a specified distance safely.

c. Peers hold the rope while others climb up half way safely.
d. Teachers hold the rope while pupils climb the rope safely to the ceiling and ring a bell with the forehead.
e. Do likewise with a peer holding the rope.

After completion of each step, the pupils should be reinforced appropriately until the target behavior (safely climbing rope) is developed. It should be noted that after a shaping procedure has been completed, a number of the former approximations are no longer distinctly relevant. In our example, the second step blends into the last step and, therefore, loses its identity and significance.

Another reinforcement technique requires a more complex behavioral response by physical educators. It involves teaching a combination of already learned pupil behaviors. When taken together, a combination of responses related to the learning of an advanced skill might be too complex for some pupils to perform (e.g., completion of a double play in baseball). Therefore, a *chaining* procedure may be advisable. In chaining, a terminal goal is broken down into small steps or links. The linkage of the determined steps then becomes the key factor in the chaining procedure.

Shaping and chaining procedures should not be confused. Whereas shaping ties approximations together always in a forward direction resulting eventually in an acquired behavior, chaining links already acquired responses usually in a backward direction since most reinforcement is realized at the completion of a task. (Forward chaining would only be recommended when the target behavior is dangerous or threatening.) Further, in shaping the emphasis is on the acquisition of one new behavior, whereas chaining links separately acquired or shaped behaviors into a more complex terminal response. If one link in a chaining procedure is not in a pupil's behavioral repertoire, it needs to be shaped first and then chaining can continue.

An example of the use of backward chaining is in a situation in which pupils know how to dress but refuse to dress properly for gymnastics. The concern is to get pupils to dress appropriately for class using the following items (shoes are usually put on last):

1. T-shirt
2. Shorts
3. White socks
4. Tennis shoes

In the hope that the four items of clothing eventually will become chained into full uniform dress behavior, the chaining process would first involve a contingency in which tennis shoes are worn in class by pupils before recognition is given. Following the chaining model, the contingency requirement would increase to the next step by requiring that both tennis shoes and white socks be worn in class. When the chaining process involves all four items of clothing, the four hierarchy items will be linked together and the end goal (proper physical education uniform worn) will be reached. It should be noted that the tennis shoes should be chosen first in the chaining procedure not only because they are typically the last article of clothing put on but also because physical educators have a natural concern for pupil safety and the condition of the gymnasium floor. This example of the use of chaining dress behavior is also practical because physical educators can realistically teach a class and also attend to one aspect of a target pupil's dressing behavior.

Prompting involves utilization of signals, cues, and other stimulus control primes to assist pupils in identifying and developing a specific behavior. Several types of prompts can be used by physical educators, including verbal, nonverbal, or written instruction,

demonstration, and physical guidance techniques. The least intrusive and most natural prompt is one that is heard or read, the next is shown (modeled), and the most intrusive is physical guidance. As a guideline, physical educators should attempt to use the most natural, least intrusive technique possible when prompting behavior, with physical guidance being the last resort.

Instructional auditory prompts are commonly used in physical education. The use of the whistle (nonverbal) and verbal directions are classic examples of such prompts. For example, when physical educators see that a behavior problem may disrupt the class, a whistle is blown. This signal provides pupils with the information that if the behavior continues, there will be a consequence. Aside from the straightforward use of words in giving instructions, the physical educator and selected pupils may also have a specific secret verbal signal that informs each pupil that the behavior exhibited is inappropriate. For instance, the teacher could call out a number, such as 10, which signals targeted pupils that the exhibited behavior should be modified. Instructions written on posters also commonly serve as reminders of class rules.

Other types of visual prompts used to manage behavior include circles painted or taped on the floor to cue pupils concerning the appropriate spot, zone, or boundary that is indicated for them. Also, picture posters provide cues related to desired behavior (e.g., cleanliness, nonuse of drugs).

Live models can demonstrate appropriate behaviors for a class or target pupil. Models or demonstrations should be expertly provided by a respected person if an effect on a target pupil is to be expected.

The most intensive type of prompt is physical guidance or manipulation. For example, if a pupil keeps turning her head away, the physical educator can gently touch the individual's chin to prompt looking straight ahead. Another physical prompt for the pupil who has problems waiting in line would be to hold his hand or place a hand on his back to ensure proper waiting. Caution is advised here not to apply too much physical pressure. Only what physical guidance is necessary to manage behavior should be used.

Techniques That Eliminate or Weaken Behaviors

There are numerous techniques that physical educators can use to eliminate or weaken an inappropriate behavior. Time-out, overcorrection, extinction, satiation, deprivation, response cost, and corporal punishment are examples. General guidelines for using these techniques include the following:

1. Define problem behaviors.
2. Identify behavior incompatible with problem behavior.
3. Determine (frequency or duration) baseline occurrence of problem behavior.
4. Record baseline occurrence of problem behavior.
5. List reinforcers for pupil.
6. Restructure environment if necessary to change occurrence of behavior.
7. List and explain rules to pupil (what must be done and how often, to get what).
8. Shape incompatible behavior.
9. Continue recording.
10. Implement selected behavior management technique.
11. Increase criterion for reinforcement.
12. Reinforce intermittently.
13. Gradually withdraw from tangible reinforcers.
14. Go on to another behavior (if necessary).

Time-out is an effective technique to eliminate or weaken problem behaviors in physical education. Specifically, this technique requires the immediate withdrawal of a pupil from a reinforcing situation (or vice versa) when he or she emits an inappropriate behavior. Inappropriate behavior is hopefully eliminated or at least weakened by placing the pupil in a totally nonreinforcing solitary environment (i.e., a neutral environment). Guidelines for using time-out include the following (Kazdin, 1980):

1. Inform the pupil specifically which behavior produced the time-out.
2. Administer time-out in a consistent and matter-of-fact manner.
3. Ensure that the removal from a situation is nonaversive and nonreinforcing. Sometimes a teacher will send the pupil to the principal's office for the purpose of time-out and the pupil becomes the secretary's office helper, spending part of the time visiting friends in other classes (very reinforcing); or a pupil is told to sit in the hall and passers-by pay attention to the pupil (very reinforcing). Be sure that the pupil is not getting out of doing an activity. Sometimes a teacher must eliminate a pupil from an activity because of misbehavior, when that is exactly what the pupil wants all along. In addition, evaluate the physical location of the time-out area very carefully to ensure that the area is void of sources of positive reinforcement. Some teachers use a bench or painted circle on the playing surface away from the activity as a time-out area. In severe cases, an inexpensive three panel screen like those used by school nurses could be placed in the gymnasium as a time-out area.
4. Keep the time-out periods relatively short. One to 5 minutes has been found to be effective (see Figure 13.5). Remember that you set the length of time, not the pupil.
5. Reinforce appropriate behaviors (when time-out is not being administered) displayed by the pupil that are incompatible with behaviors that cause time-out.

There is a hierarchy of time-out techniques (see Figure 13.6). The mildest time-out technique is ignoring an unwanted behavior for a

FIGURE 13.5 Timing a time-out.

specified short period. What this technique amounts to is the temporary social (not physical) removal of pupils from reinforcing social situations. A slightly more aversive time-out technique is relegating a pupil to a spot (e.g., circle) in the gymnasium, pool, or playground. This would be followed in severity by a time-out approach in which the pupil is placed outside the activity area and out of the sight of peers. The last step in the hierarchy would be placing a pupil in a designated time-out enclosure, hopefully in close proximity to the activity area.

Overcorrection is a technique that can be an alternative to the continual use of time-out. This technique is used to reduce or eliminate an inappropriate behavior, but it also involves an educational component. There are two elements in overcorrection. First, there is the restitutional element for situations when there is a disruption in the environment. For example, if balls are consistently left on the playground, pupils are pinpointed to bring in these balls from the playground. Second, there is the positive-

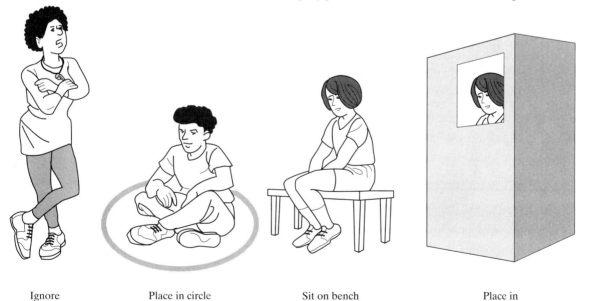

| Ignore | Place in circle near activity | Sit on bench out of view of activity | Place in time-out enclosure |

FIGURE 13.6 Hierarchy of time-out techniques.

practice element in overcorrection. This educational element involves repeated practice of a positive, desired behavior. For instance, in the same example involving balls in the playground, the same pupils would be required to retrace their steps and retrieve the same balls numerous times.

Extinction is the technique of eliminating a problem behavior by withholding specific reinforcers that maintain or increase the behavior. Many times pupils misbehave because they know that misbehavior provides more reinforcement than appropriate behavior. If they perceive this to be the case, physical educators can reduce or extinguish maladaptive behaviors simply by withholding reinforcement (extinction). Too often, teachers unknowingly pay attention to and reinforce inappropriate behavior. It should also be noted that an inappropriate pupil response could be a mistake and the pupil could have the ability to self-correct the behavior. In this case extinction would cease.

In order to use extinction the following steps should be used:

1. Identify reinforcer.
2. Completely withhold reinforcer on the emission of inappropriate behavior.
3. Concurrently (in contrast to time-out) strengthen the appearance of appropriate behavior by reinforcement.
4. Once a maladaptive behavior is eliminated, it may reappear or another maladaptive behavior may appear in the same situation. Initiate the extinction procedure again until that behavior totally disappears.

When initially using extinction, the pupil's target behavior may temporarily increase and aggressive behavior may arise. In this connection, extinction should not be the procedure of choice when, at the outset the target inappropriate behavior endangers other individuals and/or is destructive of property.

In comparison with extinction, time-out may be more appropriate in some cases because

1. Sometimes it is impossible to determine the real source or sources of reinforcement.
2. If the reinforcer is determined, it may be impossible to withhold it in a school setting.
3. Extinction is usually a slower procedure. Extinction, however, is the most effective way to remove permanently an inappropriate response when target behaviors call for its usage.

Satiation involves the loss of effectiveness of a reinforcing activity when it is given in excessive amounts. As long as it is not harmful to the pupil or to others, the teacher using satiation allows a pupil to engage repeatedly in a maladaptive behavior until he or she tires of it. As a case in point, if a pupil were caught writing on the walls, then "writing lines" in detention could be used as an effective satiation technique. Satiation could also be used if a pupil is constantly talking to a friend. In this situation, the teacher stops the class and encourages the pupil to keep talking to the friend. When the pupil stops talking, the teacher makes him or her continue talking. Because the effect of satiation is usually temporary, the physical educator should reinforce the pupil when the inappropriate target behavior is absent.

Deprivation is based on the premise that the effectiveness of a reinforcer can be increased by depriving or holding back a desired reinforcer. If physical educators deprive a pupil of food as reinforcers just before lunch, they will find it more effective than immediately after lunch when stomachs are full. In terms of amount and timing, three raisins are not effective reinforcers for pupils who have just eaten an entire bag. Deprivation is commonly used in physical education in cases where a trip to the water fountain is delayed until performance of a task or demonstration of behavior is completed.

Response cost is usually used in a token economy (see the next section for a discussion on token economy) that requires the pupil to lose some privilege or points that have already been earned. Combined with a token economy, it has been applied effectively in school settings to control various kinds of inappropriate behavior. Physical educators selecting this technique should follow these guidelines:

1. Magnitude of the cost should be determined in relationship to the maladaptive behavior exhibited by the pupils. Excessive fines could be frustrating to pupils.
2. Provide opportunities for pupils to regain the lost points or privilege following the demonstration of appropriate behavior.
3. Ensure that the pupils understand the rules that govern the removal of the reinforcing event.

Examples of the use of response cost in physical education could include the loss of a score already attained in a game or having a grade lowered. Grades can be viewed as tokens because they can be traded in for a diploma.

Corporal punishment as a disciplinary approach is probably employed more often in physical education than in any other curricular area. It is generally defined as an action inflicted on the body in order to cause physical pain. Numerous school districts have banned the use of this type of punishment. In other school districts, there are strict guidelines related to its administration.

The U.S. Supreme Court has upheld the use of corporal punishment in the public schools, no matter how severe. Yet, even with this judicial ruling, teachers *must* know what the state and local regulations are concerning corporal punishment. If guidance by the state or local school district is not provided, the following guidelines may be of assistance when deciding whether or not to administer corporal punishment as a *last resort* in behavior management.

1. Must be for a reasonable purpose
2. With a reasonable object (e.g., paddle)
3. With parental consent, if possible
4. In the presence of a witness (preferably the principal or a faculty member or otherwise appropriate person)
5. Without malice or in anger
6. Away from the head or face of any pupil or extremely delicate organs of the body
7. With consultation between principal and teacher or otherwise between appropriate school personnel
8. On a second or subsequent offense, depending on the gravity of the inappropriate behavior
9. Within established school and board policy
10. With the requirement that a corporal punishment report form be filed with the school superintendent for factual reference and that the document be regarded as confidential to be used for any possible ensuing litigation.

Although there are positive effects in using such corporal punishment to decrease the frequency and intensity of maladaptive behavior, its use also has negative results. For example, many times a pupil who is corporally punished will learn to avoid the physical environment where punishment has been administered (avoidance behavior) and/or avoid the individual who administered this punishment. Pupils may also attempt to use the same punitive technique to control peers and adults, or they may develop emotional reactions to the administration of the punishment such as tantruming or crying.

The long-term beneficial effects of consistently used positive reinforcers far outweigh the use of punitive tools in behavior management. If corporal punishment is necessary, the reinforcement of alternative appropriate responses is recommended because a pupil will then not only know what "bad" behavior is but also what "good" behavior is.

Techniques That Maintain, Strengthen, Eliminate, and Weaken Behavior

We discuss five major techniques/procedures: token economy, behavioral contract, group consequences, Premack principle, and modeling.

In a *token economy*, a pupil or group of pupils is reinforced with tokens (usually not rewarding in themselves) that can be earned for a specific behavioral response. The token, in turn, can be traded in to purchase some preferred item or activity. This technique has proven effective in maintaining or modifying a variety of behaviors, both appropriate and inappropriate.

Among the many types of tokens or exchangeables used are check marks, marbles, pennies, poker chips, stars, play money, happy faces, washers, and stickers. A point system is another token-oriented system that is quite workable in a physical education class. The type of token actually selected depends on the following prerequisites:

1. Its value is understood.
2. It is easy to give out.
3. It is easily identifiable as the property of the pupil.
4. It requires minimal bookkeeping.
5. It is dispensed frequently enough to ensure the maintenance or development of a desired response or elimination of an inappropriate behavior (by giving tokens for the emission of appropriate behavior).

Bookkeeping on token-related tally sheets is highly important. Without this information, teachers will not be able to determine pupil or squad progress. Through the use of tally sheets, quantifiable data can be collected on a specific behavior to determine if it is increasing, decreasing, or maintaining itself. If the behavior is not being modified or maintained, teachers can immediately adjust the consequence and/or conditions that set the stage for target behavior emission.

Depending on the rate of reward, different types of tally sheets are available. For instance, if reinforcement occurs every 10 minutes or less, use the types of tally sheets presented in Figures 13.7 and 13.8. Because of their small size, these cards can be carried by the pupil and handed to the teacher during the reinforcement (trade-in) period. It is advisable at times for the physical educator to use a special writing implement so that pupils will not be tempted to add extra points or checks that were not earned. Responsible pupils can tally their own marks during which time a teacher is advised to monitor pupil tallys every so often.

Other sheets are designed to tally points or tokens after pupils engage in specific activities, after engaging in target behavior during a total class period, or after emitting target behavior over a day or week. A system can be utilized with these long-term tally sheets in which either one earned check (or other symbol) is placed under each heading or a cumulative number of earned points is placed under each heading. Refer to Figures 13.9 and 13.10 for examples of long-term tally sheets applicable to a group of pupils (easily modified for use with one pupil).

Group tally sheets could also be developed where each squad earns points for developing, maintaining, or eliminating a target behavior. This type of program must be designed so that all squads can win. Squads should not compete against each other, but against themselves.

A *behavioral contract* is a written agreement between the physical educator and a pupil that specifies what each person will do related to target behavior for a specific time period. Some authorities consider behavior contracts to be the most sophisticated behavioral management technique.

Behavioral contracts are of three basic types. There is the manager-controlled con-

Behavior _____

Pupil _____

Date(s) _____

FIGURE 13.7   Point tally card (3″ X 5″ or 5″ X 8″).

	Behavior _____							
Pupil						Date(s)		
1	2	3	4	5	6	7	8	9	10
11	12	13	14	15	16	17	18	19	20
21	22	23	24	25	26	27	28	29	30
31	32	33	34	35	36	37	38	39	40
41	42	43	44	45	46	47	48	49	50
51	52	53	54	55	56	57	58	59	60
61	62	63	64	65	66	67	68	69	70
71	72	73	74	75	76	77	78	79	80
81	82	83	84	85	86	87	88	89	90
91	92	93	94	95	96	97	98	99	100

FIGURE 13.8   Numbered point tally card (3″ X 5″ or 5″ X 8″).

DAILY POINT TALLY SHEET

School _____   Date(s) _____

Pupil	Locker	Lining	Exercise	Activity	Shower	Total
Bill						
Joe						
Kelly						
Mike						
Sam						
Keith						
Tanya						

FIGURE 13.9   Daily point tally sheet.

WEEKLY POINT TALLY SHEET

School _____   Week of _____

Pupil	Monday	Tuesday	Wednesday	Thursday	Friday	Total
Janet						
Ron						
Kelly						
Niki						
Theodore						
Mike						
Dotty						
Paul						

FIGURE 13.10   Weekly point tally sheet.

tract, where the teacher/manager determines the target behavior(s) and reinforcement(s). This type of contract is referred to as a proclamation (see Figure 13.11). There is the pupil-controlled contract, where the pupil determines the task and reinforcement (see Figure 13.12). Then there is a mutual contract, where together the teacher and the pupil determine the terms of the contract (see Figure 13.13). All three types of contracts have the

---

Since <u>Rocco Neanderthal</u> has been removed from physical education class eleven (11) times for fighting in the last month, resulting in suspension twice and considerable hard feelings, <u>Rocco</u> will agree to see the school psychologist once a week for the next four school weeks, and furthermore, <u>Rocco</u> will agree to see the physical education teacher within four school days after signing this proclamation in return for a reward of a 3-minute boxing match with the teacher. This contract will have as its purpose the elimination of inappropriate fighting behavior which has caused <u>Rocco</u>'s class removal.

<u>Rocco Neanderthal</u> (date <u>5/22</u>)	<u>Ms. Sally Modify</u> (date <u>5/23</u>)	
Pupil	School Psychologist	
<u>Mr. Habit</u> (date <u>5/22</u>)	<u>Mr. A. Neanderthal</u> (date <u>5/23</u>)	
Physical Education Teacher	Parent/Guardian	

FIGURE 13.11   Sample proclamation.

I, <u>Joe Cooth</u>, agree to <u>stop swearing in physical education class</u>. If I do this for one week, starting <u>May 5</u> and ending <u>May 9</u>, I will receive <u>two items from the physical education reinforcement menu</u>.

Signed: <u>Joe Cooth</u>
                    Pupil

Witness to this contract: <u>Mr. & Mrs. Donald Cooth</u>
                    Parent/Guardian

                    <u>P. Manage</u>
                    Teacher

                    <u>Dr. Oops</u>
                    Principal

FIGURE 13.12   Sample pupil-controlled contract.

Pupil agrees to: Attend physical education class five consecutive school days starting on May 25.

Teacher agrees to: Allow pupil to announce the Junior Varsity basketball game after school on May 29 under the physical education teacher's supervision.

                    <u>Tom Truant</u>   (date 5/22)
                    Pupil

                    <u>Jim Nastics</u>   (date 5/22)
                    Teacher

FIGURE 13.13   Sample mutual contract.

potential to change or maintain behavior, particularly when combined with a token economy system (see Figure 13.14). Behavioral contracts should be viewed as a means to an end, whereby compliance with a formal written contract should eventually become pupil self-management.

Here are some specific guidelines for the use of behavioral contracts:

1. Read and explain the conditions of the contract aloud with the pupil and receive verbal affirmation.
2. Ensure that the contract is fair and suitable to all persons.
3. Design the contract in a positive way, stressing accomplishment before compliance.
4. Design the initial contract in small approximations that will lead to the target behavior. This allows for frequent reward.
5. Provide a reward that is highly prized by the pupil and is not easily obtainable outside the conditions of the contract.
6. Give reward immediately following adequate compliance with the contract.
7. A contract should always be used consistently and systematically.
8. All persons concerned should sign and receive a copy of the contract. Start the contract as soon as possible after signing.
9. The contract should be renegotiable.

Some operant conditioning techniques involve *group consequences*, which require that pupils manage each others' behavior in order to increase the probability that everyone will be reinforced. In physical education classes, squads are a natural grouping system. Each squad member can use peer pressure to affect the behavior of the other members.

Group consequences should be designed so that all squads have a possibility of being rewarded. Do not create competition between squads by allowing only one squad to win. If each can reach the appropriate level set by the teacher, all can win. This also means that no team has to lose or win.

This approach is very successful in classroom settings and in certain instances has

I, Abe Apathy, understand and agree to the following terms:	
Appropriate Behaviors in Physical Education	Points Earned
1. Being on time	3
Late	1
Absent	0
2. Dressed for class (complete uniform)	2
Incomplete uniform	1
Not dressed for physical education class	0
3. Performs all warm-up activities	2
Performs half of the warm-up activities	1
Does not perform warm-up activities	0
4. Participates in all major class activities	10
Participates in half of the class activities	5
Observes activity	1
Ignores activity	0

(Teacher aide monitors point accumulation.)

Reward: When 100 points are earned, a physical education emblem will be awarded.

Pupil   Abe Apathy   (5/22)   Teacher   B. Skinner   (5/22)

FIGURE 13.14   Sample behavior contract with token economy.

proven superior to individual reinforcement in managing behavior. One form of behavior management based on group consequences is the Good Behavior game. The following are the directions for Good Behavior using free time as a reinforcer:

1. Divide the class into squads.
2. Explain that they are going to play a game that each will try to win. The winning squad or squads will receive certain privileges.
3. Within the rules of the game all squads initially receive five points on any given day. When one team member breaks a specified rule, a point is removed from the squad's total. A squad wins if its members retain four or more points during the period, which entitles them to 5 minutes of free play at the end of class. If a team retains a specified number of points over the course of a week, they would be awarded an additional 5 minutes of extra free play the following Monday. During the free period the other team(s) continues its daily instructional program if free time was not earned.
4. If one individual of a squad loses too many points for the team in one period, the members of the team can vote to exclude that member from the group for one day, and the pupil receives other individualized tasks. This pupil then could not participate in any activities won by the team during the day he or she was excluded.

Many times material or social rewards are not necessary to develop, decrease, or maintain a target behavior. Physical activities themselves can also be used as a reinforcer. The crux of this technique, which is based on the *Premack principle*, involves the pupil engaging in a high probability physical activity (reinforcement) contingent first on the emission of a low probability physical activity target response. This principle obviously has natural application in the field of physical education. Because the Premack principle

TABLE 13.2 LOW AND HIGH PROBABILITY ACTIVITIES	
LOW PROBABILITY	HIGH PROBABILITY
Taking endurance tests	Earn 5 minutes of free play
Dancing (sometimes)	Run an errand
Competing in combative-type activities (sometimes)	Lead exercises
Dressing for class	First to participate in an activity
Showering	Run projector or record player
Entering water (phobia)	Trampoline activities
Climbing rope (phobia)	Choose activity
Doing homework	Peer teaching

is activity based, we highly recommend its use, given the variety of physical activities that naturally exist as reinforcers in physical education. This technique is, therefore, a potential boon for all physical educators. Examples of traditionally low and high probability activities are presented in Table 13.2.

Modeling is a technique in which a pupil initiates a behavior based on the observance of the consequence of exhibiting that behavior by someone else. For example, if a teacher praises a pupil (model) for not bouncing a ball while the teacher is giving the directions for a group game, another pupil who has a ball will likely listen intently to the directions as well as not bounce the ball even though he did not directly receive the original consequence (praise). The latter pupil observing the event modeled the praised pupil behavior in hopes of receiving recognition or praise.

Modeling is considered a shortcut to shaping because this technique focuses on terminal target behaviors in most cases and, therefore, requiring less time. Models can be live (teacher, peer) or symbolic (film, videotape, photograph). While live models are more effective than symbolic models, both meth-

TABLE 13.3 EXAMPLES OF THE USES OF DIFFERENT TYPES OF MODELING

Peer Modeling
1. Verbally praise pupils.
2. Appoint pupil to assist peers during practice.
3. Display name and/or picture of pupils on a bulletin board or in a local newspaper.

Adult Modeling
1. Perform the physical or motor skills with pupils.
2. Be enthusiastic and provide encouragement.
3. Enforce stated consequences.

Fictitious or Idealized Models
1. Invite local sports figures to class.
2. Use actual or animated characters from television series who demonstrate a specific behavior.
3. Encourage pupils to attend clinics conducted by local high school or college coaches or physical educators.

Source: Greenwood and French (1988).

ods have proven successful in developing, maintaining and removing behaviors. Some examples of modeling by peers, important adults, and fictitious or idealized characters are illustrated in Table 13.3.

Major guidelines in using modeling include the following.

1. Identify target behavior to be maintained, strengthened, or weakened. Make sure that this behavior is potentially in the repertoire of the pupil needing management.

2. Identify an individual(s) or a symbol(s) that will serve as an effective model in the eyes of the pupil.

3. Provide a situation(s) in which the model demonstrates the appropriate behavior in the presence of the pupil(s).

To sum up our discussion of operant conditioning and behavior management: The significance of operant techniques is based on the premise that all voluntary behaviors are learned—an approach to behavior management that has wide-reaching implications in any environment. The purpose of this chapter was to present a survey of operant management techniques that can be used in the gymnasium, pool, and playground. The techniques ranged from those that strengthen or maintain behaviors to those that weaken or eliminate behaviors.

In using the various techniques, it was stressed that positive consequences should be used whenever possible. In addition, positive reinforcers that are primary should be faded into secondary extrinsic reinforcers that are more natural in a school setting. Once the need for extrinsic reinforcers can be extinguished, intrinsic reinforcers should ultimately maintain behaviors. The goal of operant management is self-management.

Where a neutral or punitive technique is called for, the objective would be to establish a positive contingency as soon as possible. At times a punisher or neutral approach to behavior management can also be used in combination with a positive operant technique.

Operant technology requires the exact identification of a target behavior and the specifications of conditions and consequences. When a contingency is actually in operation, the effectiveness of the contingency will be a direct function of a systematic and consistent application of the selected technique.

Specific techniques selected by the physical educator should be based on the functional level of the pupil, severity of the inappropriate behavior, power of the specific reinforcer, and environmental variables. The success or failure of an operant program depends on the professional being able to effectively blend all of these variables together.

OTHER APPROACHES

Other behavior management approaches useful in physical education include the self-responsibility model, transactional analysis, reality therapy, the Foster approach, life space interviewing, assertive discipline, medication, relaxation training, and biofeedback.

The Self-Responsibility Model

Hellison (1985; Hellison & Templin, 1991) has developed a physical education model that can be utilized to help urban youth who are at risk. It is a model where the emphasis is on people and humanistic values. One of the basic premises is that self-responsibility empowers at-risk youth to take more control of their lives, to learn how to engage in self-development in the face of external forces, including socialization patterns, peer pressure, self-doubt, lack of concepts and skills, and limited vision of their own options (Hellison, 1990a, b, c). This model has been recognized by curriculum and instructional specialists as an excellent approach to teach social development, particularly self-responsibility, through physical education. The hierarchy of goals and levels of strategies in this model are the following:

- Level 0, *Irresponsibility*: Describes pupils who are unmotivated and undisciplined. Their behavior includes discrediting or making fun of other pupils, as well as interrupting, intimidating, manipulating, and verbally or physically abusing other pupils and perhaps the physical educator.
- Level 1, *Self-control:* Describes pupils who may not participate in the day's activity or show much mastery or improvement, but they are able to control their behavior enough so that they do not interfere with other pupils' right to learn or the teacher's right to teach.
- Level II, *Involvement*: Describes pupils who not only show self-control but are involved in the subject matter.
- Level III, *Self-direction*: Describes pupils

who learn to take more responsibility for their choices and for linking these choices to their own identities and are able to work without direct supervision, eventually taking responsibility for their intentions and actions.
- Level IV, *Caring:* Describes pupils who are motivated to extend their sense of responsibility by cooperating, giving support, showing concern, and helping.

Six kinds of interaction strategies can keep the levels "in front" of pupils on a regular basis (Hellison, 1985, pp. 9–10):

- *Teacher talk* simply means to explain the levels, post them, and refer to them during a teachable moment. For example, along with the rules the proper safety procedures for tumbling on the mats can be explained.
- *Modeling* attitudes and behaviors. This can be used by the teacher demonstrating waiting until the pupil is off the mat before performing a maneuver.
- *Reinforcement* is any act by the teacher that strengthens an [level-related] attitude or behavior of an individual pupil by praising the pupil or allowing free time on the apparatus.
- *Reflection time* refers to time pupils spend thinking about their attitudes and behavior in relation to the levels to allow pupils to think of reasons, while one child is allowed on the mat or apparatus at one time.
- *Student sharing* happens when pupils are asked to give their opinions about some aspect of the program or assist others in completing the skill.
- *Specific [level-related] strategies* refers to those activities that increase interaction with a specific level. For example, student contracts may help pupils operate at Level III; while reciprocal teaching, whereby pupils pair up and teach each other, may help pupils to operate at Level IV as well

as assume responsibility for safe interaction.

Transactional Analysis

Transactional analysis (TA) is a simple and easy to manage behavior management system (Harris, 1969). It is relatively free of psychological jargon, and most any professional or nonprofessional can use it. In this system, Adult/Parent/Child character transactions are represented as the essence of all human interactional behavior:

- *Adult:* Maturity and a healthy self-concept; it is the ultimate to strive for; able to focus on the best alternatives in everyday living.
- *Parent:* Teaching and commanding; interactions are closed-issue demands or requests; rules and regulations predominate.
- *Child:* Predominantly based on emotion and expression of feelings; natural curiosity is a characteristic but basically the Child character feels inferior.

The major premise of TA is that all transactions that occur within or between individuals is related to these three characters. An individual possesses all three characters, and how an individual utilizes them, verbally or nonverbally, will ultimately determine the status of his or her mental health.

Physical educators must analyze the way in which they interact with pupils. Each character could be used at different times. For example, the physical educator can function in the Parent role, particularly in situations where safety is the major consideration. The teacher then could switch to an Adult role and explain why it was not safe to do a specific activity, which is a more mature transaction. A physical educator could also function at the Child level by emitting appropriate emotions and this is appropriate. For instance, creativity and discovery activities between the physical educator and pupil should involve the interplay of all three characters with the Adult in control.

Jansma and French (1979) provide numerous guidelines for using TA in physical education settings:

1. Attempt to establish and maintain Adult transactions.
2. Demonstrate Adult behavior.
3. Assist in the transformation of pupils from a Child level to an Adult level of interaction.
4. Always be specific in discipline in relationship to a target behavior. Address the inappropriate behavior exhibited, not the pupil as a person (i.e., "You are a bad boy!").
5. Do not attempt to reason with a pupil when the pupil's Child character is in control.
6. If in doubt about giving a specific transaction, delay or eliminate it altogether.

Reality Therapy

Reality therapy (RT) is an approach to managing behaviors in school that, according to Glasser (1965, 1969), can be quickly learned and successfully applied by teachers. This approach is designed to lead pupils toward more successful dealings with the tangible and intangible aspects of the real world. RT is based on two basic human needs: the need to give and receive love and the need to have self-worth. If these two basic needs are not met, a pupil will generally resort to denial of reality and act irresponsibly. Basic steps in dealing with an inappropriate behavior are the following:

1. The educator must show that he or she cares about the pupil's behavior and wants to work with the pupil to change the behavior.

2. The pupil needs to make a value judgment and admit that the behavior needs to be changed as soon as possible.

3. The teacher and pupil commit themselves to the correction of the behavior.

4. The teacher and pupil develop a written and signed plan to correct the behavior.

5. The pupil is responsible for following the plan of action. If the plan fails, no excuses are accepted and the plan is revised.

6. The teacher confronts all irresponsible behavior that may occur until a successful plan of action results in the elimination of the inappropriate behavior and a responsible behavior is achieved.

Jansma (1980) presents numerous guidelines for physical educators who would like to consider RT in their classes. Here are some of the guidelines:

1. Attempts should be made to involve pupils who are loners by using such techniques as partners, squads, and teams.

2. Incorporate relevant physical activities into classes that apply to future living, such as fitness development and maintenance.

3. Social and emotional development must be a part of the physical education program.

4. Provide successful experiences.

5. Provide social problem-solving meetings and open-ended discussions.

6. Provide the appropriate model of responsible behavior.

7. Do not allow pupils who are disabled to let their disability be an excuse for irresponsibility.

8. Encourage coeducation, interracial, and mainstreamed physical and motor activities.

9. Comparison between different pupils' level of performance is not allowed.

10. Attempt to relate physical education to other curricular subjects to enhance relevancy in education and to life.

The Foster Approach

Foster has made a significant contribution to managing the behavior of minority pupils who are disadvantaged in his cogent and graphic book *Ribbin', Jivin', and Playin' the Dozens* (1974). The importance of such a contribution is further increased by the fact that desegregation of U.S. schools has resulted in considerably more interaction between white teachers and black pupils.

Foster offers many suggestions for white teachers to combat street corner behavior that will allow these teachers to gain a perspective about the differences between traditional white and black cultures. Among his suggestions and insights are the following:

1. Teachers must become cognizant of the different rules with which pupils who are disadvantaged were brought up (e.g., authority figures must be tough, physical and unshaken in confrontations; blacks respect this). Teachers must be in charge in order to create a relaxed atmosphere in which to learn; otherwise the pupils will be in control primarily via the use of fear and intimidation tactics.

2. Pupils must be allowed to save face in a confrontation and teachers must stay "cool."

3. Awareness and understanding of the black jive lexicon (vocabulary) is important for all teachers if open lines of healthy communication are desired. This vocabulary can also change from time to time and from place to place; the teacher must keep current. Such terms as "ribbin'," "shuckin'," "jivin'," "woofing," "signifying," "the dozens," and "working game" are clearly illustrated in Foster's work.

Life Space Interviewing

Life space interviewing (LSI) is a psycho-educational approach that may be especially helpful to a physical educator who has pupils who engage in behavioral outbursts. LSI is nonjudgmental, presents immediate concrete consequences, encourages a casual and polite "interview" atmosphere between the teacher and pupil(s), does not dwell on "why?", encourages listening on the part of the "therapist," requires teacher objectivity, and assumes that pupils can responsibly confront their problem. In the use of LSI, a teacher could be viewed as a social and behavioral traffic cop or umpire (Redl, 1959).

Assertive Discipline

Based on the writing of Canter and Canter in their *Assertive Discipline* (1976), this model describes how teachers can deal with pupil conflict. According to Wolfgang and Glickman (1986), pupils themselves will respond to conflict in a nonassertive, hostile, or assertive manner. In turn, for physical educators, the use of assertive discipline may be helpful for problem behaviors in the classroom and is compatible with other approaches to initiate new behaviors or eliminate inappropriate behaviors.

As one application, a nonassertive physical educator may plead with pupils not to swear or to complete their run around the gymnasium, whereas a hostile physical educator may respond in the same situation by verbally reprimanding pupils to just run and shut their mouths. As an alternative, the assertive physical educator would say, "Watch your language; we are all going to run and then begin the activity." The tone is nonjudgmental, but alerts the pupils to the fact that the language is inappropriate and the task to be completed is running.

Fernandez-Balboa (1990) indicates some steps to help physical educators use the assertive discipline approach:

Teacher Feelings

1. Describe the behavior nonjudgmentally.

2. Do not react to strong feelings but express feelings in relation to the behavior.

3. Deal with pupils' feelings, as well as actions.

4. Define the effects of pupil behaviors on others.

5. Designate future expectations for pupils' behavior.

6. Establish consequences for behavior and encourage positive responses for appropriate behavior.

Implementation

1. Compare a pupil's behavior to herself or himself to decrease resentment and do not ridicule the pupil.

2. Express feelings based on the behavior exhibited and do not blame pupils (e.g., I am upset because you continue to swear).

3. Allow pupils to express feelings, emotions and ask questions regarding how they feel or look (e.g., you look unhappy or frustrated).

4. Allow pupils to see the effects of their behavior on others or the class. Allow them to set standards for beginning an activity (e.g., everyone is quiet).

5. As pupils mature it is not unreasonable to delineate expectations (e.g., by the end of 6 weeks you should be able to complete this task independently).

6. Utilize behavioral principles that serve to initiate or develop appropriate behaviors, as well as eliminate inappropriate responses.

Medication

Numerous maladaptive behaviors can be managed with the use of specific medications. In fact, medication is the most common medical intervention for behavior disorders (Cullinan, Epstein, & Lloyd, 1983). This form of intervention is generally used as a temporary adjunctive technique and sometimes is not the only or even the primary treatment.

The physical educator must always remember that medications only reduce the probability of existing behaviors in a pupil's repertoire; they do not teach new behaviors. In addition, although a social-emotional behavior may be managed, the side effects of medication must also be considered. Several of the more commonly used medications not only impair cognitive functioning but also hinder physical performance.

Relaxation Training

As indicated throughout this book, the movement associated with training in fitness, fundamental motor skills, aquatics, dance, and games has its obvious place in the education of all pupils. However, aside from the various benefits of movement-oriented activities, nonmovement activities can also assist the child who is medicated, tense, or hyperactive. It is a skill to move, but it is also a skill not to move (Koehler, 1987).

Numerous relaxation techniques have been developed to serve essentially the same purpose through different methods. Their common aim is to use neuromuscular relaxation methods to manage inappropriate behavior by reducing nervousness and controlling muscular activity. The methods to achieve this purpose can be placed on a continuum from those that basically eliminate mental suggestion to those in which imagery is an integral component. Four basic techniques that can be used by physical educa-

tors are discussed here: The Jacobson technique, hatha yoga, Rathbone's relaxation method, and Yates's relaxation technique. In using any of these techniques, the instructor can facilitate relaxation by making sure there is plenty of fresh air and the room temperature is between 60° and 70° F, using dim lights in a quiet environment, speaking in a slightly slower than normal rate using words that reflect a relaxed state, and checking for a relaxed state, including slow/deep breathing and relaxed facial expression (Ballinger & Heine, 1991).

Jacobson's Conscious Relaxation Method. In the 1920s and 1930s, Jacobson developed the "progressive relaxation" procedure to help people learn to be sensitive to residual tension in the skeletal muscles. In this method, you learn to contract specific muscle groups and then to relax them. Jacobson does not emphasize imagery (imagining), particularly imagery of action, because muscles are engaged in the act imagined. Visual imagery is included at the end of some lessons, but only as a means of testing the level of relaxation that can be maintained.

A specific series of exercises has been incorporated into lessons for children and adults (Jacobson, 1944). The exercises are similar for the two groups, but those for children are presented at a much slower pace. Examples of the relaxation activities are given in Table 13.4. Practice begins with the extremities and then moves to the head and neck, followed by the trunk. Each exercise is generally performed three to four times in succession; an exception is made for breathing exercises. It takes approximately two to three months of daily practice to learn to relax properly through this technique.

In progressive relaxation, adults assume a comfortable lying position in order to perform the activities. Because pupils do not lie down in the course of their routines,

TABLE 13.4 RELAXATION EXERCISES

MOVEMENT	SUGGESTED INSTRUCTIONS
Lower Body	
Dorsiflexion of ankle joints	Bend up the feet. Pull Hard! And let go.
Plantar-flexion of ankle-joints	Push the feet down as far as you can. Push harder! And slacken off the muscles completely.
Inversion of the feet	Turn in the feet strongly. Further! And let them go.
Extension of knee and hip joints	Straighten the knees as much as possible. Now press the legs down into the mattress. Hard! Harder! And flop out.
Adduction of hip joints	Straighten the knees again. Press the legs together as tightly as you can. Grip hard! Hard!! And let the legs roll apart.
Arms, Wrists, and Hands	
Extension of fingers and wrist joints	Straighten the fingers and pull back the wrists. Pull hard! Harder than that! And let go.
Flexion of fingers, wrist, and elbow joints	Bend up the fingers and wrists. Now bend the elbows fully. A bit more! Put every ounce of effort into it! And let the muscles slacken off.
Extension of elbow joints and fingers, with adduction of shoulder joints	Straighten the fingers and elbows, and press the arms against the sides. Hard! Keep them there! And let them fall apart.
Head and Neck	
Rotation	Shut the eyes. Now roll the head slowly from side to side. It's heavy and it's rolling easily from side to side. Now stop, with the face turned forward, and rest.
Flexion	Lift the head about an inch off the mattress. Hold that position! And let the head drop back again.
Extension	Press the head back against the mattress strongly. Harder than that! And slacken off the muscles.
Temporal-mandibular joints and facial muscles	Clench the teeth together. Now "screw up" the facial muscles very tightly. Tighter! And relax.
Trunk	
Abdominal muscles	Pull in the abdominal muscles until they are quite flat. Pull a bit more! And rest.
Extensor muscles of the spine	Push the chest forward until you have hollowed the back strongly. Lift a little more! And let go.
Respiratory muscles	
(i) Very deep breathing	Breathe in and out as deeply as possible. In. And out. Force the breathing! Deeply in. And deeply out!
(ii) Deep breathing	Now slacken off the breathing, and breathe in and out more easily. In. And out. And in. And out.
(iii) Normal breathing	Breathe quite normally now, and follow your breathing movements with your thoughts. Concentrate on the breathing and put everything else out of your mind.

Source: Adapted from J. H. C. Colson, *Postural and Relaxation Training in Physio-Therapy and Physical Education,* 2nd ed. (London: William Heineman Medical Books, Ltd., 1968). Used by permission.

Jacobson has modified this method to facilitate relaxation as much as possible while activities are performed (Jacobson, 1944). This is called differential relaxation rather than progressive relaxation. In progressive relaxation, the goal is generalized conscious relaxation, whereas the goal of differential relaxation involves localized conscious relaxation. The training is basically the same for both; however, progressive relaxation occurs in a supine lying position and differential relaxation is conducted in a sitting position or in whatever position the individual assumes in a particular activity. The purpose is to reduce the effort and tension of those parts of the body that are not directly involved in the activity.

Cratty (1969) states that techniques such as conscious relaxation are a promising beginning in developing activities to manage specific inappropriate behavior. This assertion is supported by numerous testimonies sent to Jacobson by teachers who stated that the techniques can effectively quiet pupils in class and reduce behavior problems.

Hatha Yoga. Yoga is a system of physical and mental exercises developed to achieve physical and spiritual health. The basic idea of yoga originated nearly 7,000 years ago. Yoga has five major branches: karma, bhakti, jnana, raja, and hatha. Of the five, only hatha yoga has been widely accepted in the United States. It is the branch that includes the science of health and physical education.

Through hatha yoga, tension can be removed and hyperactive behavior decreased. Tension has been described as a tightness or a squeezing of the body mentally, emotionally, and physically. Yoga can effect decontraction and stop such squeezing (Hittleman, 1967). Children who have participated in hatha yoga programs have shown decreased hyperactive behavior and increased task concentration (Seiler & Renshaw, 1978).

Hatha yoga involves postures (asanas) and breath control (pranayama). These postures are usually assumed two to four times a week for a 30-minute period. Breath control consists of deep inhalation, retention of breath, and exhalation of breath. Breath control is also an integral component of all postures.

Rathbone's Relaxation Method. Rathbone (1969) contends that a comprehensive relaxation program should include not only Jacobson's techniques but also rhythmical exercises that are not too strenuous, exercises that involve moving the joints through a full range of motion, and tension-release exercises for the breathing mechanism. The rhythmical exercises include activities for the arms, legs, and trunk. Some of the activities are the following:

1. *Arms.* Slowly swing forward, sideward, and in circles, both clockwise and counterclockwise.
2. *Legs.* While sitting on the edge of a table, alternate swinging legs forward and backward and side to side in unison.
3. *Trunk.* With hands on head in a supine lying position, slowly roll from back to front; standing against wall with feet a few inches from the wall, bend at the hips and let arms droop, then sway from side to side.

Numerous exercises can be used to increase controlled behavior and the flexibility of joints. All exercises are conducted slowly and maintained in stretch position for 20 to 30 seconds. A sampling of some other exercises that Rathbone presents includes:

1. Sitting with legs crossed, push knee down by steady hand pressure.
2. Standing with hips against a wall and feet 4 inches away from the wall and approximately 18 to 20 inches apart, bend forward from the trunk and loosely hang the hands and head.

3. Standing on one foot, with the other foot straight and forward on a chair, attempt to place the head on the knee of the leg on the chair.

A relaxed diaphragm is very important for people who are usually tense. Some exercises recommended by Rathbone involve the individual lying on the back with knees bent and feet on the floor. The person takes a deep breath and then forces the air out through his or her mouth. Another exercise from the same position involves the change in thoracic and abdominal pressure caused by inhaling and filling the upper chest area, then forcing the pressure against the diaphragm, pushing the abdomen out, and retracting the abdomen while enlarging the upper chest. The last step involves a quick complete exhalation through the mouth.

Yates's Relaxation Method. Yates (1946) has developed a method of conscious relaxation called the association-set technique. It is designed to enhance a person's ability to control emotional actions and reactions by releasing neuromuscular hypertension. The first step in this procedure is to select a key word that represents a relaxed state to the person. "Calm" is chosen frequently; physical educators might also use the word "melt." Then the individual assumes a lying or sitting position with eyes closed, similar to the Jacobson technique. Muscle contraction is not used; only the tension release is used. Yates eliminated muscle contraction because she believed that overall relaxation can be attained much faster that way. When the person is relaxed, the key word is verbally associated with restful scenes. The person then imagines the scenes.

In conclusion, remember that relaxation training is not a panacea. The only claim it can make is that it may be successful in decreasing inappropriate behavior, reducing excessive psychological tension, and controlling muscular activity. The goal of relaxation training is self-control. The training may be ineffective or greatly impaired if a child has neurological lesions or behavioral disorders so severe that he or she cannot control the body or mind (Schade, 1948).

Biofeedback

Biofeedback is utilized to assist individuals control such physiological processes as muscle tension, heart rate, and blood pressure. By immediate biological feedback, individuals may be able to learn to cope behaviorally with their environment by keeping their physiological processes within safe limitations. This technique involves the use of instruments that provide the individual immediate feedback of the functioning level of specific biological processes. With this information one can begin to self-regulate these functions by incorporating techniques such as visual imagery.

The application of biofeedback in physical education to offset the high incidence of psychogenic pathology of some pupils has been suggested by Gallagher (1975). First, though, the effectiveness of this promising technique must be tested by substantial research. If it proves viable, physical educators through preservice or in-service training can develop the specific knowledge and skills to implement biofeedback in school settings.

The Educational Team Approach

Imagine parents' reactions to finding out that their child has a disability. After the initial shock, the questions come: Who can help? How soon? What's the first step? How can I help? The child may be asking questions, too. Is there something wrong with me? Who will help me? Will I have to leave my school-friends? Answers to these and other school-related questions can be found through an educational team approach.

As a growing number of children with disabilities are being identified in schools, more of them are appearing in regular and special physical education classes. As a result, physical educators are being charged with additional responsibilities and being asked to function professionally with others on an educational team for the benefit of children who are disabled.

THE IMPORTANCE OF A TEAM APPROACH

The changing role of regular and special physical educators necessitates assistance from and communication with other members of the school staff and, at times, professionals outside the school. These interactions make appropriate identification, placement, instructional programming, and evaluation of each pupil with a disability possible. In essence, an ongoing functional team of professionals from many fields is needed to address any pupil's special educational need(s).

There are a number of good reasons to use an educational team approach. First, a regular class teacher (such as a physical educator) cannot be expected to be a jack of all trades.

No one teacher knows or can hope to know how to teach within all areas of development for all pupils at all levels of functioning. For example, as a general rule, regular physical educators typically do not have the skills needed to effectively manage and teach pupils who are physically disabled. Second, the more special needs a pupil has, the greater is the number of experts required to address those needs. Third, there is usually a pool of expertise within and outside the school that should be available to each teacher. The team provides a structure in which these professionals can work. And perhaps most importantly, the more input obtained regarding a pupil's instructional needs, the better each teacher can individualize for those needs. In the end, the pupil will benefit.

Given all this, some critical questions arise. What, specifically, is this educational team approach and what is its purpose? Who is on the team? Are there any collateral benefits or issues associated with participation on an educational team? In this chapter we attempt to answer these questions.

The educational team approach refers to a joining of forces and group interaction among professionals and, at times, paraprofessionals and nonprofessionals in order to test, assess, plan, implement, evaluate, and follow up instructional programs for targeted pupils who have or are suspected of having special needs. The team operates on an ongoing basis as needs arise, from the moment of identification all the way through program follow-up. Mutual respect and open lines of communication among team members are essential (see Figure 14.1).

The educational team approach replaces the traditional self-contained approach where each teacher is responsible for all instruction-

FIGURE 14.1   An educational team in action.

related activities. The educational team is not just a child's IEP committee. The IEP committee is limited in membership and is formed only to write an approved plan of action for a child who is disabled. The educational team is a pool of all related experts, inside and outside of school, who can meet as often as needed during the academic year to serve the pupil with a disability.

The educational team can have as many members as needed, ranging from the regular classroom teacher to the physical education teacher to various support personnel from outside the school and finally to the parents and the pupil (where appropriate). Figure 14.2 diagrams the general membership and overall functions of an educational team. This broad cadre of members presents a vast variety of resources that can be used to affect all of a pupil's school experiences, not just in-class activities. Most schools can employ or in some other manner obtain the assistance of most of the personnel types listed in Figure 14.2, though some schools probably are still not taking full advantage of these human resources.

Note particularly that regular and special physical education teachers are, and should be, integral members of any educational team. In addition, theirs is not a one-way role in which they only receive information from others on the team. Membership on the team connotes a reciprocal relationship among all team members. For example, when information related to a pupil's physical education is required, the appropriate individual from whom to obtain that information is obviously the trained physical educator.

A number of side benefits result for the physical educator (and others) from participation on an educational team. Camaraderie among the school staff and the morale of all school personnel can be enhanced because of the involvement of educational teams. As a result, physical educators may interact more with others within the school and become increasingly more knowledgeable and interested in their colleagues' areas of talent. In

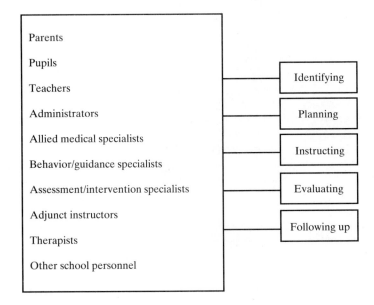

FIGURE 14.2   The educational team's general membership and functions.

addition, if some of the team's members are personnel from outside the school, valuable contacts are made between the school and community. Two possible valuable community resources for the physical educator are a recreation center and volunteer assistance. Team members may also be challenged to keep up with changes within their specialization because they need to know answers when another team member asks questions. As team members respond to this challenge, a domino or multiplier effect can take over. Again, this can only benefit pupils with special needs.

TYPES OF EDUCATIONAL TEAMS

There are two basic types of educational teams. The most common is contained within a school. In this closed system, referrals, testing, program planning, implementation, evaluation, and follow-up all take place within the school. For example, if a physical educator has a pupil with a medical problem, a referral is made to the school nurse. The nurse, in turn, seeks advice from the on-staff school physician and perhaps a physical therapist or occupational therapist. The pupil's parents may also be asked to cooperate with these team members. Key personnel within the school then meet to exchange information and ideas. During the implementation of the plan of action, there is continued dialogue concerning the pupil's medical progress.

The second type of educational team functions both in and outside a school. It is an open system and is usually used for pupils with more serious disabilities. School personnel attempt to seek outside assistance to deal with a child whose problem was originally found at the school. Take, for example, a school located near a major university that has diagnostic clinics that provide specialized educational testing and psychological

and pediatric services. The neighborhood school has a pupil who needs a full battery of orthopedic tests because the teachers suspect a serious physical disability. The specific problem and a solution to it cannot be determined by school personnel alone, and the physical educator particularly has requested immediate outside support. The school principal finds a clinic physician to join the team. The team members then pool their resources to discover the root of the pupil's problem; the child is evaluated at the clinic as well as at the school on functional tasks. The team then meets again to devise an instructional strategy during only one or two joint meetings at the school. To fulfill their role on the team, the regular classroom and physical education teachers agree to implement and evaluate the new plan of action. The clinic physician is placed on alert to follow up with additional diagnostic-prescriptive services, if and when warranted.

Educational teams, whether closed or open, can function in different ways during the identification, placement, instructional, evaluation, and follow-up processes. The multidisciplinary, interdisciplinary, and transdisciplinary team models (Hart, 1977; McCormick & Goldman, 1979; Sirvis, 1978) describe three types of functional relationships within educational teams. The important role of the special physical educator in each model is emphasized by Lavay and French (1985).

Multidisciplinary Teams

The focus of the multidisciplinary thrust is on initial testing, assessing, and planning for pupils with disabilities by various team members. In this approach, a team of experts from different disciplines is summoned by one teacher (such as a physical educator). The team is designed to pinpoint educational, psychological, or medical problems and to offer recommendations regarding a specific pupil whom the teacher has determined to be in need of special or additional services. The teacher makes the initial referral for assistance and then each team member, in turn, works with the pupil separately in order to test, assess, and plan within his or her specialty. The referring teacher is given the results (usually in a written report) by each member of the team and is then left to put the recommendations into practice. Usually there is little or no initial dialogue concerning test results and recommendations, and there is no ongoing feedback beyond the initial assessment and planning effort. The teacher is more or less left alone to deal with the recommendations.

Interdisciplinary Teams

The interdisciplinary educational team approach has all the elements of the multidisciplinary approach, but the specialists actually meet with the primary teacher to discuss their test results and recommendations. The face-to-face meeting helps control fragmentation and resolves misinterpretation and conflicts over the initial programming. Yet, when the recommendations are actually implemented, the referring teacher is again left alone. As in the multidisciplinary approach, there is no feedback on ongoing programming. The person who often has the least influence in a school (the teacher) must carry out the recommendations, some of which may call for clout on his or her part. Consequently, some of the recommendations may not be addressed, even if they are high priority.

Transdisciplinary Teams

The transdisciplinary educational team approach involves all of the elements of the interdisciplinary approach, but prompts on-going dialogue with, and feedback from, team specialists for the teacher. This provides consistent expert assistance in the actual implementation of team recommendations and evaluation of implementation strategies. The team, therefore, functions as a whole throughout the remedial process, with the teacher and pupil consistently being the center of attention. In contrast to the other two models, the transdisciplinary approach provides a more equitable distribution of responsibilities. Another advantage is that, at times, specialists can come into the pupil's regular class to provide special services without having to remove the child from class. This has come to be known as the integrated model of transdisciplinary programming. Another aspect of the integrated component is that specialists can be a source of continual in-service training for the regular teacher, and vice versa. They share their knowledge. In addition, child movement time from class to class is decreased, which adds to instructional time and the cohesiveness of overall services. We highly recommend it as the most effective educational approach to teaching pupils with disabilities.

The transdisciplinary model is the one in which most dialogue among professionals is possible. However, dialogue is a skill not automatically mastered. You must not assume, particularly at the start of any program, that the presence of several people at a meeting means a dialogue will take place. All members need to know techniques of open communication (including listening) to enhance communication and mutual respect among team members. The effort will pay off in large dividends in pupil progress. Figure 14.3 diagrams transdisciplinary team function.

Related to the transdisciplinary team concept is an increasing interest in collaboration among educators for the benefit of all pupils, including those with disabilities and those

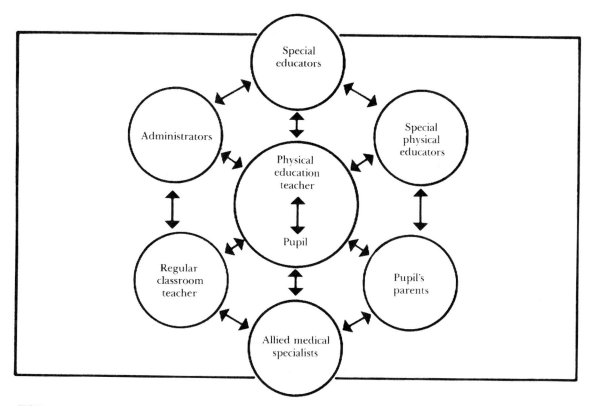

FIGURE 14.3 A model of the transdisciplinary team.

who are not disabled. In fact, "collaboration" is the buzzword for the futurists' view of the effective school beyond the year 2000 (Benjamin, 1989). Evidence of this is the current emphasis on keeping "challenging" pupils in the regular classroom through the efforts of intervention assistance teams, known by other titles as mainstream assistance teams or teacher assistance teams. These teams attempt to confront educational and behavioral pupil problems on the spot, using all the resources available in the school building, so that referrals to special education can be avoided and success in the regular classroom realized by any targeted pupil. Detailed descriptions of this assistance model, along with related research, can be found in publications from the Ohio Department of Education (1988, 1990) and in Fuchs, Fuchs, and Bahr (1990). We believe that all schools can benefit from assistance teams of this nature.

TEAM MEMBERS AND ROLES

Parents

The parents (or other primary caretakers) of a pupil with a disability should be considered potential members of any educational team because they probably know more about the child than anyone else on the team and because communication between the school and the home is so crucial. Too often in the past, all decisions concerning a child's educational program were determined only by school personnel. Parent input was typically not even sought, and parents were considered obstacles to programming. Public law 101-476 designated parents as integral members of their child's individualized educational program or individualized family service plan team, and their ideas and approval must be obtained.

In addition, parents are a valuable resource for regular and special physical educators in planning a child's everyday program at school (Henderson & French, 1992). They can serve as very effective classroom aides for the physical educator and should not be ignored as such an important hands-on resource (Folsom-Meek, 1984). Further, the best possible program for a child who requires considerable remedial work can be realized by extending the school program into his or her home where, again, parents can be a most valuable resource (see Figure 14.4). Physical education homework is to be encouraged in order to accomplish educational goals more effectively and efficiently. The only way to accomplish this is to form an ongoing bond between parents and school personnel.

Teachers

Regular Classroom Teacher. Any teacher, including a physical educator, who teaches in a traditional classroom is included here.

FIGURE 14.4 Physical education homework with parental teamwork. *(Ken Karp)*

Even though most regular teachers have not had sufficient training to teach pupils with disabilities, they should be considered resources for each other if a particular pupil needs special attention.

Unfortunately, regular teachers are sometimes expected, unrealistically, to do a little of everything with respect to pupil teaching and management, even for a pupil with a disability. Table 14.1 outlines their all-encompassing role, along with the roles of all potential team members. The receipt of a case study workup is one classic cause of teacher frustration. Many of these workups typically fail to include understandable data on a pupil's present level of performance and whether or not this information was obtained in-house or from an outside specialist. To assist the regular classroom teacher, a transdisciplinary approach is recommended.

Special Physical Educator. Special physical education is a primary educational service according to P.L. 101-476. A special physical educator could have a remedial/corrective, adapted, or developmental orientation (see Chapter 1). He or she could be employed full time or hired to serve as an itinerant teacher serving a number of schools. The remedial or corrective specialist is one who is trained to teach pupils both posture education and body mechanics through exercises. This professional, like the regular physical educator, is interested in physical fitness and lifetime activities, but also believes that posture education and body mechanics should be a permanent part of physical education programs. Posture education is provided for those recuperating from injuries and recovering from disabling diseases and as a preventive measure. The adapted physical educator concentrates on providing a diversified program of developmental activities, games, sports, and rhythms for those pupils who require special programs or adaptations within a regular class. The developmental physical educator's relationship to the regular physical educator focuses on mutual planning in order to develop needed fitness and gross motor abilities in selected pupils.

In all states special physical educators are certified to teach regular physical education. Beyond this, certification, endorsement, validation, or licensure in special physical education itself is available and required in only a minority of the 50 states. (This may change soon due to national certification efforts by the National Consortium for Physical Education and Recreation for Individuals with Disabilities.) Other unique characteristics of special physical educators include their stress on observable and measurable physical skills; their work with pupils having *any* type of disabling condition; and their emphasis on a combination of group and one-on-one teaching (with an emphasis on small group).

Special physical educators have other titles in certain localities. For example, in Ohio, the special physical educator is referred to as the physical development specialist in schools administered by the County Boards of Mental Retardation and Developmental Disabilities. In California, all special physical educators, no matter what orientation, are referred to as adapted physical educators.

Special Educator. The traditional role of the special educator has been as a teacher of children with disabilities in a self-contained classroom or special school. The special educator is responsible for conducting a program of education similar to the regular class program but presumably tailored for children with special needs. The special educator has, unrealistically, been expected to be an expert in such areas as psychoeducational testing, behavior modification strategies, perceptual-motor training, auditory discrimination training, visual perception improvement, tutor-

TABLE 14.1   SPECIFIC TEAM MEMBERS AND FUNCTIONS

	BEHAVIOR MANAGEMENT	MEDICAL/HEALTH ASSISTANCE	PSYCHOMOTOR INTERVENTION	ENVIRONMENTAL MANAGEMENT	ADMINISTRATIVE ASSISTANCE	TESTING/ASSESSING ASSISTANCE	PROGRAM PLANNING ASSISTANCE	PROGRAM IMPLEMENTATION ASSISTANCE	PROGRAM EVALUATION ASSISTANCE	FAMILY ASSISTANCE
Parents	X	X	X	X		X		X	X	
Teachers										
Regular classroom teacher	X	X	X	X	X	X	X	X	X	X
Special physical educator	X	X	X	X	X	X	X	X	X	X
Special educator	X	X	X	X	X	X	X	X	X	X
Administrators										
Principal	X	X		X	X				X	X
Director of pupil personnel					X					X
Superintendent of schools					X				X	X
Allied medical specialists										
School physician		X				X	X			X
School nurse		X	X		X	X	X	X	X	X
Occupational therapist	X	X	X			X	X	X	X	X
Physical therapist	X	X	X			X	X	X	X	X
Behavioral/guidance specialist										
School psychologist	X			X		X	X		X	X
Social worker	X	X		X	X	X	X	X	X	X
Behavior modification specialist	X			X		X	X	X	X	X
Guidance counselor	X				X	X	X		X	X
Adjunct instructors										
Peer tutor (pupil)	X		X	X				X	X	X
Volunteer	X	X	X	X	X			X	X	
Teacher aide	X	X	X	X	X			X	X	
Therapists										
Dance therapist	X		X			X	X	X	X	X
Music therapist	X		X			X	X	X	X	X
Art therapist	X		X			X	X	X	X	X
Therapeutic recreation specialist	X		X			X	X	X	X	X
Other School Personnel										
Educational/curriculum specialist			X		X	X	X		X	X
Speech/language pathologist						X	X	X	X	X
Audiologist		X				X	X	X	X	X
Librarian	X	X	X	X			X		X	
Dietician		X					X			X
Coach	X	X	X							X
Custodian				X	X					
Clerical staff member				X	X					

ing, group instruction, remedial reading, corrective arithmetic, handwriting, writing behavioral objectives, developing units of instruction, and planning highly individualized instruction.

In a number of states, special educators are also required to teach physical education, even though they are not trained in that discipline. Where certified regular and special physical educators are employed, there is a much greater opportunity to meet the needs of pupils with disabilities, particularly within the psychomotor domain. The special educator and physical educator can and should be encouraged to consult with each other about a pupil's ongoing gross motor, fitness, play, posture, and perceptual-motor needs.

Administrators

Principal. As the highest-ranking official within a specific school, the school principal is in a key position to affect immediate changes. Teachers and other staff members have a closer direct link to the principal than to the district superintendent, so the principal can provide direct, efficient, and effective assistance.

Even though the district (under the superintendent's jurisdiction) controls funds overall, most schools have some autonomy to spend their allotments as they see fit. The principal of a school is the person who should ultimately be, and usually is, the last hurdle in a funding request. The principal can be the ally of physical education if requests from physical educators are tactfully persistent, justified, timely, and well written. Administrative support of this type will enhance the function of any educational team.

Director of Pupil Personnel. The director of pupil personnel, who may also be known as the director of special services or director of special education, is the district-level ad-

ministrator responsible for delivering many services as well as accompanying administrative duties. Services commonly under the jurisdiction of the director of pupil personnel include school counseling, school psychology, social work, medical and health service delivery, special education, reading services, speech therapy, pupil testing, and pupil attendance. Knowledge of budgets is another key area of responsibility. The selection/retention of staff and fiscal management are the main responsibilities of the director of pupil personnel. The responsibilities of this position can also be subsumed within the role of superintendent of schools, depending on district organization and number of pupils within the system.

The director could affect the physical educator directly by hiring, evaluating programs, maintaining up-to-date information on pupils that could be used for research or funding, placing pupils in particular classes, controlling requisitions for equipment, and making decisions related to the building structure and the school's operating budget. Indirectly, the director selects and hires specialists, which could affect the number of resources available to the physical educator, and can contact community organizations that may be able to facilitate requests or gather pertinent information needed by the physical educator.

Superintendent of Schools. A school superintendent is the highest-ranking official and generally the most visible person within a school district. This person is the chief executive officer of a board of education in an operating local education agency or school district. He or she is accountable to the district's school board, the citizens of the district, the pupils enrolled in the school district, and to all paid and unpaid school personnel throughout the district.

Even though a physical educator does not usually have a direct link to the school district's superintendent (or even the assistant superintendent), it is obvious that this is the person to get to know. Unfortunately, the larger the school district, the more difficult this becomes.

The superintendent has the power to make any decision related to school policy, hiring/firing, purchasing, and other vital areas. Even though a person on the school district staff might be immediately responsible for certain decisions (e.g., an equipment funding decision by the director of pupil personnel), the superintendent may, and will, step in to decide matters as needed and as appropriate. The superintendent's influence and power, therefore, indirectly and directly affect the everyday operation of all teachers in the district.

Allied Medical Specialists

School Physician. The school physician plays a critical role in any program of physical education. His or her support and backing are essential for a quality program. The initial screening and assignment of pupils to special physical education are generally conducted by the regular or special physical educator along with the school physician. They should also make the final judgment on when pupils return to the regular physical education class. During the program, the school physician may be called on to do further tests on pupils or to refer them to other medical specialists for examination. In collaboration with the regular or special physical educator, these referrals may result in recommendations for change in the pupils' exercise or activity programs.

In addition, the school physician may serve on the school district's advisory committee, where he or she has the ultimate responsibility for admitting pupils into programs and adjusting pupils' schedules related to various school offerings, including physical education. The school physician can

specifically enhance the school's physical education program in the following ways:

1. Interpret the program to private physicians in the district, to parents, to pupils, and to the school staff.
2. Make referrals of pupils with special problems.
3. Fully inform the special or regular physical educator of pupils' medical conditions and recommend exercises and intensity level of activities for each pupil in collaboration with the physical education specialist.

School Nurse. The school nurse, as an integral member of the school health team, delivers direct health services to pupils; serves as a health counselor for the school; and is the medical liaison among school personnel, parents, and the school physician. The school nurse is considered the major link in school program continuity by acting not only as a family-centered professional but as a leader of nurses, a community health planning specialist, and a user of epidemiological techniques for assessment of problems within a school population.

The school nurse can be an invaluable team member to the physical educator in such specific areas as accessibility to medical case histories, in-service training related to a unique medical condition or disease, referral flow for pupils with disabilities, assistance with first aid, scheduling pupils for medical examinations, conferring with pupils and their parents, and acting as an advocate for the physical educator when programming and outright excuses from physical education class become topics of concern.

Occupational Therapist. For decades, occupational therapy has been defined as allied medicine's art and science of directing human participation in selected tasks to restore, reinforce, and enhance performance, facilitate learning of those skills and functions essential for adaptation and productivity, diminish or correct pathology, and to promote and maintain health. Its fundamental concern is a lifetime of satisfactorily performing those tasks and roles essential to productive living and to the mastery of self and the environment (American Occupational Therapy Association, 1972). Stated differently, using the American Occupational Therapy Association's more current viewpoint, occupational therapy is the "therapeutic use of self-care, work and play activities to increase independent function, enhance development, and prevent disability. May include adaptation of task or environment to achieve maximum independence and to enhance quality of life" (1986, p. 852).

Even though these definitions are quite broad, to a large extent occupational therapy stresses the clinical training of manual skills that enhance the productive independent living of clients/pupils representing a variety of disabling conditions. The hands-on work of occupational therapists is sometimes completed in conjunction with a physical therapist at a special school, clinic, or medical or psychiatric hospital. Occupational therapists are also typically certified by their national organization. In contrast to physical therapists, the work of the occupational therapist is not always directed by a medical doctor's prescription; it often centers on sensory integrative techniques (Ayres, 1972).

The main difference between the roles of the physical educator and occupational therapist is that terminal goals in physical education are limited to participation in lifetime fitness activities, recreation, and athletics, whereas in occupational therapy, the goal points toward better living generally and skills essential to that end. Such differences in the roles of the occupational therapist and the physical educator are also evident in P.L. 101-476, which specifies physical education as a primary service and occupational therapy as a related service (American Occupa-

tional Therapy Association, 1981). In addition, physical educators tend to deal with gross motor function from an educational perspective, whereas the medically oriented occupational therapist works mostly with fine motor functions of feeding, writing, and other hand and finger movements that are essential to daily living, including the world of work. Their fine and gross motor stress in programming work-related skills often concentrates on upper body function. Professionals from these two disciplines should work closely because their functions are often very related (Jansma, 1993).

Physical Therapist. Physical therapy is recognized as a related service in P.L. 101-476. Physical therapists are typically certified by their national organization, have a medical orientation, often focusing on neurodevelopmental techniques (Bobath & Bobath, 1964), are always directed by a medical specialist's prescription (usually a physiatrist or orthopedist), and concentrate on clients/pupils with physical disabilities. These professionals provide clinical service(s) to adults and pupils primarily in the area of overall neuromusculoskeletal function (in contrast to the occupational therapist's stress on the upper body). A physical therapist is involved in the evaluation of a pupil's physical function (including analysis of reflex development, range of motion, gait, and body part measurements) and prescribes and implements programs directly or on a consultation basis in hospitals, clinics, or schools. Common concerns of the physical therapist include handling and positioning, as well as developing independent use of wheelchairs, prostheses, and orthotic devices such as crutches and braces (Jansma, 1993). The adaptive equipment that they use (Campbell, Green, & Carlson, 1977), consisting of such items as prone boards, bolsters, tumble forms, Bobath balls, and wedges, are in contrast to the use or adaptation of standard equipment (adapted equipment) characteristic of special physical educators.

One simple way to describe a physical therapist's function is that this professional uses a hands-on approach to help a pupil or patient to stand and be mobile without assistance. As an extension, a physical educator's role could be described as helping the pupil to stay on his or her feet and remain mobile over time. This may occur after a pupil has left the hospital or clinic. The physical educator's approach is "hands-off," relative to extending a pupil's range of motion (flexibility), within an educational orientation.

Physical therapists have been serving pupils with disabilities, especially those with serious disabilities, in schools to a much larger extent since the passage of P.L. 94-142 (Connolly & Anderson, 1978). In this regard it is critical to realize that the physical educator and medical therapists do not serve the same role; each has his or her own professional identity. When a program of physical therapy or occupational therapy is prescribed, it should be in addition to a basic, ongoing program of physical education. Medical therapy should not supplant physical education; they should especially complement one another (not be competitive or duplicative) for the benefit of the pupil.

Behavioral/Guidance Specialists

School Psychologist. A school psychologist is a professional who has met special requirements for credentialing and follows the code of professional ethics specified by the National Association of School Psychologists. This educational team member uses specialized knowledge of assessment, learning, and interpersonal relationships to help school personnel (including physical educators) to enrich the experience and growth of all children and to identify and deal with children who are disabled. Numerous specific roles are assigned to the school psychologist, including behavioral and educational observing, testing, assessing, planning, implementing, following-up, referring, counseling, and monitoring. Aside from individual pupil concerns, the school psychologist can also serve in the capacity of parent counselor and community liaison and give input related to overall school function.

The work of school psychologists is, admittedly, global; however, their specialized services have direct relevance for physical educators at all levels. For example, because of the structure and function of physical education classes, these classes present an ideal setting in which a school psychologist can observe, assist, and interact with teachers and pupils. The school psychologist can directly work on emotional and social concerns, particularly for the pupil who is hard to handle.

Ancillary Educational Team Members

There are other supportive personnel whose involvement on the educational team may be necessary at times to implement a specific pupil's individual educational program. These can be grouped under several categories: behavioral/guidance specialists, adjunct instructors, therapists, and other school personnel. Information related to their varying roles is included in Table 14.1. The list of ancillary educational team members includes the following:

Behavioral/guidance specialists

- Social worker
- Behavior modification specialist
- Guidance counselor

Adjunct instructors

- Peer tutor (pupil)
- Volunteer
- Teacher aide

Therapists

- Dance therapist
- Music therapist
- Art therapist
- Therapeutic recreation specialist

Other school personnel

- Educational/curriculum specialist
- Speech/language pathologist
- Audiologist
- Librarian
- Dietitian
- Coach
- Custodian
- Clerical staff member

CURRENT ISSUES

It is all well and good to understand what an educational team should be and how it should function, but it is quite another thing to put one into operation. What follows is a brief discussion of some issues related to the educational team in actual practice, in regard in part to physical education.

Parent Education/Involvement

Parenting is one of the few specialized skill areas that does not require a formal education. Even more to the point, the parenting of a child with a disability has to be one of the most challenging tasks imaginable. Yet schools expect *both* parents to participate in parent/teacher associations, parent/teacher conferences, parent advisory councils, the child's homework, the child's individualized education program, and the child's individualized family service plan. Such input is expected because it is assumed that parents have a vested interest in their child's education and that parents know their child better than anyone else. In reality, too many parents show little or no interest in their child's education and, even more dramatic, too many parents cannot even be found.

At times, the reason for parent noninvolvement in a child's education is a fear of professionals. We can do a number of things to change this through various approaches to parent education and involvement. A few ideas include the following: parents can be called when their child is doing well (vs. the traditional discipline call), which has the potential for changing views toward the teacher who called; parents can be invited to class or to an assembly to see their child and teacher perform; parents can and should be listened to attentively by teachers if there is some information to share or some grievance to voice; and parents can be invited to form a parent group so that parent-to-parent strategies can be shared. Above all, parents must be treated as equal partners in the education of their child. If this "partnership principle" guides the treatment of parents by teachers and administrators, their fear of professionals has a reasonable chance of lessening.

Educators, including those who teach physical education, need to understand and be responsive to the difficult challenges faced by parents of a child who needs more than average assistance because of a disability. In fact, knowledgeable and involved parents can be the physical educator's strongest advocate for program continuation and growth within the school and within the community.

The Image of Physical Education

In order for a group of professionals to interact effectively in the interest of children with disabilities, they must have open channels of communication and respect for each other. These prerequisites apply to all team members, including physical educators. Physical education as a discipline, however, does not typically command the respect held by some other disciplines. There are several reasons for this discrepancy—the primary coaching interests of many regular physical educators, the "roll the ball out philosophy" held by some who purport to teach physical education, and the lack of knowledge of other educators about the nature of physical education and its rightful place in the school.

Special physical educators are not immune to the image problems of the field of physical education and, therefore, many sometimes face the reality of a questionable image when they first attempt to function on an educational team. It might be prudent to make a conscientious effort to inform school staff members about the function of special physical education, perhaps even before the first team meeting, through written information, dialogue, or actual demonstration of skills in the classroom, gymnasium, pool, or playground. Toward that same end, educational team members (e.g., the special physical educator and physical therapist) could even share offices. An important guideline to follow during this whole process is that actions speak louder than words.

Once functioning on an actual team of professionals, the special physical educator should try to contribute consistently to the accomplishment of team goals without being overbearing. Once communication channels are open and mutual respect is established, the physical educator will no doubt find any potential image problems to be eliminated. Of course, some of those who teach physical education to children with disabilities will not face this image problem at all, even at the outset. However, a potential problem does exist.

The Identity Dilemma

Special physical education is called by a number of other titles. Adapted physical education (perhaps the most popular), developmental physical education, physical education for the handicapped, corrective physical education, and physical education for the disabled are some synonyms for special physical education. The result of so many terms to mean essentially the same thing has resulted in confusion among educational team members. More seriously, parents and other associate special physical education (or whatever term they use) with Special Olympics, other sports activities for those with disabilities, and therapeutic recreation. This, to us, is even a more serious problem.

All of those identified as educational team members need to recognize that qualified special physical educators are, first and foremost, teachers. They are "doing their thing in the classroom" just like a qualified/certified teacher in mathematics, social science, or biology. The only primary difference is that the special physical educator does his or her work during the school day in a gymnasium, pool, multipurpose room, or school playground. One exception to this is community-based programming particularly for those pupils with serious disabilities who need a day-to-day emphasis on functional curriculum training (see Chapter 3).

Any extracurricular activities in which the physical educator participates is just that: extracurricular. Coaching and involvement in recreation programs in the community are examples of extracurricular work. And as a matter of fact, it is not uncommon for those in other areas of teaching to be involved in these types of extracurricular activities too. Yet these professionals are recognized for what they primarily are, teachers. Special physical educators should be recognized foremost as teachers of physical education for pupils with disabilities.

Community-Based Programming

The new emphasis in educational programming for pupils who are severely, profoundly, and multiply disabled is use of the functional curriculum approach (discussed in Chapter 3). Those who teach regular physical education will not, and probably should not, have to worry too much about this potential additional responsibility, but those trained in special physical education should be aware of this trend and be prepared to implement functional community-based programming in response to the needs of pupils with serious disabilities.

Yet, because the functional curriculum model is so new, most of those teaching special physical education are not competent to teach "functionally" unless more formal or informal training is made available. More importantly, this current issue needs to be addressed as soon as possible by all members of the educational team having any responsibility related to educational programming for pupils with serious disabilities. Fortunately, a few sources related to implementing the functional curriculum model in physical education are now available (Jansma, 1993).

Role Conflict and Territoriality

A common team problem is conflict over who is allowed, capable, or required to provide services within the 85,000 schools in the United States. The special needs of pupils with disabilities can be met only if all members of an educational team function within their roles while being aware of the roles of other team members. If these roles are not clearly understood, misinterpretations and role conflicts can arise. This road can lead to problems in providing services for those who are at the core to begin with—pupils with disabilities.

P.L. 101-476 defines various educational team roles to some extent. Of overriding importance to the work of the physical educator is that physical education is given one of the highest positions of prominence in this law, including a fairly detailed definition. However, in contrast to the specificity concerning physical education is the vaguely defined role of related service professionals such as physical therapists and occupational therapists. According to P.L. 101-476, the only clear difference between physical education and physical/occupational therapy is that the former is a primary service and the latter are related services to be made available when they support the delivery of special education services in school, including physical education services.

This lack of specificity has resulted in a number of unfortunate situations. For example, in some settings physical therapy and occupational therapy are being delivered in lieu of physical education and, in effect, are even considered to be physical education. As we have stressed, there is a difference between physical education and these medical therapies with respect to both training and function. Neither is to replace the other; they are to complement each other, particularly when educational services are needed by a pupil who is seriously physically disabled. We need physical therapists and occupational therapists in the schools for these challenging pupils, and they need the services of special physical educators.

In our view, when pupils are considered first, role conflict and territoriality issues are of little importance. Those on the educational team have a professional obligation to complement each other in a school. They should get on with their primary collective task—direct service to pupils who are needy.

Facilities, Equipment, and Materials

Those who teach physical education to pupils with disabilities are confronted with realities that may conflict their school districts' situations and the mandates of law. On the one hand, laws mandate that each child with a disability is to have access to facilities and is to be provided with equipment and materials to meet his or her needs as specified on the IEP. On the other hand, facilities, equipment, and materials are not always available in a local education agency (LEA) and cannot, therefore, be guaranteed, even if requested on an IEP, because of fiscal restraints. At times, even when an educational team is charged with providing services that require special facilities (such as a swimming pool) or unique materials (Braille materials, sensor devices, adapted equipment), members of the team are hard-pressed to comply adequately, if at all. They may also find themselves in competition with one another for limited funds. It is noble to plan instruction in certain settings that require specialized equipment and materials, but it is not always realistic to expect full compliance by well-intentioned specialists.

When faced with the conflict between a pupil's needs and a school's limited resources, the challenge to physical educators is to search out alternative facilities, equipment, and material sources. The physical educator can then more fully contribute to accomplishing the mission of the educational team. For example, an arrangement might be made to use the pool at the local YMCA or community center. Equipment and materials might be accumulated over time by in-school

industrial arts projects, donations from local manufacturers, or funded grants throughout the school district, the state department of education, a foundation, or a corporation. Other ideas are provided in Chapter 16.

Clearly, these sources do not appear overnight, but long-term work can eventually provide full physical education services for all pupils. Physical educators and others on the educational team should at least be committed to working toward this goal of full service, closing the gap between what the laws require, what pupils need, and the available facilities, equipment, and materials.

The Lack of Available Experts

An educational team can function best with access to a variety of experts from both inside and outside the school. Furthermore, as we have said, the interaction of these experts appears to be most effective if a transdisciplinary collaborative model is employed. In addition, P.L. 101-476 mandates that each child with a disability be served according to established need, not according to the availability of expertise. But, again, in practice not every district has funds or resources or even the administrative support needed to make all types of experts available. These issues pose a major problem in most of the approximately 17,000 school districts in the United States.

Physical educators must also face the challenge of available expertise. If a child has identified needs in the psychomotor domain, he or she should receive the expert services of teachers (and sometimes therapists) with related competencies. Yet, ironically, even though physical education is accorded such prominence in the law, there are few trained experts in special physical education and not enough are being trained. The use of well-trained and monitored volunteers, whether in the form of pupil tutors, student teachers, or teacher aides, is considered a viable solution to the problem by some. However, the real issue of substantive preservice and in-service training of physical educators remains.

Those in the field of physical education can face this challenge with at least three strategies. First, funds for special physical education training are available at a number of universities and colleges throughout the country. In approximately one year, a master's degree in special physical education can be obtained. Some LEAs (i.e., school districts) are providing sabbatical leaves to allow their physical educators to take advantage of this opportunity. Second, P.L. 101-476 mandates that each state department of education should have a comprehensive system of personnel development. Accordingly, this law's federal "flow-through" funds can be used for the purpose of special physical education in-service training. This is occurring in numerous LEAs. Finally, P.L. 101-476 funds can also be used to hire additional staff members, which could directly affect a school's physical education program. This strategy can be successful if physical educators already employed make their needs known to the person in the school district responsible for discretionary flow-through funds (often the director of pupil personnel). As with the issue of facilities, equipment, and materials, one or more of these strategies can eventually result in the availability of adequate special physical education expertise.

Meeting "Overkill"

During the process of identifying pupils with disabilities, designing their IEPs/IFSPs, and implementing these programs, a considerable amount of effort is required not only by individual teachers but also by groups of them meeting together. Many meetings are required throughout this process: of school professionals, of in-school and out-of-school professionals, with parents or guardians, and still other meetings. All of these require time, which is so important to teachers. Thus we must ask how a teacher can do the many tasks associated with directly teaching pupils and still have time for all these meetings. Unfortunately, there is no easy answer to this question. Those who teach physical education to children with disabilities must contribute in meetings to appropriately place and program for these pupils. If a physical educator does not provide assessment information, related annual goals, short-term instructional objectives, and other IEP information, the pupil cannot be appropriately served in physical education. It is best if all meetings are attended by the physical educator who will eventually be directly responsible for this child. At the very least, physical educators, including the director of physical education, need to provide educational teams with ongoing written information addressing the unique psychomotor needs of each child with a disability. In addition, the exchange of this information will minimize or eliminate the surprise placement of such a child in a physical education class (an all too frequent occurrence). And the image of physical education in general will more likely be viewed as positive by all members of the educational team.

We conclude this chapter with insights provided by Hester Henderson on the educational team as it impacts regular and special physical educators.

Hester Henderson

Dr. Hester Henderson is an associate professor in special physical education at the University of Utah, Salt Lake City.

1. How important is it for regular and special physical educators to interact with other school personnel when making placement and programming decisions?

I believe that it is critical for regular and special physical educators to interact with other school personnel such as the regular classroom teacher, the principal, the counselor, the special educator, the physical and occupational therapist, etc., when making placement and programming decisions because these individuals may be able to provide information relative to issues and concerns that need to be considered in the placement or programming process. A meeting should be held with all school personnel who are significant to the child's education so that input from all can be considered in the decision-making process. Another reason to involve these professionals at this point is to make them feel a part of the process and to open the lines of communication early on.

2. Which team approach do you believe is the best for regular and special physical educators?

The most common team approach that I see being used is the transdisciplinary team consisting of such integral members as the regular physical educator, the special educator, the special physical educator, the counselor, and the physical and occupational therapist (when the child is receiving these related services).

I believe this is the best approach because everyone works as a team to provide the pupil with an ongoing comprehensive physical education program which is designed to meet the child's individual needs. This team should meet at the beginning of the school year to determine placement and to determine the program, at least once during the year to discuss the effectiveness of the program, and at the end of the year to evaluate the program.

3. What members of a team generally are the most helpful for regular and special physical educators?

The physical therapist or occupational therapist and the special educator are generally the most helpful team members. The therapists continually evaluate the child's motor and physical abilities and can add valuable input into the programming process for the child's physical education program. The special educator sees the child on a daily basis and can provide information relative to the child's emotional well-being, his or her strengths or weaknesses in the area of physical education, and offer suggestions in the area of behavior management.

4. What do you believe the role of a regular and special physical educator should be on an ideal team?

I believe the role of both the regular physical educator and the special physical educator on the ideal team is (a) to assess the child's present level of performance in physical education and submit these data to the transdisciplinary team; (b) to plan an instructional program based on the assessed needs of the child; (c) to ensure that physical education is included in the IEP; (d) to provide input relative to the appropriate placement in physical education along a continuum of least restrictive environments; and (e) to recommend and implement changes indicated by subsequent evaluation. If the child is placed in a regular physical education class, then this becomes the role of the regular physical educator; if the child is placed in a segregated special physical education class, then this becomes the role of the special physical educator. The role may be shared if the child is placed in some combination of regular physical education and special physical education.

Testing and Evaluation

In any comprehensive educational program, data-based testing and evaluation are acknowledged as being essential in overall planning. And in order to individualize such educational programming to any real extent, it is crucial to evaluate the results of instruction by using both objective and subjective methods. Good testing and evaluation ensure effective instructional programs by providing data for such vital issues as pupil placement, feedback for the teacher for continued program planning, feedback for the pupil for learning and motivation, accountability (grading), and follow-up.

With the passage of P.L. 101-476, we must now collect ongoing data on all pupils with disabilities to determine each pupil's present level of educational performance, including psychomotor performance. Furthermore, any recommendation for a change in educational placement must be based on such data, and this information needs to be presented to and accepted by all members of each targeted pupil's IEP team. In addition, the present level of performance data is also the basis for determining the duration of a pupil's program, intensity of the program, individualized annual educational goals and short-term instructional objectives, and specific support services that may be required to reach these goals and objectives. Annual follow-up of each pupil's level of performance is also required to check on the progress toward reaching IEP goals and objectives.

A CLARIFICATION OF TERMS

Before we can delve deeper into the topic of this chapter, a clarification of terms is needed. This is important because terms such as testing, assessing, evaluating, and measuring typically create semantic problems for all concerned.

Testing is simply the gathering of data before instruction; no interpretation of data (i.e., test results) is involved. *Assessing* is an analysis of test data in order to determine the data's meaning. In education, assessment encompasses both a pupil's strengths and weaknesses. Such an analysis subsequently establishes programming priorities for a pupil. *Evaluating* occurs at the end of a specified program or period of instruction in order to determine how effective and efficient an instructional program was. The result of evaluation is accountability for grading purposes and follow-up for continued programming. The individualized instruction hierarchy (see Figure 3.5) places testing, assessing, and evaluating in an order consistent with this clarification of terms. *Measuring* is used when testing, assessing, and evaluating. Common measures (e.g., an agility score, a static balance score, a sports skills score, a posture rating score), used within the testing-assessing-evaluating process for a pupil, link directly with instruction and follow-up. Measurement, therefore, acts as the glue in each pupil's overall educational program.

TYPES OF INSTRUMENTS

There are three basic types of testing and evaluation instruments. One type is the norm-referenced instrument. This type is often used for beginning-of-term testing and end-of-term evaluation. Another way to state this is that norm-referenced instruments are often given on a pre- and post-basis with regard to a pupil's school year. Norm-referenced instruments in physical education compare an individual pupil's performance with the performance of a large group of others with the same chronological age, sex, and (if applicable) disability. The pupil's raw

scores are often converted into a statistical index that indicates his or her position relative to other matched pupils who have taken the same items. A common index is percentile ranking, which indicates the percentage of pupils scoring above and below the pupil in question.

A second type is the interpret or criterion-referenced instrument, used often on an ongoing basis during the school term. Interpret (criterion)-referenced instruments compare a pupil's performance to some external variable, such as a grade, score, or level, to describe performance along an achievement continuum. The results require interpretation and, therefore, we prefer the term *interpret-referenced*.

The third type, which should be used on an ongoing basis and at the end of a school term, is the content-referenced instrument. This type is usually not developed, field-validated, or revised by measurement experts and not administered to a norm group. Content-referenced instruments can be developed by teachers themselves for a specific situation or objective. They typically involve the testing and evaluation of a pupil's strengths and weaknesses without the use of external variables requiring interpretation or standardized data. Content-referenced instruments may be more practical and appropriate than other types of instruments because they reflect what is actually being taught on a daily basis (Gay, 1980) and focus only on raw data that reflect a pupil's precise performance. In physical education, this type of instrument determines only what a pupil can or cannot do on a specific motor skill, not in comparison to others. After giving a content-referenced test, a physical educator would begin a program for a pupil with instructional activities based on the first objective that the pupil did not master and continue working on this objective until the task is mastered. Progress by a pupil (not a class) from one developmentally and/or functionally sequenced short-term objective to another, leading to the acquisition of a major or terminal motor skill, is of central concern.

A teacher should be aware of the major differences among norm-referenced, interpret (criterion)-referenced, and content-referenced instruments in order to select or construct the most appropriate testing or evaluation strategy for a particular situation. Table 15.1 compares and contrasts these three types of instruments.

An ideal test or evaluation session employs several varied measurement instruments. Areas of strength and weakness compared to those of other pupils can be determined by using norm-referenced tools. An interpret (criterion)-referenced or content-referenced instrument could also be used to check on a pupil's acquisition of specific physical and motor skills within an area of deficiency. Further, subjective information from parents and the teacher could provide verification and support for all test or evalua-

tion results. Multiple instrument use can also reveal additional performance areas that should be assessed before making a final decision on performance level, type of physical education placement, or intensity of the program.

If only one type of instrument can be used because of time constraints, interpret (criterion)-referenced or content-referenced instruments are most appropriate to meet the purposes of the IEP or IFSP. Norm-referenced instruments usually identify only broad goals, with little guidance for specific appropriate programming. The sole use of norm-referenced tests should, therefore, be avoided. Interpret (criterion)-referenced and content-referenced instruments tend to be more specific, and their results have more direct applicability to program planning. Each can be used on a day-to-day basis to determine the specific level of a pupil's performance on an instructional objective.

In practice, a pupil could be given, for example, a norm-referenced fundamental motor skills test that determines he is below

TABLE 15.1 TYPES OF TEST/EVALUATION INSTRUMENTS

NORM REFERENCED	INTERPRET (CRITERION) REFERENCED	CONTENT REFERENCED
Uses a descriptive statistics standard (e.g., percentile).	Uses an external standard that is an arbitrary ordinal scale measure (e.g., grade, level, score) requiring interpretation.	Uses only content-referenced or raw data (e.g., "yes" or "no," number completed).
Data compared to the performance of others	Performance based on pupil's merits only. Data compared to self.	Performance based on pupil's merits only. Data compared to self.
Contains items that measure performance on a statistical scale.	Contains items that measure the achievement of the intended objective on an interpretable continuum.	Contains items that measure performance on an achievement continuum. No interpretation of scores is necessary.
Concerned more with the performance of groups.	Concerned more with the performance of an individual.	Concerned more with the performance of an individual.
Typically administered at the beginning and end of an instruction unit.	Should be administered at least at the beginning and end of an instruction unit.	Should be administered at the beginning, during, and end of an instruction unit.

his chronological age in throwing a ball overhand with correct form. Then, by using an interpret (criterion)-referenced test, the child's specific performance on throwing a ball overhand could be scored using some external variable (e.g., score) to reveal the specific level of achievement. Raw data from a content-referenced test could then be continuously gathered to determine his exact progress in achieving the specific overhand throwing performance objective. Daily progress can even be charted to inform and motivate both the pupil and teacher.

INSTRUMENT USAGE GUIDELINES

Here are some important guidelines for selecting and administering all types of test/evaluation instruments and using the collected data:

1. The most valid behavioral test data are those gathered continually. The more seriously disabled a pupil is, the more frequently he or she should be tested. More detailed measurement guidelines for use with pupils who are moderately and severely disabled are offered by Reid, Seidl, and Montgomery (1989) and Jansma (1993).

2. A definitive present level of performance should not be based on one assessment, but on multiple assessments.

3. A teacher must be thoroughly familiar with a measurement instrument before administering it.

4. The pupil should know or be familiar with the teacher giving a measurement instrument, and vice versa.

5. A measurement instrument must be valid. It must measure the skills it purports to measure. As a primary example of adherence to this vital guideline, in some of the tests discussed later in the chapter, modifications and accommodations are permitted in the administration of selected test items

in order to assess more validly the needs of a test taker who is disabled. The same component is still measured, but the avenue toward measurement is individualized.

6. A measurement instrument should be reliable. The tester or evaluator should obtain consistent results.

7. No one progression or scale fits all pupils. Developmental variability between and within pupils and resulting individual differences should always be taken into account, especially when performances are compared to norms.

8. Teachers should always be looking for more appropriate measuring instruments. Portions of different instruments can be combined to determine present levels of performance rather than limiting use to any measurement device as a whole. However, if any changes are made in the way a published instrument is given, those changes must be specified when results are reported.

9. The teacher should try to gather observational data. A pupil is then "caught" emitting target behaviors, and the need for one-to-one formal measurement becomes less necessary. Data collected by observation from the classroom teacher, parents, and significant others are often helpful in program planning.

10. In determining discrepancies between actual and normal performance levels, the major focus in testing and evaluating young children should be on developmental performance. A determination of developmental age provides relevant and immediately useful programming information with which to address normal development for young pupils. As a child ages, testing and evaluation should have a more functional focus if developmental scores become increasingly discrepant. A determination of functional psychomotor status provides relevant information for use in the individual's present and future everyday activities at home, work, or play. (See Chapter 3 for detailed

information on developmental versus functional programming.)

11. The environment must be free of distractions, as distractions can be a major source of unknown performance error. Environmental distractions are those that are not measurement related and impinge on any sense (e.g., visual, auditory, olfactory).

12. The cognitive ability of the pupil must be considered in selecting an appropriate measuring instrument. For example, if a goal is to assess motor development but the instrument directions are too complex for a given pupil, the pupil's cognitive ability, as well as level of motor development, is measured. Directions on a motor ability measuring instrument must be clearly understandable to all pupils.

13. The time requirements, amount and cost of the equipment, and the facility required to administer the instrument must be considered.

14. Testers and evaluators should realize that a pupil's medical limitations or behavioral problems can adversely affect the results of measurement. The teacher should, therefore, be aware of unique pupil behaviors, the management of these specific behaviors, the medical needs of the pupil (e.g., medications), and the communication needs of the pupil.

15. The limitations of measuring instruments and the biases of examiners themselves make measurement results tentative. Continuous measuring is important to establish a behavioral trend, which is more credible and provides clearer direction for individualized instruction.

16. Pupils should be spot-checked for retention of skills. Teachers should not assume that once a skill is learned, it will be retained. In addition, pupils may exhibit one behavior during formal testing and another in a natural setting (e.g., a softball game played in the community) related to the same skill. A variety of skill contexts must, therefore, be systematically probed in order to be sure of skill acquisition, retention, and generalization across settings.

17. Taking measurements of pupil performance should stop if the teacher or the pupil gets tired. The best data are gathered when both parties are alert and fresh.

18. If a measurement instrument does not preclude it, the teacher should model or demonstrate the skills to be measured for the pupil. This will eliminate any chance of poor performance due to lack of understanding of only verbal directions.

19. Trials and questions should be permitted before "real" trials in order to elicit the best possible performance. Related to this, repeat instructions, as necessary, and then ask the pupil to repeat your instructions so that no problem in comprehension of instructions exists. Also avoid asking pupils the question "Do you understand?" as pupils will not always admit a lack of understanding.

20. If possible, a measuring session should be made into a game. Such a tactic will more likely hold the attention of a pupil who is easily distracted. Associating fun with teaching and learning is appropriate and, usually, quite successful.

21. The pupil's needs should be met before a testing or evaluation session begins. Such needs could relate to hunger, thirst, a visit to the bathroom, clothing, familiarity with the measuring instrument, the use or nonuse of assistive devices (e.g., cane, hearing aid), and teacher/pupil rapport.

22. Several techniques should be considered for coping with large-group testing and evaluating situations. As examples:

   a. Do a mass screening, followed by one-on-one measurement for pupils with suspected problems. If available, use a video recorder to observe performance and analyze the videotape after class.

b. Use an assistant to teach three quarters of the class while measuring the other quarter.

c. Use task cards and have pupils measure themselves. The teacher just spot-checks to determine the accuracy of the information collected. For nonreaders, use illustrations.

d. Use a circuit training system with each station being a measurement site. Self-scoring or peer assistance can be used to collect the results.

e. Divide the class into squads and take measurements with one or two squads while an assistant leads the other squads in specifically assigned activities. This system would spread the gathering of measurements over a few days.

f. Use an observational system whereby the teacher observes measurement-related tasks that are intentionally included within regular physical education program activities. A pupil moves to the next measurement level when observed satisfying the prior level of performance.

23. Several techniques should be considered when administering fitness test items to pupils with disabilities. As examples:

a. When testing pupils who are mentally retarded for speed, have the finish line a few yards (meters) farther than the real finish line so that, if a runner slows down at the end, a "true" time can be obtained.

b. For burpees or squat thrusts, use a two-count and down position so that complexity of this task is not an issue for pupils who are cognitively slow or easily distracted.

c. When testing heart–lung endurance with pupils who are orthopedically disabled, use criterion-referenced measures of cycle or arm ergometry and pool "walking" in waist-high water.

d. For pupils with dynamic balance problems, substitute a vertical jump for the running long jump when testing lower body power.

e. For pupils in wheelchairs, test pull-ups or the flexed arm hang using a dowel rod or a lowered bar.

Other methodological tips are offered in each of the categorical chapters in this text. They can be creatively used to teach and test pupils with disabilities more effectively and efficiently.

RECOMMENDED INSTRUMENTS

This section is devoted to brief descriptions of several measurement instruments (listed alphabetically) that can be utilized in a special physical education program. The reader will find a mix—some instruments are disability specific and a few are intended primarily for the nondisabled population but are still applicable to those with disabilities. The recommended instruments span preschool through postschool age and are separated into the major areas of special physical education programming as specified in P.L. 101-476: physical and motor fitness, fundamental motor skills and patterns, aquatics, dance, and individual and group activities. For clarity, the recommended fitness and motor skill instruments are listed in Table 15.2. Specific information provided for each recommended test tool includes test title, bibliographical references, test type, intended population (age, gender, disability), awards (if applicable), content, administration time (only if short or long), cost (only if expensive or modest), and availability. Posture- and weight-measuring instruments are presented as separate areas. Examples of recording forms for some of the recommended instruments are found in Appendix B.

TABLE 15.2   RECOMMENDED FITNESS AND MOTOR SKILL INSTRUMENTS

Physical and Motor Fitness

AAHPER Youth Fitness Test Adaptation for the Blind
AAHPERD Functional Fitness Test for Older Adults
Data Based Gynmasium Model
FITNESSGRAM
I CAN: Health and Fitness
Kansas Adapted/Special Physical Education Test
Kraus Weber Test
Motor Fitness Testing Manual for the Moderately
    Mentally Retarded
Physical Best
Physical Fitness Battery for Mentally Retarded
    Children
President's Council on Physical Fitness and Sport
    Fitness Program
Project ACTIVE Physical Fitness Test
Project MOBILITEE
Project TRANSITION
Project UNIQUE
Special Fitness Test Manual for Mildly Mentally
    Retarded Persons

Fundamental Motor Skills and Patterns

Basic Motor Ability Tests
Behavioral Characteristics Progression
Body Image Screening Test for Blind Children
Bruininks-Oseretsky Test of Motor Proficiency
Carolina Curriculum for Preschoolers with
    Special Needs
Data Based Gymnasium Model
Denver Developmental Screening Test
Early Intervention Developmental Profile
Hawaii Early Learning Profile
Hughes Basic Gross Motor Assessment
I CAN: Body Management
I CAN: Fundamental Skills
Inventory of Early Development
Learning Accomplishment Profile
Move-Grow-Learn: Movement Skills Survey
Movement Pattern Checklist
Ohio State University SIGMA
Peabody Motor Development Scales
Portage Classroom Curriculum-CHECKLIST
Portage Guide to Early Intervention CHECKLIST
Project ACTIVE Motor Ability Test
Project MOBILITEE
Purdue Perceptual Motor Survey
Six Category Gross Motor Test
Test of Gross Motor Development
Test of Motor Impairment

Many of the instruments recommended here could also be of considerable value in designing teacher-made tests. A teacher can use any published or unpublished measurement instrument to create a content-referenced instrument for specific pupils. When doing this, simply eliminating the external variables in interpret (criterion)-referenced tests and the references to chronological age, sex, and disability in norm-referenced tests can be appropriate, too.

Physical and Motor Fitness

Several measurement instruments have been developed to assess the physical and motor fitness of those who are disabled. Some of the instruments are intended mainly for use with "normal" pupils with adaptations added for inclusion of those with disabilities.

AAHPER Youth Fitness Test Adaptation for the Blind (Buell, 1973). This norm-referenced physical fitness instrument is an adaptation of the AAHPER Youth Fitness Test (AAHPER, 1976b). It is intended for children who are blind or partially sighted (i.e., two sets of norms) between 10 and 17 years of age. Achievement and merit awards are built into the instrument. The items and norms for pull-ups (boys), flexed arm hang (girls), sit-ups, and standing broad jump are the same as in the AAHPER Youth Fitness Test. Separate norms were developed for the 50-yard dash and the 600-yard run-walk. A basketball throw was added to measure upper body power. Complete test directions and norms for the basketball throw test item are presented in Buell (1966). A medicine ball put or straight-arm or overhead medicine ball throw was also recommended to measure the upper body power component (Buell, 1982).

The AAHPER Youth Fitness Test Adaptation for the Blind can be obtained at a modest cost from AAHPERD Publication Sales, 1900 Association Drive, Reston, VA 22091.

AAHPERD Functional Fitness Test for Older Adults (Clark, 1989). This norm-referenced fitness instrument measures fitness items that address 60 year and older male and female "individuals' capacity to meet ordinary and unexpected demands of daily life safely and effectively" (p. 66). No awards are associated with this instrument, which was at its formative stage of development in 1989. The test components include a chair-to-cones shuttle walk, a sit and reach from the floor, 30-second one-arm weight lifting from chair position, soda can coordination task with preferred hand, and a half-mile walk. The cost of items needed is very modest and common items are used (e.g., stopwatch, masking tape, measuring tape, cones, chalk, light dumbbells, soda cans). Detailed information on this instrument can be obtained from Department of Health, Physical Education and Recreation, University of Kansas, Lawrence, KS 66045.

Data Based Gymnasium Model (Dunn, Morehouse, & Fredericks, 1986). This model (discussed in Chapter 3) contains a content-referenced test tool including physical fitness items for use with pupils classified as severely disabled. Fitness areas are cardiorespiratory (8 items), muscle strength and endurance (7 items), and flexibility (5 items). Each test item is task analyzed into phases and, in some cases, substeps. The phase/step analyzed skills can be used in a curriculum-embedded fashion during training, or the teacher can refer to the model's *Game, Exercise, and Leisure Sport Curriculum* (Dunn, Morehouse, & Dalke 1979) and use it as a direct resource. Use of the test items and cur-

riculum depends on appropriate usage of a behavioral system that focuses on the systematic cueing and consequating of targeted behaviors. Trained volunteers are emphasized in using the model with the low ratio of teacher-to-pupils characteristic of those with severe disabilities. Information on the test portion and the Data Based Gymnasium Model is available from Pro Ed, 8700 Shoal Creek Boulevard, Austin, TX 78758. Information on the Game, Exercise, and Leisure Sport Curriculum is available from Department of Sport and Exercise Science, Oregon State University, 214 Langton Hall, Corvallis, OR 97331-3002.

FITNESSGRAM (Institute for Aerobics Research, 1987). The FITNESSGRAM system was developed by Kenneth Cooper's Institute for Aerobics Research and is sponsored by Campbell Soup Company. Its norm-referenced test of physical fitness is designed for use with K–12 nondisabled children, but interpret-referenced allowances are made for use of standards with individual pupils who are disabled. Test items are those from either the AAHPERD Youth Fitness Test or the AAHPERD Health-Related Physical Fitness Test (1980b). A unique feature of FITNESS-GRAM is its computerized program of fitness reporting that links the pupil with the teacher and parent. Such a report includes percentile rank on each test item, a total fitness score, a physical fitness profile, and programming ideas for test scores below the 50th percentile. Pupils can qualify for three types of FITNESSGRAM awards via the FITNESS-GRAM system of reporting to school districts. Such awards are meant to reinforce ongoing health-related behaviors, not performance against other pupils. Complementing the test is a curriculum manual entitled *Teaching Strategies for Improving Youth Fitness* written by Charles Corbin and Robert Pangrazi. FITNESSGRAM is available from FITNESSGRAM, Institute for Aerobics Research, 12330 Preston Road, Dallas, TX 75230.

I CAN: Health and Fitness (Wessel, 1976d).
Within this comprehensively packaged program, specific areas of physical fitness are evaluated using an interpret-referenced approach. This measurement tool is gender, age, and disability label free. The specific areas evaluated are abdominal strength and endurance, arm/shoulder/chest strength and endurance, stamina and heart/lung strength and endurance, and trunk and leg flexibility. Based on the results of a pupil's performance, specific instructional activities and games are recommended. The task analysis–based program is designed to provide continuous evaluation of each pupil. See one example of this instrument's recording form in Appendix B1. This packaged module is relatively expensive and can be obtained from Hubbard Scientific Company, Box 104, Northbrook, IL 60062.

Kansas Adapted/Special Physical Education Test (Johnson & Lavay, 1988, 1989).
This interpret-referenced test instrument is age, gender, and disability label free. It contains four areas of content based on AAHPERD's Physical Best fitness test. Specific test items include bent-knee arms-across-chest sit-ups, sit and reach, isometric push-up (static push-up hold position) or 35-pound bench press, and aerobic movement. In the aerobic movement item, any movement is acceptable that produces a 140–180 heart rate for 12 minutes yielding a measure of pulse rate and time. Alternative substitute test items are also included in the manual, especially for use by pupils who are the most severely disabled. Awards are advocated at different levels in the form of praise during testing and tangible rewards at the participation, improvement,

achievement, and excellence levels. This test is free or inexpensive and can be obtained from the Kansas State Department of Education, Kansas State Education Building, 120 East 10th Street, Topeka, KS 66612.

Kraus Weber Test (Kraus & Hirschland, 1954).
This is an interpret-referenced physical fitness screening tool that is age free, gender free, and noncategorical. It consists of five muscular fitness items and one flexibility item. The performance items and criteria include one straight leg sit-up, one bent-knee sit-up, a 10-second double leg raise and hold from a supine position, a 10-second double leg raise and hold from a prone position, a prone trunk raise held for 10 seconds, and a straight leg toe touch held for 3 seconds. In the original test, an all-or-nothing approach to scoring was employed with all items needing to be performed completely for a passing score. If all six items are used, we recommend subscores based on fraction of sit-ups completed for items 1 and 2; number of seconds up to 10 for items 3, 4, and 5; and number of inches from the floor for item 6. Further, we recommend reducing undue lower back stress by eliminating item 1, bending the knees in item 3, and using a sit and stretch for the last item—with the same modified scoring system. This screening tool is quickly administered and no special equipment is required. The Kraus Weber Test, with the modified scoring method and test item modifications, is available from the Adapted Physical Activity Section, The Ohio State University, School of Health, Physical Education and Recreation, 341 Larkins Hall, 337 West 17th Avenue, Columbus, OH 43210-1284.

Motor Fitness Testing Manual for the Moderately Mentally Retarded (Johnson & Londeree, 1976).
The purpose of this norm-referenced test is to determine the psychomotor ability of persons who are moderately

mentally retarded. Norms are provided separately for males and females between the chronological ages of 6 and 20 years. Incentive awards are available at three levels for achievement. Specific test items include the following:

- Flexed-arm hang
- Sit-ups
- Standing long jump
- Softball throw for distance
- 50-yard dash
- 300-yard dash
- Height
- Weight
- Sitting bob-and-reach
- Hopping
- Skipping
- Tumbling progression
- Target throw

This test is available from AAHPERD, 1900 Association Drive, Reston, VA 22091.

Physical Best (AAHPERD, 1988). Physical Best is a fitness test and computer-based educational kit, with lesson plans, for implementing a comprehensive health-related fitness program. Personal goal setting is the key along with attaining standards for boys and girls 5 to 18 years of age. Therefore, the Physical Best system is both content referenced and norm referenced. Its components and test items include aerobic endurance (1-minute run/walk with options), flexibility (sit and reach), upper body strength and endurance (pull-ups), abdominal strength and endurance (bent-knee sit-ups with arms across chest), body composition (skinfold measures of triceps and calf yielding a body mass index), and three optional tests (50-yard dash, standing long jump, and shuttle run). Its unique recognition system is nonhierarchi-

cal and allows pupils, disabled or nondisabled, to earn emblems at three levels. Also to be highlighted is its contract option for pupils, which lends itself to individualized instruction (see Chapter 3). The Physical Best packet can be ordered at minimal cost from AAHPERD, 1900 Association Drive, Reston, VA 22091. See the Physical Best Report Card recording form in Appendix B2.

Physical Fitness Battery for Mentally Retarded Children (Fait, 1978). This fitness test battery is for pupils who are mildly and moderately retarded. It is norm referenced with separate tables for males and females from 9 to 20 years of age. Each of its six test items has a low correlation with intelligence so that test results reflect state of physical fitness, not a combination of ability in physical performance and instruction following. The six items are 300-yard run-walk, bent-arm hang, stork stand with eyes closed, Fleishman's 20-second leg lift test, squat thrusts without stand, and 25-yard run. Low, average, and good scores have been established for each of the test items. This physical fitness battery's norms are available from

Dunn, J., & Fait, H. (1989). *Special physical education: Adapted, individualized, developmental,* 6th ed. Dubuque, IA: William C. Brown, pp. 543–546.

The test administration instructions are provided in

Sherrill, C. (1976). *Adapted physical education and recreation: A multidisciplinary approach.* Dubuque, IA: William C. Brown, p. 484.

President's Council on Physical Fitness and Sport Fitness Program (President's Council, 1987, 1989). This program, also known as the President's Challenge Physical Fitness Program, includes a norm-referenced test of physical fitness that has separate norms for nondisabled males and females 6 to 17 years of age. Its test items provide measures of abdominal strength and endurance, arm and shoulder strength and endurance, low back/hamstring flexibility, cardiorespiratory endurance, and agility. An award standard has been set at the 85th percentile across all test items in order for a pupil to receive the Presidential Physical Fitness Award. As an alternative, the National Physical Fitness Award has been designed to motivate all youngsters to achieve a basic fitness level and is available to pupils with physical disabilities. Pupils with disabilities can also receive these awards (along with a related emblem, certificate, or decal) using the same standard, and accommodations for specified items have been given consideration by the President's Council. The test tool and related materials (e.g., awards, *Get Fit* handbook) are available at a modest cost from President's Council on Physical Fitness and Sports, 450 5th Street N.W., Suite 7103, Washington, DC 20001, or President's Challenge, Poplars Research Center, 400 East 7th Street, Bloomington, IN 47405.

Project ACTIVE Physical Fitness Test (Vodola, 1978). This fitness test (Level II) is normed on children 6 to 16 years of age by gender and mental age. It purportedly is useful with children classified as nondisabled, mentally retarded, learning disabled, and emotionally disordered. It provides a measure of arm and shoulder strength (static arm hang), abdominal strength (curl-ups), explosive leg power (standing broad jump), and cardiorespiratory endurance (200-yard dash to 12-minute run). It is available at minimal cost from Vee Inc., Box 2093, Neptune City, NJ 07753.

Project MOBILITEE (Hopewell Special Education Regional Resource Center, 1981). This project has developed a test tool and curriculum guide in special physical education for pupils classified as moderately and severely disabled. Its seven fitness items include 20-foot dash (severely disabled/wheelchair bound), 30-yard dash, wheelchair push-ups, traditional push-ups, wheelchair power push, agility run, and 5-minute walk/run. The test is interpret referenced, noncategorical, age free, and gender free. Its qualitative level system of scoring is depicted on the Wheelchair Physical Education Assessment score sheet in Appendix B3. The Project MOBILITEE manual is available at minimal cost from Consultant in Adapted Physical Education, Division of Curriculum, Instruction, and Professional Development, Ohio Department of Education, Ohio Departments Building, Room 1004, 65 South Front Street, Columbus, OH 43215.

Project TRANSITION (Jansma, McCubbin, Combs, Decker & Ersing, 1987). This interpret-referenced test and curriculum stresses functional assessment and related programming. It is gender, age, and disability category free; however, it does emphasize persons with serious disabilities. Both quantitative and qualitative (level of independence) elements are featured in the test itself, which consists of five fitness items: 300-yard run/walk for cardiorespiratory endurance, bench press for upper body strength/endurance, sit and reach for lower back and hamstring flexibility, bent-knee sit-up with arms across chest for abdominal strength/endurance, and grip strength. The assessment system is highlighted separately in the literature (Jansma, McCubbin, Decker, & Ersing, 1988), as well as the modified test equipment itself (Jansma, Decker, McCubbin, Combs, & Ersing, 1986). Ongoing specific information on Project TRANSITION can be obtained from Adapted Physical Activity Section, School of Health, Physical Education and Recreation, The Ohio State University, 341 Larkins Hall, 337 West 17th Avenue,

Columbus, OH 43210-1284. See an example of this project's score recording form in Appendix B4.

Project UNIQUE (Winnick & Short, 1985). This norm-referenced test and training curriculum originally targeted pupils from 10 to 17 years of age with orthopedic and sensory disabilities and also pupils without disabilities. Additional related Project UNIQUE research also has been completed (Winnick & Short, 1991) comparing adolescents with cerebral palsy to adolescents with cerebral palsy and mild mental retardation. Project materials contain separate norms for males and females. Its test components cover body composition (millimeters of adipose at triceps and subscapular sites), muscular strength and endurance (grip strength, bent-knee sit-ups), speed (50-yard/meter dash), flexibility (sit and reach), and cardiorespiratory endurance (9–12 minutes or 1–$1\frac{1}{2}$ mile run). The cost of the Project UNIQUE manual is moderate and can be obtained from Human Kinetics Publishers, Inc., Box 5076, Champaign, IL 61820. See this project's score recording form in Appendix B5.

Special Fitness Test Manual for Mildly Mentally Retarded Persons (AAHPER, 1976a). This norm-referenced test is a modification of the original AAHPER Youth Fitness Test (1965) and is specially designed for use with pupils who are mildly mentally retarded. Built-in awards at five levels can be earned. It is composed of seven test items: flexed-arm hang, sit-ups, shuttle run, standing long jump, 50-yard dash, softball throw for distance, and 300-yard run/walk. Minor alterations from the original AAHPER Youth Fitness Test are: (a) pull-up test for males is changed to flexed-arm hang, (b) the scoring of the sit-up test is changed from the maximum number of sit-ups that could be performed to the number performed in 1

minute, and (c) the run/walk for distance was reduced from 600 to 300 yards. Norms are provided for each test item by sex for each chronological age from 8 to 18 years. This test is available at modest cost from AAHPERD, 1900 Association Drive, Reston, VA 22091.

Fundamental Motor Skills and Patterns

Many testing instruments have been developed to assess fundamental motor skills and patterns. Some of these tests are designed for infants or children, and others are for both infants and children. Some are developmentally sequenced and task related rather than age related. And some provide specific information related to the performance of individuals with specific disabilities.

Basic Motor Ability Tests—Revised (Arnheim & Sinclair, 1979). This norm-referenced screening instrument contains 11 items designed to measure fine and gross motor skills of male and female children who are 4 to 12 years of age. This tool was developed to evaluate the selected motor responses of small and large muscle control, static and dynamic balance, eye–hand coordination, and flexibility. The 11 items are bead stringing, target throwing, marble transfer, back and hamstring stretch, standing long jump, face down to standing, static balance, basketball throw for distance, ball striking, target kicking, and agility run. A child can be screened with this instrument in approximately 15 to 20 minutes. This revised test is available from the reference cited above and also is available in a Spanish edition.

Behavioral Characteristics Progression (Vort Corporation, 1973, 1977). This test battery is an interpret-referenced, age-free, gender-free and disability label–free tool that pinpoints 59 curricular strands, each of which is subdivided into as many as 50 behavioral characteristics. Its psychomotor strands cover mobility (including wheelchair use), gross motor coordination, balance, strength, agility, swimming, posture, ambulation, flexibility, and speed. This instrument is intended to be an observational tool and does provide programming ideas. An updated version of the California Behavioral Characteristics Progression is also available (Texas Department of MH/MR, 1977). It contains 61 strands overall, with 17 related strictly to the physical education area. The behavioral characteristics associated with this refined version are behaviorally written and, therefore, more clearly understood for use in testing and programming. The Texas version, which we recommend, can be obtained from Texas Department of Mental Health and Mental Retardation, Arts, Graphics, and Education Service, Box 12668, Capital Station, Austin, TX 78711.

Body Image Screening Test for Blind Children (Cratty, 1971a; Cratty & Sams, 1968).

This content-referenced tool is targeted primarily for use by 5- to 16-year-old youngsters who are partially sighted or totally blind. It is gender free, and no curriculum is directly written for use with the tool, although selected training ideas are offered. It covers multiple items within five groupings across the following components; body planes (15 items across 3 groupings), body parts (20 items across 4 groupings), body movements (15 items across 3 groupings), laterality (15 items across 3 groupings), and directionality (15 items across 3 groupings). Test items within each grouping are arranged from easy to difficult and are scored on a pass/fail basis. The test is available from American Foundation for the Blind, 15 West 16th Street, New York, NY 10011.

Bruininks-Oseretsky Test of Motor Proficiency (Bruininks, 1978).

This is an individually administered norm-referenced test designed to assess the motor proficiency of children from $4\frac{1}{2}$ to $14\frac{1}{2}$ years of age. It is gender and disability label free. The complete battery contains eight subtests that include 46 test items. The eight subtests on the long form are running speed and agility, balance, bilateral coordination, strength, upper limb coordination, response speed, visual-motor control, and upper limb speed and dexterity. Gross motor, fine motor, and total battery scores can be obtained on a long form. There is also a short form of 14 items that provides a brief survey of overall motor efficiency. It takes approximately 45 to 60 minutes to administer the complete battery and 15 to 20 minutes to complete the short form. See this instrument's recording form in Appendix B6. This test is available, also in a Spanish edition, at some expense from American Guidance Service, Circle Pines, MN 55014.

A curriculum directly linked with this test is the Body Skills motor development curriculum for children age 3–12 (Werder & Bruininks, 1988). This curriculum covers body management, locomotion, body fitness, object movement, and fine motor skills. Its Motor Skills Inventory records ongoing progress in overall motor skill achievement.

Carolina Curriculum for Preschoolers with Special Needs (Johnson-Martin, Attermeier, & Hacker, 1990).

This revised norm-referenced battery for preschoolers (3–5) covers assessment and program planning strategies across five domains of development, including fine and gross motor skills. Items from the curriculum are arranged in 26 sequences for assessment. Skills are judged to be either passed, emerging, or failed as reflected over time on an Assessment Log and Developmental Progress Chart. Equipment required includes toys and physical education equipment found in most preschool settings. This instrument also provides specific information about selected disabilities and their effects on classroom function. The Carolina Curriculum for Preschoolers with Special Needs is reasonably priced and is available from Paul H. Brookes Publishing Company, Inc., Box 10624, Baltimore, MD 21285-0624.

Data Based Gymnasium Model (Dunn, Morehouse, & Fredericks, 1986). In addition to its physical fitness dimension, the Data Based Gymnasium Model also contains a substantive motor skills component. Its basic movement concepts involve 32 test items divided into personal movement (23 steps) and general space (9 items). Its basic game skills section contains 19 test items. See the fitness section of this chapter and Chapter 3 for more detailed information on the format, use, availability, and other characteristics of this model.

Denver Developmental Screening Test (Frankenburg, Dodds, & Fandal, 1973). This tool is intended as a norm-referenced and gender-free screening device for nondisabled children aged 0–6. It provides gross motor, language, fine motor-adaptive, and personal-social information. Its 31 gross motor items cover the areas of prelocomotion, locomotion, balance, eye–foot, and eye–hand coordination. The gross motor section can be given quickly because only those items associated with the child's chronological age are generally selected for administration. The latest version of this test is available from W. K. Frankenburg, M.D., University of Colorado Medical Center, Boulder, CO 80309. See this instrument's revised recording form in Appendix B7.

Early Intervention Developmental Profile (Schafer & Moersch, 1981a). This revised norm-referenced battery covers six areas of development, including gross motor skills. It is gender free and intended for use with nondisabled youngsters 0–3 years old. Because it is developmentally low, it is useful in assessing the skills of individuals who are older and seriously disabled. The 76 gross motor items include an emphasis on the subareas of locomotion, balance, eye–hand coordination, eye–limb coordination, eye–foot coordination, and reflexes. A one-to-one test situation is advised, yet administration time is relatively short with few items of test equipment required. Curriculum-related materials also have been developed for use with this profile's test results (Schafer & Moersch, 1981b). A similarly constructed Preschool Developmental Profile has been developed for use in the 3–6 year developmental range (D'Eugenio & Moersch, 1978). Its 56 gross motor items cover the areas of fundamental gross motor skills, body imitations, body image, and use of toys. All of these materials are available from University of Michigan Press, 839 Greene Street, Box 1104, Ann Arbor, MI 48106.

Hawaii Early Learning Profile (Feruno, O'Reilly, Hosaka, Inatsuka, & Zeisloft-Falbey, 1985). This revised interpret-referenced battery covers multiple domains of development and includes 164 developmentally sequenced gross and fine motor skills from 0 to 36 months. Its checklist format is observational, with a focus on unobtrusive play interactions, parent interviews, and the collection of maintenance data. Only common, easily obtainable equipment is required. This battery is accompanied by cross-referenced curriculum materials, including a substantial activities binder and activity sheets for use by parents. It is available at moderate cost from Vort Corporation, Box 60132, Palo Alto, CA 94306.

Hughes Basic Gross Motor Assessment (Hughes, 1979). This test is norm referenced on "normal" children aged 6 to 12. It has separate norms by age and gender. The areas of balance, eye–foot/hand coordination, and gross motor patterns are tested using the following items: standing balance, stride jump, tandem walking, hopping, skipping, throwing, yo-yo, and ball handling. Observation of gait, preferred hand, and midline is also highlighted. Only common equipment is needed. The instrument is available from Office of Special Education, Denver Public Schools, Denver, CO 80203, or G. E. Miller, Inc., 484 South Broadway, Yonkers, NY 10705.

I CAN: Body Management (Wessel, 1976b). Within the I CAN program, already introduced in this chapter, interpret-referenced tests are provided for numerous body management skills. The skills evaluated include the following:

Body Awareness

- Body parts
- Body actions
- Body planes
- Shapes and sizes
- Directions in space
- Personal space
- General space

Body Control

- Log roll
- Shoulder roll
- Forward roll
- Backward roll
- Static 2-point balances
- Static 1-point balances
- Dynamic balances
- Inverted balances
- Bounce on trampoline
- Drops on trampoline
- Airborne on trampoline

Based on the results of testing, instructional activities and games are recommended to improve the child's performance.

I CAN: Fundamental Skills (Wessel, 1976c). As in the other I CAN packets discussed in this chapter, the Fundamental Skills packet includes a series of interpret-referenced tests that cover selected motor skills and patterns. Programming-related instructional activities and games are also provided on standard I CAN sheet formats to improve a child's level of performance on these skills. The specific fundamental motor skills and patterns addressed in this packet are the following:

Object Control

- Underhand roll
- Underhand throw
- Kick
- Bounce
- Catch
- Underhand strike
- Overhand strike
- Forehand strike
- Backhand strike
- Sidearm strike

Locomotor and Rhythmic Skills

- Run
- Leap
- Horizontal jump
- Vertical jump
- Gallop
- Slide
- Skip
- Even beat
- Uneven beat
- Accent
- Communication

Inventory of Early Development (Brigance, 1978). This norm-referenced inventory is designed to test infants and children below the developmental age of 7 years. It assesses motor, speech and language, and general knowledge. Of interest to the physical educator are the preambulatory and gross motor components of the motor subtest. The preambulatory component includes the assessment of general motor behavior in supine, prone, sitting, and standing positions; the gross motor component involves the assessment of walking, stair climbing, running, jumping, hopping, kicking, balance board activities, catching, rolling and throwing, ball bouncing, rhythmic activities, and the operation of wheel toys. Based on the results of testing, the teacher can write a statement of the pupil's present level of performance and annual goals and short-term objectives. The test tool can be obtained at some expense from Curriculum Associates, Inc., 5 Esquire Road, Woburn, MA 01801.

Learning Accomplishment Profile (Sanford, 1974). This norm-referenced, gender-free battery contains normal developmental sequences for children aged 0–6. Sequences are provided across the areas of gross motor, fine motor, social, self-help, cognitive, and language development. Its 64 motor items cover locomotion, balance, eye–hand coordination, eye–foot coordination, eye–limb coordination, and rhythm. The Learning Accomplishment Profile can be given quickly, yet should be used on a one-to-one basis. It does not contain a curriculum. A similar battery has been developed for the 0–3 age range (Glover, Preminger, & Sanford, 1978): the Early Learning Accomplishment Profile for Developmentally Young Children (Early LAP). Its progression of psychomotor developmental milestones is in 163 small steps across the gross motor and fine motor areas. It also illustrates appropriate methods of

developing materials for the early education of children with disabilities. Both batteries are available from Kaplan School Supply, Box 609, Lewisville, NC 27023-0609.

Move-Grow-Learn: Movement Skills Survey (Orpet & Heustis, 1971). This test is normed for "normal" children 6 to 12 years of age, with separate norms for males and females. It is administered informally using observation. The motor areas covered include coordination and rhythm, gross motor, fine motor, eye–motor, static-dynamic-object balance, and body awareness. A curriculum in the form of a color-coded card file with activities matched to test items is available as a supplement. These materials are all available from Modern Curriculum Press, 13900 Prospect Road, Cleveland, OH 44136.

Movement Pattern Checklist (Godfrey & Kephart, 1969). This tool has both long and short versions. Both are noncategorical, gender free, and age free. The regular Movement Pattern Checklist is a summary of 18 separate fundamental motor patterns. On this longer tool, specific qualitative dimensions and deviations relative to motor patterns are noted. Its short form is a screening tool that provides a "quick read" of the same 18 fundamental motor skills, which include:

Walking	Standing	Crawling
Running	Throwing	Climbing
Jumping	Catching	Rolling
Hopping	Hitting	Pulling
Skipping	Kicking	Carrying
Sliding	Pushing	Sitting

Both versions do not have an associated curriculum, can be obtained at minimal cost, require minimal equipment, and focus on making a game out of testing. Both forms of the Movement Pattern Checklist are on pages 153–177 in the reference cited above or are available from Appleton-Century-Crofts, 292 Madison Avenue, New York, NY 10017.

Ohio State University—Scale of Intra-Gross Motor Assessment (Loovis & Ersing, 1979). This interpret-referenced tool and its accompanying curriculum are designed to provide a comprehensive individualized gross motor program applicable to preschool and elementary school children who are "normal" and mentally retarded. The manual is separated into two parts: the Ohio State University—Scale of Intra-Gross Motor Assessment (SIGMA) and the Performance Base Curriculum. The SIGMA is used to assess qualitatively 11 basic motor skills within four functional levels in a relatively short time. Equipment needs are minimal. The skills assessed include:

Walking	Hopping
Stair climbing	Skipping
Running	Striking
Throwing	Kicking
Catching	Ladder climbing
Jumping	

Based on the results of the test, a sequence of progressive instructional activities included in the manual's Performance Base Curriculum is recommended. See the scale's recording form in Appendix B8. The SIGMA is available at a modest cost from College Town Press, Box 669, Bloomington, IN 47402.

Peabody Motor Development Scales (Folio & Fewell, 1983). This tool is both norm and interpret referenced, is gender free, and includes normal developmental items that cover ages 0–7. Its 170 gross motor tasks cover reflexes, balance, nonlocomotor, locomotor, and receipt and propulsion. Its 112 fine motor tasks cover grasping, hand use, eye–hand coordination, and finger dexterity. Small groups of children can be tested at one

time using a station-testing approach. The Peabody Motor Development Scales have an accompanying curriculum that is in the form of a tab-indexed card file that matches 282 programming ideas to test items. The Peabody materials are available from DLM Teaching Resources, Box 4000, One DLM Park, Allen, TX 75002.

Portage Classroom Curriculum–CHECKLIST (Brinckerhoff, 1987). Similar to the related Portage Guide to Early Intervention CHECKLIST, this is an observation-based test battery that is multidomain, gender free, and norm referenced. It is intended for nondisabled pupils aged 2 to 6 and useful for any pupil with developmental problems. This version of the Portage covers 276 skills across five developmental domains, including 43 motor items that collectively cover large and small motor movements. Further, it is curriculum embedded (test items are subsequently taught), requires only common equipment, and stresses generalization of acquired functional skills. It is meant for use with groups within a classroom context. The Portage Classroom Curriculum and CHECKLIST is available from the same source listed for the Portage Guide to Early Intervention CHECKLIST.

Portage Guide to Early Intervention CHECKLIST (Bluma, Shearer, Frohman, & Hilliard, 1976). This is an interpret-referenced test battery that is multidomain, gender free, and norm referenced. It is intended for use with nondisabled children 0 to 6 years of age, but it is also appropriate for use with older pupils who are developmentally low. This instrument is home based in nature and is, therefore, geared toward one-on-one instruction. Its motor items are connected with a curriculum consisting of a color-coded card system with programming ideas offered for each of the 140 test items. In addition to its emphasis on infant stimulation, the items emphasize the areas of balance, posture, manipulation, fine motor, locomotion, eye–hand coordination, and strength. This instrument is available from Portage Project CESA #5, 626 East Slifer Street, Box 564, Portage, WI 53901.

Project ACTIVE Motor Ability Test (Vodola, 1974). Project ACTIVE's Motor Ability Test provides norms by chronological age, gender, and mental age across two levels. Its Level II motor ability test is for pupils 5 to 8 years of age and its Level III motor ability test covers ages 8 to 11. Both tests are meant for use with children who are classified as nondisabled, mentally retarded, learning disabled, or emotionally disordered. The five specific areas tested include gross body coordination, balance and posture, eye–hand coordination, eye–hand accuracy, and eye–foot accuracy. It is available at minimal cost from Vee, Inc., Box 2093, Neptune City, NJ 07753.

Project MOBILITEE (Hopewell Special Education Regional Resource Center, 1981). In addition to the description of Project MOBILITEE in the fitness test section of this chapter, this project also has 17 fundamental motor skill test items and associated curriculum ideas. These 17 items are outlined below.

Fundamental Motor Skill Assessment

- Throwing (standing)
- Wheelchair throw
- Catching
- Striking (standing)
- Wheelchair strike
- Running
- Wheelchair run
- Jumping
- Kicking

Motor Pattern Assessment for Low-Functioning Students

- Rolling
- Creeping/crawling
- Walking/wheelchair mobility
- Modes of movement
- Posture maintenance
- Prestriking
- Precatching
- Prekicking

The qualitative level system of scoring these items is shown on the Motor Pattern Assessment for Low-Functioning Students score sheet in Appendix B9.

Purdue Perceptual Motor Survey (Roach & Kephart, 1966). This test is interpret referenced with a four-level qualitative scoring system. It is intended for use with the general population of children 6 to 10 years old and is gender free. The survey's test areas include balance and posture, body image and differentiation, perceptual-motor match, ocular control, and form perception. These five components collectively have 22 scorable items. It is not accompanied by a curriculum. The survey is available from Psychological Corporation, 555 Academic Court, San Antonio, TX 78204. See the survey's recording form in Appendix B10.

Six Category Gross Motor Test (Cratty, 1969). This norm-referenced test is normed by disability, age, and gender. Separate norms are available for nondisabled pupils aged 4 to 12; pupils who are mildly retarded from 5 to 20 years of age; pupils who are moderately retarded from 5 to 24 years of age; and pupils classified as Down syndrome from 5 to 22 years of age. The six areas tested are body perception, gross agility, balance, locomotor agility, ball throwing, and ball tracking. This test has also been revised (Cratty, 1975). Stanine tables are provided to represent valid indices of the motor skills assessed. In an attempt to discriminate between children who are neurologically impaired and normal, norms have been established for males and females between 4 and 11 years of age. See this instrument's recording form in Appendix B11. The test is available from Charles C. Thomas, Publisher, 301-27 East Lawrence Avenue, Springfield, IL 62717.

Test of Gross Motor Development (Ulrich, 1985b). This norm-referenced test is designed for pupils 3 to 10 years of age and is meant to be individually administered. Its qualitative assessment feature also classifies it as interpret referenced. It is gender and disability label free. The test measures a dozen fundamental motor skills commonly engaged in by youngsters. Test items are grouped under the categories of locomotion and object control and specifically include

Locomotion

- Run
- Gallop
- Hop
- Leap
- Horizontal jump
- Skip
- Slide

Object Control

- Two-hand strike
- Stationary bounce
- Catch
- Kick
- Overhead throw

The cost of this tool is modest, and it can be obtained, including a Spanish version, from

Pro Ed, 8700 Shoal Creek Boulevard, Austin, TX 78758. See this instrument's recording form in Appendix B12.

Test of Motor Impairment (Stott, Moyes, & Henderson, 1984). Originally developed for use in Britain and Canada, the Test of Motor Impairment (TOMI) is a standardized means of identifying pupils who may need special motor programming even if not disabled. TOMI is norm referenced by gender for pupils aged 5 to 16 within four age bands. Qualitative assessment of motor functioning also adds to the information yield of this tool. Eight specific fine and gross motor test items are represented for each age band across the areas of manual dexterity, ball skills, static balance, and dynamic balance. Observed difficulties are also matched with factors of attitude and temperament in order to explain performance deficits more accurately and comprehensively. Guidelines for remediation are presented. TOMI is available from The Psychological Corporation, 555 Academic Court, San Antonio, TX 78204.

Aquatics

Aquatics has had a sustained history in skill test development. Since the early 1920s, more than 50 test instruments have been developed. Numerous checklists for children without and with disabilities have also been developed. Four samples of this type of test are reported here and include tools developed in connection with the American National Red Cross and the Young Men's Christian Association (YMCA), the I CAN Project, and Oregon State University's Data Based Gymnasium Model.

Recording and Evaluating Pupil Swimming Progress (American National Red Cross, 1977). The American National Red Cross has stressed the importance of monitoring pupil progress in swimming and recommends a test sheet (see Appendix B13) that is classified as content referenced and gender, age, and disability label free. The aquatics skills to be evaluated are developmentally sequenced. For each skill item, the teacher records (where appropriate) the number of times the skill was performed, the distance traveled, the amount of time taken, and the manner of performance.

YMCA Progressive Swimming Program (Arnold & Freeman, 1972). Numerous swimming tests ranging from simple to complex have been developed by the YMCA. These are skill checklists (content-referenced tests) that involve descriptive assessment regardless of age, gender, and disability label. All test items must be performed successfully in order to advance to another test level. Each test can be administered quickly, and the checklist as a whole requires very little equipment. Certificates and patches are awarded for the successful completion of each test. Following are the specific descriptive tests.*

A. Polliwog (Beginner) Test
   1. Endurance Swim—Jump feet first into chest-deep water, swim from 60 to 75 feet, any style, with flotation aid if needed, or 20 feet without flotation aid.
   2. Survival Float—Stay afloat 1 minute with flotation device if needed. Pupil is to demonstrate the ability to stay afloat for 1 minute using any one or a combination of the following: survival floating, front and/or back float, treading, or swimming.
   3. Lifesaving Skills—Elementary nonswimming throwing assists: kickboard, ball, etc. Pupil demonstrates ability to help buddy by throwing a floatable object.

*All six tests from Arnold and Freeman (1972) are reprinted by permission of National YMCA Program Materials.

Emphasis must be placed on pupil's own safety. Pupil should also be instructed to call out for additional assistance for the person in distress.
   4. Personal Safety Skill—Instructor demonstrates use of life jacket, then each pupil practices the skill. (p. 39)

B. Minnow (Advanced Beginner) Test
   1. Combination Swim—Front dive, swim one length (60 to 75 feet) front crawl stroke with rotary breathing, return one length back crawl.
   2. Survival Float—Minimum of 3 minutes on front (drownproofing).
   3. Nonswimming Assists—Reaching and extension assists from pool deck—pole, towel, etc.
   4. Mouth-to-Mouth Resuscitation.
   5. Safety Swim—Jump into deep water, swim 30 feet on front, tread and scull 10 seconds; return to starting point, using flutter back scull. (p. 42)

C. Fish (Intermediate) Test
   1. Endurance Swim (120 to 150 yards)—Two lengths each of back crawl, breaststroke, front crawl.
   2. Survival Float—7 minutes, front and/or back (minimum movement optional). Perform a (front) survival float as described in Minnow, and/or back float with minimum movement for 7 minutes.
   3. Nonswimming Assists—Extension assists, in water holding on to pool deck (pole, towel, kickboard, arm, leg, etc.).
   4. Standing Front Dive (1-meter board).
   5. Underwater Swim—Push off, glide, and swim under water for a total distance of 30 feet. (p. 48)

D. Flying Fish (Advanced Intermediate) Test
   1. Endurance Swim (200 yards) front crawl.
   2. Survival Float—15 minutes (7-1/2 minutes front and 7-1/2 minutes back); movement allowed.
   3. Treading Water—Legs only, 2 minutes; arms only, 2 minutes.

4. Front Dive with Approach and Hurdle—From 1-meter board with minimum three-step approach and hurdle.

5. Individual Medley 80 to 100 yards—20 to 25 yards each of butterfly, back crawl, breaststroke, and front crawl with start and turns. (p. 51)

E. Shark (Swimmer) Test

1. Individual Medley—160 to 200 yards. 40 to 50 yards each of butterfly, back crawl, breaststroke, front crawl, with starts and turns.

2. Survival Float—20 minutes. Arms only, 10 minutes; legs only, 10 minutes.

3. Surface Dives—Recover object in 6 to 8 feet of water; head first and feet first. (p. 54)

F. Porpoise (Advanced Watermanship) Test

1. Endurance Swim—Qualifying times are indicated for three age groups and for female swimmers as well as for male swimmers.

2. Treading kicks—Four.

3. Perform three specific strokes.

4. Individual Medley Swim (IMS)—Meet qualifying times shown for three age groups and for both sexes.

5. Racing turns—Two.

6. Drownproofing—Continue for $\frac{1}{2}$ hour.

7. Artificial respiration—Show three methods of resuscitation.

8. Safe use of small craft.

9. Perform six synchronized swimming skills.

10. Volunteer 25 hours' service in YMCA Aquatics Program. (p. 59)

I CAN: Aquatics (Wessel, 1976a). Another approach to aquatics testing is presented in I CAN: Aquatics. Similar to the other I CAN tools, the aquatics package is an interpret-referenced test tool. It is designed to assess the following areas:

Basic Swimming Skills

- Water adjustment
- Breath control
- Front buoyancy
- Back buoyancy
- Front flutter kick
- Wedge kick

Swimming and Water Entry

- Front crawl
- Back crawl
- Finning
- Elementary backstroke
- Tread water
- Survival float
- Jump into water
- Front dive

Based on the results of the assessments, appropriate aquatics instructional activities and games are recommended. The I CAN program is further detailed in other sections of this chapter.

Data Based Gymnasium (Dunn, Morehouse, & Fredericks, 1986; Dunn, Morehouse, & Dalke, 1979). Oregon State University's Data Based Gymnasium Model, already described in this chapter and in Chapter 3, also contains a section on swimming assessment in its Game, Exercise, and Leisure Sport Curriculum (Dunn, Morehouse, & Dalke, 1979). Twenty task-analyzed aquatic activities are targeted:

- Adjustment to water
- Breath holding
- Bobbing rhythmically
- Rhythmic breathing
- Jelly fish float
- Prone float

- Prone glide
- Back float
- Back glide
- Front flutter kick
- Back flutter kick
- Wedge kick
- Arm stroke
- Front crawl
- Back crawl
- Finning stroke
- Elementary backstroke
- Tread water
- Survival float
- Jump into water

Dance

Dance is probably the least frequently tested physical education area, perhaps because, even though dance is an integral component of physical education, it is often overlooked or minimally addressed in programming. Most of the tests developed to assess dance skills are designed for the secondary school pupil or college level student.

Teacher-made tests can be created by rating specific dance skills in which several pupils can be tested at one time. The following are a few examples of this skill-testing approach (Freed, 1976; pp. 144–145).

1. Pupil shall be able to perform any of the basic locomotor movements, as requested by the instructor, in appropriate form and rhythm. Example: Given a drum beat or appropriate music, the pupil will be able to perform a skip with body extended, feet pushing off from floor, arms either held in position (sideward at shoulder height) or swinging with control in opposition to legs.
2. Pupil shall demonstrate ability to perform basic axial movements, as requested by instructor, in appropriate form and rhythm, at different levels. Example: Given a drum

beat or appropriate music, the pupil will be able to perform a series of two-beat swings, emphasizing the curved line and rebound of true swinging movement. The swings may be performed at a single level (for example, standing) or at several levels in succession (for example, standing, kneeling, sitting).
3. Pupil shall perform a combination of at least three locomotor movements, either a pattern assigned by instructor or one devised by pupils. Example: Instructor assigns locomotor pattern of four skips forward, four slides to the right, two step-hops forward, four jumps in place. Pupils are graded on accuracy, grace, and quality of the movement pattern. Example: Pupil shall perform a locomotor pattern four measures in length, including at least three different locomotor movements with at least two changes of direction. The patterns may be devised and performed individually or in groups of two or three pupils.
4. Dances (or shorter patterns) shall be evaluated by class and instructor on the basis of an evaluation sheet provided by instructor. Class discussion may be substituted for written evaluation when deemed appropriate.

The testing form could be one sheet with a listing of each skill to be tested. An additional column could be provided for comments.

Robins and Robins (1968) have developed an interpret-referenced test of dance skills for pupils classified as mentally retarded. A sample of their pupil progress record form is shown in Appendix B14. The letters represent the exercises (described in the index column) that each pupil is able to perform during each lesson.

Individual and Group Activities

Numerous sports skill tests have been designed for regular physical education classes. A resourceful teacher can modify these tests or can develop new ones. Three major resources for individual and group activity tests are the following:

Collins, D. R., & Hodges, P. B. (1978). *A comprehensive guide to sports skills tests and measurements.* Springfield, IL: Charles C Thomas.

Johnson, B. L., & Nelson, J. K. (1979). *Practical measurements for evaluation in physical education,* 3rd ed. Minneapolis: Burgess.

Kirkendall, D. R., Gruber, J. J., & Johnson, R. E. (1987). *Measurement and evaluation for physical educators,* 2nd ed. Champaign, IL: Human Kinetics.

Tests analyzed in these resources cover the following sports:

- Archery
- Badminton
- Baseball
- Basketball
- Bowling
- Canoeing
- Diving
- Football
- Golf
- Gymnastics
- Handball/racquetball
- Soccer
- Softball
- Table tennis
- Tennis
- Track and field
- Volleyball

A number of resources are available specifically in special physical education. We report on four here.

I CAN: Sport, Leisure and Recreational Skill (Wessel, 1979). This packet divides common sports and recreational activities into basic components. Each component is then analyzed by subtasks that translate into a continuum of performance items. Testing activities are presented to determine where a pupil is performing on the continuum, and several activities are also listed for use in enhancing future performance. Some of the sports and recreational activities included in the packet are volleyball, basketball, softball, golf, cross-country skiing, and roller skating. The I CAN program is further detailed in other sections of this chapter.

Project MOBILITEE (Hopewell Special Education Regional Resource Center, 1981). This test and curriculum resource for pupils classified as moderately and severely disabled (already described in this chapter) has a unique aspect to its assessment scheme that relates to a pupil's ability to participate in games successfully. Successful participation in games and sports is viewed as involving more than the adequate performance of fundamental motor skills and the possession of adequate levels of physical fitness. As a reflection of this viewpoint, selected social and emotional dimensions also are assessed. To reflect this affective domain emphasis, the games portion of the Project MOBILITEE materials highlights gathering data on specific areas of behavior, such as

- Complies with rules and directions
- Impulsive behavior
- Leadership/team membership
- Teamwork
- Safety
- Self-concept

With such information, activity leaders can better address such questions as How often does a pupil comply with rules? How often does a pupil work with partners to achieve a game goal? Is a pupil excessively upset and disruptive if unable to control major aspects of a game? Is a pupil willing to accept the role of leader? Does a pupil recognize potentially dangerous situations? Is a pupil willing to take chances or try a new game?

Special Olympics Sports Skills Series (Special Olympics, 1982). Since 1979, the Kennedy Foundation has developed numerous sports skills series for use by individuals who are mentally retarded. These cover such individual and group games and sports as the following:

- Basketball
- Softball
- Figure skating
- Gymnastics
- Nordic skiing
- Roller skating
- Rowing
- Weight lifting
- Volleyball
- Alpine skiing
- Track and field
- Bowling
- Cycling
- Equestrian
- Ice hockey
- Soccer
- Handball
- Tennis

As one example, its Softball Sports Skills Program (Special Olympics, 1981) provides practitioners with test and curriculum information related to slo-pitch softball participation. The manual includes specific information on clothing, field preparation, equipment, warming up, slo-pitch softball skill content-referenced assessment at two levels, task analysis of fundamental skills for use in teacher training, lead-up activities, and modifications and adaptations. The assessments are age and gender free. The Level I assessment includes 39 items that cover throwing, catching, batting, base running, rules, and affective dimensions related to slo-pitch softball participation. Beginner, rookie, and winner classifications are given. The Level II assessment includes 38 items that cover the same areas with an additional emphasis on the skill of pitching. Champ, Superchamp, and Superstar classifications are given at this level. The softball program, or any of the other programs within the Special Olympics Sports Skills series, can be obtained at minimal cost from Kennedy Foundation, 1350 New York Avenue N.W., Suite 500, Washington, DC 20005.

Data Based Gymnasium (Dunn, Morehouse & Fredericks, 1986; Dunn, Morehouse & Dalke, 1979). Oregon State University's Data Based Gymnasium Model, already described in this chapter and in Chapter 2, also has a section on the assessment and programming of elementary games and lifetime leisure skills in its Game, Exercise, and Leisure Sport Curriculum (Dunn, Morehouse & Dalke, 1979). Its dozen task-analyzed individual and group games and sports include

- Rides push toy
- Scooter board
- Tricycle riding
- Bike riding
- Go down a slide
- Swinging
- Teeter-Totter
- Horseshoes
- Quoits
- Bowling
- Frisbee throw
- Roller skating

Posture Deviations

The testing of posture is very complex, because even experts cannot agree on what constitutes good posture. In general, though, most believe that such testing should include measures of both static and dynamic posture. Such a dual emphasis on posture testing appears warranted because good body mechanics affects performance in all physical education activities. In addition, systematic attention to posture testing is especially important during the elementary and junior high school years. The following tests are some relatively traditional posture tests currently being used in special physical education settings.

Full View Dynamic Posture Evaluation (Ersing, 1980). This is a quick content-referenced observation technique. The pupil stands at a corner of a large square on the floor and walks along the square's path on a teacher's cue. This square can be formed by cones, tape, or already existing lines on the floor. The teacher stands far enough away on one side to comfortably analyze static and dynamic posture from the front, the back, and both sides of the pupil. It is desirable to have the pupil wear a swimsuit so that the spinal column and other key anatomical checkpoints can be easily viewed. The recording form used at the Ohio State University is shown in Appendix B15.

I CAN: Health and Fitness (Wessel, 1976d). Within this packet are interpret-referenced tests of specific static and dynamic postures such as standing, sitting, walking, and ascending/descending stairs. Based on the performance of the pupil on each test, specific instructional activities and games are recommended. Standard I CAN test and activity planning formats are available for use in posture training. The I CAN system is further discussed in other sections of this chapter.

New York State Posture Test (New York State Physical Fitness Test for Boys and Girls, Grades 4–12, 1966). This interpret-referenced test involves the assessment of 13 areas of the body (see a sample recording form in Appendix B16. The teacher rates each person based on a 5-3-1 scoring system matched to body diagrams on the rating form itself. These scores can be translated into a percentile rank and an achievement level (see Table 15.3). Vodola (1973) has suggested that the posture score on this test would be more meaningful using a 7-4-1 scoring system. The maximum score would then be 91, with an additional nine points added to all raw scores, which would give a perfect score of 100 points, instead of 65 points. He also suggests that a pupil who scores 70 or below on any body area should be recommended for a thorough posture examination by the school physician.

TABLE 15.3   NORMS FOR NEW YORK STATE POSTURE TEST

ACHIEVEMENT LEVEL	PERCENTILE RANK	POSTURE SCORE
10	99	—
9	98	65
8	93	63
7	84	61
6	69	59
5	50	57
4	31	53–55
3	16	49–51
2	7	43–47
1	2	39–41
0	1	13–37

Portland State University has adapted the New York State Posture Test (Althoff, Heyden, & Robertson, 1988). Fourteen areas of the body are rated using the same 5-3-1 scoring system and associated body part diagrams. The Portland Posture Rating Form is used in connection with a posture grid, plumb line, and positional markers, and the scores placed on the form are coded for computer analysis. Appendix B17 shows the form itself. More detailed information on this posture test's variations can be obtained from Physical Education Department, Portland State University, Portland, OR 97207.

Orthopedic Screening (Ayres & Smith, 1964). This screening instrument is designed for pupils in grades 1–12. The items include the testing of the general posture, shoulders, spine, abdomen, lower extremities, feet, gait, and musculature. Only a few minutes are required to administer this screening instrument.

Pedograph (Arnheim, Auxter, & Crowe, 1977). A pedograph is an imprint of the foot bottom, made while an individual is in a full weight-bearing position or while walking across the pedograph. It can also be used to record outer foot tracings. This machine is commercially produced by the William M. Scholl Company in Chicago.

Podiascope (Arnheim, Auxter, & Crowe, 1977). This piece of equipment is used to test the plantar surface of the foot under weight-bearing conditions. It is usually homemade. A 2' X 2' box is built with 3/4" plywood. The front and top sides are left open. A thick plate of safety glass is mounted on the top of the box, and a mirror is placed inside the box on an adjustable plate at approximately a 45-degree angle. The adjustable mirror allows the teacher to view the bottom of the feet in various angles or allows pupils to view their own feet. In some podiascopes, a Polaroid camera is also mounted inside the box. The teacher can compare photographs of the same pupil during the course of a remedial program to determine how much progress is being made.

Photographic Postural Evaluation (Kelly, 1946). A photograph is taken of a pupil assuming a static posture, and then the photo is assessed using an acceptable standard. The methods of taking the photographs are discussed in detail in Kelly (1946). We also recommend use of videotape analysis, which assures static and dynamic postural assessment and the possibility of interrater reliability determinations, if desired.

Skan-a-Graf. This instrument is used to assist the teacher to determine postural improvement, if any, through the aid of an angle sight (see Figure 15.1 on page 444).

Symmetrigraf. This technique involves a screen with a plumb line (see Figure 15.2 on page 445). It is used as a quick screening device to determine normal and abnormal static posture.

Weight Problems

The most common means of estimating whether a child is underweight, overweight, or obese is to use a standard weight reference table (see Table 15.4). Such tables also exist for men and women (see Table 15.5). At a minimum, any reference table should include information on age and sex. Children are generally considered underweight if 10 percent below their peer standard, overweight if 10 percent above their peer standard, and obese if 20 percent or more above their peer standard.

TABLE 15.4   WEIGHT AND HEIGHT PERCENTILE TABLES FOR BOYS AND GIRLS, BIRTH TO AGE 18

Boys							Girls						
Weight (pounds)				Height (pounds)			Weight (pounds)				Height (pounds)		
10%	50%	90%	Age	10%	50%	90%	10%	50%	90%	Age	10%	50%	90%
6.3	7.5	9.1	Birth	18.9	19.9	21.0	6.2	7.4	8.6	Birth	18.8	19.8	20.4
8.5	10.0	11.5	1 mo.	20.2	21.2	22.2	8.0	9.7	11.0	1 mo.	20.2	21.0	22.0
10.0	11.5	13.2	2 mo.	21.5	22.5	23.5	9.5	11.0	12.5	2 mo.	21.5	22.2	23.2
11.1	12.6	14.5	3 mo.	22.8	23.8	24.7	10.7	12.4	14.0	3 mo.	22.4	23.4	24.3
12.5	14.0	16.2	4 mo.	23.7	24.7	25.7	12.0	13.7	15.5	4 mo.	23.2	24.2	25.2
13.7	15.0	17.7	5 mo.	24.5	25.5	26.5	13.0	14.7	17.0	5 mo.	24.0	25.0	26.0
14.8	16.7	19.2	6 mo.	25.2	26.1	27.3	14.1	16.0	18.6	6 mo.	24.6	25.7	26.7
17.8	20.0	22.9	9 mo.	27.0	28.0	29.2	16.6	19.2	22.4	9 mo.	26.4	27.6	28.7
19.6	22.2	25.4	12 mo.	28.5	29.6	30.7	18.4	21.5	24.8	12 mo.	27.8	29.2	30.3
22.3	25.2	29.0	18 mo.	31.0	32.2	33.5	21.2	24.5	28.3	18 mo.	30.2	31.8	33.3
24.7	27.7	31.9	2 yr.	33.1	34.4	35.9	23.5	27.1	31.7	2 yr.	32.3	34.1	35.8
26.6	30.0	34.5	2½ yr.	34.8	36.3	37.9	25.5	29.6	34.6	2½ yr.	34.0	36.0	37.9
28.7	32.2	36.8	3 yr.	36.3	37.9	39.6	27.6	31.8	37.4	3 yr.	35.6	37.7	39.8
30.4	34.3	39.1	3½ yr.	37.8	39.3	41.1	29.5	33.9	40.4	3½ yr.	37.1	39.2	41.5
32.1	36.4	41.4	4 yr.	39.1	40.7	42.7	31.2	36.2	43.5	4 yr.	38.4	40.6	43.1
33.8	38.4	43.9	4½ yr.	40.3	42.0	44.2	32.9	38.5	46.7	4½ yr.	39.7	42.0	44.7
33.5	40.5	46.7	5 yr.	40.8	42.8	45.2	34.8	40.5	49.2	5 yr.	40.5	42.9	45.4
38.8	45.6	53.1	5½ yr.	42.6	45.0	47.3	38.0	44.0	51.2	5½ yr.	42.4	44.4	46.8
40.9	48.3	56.4	6 yr.	43.8	46.3	48.6	39.6	46.5	54.2	6 yr.	43.5	45.6	48.1
43.4	51.2	60.4	6½ yr.	44.9	47.6	50.0	42.2	49.4	57.7	6½ yr.	44.8	46.9	49.4
45.8	54.1	64.4	7 yr.	46.0	48.9	51.4	44.5	52.2	61.2	7 yr.	46.0	48.1	50.7
48.5	57.1	68.7	7½ yr.	47.2	50.0	52.7	46.6	55.2	65.6	7½ yr.	47.0	49.3	51.9
51.2	60.1	73.0	8 yr.	48.5	51.2	54.0	48.6	58.1	69.9	8 yr.	48.1	50.4	53.0
53.8	63.1	77.0	8½ yr.	49.5	52.3	55.1	50.6	61.0	74.5	8½ yr.	49.0	51.4	54.1
56.3	66.0	81.0	9 yr.	50.5	53.3	56.1	52.6	63.8	79.1	9 yr.	50.0	52.3	55.3
58.7	69.0	85.5	9½ yr.	51.4	54.3	57.1	54.9	67.1	84.4	9½ yr.	50.9	53.5	56.4
61.1	71.9	89.9	10 yr.	52.3	55.2	58.1	57.1	70.3	89.7	10 yr.	51.8	54.6	57.5
63.7	74.8	94.6	10½ yr.	53.2	56.0	58.9	59.9	74.6	95.1	10½ yr.	52.9	55.8	58.9
66.3	77.6	99.3	11 yr.	54.0	56.8	59.8	62.6	78.8	100.4	11 yr.	53.9	57.0	60.4
69.2	81.0	104.5	11½ yr.	55.0	57.8	60.9	66.1	83.2	106.0	11½ yr.	55.0	58.3	61.8
72.0	84.4	108.6	12 yr.	56.1	58.9	62.2	69.5	87.6	111.5	12 yr.	56.1	59.8	63.2
74.6	88.7	116.4	12½ yr.	56.9	60.0	63.6	74.7	93.4	118.0	12½ yr.	57.4	60.7	64.0
77.1	93.0	123.2	13 yr.	57.7	61.0	65.1	79.9	99.1	124.5	13 yr.	58.7	61.8	64.9
82.2	100.3	130.1	13½ yr.	58.8	62.6	66.5	85.5	103.7	128.9	13½ yr.	59.5	62.4	65.3
87.2	107.6	136.9	14 yr.	59.9	64.0	67.9	91.0	108.4	133.3	14 yr.	60.2	62.8	65.7
93.3	113.9	142.4	14½ yr.	61.0	65.1	68.7	94.2	111.0	135.7	14½ yr.	60.7	63.1	66.0
99.4	120.1	147.8	15 yr.	62.1	66.1	69.6	97.4	113.5	138.1	15 yr.	61.1	63.4	66.2
105.2	124.9	152.6	15½ yr.	63.1	66.8	70.2	99.2	115.3	139.6	15½ yr.	61.3	63.7	66.4
111.0	129.7	157.3	16 yr.	64.1	67.8	70.7	100.9	117.0	141.1	16 yr.	61.5	63.9	66.5
114.3	133.0	161.0	16½ yr.	64.6	68.0	71.1	101.9	118.1	142.2	16½ yr.	61.5	63.9	66.6
117.5	136.2	164.6	17 yr.	65.2	68.4	71.5	102.8	119.1	143.3	17 yr.	61.5	64.0	66.7
118.8	137.6	166.8	17½ yr.	65.3	68.5	71.6	103.2	119.5	143.9	17½ yr.	61.5	64.0	66.7
120.0	139.0	169.0	18 yr.	65.5	68.7	71.8	103.5	119.9	144.5	18 yr.	61.5	64.0	66.7

Modified from G. H. Lowrey, *Growth and Development of Children*, 8th ed. (Chicago: Year Book Medical Publishers, 1986), pp. 95–96. Used with permission.

TABLE 15.5   1983 Metropolitan Height and Weight Tables

	Men				Women		
		Weight (pounds)				Weight (pounds)	
Height FT. IN.	SMALL FRAME	MEDIUM FRAME	LARGE FRAME	Height FT. IN.	SMALL FRAME	MEDIUM FRAME	LARGE FRAME
5 2	128–134	131–141	138–150	4 10	102–111	109–121	118–131
5 3	130–136	133–143	140–153	4 11	103–113	111–123	120–134
5 4	132–138	135–145	142–156	5 0	104–115	113–126	122–137
5 5	134–140	137–148	144–160	5 1	106–118	115–129	125–140
5 6	136–142	139–151	146–164	5 2	108–121	118–132	128–143
5 7	138–145	142–154	149–168	5 3	111–124	121–135	131–147
5 8	140–148	145–157	152–172	5 4	114–127	124–138	134–151
5 9	142–151	148–160	155–176	5 5	117–130	127–141	137–155
5 10	144–154	151–163	158–180	5 6	120–133	130–144	140–159
5 11	146–157	154–166	161–184	5 7	123–136	133–147	143–163
6 0	149–160	157–170	164–188	5 8	126–139	136–150	146–167
6 1	152–164	160–174	168–192	5 9	129–142	139–153	149–170
6 2	155–168	164–178	172–197	5 10	132–145	142–156	152–173
6 3	158–172	167–182	176–202	5 11	135–148	145–159	155–176
6 4	162–176	171–187	181–207	6 0	138–151	148–162	158–179

Another technique sometimes used in schools is the skinfold test. A skinfold (fat) caliper is used to measure subcutaneous and adipose (fat) tissue. There are several commonly selected sites on the body—the chest, abdomen, back of arm (triceps), thigh, calf, and scapula. These are sites where the skin and adipose can be lifted between the thumb and forefinger, away from the underlying muscle tissue. The skinfold thickness is then measured and weight problems, if any, determined (see Figure 15.3 on 446).

Standards for minimum tricep skinfold thickness (in millimeters), indicating obesity by age (5–50) for nondisabled Causasian Americans, are given in Table 15.6 on page 445. Additional skinfold standards using tricep, subscapular, and combined tricep/subscapular site measures are available for ages 10 to 17 for individuals classified as nondisabled, learning disabled, visually impaired, cerebral palsied, paraplegic, and wheelchair bound (Winnick & Short, 1985). The AAHPERD Health-Related Fitness Test (AAHPERD, 1980b) also provides body fat measures at the triceps and subscapular sites for normal boys and girls 5 to 17 years of age. And AAHPERD's Physical Best (1988) test includes skinfold measures of the triceps and calf yielding a body composition index for 5–18-year-old normal males and females.

PROGRAM EVALUATION

Evaluation is essential in order to determine the benefits derived from a special physical education program. Through continuous evaluation, a program's strengths and weaknesses can be made known, and corrections, if necessary, can occur over a reasonable time period.

There are numerous program evaluation techniques that can be used. For instance, questionnaires and checklists can be employed to impact the development and refinement of special physical programs. Such program evaluation techniques should make use of respondents including parents,

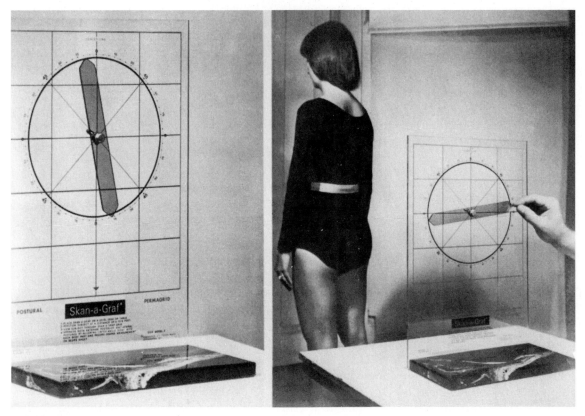

FIGURE 15.1   Skan-a-Graf. *(Courtesy of Reedco, Inc., Auburn, NY 13021.)*

teachers, administrators, and pupils themselves. And such evaluation should probe for information across numerous factors, including such things as program offerings, organization, personnel, and pupil status. We should continually seek the best evaluation devices, and, therefore, ongoing scholarly inquiry is needed to determine the characteristics of good local school district special physical education programs and to develop better instruments for assessing the extent to which a program is meeting local needs.

Toward this end, a first of its kind systematic effort to determine and prioritize school district special physical education needs evolved from the development of a program evaluation tool entitled Survey of Adapted Physical Education Needs, SAPEN (Sherrill & Megginson, 1984). This is a 50-item Likert Scale questionnaire for school district use that attempts to address the overall question: What exists and/or what should exist in the area of special physical education in your school program? The 50 questions collectively cover the area of special physical education and include, as examples, such concerns as curriculum content and availability, duration and frequency of services, pupil placement and grouping, contact with the school's administration, public relations, involvement in the IEP process, quality of personnel, pupil screening and testing, and pupil physical

FIGURE 15.2 Symmetrigraf. *(Courtesy of Reedco, Inc., Auburn, NY 13021.)*

TABLE 15.6 OBESITY STANDARDS FOR CAUCASIAN AMERICANS

AGE (YEARS)	Minimum Triceps Skinfold Thickness Indicating Obesity (millimeters)	
	MALES	FEMALES
5	12	14
6	12	15
7	13	16
8	14	17
9	15	18
10	16	20
11	17	21
12	18	22
13	18	23
14	17	23
15	16	24
16	15	25
17	14	26
18	15	27
19	15	27
20	16	28
21	17	28
22	18	28
23	18	28
24	19	28
25	20	29
26	20	29
27	21	29
28	22	29
29	22	29
30–50	23	30

Source: C. C. Seltzer and J. Mayer, "A Simple Criterion for Obesity," *Postgraduate Medicine, 38* (1965), A101–A107. Used by permission, McGraw-Hill, Inc.

activity involvement in the community. This tool also promotes interaction among different individuals and, therefore, provides different perceptions and perspectives. In fact, the original research on the use of the tool made use of feedback from administrators, physical educators, special educators, and parents that resulted in an actual special physical education service delivery action plan in a school district in Texas. An excerpt from the first part of the tool is provided in Figure 15.4 on page 447.

Toward the same end, the Ohio State University has compiled a profile of related quality program indicators for use as a checklist in evaluating special physical education

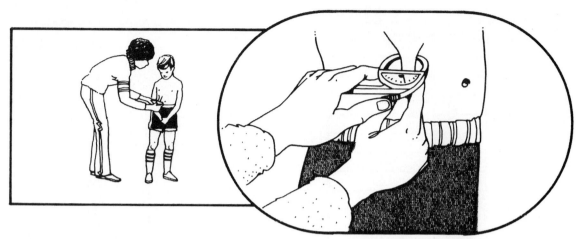

FIGURE 15.3 Abdominal skinfold measure with calipers.

programs at the school building level. This profile has a particular focus on the area of educating pupils with disabilities in the least restrictive environment. Its 23-item checklist is contained in Table 15.7 on page 448. The content of this checklist received internal approval from numerous individuals involved in special physical education programs across the country, including school building, school district, state department of education, and college/university personnel.

Some teachers not only evaluate the pupils presently in their programs but follow up their alumni as well. Another excellent technique is to invite consultants to observe and critically evaluate the program in relation to other programs within the district, state, or nation.

Regardless of the depth of the formal evaluation, the teacher should also be constantly observing what is said, seen, or even sensed. As an additional recommendation, once a year all equipment and facilities should be inspected and a formal report developed on things like unsafe equipment, hazards on the playground, and broken bleachers. There should be immediate action to alleviate *all* safety hazards. Combining these techniques and using them periodically, the teacher will be kept informed of all phases of the program for which he or she is responsible.

SURVEY OF ADAPTED PHYSICAL EDUCATION NEEDS (SAPEN)

Please circle in the left hand column the number which you feel best represents the services that now exist in your school district. Circle in the right hand column the number which best represents your opinion about what should exist. IT IS CRITICAL THAT YOU CIRCLE A NUMBER FOR EACH ITEM IN EACH COLUMN. Once you are completed, double check to see if you have responded to every item using both columns.

GIVE YOUR OPINION NOW EXIST							GIVE YOUR OPINION SHOULD EXIST					
6-Completely Agree	5-Mostly Agree	4-Slightly Agree	3-Slightly Disagree	2-Mostly Disagree	1-Completely Disagree		6-Completely Agree	5-Mostly Agree	4-Slightly Agree	3-Slightly Disagree	2-Mostly Disagree	1-Completely Disagree
6	5	4	3	2	1	1. A curriculum manual describing physical education instruction/services for the handicapped is available.	6	5	4	3	2	1
6	5	4	3	2	1	2. Elementary school handicapped students receive 150 minutes of physical education instruction per week.	6	5	4	3	2	1
6	5	4	3	2	1	3. Administrative personnel understand that adapted physical education services are separate and different from those provided by a physical, occupational, or recreational therapist.	6	5	4	3	2	1
6	5	4	3	2	1	4. Regular physical education classes with handicapped students in them have a student-staff ratio of 30 to 1 or less.	6	5	4	3	2	1
6	5	4	3	2	1	5. Evaluative criteria are available to guide administrators in monitoring the quality of adapted physical education programs.	6	5	4	3	2	1
6	5	4	3	2	1	6. Administrators are utilizing current funding alternatives for hiring adapted physical education specialist.	6	5	4	3	2	1

FIGURE 15.4 First part of SAPEN instrument.

TABLE 15.7 OHIO STATE UNIVERSITY'S PROFILE OF SPECIAL PHYSICAL EDUCATION QUALITY PROGRAM INDICATORS

QUALITY PROGRAM INDICATORS	Indicators Present		
	YES	NO	NOT SURE
Has written policies and procedures for physical education which include provisions for all pupils			
Offers a variety of placement levels to meet all pupil needs			
Determines pupil placement and programming using educational team results			
Designates special physical education entry and exit criteria and standards			
Utilizes an educational team approach			
Includes parents as members of the educational team			
Includes pupil in IEP meetings, where appropriate			
Includes special physical education and related service personnel in IEP and staff meetings			
Evaluates program effectiveness regularly			
Utilizes a zero reject philosophy			
Utilizes qualified physical education personnel			
Uses qualified related service personnel (e.g., OT, PT)			
Offers instruction in community settings (e.g., swimming pool near pupil's home)			
Systematically evaluates pupil skill retention and generalization			
Provides a variety of age appropriate curriculum alternatives in physical and motor fitness			
Provides a variety of age appropriate curriculum alternatives in fundamental motor skills and patterns			
Provides a variety of age appropriate curriculum alternatives in individual group games and sports, including lifetime and leisure time skills			
Offers extracurricular activities for all pupils			
Has appropriate facilities and resources			
Maintains appropriate teacher/pupil ratios			
Allots flexible class frequency to meet pupil needs			
Allots appropriate duration of classes to meet pupil needs			
Uses a functional curriculum approach, when appropriate			

PERSONNEL EVALUATION

Program evaluation must involve the ongoing evaluation of program personnel because when the quality of teaching is improved and maintained, pupils especially benefit. We, therefore, specifically want to address the evaluation of teachers and their assistants.

At least four options exist for the evaluation of direct-contact educational personnel. A teacher or an assistant can self-evaluate, be observed by colleagues "in-house," be evaluated by pupils, or be evaluated by outside team personnel. Technology can be incorporated in this evaluation process with more common devices such as audio- or videotape or less common means such as computer applications. Such evaluation as it relates to systematic methods of teaching and teacher analysis has been summarized in the literature (Darst, Zakrajsek, & Mancini, 1989).

Three primary teacher evaluation instruments that can be applied with teachers of special physical education include the Academic Learning Time–Physical Education (ALT–PE) system with its emphasis on percentage of a pupil's motor engagement (Siedentop, Tousignant, & Parker, 1982; Siedentop, 1991); the Cheffer's Adaptation of Flanders Interaction Analysis System with its emphasis on the quantity and quality of teacher–pupil interactions (Cheffers, 1972); and the Observational Recording Record of Physical Educator's Teaching Behavior (Stewart, 1983), as adapted for special physical educators by Miller (1985), with its concentration on the instructional climate, interaction, and teachers' behaviors.

In evaluating the effectiveness of teachers and their assistants, many areas of teaching-related behavior can be measured. Some of these are more directly indicators of pupil behavior, but reflect teaching ability too. Just a few variables are listed here:

- Percentage of time engagement
- Ratio of activity mixes
- Types of activity
- Latency time before pupils move
- Number of trials to task completion
- Frequency of phrases
- Amount of instructional time
- Downtime
- Presentation clarity
- Teacher exuberance
- Activity relevance
- Cueing behaviors properly
- Appropriate correction of pupils
- Instruction giving
- Pupil reinforcement
- Negative expressions
- Voice control
- Distracting mannerisms
- Speech tone

- Teacher participation
- Variety of methods
- Adaptability
- Uses progressions
- Breaks skills down
- Evidence of planning
- Body language
- Class logistics
- Use of humor

A key issue, however, is the objective measurement of such teaching-related variables based on precise operational definitions. Two examples of such evaluation are provided in the ALT–PE Model (Siedentop, Tousignant, & Parker, 1982) and the Data Based Gymnasium volunteer observation system in Figure 15.5 (Dunn, Morehouse, & Fredericks, 1986).

In the ALT–PE Model, measurement of a teacher's effectiveness is determined from pupil behaviors in class. The model emphasizes the components of management, transition, waiting, knowledge, activity, and off-task. Each major component, in turn, is broken down collectively into a number of other subfactors. These six major components are operationally defined as follows:

- *Management* (M): time spent devoted to class business that is unrelated to instructional activity.
- *Transition* (T): time spent listening to or performing organizational activities related to instruction.
- *Waiting* (W): time spent awaiting the next instruction or opportunity to respond; being on a team but not actively involved.
- *Knowledge* (K): time spent listening to instructions, watching a demonstration, questioning, or discussing.
- *Activity* (A): time spent appropriately engaged in motor activity by actively responding or by actively supporting.

FIGURE 15.5 The Data Based Gymnasium Volunteer Observation Form

Volunteer/Aide: _____   Observer: _____

Program: _____   Date: _____

Cue (verbal): _____   Time: _____

Instructional Setting: _____   Materials: _____

Describe Motor Response: _____   Criteria: _____

_____

Reinforcer and Schedule: _____

_____

Correction Procedure: _____

_____

Key	
Code 1	Code 2
1 = Correct 0 = Incorrect	1 = Correct F = Fail To D = Delay C = Change W = Weak Word R = Repeat L = Level

Student		Program Cues			Program Correction								Data
		Verbal			Model			Physical Assistance			Behavior Cues and Consequences		
		Cue	Consequences		Cue	Consequences		Cue	Consequences		Cue	+	−
			+	−		+	−		+	−			
	1												
	2												
	3												
	4												
	5												
	6												
	7												
	8												
	9												
	10												
	11												
	12												

Scores

Comments:

Cues: $\dfrac{\text{Correct Cues}}{\text{Correct + Incorrect Cues}}$ = ____/____ or ____ %

Consequences: $\dfrac{\text{Correct Consequences:}}{\text{Correct + Incorrect Consequences}}$ = ____/____ or ____ %

Data: $\dfrac{\text{Correct Data}}{\text{Correct + Incorrect Data}}$ = ____/____ or ____ %

Criterion: Individual 90%, Agreement 85%

- *Offtask* (O): time spent not engaged in activity in which a pupil should be engaged.

Percentage data are typically taken of these observed instruction-related components using measurement techniques such as interval recording or time sampling (Cooper, Heron, & Heward, 1987). Percent of activity (A) or activity (A) and knowledge (K) combined are commonly the final desirable measure of basic ALT–PE. The higher the percentage, the more effective is the teacher.

The Data Based Gymnasium Model incorporates a written teacher assistant or volunteer observation system that provides percentage data on the direct caregiver's ability

to cue pupils, correct pupils, and reinforce pupils, plus to consistently record pupil data. A 90 percent criterion level is the goal. The observation form on which these data are recorded is contained in Figure 15.5.

Special physical educators are urged to determine a system of teacher and teacher aide evaluation that is most conducive and applicable to their situation. A system of teacher evaluation provided in the literature or a school-designed system of evaluation are possibilities. Finally, such evaluation should be ongoing and frequent. The ultimate payoff will be safe, successful, and satisfied pupils.

We end this chapter with interview comments on testing and evaluation from Julian Stein.

Julian Stein

Dr. Julian Stein, now retired, was a professor in physical education at George Mason University in Fairfax, Virginia, and, prior to that, was the director of the American Alliance for Health, Physical Education, Recreation and Dance's Unit on Programs for the Handicapped.

1. *Which special physical education testing/evaluating area (posture, motor, fitness, or play) should receive more emphasis? Does the emphasis shift with a pupil's age? Are there other factors to be considered?*

Four areas of the psychomotor domain (i.e., posture, motor, fitness, and play) should

all receive priority consideration in programs of special physical education, including testing and evaluating activities of such programs. Percentage of emphasis, however, depends on a number of factors which include pupil's age and type/severity of disability. As examples, greater stress on posture and motor factors would be typical of the elementary level and greater stress on fitness and play (i.e., leisure-time competence) more typical of the secondary level. Of course, needs of *individual* pupils might indicate an emphasis different from the norm and these should dominate testing/evaluation thrusts employed.

2. *How much testing and evaluating is minimal in order for a physical educator to appropriately impact a child's IEP?*

Minimal testing and evaluating time cannot be estimated with any precision since this depends on factors such as IEP-related school policy, special physical educator expertise, overall time available, and motivation. The most valid and effective testing and evaluation comes from teachers, including physical educators, working with pupils in class or activity situations. Simply to use quantitative data from a norm-referenced test or number of successes and failures from criterion-referenced instruments is not sufficient. Neither of these approaches gets at types of vital information that comes from observation (20/20 assessment) tempered by understanding pupils, knowledge of each child as an individual, expertise in activities, personal experience, and sound professional judgment. In addition to observation and other informal approaches, input can be obtained from both criterion- and norm-referenced techniques, when appropriate.

Another point which needs to be made is that a pupil's curriculum and testing/evaluating cannot and should not be separated. Curriculum-embedded (i.e., where testing and teaching occur together continuously) formative approaches emphasizing criterion-referenced techniques are more productive than summative approaches emphasiz-

ing norm-referenced techniques. Many pupils with disabilities defy norming and normative data. And since curriculum and testing/evaluating are so intertwined, *every* category of activity and specific task included in the program must be guided by an ongoing curriculum-embedded thrust.

3. *What kind of testing and evaluation preservice/in-service training should be a priority for non-special physical educators who are involved in teaching physical education to pupils with disabilities?*

The most effective preservice/in-service training for non-special physical educators (i.e., regular physical educators, classroom teachers responsible for teaching physical education) should be understanding of testing/evaluating processes necessary in sound programs for all children and youth. Emphasis should be on similarities, *not differences,* among all pupils and how to test/evaluate their psychomotor performances appropriately. Within this context non-special physical educators should be aware of a variety of related instruments and specific tasks that can be used with all pupils including those with disabilities. Teachers should have experiences in administering such instruments and tasks for specific purposes in different situations with individuals of diverse ability levels and performance capabilities. When this process is coupled with opportunities and experiences that promote acceptance of these pupils, non-special physical educators become extremely creative in finding sound and appropriate ways to make accommodations in all aspects of their programs, including valid and reliable testing/evaluating techniques.

Administration of the Program

The hardest topic to teach in physical education without a doubt is program administration. This is not because the subject is irrelevant but because physical education majors are more interested in program activities and topics that directly relate to pupils who are disabled. Students taking a practicum experience in a segregated physical education setting or in a mainstreamed setting are looking for immediate techniques to survive that experience. Very seldom are these students required to become directly involved in administering the program. However, the ability to provide an organized and efficient program is based on the competency of the professionals who administer the program. Although you may never actually administer your own program, if you read, conceptual-

ize, retain, and file the information in this chapter for future use, you can be more effective in whatever role as a physical educator you eventually choose.

Administration in special physical education involves the management and conduct of related program activities to complement effective teaching and learning. To some degree, all physical educators responsible for a program that includes pupils who are disabled must perform administrative duties; particularly the special physical educator in charge of a district-wide program, a program at a self-contained special school, and even a state-wide program. The following interview is related to the consultant/administrative role of Jody Wallace when she served within Ohio's Department of Education.

Jody Wallace

Ms. Jody Wallace is the former special physical education consultant within Ohio's Department of Education. She served for 8 years in this capacity.

1. *What was your role and place as Ohio's special physical education consultant according to your State's Division of Special Education? In this regard, can you give specific examples of how Ohio's Department of Education is an advocate for special physical education?*

The Ohio Department of Education has shown strong leadership in special physical education. It is only one of a few states that employs a special physical education consul-tant. As the consultant, I viewed my "placement" in the Division of Elementary and Secondary Education as a liaison position to the Division of Special Education and a repre-sentative of the Department's philosophy that maintains an integrated approach between regular and special education.

Additionally, a special physical education validation certificate is now part of the Teacher Education and Certification Standards as of January 1, 1987. The Ohio special physical education consultant served as an advocate in the development process of the standards.

The role of the Ohio special physical education consultant is to assist school districts in improving the quality of special physical education services for pupils with disabilities by assuring implementation of state and federal law and regulations and by providing technical assistance to university and school personnel, as well as parents of pupils with disabilities.

2. *In connection with your consultant activities around the state of Ohio, what are the most common major concerns in the administration of school district special physical education programs?*

One major concern is the inconsistent involvement of physical educators and special physical educators as educational team members. Decision making (placement, scheduling, and programming) is often completed without input from physical educators. Some teachers are not even aware that they can and should participate in this process. Some teachers, who would like to participate as an educational team member, feel a sense of inadequacy due to a limited amount of experience in working in physical education with pupils who have disabilities.

3. *What advice would you give to special physical educators about the importance of such things as advocacy, public relations, compliance with the mandate to have placement options, and accountability in special physical education?*

Advocacy and public relations are areas of critical importance in special physical education. Teachers, support staff, and administrators are often unaware of the benefits which special physical education can provide. It is also confused with occupational and/or physical therapy. Even though the three disciplines can and should work together to provide a comprehensive motor program, it is imperative that all who are involved in a child's programming, including parents, have an adequate knowledge base and understanding of the scope of special physical education.

In response to another part of your question, some Ohio school districts have developed their own policies regarding criteria for placement in physical education. This may be a first step in utilizing a pupil's present level of psychomotor performance to provide an effective placement within a continuum of options.

Finally, the most recent accountability issue I can address is the fact that many districts in Ohio serving pupils with severe disabilities have adopted a "functional curriculum" model. This model requires that the community, in essence, be the classroom. As pupils move from the traditional classroom setting to the community and perhaps a vocational placement, it appears increasingly more difficult to determine program effectiveness. Perhaps this accountability issue stems from viewing special physical education in another perspective or at least with more emphasis on the functional nature of physical education. We may also be asked to redefine special physical education programming in community-based terms in order to resolve this issue of accountability.

In this chapter diverse administrative responsibilities that reflect current practices in special physical education are discussed. The responsibilities highlighted are program organization, time allotment and class size, pupil exemptions, grading, computer application, program forms, facilities and equipment, dress code, homework, financial support, itinerant teachers, legal liability, public relations, personnel development, and paraprofessional training.

PROGRAM ORGANIZATION

Before the mid-1960s there were two basic educational placements available for pupils who were disabled: either a regular or a special education class. Although both placements fell under the jurisdiction of the school district's board of education, each was basically an independently functioning administrative organization. Special education teachers, including special physical educators, and administrators communicated infrequently with their counterparts in regular education.

Today a variety of organizational patterns (as discussed in Chapter 1) is required to meet appropriately the unique physical education needs of pupils who are disabled. Each school must provide a hierarchy of alternative placements to meet the education needs of all such children. This is still mandated by Federal law even though the inclusion movement is gaining momentum across the country. Figure 16.1, which complements Figure 1.5 on page 6, depicts seven potential placements in which a physical education program might be offered to pupils who are disabled. They range from least to most restrictive: full-time regular physical education to full-time special physical education in residential and institutional settings.

A regular class setting without supportive personnel is the most common in physical education, as well as the least restrictive for any pupil who is disabled. The physical edu-

cator in this type of environment makes all the decisions regarding testing, assessment, lesson planning, implementation, administration, and evaluation. However, if a physical educator has a pupil who is disabled with special needs in a regular class setting and no access to supportive personnel, true mainstreaming is not being practiced. When school districts "dump" large numbers of pupils who are disabled into regular classes without consideration of the potential or actual need for supportive personnel, they are engaging in counterfeit mainstreaming. A better plan would be to provide the needed support services. For example, a physical educator might work with other specialists, such as an occupational therapist or a physical therapist, who have unique skills to deal with pupils who are disabled.

In the setting that provides special class and regular class flexible options, a pupil who is disabled participates in physical education activities with the regular class when success

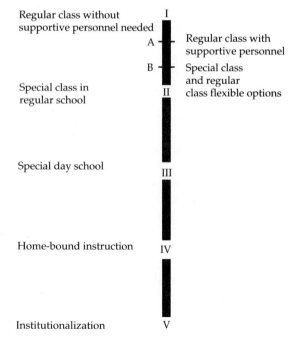

FIGURE 16.1 Continuum of least-to most-restrictive physical education environments.

is possible and participates in a specially designed program when success can be realized only in that setting. In this option, the pupil may move back and forth between the two placements throughout the school year, on either a fixed or a variable schedule, as a function of his or her successful participation in varying class activities.

Special self-contained classes in a regular school is another type of placement. Even though self-contained classes are more restrictive, placement in a regular school allows interaction with peers who are nondisabled in many contexts, such as the hallway, bus, and lunch. In physical education, only pupils who are disabled would be in a self-contained class.

The next most restrictive educational placement is the special day school to which a child is transported daily. Transportation, participation in every class, and participation in all other activities involves interaction only with pupils who are disabled. In homebound instruction, the child who is disabled is restricted to the home for all educational programs and thus is not able to interact with any pupils. The most restrictive setting is full-time placement in a residential or institutional setting. This type of setting is designed for children with extreme physical, emotional, and/or mental disorders. Although special physical educators could be of great assistance, they are generally not employed in this environment. Structured physical education, when it is provided, is generally given by the classroom teacher, an aide, or the recreational therapist.

Although most teachers and administrators would agree with the appropriateness of providing such placement options, implementation is a problem. For example, physical educators rarely have state or school building level standards to follow so they must decide for themselves reasonable cutoff scores to use in placing a pupil. The scores could be based on percentile scores, a standard deviation, or developmental scores on motor and/or fitness tests.

In regard to placement factors generally, at least 37 factors have been identified and a few have been specifically recommended to practitioners in the field for priority consideration (Jansma & Decker, 1990, 1992). These priority factors, some which have been legally mandated are motor ability test scores, developmental scale scores, reaching IEP objectives, special educator teacher recommendation, regular physical educator recommendation, activity offerings, classroom physical accessibility, and safety considerations. Of course, each physical educator's specific situation will ultimately dictate which factors are utilized.

Other program organization constraints exist. It is expensive to provide personnel to teach classes for only one or two pupils, even though by law cost is not supposed to be a determining factor in providing appropriate services. In addition, specialized media, materials, and accessible facilities add to financial realities. This overall financial burden is often one that voters are unwilling to assume. Scheduling of classes can become another monumental problem that can be solved only through the cooperation and understanding of administrators, teachers, and in some cases, numerous support personnel.

On the plus side, only a small percentage of children have disabilities so severe that they interfere with their ability to receive an appropriate education in regular physical education and, therefore, require more restrictive physical education placement. In some states, 85 percent or more of the pupils who have been identified as disabled are enrolled in regular physical education classes. Most pupils with mild mental retardation or emotional, social, or physical disabilities are placed in physical education programs without any restrictions.

TIME ALLOTMENT AND CLASS SIZE

Instructional time requirements for physical education vary from state to state. One state (Illinois) requires a specific daily requirement; others require a specific number of minutes of physical education per week. Most states have very permissive requirements. Generally, more time is required at the secondary level.

It is recommended by the Texas Association for Health, Physical Education, Recreation and Dance that physical education be required from kindergarten through the twelfth grade. From kindergarten to grade 3, there should be a minimum of 30 minutes of daily structured physical education, and for grades 4 to 8 a minimum of 45 minutes of daily instruction. From grades 9 to 12 daily physical education should be required for two years and offered on an elective basis in the third year. Further, no substitutions should be permitted such as drill team, marching bands, ROTC, vocational subjects, or any other curricular or extracurricular activity.

In most cases, the time requirements determined for pupils in regular physical educa-

tion classes are appropriate for pupils whose disabilities require added time in school. Specific time requirements should also be considered and stipulated on the IEP of a pupil who is disabled. Ideally, physical education instruction should be provided by a competent certified instructor every day.

As in time allotment, there is great variation in the class size requirements mandated by different states. The number of pupils in a special education classroom is likely to be one third to one half the size of a regular classroom. Research on class size is generally in favor of smaller class sizes. Specially related to pupils who are disabled, it has been reported that smaller class sizes are very beneficial because of increased interaction between the teacher and the pupils, and a reduction in disruptive behavior as well (Forness & Kavale, 1985).

The general rule, though, is that the more severe the disabling condition, the smaller the class size, with an accompanying increase in classroom aides. This is illustrated in the maximum class size mandated in Ohio (see Table 16.1). this pupil–teacher ratio require-

TABLE 16.1   MAXIMUM PUPIL–TEACHER RATIO IN OHIO

CATEGORY	ENROLLMENT IN SELF-CONTAINED SPECIAL CLASSES	ENROLLMENT IN REGULAR CLASSES WITH ADDITIONAL RESOURCES PROGRAM HELP
Multiple disabilities	6–8	15–30
Hearing impairment	6–10	15–30
Visual impairment	6–10	15–30
Orthopedic and/or other health impairment	6–10	15–30
Severe behavior disabled	6–12	15–30
Developmentally disabled	8–16 (El/JHS) 12–24 (HS)	15–30
Specific learning disabilities	8–16 (El/JHS) 12–24 (HS)	15–30

El = elementary. JHS = junior high school. HS = high school.

ment should also be reflected in the physical education program. The physical educator should not be given additional pupils. Further, classroom aides should be encouraged to assist in physical education and not use this time for classroom preparation or other pursuits. The classroom teacher should also be kept informed of pupil activities and progress. Any physical education involvement by the classroom teacher should be welcomed.

In Texas, the State Education Agency has stated that class sizes in physical education should be comparable with those of regular education classes. If the class size must be increased, provisions should be made for adding personnel such as paraprofessionals. This mandate should also be applied in special physical education using class size in the special education classroom as the standard.

PUPIL EXEMPTIONS

Many times pupils are excused from physical education because they do not want to participate for minor reasons (Dannaldson, 1992). Pupils may be excused by a parent note written because of pressure from the child, a short note from a family physician based on a request from a parent and/or child, or even at the general discretion of the physical educator. In one school district a physical educator stated that "the ticket out of physical education is 40 dollars, the price of a short visit to the local physician"!

Based on the Rules and Regulations of P.L. 101–476, physical education services must be provided for all pupils who are disabled. Only in extreme cases, such as communicable diseases, should a pupil be excused from physical education. Exemptions granted should be only on a temporary basis. Generally physicians today, as in the past, are opposed to excusing pupils from physical education.

Excuses from physical education which deprive a young person of desirable developmental experiences in this area should not be granted unless there is a clear and over-riding health reason wherein the student cannot participate except in a prescribed program of restricted physical activity. Currently, there is generally agreement among both physicians and educators that when good programs exist, "blanket" or overall excuses from physical education are unnecessary (Committee on Exercise, 1967, p. 113).

If a physical education exemption is prescribed by a physician, the physical educator or school nurse should personally contact the physician and explain the available program options. These options might range all the way from relaxation training to competitive contact sports. The original medical exemption might then be withdrawn or modified.

Guidelines on medical excuses have been developed jointly by physical educators, school administrators, and physicians (Bucher, 1983). These guidelines include the following:

1. Pupils, parents, and physicians should be oriented to the goals and objectives of the physical education program at an early date.
2. Develop a medical form.
3. Requests for excuses should be routed through the school physician; at the least, the school nurse should be contacted.
4. Either medical personnel or the physical educator should contact the prescribing physician.
5. Pupils with participation exemptions should have periodic reexaminations, which can reduce exemptions as much as 50 percent.
6. Conferences should be held between school medical personnel and the physical educator.
7. School administrators and classroom teachers should be familiar with the goals and

objectives of the physical education program.

GRADING

In the age of educational reform and accountability, physical education teachers are confronted with the problem of determining what is an acceptable performance in class and how that level of performance can be communicated in terms of a grade on a report card for pupils who are disabled. This is particularly true for regular physical educators, who now are responsible for grading pupils who are disabled and mainstreamed into their classes. The concern is that traditional grading techniques may victimize these pupils.

Grades should be related to the objectives of physical education and should provide absolute rather than relative grade information. The problem in physical education is that grades are not generally based on the objectives traditionally stated for physical education. Grades may be based on administrative factors such as attendance, proper dress, or vague ideals, such as effort and attitude, which are difficult to assess. This does not provide any description of what specific physical education objectives are being reached by a pupil.

What is recommended is that the grading system be related to the IEP and that the grading system be included in the IEP. The specific objectives that are on the IEP are clearly related to the definition of physical education as stated in P.L. 101–476 and these objectives are those that need to be graded. The pupil will earn a grade based on the objective that is achieved during the grading period. This type of grading system is illustrated in Table 16.2. Such a system, in effect, can be viewed as a contract in which grades are earned for accomplishing individualized physical education objectives.

COMPUTER APPLICATION

To remove some of the burden of paperwork, physical educators working with pupils who are disabled need to enter the age of computer technology. Computers can be incorporated into the assessment process, designing the IEP, individualizing instruction, and teaching sports and games (Kelly, 1987; Stein, 1984).

The Assessment Process. Related to the assessment process, there are a number of software packages that have been developed. Physical Best (AAHPERD, 1988) and the FITNESSGRAM (Lacey & Marshall, 1984) are two physical fitness tests that have software packages. Physical Best, which is criterion referenced, was designed to assess the physical fitness levels of pupils in grades K–12. The items in the test battery are 1-mile run/walk, triceps and calf skinfold measures or body mass index, sit and reach test, pull-ups, and sit-ups. The software package generates a pupil fitness profile graph, fitness recommendations, an awards list, class composites, and cumulative statistics.

FITNESSGRAM is a computerized system of scoring and reporting the results obtained by students on either the AAHPERD Youth Fitness Test or the AAHPERD Health Related Physical Fitness Test. The report contains the following information about the pupil tested: date, grade in school height, and weight; score and national percentile rank on each test item; total fitness score with the designated classifications of excellent, above average, average, below average; physical fitness profile; recommended activities to improve levels on all areas in which a score less than the 50th percentile was earned; provisions for tracking cumulative results on repeated tests; and test results for all participating pupils qualifying for the Presidential Physical Fitness Award.

Both these tests could be appropriate for most pupils who are disabled. There have

TABLE 16.2   MAINSTREAMING STUDENT GRADING CONTRACT

Statement of Annual Goals	Specific Educational and/or Related Services Needed	Present Level of Performance	Person Delivering Service		Comments
Goal 1: The student will improve abdominal strength.	Special Physical Education Consultant Services	Performs 8 bent-leg sit-ups/w assistance	Bill Bishop		
Goal 2: The student will improve static balance.	Special Physical Education Consultant Services	Stands on preferred foot for 3 seconds with arms out to the side	Bill Bishop		

Short-Term Objectives	Date Completed	Special Instructioal Methods and/or Materials		Grade	
Goal 1. Objectives 1. In the gym with assistance the student will perform 10 bent-leg sit-ups.	10–12–90	Social praise and a performance graph		C	
2. In the gym without assistance the student will perform 18 bent-leg sit-ups.	11–07–90	Social praise and a performance graph		B	
3. In the gym without assistance the student will perform 25 bent-leg sit-ups.	Progressing	Social praise and a performance graph		A	
Goal 2. Objectives 1. In the classroom, standing on preferred foot, arms out to the side, the student will stand for 8 seconds while focusing on a spot on the wall.	11–14–90	Poster of circle from the Bruininks-Oseretsky Test, social praise, and a performance graph		C	
2. In the classroom, standing on preferred foot, arms out to the side, the student will stand for 10 seconds while focusing on a spot on the wall.	11–21–90	Poster of circle from the Bruininks-Oseretsky Test, social praise, and a performance graph		B	
3. In the classroom, standing on preferred foot, hands on the hips, the student will stand for 15 seconds while focusing on a spot on the wall.	Progressing	Poster of circle from the Bruininks-Oseretsky Test, social praise, and a performance graph		A	

SIGNATURES AND TITLES OF APPROPRIATE TEAM MEMBERS (signatures indicate approval of this IEP)

(Parent)   (Teacher)   (Administrator/Supervisor) been some software packages designed for use with individuals with suspected or known disabling conditions. For example, the Hawaii Early Learning Profile (HELP) was designed with a computer to assess and develop intervention programs for infants and toddlers (Holt, 1987). HELP involves more than 650 skills in six developmental areas: cognitive, language, gross motor, fine motor, social, and self-help. If a specific deficiency is determined in one of the skill areas, up to 10 activities that are developmentally sequenced can be accessed.

Another software program is Prescribing Adapted Physical Education (PAPE) (Kelly, 1981). This program is specifically designed to assist teachers write IEPs using an I CAN instructional package. Via this program, the teacher selects from numerous options the motor skill that best describes a specific pupil's needs based on qualitative analysis. Then a series of performance objectives are presented for the teacher's consideration. Once the selections are made, instructional activities and games are provided to achieve each objective.

Designing IEPs. It has been estimated that writing an IEP takes three hours, but it takes less than two hours using computerized IEPs (Kellogg, 1984). For instance, after the evaluation, the data could be fed into the computer and long-term goals and short-term objectives stored in the computer, such as those in PAPE, could be coded and retrieved. It must always be remembered that the specific goals and objectives must be determined by the IEP team and "human decisions based on personal experience, professional knowledge, and cooperative teamwork among parent, teacher, and administrator" (Stein, 1984, p. 3).

Individualizing Instruction. Computers can be used to analyze physical and motor performance. For example, criteria reached for different types of fundamental motor skills and sports, weight training progressions, and pace in jogging could be analyzed. The teacher then could use the information to adjust or revise a pupil's program. The information could also be graphed for the pupil and/or parents.

Teaching Sports and Games. Numerous aspects of sports and games can be taught through the use of the computer and generally in a manner more motivational than a lecture from the teacher. Fundamental skills, rules, strategies, and courtesies are just a few examples.

Computers have also been used in the preparation of physical educators to teach pupils who are disabled in the college classroom and in practical settings. Computer-assisted instruction (CAI) has been effectively incorporated in the classroom instructional process. CAI involves the use of computers to supplement classroom instruction, allowing the student to obtain the information on their own in the computer laboratory instead of the lecture room. This method of instruction has been used to teach basic behavior management techniques to undergraduate physical educator majors. Based on the research findings of Montelione (1984), CAI is just as effective as the lecture form of instruction.

Systematic observation techniques have also been developed to describe teaching behaviors and then used to improve teaching skills. One observation technique that has been recommended for use in special physical education settings (Rich, Wuest & Mancini, 1988) is the Cheffers Adaptation of Flanders Interaction Analysis System (CAFIAS). This system (Cheffers, 1972) is designed to code both verbal and nonverbal behaviors while focusing on numerous teaching-related factors, such as the teacher, pupil(s), and environment, while accounting for differences in class structure.

Another computerized observational system (see Figure 16.2) is OARS (observational,

FIGURE 16.2 College supervisor using OARS.

analysis, and recording system). The program runs on an MS-DOS compatible laptop computer with either 3.5 or 5.25 disk drive such as IBM, Sharp, Toshiba, or Zenith. The program can be used to record frequency and temporal duration data on as many as 10 behaviors or events concurrently. Some of the behaviors or events that can be timed are managerial, instructional time, general feedback, negative feedback, pupil waiting, lesson introduction, and lesson body. Comments can also be entered at any time during the recording session and summary

comments can be entered at the end of each session. At the end of the session a graphic summary of all categories across time can be immediately produced. The OARS program can be obtained from MAZE Products, 8 Randolph Court, Charlottesville, VA 22901.

PROGRAM FORMS

Steps must be taken to ensure the correct placement of each pupil in the least restrictive physical education setting (see Figure 16.3). Developing proper admissions/referral

FIGURE 16.3 Steps in the referral process for placement in adapted (special) physical education programs.

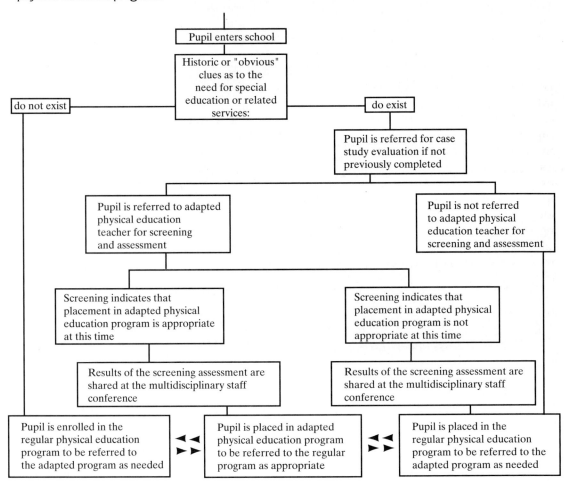

procedures is very important. Careful attention to admissions/referral procedures will, for example, alleviate problems of receiving numerous inappropriate referrals. During the beginning of each fall session, a workshop should be held to discuss with teachers the basic criteria for placement into a special class environment to reduce the number of inappropriate referrals. Special physical educators could provide teachers with a checklist of skills pupils should possess at different age levels, so they can have some initial basis for referral. Yet very few teachers, particularly regular physical educators, refer pupils for special physical education. This is generally, however, where the referral request should originate. It is incumbent upon the educator responsible for providing the physical education program to refer needy pupils for testing.

A teacher should also know the general nature of the pupil's problem beforehand in order to ensure proper direction during admissions/referral testing. For instance, it is important to know if the pupil is a behavior problem or is in a wheelchair. Different assessment instruments would be needed to test a pupil who is behavioral disordered as opposed to a pupil who is in a wheelchair. In addition, testing is very time consuming during the initial referral progress, so knowing specific problems can reduce the time. For example, if the physician states the pupil has an inner ear problem, the tester would be aware of and could look for possible balance problems.

At each step of this admission/referral process, there should be written communication between parents, educators, and support personnel. Many districts use standard forms to record these communications in order to protect the rights of the pupil, the parents, school personnel, and the school district. Some forms are presented here; examples of others discussed are given in Appendix A.

Initially, written permission from parents is required before a pupil can be evaluated (see Appendix A2). A written physical education referral (see Figure 16.4) by the family physician may also be requested from the parents at this time, as well as permission from the parents for a school physician to examine the pupil (see Appendix A3). The school physician completes a reference form similar to that completed by the family physician. This form must provide a place for the physician to address what medications the pupil takes and any side effects of the medications that could influence participation in physical education. For instance, some possible side effects of medication taken by pupils with hyperactivity (attention deficit disorder) could be muscle weakness, faintness, mental confusion, dizziness, visual abnormalities, disorientation, fatigue, and depression.

Regardless of the type of medical form used, information on medical background should be requested. Physicians should not be asked at this point to make judgments about the types of physical activities in which a pupil may or may not participate. Further medical information may be collected by the special physical educator from pupils' school records. All pertinent medical information collected from these records, with the source and date of examination identified, could be entered on a medical information sheet (see Appendix A4).

With psychomotor, medical, and all other sources of information collected, a decision on the type of physical education placement for the pupil is determined by the IEP team. If special physical education placement is required, an IEP is designed around the basic information. Examples of IEP forms used in Ohio and Texas are given in Appendixes A5 and A6. (An actual IEP is provided in Chapter 3.) If a pupil's performance changes in the future to a level that warrants placement in another educational setting, another medical examination should be requested (see

FIGURE 16.4 American Medical Association approved prescription form. (From *Adapted Physical Education: Related Legislation, IEP Development, and Programmatic Considerations for Illinois.* Springfield: Illinois Office of Education, Department of Specialized Educational Services, 1978, pp. E1 & E2. Funded in part by the Area Learning Resource Center. Contract #300-75-0038, Project #446-AH660014, and Public Law 94-142. Used by permission.)

AMERICAN MEDICAL ASSOCIATION (AMA) APPROVED PRESCRIPTION FORM

ANY CITY PUBLIC SCHOOLS
SCHOOL HEALTH DEPARTMENT
PHYSICAL EDUCATION DIVISION

Physical Education Medical Referral Form
ASAW No. 1313-1975

Dear Dr. _____ :

(This space can be used for information about state/local physical education requirements, rationale of adapted physical education, objectives and benefits of local programs, organization and administration of local classes, purposes, and uses of this form and related areas to improve understanding and communication among physicians, physical education teachers, parents, and others concerned with and involved in the education, health, and welfare of the student. Procedures for returning the form can be included in this section or at the end of the form.)

John J. Jones, M.D.   George T. Smith, Supervisor
Director, School Health Department   Division of Health, Physical
                                                                Education, and Athletics

STUDENT INFORMATION

Name _____
School _____
Home Address _____
City _____
State _____
Zip _____
Home Telephone (_____) _____
Grade and Section _____

CONDITION

Brief description of condition

Condition is   permanent   temporary

Comments _____
_____
_____

If Appropriate:
Comments about student's medication and its effects on participation in physical activities:

Student may return to unrestricted activity _____ , 19___ .
Student should return for reexamination _____ , 19___ .

(Continued)

FIGURE 16.4 *Continued.*

FUNCTIONAL CAPACITY

Unrestricted – no restrictions relative to vigorousness of types of activities
Restricted – Condition is such that intensity and types of activities need to be limited (check one category below):
   Mild – ordinary physical activities need not be restricted but unusually vigorous efforts need to be avoided
   Moderate – ordinary physical activities need to be moderately restricted and sustained strenuous efforts avoided
   Limited – ordinary physical activities need to be markedly restricted

ACTIVITY RECOMMENDATIONS

Indicated body areas in which physical activities should be minimized, eliminated, or maximized.

						Comments, including any medical contraindications to physical activities
Neck						
Shoulder Girdle						
Arms						
Elbows						
Hands & Wrists						
Abdomen						
Back						
Pelvic Girdle						
Legs						
Knees						
Feet & Ankles						
Toes						
Fingers						
Other (specify)						

REMEDIAL

Condition is such that defects or deviations can be improved or prevented from becoming worse through use of carefully selected exercises and/or activities. The following are remedial exercises and/or activities recommended for this student. (Please be specific)

Signature of M.D. ——————————————————————————————
Address ———————————————————————————————————
Telephone ( )
Date ————————————————————————————————————

Appendix A7). If no medical restrictions require the continued placement in the same setting, the pupil should be transferred (see Appendix A8). Parents should be notified of any transfer with a form similar to the one used in the original notification of special class placement.

FACILITIES AND EQUIPMENT

Two major responsibilities of the physical educator involve facilities and equipment. School facilities should be built or remodeled to be accessible to all pupils who are disabled to provide for program accessibility. It must be made clear that this does *not* mean that *all* existing structures must be accessible, but that pupils who are disabled must have access to each part of a program. This could involve providing a paraprofessional to assist a pupil, assigning classes in an accessible location, or modifying some structures. It must always be stressed that individuals who are disabled represent a large segment of the population and have the right to program access. It is estimated that one out of eight individuals in the United States are disabled (Bronzan, 1980).

Physical educators should be knowledgeable about facility planning and be willing to serve on committees charged with designing new facilities or renovating part of an existing facility. Some general guidelines in planning and construction of a facility are the following (Bookwalter, 1964, pp. 84–87):

1. *Validity.* Standards for space, structure, and fixtures must be compatible with the rules essential for the effective conduct of the program.
2. *Utility.* Facilities should be adaptable for different activities and programs without affecting safety and effective instruction.
3. *Accessibility.* Facilities should be readily and directly accessible for all individuals.
4. *Isolation.* Facilities should be planned to reduce distractions, offensive odors, noise, and undesirable activities to a minimum.
5. *Departmentalization.* Functionally related services and activity areas should be continuous or adjacent for greatest economy and efficiency.
6. *Safety, hygiene, and sanitation.* The maintenance of proper health standards and the elimination of hazards should be major considerations in all facility planning.
7. *Supervision.* Facilities should take into consideration the need for proper teacher supervision of activities. Therefore, visibility and accessibility are essential.
8. *Durability and maintenance.* Facilities should be easy and economical to maintain and should be durable.
9. *Beauty.* Facilities should be attractive and aesthetically pleasing, using good color dynamics and design.
10. *Flexibility and expandability.* Changes in program and other considerations for future expansion should be considered. Modern thinking stresses flexibility in physical education facilities. Flexibility should provide for immediate change through folding partitions that divide gymnasia, for overnight change with very little effort in cases in which partitions cannot be removed immediately, and for greater change that can be made within a period of one to two months, such as during the summer vacation.
11. *Economy.* The best use of funds, space, time, energy, and other essential factors should be considered as they relate to facility planning.

Facilities built in the past for able-bodied pupils will usually meet the needs of most pupils who are disabled. Modifications may only be minor, such as for lockers with key locks for pupils who are blind, learning disabled, or mentally retarded or large lockers to enable a pupil with an amputation to store a prosthesis or crutches/braces.

One major consideration in facility planning and use is accessibility for people in wheelchairs. There are several approaches to compliance with accessibility standards. Accessibility can be increased by structural changes, equipment modification (e.g., a portable ramp), providing aides, or reassigning the pupil to another program that has an accessible facility.

Bronzan (1980) presents a checklist to use when designing functionally barrier-free facilities in either new or existing physical education structures. This basic checklist provides guidelines for planning facilities for individuals who use wheelchairs and those who are visually impaired. Ideally, the response to each statement should be "yes."

Site

1. Facility is easily accessible by foot, wheelchair, or vehicle.
2. Facility is located so the pupil who is disabled may go to and from the physical education/sports facility and academic buildings within the typical class-changing time.

Access to Building

1. All walkways leading to the facility are at least 48 inches wide.
2. All walkways are smooth, firm, free of cracks and ruts, and without abrupt change in level.
3. The main entrances to the facility are at ground level.
4. All ramps, walkways, or other approaches are no steeper than a 1 foot–12 feet ratio.
5. All ramps, walkways, or other approaches are provided with at least one handrail on one side, 32 inches above surface level, that extends 1 foot beyond their top and bottom.

Entrance to Building

1. Doorways have at least a 36-inch clearance.
2. Door can be opened with a single effort.

3. Door automatically activates.
4. Door is provided with a delayed closing-time mechanism.
5. Entrances are provided with emergency manually operated doors adjacent to or near the automatically activated door.
6. Doors are provided with both push and pull bars.
7. Doors are provided with a shatterproof glass insert.
8. Doors allow for a small person in a wheelchair to see through to the other side or be seen from the other side.
9. Thresholds and door saddles are flush with the floor or no more than a half-inch high.

Ramps

1. Ramp surface is smooth, hard and nonslip.
2. Ramp width is 5 feet or more so as to allow two wheelchairs to pass safely in opposite directions.
3. Ramp is no steeper than 1 foot in height for each 12 feet horizontally.

Stairs

1. Risers are 7 inches or less.
2. At least one handrail, 32 inches as measured from tread at the face of the riser, is provided.
3. Treads are provided with nonslip surfacing.

Elevators

1. All facilities with more than one level or floor have at least one passenger elevator.
2. Elevator call button is no more than 48 inches above the floor.
3. Elevator is provided with a delayed-closing door.
4. Elevator control board button is no more than 48 inches above the elevator floor level.
5. Elevator emergency telephone is not more than 48 inches above elevator floor level.

6. Emergency stop button or switch is no more than 48 inches above the elevator floor level.

Rest Rooms

1. Rest room entrance is at least 36 inches wide at all points.
2. Doors automatically activated or lever door handles.
3. There is at least a 5 foot by 5 foot clear area inside the rest room.
4. There is at least one toilet stall with a door that swings outward, creating at least a 32-inch opening.
5. Lavatories are wall-mounted, with narrow aprons.

Water Fountains

1. Water fountains or coolers have up-front spouts and controls.
2. Water fountains and coolers are hand- or foot-operated.
3. Wall-mounted, hand-operated water fountains or coolers are mounted 33 inches above the floor.

Telephones

1. Dial and handset heights are no more than 48 inches.
2. Handset cord is at least 42 inches in length.
3. If the speaker unit is fixed, it is no more than 48 inches above the floor level.
4. Dial numerals are raised for the individuals who are visually disabled.

Aquatic Facilities

1. Water temperature can be adjusted conveniently to reach 80°-90°F.
2. Dressing/shower/toilet facilities are convenient to pool.
3. Provisions are included to facilitate movement of wheelchair from shower room to pool deck.

4. Pool water depths are adjustable.
5. Deck is slip-resistant.
6. Deck is close to water level.

Locker-Shower Rooms

1. There are provisions made for locking devices that are easy for pupils who are physically or visually disabled to manipulate.
2. Shower heads and their controls are placed so they may be used while seated in a wheelchair.
3. Shower facilities are equipped with approved grab rails.
4. Lockers for pupils who are disabled are free from impediment by benches, etc.
5. Lockers have key locks, large lockers are available to store a prosthesis, and there are wide aisles.
6. Doors are automatically activated or there are lever doors.

Specific Provisions for Those Who Are Blind and Visually Impaired

1. Raised letters or numerals and Braille used to identify rooms and offices.
2. Light-colored characters, numerals and Braille symbols are used on low reflecting dark backgrounds to heighten visibility.
3. Room and office signs are placed on the wall to the left of the door at a height between 4'6" and 5'6", preferably 5 feet.
4. Persons with guide dogs are provided entrances other than revolving doors.
5. There is a tactile orientation map, indicating building location, on the nearest wall to the left of the main entrance way or lobby, at a height of 5 feet.
6. Vending machines have tactile signs adjacent to the coin insert that indicates contents and prices.

7. Regular signs and other amenities are painted in colors that aid individuals who are visually impaired.

Today all states have passed legislation that requires architectural accessibility in public buildings. Access is also required by federal law through the Americans with Disabilities Act of 1990 (P.L. 101–336). Most states have adopted the American National Standards Institute (1980) standards specifications for making buildings and facilities accessible to and usable by people who are physically disabled.

The purchase of any equipment for special physical education must be based on the goals of the program, the specific population, and appropriateness for the facilities. When individual needs and program goals are determined, enough equipment should be obtained to provide optimum appropriate activity for all pupils. A pupil should, for example, not have to wait for a long time for a turn to jump a rope or bounce a ball. Schools should purchase only quality equipment, designed for the safety and protection of the child who will be using it (see Figure 16.5).

Equipment needed for special physical education programs will vary according to age, type of disability, and severity of the disability of the pupils. The following are illustrative lists of items generally considered necessary for a viable program.

Exercise Room

- Mats
- Stall bars
- Incline board
- Dynamometer
- Universal gym machine
- Wheelchair and bicycle

- Ergometers
- Wall mirrors
- Postural screens
- Skin calipers
- Stopwatch
- Medicine balls of various weights
- Mini trampoline
- Bulletin board
- Anatomical chart
- Sand bags
- Dynabands
- Balance beams of various widths
- Climbing ropes

Game Equipment

- Beanbags
- Record/tape player
- Bats
- Rackets/paddles
- Cargo nets
- Balls of varying types/sizes/colors
- Automobile/truck tires
- Scooter board
- Jump ropes
- Bowling ball/pins
- Lumni sticks
- Tricycles/bicycles
- Stopwatch
- Percussion instruments
- Records/tapes
- Bases
- Hula hoops
- Parachute
- Football flags
- Cones
- Goal ball/beep
- Baseball/beep

(a) Universal Gymnasium.

(b) Hand-cranked tricycle. Courtesy Janssen Handcycle Co.

(c) Stationary exercise bicycles.

(d) Therapeutic pool.

(e) Batting tee and ball.

(f) Vertical peg board.

(g) Varied balls.

FIGURE 16.5   Equipment suggested for use in special physical education programs.

FIGURE 16.5   *Continued.*

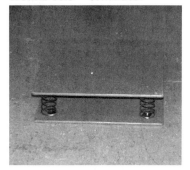

(h) Spring bouncer.

(i) Rocker board.

(l) Semipermanent Hoyer hydraulic pool lift. Courtesy of Guardian Products, Simi Valley, CA.

(j) Mini-trampoline.

(k) Standard scooter.

(m) The third hand. Courtesy of Snitz Manufacturing Company.

(n) Spring-loaded handle-grip bowling ball. Courtesy of Snitz Manufacturing Company.

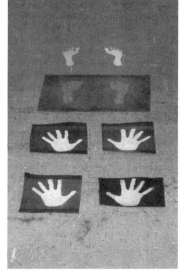

(o) Hand and foot prints.

FIGURE 16.5 *(Continued).*

(p) Inflatable swimming suit.

(q) Stegel.

(r) Stall bars.

(s) Varied striking implements.

(t) Lind Climber (Stegel).

(u) Foot-propelled treadmill.

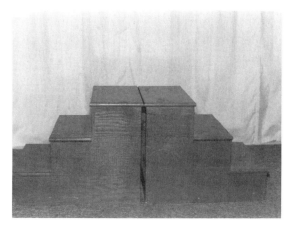

(v) Mobile mat. Courtesy of Snitz Manufacturing Company.

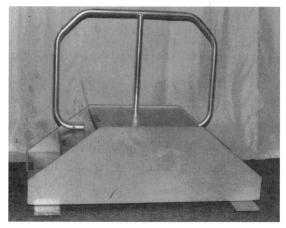

(w, x, y) Climbing stairs–three variations.

Pool

- Hydraulic lift
- Resting table
- Flotation devices
- Kickboard
- Goggles/masks/noseclips
- Swim fins/hand paddles
- Inflated paddles
- Water balls

Numerous companies sell special physical education equipment. Here is a sampling.

Educational Toys and Games

Educational Activities
Box 392
Freeport, NY 11520

American Athletic Equipment
American Avenue
Jefferson, IA 50129

Gopher Industries Inc.
35047 31st Street
Long Island City, NY 11106

Jayfro Corporation
976 Hartford Turnpike
Box 400
Waterford, CT 06385

J. A. Preston Corporation
744 W. Michigan Avenue
Jackson, MI 49204

Sporttime
One Sporttime Way
Atlanta, GA 30340

Snitz Manufacturing
2096 South Church Street
Box 76
East Troy, WI 53120

Passon's/North American Elementary
Box 49
Jenkintown, PA 19046

Innovator of Disability Equipment and
   Adaptation, Inc.
1393 Meadow Creek Drive
Suite 2
Pewaykee, WI 53072

Things from Bell
Box 26
Homer, NY 13077

Quality equipment may not always have to be purchased. Many items can be constructed at low cost by the teacher, the school's parent–teacher association, instructional art classes, industrial arts classes, or local service groups. Potential advantages of homemade equipment, in addition to low cost, are (Information and Research Utilization Center, 1973):

1. The teacher becomes more effective when teaching.
2. Innovative design and construction may lead to innovative use.
3. Increased interest stimulated by innovation and adaptation by the educator could be contagious.
4. Pupils have pride in maintenance and use of the equipment they create.
5. Special needs of a pupil with particular disabilities can be met.
6. Joint projects between physical education and industrial arts personnel may enhance professional team cooperation.
7. Large projects enhance cross-disciplinary cooperation and multiagency coordination between the school and the community.

Batons, balance beams and boards, batting tees, ladders, gymnasium scooters, and vaulting boxes can all be constructed with materials purchased at local hardware stores or lumber yards. Old tires can be cleaned, painted, and used as field markers or to jump into, crawl through, or roll. Carpet remnants can be used to pad equipment, and a pile of galvanized pipe can be transformed into a horizontal or parallel bar.

When designing and constructing this or any other physical education equipment, the teacher must consider if it is safe, if it is durable, if it is right for the pupil's developmental and chronological age, if it will contribute to the program's objectives, and if the paint is nontoxic (Information and Research Utilization Center, 1973). There are numerous sources that provide instructions on how to build homemade physical education equipment. We list a few here.

- Corbin, C. (1976). *Inexpensive equipment for games, play and physical activity*, 2nd ed. Dubuque, IA: William C. Brown.
- Kirchner, G. (1989). *Physical education for elementary school children*. Dubuque, IA: William C. Brown, pp. 596–612.
- Physical Education and Recreation for the Disabled: Information and Research Utilization Center (IRUC). (1973). *Homemade innovative play equipment for activities in physical education and recreation for impaired, disabled, and handicapped participants*. Washington, DC.: American Association for Health, Physical Education, and Recreation.
- Sosne, M. (1972). *Handbook of adapted physical education equipment and its use*. Springfield, IL: Charles C Thomas.
- Werner, P., & Rini, L. (1976). *Perceptual-motor development equipment*. New York: Wiley.

- Werner, P., & Simmons, R. A. (1990). *Inexpensive physical education equipment for children*. Minneapolis, MN: Burgess.

DRESS CODE

In most cases dress codes for pupils who are disabled should be the same as for other pupils in a physical education class. In observing many mainstreamed and segregated physical education classes, we note that pupils who are disabled are participating in physical activities wearing their daily clothing. This has included boys wearing boots and girls wearing plastic sandals and dresses. Further, clothing is worn with offensive words or phrases and/or designs imprinted on them or that advertise alcohol, tobacco, or illegal products. It seems that some physical educators or the classroom teachers responsible for providing the physical education program are pleased that these pupils are participating at all and do not seem to be concerned with this type of dress.

In the accompanying interview, Paul Bishop discusses dress codes, as well as many other administrative issues.

Paul Bishop

Dr. Paul Bishop is a professor of special physical education at the University of Nebraska at Kearny.

1. *What do you think about having a dress code in physical education?*

I think there needs to be a standard dress code, if not from school district to school district, at least from school to school within a school district. This may neutralize differences between pupils based on clothing. In addition, the major factor of the clothes should not be style because many times the dominant styles are not con-ductive to the participation in physical activi-ties. The key factor should be safety. Specifically related to pupils who are dis-abled, in most cases these pupils should be required to wear the same clothes as other pupils particularly if normalization is a con-cern. There could be some exceptions of course. For example, a pupil with spina bifida who uses a wheelchair and may require the use of an external urine collection bag could be allowed to wear sweat pants for social reasons.

2. What are your thoughts on legal liability in physical education environments?

The topic of legal liability must be addressed in preservice training for those who will be working in physical activity set-tings, and particularly in settings that involve individuals who are disabled. The topic should then be reinforced through continual in-service training. Physical edu-cators must be able to provide safe and meaningful instruction, which takes consid-erable planning. In addition, in some cases they also must be able to utilize support services such as occupational and physical therapists. For instance, persons who pro-vide physical education to pupils who are nonambulatory may need to be aware of any potential injury that could occur if the pupil participates in certain physical activi-ties. To cite just one example, in one school recently, range of motion exercises were being provided a child who was multiply disabled and too much force was applied while doing one of the exercises. This caused a fracture. Maybe if prior consulta-tion with an occupational therapist was pro-vided it could have prevented this injury.

3. *What do you think about grading pupils who are disabled and enrolled in physical education?*

We need to move away from the idea that just a letter or number grade is an appropriate way to grade, particularly pupils who are disabled. There is a need for an accompanying narrative report, tabular form, and/or graphic which provides more information than the pupil's attitude, num-ber of days dressed, and attendance record. The teacher must be more accountable about providing information on the child's achievements in reaching stated objectives derived from some type of systematic eval-uation.

4. *What is your opinion on the use of com-puters in special physical education?*

Computers are excellent tools to as-sist in several administrative functions. For instance, computers can facilitate in the grading process by monitoring how many steps and what percentage of the steps on an objective was reached. Computers can also be utilized to collect heart rate data and other physiological responses as a pupil is performing different physical activi-ties. This information is collected over the semester and then graphed. The graph and an accompanying explanation are provided to the parents and pupils as part of the report card. Computers are also being effec-tively utilized in the physical education classroom settings at the university level to provide computer-assisted instruction and in student teaching settings to collect data and evaluate performance.

There are numerous reasons why a common dress code should be developed for all pupils and only modified—not eliminated—in special cases, such as for a pupil who is in a wheelchair or a pupil who is mentally retarded and may need a little more time to dress for class. Some of the reasons for using a common dress code for all pupils are (Bucher, 1983):

1. The pupil who is disabled does not stand out because he or she is not dressed as other pupils for class. This could aid in morale and promote equality.
2. Such a practice enhances comfort and safety.
3. More freedom of movement is allowed.

The dress code does not have to be elaborate, but it should address type of shoe, socks, shorts, blouses/shirts, and undergarments worn. Whatever the dress code, the physical educator must establish a policy that highlights clean clothes and hygienic maintenance standards for all pupils.

The dress code must be appropriate and not extreme; pupils have rights, too. Dress can be regulated as long as the regulations are reasonable and do not infringe on free expression, including symbolic. Pupils do not have to purchase a particular uniform, but can be required to wear appropriate clothes that enable them to perform the physical activities in class.

A special concern in the dress code must be footwear. Requiring pupils to wear tennis shoes and socks is a great start but not enough. Improper footwear can cause numerous foot disorders such as hallus valgus, skin and nail abnormalities, calluses, and blisters. In many cases pupils will not complain about or may be unable to communicate problems associated with such conditions, which will only compound the problem further.

To counter such issues, physical educators should have parents periodically check their child's feet, looking for blisters, calluses, bright red spots, or nail irritations. These are all indicators that the shoe may not be fitted correctly. The bottoms of the shoes should be examined. If the outer part of the shoe is worn, then the foot is supinating, which can cause excessive ankle and knee injuries. If the inner heel is wearing, this may indicate a pronated foot that could cause lower leg or lower back problems.

Besides knowing how to check for foot disorders, parents need to be informed about what should be considered when purchasing shoes. This could be in the form of a note sent home at the beginning of the school year, personal communication in a parent conference, or by telephone. Some of the considerations to be addressed are (French, Stranathan, & Silliman, in press):

1. The length on the shoe should never be longer than 1/2 inch between the toe and the end of shoe. In contrast, shoes that are too small do not "break in"; if they do, it happens when the foot breaks down due to injury. Further, when feeling for length, the child should stand with the shoe snuggly tied and the tongue not creased.
2. Girls need to be fitted in shoes designed for girls. Girls' feet are generally narrower than boys'.
3. Have the child move around and notice if the heel moves up and down more than 1/8 inch. If it does, the shoe is too large.
4. Children with flat feet or high arches need appropriate support for their arches.
5. Expensive shoes are not always the best. Consider the guidelines just listed and purchase the best shoe for the wear.

Another consideration regarding footwear is socks. Information about proper socks must also be communicated to parents and physical educators. As with inappropriate shoewear, inappropriate socks can also cause skin and nail irritations. Socks must be worn at all times in physical education. The sock should be no longer than the shoe and the seam at the end of the toes. When wearing socks and shoes, the foot should be able to move slightly in the shoe.

HOMEWORK

Homework is defined as a pedagogical technique used by a teacher that involves the assigning of a task to be completed outside of class. The major purpose of homework is to review and reinforce selected skills and subject matter. It can also be used to complete tasks that are not finished during class time, teach independent work habits, and communicate to parents the skills and material being taught in class (Armstrong & McPherson, 1991). Classroom teachers, because of the amount of information that needs to be learned by pupils and the small amount of class time to acquire the information, use homework as a supplement to their classroom teaching (Mims, Harper, Armstrong, & Savage, 1991).

The use of homework in physical education, while not often part of the curriculum, is just as necessary in this area of instruction as in the classroom. More to the point, homework seems essential when working with pupils with disabling conditions because, by definition, they are behind in some aspect of development compared to their peers. Therefore, they need some type of support technique, such as homework, that can enhance their quality and quantity of learning. Further, any such assignment should closely parallel the goals and objectives designated in the pupils' IEP.

There are numerous types of assignments that could be used by a physical educator for the total class, for a small group, or for an individual who needs extra assistance (Docheff, 1990). Here are a few.

1. Perform specific physical fitness and/or motor skills.
2. Attend a sporting event and keep score.
3. Coach or officiate a game.
4. Watch a specific sporting event on television and write a report.
5. Use the newspaper and follow a specific team throughout the season.
6. Study for a quiz or test.
7. Interview a sports figure.

In any homework assignment, the pupil should be provided the following information: value of the assignment, steps required to complete assignment, format of the assignment, assignment due date, materials needed to complete the assignment, and type of assistance from others that is allowed in order to complete the assignment.

Parents can be instructed in monitoring the homework process. As part of this, the physical educator must instill in them the positive aspects of homework in physical education. To alleviate any negative aspects of homework, the physical educator could

1. Send home handouts that explain what is being taught during the semester or the unit.
2. Give parents the opportunity to observe the program.
3. Hold mini in-services or present at the PTA meeting new approaches or materials that are going to be taught.
4. Provide question and answer time to discuss with parents any concerns regarding homework.
5. Provide a suggestion box to allow parents an anonymous opportunity to raise ques-

tions related to homework. Answers could be in the form of a newsletter to all parents.

Parents require specific suggestions in order to assist their children effectively in completing homework assignments. These suggestions should be provided early in the school year. Some suggestions are

1. Provide specific time each day when homework is to be done.
2. Provide a specific place to do the homework assignment.
3. Assist child by making sure the assignment is understood, provide a demonstration of the task, provide feedback on how the task is being done, praise the child for completing the assignment, and support the child when he or she is having difficulty with the assignment.

Each homework assignment should be evaluated by the physical educator in order to provide timely feedback to the pupil, make any needed modification in instruction, or change the type of homework assignment for a pupil. Grades could also be given for each assignment. The grades can be used in determining part of a report card grade.

One homework technique that has proven effective in enhancing physical and motor skills is the use of task cards (Arbogast & Misner, 1990). Figure 16.6 is an example of a letter to parents that introduces a homework assignment to improve their child's abdominal strength. The task cards that are used to explain the bent-leg sit-up task and the evaluation procedures are presented in Table 16.3.

FIGURE 16.6 Homework letter to parents.

Dear Mr. and Mrs. Jones,

I am Mrs. Goldsmith, your son John's physical education teacher. Presently his class is in a physical fitness unit. While he is putting forth his best effort and is really showing improvement in his upper body strength and overall flexibility, John does have some problems performing sit-ups because of his weak abdominal strength. If he can improve his abdominal strength, it will be easier for him to perform the skills in upcoming physical education unit activities.

To assist John to develop his abdominal strength, I have enclosed a homework assignment to supplement the activities performed in class. I have enclosed a brief instruction sheet and a task card with this letter. Please read the instructions on how to perform the crunch sit-ups and then decide the four days a week that you can assist John

on his assignment. The two-week goal is to perform 10 crunch type sit-ups with a 3-second hold in the up position. You will need to record on the task chart enclosed the number of sit-ups performed each session. Begin recording on the score card on November 1st and return the completed card about November 15th.

If you have any questions, please contact me at school between 9:45 and 3:15. My telephone number is 222-3333. I hope you will enjoy working with John as much as I do teaching him in my class.

Yours,

Physical Educator

TABLE 16.3   HOMEWORK INSTRUCTION SHEET AND EVALUATION FORM

INSTRUCTIONS FOR TASK
(FRONT OF CARD)

John will perform 10 crunch sit-ups with a 3-second hold in the up position.

1. Lie on the back with the knees bent, feet flat on the floor together.
2. Arms crossed across the chest.
3. With abdominals, raise uppor back off the floor.
4. Lower upper back to floor slowly; control with the abdominal muscles.

* It is very important that the knees remain bent!

Score Chart

Task Card—John Jones

Days of the 1st Week:

Do 10 crunch sit-ups, holding
the up position for 3 seconds.

1 ——	1 ——	1 ——	1 ——
2 ——	2 ——	2 ——	2 ——
3 ——	3 ——	3 ——	3 ——
4 ——	4 ——	4 ——	4 ——
5 ——	5 ——	5 ——	5 ——
6 ——	6 ——	6 ——	6 ——
7 ——	7 ——	7 ——	7 ——
8 ——	8 ——	8 ——	8 ——
9 ——	9 ——	9 ——	9 ——
10 ——	10 ——	10 ——	10 ——

Task Card—John Jones

Days of the 2nd Week:

Do 10 crunch sit-ups; holding
the up position 3 seconds.

1 ——	1 ——	1 ——	1 ——
2 ——	2 ——	2 ——	2 ——
3 ——	3 ——	3 ——	3 ——
4 ——	4 ——	4 ——	4 ——
5 ——	5 ——	5 ——	5 ——
6 ——	6 ——	6 ——	6 ——
7 ——	7 ——	7 ——	7 ——
8 ——	8 ——	8 ——	8 ——
9 ——	9 ——	9 ——	9 ——
10 ——	10 ——	10 ——	10 ——

FINANCIAL SUPPORT

To maintain and further develop a physical education program, the physical educator must constantly be aware of the district's current and proposed budgets and then lobby for appropriate funding. There are many external sources that can also be used for potential funds. Within the school system, physical educators or directors of physical education should personally know the person primarily responsible for the disbursal of discretionary funds (often the director of special education, the director of special services, or the director of pupil personnel). By knowing the person in charge, they can find out when funds are available from district or state allocations and how to apply for money. If physical educators are knowledgeable about laws, can justify and document their program's needs, time their requests well, know funding coordinators in their school district or at the state level, and are persistent, they may well be successful.

Outside the education system, numerous civic groups, such as Civitan, Elks, Lions, Kiwanis, Moose, and Veterans of Foreign Wars, are willing to provide funds for education projects. For example, we know of one special physical educator who obtained a bowling ramp for a pupil who was physically disabled, another received wood and supplies to build an obstacle course for pupils who were visually impaired, and another received funds for transporting individuals to program sites. A word to the wise: Often these groups have funds but do not know appropriate projects to support!

There are more than 5,000 foundations in the United States that provide support for projects. Some of these specifically target their funds to projects related to individuals who are disabled. The following are just a few of the foundations whose primary purpose is to fund projects related to physical education and/or individuals with disabilities (Olsen, 1989) (see Table 16.4).

TABLE 16.4 FOUNDATIONS THAT SUPPORT PROJECTS RELATED TO PHYSICAL EDUCATION AND/OR INDIVIDUALS WITH DISABILITIES

Levitt Foundation
 8484 Wilshire Boulevard
 Beverly Hills, CA 90211

Kraft Foundation
 Kraft Court
 Glenview, Il 60025

Aber D. Unger Foundation
 233 East Redwood Street
 Baltimore, MD 21202

Jefferson Lee Ford III Memorial Foundation, Inc.
 9600 Collins Avenue
 Box 546487
 Bal Harbor, Fl 33154

ITINERANT TEACHERS

Numerous special physical educators are increasingly assuming the role of itinerant teacher, traveling to various schools to provide direct instruction or consultant services. Itinerant physical educators have a special set of administrative problems that must be overcome compared to special physical educators who teach at just one instructional site. Related strategies that can be used by itinerant special physical educators to function more efficiently and effectively within such a service delivery model include the following (French, Lavay, & Montelione, 1986):

1. Initiate informal dialogue with regular physical educators, special educators, regular educators, administrators, and support personnel.
2. Provide an in-service in which their job functions are defined.
3. Work together with other teachers and support personnel to arrange desired schedule.
4. Check the regular physical education schedule to determine the times when specific instructional settings are available.
5. Design schedule to minimize time spent traveling between schools.
6. Secure your own set of keys for facilities at the schools where you are teaching. Do not depend on the custodians or secretaries.
7. Obtain a mailbox at each school where you provide services.
8. When possible, attend departmental meetings in physical education and special education, faculty meetings, and other social events.
9. Determine what equipment is available at each school and when it will be used by regular physical educators.
10. Consider team teaching with the regular physical educator during certain activities/units.
11. Public relations is a must. Some techniques that can be used:

a. Invite the principal and other administrators to observe your class.

b. Plan special demonstrations for school administrators, teachers, and pupils.

c. Communicate with parents about their child's progress and the general special physical education program.

LEGAL LIABILITY

Liability is defined as being legally responsible or under obligation to act in a specific manner. Lawsuits have become a way of life, as the public attitude seems to be to get as much as one can from an accident or injury. Educators responsible for conducting physical education programs must, therefore, be knowledgeable about program considerations and the precautions that are needed to avoid legal liability in the case of an accident. This is particularly true when programming for pupils who are disabled and may have medical problems (Aufsesser, 1986).

It is important to note that approximately 50 percent of all school lawsuits are related to accidents that occur in physical education programs. It has been reported that a teacher in 1970 had a 1 in 100,000 chance of being involved in a legal incident. In contrast, in the 1980s, a teacher had a 1 in 5 chance of being involved in a legal incident (Blucker & Pell, 1986). Further, it is estimated that 1 out of every 33 pupils will sustain an injury during his or her school career (Bucher, 1983).

A teacher can be held legally liable for negligence for either action, nonaction, or inappropriate action. If the action or inaction results in a direct or indirect injury to another person or property, it is referred to in legal terms as a tortious act. The major areas of potential legal negligence are (Carpenter & Acosta, 1982):

1. Inappropriate activities are selected that are beyond the capabilities of a pupil.

2. Standard protective equipment is not required by the instructor.

3. Possible hazards in play areas are not removed.

4. Unsafe equipment is used.

5. Supervision is inadequate.

6. Unverified confidential personal or instructional information about a pupil is released.

7. Class organization is improper. For example, if pupils on the offensive team in a softball game are not seated behind the backstop, or if only one mat is used when the pupils are required to perform a series of forward rolls, an accident might result.

8. Eligibility rules for athletic participation by pupils who are disabled are improper.

9. Attention to attractive nuisances is inappropriate. Some equipment, such as swings, climbing ropes, and trampolines, and facilities, such as the swimming pool, are very attractive to some pupils. This equipment must be put away or made inoperable and facilities locked when not in use. "No trespassing" signs are usually not sufficient legal protection from a lawsuit if an accident occurs. Generally to avoid negligence liability and avoid injuries caused by negligent behavior, adequate supervision must be provided, good judgment must be exercised, and proper instruction must be given. Further, there should be a conscientious review of potential risks and a comprehensive evaluation of reasonable and prudent means to prevent or reduce these risks. Specifically, more care must be exercised by the physical educator as the risks involved in an activity increase, such as football and gymnastics.

Physical educators must also be aware of problems related to the use of liability waivers. Such releases of liability, consent forms or permission slips, purportedly are used to release the teacher, the school, and the school district from liability related to pupil injury. Signing such waivers typically is required before a pupil can participate in special events and specific sports programs.

Specifically related to the inclusion of pupils with a disabling condition in these events and programs, physical educators must be aware that waivers generally are not useful in a court of law. Using such waivers may decrease the possibility of a lawsuit, but a liability waiver will not protect the physical educator from negligence. The only thing a carefully drafted liability waiver may do is to discourage an injured party from filing a lawsuit and enhance other legal defenses by increasing participant awareness of program risks and hazards (Kaiser, 1967). In this connection, physical educators need to know physical activity indications and nonindications and operate within a medical margin of safety with each pupil in a program.

In all cases that involve a significant injury, an accident report should be completed as soon as possible. Figure 16.7 shows a standard accident report form. After the form is completed, the teacher should retain the original form and submit a copy to the appropriate supervisor.

Many kinds of insurance policies are available to schools and individual employees to protect against liability and medical health problems. Each physical educator should review the school policy to determine the insurance coverage and the amounts designated because the policy may need revision. The teacher may also want to purchase tax-deductible personal liability insurance. AAHPERD provides substantial individual coverage at minimal rates. We advise professional liability umbrella coverage of about $1 million for any special physical educator.

PUBLIC RELATIONS

Public relations primarily involves providing the community with information in order to retain or modify attitudes and actions. It can be used to develop understanding and goodwill between the physical educator and other school personnel and the community. Within a special physical education program, public relations can encompass providing information about school activities, promoting confidence in the program, gathering support for the program, stressing the value of physical education for individuals who have disabilities, and correcting misunderstandings and misinformation about the goals and objectives of the program (Bucher, 1983). This information can be communicated through letters to parents, presentations to the PTA, school and community demonstrations, school publications, programs where parents are physically involved, window displays, report cards, sports days, local newspapers, radio, and television.

Special physical educators must think about public relations if they wish to maintain and build their programs. They have at least two problems when dealing with the public. First, programming for pupils who are disabled is probably one of the least understood school-related concerns, yet it is one of the most expensive per capita. Second, many people would like to see only academic subjects retained and physical education eliminated for all pupils.

PERSONNEL DEVELOPMENT

In-Service Training

The techniques available for providing direct services to children who are disabled,

FIGURE 167   A standard accident report form.

STANDARD ACCIDENT REPORT

Injured person's name: _____ School: _____ Grade: _____

Accident setting: _____ Date & time of accident: _____

Teacher: _____ Other witnesses: _____

_____

1.   Describe the injury (type, severity, body parts affected):

2.   Describe the activity at time of injury:

3.   Describe the accident's cause:

4.   Describe first aid and/or any corrective action offered:

Person completing form: _____ Title: _____ Date: _____

Administrator: _____ Title: _____ Date: _____

(USE OTHER SIDE OF FORM FOR ADDITIONAL DETAILS RELATED TO THIS ACCIDENT.)

as well as the indirect services involving organization and administration, are constantly evolving. Thus we need systems to educate or reeducate the teachers responsible for providing physical education to such pupils. One such system is in-service training. Short-term training involves an afternoon, one-day or two-day workshop. Generally these workshops include a large number of teachers; the topic is often an awareness or basic understanding of one or several related issues. Long-term in-service training frequently involves consultation or direct guidance provided to one or two teachers to help them develop new skills. Visits could be on a weekly or monthly basis over the course of a semester or even a school year. Other systems to educate or reeducate teachers include college courses and attendance at state and national conferences.

No matter what system is used, incentives should be provided to ensure teacher attendance. Incentives could include school release time, promotion, or increased salary.

Preservice Preparation

At the preservice level, introductory courses in special physical education are being required by more state boards of education not only for majors in physical education but also for special educators before a teaching certificate is awarded. In addition, some colleges and universities are now offering physical education majors specialized courses of study emphasizing programs for children with severe and profound disabling conditions (see Figure 16.8). In fact, some states now even require physical educators to earn a special teaching certificate beyond the regular certificate in order to teach children who are disabled in segregated settings.

Which professionals are assigned to provide physical education for pupils who are disabled usually depends on pupils' educational placement. If a pupil who is disabled is integrated into a regular elementary school class, the physical education program would probably be provided by the classroom

FIGURE 16.8 Developing physical education programs for pupils with disabilities is of special interest to physical education majors.

teacher or a physical education specialist. At the secondary level, the class would probably be conducted by a physical educator. In segregated classes or segregated facilities for such pupils, the special educator and special physical educator typically would provide the program.

A committee within AAHPERD (Adapted Physical Activity Council, 1993; Hurley, 1981) revised guidelines related to competencies for both the physical education generalist and the special physical educator. The categories within which competencies were identified are biological foundations, sociological foundations, psychological foundations, historical-philosophical foundations, assessment and evaluation, and curriculum planning, organization, and implementation.

To ensure adequate preparation of individuals teaching physical education to pupils with disabilities, certification in special physical education has been supported. For instance, the state of California, as well as approximately 13 other states, now require physical educators to be certified in special physical education in order to teach in segregated classes. Other states are considering similar certifications. California's certification requirements include skills in foundations and understanding of special physical education, teaching methods specific to disabling conditions, behavior management techniques, assessment techniques, writing individual educational programs, designing individual specialized activities, knowledge of the interdisciplinary approach, and success in field and student teaching experiences.

Recently, the U.S. Department of Education has funded a project to achieve two major goals. These goals are to develop national standards for special physical education and develop a competency-based exami-

nation to evaluate the standards (Kelly, 1993).

PARAPROFESSIONAL TRAINING

One of the most effective means to increase both program efficiency and the skill levels of pupils who are disabled is the use of paraprofessionals. Paraprofessionals work under the supervision of the physical educator. Based on their training, they can administer screening tests, secure needed materials and equipment, provide one-to-one instruction, and perform clerical duties (Vogler, French, & Bishop, 1989).

At least five basic rules can be followed in training and retaining competent paraprofessionals (Dunn, Morehouse, & Fredericks, 1986):

1. Take the time to train paraprofessionals.
2. Give paraprofessionals tasks that are appropriate to their level of training.

FIGURE 16.9 Peer tutors assist in a special physical education class.

3. Establish a system of feedback regarding the paraprofessional's performance.

4. Develop a system of minimal communication between the physical educator and paraprofessional.

5. Maintain a system of flexible scheduling for the volunteers.

Sources of paraprofessionals can be individuals from the community or parents. An oftentimes overlooked source is peer tutors (see Figure 16.9). To obtain pupil paraprofessionals to assist in special physical education classes, recruit pupils in classes who demonstrate appropriate attitudes and skills, advertise in your school literature and include a screening interview, and request nominations from teaching staff and counselors.

Extracurricular Activities

Federal law requires that school personnel provide physical education for all pupils with disabilities. It does not stop there. Additionally, the law calls for the provision of extracurricular activities that support and extend the delivery of special education services. Further, these services need to stress the integration of individuals having disabilities with those who are not disabled in the least restrictive environment. Such programming will better prepare pupils for life both during and after school.

Stated in different terms, all individuals with disabilities have psychomotor needs (posture, motor, fitness, play) that should be addressed not only within the context of the school curriculum but also through extracurricular physical activity programming at school and even beyond the school years. Those leisure time physical skills learned, in turn, are essential if these individuals are to

make a full, permanent transition into the mainstream of modern life. It is no longer acceptable simply to integrate all individuals with disabilities into specific "mandated" curricula or postschool segregated programs; they must have opportunities to play, recreate, and even compete in the mainstream of society. Whether it be an elementary school pupil who is severely mentally retarded learning to swim in a modified fashion independently for the first time, an elite athlete in a wheelchair competing internationally, or a senior citizen competing against peers, this principle of access to and programming in extracurricular activities equally applies.

To address this issue of extracurricular activities for persons with disabilities, we propose the use of a continuum of extracurricular activities (see Figure 17.1), ranging from completely segregated to completely integrated. Additionally this model assimi-

FIGURE 17.1   Continuum of extracurricular activities.

AMATEUR ATHLETICS	INTEGRATED
	SEGREGATED
INTERSCHOLASTIC and INTERCOLLEGIATE ATHLETICS	INTEGRATED
	SEGREGATED
EXTRAMURALS	INTEGRATED
	SEGREGATED
INTRAMURALS	INTEGRATED
	SEGREGATED
LEISURE ACTIVITIES (Noncompetitive)	INTEGRATED
	SEGREGATED

lates developmental stages of physical activity participation, from cooperative leisure time activities to highly competitive athletics. The most restrictive level is cooperative leisure activities in a segregated environment. The next step is cooperative leisure activities integrating individuals with and without disabilities. Competitive activities begin with intramurals, and this competitive element is reflected throughout the remainder of the continuum. Intramurals (physical activity competition within a school) and extramurals (physical activity competition between pupils of different schools) can be both segregated or integrated. Interscholastic and intercollegiate athletics primarily focus on higher level competition between a number of schools or agencies, which can take place in a segregated or integrated fashion. Lastly, amateur athletics may be participated in both during and after the school years, within a segregated or integrated context, and can be local, regional, national, or international. Keep in mind that physical education programs form the base on which our extracurricular activities model is built.

After discussion of the impact of federal law on extracurricular physical activities for special populations, the remainder of this chapter surveys specific extracurricular activity programs. The programs are presented in the order as in Figure 17.1, from noncompetitive segregated leisure activities to competitive integrated amateur athletics. Additional key resources for more comprehensive information on recreation and sports for individuals with disabilities include the following:

Adams, R. C., & McCubbin, J. A. (1991). *Games, sports, and exercises for the physically disabled*, 4th ed. Philadelphia: Lea & Febiger.

Guttmann, L. (1979). *Textbook of sport for the disabled*. Aylesburg, England: HM&M.

Jones, J. (Ed.). (1988). *Training guide to cerebral palsy sports*, 3rd ed. Champaign, IL: Human Kinetics.

Paciorek, M. J., & Jones, J. A. (1989). *Sports and recreation for the disabled: A resource manual*. Indianapolis, IN: Benchmark Press.

IMPACT OF LEGISLATION

The Rules implementing P.L. 101–476 and P.L. 93–112, Section 504, clearly affect programs that receive federal financial assistance. These Rules specify the provision of recreational, athletic, leisure time, club sport, and intramural activities for individuals with disabilities. The following extracts from these Rules reflect this extracurricular emphasis.

P.L. 101-476

As used in this part, the term "related services" means transportation and such developmental, corrective, and other supportive services as are required to assist a child with a disability to benefit from special education, and includes . . . recreation, including therapeutic recreation (p. 44803).

Recreation includes:

1. Assessment of leisure function;
2. Therapeutic recreation services;
3. Recreation programs in schools and community agencies; and
4. Leisure education (p. 44803).
   (a) Each public agency shall take steps to

provide nonacademic and extracurricular services and activities in such a manner as is necessary to afford children with disabilities an equal opportunity for participation in those services and activities.

(b) Nonacademic and extracurricular services and activities may include . . . athletics . . . recreational activities (p. 44813).

In providing or arranging for the provision of nonacademic and extracurricular services and activities, . . . each public agency shall insure that each child with a disability participates with nondisabled children in those services and activities to the maximum extent appropriate to the needs of that child (p. 44824).

P.L. 93–112 (Section 504)

(a) No qualified handicapped student shall, on the basis of handicaps, be excluded from participation in, be denied the benefits of, or otherwise be subjected to discrimination under any . . . athletics, recreation, . . . other extracurricular, or other. . . program or activity to which this subpart applies (p. 22684).

(b) Physical education and athletics.
   (1) In providing physical education courses and athletics and similar programs and activities to any of its students, a recipient to which this subpart applies may not discriminate on the basis of handicap. A recipient that offers physical education courses or that operates or sponsors intercollegiate, club, or intramural athletics shall provide to qualified handicapped students an equal opportunity for participation in these services.
   (2) A recipient may offer to handicapped students physical education and athletic activities that are separate or different only if separation or differentiation is consistent with the requirements of [operating its programs and activities in the most inte-

grated setting appropriate] and only if no qualified handicapped student is denied the opportunity to compete for teams or to participate in courses that are not separate or different (p. 22684).

According to a position statement prepared by several physical educators (Auxter, Jansma, Sculli, Stein, Weiss, & Winnick, 1980), extracurricular activities (including intramurals/extramurals and interscholastic programs) are clearly governed by the mandates of Section 504. No qualified individual with a disability is to be excluded from, denied benefits of, or discriminated against in any extracurricular program sponsored by a recipient of federal funds. This is especially applicable to schools because almost all public schools are recipients of federal funds. More simply, no pupil is to be kept from any extracurricular program offered to nondisabled pupils; and, once in such a program, no pupil is to be denied equal opportunity to succeed. In accomplishing both objectives, extracurricular programs must be physically accessible (buildings, transportation), accommodations such as auxiliary aids and rule changes must be made available, opportunities to succeed must be as effective as those offered to nondisabled pupils, and extracurricular activities must be offered in the most normal setting possible. Public Law 101–336 (the Americans with Disabilities Act of 1990) also adds weight to the mandates of P.L. 93–112.

Further, the provision of extracurricular physical activities for individuals with disabilities has been affected by the passage of P.L. 95–606, The Amateur Sports Act of 1978. Public Law 95–606 is based largely on the Report of the Presidential Commission on Olympic Sports (1977), building on the impetus of P.L. 93–112 and P.L. 94–142 to mandate the inclusion of individuals with disabilities (school-aged and non-school-aged) into amateur athletics in the United States. The commission found that individuals with disabilities were strikingly underrepresented in sports. The commission also found that those sport programs that did include individuals with disabilities typically occurred outside the mainstream of American athletics. To remedy this situation, the Commission sought to restructure the U.S. Olympic Committee (USOC).

Public Law 95–606 mandates the following among the objectives and purposes of the USOC:

> Sec. 104. (13) to encourage and provide assistance to amateur athletic programs and competition for handicapped individuals, including, where feasible, the expansion of opportunities for meaningful participation by handicapped individuals in programs of athletic competition for able-bodied individuals (p. 3046).

As one result, a standing Handicapped in Sports Committee (now the Committee on Sports for the Disabled) was created as well as USOC Group E membership status for the major national governing bodies dealing with sports for those who are disabled. At present there are eight national governing bodies represented on the USOC Committee on Sports for the Disabled:

- American Athletic Association for the Deaf
- Dwarf Athletic Association of America
- National Handicapped Sports and Recreation Association
- National Wheelchair Athletic Association
- Special Olympics
- United States Amputee Athletic Association
- United States Association for Blind Athletes
- United States Cerebral Palsy Athletic Association

Even though in existence only a short time, the USOC Committee on Sports for the Disabled has successfully increased the visibility and participation of individuals with disabilities in the mainstream of American sports. The mandated use of USOC training centers by athletes who are disabled, the mandated inclusion of qualified individuals with disabilities in competitions for able-bodied athletes, and the participation of athletes with disabilities in the U.S. Olympic Festival are reasons for and concrete evidence of this success.

The laws and their Rules imply several specific considerations for organizers of extracurricular activities and for pupils and post-school-aged individuals engaging in leisure, intramural/extramural, interscholastic/intercollegiate, and amateur athletic activities. A number of these considerations are highlighted by Auxter et al. (1980).

Training

- Coaches and athletic trainers should be knowledgeable about the provision of equal opportunities for athletes with disabilities (see Figures 17.2 and 17.3).
- Coaches should be up to date on advances and research in coaching techniques for individuals with disabilities. A few examples include weight training for people with mental retardation (Weber & French, 1988), the selection of sports wheelchairs (Higgs, 1983), biomechanical analyses of runners who are visually impaired (Pope, McGrain, & Arnhold, 1986), and expected performances of athletes with cerebral palsy who are in a wheelchair (Davis, 1985).

Accessibility

- Swimming areas may need an enlarged shallow water area for training, adjusted facility schedules to allow increased time

FIGURE 17.2   A coach teaches passing skills to basketball players in wheelchairs.

for practice, and ramps and lifts for pupils to enter and exit the pool area.

- Gymnasium areas may need to include Brailling on bulletin boards, eliminate stairs to all areas (out-of-doors, lockers, entrance/egress to hallways), and provide safe spaces for spectators in wheelchairs for sporting events.

- Playing fields need to be clear of obstacles (ruts, steep hills, sandy surfaces) so that the participants in wheelchairs can freely engage in activities.

- Lockers, showers, and bathrooms may require widened access and well-placed rails for wheelchair mobility and transferring.

Equal Opportunity

- Authorities excluding a pupil who is disabled from an extracurricular activity because of low academic standards or grades, poor performance on rules and strategies tests, or failure in tests of psychomotor ability may be unduly discriminating against the pupil.

FIGURE 17.3   A tennis player in a wheelchair practices ball control.

- Authorities excluding a team from competition because its school is not a member of their state high school athletic or activities association may be unduly discriminating against a team made up of athletes with special needs (D'Alonzo, 1976).

- Authorities excluding an individual because of a unilateral physical disability (below the knee amputee, visually impaired in one eye) may be unduly discriminating against the person.

- Schools (or any other recipient of federal funds) offering basketball to nondisabled pupils must offer wheelchair basketball for pupils who are in a wheelchair when the need exists.

- If a team only for pupils with disabilities is desirable and an individual school does not have enough participants, schools

within the school district should collaborate to form a combined school team.

- Even such activities as high rope courses, mountain climbing (see Figure 17.4), and water skiing can be made available to individuals with disabilities through the use of adapted equipment and combination with nondisabled partners.

- Athletic teams consisting partly or totally of participants with disabilities should receive similar equipment, supplies, travel expenses, and officials as "regular" teams do.

- If late buses are provided to take nondisabled pupils home after extracurricular activities, similar arrangements must be made for pupils with disabilities, including those who require special transporta-

FIGURE 17.4   A mountain climber without legs.

tion (e.g., buses equipped with wheelchair lifts).

• For many individuals with disabilities, adapted devices are the only modification required to ensure safe, successful, and satisfying participation in least restrictive environments. Examples of these devices include special handle bowling balls for individuals with cerebral palsy, arthritis, missing fingers, poor coordination, low hand and arm strength; bowling ramps for those with cerebral palsy, paraplegia, quadraplegia, and multiple disabilities; a specially designed Braille compass for the pupil with a visual impairment who is orienteering (see Figure 17.5); swivel seats on carts for golfers requiring them; outriggers for skiers who are amputees; and countless other items, according to the individual interests, needs, and abilities of participants.

FIGURE 17.5 A specially designed Braille compass for orienteering by those who are visually impaired.

• Those with prosthetic devices should be allowed to play in contact sports with nonamputees as long as the prostheses create no more danger than other participants' natural limbs.

• Wrestlers who are visually impaired may be allowed constant finger contact when wrestling sighted peers, with initial contact in a neutral and frontal position. Only during the moment when a takedown is attempted with forward motion are they permitted to lose contact.

• Participants in wheelchairs entered in marathons and other road races should be allowed to begin prior to the start of the nondisabled racers to avoid potentially dangerous situations caused by congested conditions.

• Rules should permit starting guns to be held low when shot so that athletes with hearing problems can see the smoke signal and, therefore, compete more equitably in such activities as track, cross-country, and swimming.

• Rules should permit a football team of athletes classified as hearing impaired to have signals keyed by means of bass drum rhythms originating from out-of-bounds.

As a final note related to equal opportunity, individuals who are disabled should not be allowed to take advantage of their disabilities by unnecessarily modifying movements like their swimstrokes or pitching style in order to improve their performance. As another example, prosthetic devices cannot be used to the advantage of able-bodied competitors.

LEISURE TIME ACTIVITIES

Leisure-time activities include numerous noncompetitive, voluntary, and physically active programs that can be further charac-

FIGURE 17.6   All kinds of people enjoy fishing.

FIGURE 17.7   Horseback riding can be safe and fun for all.

terized as any satisfying and socially sanctioned recreation and play. These activities can take place at schools (during nonclass periods), churches, community centers, residential facilities, or places of business. Traditional examples include arts and crafts; outdoor activities such as hiking, orienteering, and nature study; home-oriented projects such as gardening and cooking; fishing (see Figure 17.6); horseback riding (see Figure 17.7); roller skating (see Figure 17.8); cards; travel; and hobbies such as photography and stamp collecting.

Training in leisure time skills has proven to be one of the most effective means of integrating individuals with disabilities in least restrictive environments. One reason for this is that leisure time extracurricular activities are typically ranked among the most satisfying by individuals with disabilities. The American Academy of Pediatrics Joint Committee on Physical Fitness, Retardation, and Sports Medicine wrote a position statement with respect to the importance of recreation and leisure time activities for those who are mentally retarded, which can be applied to individuals with all types of disabling conditions.

Every effort should be made to include the mentally retarded child in all appropriate

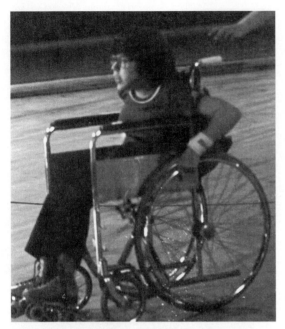

FIGURE 17.8 Wheelchair roller skating.

recreational activities. Were this the case, many of the problems of the mentally retarded (e.g., poor physical fitness, boredom, restlessness, and hyperactivity) would be lessened. They, their families, and the entire community could share in a sense of accomplishment (1974, p. 377).

Some pupils in special education need both physical education and recreation programming, particularly during the last few years of school. If indicated on a pupil's IEP, both the primary service of physical education and possibly the related service of recreation or therapeutic recreation must be provided. Yet, legal mandate aside, for a pupil whose immediate or future vocational options are limited, the establishment of a well-grounded foundation of generalized leisure time skills is essential. This kind of training is especially important for those with serious disabilities, including individu-

als with severe/profound mental retardation, who must be taught to play.

When leisure time or therapeutic recreation training takes place as part of a child's education, it is a programmed activity to support the child's special education. It is not necessarily voluntary, and may be considered as essential as other related services such as physical, occupational, and speech therapy. Some individuals with disabilities not only do not seek out leisure time training or therapeutic recreation, but do not find it initially satisfying. Over time, however, voluntary and enjoyable participation is the educational and therapeutic goal. Ultimately, training in leisure time pursuits should not only be associated with learning but should be fun, so that the pupil wants to continue the activity.

The array of alternative leisure time, play, and recreation activities for those who are disabled is broad. Identified programs include participation in school and summer programs conducted at community agencies (Jewish community centers, YMCAs, and YWCAs), local parks, schools, or in the home; camping and scouting for those who are disabled; and such outdoor education offerings as:

- Boating
- Fishing
- Orienteering
- Backpacking
- Hiking
- Water skiing
- Bird watching
- Tobogganing
- Gardening
- Mountain climbing
- Ropes course exploring
- Horseback riding
- Snow skiing

Considerable success and satisfaction have been realized by participants in these activities. As one example, see Huber's account (1991) of the first person with blindness to hike the Appalachian Trail.

The most recent "grow through play" resource is the Kennedy Foundation's second edition of *Creative Play Activities for Children with Disabilities* (Rappaport-Morris & Schulz, 1989). This guide for teachers and parents contains 250 games and activities for the 0–8 age group, with suggested adaptations for a variety of disabilities. Another play-oriented home program for children with disabilities is the Kennedy Foundation's Let's Play to Grow Program (see Chapter 5 for details). A similar play-oriented program, but not field-tested as extensively as Let's Play to Grow, is *Sensory Motor Experiences for the Home* (Seaman & DePauw, 1979), specially written for parent use with any child who needs consistent attention to sensorimotor activity modification. A nationally recognized source of related ideas for teachers interested in leisure time play activities and recreation skill development with those who are disabled is the I CAN: Sport, Leisure, and Recreation Skills Program (Wessell, 1979). Within this four-module program are two key modules:

1. Backyard and Neighborhood Activities Module
   - Badminton playing
   - Horseshoe playing
   - Tetherball playing
   - Roller skating
2. Outdoor Activities Module
   - Camping
   - Hiking
   - Backpacking
   - Cross-country skiing

All of these programs must be physically accessible to participants. A clear example of attention to the needs of those with disabilities in this respect is the increased number of accessible play areas now available to the public.

Camping for individuals who are disabled has grown in size and scope, particularly within the last two decades and, therefore, deserves separate recognition. The type of camp ranges from day camp to residential camp and from one-site to multiple-site camp. Campers come in both sexes and most ages, and camps are both integrated and disability specific. Some camps also award "camperships," which permit a child or adult to attend at a limited or no cost. Private and public agency and school camps exist to serve those with a variety of disabilities.

According to the American Camping Association (1973), critical considerations for camp programs include the modification of the environment inside and outside in order to permit full accessibility, the specialized training of personnel, an increased ratio of staff to campers when campers who are seriously disabled are to be accommodated, and careful liability insurance planning. Exemplary summer programs, which address these and other issues, are cited in the *Exceptional Parent* journal (March 1989). These include

Summer Program Award Winners

Timber Trails
Connecticut Valley Girl Scout Council
74 Forest Street
Hartford, CT 06105

C.A.M.P.
Lackland Air Force Base
San Antonio, TX 78236

HASC Summer Program
Box 119
Brooklyn, NY 11219

YMCA New Horizons
New Horizons Building
205 West Civic Center Drive
Santa Ana, CA 92701

Summer Program Commendations

Bay Cliff Health Camp
102 West Washington Street
Marquette, MI 49855

Helping Hands Day Camp
520 26th Street
Virginia Beach, VA 23451

Rutherford County Camp B.E.S.T.
Smyrna, TN 37167

The Special Needs Day Camp
City of Middletown Parks
  and Recreation Department
Lawrence School
Middletown, CT 06457

Search Day Program, Inc.
73 Wickapecko Drive
Ocean, NJ 07712

UP with Kids
University of Portland
School of Education
5000 North Willamette Boulevard
Portland, OR 97203

Additional options and better quality leisure time experiences are goals to be established for individuals of all ages who are disabled. Fortunately, leisure time programming and therapeutic recreation are among the most rapidly growing professions. Key organizations to look for leadership in these growth areas include the National Therapeutic Recreation Society of the National Recreation and Park Association (Arlington, Virginia) and the National Handicapped Sports and Recreation Association (Denver, Colorado). In addition, the single most comprehensive source for continuing written information on leisure time activities for special populations has been the *Special Recreation Digest*, produced at the University of Iowa and conceived by John Nesbitt, professor emeritus of therapeutic recreation at the university. In Nesbitt's interview, his futuristic views are given in response to one critical question.

John Nesbitt

Dr. John Nesbitt is professor emeritus of therapeutic recreation at the University of Iowa, Iowa City.

The decade of the '80s has seen an explosion of leisure opportunities for individuals of all ages with disabilities. How do you envision these individuals' need for and access to recreational opportunities in the 1990s and beyond?

I'd like to go back a little farther in time, if I may, because of important historical perspective. The role of special populations recreation specialists in 1990 is essentially the same as it was in the first decade of this century. During that decade, the play and recreation deprivation of immigrants, the poor, those labeled disabled and others in need motivated the formation of the Playground Association of America (PAA) and the PAA Committee on Play in Institutions (disabled, ill, immigrants, offenders, and poor). The PAA is now called the National Recreation and Park Association and the Committee has evolved in upwards of 50 organizations that address the play and recreation needs of special populations.

In the 1950s, national experts indicated that 3 to 5 percent of the people with disabilities were able to achieve high-quality recreation participation. Through the 1960s and 1970s, extraordinary development occurred in both special recreation and therapeutic recreation. By the 1980s, high-quality recreation experience was achieved by 10 percent of people labeled disabled through programs such as Special Olympics, international and national sports for those with disabilities, Very Special Arts, special recreation, and a wide range of consumer organizations for those with disabilities. Development of the special recreation movement will continue in the 1990s to the point where 20 percent of those within special populations will achieve high-quality participation.

Therapeutic recreation service rendered

in medical- and treatment-oriented service has experienced growth as well. Prior to the 1960s, the specialization relied on a voluntary registration system. In the 1960s, three major developments were initiated: (a) a national professional society, (b) a national educational program accreditation system, and (c) a nationally recognized certification system. There are currently 12,000 "certified therapeutic recreation specialists." During the 1990s, this professionally certified work force is projected to increase to 20,000. In turn, this work force will directly address the treatment needs of those who are disabled.

These projections are particularly important since unemployment is an increasingly difficult problem for those with disabilities. Approximately 65 percent of adults with disabilities are unemployed now and 75 percent of children and youth with disabilities are tracking to unemployment in the 1990s. Further, it must be recognized that Americans who are disabled live recreationally impoverished lifestyles in a nation which experiences extraordinary recreation extravagance as compared with the rest of the world. This recreation extravagance is enjoyed particularly by America's 50 billionaires, 36,000 millionaires, and 47 million shareholders. Therefore, the wise and healthy use of free time is and will continue to be a chief concern for special needs populations.

Relatedly, I believe that existing barriers to the "recreation normalization" of those labeled disabled will be further addressed at various levels of advocacy in the 1990s from the individual to the federal government. These barriers include, in approximate rank order, the following: lack of transportation, inadequate funding, architectural barriers, inadequate outreach to those who are disabled, negative community attitudes, nonemployment of those with disabilities in recreation service, insufficient training of regular staff, negative staff attitudes, and bureaucratic barriers such as insurance.

To make all this happen, there is a basic need for all helping specializations to work together in a cooperative and coordinated manner. The skills and insights of special physical education, therapeutic recreation service, special education, the therapies (art therapy, physical therapy, dance therapy, occupational therapy, music therapy) and so on are all needed in addressing the needs and rights of individuals who are disabled. Only by working together can opti-

mal use be made of the individual skills and insights and the resources of the respective organizations.

The recreation needs of special populations in the last decade of this century call for the same sense of mission and commitment that was needed in the first decade of the century. As stated, the adornments of modernity abound and they can obscure reality. The reality is that only partial success has been realized in meeting the recreation needs of people who are disabled. The role of therapeutic recreation specialists, special physical educators (and related others), in the 1990s is to address this awesome reality together.

INTRAMURALS AND EXTRAMURALS

Intramurals are a conceptual outgrowth of the basic physical education instructional program and fill the gap between instructional programs and interscholastic competition. Thus participation in intramurals is not as demanding as interscholastic and intercollegiate athletic competition. Intramurals take place within one school and are voluntary.

Intramurals for those who are disabled can be integrated or segregated. Where appropriate, such pupils should be integrated with their nondisabled peers. Clearly, the least restrictive environment mandates of P.L. 101–476 and Section 504 of P.L. 93–112 apply to all types of extracurricular activities such as intramurals. For those pupils who cannot participate safely, successfully, or with satisfaction in integrated intramural activities, a hierarchy of options should be provided. These options could involve participation within a specified division, class, or level. According to Sherrill,

Ideally, an intramural program should be organized with A, B, C, D ad infinitum leagues, thereby providing an opportunity for every student—regardless of this level of skill—to compete with students of like abilities. Handicapped students should be integrated into an intramural program which is organized in accordance with this "ideal" (1976, p. 40).

Pupils with disabilities should also be challenged to be resourceful by planning and implementing their own intramural events (see Figure 17.9), supported by administrators and physical educators. Their involvement can also include officiating for themselves. Section 504 encourages such efforts to combat discrimination against those who are disabled. By law, administrators and other program planners must support any organizations that provide options for all in an activity like intramurals.

Extramurals are an extension of intramural competition beyond only one school.

FIGURE 17.9 A player/coach reviews wheelchair basketball strategies.

Pupils from more than one school participate against peers from other schools in physical activity competitions, which usually stress winning. One objective of extramurals, which are often called "sports day" or "sports festival," is to actively involve the greatest number of participants possible. This obligation extends to the involvement of pupils with disabilities. Again, an important consideration is equalization of competition. By equalizing competitors by functional skill level, many pupils with disabilities can be included (see Figure 17.10). Where competition by individuals who are severely disabled is precluded in a fully integrated context, extramural organizers should also provide them with competitive experiences at more restrictive levels.

INTERSCHOLASTIC AND INTERCOLLEGIATE ATHLETICS

Freshman, junior varsity, and varsity interscholastic and intercollegiate athletics represent highly organized athletic programs.

Although these programs are a natural extension of the less competitive intramurals and extramurals, they are distinguished by high skill levels and a concentration on position/activity specialization. Intramurals and extramurals emphasize participation and enjoyment, whereas interscholastic and intercollegiate athletics are limited to a relatively small

FIGURE 17.10 A game of Nerf football.

number of individuals and emphasize competitiveness.

Typically, regular schools have great difficulty in fielding segregated interscholastic teams composed of pupils with disabilities, even when pupils from a number of schools are combined to form a school district–wide team. One obvious problem is that even if such a team is formed, there remains the dilemma of a lack of similar teams to compete against. Another significant dilemma for those schools with both the pupils and desire to create segregated interscholastic athletic teams is the identification and retention of qualified coaches.

At least one example of successful segregated interscholastic team competition can, however, be cited. Since the 1980s the Minnesota Association for Adapted Athletics (MAAA) has provided modified sport competitive experiences for seventh- to twelfth-grade male and female pupils with physical disabilities. School athletic letters were earned in indoor soccer, indoor softball, and floor hockey. More significantly, in November 1992 the Minnesota High School League (MHSL) became the first high school league in the U.S. to sanction interscholastic athletics for junior and senior high school pupils with disabilities. The MHSL now incorporates MAAA into its league structure and will conduct events for *all* athletes complete with awards, banners, letters, etc. Dave Stead, MHSL's executive director, and George Hanson, health and physical education specialist in the Minnesota State Department of Education, have been instrumental in this movement.

Segregated intercollegiate athletics also exist. For example, the National Intercollegiate Wheelchair Basketball League holds an annual tournament to crown a national champion. Further discussion of related interscholastic\intercollegiate sport offerings can be found in Winnick and Short (1981).

It is not that uncommon, however, for specialized schools to field integrated interscholastic athletic teams (e.g., basketball, baseball, football, track and field). For instance, the Ohio School for the Deaf competes in a regular basketball league. Related to this, some individuals with disabilities individually earn positions on regular interscholastic and intercollegiate athletic teams. Buell (1986) estimates that 5,000 sighted wrestlers compete against athletes who are visually impaired annually. Jim Abbott, who was born with only rudimentary fingers on his right hand, was an award-winning football quarterback and baseball pitcher at his Flint, Michigan, high school. Abbott also starred as a pitcher for the University of Michigan and won the Sullivan Award, signifying him as America's best amateur athlete. After college, Abbott successfully joined the California Angels (now the New York Yankees), which potentially adds "professional athletics" to our continuum of extracurricular activities model (refer to Figure 17.1).

Yet such individual situations are exceptions rather than the norm. Numerous petitions to participate in integrated interscholastic and intercollegiate athletics for otherwise qualified individuals with disabilities have been denied by school boards and colleges nationwide (Appenzeller, 1983). On occasion such rulings have been overturned in civil court; yet there has been relatively little opportunity in schools and colleges for athletes with disabilities to openly and freely compete.

On the bright side and in addition to the force of law, professional organizations do espouse the value of athletics for all participants, including those who are disabled. The American Alliance for Health, Physical Education, Recreation and Dance has led a movement toward establishing a "Bill of Rights for Young Athletes" that affects all pupils. This Bill of Rights, promoted specifically by AAHPERD's National Association for Sport and Physical Education (NASPE), includes the following (Thomas, 1977, p. 140):

- Right of the opportunity to participate in athletics regardless of ability level
- Right to participate at a level that is commensurate with each child's developmental level
- Right to have qualified adult leadership
- Right to participate in safe and healthy environments
- Right of each child to share in the leadership and decision making of their sport participation
- Right to play as a child and not as an adult
- Right to proper preparation for participation in the athletic event
- Right to an equal opportunity to strive for success
- Right to be treated with dignity by all involved
- Right to have fun through athletics

The American Academy of Pediatrics Joint Committee on Physical Fitness, Rehabilitation, and Sports Medicine (1974) also holds that participation by the child who is mentally retarded in regular exercise and athletic activities is essential to wholesome growth. Their position statement can be extrapolated to all those with special needs:

> Every retarded child needs a continuing program of physical maintenance with regular exercising and supervised athletic activities. If he is not able to participate in basketball, football, or baseball, he may be able to compete in track and field events or in the basic skills such as throwing baskets, kicking, or playing catch. Swimming, hiking, camping, archery, soccer, trampoline jumping, tennis, bicycling, folk dancing, and boating are examples of . . . activities that can give a

retarded youngster the satisfaction, the sense of participation, the social contacts, and the physical exercise that can be profitable for him (pp. 376–377).

Lastly, we would be remiss if we did not mention the possibility of interagency competitive adapted sports for the older adult. Older adults, with or without disabilities, are often assumed to be too frail for such active competitive programs and should only be spectators. This is not the case because adapted sport can be instrumental in skill and fitness maintenance and a sustained quality of life for this population.

One example of such sport competition can be found among a series of Northern Virginia Adult Day Health Care Centers as reported by D'Urso and Logue (1988). Five centers established an adapted volleyball league, and the participants themselves designed the appropriate net height (5 feet), court size (20 feet by 10 feet), rules (e.g., playing in chairs), ball (elasticized punch ball), number of players per team (9), the season schedule (8 games each team), a playoff schema, and awards. This program permitted these adults to associate more with a variety of peers, to identify more with their facility and others, and to be a greater part of their community.

AMATEUR ATHLETICS

The number and variety of amateur athletic opportunities for individuals with disabilities have exploded in recent years and will continue to do so. This is due, in part, to the increased attention given to individuals with disabilities in P.L. 101–476, P.L. 93–112, and especially P.L. 95–606. Opportunities for both segregated and integrated amateur athletics now exist for those with special needs. We highlight some of them.

Segregated Amateur Athletics

For those individuals with disabilities who want to compete in amateur athletics but for whom total integration would be inappropriate, a variety of opportunities are available. In addition to increased organizational support for such athletic opportunities at the local level, the number of state, regional, and international segregated amateur competitions has also significantly increased. We profile three of the most well known: The Special Olympics, Wheelchair Athletics, and the Deaf Games. Keep in mind that participation in these more restrictive athletic options is not illegal under federal law, as long as opportunities also exist in more normalized environments.

Special Olympics. The Special Olympics is the most widely known amateur athletic competition for those who are disabled. About 1 million individuals participate in the United States supported by more than 500,000 volunteers and 100,000 qualified coaches. Internationally, more than 100 countries have active programs, including China and Russia. Created in 1968 by the Joseph P. Kennedy, Jr., Foundation, with Eunice Kennedy Shriver as the driving force, the Special Olympics has as its purpose to provide year-round Olympics-style sports training and competition for individuals with mental retardation. Inherent in the goals of the program is the development of participants' human potential by affording them activities to improve their physical skills, strengthen their character, and display their talents (see Figure 17.11). The essence of the program is exemplified by the Special Olympics Oath, which is repeated by all participants prior to each competition:

> Let me win
> But if I cannot win
> Let me be brave
> in the attempt

FIGURE 17.11 They're all winners.

Individuals with an IQ of 76 or less who are 8 years or older (including the aged) are eligible to participate in the Special Olympics. Members of regular interscholastic or intramural teams are not eligible to compete. Many Special Olympics participants are both mentally and physically disabled; some are in wheelchairs.

The Special Olympics participant has a choice of numerous games and athletics in which to compete, and these are being added to on a regular basis. Special Olympics sports are categorized into Summer Games, Winter Games, Demonstration Sports, and Senior Sports. Here is a sampling of the key competitions in these four categories:

Summer Games

- Aquatics
  Swimming
  Diving
- Track and field
- Basketball
- Bowling
- Gymnastics
- Soccer
- Volleyball
- Roller skating
- Softball
- Equestrian

Winter Games

- Hockey
  Floor
  Poly
- Skating
  Figure
  Speed
- Skiing
  Alpine
  Nordic

Demonstration Sports

- Bocce
- Cycling
- Table tennis
- Tennis
- Team handball
- Power lifting

Senior Sports

- Bocce
- Croquet
- Horseshoes

Special Olympics games are held locally year-round. State-wide Summer and Winter Games (where appropriate) are held yearly. International Summer and Winter Games are held every four years. The International Summer Games are held in the year prior to the regular Olympics (see Figure 17.12), and the Winter Games are held the year following the regular Olympics (see Figure 17.13). In 1991, the Eighth International Summer Special Olympics were held in Minneapolis–St. Paul. Competitors representing every U.S. state and territory and more than 100 countries participated. The International Winter Special Olympics Games were last held in Austria in 1993; they began in 1977 in Steamboat Springs, Colorado.

Special Olympics competition exemplifies the least restrictive environment philosophy by means of graduated ability groups. Athletes ranging from the best to the poorest performers are grouped in divisions by age and sex, thus providing the overall frame-

FIGURE 17.12 Lighting the Special Olympics torch at the International Games.

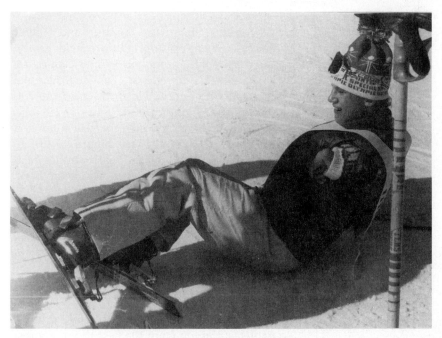

FIGURE 17.13   Down, but not out, at the Winter Games.

work of the games. The number of groups is based on the total number and ability of participants. Each ability group is limited to a maximum of a 10 percent differential in ability score, therefore, effectively equalizing competition for all participants. Within this system, each individual competes to the best of his or her ability and is constantly encouraged to improve performance. This allows for equalized competition for those with even the most serious disabilities. To support the goal of improved performance across all levels of ability, a series of Special Olympics Sports Skills Guides have been developed by the Special Olympics organization that cover each of the official and demonstration sports (see Chapter 15 for further discussion).

In terms of improved performances and least restrictive environments, Eunice Shriver views the participation of athletes who are mentally retarded along a continuum from Special Olympics programming to regular sports to the Olympic Games themselves. In fact, Kennedy Foundation personnel have estimated that approximately 90 percent of the competitors in the Special Olympics' highest level of competition could compete satisfactorily against the nondisabled, including winning Junior Olympic medals. As an outgrowth of this thinking, Special Olympics has introduced to a majority of the states its Unified Sports Program (Special Olympics, 1989; Smith, 1991), which emphasizes the matched combination of athletes who are mentally retarded and nondisabled athletes in sport training and competition. Team sports include basketball, bowling, soccer, softball, volleyball, and long distance running. This provides a choice between, for example, regular softball teams and participation on a segregated Special Olympics softball team. Of note is that the Unified Sports of basketball, soccer, softball, and volleyball were represented at the International Special Olympics in 1991 (Webster, 1991).

Unified Sports programs have also evolved within schools, along with sport partnership and partner clubs programs at the high school level (Krebs, Smith, & Martch, 1991). Sport partnerships involve a one-to-one pairing of athletes, one who is nondisabled and one who is mentally retarded. Each twosome trains and sometimes competes on junior varsity and varsity teams. Partner clubs involve similar matchups that provide an outlet for the partners to compete, recreate, and socialize. The nondisabled athlete serves as a role model, friend, and confidant to the athlete who is mentally retarded.

Two cautionary notes related to Special Olympics programs must be mentioned:

1. The Special Olympics should not replace the physical education programs of school-aged athletes. Rather, Special Olympics should supplement and complement the programs.

2. In the conduct of the Special Olympic Games, a normalized atmosphere including age-appropriate noncompetitive activities should be maintained. Therefore, the presence of clowns and a near-carnival atmosphere should be avoided.

Wheelchair Amateur Athletics. A number of sports and related organizations have been developed to serve the interests of athletes who are in a wheelchair. A primary example is the National Wheelchair Athletic Association (NWAA), founded in 1956 as a result of increasing interest shown by individuals having amputations and individuals with spinal cord lesions. Over the years the NWAA has stressed competitive athletics, and it currently sponsors competitions in air guns, archery (see Figure 17.14), track and field (see Figures 17.15 and 17.16), swimming, table tennis (see Figure 17.17), and weight lifting (see Figure 17.18).

In order to equalize competition, a medical system based on each individual's muscle functioning ability and a vertical spinal column analysis are used to classify each participant. The NWAA system (see Figure 17.19) contains seven classes (one additional class is

FIGURE 17.14 Wheelchair archery.

FIGURE 17.15   Wheelchair track competition.

FIGURE 17.16   Wheelchair shot put throw.

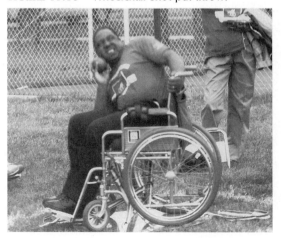

used for swimming events only). Even though some juniors and adults are difficult to classify due, as examples, to the nature of their injury or unequal functioning bilaterally, the classification system remains one of the strengths of the NWAA program.

The NWAA sponsors national championships annually. Additionally, athletes are chosen to compete internationally at the Stoke Mandeville Games for the disabled held annually in England. The NWAA places increasing emphasis on the development of training and coaching techniques specifically for the athlete (see Figures 17.20 and 17.21). The results of these efforts can be seen at the junior level (athletes 5 to 18 years of age) where both the number and level of performance of competitors have been rapidly rising.

The National Wheelchair Basketball Association (NWBA) utilizes a similar classification, adding points for each level of impair-

FIGURE 17.17 Wheelchair table tennis.

FIGURE 17.18 Wheelchair weight lifting.

ment in order to equalize competition among teams. For the most part NWBA rules are identical to those followed by able-bodied players with the following exceptions:

1. The participants must remain in the chair at all times during "live" play.
2. Traveling is called when more than two wheel pushes occur between dribbles on the court or before passing or shooting.
3. A player can stay within the foul line for a maximum of 6 seconds during active play.

The NWBA sponsors annual championship tournaments for both men's and women's teams (see Figure 17.22).

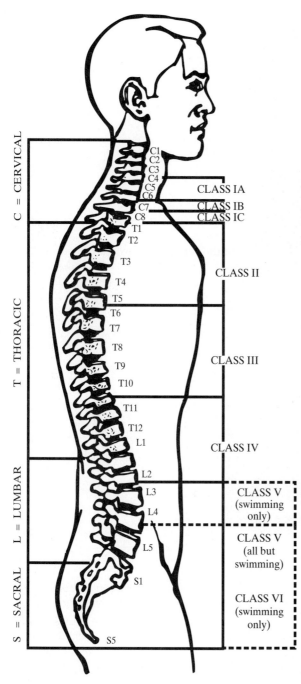

FIGURE 17.19   The NWAA classification system.

Class 1A—All cervical lesions with complete or incomplete quadriplegia who have involvement of both hands, weakness of triceps (up to and including grade 3 on testing scale) and with severe weakness of the trunk and lower extremities interfering significantly with trunk balance and the ability to walk.

Class 1B—All cervical lesions with complete or incomplete quadriplegia who have involvement of upper extremities by less than 1A with preservation of normal or good triceps (4 or 5 on testing scale) and with a generalized weakness of the trunk and lower extremities interfering significantly with trunk balance and the ability to walk.

Class 1C—All cervical lesions with complete or incomplete quadriplegia who have involvement of upper extremities but less than 1A with preservation of normal or good triceps (4 or 5 on testing scale) and normal or good finger flexion and extension (grasp and release) but without intrinsic hand function and with a generalized weakness of the trunk and lower extremities interfering significantly with trunk balance and the ability to walk.

Class II — Complete or incomplete paraplegia below T1 down to and including T5 or comparable disability with total abdominal paralysis or poor abdominal muscle strength (0–2 on testing scale) and no useful trunk sitting balance.

Class III — Complete or incomplete paraplegia or comparable disability below T5 down to and including T10 with upper abdominal and spinal extensor musculature sufficient to provide some element of trunk sitting balance but not normal.

Class IV — Complete or incomplete paraplegia or comparable disability below T10 down to and including L2 without quadriceps or very weak quadriceps with a value up to and including 2 on the testing scale and gluteal paralysis.

Class V — Complete or incomplete paraplegia or comparable disability below L2 with quadriceps in grade 3–5.

Swimming Events Only

Class V — Complete or incomplete paraplegia or comparable disability below L2 with quadriceps in grades 3–5 and with up to and including 39 points on the point scale.

Class VI — Complete or incomplete paraplegia or comparable disability below L2 and with 40 points and above on the point scale.

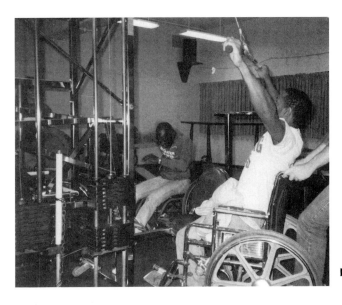

FIGURE 17.20   Athletes in wheelchairs using strength training equipment.

FIGURE 17.21   An athlete in a wheelchair works on flexibility.

FIGURE 17.22   Wheelchair basketball.

Other organizations representing athletes who are in a wheelchair include: National Foundation of Wheelchair Tennis, National Wheelchair Racquetball Association, American Wheelchair Bowling Association, and National Wheelchair Softball Association. One of the fastest growing organizations is the International Wheelchair Road Racers Club, Inc. Road racers from this group are regularly included in marathons and shorter races throughout the United States and other countries. Surprising to most, these racers regularly complete marathons in shorter times than able-bodied runners. Additionally, athletes in wheelchairs were showcased through races at the 1988 and 1992 Olympic Games.

Much of the success of athletes in wheelchairs can be traced to substantially improved technology in wheelchair design. Wheelchairs typically weighed between 45 and 50 pounds when the NWAA was established. In contrast, the influence of rule changes, lightweight materials, aerodynam-

ics, and the results of applied research have now produced sport wheelchairs weighing as little as 12 pounds (see Figure 17.23) and specifically designed for selected events (e.g., road racing, track racing, field events, basketball). See Appendix C for a listing of lightweight wheelchair manufacturers. *Sports 'n' Spokes*, a magazine that chronicles wheelchair sports and recreational activities, annually publishes a survey of the latest in lightweight recreational and athletic wheelchairs. These advances, along with increased access to training facilities and sports medicine specialists located at United States Olympic Committee (USOC) training centers, have significantly improved the performance of athletes in wheelchairs and account for the fantastic times in such events as the marathon. In addition, more sophisticated analysis of wheelchair racing performance is now the norm, with such factors as types of performance errors, biomechanical problems, environmental performance limitations, and performer-imposed limitations

FIGURE 17.23 A lightweight racing wheelchair.

being observed more systematically (Pope, Wilkerson, & Ridgway, 1992).

The Deaf Games. In 1924, the World Games for the Deaf (Summer) began in Paris, France, and have been held approximately every four years since. Competition in the following events is sanctioned:

- Track and field
- Wrestling
- Tennis
- Swimming
- Basketball
- Volleyball
- Cycling
- Water polo
- Soccer
- Shooting
- Table tennis
- Field hand ball
- Judo

The standards of performance and the rules governing competitions for school-aged and adult athletes who are deaf are comparable to those for able-bodied individuals. Pan American Games are also held, in addition to regional and local competition. The International Committee of Silent Sports also sponsors the World Winter Games for the Deaf, which originated in 1949. As with the Summer Games, these games are held approximately every four years. The Twelfth World Winter Games for the Deaf were held in Banff, Alberta, Canada. Since 1945, the American Athletic Association for the Deaf (Cheverly, Maryland) has promoted and sanctioned most athletic competition at home and abroad for American athletes who are hearing impaired.

Other Organizations. Several other organizations for athletes with disabilities are worthy of note. The National Handicapped Sports and Recreation Association (NHSRA) is dedicated to individuals with various physical disabilities. The NHSRA is active in such sports as snow and water skiing, swimming, scuba diving, sailing, canoeing, river rafting, tennis, hiking, biking, horseback rid-

ing, climbing, and sky diving. Much of this organization's activity is centered on alpine skiing, an activity in which annual national championships are held.

The United States Cerebral Palsy Athletic Association (USCPAA) provides competitive sports opportunities for individuals with cerebral palsy and similar physically disabling conditions. The USCPAA utilizes a functional classification system to equalize competition that combines measures of coordination, range, and speed of muscle movement and whether the athlete is ambulatory, on crutches, or in a wheelchair. This organization sponsors a variety of sports, including

- Archery
- Bocce
- Bowling
- Cross-country
- Cycling
- Equestrian
- Field events
- Power lifting
- Shooting
- Slalom
- Swimming
- Handball
- Table tennis
- Track

The United States Association for Blind Athletes (USABA) holds competition in alpine and nordic snow skiing, marathon running, gymnastics, power lifting, swimming, track and field, and wrestling. All athletes associated with the USABA are organized into one of three classes based on their visual acuity and visual field. Two unique activities sponsored by the USABA are goal ball and beep baseball (see also Chapter 9). Goal ball is played indoors on a basketball court. All players are blindfolded. The court is divided in half with each team commanding one end. The object is to roll an audible ball past all the members of the opposing team. Beep baseball also uses an audible ball. Players are positioned similarly as in regular baseball, with the exception that there are only two bases (see Figure 17.24). A sighted pitcher throws the ball to the person at bat. When the

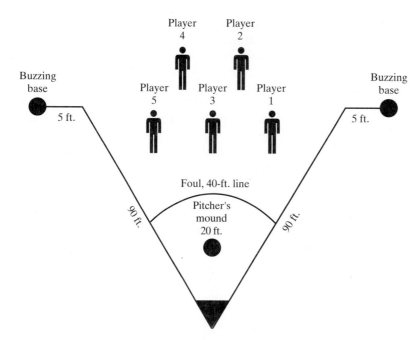

FIGURE 17.24   Field diagram for beep baseball.

ball is struck, a sighted referee turns on an audible sound (usually buzzing) in one of the two bases. In order to score a point, the batter must reach the buzzing base before the ball is retrieved by the team in the field.

The United States Amputee Athletic Association (USAAA) sponsors national games in air pistol, archery, basketball, discus, high jump, long jump, javelin, pentathlon, swimming, table tennis, track, and weight lifting. The USAAA utilizes a nine-level medical classification system. This system of classification and systems for other similar organizations are explained more fully in Shephard's *Fitness in Special Populations* (1990).

Multisport Competitions. Recent years have seen an increase in the number of multisport competitions for athletes with disabilities. The New York State Games for the Physically Challenged, initiated in 1984, brings together athletes with various disabilities including the hearing impaired, spinal cord injured, cerebral palsied, athletes with amputations, and les autres (all others). Another significant event occurring in New York was the 1984 International Games for the Disabled. President Ronald Reagan opened the games, which included athletes from 44 nations representing four disability categories (amputee, visually impaired, cerebral palsied, and les autres). The 1992 Paralympics were held in Barcelona, Spain with approximately 4,000 athletes from more than 60 countries involved. More than 400 athletes from the NWAA, USAAA, USABA, and USCPAA competed.

Integrated Amateur Athletics

We believe that an increasing number of school-aged and nonschool-aged individuals with disabilities will participate in regular athletic competition. As Lindstrom (1992) states, the "integration of able bodied and athletes with disabilities in sport movement" is on. Such competition may involve one or more participants with a disability on one or both sides in a regulation athletic event, or one complete team consisting entirely of players who are disabled competing against a team of nondisabled athletes. In both situations some accommodations and rule changes might or might not be required.

The Special Olympics Unified Sports Program is a prime example of integrated athletics. In 1989, more than 15 states had Unified Sports demonstration programs. It is the hope of the Kennedy Foundation that successful Unified Sports programs will become reality nationwide, providing a significant addition to the continuum of least restrictive athletic environments for individuals who are mentally retarded.

Another example of integrated athletics is the wheelchair division of the Boston Marathon, which also adds an international dimension. This event also provides evidence of increased participation and quality in wheelchair athletics. In 1975, Bob Hall became the first athlete to complete the Boston Marathon in a wheelchair, finishing in 2 hours and 58 minutes. In 1989, 32 men and 8 women completed the marathon in wheelchairs. Even more exciting, in 1993 Jean Driscoll completed the Boston Marathon in 1 hour, 34 min-

utes, and 50 seconds—an average of about three and a half minutes per mile! The awarding of prize monies in the wheelchair division, as is done in the able-bodied divisions, is a further indication of the acceptance of athletes with disabilities. The 1989 Boston Marathon wheelchair division winners were awarded prize monies as follows: $7,000 for first place, $7,500 for breaking a course rec-ord, and $10,000 for breaking a world record.

Pupils who are hearing impaired have been successfully integrated into swimming, soccer, football, and basketball competition. Similarly, pupils with amputations have demonstrated outstanding ability in such integrated athletic events as football and swimming. Suffice it to say that many similar scenarios are anticipated, and should be expected.

As another form of integration, it is now common to incorporate events for those who are disabled into regular games or sports festivals. As an example, in addition to the Olympic Games' wheelchair races, adapted skiing was on display at the 1988 Winter Olympics in Calgary, Canada. And, since 1985, adapted athletic events have been included in the annual United States Olympic Festival.

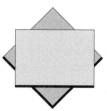

References

A clarification of terms. (1971). *Journal of Health, Physical Education, and Recreation, 42,* 63–66.

Adams, G. (1984). *Comprehensive test of adaptive behavior.* Columbus, OH: Merrill.

Adams, R., & McCubbin, J. (1991). *Games, sports, and exercises for the physically disabled,* 4th ed. Philadelphia: Lea & Febiger.

Adapted Physical Activity Council. (February 1993). Competencies for adapted (special) physical education. *Update,* 7.

Allen, J. (1980). Jogging can modify disruptive behaviors. *Teaching Exceptional Children, 12*(2), 66–70.

Althoff, S. A., Heyden, S. M., & Robertson, L. D. (1988). Back to the basics: Whatever happened to posture? *Journal of Physical Education, Recreation, and Dance, 59*(7), 20–24.

American Academy of Pediatrics, Joint Committee on Physical Fitness, Retardation, and Sports Medicine. (1974). Athletic activities for children who are mentally retarded. *Pediatrics, 54,* 376–377.

American Alliance for Health, Physical Education, Recreation and Dance. (1980a). P.L. 94-142 regulations clarified. *Update.* Reston, VA.

———. (1980b). *Lifetime health related physical fitness test manual.* Reston, VA.

———. (1988). *Physical best.* Reston, VA.

American Association for Health, Physical Education, and Recreation. (1965). *AAHPER youth fitness test manual.* Reston, VA.

———. (1976a). *Special fitness manual for mildly mentally retarded persons.* Reston, VA.

———. (1976b). *AAHPER youth fitness manual,* rev. Reston, VA.

American Camping Association. (1973). *Camp standards with interpretations.* Martinsville, IN.

American Dance Therapy Association. (1974). *Proceedings of the 9th Annual Conference,* 4.

American Heart Association. (1982). *If your child has a congenital heart defect.* Dallas, TX: American Heart Association, Office of Communications.

American National Red Cross. (1977). *Adapted aquatics.* Garden City, NY: Doubleday.

American National Standards Institute. (1980). *American national standard specification for making buildings and facilities accessible to, and usable by, the physically handicapped*. New York.

American Occupational Therapy Association (1972). Occupational therapy: Its definition and functions. *American Journal of Occupational Therapy, 26,* 204.

———. (1981). The role of occupational therapy as an education-related service. *American Journal of Occupational Therapy, 35,* 811.

———. (1986). Dictionary definition of occupational therapy. *American Journal of Occupational Therapy, 40,* 852.

American Psychiatric Association. (1987). *Diagnostic and statistical manual of mental disorders*, 3rd ed., rev. Washington, DC.

Anderson, L. E. (Ed.). (1970). *Helping the adolescent with the hidden handicap*. Los Angeles: California Association for Neurologically Handicapped Children.

Appenzeller, H. (1983). *The right to participate: The law and individuals with handicapping conditions in physical education and sports*. Charlottesville, VA: Michie.

Arbogast, G., & Misner, J. (1990). Homework "how-to-do's." *Strategies, 4,* 12–15.

Armstrong, S. W., & McPherson, A. (1991). Homework as a critical component in social skills instruction. *Teaching Exceptional Children, 24*(1), 45–47.

Arnheim, D. D., Auxter, D., & Crowe, W. C. (1977). *Principles and methods of adapted physical education and recreation*, 3rd ed. St. Louis, MO: Mosby.

Arnheim, D. D., & Sinclair, W. A. (1979). *The clumsy child: A program of motor therapy*, 2nd ed. St. Louis, MO: Mosby.

———. (1985). *Physical education for special populations*. Englewood Cliffs, NJ: Prentice Hall.

Arnold, L. C., & Freeman, R. W. (Eds.). (1972). *Progressive swimming and springboard diving program*. New York: National YMCA Program Materials.

Aufderheide, S., Knowles, C., & McKenzie, T. (1981). Individualized teaching strategies and learning time: Implications for mainstreaming. *The Physical Educator, 38*(1), 20–26.

Aufsesser, P. (1986). *Liability: And its implications in adapted physical education*. Paper presented at 15th National Conference on Physical Activity for Exceptional Individuals, Woodland Hills, CA, October.

———. (1991). Mainstreaming and the least restrictive environment: How they differ? *Palaestra, 7*(2), 31–34.

Auxter, D. (1971). *Perceptual motor developmental programs for an individually prescribed instructional system*. Slippery Rock, PA: Slippery Rock College.

———. (1976). *Diagnostic prescriptive individualized programming*. Paper presented at National Conference of the American Association for Health, Physical Education and Recreation, Milwaukee, WI.

Auxter, D., Jansma, P., Sculli, J., Stein, J., Weiss, R., & Winnick, J. P. (1980). Implications of Section 504 of the Rehabilitation Act as related to physical education instruction, personnel preparation, intramural and interscholastic/intercollegiate sports programs. *Practical Pointers, 3,* 1–20.

Auxter, D., Pyfer, J., & Huettig, C. (1993). *Principles and methods of adapted physical education and recreation*, 6th ed. St. Louis, MO: Times Mirror/Mosby.

Auxter, D., Zahar, E., & Ferrini, L. (1967). Body image development of emotionally disturbed children. *American Corrective Therapy Journal, 21,* 154–155.

Axline, V. M. (1947). *Play therapy*. Boston: Houghton Mifflin.

Ayres, G., & Smith, H. C. (1964). Orthopedic screening in Delaware. *Journal of Health, Physical Education and Recreation, 35,* 30–31.

Ayres, J. A. (1969). *Southern California perceptual-motor tests*. Los Angeles: Western Psychological Services.

———. (1972). *Sensory integration and learning disorders*. Los Angeles: Western Psychological Services.

Bailey, D. (1976). The growing child and the need for physical activity. In J. Albinson and G. Andrews (Eds.), *Child in sport and physical activity*. Baltimore: University Park Press.

Bailey, D., & Wolery, M. (1984). *Teaching infants and preschoolers with handicaps*. Columbus, OH: Merrill.

Ballinger, D. A., & Heine, P. L. (1991). Relaxation training for children—A script. *Journal of*

Physical Education, Recreation, and Dance, 62(2), 67–70.

Bar-Or, O., Inbar, O., & Spira, R. (1976). Physiological effects of a sports rehabilitation program on cerebral palsied and post-poliomyelitic adolescents. *Medicine and Science in Sports and Exercise, 8*, 157–161.

Barsch, R. H. (1968). *Achieving perceptual motor efficiency*. Seattle: Special Child Publications.

Barton, B. (1982). Aerobic dance and the mentally retarded—A winning combination. *The Physical Educator, 39*(1), 25–29.

Beals, P. (1978). *Parents' guide to the childbearing year*, 6th ed. Rochester, NY: The International Childbirth Education Association.

Bender, N. S. (1992). Are today's students falling behind in the quest for physical fitness? *Association of Texas Professional Educators, 12*(5), 12–15.

Benjamin, S. (1989). An ideascape for education: What futurists recommend. *Educational Leadership, 47*, 8–14.

Billig, H. E., Jr. (1943). Dysmenorrhea: The result of a postural defect. *Archives of Surgery, 46*, 611–613.

Birch, J. W. (1975). *Hearing impaired pupils in the mainstream*. Minneapolis: University of Minnesota, Leadership Training Institute/Special Education.

Bishop, P., & Donnelly, J. E. (1987). Home based activity program for obese children. *American Corrective Therapy Journal, 41*(1), 12–19.

Blatt, B., & Kaplan, F. (1966). *Christmas in purgatory*. Boston: Allyn & Bacon.

Blatt, B., Ozolins, A., & McNally, J. (1980). *The family papers: A return to purgatory*. New York: Longman.

Block, M. E. (1989). *Special Olympics: Motor activities training program*. Washington, DC: Special Olympics International.

———. (1991). Motor development in children with Down syndrome: A review of the literature. *Adapted Physical Activity Quarterly, 8*, 179–209.

Block, M. E., & Krebs, P. L. (1992). An alternative to least restrictive environments: A continuum of support to regular physical education. *Adapted Physical Activity Quarterly, 9*, 97–113.

Blucker, J. A., & Pell, S. W. (1986). Legal and ethical issues. *Journal of Physical Education, Recreation, and Dance, 57*(4), 19–22.

Bluma, S., Shearer, M., Frohman, A., & Hilliard, J. (1976). *The Portage guide to early education*, rev. ed. Portage, WI: Cooperative Educational Service Agency #12.

Bobath, B. (1971). *Abnormal postural reflex activity caused by brain lesions*, 2nd ed. London: Heinemann/Chartered Society of Physiotherapy.

Bobath, B., & Bobath, K. (1975). *Motor development in the different types of cerebral palsy*. London: Heinemann.

Bobath, K., & Bobath, B. (1964). The facilitation of normal postural reactions and movements in the treatment of cerebral palsy. *Physiotherapy, 50*, 246–262.

Bookwalter, K. W. (1964). *Physical education in secondary schools*. Washington, DC: Center for Applied Recreation in Education.

Boswell, B. (1989). Dance as a creative expression for the disabled. *Palaestra, 6*(1), 28–30.

Brandon, J. E., Eason, R., & Smith, T. L. (1986). Behavioral relaxation training and motor performance of learning disabled children with hyperactive behaviors. *Adapted Physical Activity Quarterly, 3*(1), 67–79.

Brannan, S. A. (Ed.). (1979). *Project EXPLORE*. Portland, OR: Portland State University, Special Education Department.

Brigance, A. H. (1978). *Brigance diagnostic inventory of early development*. Woburn, MA: Curriculum Associates.

Brinckerhoff, J. (1987). *The Portage classroom curriculum—CHECKLIST*. Portage, WI: Cooperative Educational Service Agency #5.

Brink, J. D., Imbus, C., & Woo-Sam, J. (1980). Physical recovery after severe closed head trauma in children and adolescents. *Journal of Pediatrics, 97*, 721–729.

Britton, C. B., & Miller, J. R. (1984). Neurological complications in acquired immunodeficiency syndrome (AIDS). *Neurologic Clinics, 2*, 315–319.

Bronzan, R. T. (1980). A comprehensive guide to planning facilities for the handicapped. *Athletic Purchasing & Facilities, 4*(8), 12–17.

Brooks, D. M., & Boatwright, J. D. (1992). Southeast Texas high school coaches' knowledge of amenorrhea. *Texas Association of Health, Physical Education, Recreation, and Dance, 55*(2), 18–23.

Brownell, K. D., & Kaye, F. S. (1982). A school-based modification, nutrition education, and physical activity program for obese children. *American Journal of Clinical Nutrition, 35,* 277–283.

Bruininks, R. H. (1978). *Bruininks-Oseretsky test of motor proficiency.* Circle Pines, MN: American Guidance Service.

Bucher, C. A. (1983). *Administration of physical education and athletic programs,* 8th ed. St. Louis, MO: Mosby.

Buell, C. E. (1966). *Physical education for blind children.* Springfield, IL: Thomas.

———. (1973). *Physical education and recreation for the visually handicapped.* Washington, DC: American Association for Health, Physical Education, and Recreation.

———. (1982). *Physical education and recreation for the visually handicapped,* (2nd ed.) Reston, VA: American Alliance for Health, Physical Education, Recreation and Dance.

———. (1986). Blind athletes successfully compete against able-bodied opponents. In C. Sherrill (Ed.), *Sport and disabled athletes* (pp. 217–224). Champaign, IL: Human Kinetics.

Bundschuh, E. (Ed.). (1985). *Position paper on adapted physical education.* Report submitted to the U.S. Department of Education, Office of Special Education Programs, Washington, DC.

Bundschuh, E., Williams, W., Hollingworth, J., Gooch, S., & Shirer, C. (1972). Teaching the retarded to swim. *Mental Retardation, 10*(3), 14–17.

Buntke, C. F. (1990). Medical advances in the treatment of brain injury. In J. S. Kreutzer & P. Wehman. *Community integration following traumatic brain injury* (pp. 3–13). Baltimore: Brookes.

Butterfield, S. (1987). The influence of age, sex, hearing loss, etiology, and balance ability on the fundamental motor skills of deaf children. In M. Berridge & G. Ward (Eds.), *International perspectives in adapted physical activity* (pp. 43–51). Champaign, IL: Human Kinetics.

———. (1991). Physical education and sport for the deaf: Rethinking the least restrictive environment. *Adapted Physical Activity Quarterly, 8,* 95–102.

Campbell, J. (1978). Evaluation of physical fitness programs for retarded boys. *Journal for Special Educators of the Mentally Retarded, 14,* 78–83.

Campbell, P., Green, K., & Carlson, L. (1977). Approximating the norm through environmental and child-centered prosthetics and adaptive equipment. In E. Sontag (Ed.), *Educational programming for the severely and profoundly handicapped.* Reston, VA: Council for Exceptional Children.

Canter, L., & Canter, M. (1976). *Assertive discipline: A take-charge approach for today's educator.* Seal Beach, CA: Canter and Associates.

Carpenter, L. J., & Acosta, R. V. (1982). Negligence. What is it? How can it be avoided? *Journal of Physical Education, Recreation, and Dance, 53*(2), 51–52, 89.

Charest-Lilly, P., Sherrill, C., & Rosentswieg, J. (1987). Body composition of women with anorexia nervosa: A pilot study. *Adapted Physical Activity Quarterly, 4,* 126–136.

Chasnoff, I., & Burns, K. A. (1986). Cocaine use in pregnancy. *New England Journal of Medicine, 9*(1), 291–293.

Cheffers, J. (1972). *The validation of an instrument designed to expand the Flanders system of interaction analysis to describe nonverbal interaction, different varieties of teacher behavior, and pupil responses.* Unpublished dissertation, Temple University.

Churton, M. (1984). I'M SPECIAL: A review of the videotape series. *Adapted Physical Activity Quarterly, 1*(1), 89–94.

———. (1987). Impact of the Education of the Handicapped Act on adapted physical education: A 10-year overview. *Adapted Physical Activity Quarterly, 4*(1), 1–8.

Clark, B. (1989). Tests for fitness in older adults. AAHPERD fitness task force. *Journal of Physical Education, Recreation, and Dance, 60*(3), 66–71.

Cockrell, J. C., Chase, J., & Cobb, E. (1990). The rehabilitation of children with traumatic brain injury. In J. S. Kreutzer & P. Wehman (Eds.), *Community integration following traumatic brain injury* (pp. 287–300). Baltimore: Brookes.

Cole, E. L. (1978). *Swimming and hyperactivity: The influence of water temperatures.* Unpublished thesis, Texas Woman's University.

College of obstetricians and gynecologists exercise during pregnancy at the postpaternal period. (1986). Washington, DC: ACOG.

Collier, D., & Reid, G. (1987). A comparison of two models designed to teach autistic children a motor task. *Adapted Physical Activity Quarterly, 4,* 226–236.

Collins, C., & Curet, L. B. (1985). Fetal heart rate to maternal exercise. *American Journal of Obstetric Gynecology, 151*(4), 498–501.

Committee on Adapted Physical Education. (1952). Guiding principles for adapted physical education. *Journal of Health, Physical Education, and Recreation, 23*(4), 15–28.

Committee on Cross-Categorical Resource Programs of the Association for Children and Adults with Learning Disabilities. (1982). *Final report*. Pittsburgh.

Committee on Exercise and Physical Fitness. (1967). Classification of students for physical education. *Journal of the American Medical Association, 199*, 113–115.

Connolly, B., & Anderson, R. (1978). Severely handicapped children in the public schools: A new frontier for the physical therapist. *Physical Therapy, 58*, 433–438.

Connor, F. (1990). Physical education for children with autism. *Teaching Exceptional Children, 23*(1), 30–33.

Cooper, J. O., Heron, T. E., & Heward, W. L. (1987). *Applied behavior analysis*. Columbus, OH: Merrill.

Coram, S. J., & Mangum, M. (1986). Exercise risks and benefits: A review. *Adapted Physical Activity Quarterly, 3*, 35–57.

Cordellos, H. (1987). *Aquatic recreation for the blind*. Berkeley: LaBuy Printing.

Costonis, M. N. (Ed.). (1977). *Therapy in motion*. Urbana: University of Illinois Press.

Council for Exceptional Children, Teacher Education Division. (1987). The regular education initiative. *Journal of Learning Disabilities, 20*(5), 289–293.

Cowden, J. (1980). *Administrator inservice training for program implementation in adapted and developmental physical education*. Unpublished doctoral dissertation, Texas Woman's University.

Cowden, J. E., & Eason, B. L. (1991). Pediatric adapted physical education for infants, toddlers, and preschoolers: Meeting IDEA-H and IDEA-B challenges. *Adapted Physical Activity Quarterly, 8*, 263–279.

Cratty, B. J. (1966). *Perceptual-motor attributes of mentally retarded youth*. Los Angeles: Mental Retardation Services Board of Los Angeles County.

———. (1969). *Motor activity and the education of retardates*. Philadelphia: Lea & Febiger.

———. (1971a). *Active learning: Games to enhance academic abilities*. Englewood Cliffs, NJ: Prentice Hall.

———. (1971b). *Movement and spatial awareness in blind children and youth*. Springfield, IL: Thomas.

———. (1972). *Physical expressions of intelligence*. Englewood Cliffs, NJ: Prentice Hall.

———. (1973). *Intelligence in action: Physical activities for enhancing intellectual abilities*. Englewood Cliffs, NJ: Prentice Hall.

———. (1974). *Motor activity and the education of retardates*, 2nd ed. Philadelphia: Lea & Febiger.

———. (1975). *Remedial motor activity for children*. Philadelphia: Lea & Febiger.

———. (1979). *Perceptual and motor development in infants and young children*, 2nd ed. Englewood Cliffs, NJ: Prentice Hall.

———. (1990). Motor development of infants subject to maternal drug use: Current evidence and future research strategies. *Adapted Physical Activity Quarterly, 7*(2), 110–125.

Cratty, B. J., Cratty, I., & Cornell, S. (1986). Motor planning abilities in deaf and hearing children. *American Annals of the Deaf, 131*, 281–284.

Cratty, B. J., & Sams, T. A. (1968). *The body-image of blind children*. New York: American Foundation for the Blind.

Criteria Committee of the New York Heart Association. (1964). *Diseases of the heart and blood vessels: Nomenclature and criteria for diagnosis*, 6th ed. Boston: MA: Little, Brown.

Croce, R. V. (1987). Exercise and physical activity in managing progressive muscular dystrophy: A review for practitioners. *Palaestra, 9*–15.

Croce, R. V., DePaepe, J., & McGuire, P. (1987). *Motor development of children with special needs: Scientific and systematic instruction*. Special P.E. Monograph #1. Durham: University of New Hampshire, Department of Special Education.

Cullinan, D., Epstein, M. H., & Lloyd, J. W. (1983). *Behavior disorders of children and adolescents*. Englewood Cliffs, NJ: Prentice Hall.

Curtis, K. A. (1982). Athletic injuries. *Sports 'n' Spokes, 7*(5), 20–24.

D'Alonzo, B. J. (1976). Rights of exceptional children to participate in interscholastic athletics. *Exceptional Children, 43*, 86–92.

Dannaldson, D. J. (1992). Why I can't take P.E. *Strategies, 6*(3), 13–16.

Darst, P. W., Zakrajsek, D. B., & Mancini, V. H. (1989). *Analyzing physical education and sport instruction*, 2nd ed. Champaign, IL: Human Kinetics.

Davis, K. (1990). *Adapted physical education for students with autism.* Springfield, IL: Thomas.

Davis, R. (1982). An elementary fitness program that works. *Health Education, 13,* 54.

———. (1985). *Qualitative analysis of backward wheelchair propulsion performance by elite class II cerebral palsied athletes.* Paper presented at National Convention of the American Alliance for Health, Physical Education, Recreation, and Dance, Atlanta.

Delacato, C. H. (1964). *The diagnosis and treatment of speech and reading problems.* Springfield, IL: Thomas.

DeLorme, T. L., & Watkins, A. L. (1951). *Progressive resistance exercise.* New York: Appleton-Century-Crofts.

Deno, E. (1970). Special education as developmental capital. *Exceptional Children, 37,* 229–237.

Department of Health, Education and Welfare. (1977). *Education of Handicapped Children: Implementation of Part B of the Education of the Handicapped Act. Federal Register,* August 23.

DePauw, K. (1984). Total body mass centroid and segmental mass centroid locations found in Down's syndrome individuals. *Adapted Physical Activity Quarterly, 1,* 221–229.

D'Eugenio, D. B., & Moersch, M. S. (Eds.). (1978). *Preschool developmental profile.* Ann Arbor: Institute for the Study of Mental Retardation and Related Disabilities, University of Michigan.

Diet and Cancer. (1986). Statement from the National Cancer Institute, National Institutes of Health, Bethesda, MD.

DiRocco, P. (1981). Cardiopulmonary effects of scoliosis. *American Corrective Therapy Journal, 35*(2), 38–40.

Docheff, D. (1990). Homework . . . in physical education. *Strategies, 4*(1), 10–11.

Doremus, W. A. (1992). Developmental aquatics: Assessment and instructional programming. *Teaching Exceptional Children, 24*(4), 6–10.

Dresen, M. (1985). Physical training of handicapped children. In R. Binkhorst, H. Kempter, & W. Saris (Eds.), *Children and exercise XI* (pp. 203–209). Champaign, IL: Human Kinetics.

Drew, C. J., Logan, D. R., & Hardman, M. L.

(1990). *Mental retardation,* 4th ed. Columbus, OH: Merrill.

Dunn, J. M., & Craft, D. (1985). Mainstreaming theory and practice. *Adapted Physical Activity Quarterly, 2*(4), 273–276.

Dunn, J. M., Morehouse, J. W., & Dalke, B. (1979). *Game, exercise, and leisure sport curriculum.* Corvallis: Oregon State University.

Dunn, J. M., Morehouse, J. W., & Fredericks, H. (1986). *Physical education for the severely handicapped: A systematic approach to a data-based gymnasium.* Austin, TX: Pro-Ed Publishers.

D'Urso, M., & Logue, G. (1988). Competitive adapted sports for impaired older adults. *Therapeutic Recreation Journal, 22*(4), 56–64.

Eames, P., & Wood, R. L. (1989). The structure and content of a head injury rehabilitation service. In R. Wood & P. Eames, *Models of brain injury rehabilitation* (pp. 31–47). Baltimore: Johns Hopkins University Press.

Eichstaedt, C. B., & Kalakian, L. H. (1993). *Developmental/adapted physical education.* New York: Macmillan.

Eichstaedt, C. B., & Lavay, B. L. (1992). *Physical activity for individuals with mental retardation: Infancy through adulthood.* Champaign, IL: Human Kinetics.

Eichstaedt, C. B., Polacek, J. J., Wang, P. Y., & Dohrmann, P. F. (1991). *Physical fitness and motor skill levels of individuals with mental retardation: Mild, moderate, and Down syndrome.* Normal: Illinois State University Printing Services.

Eichstaedt, C. B., & Seiler, P. J. (1978). Singing: Communicating with hearing impaired individuals in physical education. *Journal of Physical Education and Recreation, 49,* 19–21.

Ekstein, R., & Caruth, E. (1976). On the structure of inner and outer spielrauns—The play space of the schizophrenic child. In E. Schapler & R. Reichert (Eds.), *Psychopathology and child development: Research and treatment.* New York: Plenum.

Ellis, D. (1980). Fat, fun, and fitness. *Journal of Physical Education and Recreation, 51,* 77.

Emes, C., Velde, B., Moreau, M., Murdoch, D., & Trussell, R. (1990). An activity based weight control program. *Adapted Physical Activity Quarterly, 7,*(4) 314–324.

Ersing, W. F. (1980). *Guidelines for adapted physical*

education. Columbus: Ohio State University Press.

Ersing, W. F., & Huber, J. H. (1992). Considerations for clinical programs in adapted physical education. *Palaestra, 9*, 38–41.

Ersing, W. F., Loovis, E., & Ryan, T. (1982). On the nature of motor development in special populations. *Exceptional Education Quarterly, 31*(1), 64–72.

Fait, H. (1978). *Special physical education*: adapted, corrective, developmental, 4th ed. Philadelphia: Saunders.

Federal Register. Tuesday, September 29, 1992, *57*(189), 44802.

Feingold, B. F. (1974). *Why your child is hyperactive*. New York: Random House.

————. (1976). Hyperkinesis and learning disabilities linked to the ingestion of artificial food colors and flavors. *Journal of Learning Disabilities, 9*, 551–559.

Fernandez-Balboa, J. (1990). Helping novice teachers handle discipline problems. *Journal of Physical Education, Recreation, and Dance, 62*(7), 50–54.

Feruno, S., O'Reilly, K., Hosaka, C., Inatsuka, T., & Zeisloft-Falbey, B. (1985). *The Hawaii early learning profile*. Palo Alto, CA: Vort.

Finholt, J. M., Peterson, B. A., & Colvin, N. R. (1987). *Guidelines for physical educators of mentally handicapped youth*, 2nd ed. Springfield, IL: Thomas.

Finnie, N. R. (1975). *Handling the young cerebral palsied child at home*, 2nd ed. New York: Dutton.

Fitness and Amateur Sport Secretary of State of Canada. (1980). *Take it easy*. Minister of Supply and Services, Canada. Cat. No. H93-561i980e.

Fluegelman, A. (1981). *More new games*. Garden City, NY: Doubleday.

————. (Ed.). (1976). *The new games book*. Garden City, NY: Doubleday.

Foederer, R. (1987). *Adapted physical education inservice needs of physical educators, special educators, and aides*. Unpublished thesis, Texas Woman's University.

Folio, M. R., & Fewell, R. (1983). *Peabody developmental motor scales and activity cards*. Allen, TX: DLM Teaching Resources.

Folsom-Meek, S. L. (1984). Parents: Forgotten teacher aides in adapted physical education. *Adapted Physical Activity Quarterly, 1*, 275–281.

Forness, S., & Kavale, K. (1985). Effects of class size on attention, communication, and disruption of mildly mentally retarded children. *American Educational Research Journal, 22*(3), 403–412.

Foster, H. (1974). *Ribbin', jivin', and playin' the dozens*. Cambridge, MA: Ballinger.

Francis, R. J., & Rarick, G. L. (1959). Motor characteristics of the mentally retarded. *American Journal of Mental Deficiency, 63*, 792–811.

Frankenburg, W., Dodds, J., & Fandal, A. (1973). *Denver developmental screening test*. Denver: LADOCA.

Freed, M. (1976). *A time to teach, a time to dance. A creative approach to teaching dance*. Sacramento, CA: Jamar Press.

Fremion, A. S., Marrero, D. G., & Golden, M. P. (1987). Maximum oxygen uptake determination in insulin-dependent diabetes mellitus. *The Physician and Sportsmedicine, 15*(7), 119–126.

French, R. (1991). *Survey of the special physical education needs in Texas*. Unpublished manuscript, Texas Woman's University.

French, R., Folsom-Meek, S., Cook, C., & Smith, D. (1987). The use of electrical response devices to motivate nonambulatory profoundly mentally retarded children. *American Corrective Therapy Journal, 41*(3), 64–68.

French, R., Henderson, H., & Horvat, M. (1992). *Creative approaches to managing student behavior*. Park City, UT: Family Development Resources.

French, R., & Horvat, M. (1983). *Parachute movement activities*. Bryan, CA: Front Row Experience.

French, R., & Jansma, P. (1981). Medication, learning disabilities and physical education. *American Corrective Therapy Journal, 35*(1), 26–30.

French, R., Lavay, B., & Montelione, T. (1986). Survival strategies: Itinerant special physical educators. *Journal of Physical Education, Recreation, and Dance, 57*(8), 84–86.

French, R., Stranathan, P., & Silliman, L. M. (in press). Decreasing possible foot disorders of students through student and parent education. Nebraska Association for Physical Education, Recreation, and Dance.

Frisch, R. E., Wyshak, G., & Albright, N. L. (1985). Lower prevalence of breast cancer and cancer of the reproductive system among former college athletes compared to nonathletes. *British Journal of Cancer, 52*, 885–891.

Frostig, M. (1970). *Movement education: Theory & practice*. Chicago: Follett.

Frostig, M., Lefever, W., & Whittlesey, J. R. B. (1966). *The Marianne Frostig developmental test of visual perception*, rev. ed. Palo Alto, CA: Consulting Psychologists Press.

Fry, E. (1968). Do-it-yourself terminology generator. *Journal of Reading, 11*, 428.

Fuchs, D., Fuchs, L. S., & Bahr, M. W. (1990). Mainstream assistance teams: A scientific basis for the art of consultation. *Exceptional Children, 57*, 128–139.

Gallager, J. J. (1975). *The application of child development research to exceptional children*. Reston, VA: Council for Exceptional Children.

Gallagher, J. R. (1977). Concept paper on device to train blind people to run. *Journal of Physical Education and Recreation, 48*, 36.

Gardner, L. (1985). Low vision enhancement: The use of figure–ground reversals with visually impaired children. *Journal of Visual Impairment and Blindness, 79*(2), 64–69.

Gauthier, M. M. (1980). Can exercise reduce cancer? *The Physician and Sports Medicine, 14*(10), 171–178.

———. (1986). Guidelines for exercise during pregnancy: Too little or too much? *Physician and Sports Medicine, 14*(4), 162–169.

Gay, L. R. (1980). *Educational evaluation & measurement*. Columbus, OH: Merrill.

Geddes, D. (1978). *Physical activities for individuals with handicapping conditions*, 2nd ed. St. Louis, MO: Mosby.

Georgiadis, N. (1990). Does basketball have to be all W's and L's? An alternative program at a residential boys' home. *Journal of Physical Education, Recreation and Dance, 61*(6), 44–45.

Getman, G. N., & Kane, E. R. (1964). *The physiology of readiness*. Minneapolis: Programs to Accelerate School Success.

Geuze, R., & Borger, H. (1993). Children who are clumsy: Five years later. *Adapted Physical Activity Quarterly, 10*, 10–21.

Glasser, W. (1965). *Reality therapy: A new approach to psychiatry*. New York: Harper & Row.

———. (1969). *Schools without failure*. New York: Harper & Row.

Glover, M. E., Preminger, M. A., & Sanford, A. (1978). *The early learning accomplishment profile for developmentally young children*. Chapel Hill: University of North Carolina–Chapel Hill Training Outreach Project.

Godfrey, B. B., & Kephart, N. C. (1969). *Movement patterns and motor education*. New York: Appleton-Century-Crofts.

Golub, L. J. (1959). A new exercise for dysmenorrhea. *American Journal of Obstetrics and Gynecology, 78*, 152–155.

Greenwood, C. M., Dzewaltowski, D., & French, R. (1990). Self-efficacy and psychological well-being of wheelchair tennis participants and wheelchair nontennis participants. *Adapted Physical Activity Quarterly, 7*, 12–21.

Greenwood, M., & French, R. (1988). Modeling: One approach to improve teaching efficiency. *Catalyst, 18*(1), 12–13.

Greenwood, P., & Turner, S. (1983). *The Vision Quest program: An evaluation*. Santa Monica, CA: Rand Corporation.

Greer, J. (1988). No more noses to the glass. *Exceptional Children, 54*(4), 294–295.

Grosse, S. (1985). Instruction of a deaf-blind swimmer. *National Aquatics Journal, 1*(3), 14–16.

Grosse, S., & Gildersleeve, L. (1984). *The Halliwick method: Water freedom for the handicapped*. Milwaukee, WI: Milwaukee Public Schools.

Grossman, H. J. (Ed.). (1983). *Manual on terminology and classification in mental retardation*, 8th rev. Washington, DC: American Association on Mental Deficiency.

Guttmann, L. (1979). *Textbook of sport for the disabled*. Aylesburg, England: HM&M.

Hahn, A. G. (1985). The nature and causes of exercise-induced asthma. *Australian Journal of Science and Medicine in Sport, 17*(2), 3–10.

Halle, J., Gabler-Halle, D., McKee, M., Bane, S., & Boyer, T. (1991). *Enhancing the aerobic fitness of individuals with moderate and severe disabilities: A peer-mediated conditioning program*. Champaign, IL: Sagamore.

Hallgren, B. (1950). Specific dyslexia (congenital word-blindness): A clinical and genetic study. *Acta Psychiatrica et Neurologica*, Supplement 65, 1-287.

Haring, N. G. (Ed.). (1978). *Behavior of exceptional children*, 2nd ed. Columbus, OH: Merrill.

Harkins, S., & Chrietzberg, A. (1983). *Project Hearty Heart*. Paper presented at Contemporary Elementary and Middle School Physical Education Conference, Georgia State University, Atlanta, January 13.

Harris, T. (1969). *I'm OK, You're OK.* New York: Harper & Row.

Hart, V. (1977). The use of many disciplines with the severely and profoundly handicapped. In E. Sontag, N. Certo, & J. Smith (Eds.), *Educational programming for the severely and profoundly handicapped.* Reston, VA: Council for Exceptional Children.

Hellison, D. (1985). *Goals and strategies for teaching physical education.* Champaign, IL: Human Kinetics.

———. (1990a). Physical education for disadvantaged youth. *Journal of Physical Education, Recreation and Dance, 61*(6), 37.

———. (1990b). Teaching PE to at-risk youth in Chicago—A model. *Journal of Physical Education, Recreation and Dance, 61*(6), 38–39.

———. (1990c). Making a difference: Reflections on teaching urban at-risk youth. *Journal of Physical Education, Recreation and Dance, 61*(6), 44–45.

Hellison, D. R., & Templin, T. J. (1991). *A reflective approach to teaching physical education.* Champaign, IL: Human Kinetics.

Henderson, D., & Gillespie, R. D. (1956). *A textbook of psychiatry for students and practitioners,* 8th ed. New York: Oxford University Press.

Henderson, H. L., & French, R. (1992). The parent factor. *Strategies, 5*(6), 26–29.

Heward, W., & Orlansky, M. (1992). *Exceptional children,* 4th ed. New York: Macmillan.

Hewett, F. M. (1974). *Education of exceptional learners.* Boston: Allyn & Bacon.

———. (1977). *Education of exceptional learners,* 2nd ed. Boston: Allyn & Bacon.

Higgs, C. (1983). An analysis of racing wheelchairs used at the 1980 Olympic Games for the Disabled. *Research Quarterly for Exercise and Sport, 54*(3), 229–233.

Hill, K. (1976). *Dance for physically disabled persons: A manual for teaching ballroom, square, and folk dances to users of wheelchairs and crutches.* Washington, DC: American Alliance for Health, Physical Education, and Recreation.

Hilsendager, D. R., Jack, H., & Mann, L. (1968). The Buttonwood farms project. *Journal of Health, Physical Education and Recreation, 39,* 46–48.

Hittleman, R. L. (1967). *Yoga for physical fitness.* New York: Warner.

Holt, T. D. (1987). Using the Hawaii Early Learning Profile (HELP) with computers for assessment and intervention. *Proceedings from the 16th National Conference on Physical Activity for Exceptional Individuals.* Los Angeles.

Hopewell Special Education Regional Resource Center. (1981). *Project MOBILITEE.* Columbus: Ohio Department of Education.

Hopkins, H. L., & Smith, H. D. (Eds.). (1988). *Willard and Spackman's occupational therapy,* 7th ed. Philadelphia: Lippincott.

Hopkins, W., Gaeta, H., Thomas, A., & Hill, P. (1987). Physical fitness of blind and sighted children. *European Journal of Applied Physiology, 56,* 69–73.

Horvat, M. (1991). *Program competencies for training personnel in adapted physical education: Task force report.* Presented at the national convention of the American Alliance for Health, Physical Education, Recreation and Dance, San Francisco.

Horvat, M., & Carlile, J. R. (1991). Effects of progressive resistance exercise on physical functioning and self-concept in cystic fibrosis. *Clinical Kinesiology, 45*(2), 18–23.

Hsu, P., & Dunn, J. (1984). Comparing reverse and forward chaining instructional methods on a motor task with moderately mentally retarded individuals. *Adapted Physical Activity Quarterly, 1,* 240–246.

Huber, J. H. (1991). An historic accomplishment: The first blind person to hike the Appalachian Trail. *Palaestra, 7*(4), 18–23.

Huettig, C. (January 1989). Health related fitness and health promotion for the differently abled. Seminar in Physical Activity for the Differently Abled, Texas Woman's University.

Hughes, J. (1979). *Hughes basic gross motor assessment.* Golden, CO.

Humphrey, J. (1965). *Child learning through elementary school physical education.* Dubuque, IA: Brown.

Humphrey, J., & Sullivan, D. D. (1970). *Teaching slow learners through active games.* Springfield, IL: Thomas.

Hunsucker, G. (1988). *Attention deficit disorder.* Abilene, TX: Forrest Publishing.

Hurley, D. (1981). Adapted physical education guidelines. *Journal of Physical Education, Recreation, and Dance, 52*(6), 43–45.

Information and Research Utilization Center. (1973). *Homemade innovative play equipment for activities in physical education and recreation for impaired, disabled, and handicapped*. Washington, DC: American Association for Health, Physical Education, and Recreation.

Institute for Aerobics Research. (1987). *FITNESS-GRAM: User's Manual*. Dallas.

Itard, M. J. (1962). *The wild boy of Aveyron*, G. Humphrey & M. Humphrey, trans. Englewood Cliffs, NJ: Prentice Hall.

Jackson, S., French, R., & Pope, C. (1986). *Texas special education directors' needs for adapted physical education personnel*. Unpublished manuscript, Texas Woman's University.

Jacobson, E. (1944). *Progressive relaxation*, 3rd ed. Chicago: University of Chicago Press.

———. (1973). *Teaching and learning new methods for old arts*. Chicago: National Foundation for Progressive Relaxation.

Jansma, P. (1978a). Mainstreaming in archery at the secondary level for the blind. In J. P. Winnick & P. Jansma (Eds.), *Physical education inservice resource manual for the implementation of the Education for All Handicapped Children Act (P.L. 94-142)*. Brockport, NY: State College at Brockport.

———. (1978b). Operant conditioning principles applied to disturbed male adolescents by a physical educator. *American Corrective Therapy Journal, 32*(3), 71–78.

———. (1980). Reality therapy: Another approach to managing inappropriate behavior. *American Corrective Therapy Journal, 34*, 64–69.

———. (1988). Teaching the introductory adapted physical education course. C. Sherrill (Ed.), *Leadership training in adapted physical education* (pp. 301 to 309). Champaign, IL: Human Kinetics.

———. (Ed.) (1993). *Psychomotor domain training and serious disabilities*, 4th ed. Washington, DC: University Press of America.

Jansma, P., & Combs, S. (1987). The effects of fitness training and reinforcement on maladaptive behaviors of institutionalized adults, classified as mentally retarded/emotionally disturbed. *Education and Training in Mental Retardation, 22*(4), 268–279.

Jansma, P., & Decker, J. (1990). *Project LRE/PE: Least restrictive environment usage in physical education*. Final Report, Grant No. G008730022. Columbus: Ohio State University.

Jansma, P., & Decker, J. T. (1992). An analysis of least restrictive environment placement variables in physical education. *Research Quarterly for Exercise and Sport, 63*(2), 171–178.

Jansma, P., Decker, J., McCubbin, J., Combs, S., & Ersing, W. (1986). Adapted equipment for improving the fitness of severely retarded adults. *American Corrective Therapy Journal, 40*(6), 136–141.

Jansma, P., & French, R. (1979). Transactional analysis: An alternative approach to managing inappropriate behavior. *American Corrective Therapy Journal, 33*, 155–162.

Jansma, P., McCubbin, J., Combs, S., Decker, J., & Ersing, W. (1987). *Fitness and hygiene programming for the severely handicapped: A curriculum-embedded assessment guide*. Worthington, OH: Moody's.

Jansma, P., McCubbin, J., Decker, J., Combs, S., & Ersing, W. (1988). A fitness assessment system for individuals with severe mental retardation. *Adapted Physical Activity Quarterly, 5*(3), 223–232.

Johnson, B. L., & Londeree, B. (1976). *Motor fitness testing manual for moderately mentally retarded*. Washington, DC: American Association for Health, Physical Education, and Recreation.

Johnson, R. E., & Lavay, B. (1988). *Kansas adapted/special physical education test manual*. Topeka: Kansas State Department of Education.

———. (1989). Fitness testing for children with special needs—An alternative approach. *Journal of Physical Education, Recreation, and Dance, 60*(6), 50–53.

Johnson-Martin, N., Attermeier, S., & Hacker, B. (1990). *Carolina curriculum for preschoolers with special needs*. Baltimore: Brookes.

Jones, J. (Ed.). (1988). *Training guide to cerebral palsy sports*, 3rd ed. Champaign, IL: Human Kinetics.

Joseph P. Kennedy, Jr. Foundation (1977). *Let's play to grow*. Washington, DC.

Kaiser, W. (1967). *Baby gymnastics*. Oxford: Pergamon.

Karp, J. (1987). *ACTIVE Newsletter*. Kelso, WA: Project ACTIVE.

Karp, J., & Adler, A. (1991). *ACTIVE*. Woodinville, WA.

Karper, W., & Martinek, T. (1985). The integration

of handicapped and nonhandicapped children in elementary physical education. *Adapted Physical Activity Quarterly, 2*(4), 314–319.

Kaufman, A., & Kaufman, N. (1983). *Kaufman assessment battery for children.* Circle Pines, MN: American Guidance Service.

Kavale, K., Forness, S., & Bender, M. (Eds.). (1987). *Handbook of learning disabilities.* Boston: College-Hill Press.

Kazdin, A. E. (1980). *Behavior modification in applied settings,* 2nd ed. Homewood, IL: Dorsey Press.

Kellogg, R. C. (1984). *Computerized individualized educational plans: One way.* Paper presented at Computer Technology for the Handicapped Conference, Minneapolis, MN, September.

Kelly, E. (1946). Taking posture pictures. *Journal of Health, Physical Education and Recreation, 17,* 464–465, 504.

Kelly, L. (1987). Computer management of student performance. *Journal of Physical Education, Recreation, and Dance, 58*(8), 12–13, 82–85.

———. (1981). *Microcomputer assistance for educators in prescribing adapted physical education.* Unpublished doctoral dissertation, Texas Woman's University.

———. (February 1993). National standards for adapted physical education. *Update,* 10.

Kephart, N. C. (1971). *The slow learner in the classroom,* 2nd ed. Columbus, OH: Merrill.

Kern, K. (1987). Teaching circulation in elementary PE classes: A circulatory system model. *Journal of Physical Education, Recreation, and Dance, 58*(1), 62–63.

Killian, K., Joyce-Petrovich, R., Menna, L., & Arena, S. (1984). Measuring water orientation and beginner swim skills of autistic individuals. *Adapted Physical Activity Quarterly, 1,* 287–295.

King, F., & Herzig, W. F. (1968). *Golden age exercises.* New York: Gramercy.

Kirby, E. A., & Grimley, L. K. (1986). *Understanding and treating attention deficit disorders.* New York: Pergamon.

Knitzer, J., Steinberg, A., & Fleisch, B. (1990). *At the school house door: An examination of programs and policies for children with behavioral and emotional problems.* New York: Bank Street College of Education.

Koehler, G. (1987). Stress management for children. *Strategies, 1*(2), 23–24.

Komp, D., & Adams, R. (1972). The role of athletics in the total care of the hemophiliac. *Journal of Health, Physical Education and Recreation, 43,* 53–54.

Kratz, L. E., Tutt, L. M., & Black, D. A. (1987). *Movement and fundamental motor skills for sensory deprived children.* Springfield, IL: Thomas.

Kraus, H., & Hirschland, R. P. (1954). Minimum muscular fitness tests in school children. *Research Quarterly, 25,* 178–188.

Krebs, P. L., & Block, M. E. (1992). Transition of students with disabilities into community recreation. The role of the adapted physical educator. *Adapted Physical Activity Quarterly, 9,* 305–315.

Krebs, P., & Cloutier, G. (1992). Unified Sports: I've seen the future. *Palaestra, 8*(2), 42–44.

Krebs, P. L., Smith, G. W., & Martch, T. (1991). *Special Olympics unified sports activities.* Washington, DC: Special Olympics International.

Kreutzer, J. S., Zasler, N. D., Camplair, P. S., & Leininger, B. E. (1990). A practical guide to family intervention following adult traumatic brain injury. In J. S. Kreutzer & P. Wehman, *Community integration following traumatic brain injury* (pp. 249–273). Baltimore, MD: Brookes.

Kudlac, R. S. (1978). *Scoliosis: Its incidence in nonambulatory mentally retarded persons.* Unpublished master's thesis, Texas Woman's University.

Kurtzke, J. F. (1965). Further notes on disability evaluation in multiple sclerosis with scale modification. *Neurology, 15,* 654–661.

L'Abate, L., & Curtis, L. T. (1975). *Teaching the exceptional child.* Philadelphia: Saunders.

Lacay, E., & Marshall, B. (1984). Fitnessgram: An answer to physical fitness improvement for school children. *Journal of Physical Education, Recreation, and Dance, 55*(1), 18–19.

Lasko, P., & Knopf, K. G. (1988). *Adapted exercises for the disabled adult: A training manual,* 2nd ed. Dubuque, IA: Eddie Bowers.

Lavay, B., & French, R. (1985). The special physical educator: Meeting educational goals through a transdisciplinary approach. *American Corrective Therapy Journal, 39*(4), 77–81.

Lavay, B., & Marshall, B. (1984). *FITNESSGRAM:* An answer to physical fitness improvement for school children. *Journal of Physical Education, Recreation, and Dance, 55*(1), 18–19.

Lavay, B., Reid, G., & Cressler-Chaviz, M. (1990). Measuring the cardiovascular endurance of persons with mental retardation: A critical review. In K. Pandolf (Ed.), *Exercise science sport review* (pp. 263–290). Baltimore: Williams & Wilkins.

Lee, M., & Wagner, M. M. (1949). *Fundamentals of body mechanics and conditioning*. Philadelphia: Saunders.

Leitner, M. J., & Leitner, S. F. (1985). *Leisure in later life: A sourcebook for the provisions of recreational services for the elders*. New York: Haworth.

Lemme, S. A., & Looney, M. A. (1986). *Heartland gross motor evaluation*. Iowa City: University of Iowa.

Leviton, D., & Campanelli, L. (1980). *Health, physical education, recreation and dance for the older adult: A modular approach*. Reston, VA: American Alliance for Health, Physical Education, Recreation and Dance.

Lewis, S. M. (1985). Therapeutic swimming: A different kind of nursing. *Journal of Nursing Education, 24*(3), 125.

Licht, S. (1965). History. In S. Licht (Ed.), *Therapeutic exercise*. Baltimore: Waverly Press.

Lifka, B. (1990). Hiding beneath the stairwell: A dropout prevention program for hispanic youth. *Journal of Physical Education, Recreation and Dance, 61*(6), 42–43.

Lilly, M. (1988). The regular education initiative: A force for change in general and special education. *Education and Training in Mental Retardation, 23*(4), 253–260.

Lindsey, B. J., & Janz, K. (1985). Helping physical educators address eating disorders. *Journal of Physical Education, Recreation, and Dance, 56*(9), 41–44.

Lindstrom, H. (1992). Integration of sport for athletes with disabilities into sport programs for able-bodied athletes. *Palaestra, 8*(3), 28–32, 58–59.

Little, R. E., Anderson, K. W., Ervin, C. H., Worthington-Roberts, B., & Clarren, S. K. (1989). Maternal alcohol use during breast-feeding and infant mental and motor development at one year. *New England Journal of Medicine, 321*, 425–430.

Londeree, B. R., & Johnson, L. E. (1974). Motor fitness of TMR vs EMR and normal children. *Medicine Science and Sport, 6*, 247–252.

Long, E., Irmer, L., Burkett, L., Glasenapp, G., &

Odenkirk, B. (1980). PEOPEL. *Journal of Physical Education and Recreation, 51*(7), 28–29.

Loovis, E. M., & Ersing, W. F. (1979). *Assessing and programming gross motor development for children*, 2nd ed. Bloomington, IN: College Town Press.

Los Angeles City School District. (1957). *Playground guide*. #487. Los Angeles City School District Division of Instructional Services.

Luckasson, R., Coulter, D. L., Polloway, E., Reiss, S., Schalock, R. L., Snell, M. E., Spitalnik, D. M., & Sark, J. A. (1992). *Mental retardation: Definition, classification, and systems of supports*, 9th ed. Washington, DC: American Association on Mental Retardation.

Luke, M. D. (1989). Research on class management and organization: Review with implications for current practice. *Quest, 41*, 55–67.

McCormick, L., & Goldman, R. (1979). The transdisciplinary model: Implications for service delivery and personnel preparation for the severely and profoundly handicapped. *AAESPH Review, 4*, 152–161.

McCubbin, J., & Jansma, P. (1987). The effects of training selected psychomotor skills and the relationship to adaptive behavior. In M. Berridge & G. Ward (Eds.), *International perspectives on adapted physical activity* (pp. 119–126). Champaign, IL: Human Kinetics.

Mackie, R. (1945). *Crippled children in American education*. New York: Bureau of Publications, Teachers College, Columbia University.

Mallick, M., Whipple, T., & Huerta, E. (1987). Behavioral and psychological traits of weight-conscious teenagers: A comparison of eating disordered patients and high- and low-risk groups. *Adolescence, 22*, 85.

Malone, J. J., & Rosenbloom, A. (1981). Put the pleasure back into parenting. *Diabetes Forecast*. New York: American Diabetes Association, pp. 1–4.

Malone, M. J. (1989). *Kids weigh to fitness*. Reston, VA: American Alliance for Health, Physical Education, Recreation and Dance.

Marin, R. (1985). Lose to win: A goal-oriented group for overweight children. *School Counselor, 32*, 219–223.

Marlowe, M. (1980a). Games analysis intervention: A procedure to increase peer acceptance of socially isolated children. *Research Quarterly, 51*(2), 422–426.

———. (1980b). Games analysis: Designing games

for handicapped children. *Teaching Exceptional Children, 12*(2), 48–51.

———. (1981). Motor experiences through games analysis. *Journal of Physical Education and Recreation, 52*(1), 78–80.

Martin, J. (1981). The Halliwick method. *Physiotherapy, 67*(10), 288–291.

Mayer, J. (1968). *Overweight: Causes, cost, and control.* Englewood Cliffs, NJ: Prentice Hall.

Mayse, J. (1991). Aquacise and aquafitness for adapted aquatics. *Palaestra, 7*(2), 54–56.

Mercer, C. D. (1987). *Students with learning disabilities,* 3rd ed. Columbus, OH: Merrill.

Messick, S. (1983). Assessment of children. In P. H. Mussen (Ed.), *Handbook of child psychology: History, theory, and methods* (Vol. 1, pp. 477–526). New York: Wiley.

Mestre, R. (1986). *Physical fitness of learning disabled and normal adolescent males.* Unpublished thesis, Texas Woman's University.

Meyen, E. L. (1978). *Exceptional children and youth.* Denver, CO: Love.

Mikkelsen, M., & Stene, J. (1970). Genetic counseling in Down's syndrome. *Human Heredity, 20,* 457.

Miller, B. E. (1985). *A descriptive-analysis of academic learning time and teacher behaviors in regular, mainstreamed, and adapted physical education classes.* Unpublished dissertation, Ohio State University.

Miller, S. E., & Schaumberg, K. (1988). Physical education activities for children with severe cerebral palsy. *Teaching Exceptional Children, 20*(2), 9–11.

Millikan, T., Morse, M., & Hedrick, B. (1991). Prevention of shoulder injuries. *Sports 'n' Spokes, 17*(2), 35–38.

Mims, A., Harper, C., Armstrong, S. W., & Savage, S. (1991). Effective instruction for students with disabilities. *Teaching Exceptional Children, 24*(1), 42–44.

Minner, S., & Knutson, R. (1982). Mainstreaming handicapped students into physical education: Initial considerations and needs. *The Physical Educator, 39*(1), 13–15.

Montelione, T. L. (1984). *Computer assisted instruction in behavior management for the physical education setting.* Unpublished dissertation, Texas Woman's University.

Montessori, M. (1912 / 1964). *The Montessori method.* New York: Schocken Books.

Moore, M. (1988). Caring for the elderly: Public/private sector responsibilities. *Federation of American Health Systems Review, 21,* 28–29.

Moran, J., & Kalakian, L. (1977). *Movement experiences for the mentally retarded or emotionally disturbed child,* 2nd ed. Minneapolis, MN: Burgess.

Morris, G. S. (1980). *How to change the games children play,* 2nd ed. Minneapolis, MN: Burgess.

Morris, G. S., & Stiehl, J. (1989). *Changing kids' games.* Champaign, IL: Human Kinetics.

Morris, T. (1973). Hearing impaired cerebral palsied children and their education. *Public Health, 88,* 27–33.

Morse, M., Hedrick, B., & Hart, A. (1992). Medicine ball drills. *Sports 'n' Spokes, 17*(5), 52–54.

Mosher, C. D. (1914). A physiologic treatment of congestive dysmenorrhea and disorders associated with the menstrual function. *Journal of the American Medical Association, 62,* 1297–1301.

Mosston, M. (1981). *Teaching physical education,* 2nd ed. Columbus, OH: Merrill.

Mulholland, R., & McNeill, A. (1985). Cardiovascular responses of three profoundly retarded, multiply handicapped children during selected motor activities. *Adapted Physical Activity Quarterly, 2,* 151–160.

Muss, R. E. (1985). Adolescent eating disorders: Anorexia nervosa. *Adolescence, 20*(79), 525–535.

Myklebust, H. R. (1964). *The psychology of deafness,* 2nd ed. New York: Grune & Stratton.

Nagel, K. L., & Jones, K. (1991). Eating disorders. *Strategies, 4*(3), 24–26.

Nagel-Murray, K. L. (1989). *A study investigating how concepts associated with eating disorders are addressed in a preventive context in the home.* Unpublished doctoral dissertation, University of Georgia.

NASDSE. (1991). Physical education and sports: The unfulfilled promise for students with disabilities. *Liaison Bulletin, 17*(6), 1–10.

National Association for State Boards of Education. (1992). *Winners all: A call for inclusive schools.* Alexandria, VA.

National Dissemination Study Group. (1988). *Educational programs that work: A collection of proven exemplary educational programs and practices,* 14th ed. Longmont, CO: Sopris West.

———. (1992). *Educational programs that work: A collection of proven exemplary educational pro-*

grams and practices, 18th ed. Longmont, CO: Sopris West.

National Hemophilia Foundation and American Red Cross. (n.d.). *Hemophilia and sports.* New York.

National Information Center on Deafness. (1984). *Deafness: A fact sheet.* Washington, DC: Gallaudet College.

National Institute of Handicapped Research. (1988). Speech-impaired clients: Working with nonspeaking people. *Rehab Brief, 9*(1),1–4.

National Society for Autistic Children. (September, 1977). A short definition of autism. *Newsletter.*

National Society for the Prevention of Blindness. (1966). *NSPB fact book.* New York.

New York state physical fitness test for boys and girls, grades 4–12. (1966). Albany: New York State Education Department.

Nihira, K., Foster, R., Shellhaas, M., & Leland, H. (1974). *AAMD adaptive behavior scale,* rev. Washington, DC: American Association on Mental Deficiency.

Nissen, H. (1947). *Practical massage and corrective exercises with applied anatomy.* Philadelphia: Davis.

Ogden, E. H., & Germinario, V. (1988). *The at-risk student: Answers for educators.* Lancaster: Technomic Publishing.

Ohio AIDS education package. (1987). Columbus: Ohio Department of Health.

Ohio Department of Education. (1988). *Intervention assistance team models.* Columbus.

———. (1990). *Secondary-level intervention assistance team models.* Columbus.

Olsen, S. (1989). *The foundation directory.* New York: Foundation Center.

Orpet, R. E., & Heustis, T. L. (1971). *Move-grow-learn movement skills survey.* Chicago: Follett.

Osler, W. (1961). *The evolution of modern medicine.* London: Yale University Press.

Paciorek, M. J., & Jones, J. A. (1989). *Sports and recreation for the disabled: A resource manual.* Indianapolis: Benchmark Press.

Paulsen, P., French, R., & Sherrill, C. (1991). Comparison of mood states of college able-bodied and wheelchair basketball players. *Perceptual and Motor Skills, 73,* 396–398.

Peganoff, S. A. (1984). The use of aquatics with cerebral palsied adolescents. *American Journal of Occupational Therapy, 38*(7), 469–473.

Peterson, N. (1987). *Early intervention for handicapped and at-risk children.* Denver: Love.

Pierce, C., & Risley, R. (1974). Recreation as a reinforcer: Increasing membership and decreasing disruptions in an urban recreation center. *Journal of Applied Behavior Analysis, 7*(3), 403–411.

Plimpton, C. E. (1987). Childhood obesity: A concern for the physical educator. *Journal of Physical Education, Recreation, and Dance, 58*(8), 24–27.

Polacek, J., Wang, P., & Eichstaedt, C. (1985). *A study of physical and health related fitness levels in mild, moderate, and Down syndrome students in Illinois.* Normal: Illinois State University Press.

Ponichtera-Mulcare, J. A., Glaser, R. M., Mathews, T., & Camaione, D. N. (1993). Maximal aerobic exercise in persons with multiple sclerosis. *Clinical Kinesiology, 46*(4), 12–21.

Pope, C., McGrain, P., & Arnhold, R. (1986). Running gait of the blind: A kinematic analysis. In C. Sherrill (Ed.), *Sport and disabled athletes* (pp. 173–177). Champaign, IL: Human Kinetics.

Pope, C., Wilkerson, J., & Ridgway, M. (1992). Wheelchair racing: A second look. *Palaestra, 8*(4), 21–27.

Poynter, F. N. L., & Keele, K. D. (1961). *A short history of medicine.* London: Butler & Tanner.

President's Committee on Mental Retardation. (1969). *The six-hour retarded child.* Washington, DC: U.S. Department of Health, Education and Welfare.

President's Council on Physical Fitness and Sports. (1987). *The presidential physical fitness award program: Instructor's guide.* Washington, DC.

———. (1989). *President's challenge physical fitness program.* Bloomington, IN: Poplars Research Center.

Pyfer, J. (1988). Teachers, don't let your students grow up to be clumsy adults. *Journal of Health, Physical Education, Recreation, and Dance, 59,* 38–42.

Questions and answers: P.L. 94-142 and Section 504. (November 1977). *Update, 5.*

Rappaport, L. (1986). *Recipes for fun: Play activities and games for young children with disabilities and their families.* Washington, DC: Joseph P. Kennedy, Jr., Foundation.

Rappaport-Morris, L.,& Schulz, L. (1989). *Creative play activities for children with disabilities.* Champaign, IL: Human Kinetics.

Rarick, G. L., & Beuter, A. (1985). The effect of mainstreaming on the motor performance of mentally retarded and nonhandicapped students. *Adapted Physical Activity Quarterly, 2*(4), 277–282.

Rarick, G. L., Dobbins, D. A., & Broadhead, G. D. (1976). *The motor domain and its correlates in educationally handicapped children.* Englewood Cliffs, NJ: Prentice Hall.

Rarick, G. L., & McQuillan, J. P. (1977). *The factor structure of motor abilities of trainable mentally retarded children: Implications for curriculum development.* Final Report, Project No. H23-2544 for the Department of Health, Education and Welfare, U.S. Office of Education, Bureau of Education for the Handicapped. Berkeley: University of California, Department of Physical Education.

Rash, G. S., & Rash, T. L. (1988). Understanding diabetes and exercise. *Physical Educator, 45*(3), 124–128.

Rathbone, J. L. (1969). *Relaxation.* Philadelphia: Lea & Febiger.

Redl, F. (1959). The concept of the life space interview. *American Journal of Orthopsychiatry, 29,* 1–18.

Redlich, F. C., & Freedman, D. X. (1966). *The theory and practice of psychiatry.* New York: Basic Books.

Reid, G., Collier, D., & Morin, B. (1983). The motor performance of autistic individuals. In R. Eason, T. Smith, & F. Caron (Eds.), *Adapted physical activity: From theory to application* (pp. 201–219). Champaign, IL: Human Kinetics.

Reid, G., Seidl, C., & Montgomery, D. (1989). Fitness tests for retarded adults: Tips for test selection, subject familiarization, administration and interpretation. *Journal of Physical Education, Recreation and Dance, 60*(6), 76–78.

Reinert, H. (1980). *Children in conflict.* St. Louis, MO: Mosby.

Report of the President's Commission on Olympic Sports. (1977). Washington, DC: U.S. Government Printing Office.

Reynolds, M. (1962). A framework for considering some issues in special education. *Exceptional Children, 28*(7), 367–370.

Reynolds, M. (1988). A reaction to the JLD special series on the regular education initiative. *Journal of Learning Disabilities, 21*(6), 352–356.

Ribaldi, H., Rider, R., & Toole, T. (1987). A comparison of static and dynamic balance in congenitally blind, sighted and sighted blindfolded adolescents. *Adapted Physical Activity Quarterly, 4,* 220–225.

Rich, S. M., Wuest, D. A., Mancini, V. H. (1988). CAFIAS: A systematic observation tool to improve teaching behaviors. In C. Sherrill (Ed.), *Leadership training in adapted physical education* (pp. 373–384). Champaign, IL: Human Kinetics.

Rimel, R. W., & Jane, J. A. (1983). Characteristics of the head injured patient. In M. Rosenthal, E. R. Griffith, M. R. Bond, & J. D. Miller (Eds.), *Rehabilitation of the head injured adult* (pp. 9–22). Philadelphia: Davis.

Rimmer, S. H. (1989). An exercise prescription for persons with arthritis. *Clinical Kinesiology, 43*(1), 20–23.

Riordan, A. (1980). A conceptual framework for teaching dance to the handicapped. In S. Fitt, & A. Riordan (Eds.), *Focus on dance IX: Dance for the handicapped* (pp. 13–19). Reston, VA: American Alliance for Health, Physical Education, Recreation and Dance.

Roach, E. G., & Kephart, N. C. (1966). *The Purdue perceptual-motor survey.* Columbus, OH: Merrill.

Robins, F., & Robins, J. (1968). *Educational rhythmics for mentally and physically handicapped children.* Chicago: Association Press/Follett.

Robinson, V. (1944). *The story of medicine.* New York: New Home Library.

Robson, P. (1968). The prevalence of scoliosis in adolescents and young adults with cerebral palsy. *Developmental Medicine and Child Neurology, 10,* 447–452.

Rodman, M., Karch, A., Boyd, E., & Smith, D. (1985). *Pharmacology and drug therapy in nursing,* 3rd ed. Philadelphia: Lippincott.

Rosenthal, R., & Jacobson, L. (1968). Teacher expectations for the disadvantaged. *Scientific American, 218,* 19–23.

Ruhlig, B. (February 1987). Physical education for pre-school cerebral palsied children. *Proceedings of the Civitan-I'm Special Network International Conference on Physical Education and Sport for Disabled Persons.* Tampa: University of South Florida, pp. 97–98.

Sanders-Phillips, K. (1990). *Developmental outcomes*

of drug and alcohol exposed infants. Downey, CA: Los Angeles County Office of Education, Adapted Physical Education Inservice Program.

Sanford, A. (1974). *Learning accomplishment profile.* Chapel Hill: University of North Carolina.

Santarcangelo, S., Dyer, K., & Luce, S. (1987). Generalized reduction of disruptive behavior in unsupervised settings through specific toy training. *Journal of the Association for Persons with Severe Handicaps, 12*(1), 38–44.

Savage, R. C. (1987). Educational issues for the head injured adolescent and young adult. *Journal of Head Trauma and Rehabilitation, 2,* 1–10.

Schafer, D. S., & Moersch, M. S. (Eds.). (1981a). *Early intervention developmental profile,* rev. Ann Arbor, MI: Institute for the Study of Mental Retardation and Related Disabilities.

———. (Eds.). (1981b). *Stimulation activities,* rev. Ann Arbor, MI: Institute for the Study of Mental Retardation and Related Disabilities.

Schleichkorn, J. (1977). Physical activity for the child with cystic fibrosis. *Journal of Physical Education and Recreation, 48*(1), 50.

Schmidt, S., & Dunn, J. M. (1980). Physical education for the hearing impaired: A system of movement symbols. *Teaching Exceptional Children, 12,* 99–102.

Seaman, J. A. (1976). *Success is physical activity for spina bifida children.* Paper presented at convention of the Spina Bifida Association, Chicago, January.

Seaman, J., & DePauw, K. (1979). *Sensory-motor experiences for the home.* Los Angeles: Trident Shop.

Seelye, S. (1983). Physical fitness of blind and visually impaired Detroit public school children. *Journal of Visual Impairments and Blindness, 77*(3), 117–118.

Seiler, G., & Renshaw, K. (1978). Yoga for kids. *Elementary School Guidance and Counseling, 12,* 229–237.

Select Committee on Youth, and Families, U.S. House of Representatives. (November 1989). No place to call home: Discarded in America. Washington, DC: U.S. Government Printing Office.

Seltzer, C., & Mayer, J. (1970). An effective weight control program in a school system. *American Journal of Public Health, 68,* 679–689.

Serfass, R. (1980). Physical exercise and the elderly. In G. A. Still (Ed.), *Encyclopedia of physical education, fitness and sports.* Salt Lake City, UT: Brighton.

Shade, M. L. (1948). *Relaxation.* Unpublished master's thesis, University of Wisconsin.

Share, J., & French, R. (1993). *Motor development of Down syndrome children: Birth to six years.* Kearney, NE: Educational Associates.

Sheldon, W. H., Dupertius, C. W., & McDermott, E. (1954). *Atlas of men.* New York: Harper & Row.

Shephard, R. (1990). *Fitness in special populations.* Champaign, IL: Human Kinetics.

Sherrill, C. (1976). *Adapted physical education and recreation: A multidisciplinary approach.* Dubuque, IA: Brown.

———. (1979). *Psychomotor development for the deaf-blind.* Paper presented to the North Texas State University Deaf-Blind Project, Denton, TX.

———. (1986). *Adapted physical education and recreation: A multidisciplinary approach,* 3rd ed. Dubuque, IA: Brown.

———. (Ed.). (1988). *Leadership training in adapted physical education.* Champaign, IL: Human Kinetics.

Sherrill, C., & Megginson, N. (1984). A needs assessment instrument for local school district use in adapted physical education. *Adapted Physical Activity Quarterly, 1*(2), 147–157.

Sherrill, C., & Pyfer, J. L. (1985). Learning disabled students in physical education. *Adapted Physical Activity Quarterly, 2*(4), 284–291.

Siedentop, D. (1991). *Developing teaching skills in physical education,* 3rd ed. Palo Alto, CA: Mayfield.

Siedentop, D., Mand, C., & Taggart, A. (1986). *Physical education: Teaching and curriculum strategies for grades 5–12.* Palo Alto, CA: Mayfield.

Siedentop, D., Tousignant, M., & Parker, M. (1982). *Academic learning time–physical education–1982 revision manual.* Columbus: School of Health, Physical Education and Recreation, Ohio State University.

Sigerist, H. (1961). *A history of medicine,* Vol. 2. New York: Oxford University Press.

Silberman, R., & Tripodi, V. (1979). Adaptation of project "I CAN" primary skills: Physical education program for deaf-blind children. *Visual Impairment and Blindness, 73*(7), 270–276.

Silliman, L. M., French, R., & Ben Ezra, V. (1989). High blood pressure: Activity considerations in elementary school. *Physical Educator, 46*(3), 154–160.

Silliman, L. M., & Sherrill, C. (1989). Self-actualization of wheelchair athletes. *Journal of Clinical Kinesiology, 43*(3), 77–82.

Singer, C. (1928). *A short history of medicine*. New York: Oxford University Press.

Sirvis, B. (1978). Developing IEPs for physically handicapped students: A transdisciplinary viewpoint. *Teaching Exceptional Children, 10*, 78–82.

Skinner, B. F. (1968). *Technology of teaching*. Englewood Cliffs, NJ: Prentice Hall.

Skrobak-Kaczynski, J., & Varik, T. (1980). Physical fitness and trainability of young male patients with Down's syndrome. In K. Berg & B. Erickson (Eds.), *Children and exercise IX* (pp. 300–316). Baltimore: University Park Press.

Smith, G. W. (1991). Unified Sports: Helping meet the mission of Special Olympics. *Special Olympics International Coaches Quarterly* (Spring), 1.

Solberg, E. (1988). Can I be excused from gym? I'm pregnant. *Physical Educator, 45*(2), 109–111.

Sparrow, S., Balla, D., & Cicchetti, D. (1984). *Vineland adaptive behavior scales*. Circle Pines, MN: American Guidance Service.

Special Olympics. (1981). *Special Olympics softball sports skills program*. Washington, DC: Special Olympics International.

———. (1982). *Sports skills instructional program*. Washington, DC: Kennedy Foundation.

———. (1989). *Special Olympics Unified Sports handbook*. Washington, DC.

Stainback, W., & Stainback, S. (1990). *Support networks for inclusive schooling: Interdependent integrated education*. Baltimore: Brookes.

Stein, J. (1978). Tips on mainstreaming: Do's and don'ts in activity programs. *Practical Pointers, 1*(10), 1–16.

———. (1979). The mission and the mandate: Physical education, the not so sleeping giant. *Education Unlimited, 1*(2), 6–11.

———. (1980). From the director. *IRUC Briefings, 5*, 2, 7.

———. (February 1984). Using the microcomputer to promote the physical proficiency and motor development of handicapped students. *Physical Education Newsletter*, (158), 2–4.

Stewart, M. J. (1983). Observational recording record of physical educator's teaching behavior (ORRPETB). In P. W. Darst, V. H. Mancini, & D. B. Zakrajsek (Eds.), *Systematic observation instrumentation for physical education*. West Point, NY: Leisure Press.

Stoker, B. (1977). *The postural characteristics of the severely mentally retarded*. Unpublished master's thesis, Texas Woman's University.

Stott, S. H., Moyes, F. A., & Henderson, S. E. (1984). *Test of motor impairment*. San Antonio, TX: Psychological Corporation.

Strauss, A. A., & Lehtinen, L. E. (1947). *Psychotherapy and education of the brain-injured child*. New York: Grune & Stratton.

Strauss, R., & DeOreo, K. (1979). *AIMS, assessment manual and activities manual*. Austin, TX: Education Service Center.

Surburg, P. R. (1988). Are adapted physical educators ready for the student with AIDS? *Adapted Physical Activity Quarterly, 5*, 259–263.

———. (1990). Other health-impaired and non-handicapped students in adapted physical education. In J. Winnick (Ed.), *Adapted physical education and sport* (Chap. 17, pp. 269–297). Champaign, IL: Human Kinetics.

Surburg, P. R., & Jansma, P. (1991). *Doctoral competencies for training personnel in adapted physical education: Task force report*. Paper presented at National Convention of the American Alliance for Health, Physical Education, Recreation, and Dance, San Francisco, April.

Talbot, M. E. (1964). *Edward Seguin: A study of an educational approach to the treatment of mentally defective children*. New York: Columbia University, Bureau of Publications.

Talbott, R. (1989). The brain-injured person and the family. In R. Wood & P. Eames, *Models of brain injury rehabilitation* (pp. 3–16). Baltimore: Johns Hopkins University Press.

Task Force on Blood Pressure Control in Children. (1977). Report of the Task Force on Blood Pressure Control in Children. *Pediatrics, 59*, pt. 2, 797–818.

Terman, L. M., & Merrill, M. A. (1973). *Stanford–Binet intelligence scale: Manual for the third revision, form L-M*. Boston: Houghton Mifflin.

Texas Department of MH/MR. (1977). *Behavioral characteristics progression*, rev. Austin.

Thomas, J. R. (Ed.). (1977). *Youth sports guide for*

coaches and parents. Washington, DC: National Association of Sport and Physical Education and American Association for Health, Physical Education, and Recreation.

Tomberlin, J. (1990). Physical therapy in community reentry. In J. S. Kreutzer and P. Wehman (Eds.), *Community integration following traumatic brain injury* (pp. 29–46). Baltimore: Brookes.

Tower, C. C. (1987). *Child abuse and neglect,* 2nd ed. Washington, DC: National Education Association.

Tucker, L. A. (1986). The relationship of television viewing to physical fitness and obesity. *Adolescence, 21*(84), 797–806.

Tymeson, G. (1977). *Haptic learning center: Developmental gross motor ability training circuit for deaf-blind children.* Unpublished synthesis project, Brockport State College, New York.

———. (1988). In-service teacher education: A review of general practices and suggested guidelines for adapted physical education teacher trainers. In C. Sherrill (Ed.), *Leadership training in adapted physical education* (pp. 401–409). Champaign, IL: Human Kinetics.

Ulrich, D. (1985a). *Current assessment practices in adapted physical education.* Paper presented at Annual Meeting of the National Consortium on Physical Education and Recreation for the Handicapped, New Carrollton, MD.

———. (1985b). *Test of gross motor development.* Austin, TX: Pro-Ed.

Ultmann, M. H., Belman, A. L., Ruff, H. A., Novick, B. E., Cone-Wesson B., Cohen, H. J., & Rubinstein, A. (1985). Developmental abnormalities in infants and children with acquired immune deficiency syndrome (AIDS) and AIDS-related complex. *Developmental Medicine & Child Neurology, 27,* 563–571.

U.S. Congress. House of Representatives. (1975). House Report No. 94-332, p. 9.

U.S. Department of Commerce. (1990). Persons arrested by crime, sex, and age: 1988. *Statistical abstracts of the U.S.,* p. 177. Washington, DC.

U.S. Department of Health and Human Services. (1992). *Healthy children: 2000.* Boston: Jones and Bartlett.

U.S. Office of Special Education and Rehabilitative Services. (1992). *Fourteenth annual report to Congress on the implementation of the Individuals with Disabilities Education Act.* Washington, DC.

Van Dalen, D. B., Mitchell, E. D., & Bennett, B. L.

(1953). *A world history of physical education.* Englewood Cliffs, NJ: Prentice Hall.

Vodola, T. (1973). *Individualized physical education program for the handicapped child.* Englewood Cliffs, NJ: Prentice Hall.

———. (1974). *Project ACTIVE level II–III motor ability tests.* Oakhurst, NJ: Township of Ocean School District.

———. (1976). *Project ACTIVE.* Oakhurst, NJ: Township of Ocean School District.

———. *Project ACTIVE level II physical fitness test.* Oakhurst, NJ: Township of Ocean School District.

Vogler, E. W. (1981). The effects of a group-oriented contingency management system on behaviorally disordered students in physical education (doctoral dissertation, University of Utah). *Dissertation Abstracts International, 41,* 4331A.

———. (1990). Fitness data of children with ostomy. *Adapted Physical Activity Quarterly, 7,* 259–264.

Vogler, E. W., & Bishop, P. (1990). Management of disruptive behavior in physical education. *Physical Educator, 47*(1), 16–26.

Vogler, E. W., French, R., & Bishop, P. (1989). Paraprofessionals: Implications for adapted physical education. *Physical Educator, 46*(2), 69–76.

Vogler, E. W., van der Mars, H., Darst, P.,& Cusimano, B. (1990). Relationship of presage, context, and process variables to ALT-PE of elementary level mainstreamed students. *Adapted Physical Activity Quarterly, 7,* 298–313.

———. (1992). Experience, expertise, and teaching effectiveness with mainstreamed and nondisabled children in physical education. *Adapted Physical Activity Quarterly, 9,* 316–329.

Vort Corporation. (1973). *Behavioral characteristics progression.* Palo Alto, CA.

———. (1977). *Behavioral characteristics progression method book #107—motor skills.* Palo Alto.

Way, J. (1981). Project SuperHeart: An evaluation of a heart disease intervention program for children. *Journal of School Health, 51,* 16–19.

Webb, R. (1969). Sensory-motor training of the profoundly retarded. *American Journal of Mental Deficiency, 74,* 283–295.

Webber, J., & Scheuermann, B. (1991). Accentuate the positive. Eliminate the negative! *Teaching Exceptional Children, 24*(1), 13–19.

Weber, R. (1989). Motivating and teaching disabled students. *Journal of Physical Education, Recreation, and Dance, 60*(2), 85–87.

Weber, R., & French, R. (1988). Down's syndrome adolescents and strength training. *Clinical Kinesiology, 42*(1), 13–21.

Webster, G. (Ed.). (1991). International Summer Special Olympics Games. [Special issue]. *Palaestra, 8,* 8.

Weideger, P. (1976). *Menstruation and menopause.* New York: Knopf.

Weiss, L., Katzman, M., & Wolchik, S. (1985). *Treating Bulimia.* New York: Pergamon.

Werder, J. K., & Bruininks, R. H. (1988). *Body skills: A motor development curriculum for children.* Circle Pines, MN: American Guidance Service.

Weschler, D. (1974). *Manual for the Wechsler intelligence scale for children—Revised.* New York: Psychological Corporation.

Wessel, J. (1976a). *I CAN: Aquatics.* Northbrook, IL: Hubbard.

———. (1976b). *I CAN: Body management.* Northbrook, IL: Hubbard.

———. (1976c). *I CAN: Fundamental skills.* Northbrook, IL: Hubbard.

———. (1976d). *I CAN: Health and fitness.* Northbrook, IL: Hubbard.

———. (1979). *I CAN: Sport, leisure, and recreational skills.* Northbrook, IL: Hubbard.

Wessel, J., & Kelly, L. (1985). *Achievement-based curriculum development in physical education.* Philadelphia: Lea & Febiger.

Weston, A. (1962). *The making of American physical education.* New York: Appleton-Century-Crofts.

Wheeler, R. H., & Hooley, A. M. (1969). *Physical education for the handicapped.* Philadelphia: Lea & Febiger.

White, K., Snyder, J., Bourne, R., & Newberger, E. (1989). *Treating child abuse and family violence in hospitals.* Lexington, MA: Lexington Books.

White House Conference on Child Health and Protection. (1932). *Report of the sub-committee on orthopedic and body mechanics.* New York: Appleton-Century-Crofts.

Wide, A. (1899). *Handbook of medical gymnastics.* London: Sampson Low, Marston.

Wilson, E. W., & Rennie, P. I. C. (1976). *The menstrual cycle.* London: Lloyd-Luke.

Wilson, K. (n.d.). *Twinges in the hinges.* Whittier, CA: Whittier YMCA.

Winnick, J. P. (1978). Techniques for integration. *Journal of Physical Education and Recreation, 49,* 22.

———. (1979). *Early movement experiences and development: Habilitation and remediation.* Philadelphia: Saunders.

Winnick, J. P., & Short, F. (1981). *Special athletic opportunities for individuals with handicapping conditions.* Brockport, NY: SUNY College at Brockport.

———. (1982). *The physical fitness of sensory and orthopedically impaired youth: Project UNIQUE final report.* Brockport, NY: SUNY College at Brockport, Physical Education Department.

———. (1985). *Physical fitness testing of the disabled: Project UNIQUE.* Champaign, IL: Human Kinetics.

———. (1986). Physical fitness of adolescents with auditory impairments. *Adapted Physical Activity Quarterly, 3,* 58–66.

———. (1991). A comparison of the physical fitness of nonretarded and mildly mentally retarded adolescents with cerebral palsy. *Adapted Physical Activity Quarterly, 8,* 43–56.

Winningham, M. L., & MacVicar, M. G. (1985). Response of cancer patients on chemotherapy to a supervised exercise program. *Medicine and Science in Sports and Exercise, 17,* 282.

Winningham, M. L., MacVicar, M. G., & Burke, C. A. (1986). Exercise for cancer patients: Guidelines and precautions. *The Physician and Sportsmedicine, 14*(10), 125–134.

Winther, N., & Currie, P. (1987). *Northern fly-in sports camps: A joint sport development/crime prevention project.* Paper presented at North American Society for the Sociology of Sport Conference, Edmonton, Alberta.

Wisher, P. R. (1969). Dance and the deaf. *Journal of Health, Physical Education and Recreation, 40,* 81–84.

Wolfgang, C., & Glickman, C. D. (1986). *Solving discipline problems,* 2nd ed. Boston: Allyn & Bacon.

Wright, J. (1986). *CREOLE: Leisure and recreation curriculum for severely handicapped secondary students.* Gretna, LA: Jefferson Parish Public Schools.

Yates, D. (1946). Relaxation in psychotherapy. *Journal of General Psychology, 34,* 213–238.

Ziter, F. A., & Allsop, K. G. (1976). The diagnosis and management of childhood muscular dystrophy. *Clinical Pediatrics, 15,* 540–548.

APPENDIX A
ADMINISTRATION AND ORGANIZATION FORMS

APPENDIX A1
Heartland Education Agency Forms.

HEARTLAND EDUCATION AGENCY
PART I — PRE-EVALUAION CONFERENCE/REFERRAL

PUPIL: _____ _____ _____ _____ Sex: M / F Race: 1 – 2 – 3 – 4 – 5
    Last   First   MI   AKA   Circle One   Circle One (Optional)

B.D.: ___ / ___ / ___
      MM   DD   YY

Grade/Level: _____ Teacher(s): _____

Dominant Language (if not English): _____

Legal Parent(s): _____ Address/City/State: _____

Legal Parent(s) Phone:(Home) _____ (Work) _____ (Zip)

Foster Parent(s) _____ Foster Parent(s) Phone:(Home) _____ (Work) _____ (Zip)

Legal Parent's School District: _____ Address/City/State: _____

District/Building Student Attends: _____

A. CONCERNS (CURRICULUM AREAS)

__ (CN) Consumer Economics	__ (MA) Mathematics	__ (SP) Speech & Language	**PRESCHOOL**
__ (CO) Community Mobility	__ (PL) Personal Living	__ (SS) Study Skills	__ (CS) Cognitive Skills
__ (CV) Career Vocational Skills	__ (RE) Reading	__ (SW) Social Work	__ (FM) Fine Motor
__ (FS) Funcional Skills	__ (RL) Recreational/Leisure	__ (VI) Vision	__ (SE) Social Emotional
__ (HM) Household Management	__ (SB) Social Behavior	__ (WE) Written Expression	__ (SH) Self Help
__ (HS) Health/Safety	__ (SC) Science Elem/Sec		__ (SI) Science-Preschool
__ (LA) Language Arts	__ (SO) Social Studies		__ (VS) Visual

OT-PT-APE
__ (DL) Activity for Daily Living
__ (FI) Fine Motor
__ (GM) Gross Motor
__ (NM) Neuromuscular
__ (PV) Prevocational
__ (SM) Sensorimotor

SEVERE/PROFOUND
__ (AQ) Swimming
__ (CM) Communication
__ (HL) Home Living Skills
__ (MU) Music
__ (PE) Physical Education
__ (QS) Self-Help Skills

SEVERE/PROFOUND
__ (RD) Readiness
__ (VE) Vocational Ed
HEARING
__ (HA) Hearing Aid
__ (HE) Hearing
__ (SR) Speechreading

B. SPECIFIC DESCRIPTIONS THAT SUPPORT ABOVE CONCERN (LIST GOAL CODES IN GROUPS BY THE ABOVE CURRICULUM AREAS:

Comments:

C. INTERVENTIONS PREVIOUS TO THIS REQUEST (CHECK APPPROPRIATE ITEMS)

Y = TRIED AND SUCCESSFUL   N = TRIED AND NOT SUCCESSFUL #1 thru #19

ACADEMIC/INSTRUCTIONAL
__ (1) Alternate Methods/Materials
__ (2) Individual Instruction/Tutor
__ (3) Schedule Change
__ (4) Room Arrangement
__ (5) Classroom Management Program
__ (6) Special Education Class

SUPPORT SERVICES
__ (7) Other
__ (8) Counseling
__ (9) Peer Assistance
__ (10) Volunteer/Aide Asst.
__ (11) Remedial (Chapt. 1)
__ (12) AEA Support (types)

OTHER ACTIVITIES
__ (13) Student/Teacher Conference
__ (14) Behavior Management System
__ (15) Home/School Management System
__ (16) Medication
__ (17) Retention
__ (18) Suspension/Expulsion
__ (19) Outside Agencies

PARENT CONTACTS ABOUT CONCERNS
Y = CONTACT   N = NO CONTACT
__ (20) Phone Contacts
__ (21) Written Reports
__ (22) Parent Conference

D. RECORD VIEW: Check areas that indicate evaluation results are in the student's record
__ Health Status __ Academic Status __ Vision __ Behavioral Observation __ Speech & Language __ Social Functioning __ Motor Functioning __ Educational History __ Hearing __ Intellect __ Adaptive Behavior __ Career Vocational

E. REFERRING PERSON: _____ Position _____

F. ACTIONS RECOMMENDED:

___ / ___ / ___ Regular Education Intervention By: _____ Position- _____

___ / ___ / ___ Support Team Pre-evaluation Intervention By: _____ Position- _____

___ / ___ / ___ Defer Further Action Until — Date: ___ MM / ___ DD / ___ YY Reason: _____

___ / ___ / ___ Evaluation Requested - Type(s) _____

___ Comments:

Participants' Signatures: _____

Priciple's Signature: _____ Pre-Evaluation/Referral Meeting Date: ___ MM / ___ DD / ___ YY

HEARTLAND EDUCATION AGENCY
PART II — PARENT CONSENT FOR EVALUATION

PUPIL: _____ / _____ / _____

    (Last)   (First)   (MI)   (AKA)

BIRTHDATE: _____ / _____ / _____
            MM   DD   YY

SCHOOL DISTRICT: _____ BUILDING: _____ GRADE: _____

REASON FOR REFERRAL: _____

I understand that an individual evaluation may provide useful information for school planning. In order to obtain this additional information, I hereby grant my permission for the following indicated evaluation.

_____ **SPEECH AND LANGUAGE** — The evaluation includes an overall assessment of oral communication skills. It could include the assessment of sound production, verbal expression, fluency and voice quality.

_____ **HEARING** — The evaluation consists of a measurement of hearing ability. It may include a screening for common ear problems (middle ear fluid, ear infections).

_____ **HEALTH HISTORY** — It includes prenatal and birth factors, early growth and developmental, personal care, home environment and medical information.

_____ **VISION** — This screens visual acuity.

_____ **SOCIAL FUNCTIONING** — This is an assessment of functioning in the areas of developmental/medical influences, the family environment, social skills and behaviors in home, school and community.

_____ **INTELLECT** — The evaluation is designed to determine general intellectual level, as well as strengths and weaknesses, in a number of ability areas.

_____ **MOTOR FUNCTIONING** — Tests and observations of fine and gross motor functioning measure physical development, eye-hand coordination and ability to plan and carry out a broad range of motor activities. Classroom skills such as handwriting, dexterity and phsycial education may be included.

_____ **ACADEMIC STATUS** — The evaluation will provide a current assessment of performance in the home and/or in school. The following areas may be included: social/emotional development, self-help skills, concept development and academic skills.

_____ **BEHAVIORAL OBSERVATION** — A direct observation of relevant school behaviors and a comparison of other students with the same behaviors in similar environments.

_____ **EDUCATIONAL HISTORY** — A review of records to determine previous academic growth, individual and/or group evaluations, school attendance, number of schools attended, and any previous special assistance offered. This review will also include any formal records related to problems of school adjustment.

_____ **CAREER VOCATIONAL** — This assessment indicates the need for training in the following areas: career awareness, recognizing unique interests and abilities in relation to careers, exploring jobs and learning specific skills (if needed).

_____ **COMPREHENSIVE** — Includes all of the above. Required if considering placement/assignment into a special instructional program. Speech-language, intellect, academic status, behavioral observation and social functioning assessments include ADAPTIVE BEHAVIOR which measures the ability to cope with the demands of the environment in both school and community settings.

_____ **OTHER**

_____   _____
Signature of person initiating referral   Position

*Signature of parent/guardian giving consent for evaluation   Date: (M) ___ (D) ___ (Y) ___

Address _____ Home Phone: _____ Work Phone: _____

Principal _____ Date: (M) ___ (D) ___ (Y) ___

*See **"PARENTAL RIGHTS IN SPECIAL EDUCATION"** on reverse side.
DISTRIBUTION: (1) AEA (white) (2) School (yellow) (3) Parent (pink) (4) Photo copy to resident district if different

806-095

540

COMMUNITY SCHOOL DISTRICT
PARENT NOTICE OF SPECIAL EDUCATION RE-EVALUATION AND/OR REVIEW OF RECORDS

PUPIL: (Last) _____ (First) _____ (MI) _____ /(AKA) _____ B.D.: MM ___ /DD ___ /YY ___ Sex: (Circle One) M / F

Grade/Level: _____ Teacher(s): _____

Legal Parent(s): _____ Address/City/State: _____ (Zip) _____

Legal Parent(s) Phone: (Home) _____ (Work) _____ Foster Parent(s) Phone: (Home) _____ (Work) _____ (Zip) _____

Foster Parent(s): _____ Address/City/State: _____

Legal Parent's School District: _____ District/Building Student Attends: _____ / _____

Dear Parent(s)/Guardian(s):

The school is planning in the near future to initiate a re-evaluation/review of records of your child. The purpose is to determine if a change is needed in the current special education instructional program. The activity for which this notice applies is (x) below.

A. ANNUAL REVIEW AS REQUIRED BY LAW—A review of your child's educational program and current Individual Educational Plan (IEP) is required at least annually. It may result in a change of goals within the IEP curriculum area, instructional objectives within a goal and/or a change of time allocation in regular or special education. Check type of evaluation(s) below:

B. THREE-YEAR RE-EVALUATION AS REQUIRED BY LAW—A complete examination of your child's eligibility and need for special education services is required at least every three years. It may result in a staffing at which time your child's designated disability, program, and/or curriculum areas may be changed.

C. OTHER RE-EVALUATION(S)—Give reason and check type of evaluation(s) below; REASON _____

The re-evaluation and/or review of records will be initiated by the special education staff members and general education staff as appropriate. The re-evaluation and/or review of records to be conducted will involve consultation with school staff, parent interviews, observation, records review, and as appropriate, formal and informal tests or screening of your child's (1) current educational performance, (2) progress toward attainment of current IEP goals and objectives, (3) adaptive behavior and (4) functioning in areas related to educational performance including:

___ **SPEECH AND LANGUAGE**—The evaluation includes an overall assessment of oral communication skills. It could include the assessment of sound production, verbal expression, fluency and voice quality.

___ **HEARING**—The evaluation consists of a measurement of hearing ability. It may include a screening for common ear problems (middle ear fluid, ear infections).

___ **HEALTH HISTORY**—It includes prenatal and birth factors, early growth and development, personal care, home environment and medical information.

___ **VISION**—This screens visual acuity.

___ **SOCIAL FUNCTIONING**—This is an assessment of functioning in the areas of developmental/medical influences, the family environment, social skills and behaviors in home, school and community.

___ **INTELLECT**—The evaluation is designed to determine general intellectual level, as well as strengths and weaknesses, in a number of ability areas.

___ **MOTOR FUNCTIONING**—Tests and observations of fine and gross motor functioning measure physical development, eye-hand coordination and ability to plan and carry out a broad range of motor activities. Classroom skills such as handwriting, dexterity and physical education may be included.

___ **ACADEMIC STATUS**—The evaluation will provide a current assessment of performance in the home and/or in school. The following areas may be included: social/emotional development, self-help skills, concept development, and academic skills.

___ **BEHAVIORAL OBSERVATION**—A direct observation of relevant school behaviors and a comparison of other students with the same behaviors in similar environments.

___ **EDUCATIONAL HISTORY**—A review of records to determine previous academic growth, individual and/or group evaluations, school attendance, number of schools attendend, and any previous special assistance offered. This review will also include any formal records related to problems of school adjustment.

___ **CAREER VOCATIONAL**—This assessment indicates the need for training in the following areas: career awareness, recognizing unique interests and abilities in relation to careers, exploring jobs, and learning specific skills.

THIS IS NOT A PARENT NOTICE TO ATTEND AN ANNUAL OR A 3-YEAR PROGRAM REVIEW. WHEN ALL NECESSARY INFORMATION HAS BEEN COLLECTED, YOU WILL BE INVITED AT A LATER DATE TO PARTICIPATE WITH SCHOOL STAFF IN A MEETING AT WHICH TIME YOUR CHILD'S CONTINUED ELIGIBILITY AND NEED FOR SPECIAL EDUCATION SERVICES WILL BE CONSIDERED. At that time, the IEP will also be revised so appropriately provide for the special education needs. The meeting will be scheduled at a time and place convenient to you. No changes in your child's current educational placement or IEP will be made prior to that meeting or without you being fully informed. Please carefully review the information contained in this Notice and your rights as a parent/legal guardian which are explained on the back of this Notice. If you have any questions or concerns regarding the re-evaluation or review to be conducted, please contact me.

Signature: _____ Date: MM ___ /DD ___ /YY ___ Ph: _____
Building Administrator

Notice delivered to parent(s)/guardian via: ___ mail ___ meeting By: _____ Date: MM ___ /DD ___ /YY ___
Name/Position

DISTRIBUTION: (1) AEA (white)   (2) School (yellow)   (3) Parent (pink)

806-094

PARENT REQUEST FOR SPECIAL EDUCATION SERVICES

PUPIL: _____   SCHOOL: _____   GRADE/LEVEL: _____

    (Last)   (First)   (MI)

I understand that after a formal evaluation of my child's educational needs, special educational services are recommended. The type of service that is felt appropriate and beneficial at this time has been discussed with me by the principal and various Area Education Agency personnel.

OPTION 1   RESOURCE TEACHING PROGRAM

An educational program for pupils requiring special education who are enrolled in a general education curriculum for a majority of the school day, but who require special education in specific skill areas on a part-time basis. Pupils enrolled in this type of program require special education for a minimal average of 30 minutes per day. This program shall include provisions for ongoing consultation and demonstration with the pupil's teachers and may be operated on a multicategorical basis.

OPTION II   SPECIAL CLASS WITH INTEGRATION

An educational program for pupils requiring special education who have similar educational needs and who can benefit from participation in the general education curriculum in one or more academic subjects with pupils who are not handicapped. This program shall include provisions for ongoing consultation and demonstration with the pupil's teachers. Programs of this type may be operated on a multicategorical basis, with approval of the AEA Director of Special Education.

OPTION III   SELF-CONTAINED SPECIAL CLASS WITH LITTLE INTEGRATION

An educational program for pupils with similar educational needs who require special education, but who can benefit from limited participation in the general education curriculum with nonhandicapped pupils. Preschool programs of this type may be operated on a multicategorical basis.

OPTION IV   SELF-CONTAINED SPECIAL CLASS

An educational program for pupils with similar educational needs who are severely handicapped and whose instructional program is provided by a special education teacher. The pupils shall be offered opportunities to participate in activities with nonhandicapped peers and adults. Preschool programs of this type may be operated on a multicategorical basis.

OPTION V   ITINERANT TEACHER INSTRUCTIONAL SERVICES

The services offered by the itinerant teacher are designed to provide special instruction in designated disability areas in the school or home.

OPTION VI   SUPPLEMENTARY ASSISTANCE PROGRAM

a. Special Education Aide
b. Special Education Aids
c. Homebound/Hospital Instruction
d. _____

OPTION VII   RELATED SPECIAL SERVICES PROVIDED BY THE SUPPORT STAFF

a. Clinical Speech and Language Services
b. Physical Therapy
c. Occupational Therapy
d. Adapted Physical Education
e. Counseling
f. _____

*See **"PARENTAL RIGHTS IN SPECIAL EDUCATION"** on reverse side. I give my permission and request that (Child's Name) _____

Birthdate: _____ be enrolled in the special education instructional program or services indicated by **OPTION NUMBER(S):** _____

I am hereby notified that my child will be assigned to District _____ Facility/Building _____

*Parent's Signature: _____ Date: _____

Principal's Signature: _____ Date: _____

School District: _____

DISTRIBUTION: (1) AEA (white)   (2) School (yellow)   (3) Parent (pink)

APPENDIX A2

Program Description and Permission for Assessment.   This letter is used to notify parents that their child may be eligible for special physical education. It describes the program under consideration and requests permission from the parents to gather assessment data by reviewing existing medical health records or conducting motor assessment. The parent has the right to stop all consideration at this point by checking the appropriate box.

(From Process for Identification, Assessment, Planning and Placement of Individuals with Exceptional Needs into Physical Education. *Office of the Los Angeles County Superintendent of Schools, 1979, p. 13. Used by permission.)*

OFFICE OF THE LOS ANGELES COUNTY
SUPERINTENDENT OF SCHOOLS

DIVISION OF SPECIAL EDUCATION

ADAPTED PHYSICAL EDUCATION PROGRAM DESCRIPTION
and
PERMISSION FOR ASSESSMENT

Re: _____

Dear Parent,

We are pleased to inform you that classes in Adapted Physical Education are being offered at your school. Small classes such as these provide an opportunity for more individual physical education, taught by a trained adapted physical education specialist.

Class instruction is designed to aid the student in increasing his efficiency in the areas of movement, coordination, and the realization of physical potential. This may be achieved through corrective work according to specific physical needs; movement education related to general language development., behavior management, or adaptation of games and activities.

Your child has been referred to us and may be eligible to participate in this specialized physical education program. Admission to the Adapted Physical Education class is dependent upon the recommendation of an Eligibility and Planning Commitee. In order to determine eligibility and specific educational needs, it will be necessary to conduct an assessment. This assessment will be done by appropriately qualified staff in the area of adapted physical education. The assessment may include pupil observation in a group setting; a review of any reports you have authorized us to request, or that already exist in current school records; or the use of specific tests designed to measure how well an individual coordinates body movements in both small and large muscle activities.

We believe that you, as a parent, will consider this a real opportunity for your child, and can aid us in qualifying your child by granting permission for our staff to conduct thie assessment described above.

Following the collection of this information, an Eligibility and Planning Commitee will meet to consider the appropriate physical education placement for your child. You will be notified of the time and place of the commitee meeting and invited to attend. No placement will be made without your permission.

If we can provide you with any additional information, please feel free to contact our physical education specialist.

If you do not wish your child considered for Adapted Physical Education, please check here. ☐

_____   _____
Physical Education Specialist   Parent Signature

_____   _____
School, Address, Telephone   Date

PLEASE SIGN AND RETURN WHITE COPY TO YOUR SCHOOL

FORM NO 301-546   DISTRIBUTION, WHITE-Site;   YELLOW, Parent
Rev 7/79

APPENDIX A3

Notice of Physical Examination To Be Given. This form is used to secure parent permission for a physical examination to be given by the school physician. The bottom portion must be signed by the parent and returned prior to the examination.

(From Process for Identification, Assessment, Planning and Placement of Individuals with Exceptional Needs into Physical Education. *Office of the Los Angeles County Superintendent of Schools, 1979, p. 28. Used by permission.)*

OFFICE OF THE LOS ANGELES COUNTY
SUPERINTENDENT OF SCHOOLS

DIVISION OF SPECIAL EDUCATION

_____
SCHOOL

NOTICE OF PHYSICAL EXAMINATION TO BE GIVEN
(ADAPTED PHYSICAL EDUCATION)

_____
date

Dear _____ ,

It is a pleasure to inform you that we are able to provide a physical examination for your child, _____ . The examination will be performed by a licensed physician and will take place at school during school hours. There is no charge for the examination, but *we must ha e your signed permission for the ser ices.*

Your child's examination is scheduled for _____ _____ _____
day   date   time

_____
Signature and Title

_____
Telephone

Please complete the lower portion of this page, and return it to school the day after you receive it. Do not hesitate to call us if you have any questions about this exam.

- -

_____
date

Dear _____ ,

This is an authorization for my child, _____ , to be examined by a licensed physician at school:

YES ☐   NO ☐

_____
Signature of Parent or Guardian

_____
Address

_____
Telephone

Form NO. 301-391
5/1/77

543

APPENDIX A4

Medical Information Sheet. This form is used by the special physical education teacher to gather medical data from existing health records. No action may be taken prior to receipt of written permission by the parent.

(From Process for Identification, Assessment, Planning and Placement of Individuals with Exceptional Needs into Physical Education. *Office of the Los Angeles County Superintendent of Schools, 1979, p. 15. Used by permission.)*

OFFICE OF THE LOS ANGELES COUNTY SUPERINTENDENT OF SCHOOLS
DIVISION OF SPECIAL EDUCATION

ADAPTED PHYSICAL EDUCATION PROGRAM—MEDICAL INFORMATION SHEET

NAME OF PUPIL			BIRTHDATE	HEIGHT	WEIGHT
NAME OF PARENT		ADDRESS			TELEPHONE

DIAGNOSIS

CONDITION	SOURCE	DATE
Neurological Disorder (seizures, medication, hyperactivity, coordination problems, etc.)		
Heart and Lung Condition		
Orthopedic Condition (Indicate area and extent of disability)		
Language Problems		
Hearing Problems		
Vision Problems		
Emotional Problems		
Other Problems (specify)		

NOTE: All information taken from health records should identify sources (Physician, Psychiatrist) and date of examination.

ADAPTED PHYSICAL EDUCATION TEACHER	DATE

Form No. 301.643 Rev. 7/78   DISTRIBUTION: First Copy, County Office; Second Copy, School Office

DUBLIN CITY SCHOOLS SPECIAL EDUCATION	Individualized Education Program Form #8	Initial Placement Date _____ Annual Review Schedule _____ Next Multifactored Evaluation Date _____

I. IDENTIFYING DATA

Student _____ DOB _____ Age _____ School Year _____ Grade _____ SS# _____

Address _____ Custodial Parent/Guardian _____ Phone (H) _____
(B) _____
City _____ Zip _____ (B) _____

District of Residence _____ District or Educational Agency of Attendance _____ Building _____

II. PRESENT LEVELS OF PERFORMANCE
(Include both strengths and weaknesses from the following areas as appropriate: cognitive, academic, physical condition, communicative status, motor skills/physical education, work habits, adaptive behavior, vocational/occupational skills, behavior/ social skills.)

III. SPECIFIC EDUCATIONAL PROGRAM

☐ Initial Placement   ☐ Annual Review
☐ Change in placement   ☐ Change in Goals/Objectives/ Time, etc.
☐ Other _____

A. Primary Special Education Program Check only one (1)

☐ Specific Learning Disabilities
☐ Developmentally Handicapped
☐ Severe Behavior Handicapped
☐ Orthopedically Handicapped and Other Health Impaired
☐ Other _____

B. Other Services – Check each that applies

☐ Attendant
☐ Adapted Physical Education
☐ Occupational Therapy
☐ Physical Therapy
☐ Speech and Language
☐ Work/Study
☐ Other

	Date to be Initiated	Anticipated Duration

545

Student's Name _____ School Year _____

Program Options

	Yes	No	COMMENTS (If "no" is marked)
Can this student be educated in			
Regular Classroom with no modification			
Regular Classroom with supplemental services			
Regular Classroom with individual/ small group instruction			
Special Class/Learning Center (in a district school building)			
Special Class/Learning Center (in another public school district)			
*Special Class/Learning Center (in a separate facility)			
Home Instruction			

*Include a statement of needs when placement is in a separate facility

IV. REGULAR EDUCATION PARTICIPATION

A. Academic and Nonacademic Areas

B. Competency Based Testing

Competency Areas	CHECK EXTENT OF PARTICIPATION FOR EACH AREA				
	Total	None	Modified:	Specify Modification	
Math					
Reading					
English Comp.					

V. PLACEMENT/IEP CONFERENCE PARTICIPANTS

This IEP was developed cooperatively by the following conference participants (must include both name and title).

Parent(s) _____ Date _____

Teacher _____ Date _____

District Representative _____ Date _____

Name/Title _____ Date _____

Name/Title _____ Date _____

Name/Title _____ Date _____

Name/Title _____ Date _____

Name/Title _____ Date _____

VI. PARENT RESPONSE

☐ I have had the opportunity to participate in planning the program

☐ I accept the program and placement recommendations

☐ I do not accept the program and placement recommendation

☐ I waive my right to receive the notification of the proposed placement by certified mail.

Date	Signature of Parent(s)/Guardian	Relationship to Student

State and Federal Rules and Regulations mandate that every handicapped child be re-evaluated at least every three years. THIS IS TO NOTIFY YOU that your child will be provided that mandated reevaluation prior to his/her next periodic review.

Applicable if this box is checked ☐

Parent Information Booklet provided ☐

☐ Parent not present at conference, attempts to contact parents all documented in special education file

Date IEP given/sent to parent/guardian _____

Student's Name _____ School Year _____

VII. GOALS AND OBJECTIVES

Annual Goals	Short Term Instructional Objectives	To be completed at time IEP is developed — METHOD OF EVALUATION					To be completed at Annual Review — EVALUATION OF PERFORMANCE			
		Observation	Work Samples	Teacher Made Test	Standardized Test	Criteria or Other	Objective Achieved	Progress Made	Objective Not Achieved	Comments

547

VIII. OTHER SERVICES

Student's Name _____ Service _____ School Year _____

Present Levels of Performance _____

	To be completed at time IEP is developed						To be completed at Annual Review			
	METHOD OF EVALUATION						EVALUATION OF PERFORMANCE			
	Observation	Work Samples	Teacher Made Test	Standardized Test	Criteria or Other		Objective Achieved	Progress Made	Objective Not Achieved	Comments
Short Term Instructional Objectives										
Annual Goals										

APPENDIX A6
Denton, Texas Individualized Education Program Materials.

Admission ☐
Annual Review ☐
Called Review ☐
Dismissal ☐
Re-eval Date ☐
☐

DENTON INDEPENDENT SCHOOL DISTRICT
DENTON, TEXAS

ADMISSION, REVIEW, & DISMISSAL (ARD)
INDIVIDUAL EDUCATION PROGRAM (IEP)

Speech ____ O.T. ____
A.P.E. ____ P.T. ____
Spec. Trans.__ P.S. ____
H.C. Code __ S.W. ____
Inst. Arngmnt. _____
Contact Hour Code ____

NAME _____ SCHOOL_____ I.D.# _____ DATE _____

BIRTHDATE _____ AGE ____ RACE ___ GRADE ___ TEACHER _____

☐ *An interpreter was used in conducting the meeting. If YES, specify language:

*REVIEW OF ASSESSMENT DATA   (Check ☐ if applicable)
☐ Assessment reports:
  ☐ Comprehensive Individual Assessment
  ☐ Assessment for Related Services: Name of Services   Date
    _____   _____
    _____   _____
    _____   _____

  ☐ Vocational Assessment _____   _____

☐ Records from other School Districts:

☐ Information from Parents/Students:

☐ Information from School Personnel:

☐ Information/Records from other Agencies or Professionals

☐ ☐ Additional assessment was discussed.
Yes No

☐ ☐ *Additional assessment is needed. Specify timeline for assessment to be
Yes No   completed. _____

*DETERMINATION OF ELIGIBILITY (check ☐ if applicable)
Based on the assessment data reviewed, the committee has determined that the student:
  ☐ does not meet eligibility criteria as a handicapped student.

  ☐ meets eligibility criteria for: _____
                        Handicapping Condition(s)
*DENOTES REQUIRED ITEMS

1/90   TEA-52   ARD-1

549

DEVELOPMENT OF THE INDIVIDUAL EDUCATION PLAN (IEP)

☐ ☐   *The ARD committee reviewed achievement on each previous year's short-term objectives on the IEP (applicable to all but initial ARD Meetings).

PRESENT COMPETENCIES:

*Physical, as it affects participation in instructional setting

☐ No physical limitations: no modification of regular class needed
☐ Some physical impairment, but can participate with no modifications.
☐ Needs modifications, because of what impairment? _____
    Describe modifications needed:

*Physical, as it affects physical education

☐   ☐   The student is capable of receiving instruction in the essential elements of physical education through
Yes   No   the regular program without modification. If no, describe modifications needed:

*Behavioral, as it affects educational placement and programming:

☐   Normal for age and cultural group. May be treated the same as a non-handicapped student:

☐   Student has some characteristics which may affect learning, requiring adjustments within regular and special education classes. ARD Committee offers the following suggestions to increase student's appropriate behavior.

—— follow a daily schedule
—— prepare student for a change in routine
—— model appropriate behavior
—— restructure the program
—— communicate with humor
—— provide individual help
—— simplify expectations, check for
    understanding frequently
—— assign added responsibilities to channel energies

—— demonstrates specific interest
—— provide nonacademic activities\
—— emphasize consistency
—— provide a reinforcement menu
—— practice appropriate behavior
—— physically guide student
—— conference with parent
—— provide increased structure
—— minimize distractions
—— others (specify):

Ability to follow discplinary rules:

☐   Normal for age and cultural group. May be treated the same as non-handicapped student. Student should be able to follow the District's Discipline Management Plan. Use of alternative educational placement and suspension as per TEA regulations is appropriate. Student is responsible for school board rules and campus policies.

☐   This student is responsible for school board rules and campus procedures. A modified Discipline Plan will be necessary. The following special approaches are suggested to decrease inappropriate behavior and to increase student cooperation/compliance.

—— ignore the behavior
—— stand near student
—— present verbal reminder
—— praise a behaviorally appropriate student
—— directly request student compliance
—— have student graph behavior
—— withhold reinforcement
—— simplify rules and/or act out consequences
—— conference with parents
—— physically restrain student
—— remove student to time out
—— praise a behaviorally appropriate action
—— other:

—— signal nonverbal disapproval
—— withhold reinforcer, privileges
—— remove distractors
—— use of corporal punishment
—— practice appropriate behavior
—— subtract earned reinforcers
—— allow for logical consequences
—— allow for peer pressure
—— request isolation or sit out
—— avoid strong criticism/confrontation
—— use suspension according to TEA
    requirements (administrative action)
—— call parent
—— call police (administrative action)
—— other (specify):

*Prevocational/vocational skills (when appropriate): _____

Academic/Development (grade or age levels not acceptable)
*Indicate the content areas in which the student **CAN** receive instruction in the essential elements in the **REGULAR** or remedial programs **WITHOUT** modifications:

☐ All subjects	☐ Math	☐ Reading	☐ Spelling
☐ Language/English	☐ Science	☐ Health	
☐ Social Studies/History	☐ Music	☐ Art	☐ Vocational Education
☐ Physical Education:	☐ Other:		

---

*Indicate the content areas in which the student **CAN** ▆▆▆ receive instruction in the essential elements in the **REGULAR** compensatory programs **WITH** modifications:

CONTENT AREAS	COMPETENCIES

*Indicate the content areas in which the student **CANNOT** benefit from instruction (in the essential elements) **WITHOUT** modification or support from **SPECIAL EDUCATION:**

CONTENT AREAS	COMPETENCIES

Goals and Objectives should reflect essential elements where the ARD Committee deems appropriate. If instruction in the essential elements for the assigned grade level/content area is NOT appropriate at the present time, indicate the appropriate content area by (*) asterisk. The instructional program is designed to meet the specific needs of the student. The program is designed to provide the least restrictive environment and to promote a well-balanced curriculum that develops maximum competencies for each student. Modification relates directly to the degree of individualization prescribed for a student and the intensity of the student's problems. _____, the educational liason, will make all of the student's teachers aware of the modifications deemed appropriate by the ARD Committee. Students will be suspended from extracurricular activities if they make a six week grade below 70 in any academic class. However, if the ARD Committee determines that the student's handicap interferes with the ability to meet regular academic standards, his modifications will be reviewed. Suspension from extracurricular activities will be based on failure to meet those modified standards.

GRADUATION PLAN (check one)	ANTICIPATED GRADUATION DATE
☐ Method 2----Regular Credit (Same as nonhandicapped)	
☐ Method 3A--Full Time Employment and Self-Help Skills without support	
☐ Method 3B--Completion of vocational program and part time employment	
☐ Method 3C--Access to service not within responsibilities of public education	
☐ Method 6----Reaches maximum age limit. SBOE 89.235	

STUDENT _____ GRADE _____ ARD DATE _____ PAGE ____ OF __

<u>MODIFICATION PLAN</u>

*ACCOMODATIONS OR MODIFICATIONS TO BE UTILIZED TO FACILITATE MASTERY OF THE
ESSENTAL ELEMENTS AND NEEDED TO ENSURE SUCCESS IN REGULAR, REMEDIAL AND
SUPPORTIVE PROGRAMS INCLUDING ELIGIBILITY FOR PARTICIPATION IN EXTRA CURRICULAR
ACTIVITIES.

PACING

_____ extended time requirments

_____ allow breaks, vary activity often

_____ omit assignments requiring copying in a timed
     situation

_____ other:

ENVIRONMENT

_____ preferential seating

_____ alter physical room arrangement

_____ define limits (physical/behavioral)

     ___ visual ___ auditory ___ both

_____ other:

PRESENTATION OF SUBJECT MATTER

_____ emphasize teaching approach

     ___ auditory ___ visual ___ multi

_____ tactile

_____ individual/small group instruction

_____ utilize specialized curriculum

_____ tape lectures for replay

_____ present demonstration

_____ utilitze manipulatives

_____ emphasize critical information

_____ pre-teach vocabulary

_____ other:

MATERIALS

_____ taped texts, work sheets

_____ highlighted texts, study guides

_____ use supplementary materials

_____ note taking assistance: carbon copy notes of
     regular student

_____ type handwritten teacher material

_____ special equipment:_____

_____ use of laminated materials

_____ use of adapted or simplified texts

_____ use of calculator/computer

DOCUMENT PROCEDURE:

_____ Grade Book

_____ Other:

1/90

ASSIGNMENTS

_____ give directions in small, distinctive steps

_____ allow copying from paper/book, not board

_____ use written back up for oral directions

_____ lower difficulty level

_____ shorten assignment

_____ reduce paper and pencil tasks

_____ read directions to students

_____ give oral cues or prompts

_____ record or type assignment

_____ adapt work sheets, packets

_____ maintain assignment notebook

_____ utilize compensatory procedures by providing
     alternate assignment/strategy when demands of
     class conflict with student capabilities

_____ avoid penalizing for spelling errors

_____ other:

REINFORCEMENT AND FOLLOW THROUGH

_____ use positive reinforcement

_____ use concrete reinforcement

_____ check often for understanding/review

_____ peer tutoring

_____ request parent reinforcement

_____ go to Content Mastery Center

_____ have student repeat directions

_____ make/use vocabulary files

_____ teach study skills

_____ use study sheets to organize material

_____ reinforce long term assignment time lines

_____ other:

TESTING ADAPTATIONS

_____ oral _____ taped _____ short ans. _____ m.ch.

_____ read test to student

_____ modify format _____ shorten length

_____ other:

GRADING

_____ pass/fail contract

_____ modify weights of course components

_____ (alter percentages; delete inappropriate)

TEA-54B

ARD-3-A

STUDENT_____ ARD DATE_____ PAGE ____ OF _____

GRADE _____

MODIFICATION PLAN (SPEECH HANDICAPPED)

Regular teachers may use, but are not limited to, any of the following modifications to enable the student to maintain successful perfomances when the problems are related to the student's handicapping condition.

The checked adaptations have been approved by the ARD committee:

_____ Provide small group or individualized instruction
_____ Assign tasks at appropriate level
_____ Identify target phonemes in spelling words
_____ Provide opportunity to use target phoneme
_____ Avoid penalizing for spelling errors
_____ Provide appropriate speech model
_____ Provide praise for good speech
_____ Maintain supportive environment
_____ Face student when speaking
_____ Slow rate of speech during instruction
_____ Give ample time for the student to answer
_____ Don't call on student in round robin fashion
_____ Give speeches using tape recorder, in private, or written report
_____ Reinforce verbal instruction with written instruction
_____ Give explanation in small distinct steps
_____ Shorten the amount of time required to listen to the teacher
_____ Monitor closely as student begins work to assure understanding
_____ Ask questions requiring short answers or choral responses
_____ Have the child repeat instructions before starting an assignment
_____ Pre-teach vocabulary
_____ Stress major points in the regular assignment
_____ Use visual cues
_____ Use the "buddy system" to aid the student and clarify directions
_____ Peer tutoring
_____ Parents: review speech homework
_____ Avoid assignments requiring oral presentations
_____ Give work in small amounts
_____ Review speech flashcards
_____ Check hearing aid batteries regularly
_____ Special Equipment
_____ Other

Regular education teachers are responsible for notifying special education teachers/speech therapist of student's failure to meet mastery criteria for each six-weeks reporting period.
70% mastery is required for passing/participating in extra-curricular activities.

ARD-3-B

1/90

553

NAME _____ GRADE _____ PAGE _____ OF _____

Indicate the content areas in which the student *CANNOT* receive instruction *WITHOUT* Special Education.

_____ *Instructional Services (Academic, VH, Speech, APE)
_____ *Related Services   Specify: _____   _____ Draft,_____
            Speech, Social Work, Psychological Services   Date
            Service Duration from _____ to _____
_____ Accepted by ARD Committee   _____
                                                                        Date

INDIVIDUAL EDUCATIONAL PLAN (IEP)

*Goal: _____

_____

SPECIAL CONSIDERATION FOR AWARDING GRADES OR CREDITS: _____

_____

PRESENT COMPETENCIES	SHORT-TERM OBJECTIVES The student will be able to......	*Criteria and Evaluation Procedures (Mastery Level)	Schedule	Met ( )

Position Responsible for Implementation (*Required for related services): _____

_____

DETERMINATION OF PLACEMENT:

*Placement Alternative Reviewed and Additional Services were discussed: (include consideration of occupational training needs for students at or before entry into high school)   (circle)

regular	compensatory education	regular education counseling	resource
content mastery	self-contained	part. self-contained	trans. unit
vocational program	homebound/hospital	home based	

---

*The committee determined that the student's placement will be at:

_____   _____
NAME OF SCHOOL CAMPUS   NAME OF INSTRUCTIONAL OPTION

[ ] [ ]   *This is the campus which the student would attend if not handicapped.
Yes No

[ ] [ ]   *This is the campus that is as close as possible to the student's home. If
Yes No   NO explain:

Justification that the above placement is the least restrictive environment:
*Evidence that placement is based upon the needs of the student and is in the least
 restrictive environment:

*The following considerations were given to any potentially harmful effects on the
 student or the quality of services which he or she needs:

*Evidence that special classes, separate schooling, or other removal of the student
 from the regular education environment occurs only when education with the use of
 supplementary aids and services cannot be achieved satisfactorily:

*Opportunities for this student to participate with nonhandiapped peers in nonacademic activities on a regular basis:

*Opportunities for this student to participate with nonhandicapped peers in extracurricular activities on a regular basis:

ASSURANCES

The committee assures that special education placement. . .

*for national origin minority group students or linguistically different students, is not based on criteria which were developed solely on command of the English language.

      *Basis for assurance: _____ adaptation in testing procedures
                       _____ review of parent/student information
                       _____ review of language assessment
                       _____ use of interpreter

*is not based on deficiencies indentified as directly attributable to a different culture or a lifestyle or lack of educational opportunities.

      *Basis for assurance: _____ review of parent/student information
                       _____ review of sociological assessment

The committee assures that all instructional and related services specified in the IEP will be provided to the student at no cost. Fees normally charged to nonhandicapped students or their parents, as part of the general education program, may be charged (i.e., art or laboratory fees).

SPECIFIC LIMITATION: Are there any specific limitation(s) needed for this student? (activity, food restrictions, medication, prostheses, etc.)

SERVICES TO BE PROVIDED

SCHOOL _____ DATE _____

Instruction Course/ Curriculum Area	Regular Education		Sp. Ed. Time	Progress/Grade		Determined By:
	Modi-fied	Time		Reg. Ed.	Spec. Ed.	Joint

If times vary from requirements in 19 TAC 75 21.101, give justification:

*Related Services	*Amount of Time Per Week

Special Transportation   YES ☐   NO ☐
*If YES, cite justification:

COORDINATION BETWEEN REG. ED. AND SP. ED.
Responsibility for monitoring student's performance in
regular education: _____
_____

Frequency: _____

Method: _____

Schedule for evaluating progress for participation in
extracurricular activities will be:
    3 wks _____   6 wks _____   other _____

*TEAMS TEST:
The student _____ will take the complete test without modifications
               _____ will take in the following areas: (circle) for grade   1, 3, 5, 7, 9
          Reading   Writing   Math   No Areas (exemption)
   For grade 11 (exit level):   English/Language Arts   Math   No Areas (exemption)
*If student is taking part or parts, check modifications needed:
     _____ increased time   _____ real response   _____ large print or Braille
     _____ taped (Math only)   _____ individual administration   _____ interpreter for instruction
If student is exempted from TEAMS, state justification(s):
  ☐ Handicap prevents mastery of all competencies   ☐ Reading level deficit more than two grade levels
     ☐ Other

ARD/IEP   STUDENT _____   PAGE _____ OF _____
    [ ]   Decisions made by this ARD Committee were made by mutual agreement
    [ ]   Decisions were NOT made by mutual agreement and the ARD Committee agrees to recess
          until:

_____   _____   _____

DATE   TIME   PLACE   (Not to exceed 10 school days from current ARD date)

     [ ]   Despite a 10 day recess, this ARD Committee has been unable to reach mutual agreement.
           The district will implement the IEP which it has determined to be appropriate for the
           student and the parents have been notified of their opportunity for mediation or a due
           process hearing.

SIGNATURES OF COMMITTEE MEMBERS   COMMITTEE   DECISIONS   POSITION
        SIGNATURE   AGREE   DISAGREES

SIGNATURE	COMMITTEE AGREE	DECISIONS DISAGREES	POSITION
			*PARENT/STUDENT
			*ADMINISTRATION
			*INSTRUCTION
			*SPECIAL EDUCATION
			*ASSESSMENT (*)

NOTE: If a committe member disagrees with the decisions reflected in this report, he/she
        may submit a separate statement, presenting his/her reasons for disagreeing. (*) Assessment
        personnel are required when interpretations of assessment data are being considered.

        *Your rights were explained to you when you received the current copy of this booklet,   SPECIAL
EDUCATION: PARENT AND STUDENT RIGHTS.   Please refer to the following section of this booklet
for information on procedural safeguards.

SECTIONS IN BOOKLET	PAGE NUMBER
Prior Notice	Page 2, 4
Consent	Page 2, 4
Parents Rights in the Assessment Process	Page 5, 6
Education Records	Pages 13-14
Complaint Process (mediation hearings)	Pages 15-17
Least Restrictive Environment	Page 10

*FOR INITIAL PLACEMENT
[ ]   [ ]   *I have received and reviewed the admission, review, and dismissal (ARD) Committee
Yes   No   report, dated _____, that has been prepared for: _____
                                        Name of Student
[ ]   [ ]   *I agree with the ARD Committee's decision and do give my permission for the educational
Yes   No   placement that has been proposed for my child/me.
[ ]   [ ]   However, if I revoke consent after initial placement, my child's placement will not change
Yes   No   unless:
           (a) the school and I agree otherwise (following ARD Committee procedures), or
           (b) a due process hearing resolves the dispute.
[ ]   [ ]   I request a waiver of the five day waiting period for the implementation of the program for
Yes   No   my child as agreed upon by this committee.

_____   _____

SIGNATURE OF PARENT, GUARDIAN, OR SURROGATE PARENT   DATE

SEMS   sheet done [ ]   Yes   [ ]   No   Date sent to Special Education _____

**DENTON INDEPENDENT
SCHOOL DISTRICT**

NAME OF STUDENT

DATE OF MEETING

**ARD/IEP SUPPLEMENT
EXTENDED YEAR SERVICES PROGRAM (EYS)**

EYS consideration recommended by: (check ☐ appropriate box)
    ☐ Parent/guardian   ☐ Parent's designated representative
    ☐ School district personnel directly involved in student's educational program

Need for EYS demonstrated by evidence of one or more of the following:
    Description of formal evaluation results (comprehensive assessment report, achievement test
    including TEAMS, etc.):

    Description of informal evaluation results (progress reports, work samples, etc):

    Description of recorded observations by parents (behavioral observations/information):

Based on the evidence presented above, describe the critical areas in the current IEP objectives which will show severe or substantial regression and recoupment problems unless EYS is provided:

Check (☐) one or more of the following occurrences which will prevail at the end of the first eight weeks of the next school year if EYS is not provided:

    ☐ placement in a more restrictive enviroment
    ☐ the student becoming significantly less self-sufficient in daily living skill areas as
            evidenced by an increase in the number of direct service staff and/or amount
            of time required to provide special education or related services
    ☐ the loss of access to an independent living environment provided by other sources
    ☐ the loss of access to one-the-job training, sheltered work, and/or productive employment

Attach revised individual educational plan (ARD-4) to include daily schedule. The committee determined that the student will require an extended year program and that the student's placement will be at:

NAME OF INSTRUCTIONAL OPTION

NAME OF SCHOOL CAMPUS

1/90

ARD SUP-EYS

ARD/IEP STUDENT _____ PAGE _____ OF _____

MINUTES/RECOMMENDATIONS

_____

_____

_____

_____

_____

_____

_____

_____

_____

_____

_____

_____

_____

_____

_____

_____

_____

_____

_____

_____

_____

_____

_____

_____

APPENDIX A7

Request for Re-examination Form.

(Modified from Adapted Physical Education: Related Legislation, IEP Development and Programmatic Considerations for Illinois. *Springfield, Ill.: Illinois Office of Education, 1978, p. E5. Used by permission.)*

REQUEST FOR RE-EXAMINATION

To: _____   Date: _____

From: J. J. Doe, Coordinator
        Special Physical Education

_____ has been participating in the special

physical education program per your recommendations and guidance since

_____ 19 ___ .   Although you indicated no re-examination was

necessary until _____ , 19 ___ ,   observations, analysis of performance

and progress, and monitoring of this pupil's individualized progress

indicate that medical re-evaluation may be appropriate now.   Please

review the attached Physical Education Medical Referral Form after re-

examining the pupil and provide the following information:

_____ No change in status or recommendations from those of

_____ , 19 ___

_____ Change status and program recommendations as follows:

_____

_____

_____

_____ Place in unrestricted activity status.

This pupil should return for further re-examination _____ , 19 ___

Thank you for your cooperation and assistance in providing this addi-

tional information so that this pupil's needs can be met more effectively

through the comprehensive physical education program.

_____   _____
Physician's Signature   Date

APPENDIX A8

Recommendation for Discharge/transfer. This form is used whenever it is believed that a pupil has made adequate progress in the special physical education class, or that his or her needs could better be met in another type of physical education program. The form can be initiated by anyone and signed by personnel concurring with the recommendation. Parents must be notified of this recommendation for discharge and invited to attend an Eligibility and Planning Conference to discuss it.

(From Process for Identification, Assessment, Planning and Placement of Individuals with Exceptional Needs into Physical Education. *Office of the Los Angeles County Superintendent of Schools, 1979, p. 26. Used by permission.)*

OFFICE OF THE LOS ANGELES COUNTY SUPERINTENDENT OF SCHOOLS

DIVISION OF SPECIAL EDUCATION
9300 East Imperial Highway, Downey, California 90242
Telephone: (213) 922-6263

RECOMMENDATION FOR DISCHARGE/TRANSFER
ADAPTED PHYSICAL EDUCATION

Name of
Pupil _____ Program _____
        Last Name   First   Middle

Living at _____
        Street   City   State   Zip Code

School _____ District _____ Grade _____

The California Administrative Code, Title 5, Education requires that pupils shall be assigned to or removed from instruction in adapted physical education only upon the recommendation of an Eligibility and Planning Committee. (Section 3631)

In the space below, please provide as much information as possible pertaining to your recommendation for dismissal of this pupil from adapted physical education instruction.

Recommended by:

_____
      Name   Position   Date

_____
      Name   Position   Date

_____
      Name   Position   Date

APPENDIX B
TESTING AND EVALUATION FORMS

APPENDIX B1
I CAN Recording Form (example).

I CAN

CLASS PERFOMANCE SCORE SHEET
PERFORMACE OBJECTIVE: Abdominal Strength And Endurance

SCORING

Assessment:
X = Achieved
O = Not achieved

Reassessment:
⊗ = Achieved
∅ = Not achieved

FOCAL POINTS	STD.
a Starting position	
b Curl-up	2/3 times
c Returning	
a Starting position	
b Curl-up	2/3 times
c Returning	
Bent leg sit-up	100%
a Beginning and stopping	100%
b Minimal performance criteria	
Maintenance	12 weeks
Primary Responses*	

*PRIMARY RESPONSES

N - Nonattending
NR - No response
UR - Unrelated response
O - Other (specify in comments)

NAME	a	b	c	a	b	c		a	b		COMMENTS
1.											
2.											
3.											
4.											
5.											
6.											
7.											
8.											
9.											
10.											
11.											
12.											
13.											
14.											
15.											

(From "Fitness and Growth," I CAN: Primary Skills, Janet A. Wessel, Project Director. Copyright 1976 by Michigan State University. Reprinted by permission of Hubbard Scientific Company, Publishers.)

REPORT CARD

_____
NAME

_____
AGE

_____
GRADE

FITNESS COMPONENT	TEST ITEM		SCORE DATE: _____	MY GOAL	SCORE AFTER TRAINING DATE: _____
AEROBIC ENDURANCE	DISTANCE RUN (check one) Mile _____ 1/2 Mile _____ other _____				
BODY COMPOSITION	Skin folds (check those used)	1. Subscapular			
		2. Triceps			
		3. Calf			
		Sum of 2. & 3.			
	OR BMI				
FLEXIBILITY	Sit and Reach				
ABDOMINAL STRENGTH/ENDURANCE	Sit-ups				
UPPER BODY STRENGTH/ENDURANCE	(check one) Pull-ups _____ OR Modified Pull-ups _____				

(American Alliance for Health, Physical Education, Recreation and Dance)

564

APPENDIX B3
Project MOBILITEE Recording Form (example).

Name _____ Date Evaluated _____

School _____ Evaluator _____

PART A: PHYSICAL / MOTOR FITNESS

Directions: Administer all test items. Teachers should informally assess students to determine whether the 20-foot dash or 30-yard dash is most appropriate for an individual student. Students who take excessive lengths of time to ambulate or propel themselves a short distance should be administered the 20-foot dash.

All wheelchair students should be administered the wheelchair push. Individuals with known cardiac or respiratory problems should obtain medical approval before the 5-minute walk/run is administered.

	1	2	3	4
1. 20-Foot Dash (p. 28)	1.1 more than 20 seconds	1.2 15–20 seconds	1.3 10–14 seconds	1.4 less than 10 seconds
2. 30-Yard Dash (p. 30)	2.1 more than 40 seconds Time:_____sec.	2.2 31–40 seconds Time:_____sec.	2.3 20–30 seconds Time:_____sec.	2.4 less than 20 seconds Time:_____sec.
3. Wheelchair Push (p. 33)	DISTANCE TRAVELED Trial 1 _____	Trial 2 _____	Trial 3 _____	
4. Wheelchair Push-ups (p. 36)	4.1 0–4 Total:_____	4.2 5–9 Total:_____	4.3 10–14 Total:_____	4.4 15 or more Total:_____
5. Agility Run (p. 38)	5.1 less than 8 cones Cones:_____	5.2 8–15 cones Cones:_____	5.3 16–22 cones Cones:_____	5.4 23 or more cones Cones:_____
6. 5-Minute Walk/Run (p. 40)	6.1 less than 1 lap Time:_____min.	6.2 1 lap in 5 minutes Time:_____min.	6.3 more than 1 lap but less than 5 minutes Time:_____min.	6.4 entire 5 minutes Time:_____min.

565

APPENDIX B4
Project TRANSITION Score Sheet for Upper Body Strength/Endurance (example).

NAME_____

DATE_____

SCORER_____

TEST_____

Abbreviated Curriculum Steps

1.1 Sit on mats
1.2 Supine position
1.3 Bar over mid-sternum
2.1 One hand grasp
2.2 Two hand grasp
2.3 Lift
2.4 Return
3.1 Lift x 2
3.2 Lift x 4
3.3 Lift x 6
3.4 Lift x 8

LEVELS OF INDEPENDENCE

STEPS	UO (0)	HI PHY+ (1)	MIN PHY+ (2)	HI V/M (3)	MIN V (4)	IND (5)	TOTAL INDEPENDENCE
1.1							
1.2							
1.3							
2.1							
2.2							
2.3							
2.4							
3.1							
3.2							
3.3							
3.4							
Sub-totals							

Scoring Key

Unobserved Will not attempt (0 points)

High Physical+ Constant physical prompt, in addition to verbal prompting w/modeling (1 point)

Minimal Physical+ Physical to initiate, in addition to verbal w/modeling (2 points)

High Verbal/Modeling Verbal and modeling (3 points)

Minimal Verbal Verbal direction throughout steps (4 points)

Independence Verbal direction to initiate (5 points)

- -

Total Independence Self initiation of skill, not to be considered in scoring.

____% Task Score $\left(\dfrac{\text{\# Steps Ind.}}{11}\right) \times 100$

____ Ave. Ind. Score $\left(\dfrac{\text{Sum Points}}{55}\right) \times 100$

____Performance Score

Observations:_____

_____

Reinforcer:_____

_____

Reinforcement Schedule:_____

_____

Name _____ School _____

Grade _____ Sex _____ Date of Birth _____

Generic Handicapping Condition, if any (see reverse side): _____

Specific Handicapping Condition, if any (see reverse side): _____

	AGE	DATE	HEIGHT (IN.)	WEIGHT (LBS.)	TESTER
Test 1	_____	_____	_____	_____	_____
Test 2	_____	_____	_____	_____	_____

PHYSICAL FITNESS COMPONENT	TEST ITEM	RAW SCORE		PERCENTILE			
				TEST 1		TEST 2	
		TEST 1	TEST 2	R	A	R	A
Body Composition	Triceps						
	Subscapular						
	Sum of Triceps and Subs.						
Muscular Strength/ Endurance	Right Grip						
	Left Grip						
	Sum of Grips						
	Sit-ups						
	Dash						
	*Softball Throw						
	*Standing Broad Jump						
	*Arm Hang						
Cardiorespiratory Endurance	Long Distance Run						
Flexibility	Sit & Reach						

*The softball throw for distance is a basic test item only for girls with cerebral palsy. The broad jump, arm hang, and softball throw are suggested substitute test items.

Anecdotal Remarks:

Run Codes:

Dash _____

Long Distance Run _____

R = Regular Norms
A = Adapted Norms

APPENDIX B6
Bruininks-Oseretsky Test of Motor Proficiency
Recording Form.

NAME _____ SEX: Boy☐ Girl☐ GRADE _____

SCHOOL/AGENCY _____ CITY _____ STATE _____

EXAMINER _____ REFERRED BY _____

PURPOSE OF TESTING _____

Arm Preference: *(circle one)*

    RIGHT   LEFT   MIXED

Leg Preference: *(circle one)*

    RIGHT   LEFT   MIXED

	Year	Month	Day
Date Tested	____	____	____
Date of Birth	____	____	____
Chronological Age	____	____	____

Complete Battery: _____

SUBTEST	POINT SCORE Maximum Subject's	STANDARD SCORE Test (Table 23)	Composite (Table 24)	PERCENTILE RANK (Table 25)	STANINE (Table 25)	OTHER _____
GROSS MOTOR SUBTESTS:						
1. Running Speed and Agility	15 ____	____				____
2. Balance	32 ____	____				____
3. Bilateral Coordination	20 ____	____				____
4. Strength	42 ____	____				____
GROSS MOTOR COMPOSITE		☐ SUM	☐	☐	☐	☐☐☐
5. Upper-Limb Coordination	21 ____	☐				____
FINE MOTOR SUBTESTS						
6. Response Speed	17 ____	____				____
7. Visual-Motor Control	24 ____	____				____
8. Upper-Limb Speed and Dexterity	72 ____	____				____
FINE MOTOR COMPOSITE		☐ SUM	☐	☐	☐	☐☐☐
BATTERY COMPOSITE.................		☐ SUM	☐	☐	☐	☐☐

*To obtain Battery Composite: And Gross Motor Composite. Subtest 5 Standard Score, and Fine Motor Composite. Check result by adding Standard Scores on Subtests 1-8.

Short Form:

	POINT SCORE Maximum Subject's	STANDARD SCORE Test (Table 23)	Composite (Table 24)	PERCENTILE RANK (Table 25)	STANINE (Table 25)
SHORT FORM:	38 ____	☐	☐	☐	

DIRECTIONS

Complete Battery:

1. During test administration, record subject's response for each trial.

2. After test administration, convert performance on each item (item raw score) to a point score, using scale provided. For an item with more than one trial, choose best performance. Record item point score in circle to right of scale.

3. For each subtest, add item point scores, record total in circle provided at end of each subtest and in Test Score Summary section. Consult *Examiner's Manual* for norms tables.

Short Form:

1. Follow Steps 1 and 2 for Complete Battery, except record each point score in box to right of scale.

2. Add point scores for all 14 Short Form items and record total in Test Score Summary section. Consult Examiner's Manual for norms tables.

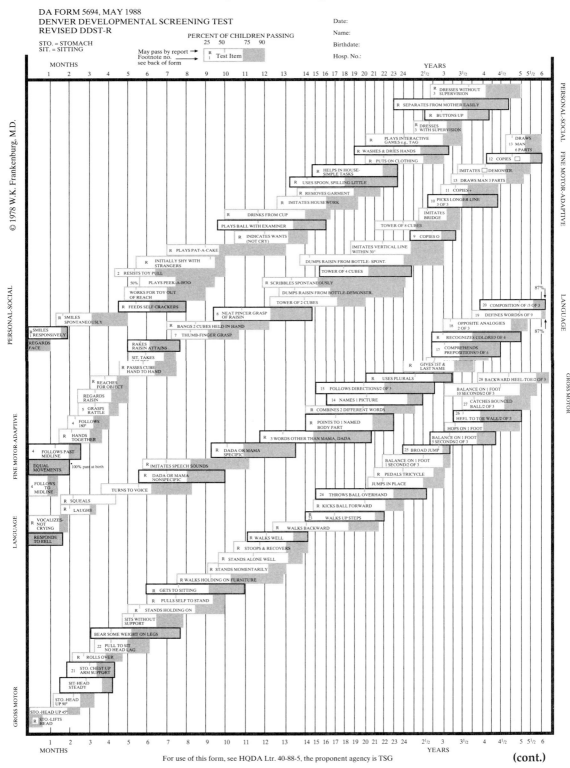

For use of this form, see HQDA Ltr. 40-88-5, the proponent agency is TSG

(cont.)

DIRECTIONS

1. Try to get child to smile by smiling, talking or waving to him. Do not touch him.
2. When child is playing with toy, pull it away from him. Pass if he resists.
3. Child does not have to be able to tie shoes or button in the back.
4. Move yarn slowly in an arc from one side to the other, about 6" above child's face. Pass if eyes follow 90° to midline. (Past midline; 180°)
5. Pass if child grasps rattle when it is touched to the backs or tips of fingers.
6. Pass if child continues to look where yarn disappeared or tries to see where it went. Yarn should be dropped quickly from sight from tester's hand without arm movement.
7. Pass if child picks up raisin with any part of thumb and a finger.
8. Pass if child picks up raisin with the ends of thumb and index finger using an over hand approach.

9. Pass any en-closed form. Fail continuous round motions.
10. Which line is longer? (Not bigger.) Turn paper upside down and repeat. (3/3 or 5/6)
11. Pass any crossing lines.
12. Have child copy first. If failed, demonstrate.

When giving items 9, 11, and 12, do not name the forms. Do not demonstrate 9 and 11.

13. When scoring, each pair (2 arms, 2 legs, etc.) counts as one part.
14. Point to picture and have child name it. (No credit is given for sounds only.)

15. Tell child to: Give block to Mommie; put block on table; put block on floor. Pass 2 of 3. (Do not help child by pointing, moving head or eyes.)
16. Ask child: What do you do when you are cold?..hungry?..tired? Pass 2 of 3.
17. Tell child to: Put block on table; under table; in front of chair; behind chair. Pass 3 of 4. (Do not help child by pointing, moving head or eyes.)
18. Ask child: If fire is hot, ice is ?; Mother is a woman, Dad is a ?; a horse is big, a mouse is ?. Pass 2 of 3.
19. Ask child: What is a ball?..lake?..desk?..house?..banana?..curtain?..ceiling? ..hedge?..pavement? Pass if defined in terms of use, shape, what it is made of or general category (such as banana is fruit, not just yellow). Pass 6 of 9.
20. Ask child: What is a spoon made of?..a shoe made of?..a door made of? (No other objects may be substituted.) Pass 3 of 3.
21. When placed on stomach, child lifts chest off table with support of forearms and/or hands.
22. When child is on back, grasp his hands and pull him to sitting. Pass if head does not hang back.
23. Child may use wall or rail only, not person. May not crawl.
24. Child must throw ball overhand 3 feet to within arm's reach of tester.
25. Child must perform standing broad jump over width of test sheet. (8-1/2 inches)
26. Tell child to walk forward, ⌒⌒⌒⌒➤ heel within 1 inch of toe. Tester may demonstrate. Child must walk 4 consecutive steps, 2 out of 3 trials.
27. Bounce ball to child who should stand 3 feet away from tester. Child must catch ball with hands, not arms, 2 out of 3 trials.
28. Tell child to walk backward, ◄⌒⌒⌒⌒ toe within 1 inch of heel. Tester may demonstrate. Child must walk 4 consecutive steps, 2 out of 3 trials.

DATE AND BEHAVIORAL OBSERVATIONS (how child feels at time of test, relation to tester, attention span, verbal behavior, self-confidence, etc.):

BASIC SKILL	LEVEL I	LEVEL II	LEVEL III	LEVEL IV
Walking	Ten-second stand	Cruising	Walks—one support	Opposition walk
Stair climbing	Creeps or animal walk	Two-foot landing up, any down!	Alternate up, two-foot landing down	Alternate up and down
Running	Rapid walk	Wide base, wide arms	Egg beater	Nonsupport
Throwing	Two-hand push	Arm only, no foot movement	One sided/ homolateral	Opposition throw
Catching	Arm stretch	Scoop	Vice squeeze	Cup fashion
Kicking	Part of walk	Stiff leg	Knee action kick	Knee action kick with follow-through
Jumping	Jumps down	Jump in place, no arms	Jump, improper arm action	Jump with arm action
Hopping	Jump	Raises up on toe	Leg lift hop	Body lift hop
Skipping	Runs/hops/ leaps/gallops	Same side skip	Segmented alternate skip	Alternate skip
Striking	One-hand chopping	Two-hand chopping with waist bending	Rocking swing	Twisting swing
Ladder climbing	Climbs one step	Two-step climb	Alternate up, two down	Alternate step up and down

Project MOBILITEE Motor Pattern Assessment for Low-Functioning Students.

Name _____ Date Evaluated _____

School _____ Evaluator _____

PART D: LOW INCIDENCE MOTOR PATTERN ASSESSMENT

Directions: Administer those test items you feel are appropriate for your student. An informal assessment should determine which of the tests to administer.

	1	2	3	4
Rolling (p. 92)	22.1 little or no attempt	22.2 supine to side	22.3 supine to prone	22.4 prone to supine
Creeping/ Crawling (p. 94)	23.1 little or no movement	23.2 arms to pull	24.3 elbows flexed, legs under	23.4 contra-lateral extremities
Walking/ Wheelchair Mobility (p. 96)	24.1 50–60 seconds	24.2 40–49 seconds	24.3 30–39 seconds	24.4 20–29 seconds
Movement	INDIVIDUAL MODE—OBSERVATION SHEET ONLY (on reverse side of score sheet)			
Maintenance of Posture (p. 100)	26.1 10 seconds or less	26.2 11–30 seconds	26.3 31–45 seconds	26.4 46–60 seconds
Pre-Strike (p. 102)	27.1 little or no movement	27.2 arm above with assistance	27.3 arm above without assistance	27.4 one hand chopping with assistance
Pre-Catch (p. 104)	28.1 little or no movement	28.2 arms in front of body	28.3 arms move to object	28.4 stop or trap object
Pre-Kick (p. 106)	29.1 little or no movement	29.2 hip/knee flexion	29.3 hip/knee extension, contact	29.4 flexion, extension, ball contact

	Score					
	4	3	2	1		
Walking Board: Forward					Balance and Posture	
Backward						
Sidewise						
Jumping						
Indentification of Body Parts					Body Image and Differentiation	
Imitation of Movement						
Obstacle Course						
Kraus-Weber						
Angels-in-the snow						
Chalkboard Circle					Perceptual-Motor Match	
Double Circle						
Lateral Line						
Vertical Line						
Rythmic writing Rhythm						
Reproduction						
Orientation						
Ocular Pursuits Both eyes					Ocular Control	
Right eye						
Left eye						
Push-up						
Visual Achievement Forms Form					Form Perception	
Organization						

APPENDIX B11
Six Category Gross Motor Test Recording Form.

Date _____   Name _____   Age _____   Sex _____

Motor Problem? _____   Diagnosed as _____
                  Yes–No

Degree of Retardation _____ I.Q. _____

	Level I	*SCORES*	*Level II*	
Test 1:	Body Perception		Body Perception	
	a. Stomach–front _____		a. Left arm _____	
	b. Back _____		b. Left leg _____	
	c. Stomach–legs _____		c. Right arm _____	
	d. Nearest tester side _____		d. Left albow _____	
	e. Left-side _____		e. Left knee _____	
	Total Score _____		Total Score _____	
Test 2:	Gross Agility (quick get-up)		Gross Agility (kneel and rise)	
	Total points _____		Total points _____	
Test 3:	Balance (eyes open)		Balance (arms folded, eyes closed)	
	Total points _____		Total points _____	
Test 4:	Locomotor Agility (crawl-hop)		Locomotor Agility (pattern jump-hop)	
	Total points _____		Total points _____	
Test 5:	Ball Throwing (form)		Ball Throwing (at target)	
	Total points _____		Total points _____	
Test 6:	Ball Tracking (swinging ball)		Ball Tracking (catching)	
	Total points _____		Total points _____	

Total Points in Battery: _____   Level I _____   Level II _____

Average Score Level I _____   Average Score Level II _____

TOTAL SCORE, TOTAL BATTERY _____

AVERAGE SCORE, TOTAL BATTERY _____

APPENDIX B12
Test of Gross Motor Development Recording Form.

Name _____

School/Agency _____

Sex: Male _____ Female _____ Grade _____

TESTING INFORMATION

1ST TESTING	Year	Month	Day
Date Tested	_____	_____	_____
Date of Birth	_____	_____	_____
Chronological Age	_____	_____	_____

Examiner's Name

Examiner's Title

Purpose of Testing

2ND TESTING	Year	Month	Day
Date Tested	_____	_____	_____
Date of Birth	_____	_____	_____
Chronological Age	_____	_____	_____

Examiner's Name

Examiner's Title

Purpose of Testing

RECORD OF SCORES

1ST TESTING

Subtests	Raw Scores	%iles	Std. Scores
Locomotor Skills	_____	_____	_____
Object Control Skills	_____	_____	_____

Sum of Standard Scores = _____

Gross Motor Development Quotient (GMDQ) = _____

2ND TESTING

Subtests	Raw Scores	%iles	Std. Scores
Locomotor Skills	_____	_____	_____
Object Control Skills	_____	_____	_____

Sum of Standard Scores = _____

Gross Motor Development Quotient (GMDQ) = _____

COMMENTS/RECOMMENDATIONS

_____

_____

575

NAME   DIAGNOSIS

MOVEMENTS INDICATED   MOVEMENTS CONTRAINDICATED

Skills	Number of Times	Distance	Amount of Time	Manner
Entering pool				
Walking across pool				
Putting face in water				
Blowing bubbles				
Bobbing				
Face float, assisted				
Back float, assisted				
Kicking with board				
Beginner arm motion				
Face float alone				
Back float alone				
Use of lifejacket				
Beginning crawl				
Safety skills				

Instuctor's Comments: Date:

(From the American National Red Cross, Adapted Aquatics. *Garden City, NY: Doubleday & Company, Inc., 1977, p. 100. Copyright 1977 by The American National Red Cross. Used by permission.)*

APPENDIX B14
Dance Progress Recording Form.

Name	I.Q.	1st lesson	2nd lesson	3rd lesson	4th lesson	5th lesson	6th lesson	7th lesson	8th lesson	9th lesson	Index	Remarks
J. Jones	50	ABE	ABC EG	ABC EGH	ABCD EGH	ABCD EFGH	etc.				*A* Arms straight up	
S. Brown	35			C	C	ABC	ABC	ABCG	ABC GE		*B* Turns in circle	
T. Hall	15				A	A	AC	AC	AC	ACE	*C* Kneels on the knee	
											D Counter-movement	
											E Jumps without help	
											F Running	
											G Heel-digs	
											H Toe-digs	
											I Stamp-clap	
											J Elbow, two claps, arms up	

Note: The above design is a suggestion for a chart, indicating the individual progress of each child. As each child achieves a certain movement, put the corresponding alphabetical letter under the proper lesson, beside the child's name. For instance: T. Hall could do nothing alone until the 4th lesson, when he managed A . . . to get his arms up!

Note: With further progress, add more movements in alphabetical sequence

(From F. Robins & J. Robins, Educational Rhythmics for Mentally and Physically Handicapped Children. *(Chicago: Association Press/Follett Publishing Company, 1968), pp. 28–29. Used by permission.)*

APPENDIX B15
The Ohio State University Posture Recording Form.

Name _____ Age _____ Height _____ Weight _____

Scoring: Slight = S   Marked = M   Right = R   Left = L   Bilateral = B

STANDING	Date(s)												
Lateral Imbalances–Anterior													
Overweight													
Underweight													
Lateral Head Tilt													
Pigeon Breast													
Shoulders Uneven													
Hips Uneven													
Knock Knee													
Bow Legs													
Foot Pronation													
Toe Deformity													
Lateral Imbalances–Posterior													
Shoulders Uneven													
Scoliosis													
Winged Scapula													
High Hip													
Achilles Deviation													
A.-P. Imbalances													
Forward Head													
Pes Planus													
Pes Cavus													
Round Shoulders													
Kyphosis													
Round Back													
Lordosis													
Kypholordosis													
Abdominal Ptosis													
Hyperextended Knees													

WALKING	Date(s)												
Pelvic Oscillation													
Side Lean													
Toeing Out													
Toeing In													
Forward Lean													
Back Lean													
Tension (Rigid)													

POSTURE RATING CHART

Grade | 4 | 5 | 6 | 7 | 8 | 9 | 10 | 11 | 12 |

Rater's Initials

Date of Test

5	3	1
HEAD ERECT GRAVITY LINE PASSES DIRECTLY THROUGH CENTER	HEAD TWISTED OR TURNED TO ONE SIDE SLIGHTLY	HEAD TWISTED OR TURNED TO ONE SIDE MARKEDLY
SHOULDERS LEVEL (HORIZONTALLY)	ONE SHOULDER SLIGHTLY HIGHER THAN OTHER	ONE SHOULDER MARKEDLY HIGHER THAN OTHER
SPINE STRAIGHT	SPINE SLIGHTLY CURVED LATERALLY	SPINE MARKEDLY CURVED LATERALLY
HIPS LEVEL (HORIZONTALLY)	ONE HIP SLIGHTLY HIGHER	ONE HIP MARKEDLY HIGHER
FEET POINTED STRAIGHT AHEAD	FEET POINTED OUT	FEET POINTED OUT MARKEDLY ANKLES SAG IN (PRONATION)
ARCHES HIGH	ARCHES LOWER, FEET SLIGHTLY FLAT	ARCHES LOW FEET MARKEDLY FLAT

Total Page One

(Source: *Courtesy of the New York State Education Department.*)

(cont.)

APPENDIX B16 (cont.)

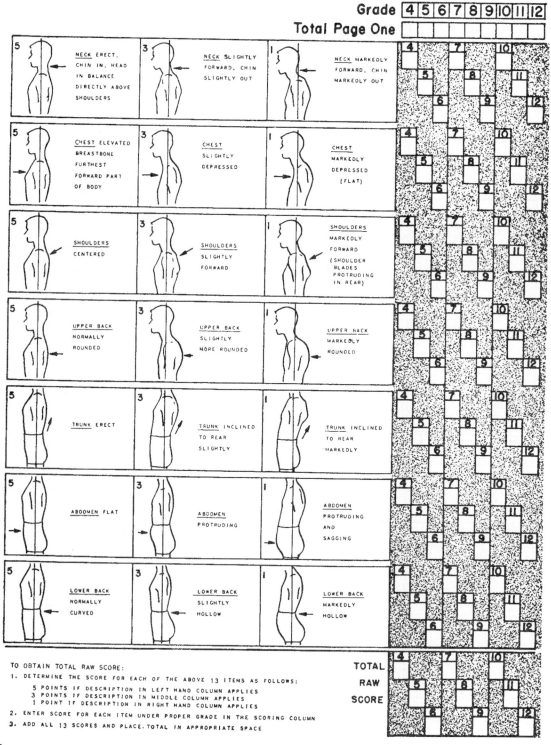

Grade: 4 5 6 7 8 9 10 11 12

Total Page One

	5	3	1
NECK	NECK ERECT, CHIN IN, HEAD IN BALANCE DIRECTLY ABOVE SHOULDERS	NECK SLIGHTLY FORWARD, CHIN SLIGHTLY OUT	NECK MARKEDLY FORWARD, CHIN MARKEDLY OUT
CHEST	CHEST ELEVATED BREASTBONE FURTHEST FORWARD PART OF BODY	CHEST SLIGHTLY DEPRESSED	CHEST MARKEDLY DEPRESSED (FLAT)
SHOULDERS	SHOULDERS CENTERED	SHOULDERS SLIGHTLY FORWARD	SHOULDERS MARKEDLY FORWARD (SHOULDER BLADES PROTRUDING IN REAR)
UPPER BACK	UPPER BACK NORMALLY ROUNDED	UPPER BACK SLIGHTLY MORE ROUNDED	UPPER BACK MARKEDLY ROUNDED
TRUNK	TRUNK ERECT	TRUNK INCLINED TO REAR SLIGHTLY	TRUNK INCLINED TO REAR MARKEDLY
ABDOMEN	ABDOMEN FLAT	ABDOMEN PROTRUDING	ABDOMEN PROTRUDING AND SAGGING
LOWER BACK	LOWER BACK NORMALLY CURVED	LOWER BACK SLIGHTLY HOLLOW	LOWER BACK MARKEDLY HOLLOW

TO OBTAIN TOTAL RAW SCORE:

1. DETERMINE THE SCORE FOR EACH OF THE ABOVE 13 ITEMS AS FOLLOWS:

    5 POINTS IF DESCRIPTION IN LEFT HAND COLUMN APPLIES
    3 POINTS IF DESCRIPTION IN MIDDLE COLUMN APPLIES
    1 POINT IF DESCRIPTION IN RIGHT HAND COLUMN APPLIES

2. ENTER SCORE FOR EACH ITEM UNDER PROPER GRADE IN THE SCORING COLUMN

3. ADD ALL 13 SCORES AND PLACE TOTAL IN APPROPRIATE SPACE

TOTAL RAW SCORE

580

Posture Analysis

Portland State University

H.P.E. 298 Name _____ Instr. _____

ID   Tr   Yr
□ □ □   □   □
1   2   3   5   6   7

Neck	1	3	5	□ 9 □ 10	1 - Female 2 - Male
Upper Back	1	3	5	□ 11	Height ft □ 12 inches □ 13 □ 14 Weight □ 15 □ 16 □ 17
Trunk	1	3	5	□ 18 Age □ 19	1 - Under 25 2 - 25 – 34 3 - 35 – 44 4 - 45 – 54 5 - 55+
Abdomen	1	3	5	□ 20 □ 21	Problems Known Already 1 - No 2 - Yes, all 3 - Yes, some
Lower Back	1	3	5	□ 22	Posture Related Activities □ 23 □ 24 □ 25 □ 26 □ 27
Back~ Knees	1	3	5	□ 28 □ 29	Value
Head	1 2 3 4 5			□ 30	
Shoulders	1 2 3 4 5			□ 31	
Spine	1 2 3 4 5			□ 32	
Hips	1 2 3 4 5			□ 33	
Bow~ Legs	1	3	5	□ 34	
Knock~ Knees	1	3	5	□ 35	
Ankles Pronation	1	3	5	□ 36	
Ankles Supination	1	3	5	□ 37	

581

APPENDIX C
LIGHTWEIGHT WHEELCHAIR MANUFACTURERS

Activeaid, Inc.
One Activeaid Road
Box 359
Redwood Falls, MN 56283-0359

Eagle Sportschairs
2351 Parkwood Road
Snellville, GA 30278

Elite Wheelchair Products, Inc.
2884 Melissa Court
Snellville, GA 30278

Enabler Wheelchairs, Inc.
310 East Easy
Simi Valley, CA 93065

ETAC Use
2325 Parklawn Drive, Suite P
Waukesha, WI 53186

Everest & Jennings
1110 Corporation Square Drive
St. Louis, MO 63132

Fortress Lite-Style Wheelchairs, Inc.
827 Jefferson
Clovis, CA 93612

Hall's Wheels
Box 784
Cambridge, MA 02238

Invacare Corporation
899 Cleveland Street
Box 4028
Elyria, OH 44036

Top End
6551 44 Street North, #5002
Pinellas Park, FL 34665

Iron Horse Productions
2624 Conner Street
Port Huron, MI 48060

K-Chair Corporation
105 West Dakota, #114
Clovis, CA 93612

Kuschall of America
753 Calle Plano
Camarillo, CA 93010

Magic in Motion
239 West Stewart Avenue
Puyallup, WA 98371

Motion Designs/Sunrise Medical
2842 Business Park Avenue
Fresno, CA 93727-1328

Ortho-Kinetics, Inc.
Box 1647
Waukesha, WI 53187

Redman
3840 South Palo Verde
Tucson, AZ 85714

Rowcycle
3188 North Marks, #120
Fresno, CA 93722

Scott Therapeutic Design, Inc.
1132 Ringwood Court
San Jose, CA 95131

Wheel Ring, Inc.
199 Forest Street
Manchester, CT 06040

XL Manufacturing Company, Inc.
4950 Cohasset Stage Road
Chico, CA 95926

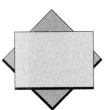

Index

T